# SHIRLEY
# HAZZARD

ALSO BY BRIGITTA OLUBAS

*Shirley Hazzard: Literary Expatriate*
*and Cosmopolitan Humanist*

EDITED BY BRIGITTA OLUBAS

*We Need Silence to Find Out What We Think:*
*Selected Essays* by Shirley Hazzard

*Collected Stories* by Shirley Hazzard

# SHIRLEY HAZZARD
## A Writing Life

### BRIGITTA OLUBAS

virago

VIRAGO

First published in the US in 2022 by Farrar, Straus and Giroux
First published in Great Britain in 2022 by Virago

1 3 5 7 9 10 8 6 4 2

Copyright © Brigitta Olubas 2022

The moral right of the author has been asserted.

A CIP catalogue record for this book
is available from the British Library.

Hardback ISBN 978-0-349-01288-9
Trade Paperback ISBN 978-0-349-01287-2

Printed and bound in Great Britain
by Clays Ltd, Elcograf S.p.A

Papers used by Virago are from well-managed forests
and other responsible sources.

Virago Press
An imprint of
Little, Brown Book Group
Carmelite House
50 Victoria Embankment
London EC4Y 0DZ

An Hachette UK Company
www.hachette.co.uk

www.virago.co.uk

*In memory of my parents, Gloria Rainbow and Edvardas Olubas,*

*and of my sisters, Mariana and Katharine*

When the territory is charted, its eventual aspect may be quite other than what was hoped for. One can only say, it will be a whole—a region from which a few features, not necessarily those that seemed prominent at the start, will stand out in clear colours. Not to direct, but to solace us; not to fix our positions, but to show us how we came.

—*The Bay of Noon*

# CONTENTS

Prologue: Only for Love     3

## I

1. Reggie's Daughter: 1931–1947     17
2. A First Glimpse of the Unknown: 1947–1948     53
3. Sea-Girt, Southerly, Sundered: 1948–1951     82

## II

4. New York: 1951–1957     113
5. A Larger Life: 1957–1958     140
6. *Sì, Scrivo!*: 1958–1963     171

## III

7. Francis: 1906–1963     201
8. *Amitié Littéraire*: 1963–1966     243

## IV

9. Small Masterpieces: 1966–1970     277
10. *The Transit of Venus*: 1970–1980     308
11. A Fated Connection: 1980–1985     346

## V

12. The Room Not as I Thought It Was: 1981–1994          389

13. *Sola Solissima*: 1995–2016                                        427

SOURCES   469

NOTES   473

ACKNOWLEDGMENTS   537

INDEX   541

# SHIRLEY HAZZARD

# PROLOGUE

## ONLY FOR LOVE

**AMONG SHIRLEY HAZZARD'S** papers at the Columbia University Rare Book and Manuscript Library on the Upper West Side of Manhattan are several boxes of small appointment diaries, four for each year. These are small, palm- or pocket-size, with clear plastic covers and shiny metallic spiral bindings. They are made by Hermès, the dates are in French, and they go back to the 1950s. They were bought each year, first by Shirley Hazzard's husband, the biographer and translator Francis Steegmuller, whose distinctive, often illegible hand records the bare bones of meetings, dinners, flights, and occasionally a flurry of details of a scene from his travels or notes about a dream he wanted to remember. In later years of their marriage, some of the entries are by Hazzard. Her handwriting is (a little) more legible, her notes and descriptions more detailed, less reserved, less diffident. After Steegmuller's death, in 1994, she took over the diaries and wrote in them until a decade or so before she died. The 4ème Trimestre diary from 2003 has a pencilled appointment for Novembre 19: "National Book Awards. Black Tie. Marriott Marquee Times Square. Shubert Alley 'red carpet' arrival, 45th St Reception 6:30–7:30 dinner—then the announcement. (Press conference later for winners.) Prepare putative remark. Ceremony concludes 10:15." Then, over the top, in red marker pen: "I won the National Book Award."

The National Book Award is one of the premier literary prizes in the United States. It is open only to U.S. writers but carries international distinction. Shirley Hazzard had twice before been nominated, first in 1971 for *The Bay of Noon* and again in 1981 for *The Transit of Venus*. The 2003 award was for *The Great Fire*, her fourth novel. It had been completed just half a year earlier and published only the previous month, but for all that haste had been long awaited. The reviews made much of this: "More than two decades have passed since the publication of Shirley Hazzard's *The Transit of Venus*"; "For years her admirers have been awaiting what would be next"; "For Shirley Hazzard—not to mention her readers and her publisher—it has been a long wait"; "In the 22 years since the publication of *The Transit of Venus*, readers and critics who declared that novel a modern classic . . . have kept a Penelope-like vigil for a new novel from Shirley Hazzard. At last, there is *The Great Fire*." And: "Few writers are worth this long a wait. The great Shirley Hazzard is one of them."

The award announcement was made before a crowd of some nine hundred people in the Marriott ballroom. There was an unusually large media contingent because the novelist Stephen King was to receive a medal for Distinguished Contribution to American Letters. Commentators had noted that King, as a writer of popular fiction, was an unusual choice for the medal, which had previously been awarded to such literary authors as Saul Bellow, Eudora Welty, and Philip Roth. There had been some heated public discussion, with Harold Bloom, tireless champion of high culture, lamenting King's award as a "dumbing down," drawing in turn the response that his "carping" demonstrated "an elitism that borders on a death wish." Stephen King took up these terms in his acceptance speech. He asked, provocatively, of his audience, "What do you think? You get social or academic brownie points for deliberately staying out of touch with your own culture?" and he listed a number of popular novelists, authors who he felt had been overlooked by august literary institutions like the National Book Award.

If Shirley Hazzard had indeed prepared a "putative remark," as flagged in her diary, she must have decided to set it aside. Instead, she addressed Stephen King's words directly: "I don't think giving us a reading list of those who are most read at this moment is much of a satisfaction," she said. "We read in all the ages." We have "mysterious inclinations. We have our own intuitions, our individuality toward what we want to read, and we developed that from childhood." Even the most ancient works, she continued, in moving us, become part of our immediate experience. The most important thing that literature brings is "Pleasure . . . the true pleasure." Her comments were spontaneous, unrehearsed, but at the same time this was a speech she could have made at any stage in her adult life, long given over to the deep rewards of reading and of writing.

There was in her devotion to literature something that set Shirley Hazzard aside, quite consciously, from the contemporary world, something that was certainly apparent to her readers. *The Great Fire*, one reviewer wrote, "is timeless as opposed to timely"; it read, another felt, "like the last masterpiece of a vanished age of civility, even of a certain understanding of civilization." The judges for the Miles Franklin Award, Australia's most prestigious literary prize, which the novel went on to win in 2004, commented that "*The Great Fire* is a reminder of why, in a digital age, the novel still matters." There was also to be found in her writing, reviewers wrote, great intellectual depth and an utterly singular style, "a clarity only possible to a writer of fastidious intellectual assurance. A style as complex and lucid as this constitutes a species of moral achievement." Some years later, the biographer Stacy Schiff described this aspect of Hazzard's work. The erudition, she wrote, "shimmers through the prose . . . like a demure, decorous spice: You may only dimly register its presence. You may mistake it for something else . . . Some will thrill to the imported line of Browning, the nod to Wordsworth, the classical allusions and painterly touches. They are hardly necessary to the enjoyment of the novel." Schiff quoted an observation from *The Transit of Venus*: "Knowledge was for some a range of topics; for others, depth of perception," adding that "Hazzard herself managed both. While she is in a league with Muriel Spark and Elizabeth Bowen, she is more muscular than either." Some readers pointed out that the erudition itself created difficulties of fictional voice, noting that several of the characters in *The Great Fire* spoke in ways that were impossibly learned, overly similar to each other, and too close, too, to the diction of the narrator.

On the other hand, Thomas Mallon made the point that the dialogue "never forces a suspension of disbelief, because Hazzard's narration is more articulate than almost anything we're now accustomed to reading: what's within quotation marks seems credible simply by the standard of what's without." This is a point made often and in different ways by her readers: within the world of Shirley Hazzard's novels it is precisely the distinctiveness and the distinction of the prose, the sentences, that compels us. No one else writes like this. The novelist Alice Jolly called it "Hazzard-land."

A couple of weeks before the National Book Award ceremonies, Shirley Hazzard gave a reading at the Unterberg Poetry Center at the 92nd Street YMHA. She was introduced by the poet J. D. McClatchy, who spoke of "a special shrine to Shirley Hazzard" beside which he had "moped" for the past twenty years, waiting for her next book. He had, he said, turned for consolation through that time to words by Flannery O'Connor, words that might seem to have constituted in advance a rebuttal of Stephen King's speech, a defence of high literature that addressed the larger currency, the presentness, of complex art. Alongside the insistent temporality of what Hazzard had called reading "in all the ages," these words set a sense of literature's achievement as something always speculative, unknowable in advance:

> The great novels we get in the future are not going to be those that the public thinks it wants, or those the critics demand. They are going to be the kind of novels that interest the novelist. And the novels that interest the novelist are going to be those that have not already been written. They are those that put the greatest demands on him, that require him to operate at the maximum of his intelligence and his talents, and to be true to the particularities of his own vocation. The direction of many of us will be towards concentration, and the distortion that is necessary to get our vision across. It will be more toward poetry than toward the traditional novel.

McClatchy added that O'Connor's statement "almost precisely, indeed uncannily, describes Shirley Hazzard's new novel *The Great Fire*, so long in the making, so brilliant now, at last, in our hands." She was, he said "a novelist's novelist's novelist."

*The Great Fire* tells the story—somewhat improbable perhaps, but largely true, at least in its main events—of a love affair between a man, older, a war hero, and a much younger woman in the wake of the Second World War. It directs itself not to the world of the plausible but rather, as McClatchy has it, to an existence "out of space and time, at once fraught and miraculous," or, as Joan Didion wrote, it is "a hypnotic novel that unfolds like a dream." Along with this otherworldliness, *The Great Fire* is immersed in time and place. It re-creates, impeccably, the postwar years in colonial Hong Kong, occupied Japan, England, and New Zealand. The fineness and liveness of these highly circumscribed novel worlds are, as Hazzard herself was quick to point out, steeped in her own memories. With previous novels she had always been rather circumspect about the sources of characters and events, but now in interviews she returned again and again to her youth spent in those places and to the heartbreak of first love experienced there. She wanted, she said, with this novel to bear witness to that past. "That atmosphere after the war, it's still so strong in me," she told one interviewer, "I wanted not to let it evaporate." She was speaking, certainly, about the historical events, and the mood and atmosphere after the war—what her protagonist Aldred Leith records in his diary as "Sunday, *grisaille*. Suspension," and the sense of "precariousness of what the world had become," and "the feeling of hope that was among us, especially young people, that mankind could learn to live without an enemy." In the process of recollecting that time, she said, "I retrieved a part of my life that was waiting for me": her own story, a love story, intense, thwarted. The long making of *The Great Fire* was, then, even longer than it had seemed, for it reached back into its author's lingering past. At the same time, she took issue with the confining of her novel, or any novel, within the limits of autobiography, or indeed of history, or fact. "The world," she told her audience at the Y that November, "likes to trace the author's life in the novel but the obvious isn't always true. Something that was very close to you and resembles your experience isn't necessarily the deepest version of the story." That, she believed, was the work that is done by fiction. "One has imagined things in novels one has never experienced. We are all cheek by jowl on the globe and have experiences which are not quite vicarious. One feels for another person. One observes. One imagines."

Aligned with that project of feeling, observing, imagining—the novelist's work—is the human and poetic matter of love. She explained that she had wanted to write "a story of falling in love," to tell truthfully "the accidental meeting of man and woman and a sense of destined engagement that would possibly last out their lives. This, to serve as a counterweight to the huge disillusion of a ravaged world. I will let myself in for derision, whatever I say on this theme, I suppose. Yet I think that such a story is not necessarily idealized, and that the dream, at least, of such love still supplies the poetry of all manner of unpoetic lives." This statement of large belief in romantic and sexual love stands behind all Shirley Hazzard's writing. It is aligned with her sense of human connectedness and above all with poetry, which is at heart for her a way of being human. She put it like this in one of her last public appearances: "Poetry comes in different forms, it can come in mere feeling, I think, people realize within themselves that they have deeper feelings than language always allows them to express. And poetry can save very much the souls of people who feel that way—who feel cut off from a deeper thing within themselves and having to fit in with much more daily forms of expression." Some years earlier, she had recorded in her diary how after a performance, "stupendously beautiful," of *Lucia di Lammermoor*, with Joan Sutherland and Alfredo Kraus, her friend the art historian John Pope-Hennessy had observed, "It treats Romantic love as an ideal," and how she had responded, in words that expressed her sense of the irreducible and necessary power of love, "A principle, almost. Something elevated and supreme, transcendent over reason, ambition, loyalty, even decency."

The publication of *The Great Fire* in 2003 and the attention it received brought Shirley Hazzard back into public awareness. She was read and admired all over again, interviewed and talked about. Those public appearances and commentaries tell us a lot about how her readers saw her, what they valued, and how she had come, already, to be remembered. They also allowed her to speak about her past, to add details about her youth and her youthful love affair to the stories she had been telling about her life since she first became a writer back in the early 1960s—stories about being born in Australia, about coming to New York, going to Italy, writing for *The New Yorker*, and meeting Francis Steegmuller. These stories were well rehearsed. They were for the most part true but, as tends to happen, had been burnished over the years of their telling. They told of a singular life that chimed with the striking uniqueness, the sui generis qualities of her writing and its aesthetic untimeliness, the longevity of her achievement, and the sparseness, overall, of her output: half a century of writing and just six books of fiction. This singularity was also a feature of her comportment. She herself made much of the untimeliness of her bearing and inclination. She spoke dismissively, still, of outdated technology such as telephone answering machines or "the telly," and be-musedly of computers and cell phones as artifacts of a present day she would never actually inhabit. (She said to one interviewer, "WWW Dot. I hear about it on the radio . . . WWW Dot means to me William Words-worth and his sister Dorothy! And I'm laughing away at this, thinking, Oh well, that's a way of exorcising the *horror* of all those buttons!") This was part of a larger identification with an idealised yesteryear; her friend and publisher Jonathan Galassi described her as someone who "willed to be out of a (non-existent) past." One evening in her later years, in Rome, walking up the steps that lead up to the Spanish Steps with her friend the literary scholar Robert Harrison, speaking of the past, or of the present, she stopped walking and, turning to him, said with great earnestness, "I hate change." The moment was made, Harrison remembered, "dramat-ically emphatic by the complete suspension of our movement. It was so heartfelt. A sincere speech act."

She was known for her impeccable grooming—Missoni jackets, Fer-ragamo shoes, the upswept hairstyles that leant back to the early 1960s— or seen, less kindly, as "preposterously prim." She wrote in *The Great Fire* of an older woman, the gracious Mrs. Fry, in words that also pic-tured her present, older self: "Beauty, long since drained of erotic appeal, had remained a habit." The writer Alec Wilkinson remembered her as a great feminine presence, "Some version of almost Jungian femininity realised. Powerful, brilliant, strong, moral." When she spoke, her expres-sion was formal and articulate; she spoke in full paragraphs, each one a pronouncement. She had an extraordinary memory for poetry and would recite, often at length, with the least inducement. Her voice and intonation were quite particular, her accent some combination of an Englishness cut loose from England, with a trace of Scots and the from-nowhere tones of mid-century middle-class Australia, an accent heard nowadays only in old newsreels. There was something unlocatable about it all. In his letter supporting her candidacy for the Century Association in New York in 1995, the art historian John Russell wrote, memorably, "If a highly intelligent and principled moth were able to talk, that is what she would sound like." For all her polish, though, there was always the trace of an outsider. Patrick White maintained that she had come from money; "he thought she was an heiress," but she was far from that. Alec Wilkinson expressed something of the flicker of contradictions around what she revealed and what she concealed about herself and her life: "You would never have understood how bruising that raising up was; the amount of territory covered. You never would have thought that she was Australian, from so far away."

Shirley Hazzard had indeed come from far away, had come a long way, had transformed, indeed created, herself. Her friend the art historian Alison West commented that she had "achieved her life through sheer power of mind"; she was somebody with "a capacity to absorb tremendous amounts of knowledge and to savour it in a certain way as a representation of who they are." This was a function of her intellect, of course, but also of the acuteness of her sensibility, as another friend, Elizabeth Archibald, observed, her "extraordinary ear for language, ability to hear and notice tiny phrases, the way people talk, the words people use. She was paying attention to every detail. She had a kind of heightened sensitivity, a kind of lived knowledge as well as erudite knowledge."

The Auden scholar Edward Mendelson described her as, above all, civilised: "There was a sense Shirley had, it was not courtesy, it was a sense of your value as a human being. It wasn't a demand, it was that she assumed good motives on your part, civilised motives." The intimacy of her conversation or friendship was itself reserved; "One loved her," Mendelson said, "without there being a centre of herself that one loved.

One loved her attributes—generosity, her sweetness, her learning, her sense that you were better than you were." She also had "an absence of irrational hatreds and passions," a commitment to "see in everyone the best they have." She made a similar observation herself about her friend the poet James Merrill: "He had the generous talent of bringing out the best in his friends; one rose to his articulate occasion." There was also a sense of serenity about her own place in the world, Mendelson felt: "She didn't seem to care if you admired her work or not . . . She didn't want anything from you. She wanted a sense of being part of your world of excellence . . . It was not that she felt 'I am a famous person and I am being generous to you,' she was absolutely at peace with herself." That serenity embraced a notable reserve; despite her loquacity and her generosity, it was clear that there were things she chose not to disclose. The writer Matthew Specktor recalled her as "very very well defended" and described her use of conversation, admiringly—"she spoke in arias"—as a form of filibuster. Amanda Vaill, one of her editors at Viking, saw some of *The Transit of Venus*'s Caro Bell in her, a quality not exactly of reserve or aloofness but more of "being able to hold herself apart from a discussion . . . It was observant . . . She wasted nothing. She didn't throw things away. She kept them." And, Alec Wilkinson noted, she made judgments: "There was something so avid about her intellect; an intelligence that couldn't help but take the measure of all it saw."

Shirley Hazzard embarked early on a project of self-cultivation and self-creation through extensive and passionate reading. Throughout her adult life she mixed in elevated cultural circles, seeking out people to admire and learn from. This all culminated, in a way, in her marriage in 1963 to Francis Steegmuller, a marriage described by their friend the poet and translator Richard Howard as "a conjugal version of literary high life." Francis was significantly older than Shirley. He had lived through the exhilarating years of the American "discovery" of Paris and of European art in the interwar years. He was a biographer and translator, an independent scholar with a private income and a private art collection, qualities he would lend to *Transit*'s Adam Vail: "He had lent the picture, which belonged to him." The Steegmullers were close in sensibility and temperament and were devoted to each other. Shirley delighted in the worlds her marriage opened up for her, but the marriage was also, importantly, daily, intimate, practical. Francis helped her manage the tribulations—which were considerable—of her mother, and in his later years, as his memory began to fail, she set her own writing aside to care for him, helping him write his last books. He had been married before, happily, for thirty years to a wealthy amateur painter, Beatrice Stein Steegmuller, and he brought not just financial security. When Shirley first met him, she thought "he looked like a person who had learnt, who had suffered and learnt and who had enjoyed life in a very deep way. There was a lot to be seen in his face."

In his acclaimed biography of Jean Cocteau, Francis wrote about the veiled revelation of self that is implicit in the writing of lives. To Cocteau's suggestive claim "I am a lie that always tells the truth," he added a gloss: "But a lie, even one that tells the truth, implies a truth that is not told. In Cocteau's case the lie, the myth, and the two kinds of truth, the one that is told and the one that is not, make a fascinating amalgam." If there are truths to be told, and not told, about Shirley Hazzard's life and work, they come together at the point where, to turn Richard Howard's lovely phrase a little, the conjugal meets the literary—the point where the writer lives. A few months after Francis's death, Shirley published a brief memorial, just a page long, in *The New York Times*, a telescoping of their times on the island of Capri, where they spent part of each year from the late 1960s. It is a kind of intimate obituary, a window onto the life they had shared, and it provides an eloquent point of entry into the story of her life:

> Francis's worktable barely held his typewriter. He often wrote in bed—yellow pad on lap, pencil in beautiful hand, cat dozing alongside—in a small, high room with luminous views of sea, sky, mountain. In the early mornings we read aloud: Shakespeare, Gibbon, Byron's "Don Juan," Clough's "Amours de Voyage," Thucydides, Seneca, Auden, Delacroix's journals, Leopardi's "Canti." We took our books on walks and read them in silence by the sea. In an outdoor restaurant, Francis once read an entire novel, Muriel Spark's "Robinson," while I finished Conrad's "Victory." He said,

"Curious that both books are set on islands," and as we named other 'island' works, mentioned Melville's poem "To Ned," about the coming doom of desert islands.

Last summer, Vladimir Nabokov was remembered in the press as having told his students: "You have to saturate yourself with English poetry in order to compose English prose . . . You must study the poets."

I read this to Francis and he said: "Exactly. Still, one cannot truly do it for a 'purpose.' Only for love."

# REGGIE'S DAUGHTER

## 1931-1947

**SHIRLEY HAZZARD LOVED** to tell the story of how she became a writer. It is a story that began with poetry, and a broken heart, and Italy, and in the course of being retold came to stand in for the story of her life and to encapsulate the largeness of her imaginative being. This is one version:

Auden said in that beautiful poem about Yeats that poetry altered nothing, that all the savagery of the world would be the same if no poet had ever written. But I know from my own small experience that it can change life radically. Poetry gave me companionship; it opened my mind and my heart—as far as they could be opened. It also changed the facts of my life.

When I was living in New Zealand in 1949–50, I read poems of Leopardi in translation by John Heath-Stubbs and I wanted to learn the originals: they were so beautiful. I remember it was a blue book.

I began to read Italian, 12,000 miles away without expectation of going to Italy. Later, it was because I had studied Italian that I was sent there by the United Nations and everything changed.

She would return over and over to this story of escape from terrible origins, the writing life that allowed her to save her life: "There was the idea that transformation in our lives would come through marriage, through falling in love and marrying, and the idea of rescue . . . I would have liked to be rescued but no one was going to rescue me, and I finally realized that I would have to rescue myself. And the only means . . . that I could see was to use the thing that was closest to my spirit, which was the literary life, the use of the word . . . I can say I lived happily ever after."

She would return, too, to the importance of Italy in that rescued life: "In Italy, the mysteries remain important: the accidental quality of existence, the poetry of memory, the impassioned life that is animated by awareness of eventual death." And she would give the delightful particulars of the transformation of her life—a villa outside Siena owned by a spirited and cultivated family who became her friends and prompted her to write. "In 1960 I wrote a story—a simple story of a young poet, derived from an evening in that Italian garden. I sent it to the *New Yorker*, without keeping a copy. It was accepted by William Maxwell, and I received his letter standing in the big, old kitchen of my friends' villa. Moments like that don't come twice: *The Order of Release*." It is a compelling story, and true as far as it goes, but it glances over what was a more prolonged and laborious commencement to her writing life. Although the story about the young poet was indeed the one accepted by William Maxwell in the summer of 1960, it was not the first story she had sent to the magazine, nor was it the first published. That, appearing in April 1961, was a story set in Australia, about a child, a little girl, in suburban Sydney, where Shirley Hazzard had grown up and where her writer's story really began.

"Woollahra Road" takes readers into the world of its author's childhood: provincial, domestic, and shaped by forces just beyond the child's grasp. It is signed with her birth date—"It was 1935, and Ida was four years old"—and with the time frame of the Great Depression. Shirley Hazzard was born on January 30, 1931, at the Bungalow Private Hospital in Chatswood on Sydney's North Shore. Shortly after, she joined her parents, Reginald and Catherine, and sister Valerie, then two years old, in the family home in Bay Road, Waverton, close to the north pylon of the soon-to-be-completed Sydney Harbour Bridge. A year or two later the family moved a little farther out to the suburb of Willoughby, to a sizable, if unremarkable, suburban bungalow on a large block of land, where they lived until 1937. The house and garden were very like those described in some detail in "Woollahra Road," a domestic haven edged by ever-encroaching remnants of native bushland:

The front garden . . . was on the shady side of the house, but even there the soft turf had died in the drought and been replaced by crisp, resistant buffalo grass, which also grew on the more exposed sides of the house. The steps were bordered with pink and blue hydrangeas, and with beds of fuchsia and daphne. Palm trees stood on the lawn. At the end of the soft drive were red hibiscus and trees of wattle and frangipani. At the side, a wall covered with wilted Dorothy Perkins roses separated this house from the [house next door] . . . The back garden was huge, and had beds of flowers and vegetables and an orchard. A swing had been built in the orchard, and if you were swung high enough you could touch the mandarin trees by extending your feet. Beyond the orchard was a field of high grass forbidden to children because of snakes. The snakes occasionally came into the garden and had to be killed with a heavy stick that was kept in the garage for the purpose. The grass of the field was cut down from time to time by Alfie, the man who did the garden, and lost cricket balls would turn up then, or an old kite, or singed rocket butts left over from Empire Night. The grass was never burned off now, because of the danger of fire. Even the orchard and the garden had their perils. There were bees in the grove of Buddleia. In the mornings, kookaburras perched on the lowest branches of the trees, looking for lizards or worms, and would burst out laughing right over your head. And there was a grey goanna, like a short, thick snake, harmless but horrible, that came to the kitchen door to be fed by the maid, Marge, with raw eggs.

The house was on McClelland Street, across from St. John's Church, where Shirley attended nursery school. She remembered these times and places in a long oral history interview she gave in 2000: "There was what we called the paddock at the back beyond the garden, and it had knee-high grass or at least knee-high to a little child, and was mown every so often . . . And that atmosphere of childhood was, I can't say a frontier town, but the bush was very close, and there was no feeling of this congestion that now any big city immediately generates." This was not, of course, the big city in any sense. Up until the late 1920s Willoughby was semirural, with orchards, market gardens, dairies, small farms, and even tanneries, but these were decades of urban expansion, and the opening of the Sydney Harbour Bridge in 1932 saw the area quickly become suburban, most likely with such residual wildlife as goannas, kookaburras, snakes, and scope for long-remembered summer freedoms. A photograph of Shirley, aged about four years old, smiling happily with a doll cradled in each arm, a rough wooden fence behind, and scrubby grass all around, certainly conveys the country-town character of her first home. There is a sense of being somehow close to the bush, too, in "Woollahra Road," with the arrival at the house of "a hawker . . . a man selling clothes props. The decrepit cart was laden with saplings of eucalyptus, roughly stripped and forked at one end." Shirley returned to this memory as she began drafting *The Great Fire* in the early 1980s, a scene later discarded:

> She remembered a morning when, kept home from nursery school for some childish ailment, she had lain in her little white bed secure in her special standing, her mother's love, the bright day without and quiet shade within; the irruption, once in a while, of some sound from the quiet street—significant because isolated—a man with a horse and cart, selling clothes props for tuppence each. These, the scarcely honed saplings of new green; the rumble of a car. Realised that she was a child and would grow; but at this moment the world needed her for its (rightness). She fitted the scheme. Also, the sense of special indulgence. Of leisure, enhanced by contrast with general obligation to toil—of "getting away with it."

Even then, she was alert to a sense of how remote was her location in the world:

I was three, I think, when I began to remember, to be there, and the sense of it, although a child doesn't reason this way, the sense, the atmosphere of the place must have been very strong because I remember being aware that we were in a place that was far from somewhere else; "somewhere else" being the world, really. There really was the tyranny of distance that was borne in on one and we were on the edge of the bush, which as I grew up I understood it was also the desert, the edge of the dead heart of the continent, and that certainly was pervasive.

While she is drawing here on familiar tropes of Australia—desert, dead heart, "the tyranny of distance"—what prevails is her conviction that her early life was lived in a place that, because it remained unrecorded in literature, set its inhabitants "in perpetual, flagrant violation of reality." The Australia into which she was born was itself a recent invention. The colonies established through British imperial expansion through the late eighteenth and early nineteenth centuries had federated just three decades earlier, in 1901, and the national parliament had only just moved from Melbourne to the new "Bush Capital" at Canberra, three hours south of Sydney, in 1927. The legacies of Australia's colonial origins were everywhere to be found through the interwar decades, including in the makeup of the population. From the mid-nineteenth century, emigration to Australia was almost wholly confined to British subjects, and this pattern continued for more than another century, sustained by the "White Australia policy," the name popularly given to a series of restrictive acts of parliament defining the new nation as Anglo and European, beginning with the Immigration Restriction Act, which gave immigration officials enormous latitude to refuse entry into Australia on racial grounds. The first attorney general, Alfred Deakin, announced to the Parliament of Australia in 1901, "At the very first instant of our national career we are as one for a white Australia."

After the establishment of the early colonies with populations largely comprised of convicts and military personnel, the European population in Australia had been controlled by the British Colonial Land and Emigration Office, which organised the funding of passages to Australia according to the principle that "the proportions sent out (as between English, Scottish and Irish) should be the same as in the home population," with the aim of producing a "new Britannia" in the colonies. At Federation in 1901, the Australian population was 95 percent of British descent. Frontier wars between settlers and Indigenous people were sustained until the early decades of the twentieth century; Indigenous Australians were largely excluded from the franchise at Federation and were mostly not included in the national census until 1967. All this matters for Shirley Hazzard's story, first because she makes much of the White Australia policy in *The Great Fire*—"We've had racial laws in Australia for generations," Peter Exley tells Archie Crindle, who is concerned about the rise of fascism in Italy—but also because it speaks to the overwhelmingly Anglo-Australian world in which she grew up. It is difficult to over-emphasize the importance of these colonial and racial legacies in the Australia of her early years, legacies that had been confirmed and consolidated by the First World War. In his history of modern Australia, Tom Keneally observes that that war, "instead of repelling Australians from the arms of the Empire, drove them more firmly into it. Apart from the undeniable convictions of the great majority, this was also for the sake of a White Australia." The historians Mark Peel and Christina Twomey describe the "defensive project" of Australia in these years, an "insularity" that yet maintained a decisive "sentimental attachment to Britain."

Shirley would later recall the deep identification of her family and social world with the ideals and dominance of the British Empire: "the globe marked out in pink" and the foldout coronation poster displayed at school—"jingoistic," she said, "like some great protective thing over us . . . And suddenly it pulverised." Her memories also turned to the darker aspects of the nation's history, characterised by what she felt to be "ignoble endurance," stemming from the conditions of its founding as a penal colony: "hardship, awfulness and no sense of pleasure." Nor was there any sense, in the popular consciousness of her family and class, or in the reaches of her own imagination, of the immensity of the country's Indigenous history, nor of the continuing presence of Indigenous people and cultures. And even while she would go on, in essays and lectures, to criticise the treatment of the First Australians by successive national governments, the language in which she evoked 1930s and 1940s Australia in *The Transit of Venus*—"a parched unvisited mystery, a forlorn horizon strung on a strand of slack barbed wire"—and her evocation of white Australians' unfamiliarity with Indigenous people are themselves grounded in an incapacity to recognise these realities. In *The Transit of Venus*, Caro and Grace Bell learn that "Australia's history soon terminated in unsuccess," that it "was engulfed in a dark stench of nameless prisoners whose only apparent activity was to have built, for their own incarceration, the stone gaols, now empty monuments that little girls might tour for Sunday outings," and that it "dwindled into the expeditions of doomed explorers, journeys without revelation or encounter endured by fleshless men whose portraits already gloomed, beforehand, with a wasted, unlucky look—the eyes fiercely shining from sockets that were already bone." There was, it seems, to be no moving past these determinants, no other way of belonging to this place.

While Australians at this time looked mostly to its colonial past for their cultural moorings, the nation also participated in the global rush to modernity. Sydney, Australia's largest city, older than the nation by more than a century, exemplified the attraction of city life after World War I, collecting an increasing proportion of New South Wales's inhabitants, so that its population more than doubled from less than half a million at Federation to more than a million the year Shirley was born. Sydney was also more international, more energetically connected to the rhythms and opportunities of the modern world than was the second major city, Melbourne, which had built its wealth in the gold rushes of the previous century and remained the establishment city. In 1927 the artist Sydney Ure Smith described Sydney's vitality: "grinding trams and busy motor cars and . . . uncompromising flats . . . and always the patch of blue harbour. Hills, noise, traffic, careless pedestrians, yellow cabs . . . ferries darting in a tangle into the harbour from Circular Quay. Tall buildings, ugly buildings . . . wharves, masses of deep sea liners, cargo boats, ships from everywhere . . . crowded houses on the foreshore . . . excitement, bustle and movement . . ." All these elements might be found, of course, in descriptions of any world city of the period, apart perhaps from the defining note of the harbour, described in 1916 by the architect

John Sulman as "a great lung . . . which can never be closed." Sydney has always been identified with its harbour, and by the Pacific Ocean into which the harbour opens, as in this paean from the city's 1938 sesquicentenary: "Golden beaches. Sun-tanned men and maidens . . . Red-roofed villas terraced above the blue waters of the harbour . . . Even Melbourne seems like some grey and stately city of Northern Europe compared with Sydney's sub-tropical splendours."

Shirley's childhood was spent in full view of those splendours and blue waters and, like the city, was defined by the opportunities they provided. By the year of her birth, Sydney was in the process of being transformed by the construction of the iconic bridge, symbol of prosperity and the future. The bridge carried a particular resonance for the Hazzards, as Reginald and Catherine, known as Kit, had met in the bridge works office. Both were working for Dorman Long, the British engineering firm charged with the bridge's construction—Reg in the post of secretary to the director of construction, Lawrence Ennis, whom Shirley remembered as "a dim, presiding figure of my infancy," and Kit in the office of the chief engineer, Sir Ralph Freeman. Australia had been hit hard by the Great Depression, but because of the bridge, one of the very few construction projects to survive the downturn, the consequences of the 1929 crash took some years to hit Sydney. The completion of the bridge in 1932 meant an end to this cushioning, and the city saw a collapse worse than anywhere else in the country. By 1933 Australia's unemployment rate was one of the highest in the world. Although the Hazzards were not directly affected, the larger deprivations were clear even to the very young Shirley: "I was lucky that my family did not actively suffer during the Depression, which was terrible in Australia. It's not something a child lives through and ever forgets. It becomes a yardstick really for human experience when you've seen an entire populace humiliated, compounded by the penury of veterans of the First World War." Those veterans too were burned into her consciousness, "spectres," "apparitions," standing alone or in groups around the city streets. "Who or what they had singly been . . . sunk in the delved sameness of the eyes. Nothing more could be done to them, but their unsurpassed worst would be sustained forever and ever." She retained more domestic images of the bleakness of Depression-era suburbia, for instance the local shop where she and Valerie would be sent, "with those windows, no one thought of dressing them up, those windows in the summer with dead flies and bleached packets of this and that."

Throughout her life Shirley Hazzard was at pains to establish a sense of distance from the country and the circumstances of her birth, claiming that "my temperament is not a very national one." She was particularly oblique about the question, writing to her first UK publisher, "I have never lived in the UK, although my passport is certainly British and I expect that I am too . . . However, these things are perhaps more mysterious than I realise." Her criticisms of Australia were pointed and sustained, but more than this, she was unwilling to saddle herself with its colonial burden, expressed sardonically by *Transit*'s narrator: "Australia required apologies, and was almost a subject for ribaldry. Australia could only have been mitigated by unabashed fortune from its newly minted sources—sheep, say, or sheep-dip." At the same time, in her writing and in her memories can be found a profound connection to the locations of her childhood, in particular to the quality of light and the topography of Sydney's North Shore, which set in place one of the essential coordinates of her lifelong visual imaginary: the sea. From the age of about five she lived in scenic Mosman, just above Balmoral Beach, on a high-ridged peninsula jutting out into Sydney's Middle Harbour, rising some seventy or eighty feet (20–25 metres) above the sea, with nearly eleven miles (18 kilometres) of coastline, cliffs of dark yellow and white Hawkesbury sandstone, and beaches, many of them still, then, surrounded by untouched bushland.

She recalled that even before the family moved to Mosman, on hot afternoons her mother would drive her and Valerie from Willoughby to Balmoral to paddle in the sea. They would arrive at the beach "down a winding road whose asphalt was edged with morning glory" and return "by the sheer ascent of Awaba Street, in terror that the brake might fail." She came to understand the sea as an essential part of her life: "All through my life I've lived near the sea and I think, sometimes, how difficult it would be for me to be landlocked." On the one hand she recognised and looked to a distant and "authoritative world where seasons were reversed (it was implied, correctly)," but she also felt a forceful sense of connection to place and to the particular lived places of her childhood, to the mesmerizing detail of a world she was inventing, imagining for herself. We can see this in *The Transit of Venus*, where despite the imaginative and aesthetic circumscriptions of colonial society, the young Caro nonetheless apprehends another world yet to be verified, glimpsed in unknowing fragments:

> There was nothing mythic at Sydney: momentous objects, beings, and events all occurred abroad or in the elsewhere of books. Sydney could never take for granted, as did the very meanest town in Europe, that a poet might be born there or a great painter walk beneath its windows. The likelihood did not arise, they did not feel they had deserved it. That was the measure of resentful obscurity: they could not imagine a person who might expose or exalt it . . . There was the harbour, and the open sea. It was an atmosphere in which a sunset might be comfortably admired, but not much else. Any more private joy—in light or dark, in leaf or gatepost—savoured of revelation and was uncountenanced; even in wisteria or wattle on mornings newer, surely, than anywhere else could by now achieve. There was a stillness on certain evenings, or a cast to rocks, or a design of languid branch against the sky that might be announcing glory. Though it could hardly be right to relish where Dora was aggrieved, the girls put their smooth faces to gardenias, inhaling December for a lifetime.

That a poet might be born there. From her earliest responses to the topography of Sydney Harbour, its green folds and sandstone tracks, its gardens and blue vistas, the "private joy" it offered, Shirley Hazzard announced herself a writer. The poetic charge of these lines derives not only from their evocative precision but also from a sense that these images are being encountered for the first time. There is a tight enfolding of poetry with childhood memory, a combination of prospect and retrospect that is strikingly her own. The sensual experience of stillness, or of gardenias, is already washed with lost time, and what we are being given access to is not simply a past and a particular place and moment—

the summer December scents of a 1930s Sydney childhood—but also a
landscape of poetic and bodily apprehension. She later reflected on this
not so much as a quality of her writing but as a phenomenon of memory
itself. In 1984, on returning to Sydney to deliver a series of lectures, she
told an interviewer that she had been struck by the particularity of place
and time—a winter's day in August—and by the alignment of a certain
quality of light with memory. Struck by the gap of thirty years since she
had last encountered the city in midyear, and struck, surely, after all this
time, by the antipodean surprise of winter sunshine in August, just as by
the scent of gardenias in December, she discovered that "light has properties of memory, like the scents of flowers. I find myself walking along
and looking at Sydney and having memories pour over me. The whole
content of one's youth and one's experience that's lingering somewhere
in one's mind is brought to attention by this quality of light." It's as if
her early years were lived primarily, imaginatively, as a process of setting
down memory, of lyrical but as yet unvoiced response to the world around
her, above all to the light and the sea. Even the city impressed her with
its radiance; she remembered being driven there in early mornings, its
towers "came into sight as one crossed the bridge. There was in fact a
golden sun—sheer radiance!—on top of the building that housed the
Sydney Sun. The whole thing, always, enchanted place to me when it
suddenly appeared. (Then, few minutes later, descent into the narrow
dark of George, Pitt, and Castlereagh, toast-rack trams, smell of sooty-
city, lights on sometimes on winter mornings . . . )."

If the harbour at Mosman, the light, and the foliage could suggest the
possibility of "glory" to her protagonist Caro years later, they were not
able to deliver anything like that in the present tense of Shirley's own
childhood. She was eloquent about the misery of family life, aware as a
child that both her parents had had hard beginnings. She described them
as "scarred for life" by what they had undergone, as "fixated on money
by their childhoods," and as each selfishly battling to thwart the desires
and pleasures of the other, with their two daughters caught miserably in
the middle. From the age of about ten she witnessed what she recalled as
a "terrible situation between my parents," with arguments and constant
raised voices. Before this, she felt, "in the early years of their marriage,"

there had been some happiness and harmony between Kit and Reg. She described them as "both very good-looking, in their Celtic way—dark hair, blue eyes, fair skin, fairly tall. My mother was strikingly beautiful even into later life, and had fine taste in clothes." (Here she might have been describing herself.) Their attractiveness to each other was evident to her, but also their wretched drive to separation, their selfishness and vindictive cruelty.

In assessing their almost lifelong incompatibility, Shirley acknowledged her parents' difficult pasts and understood that they "in their best selves rejoiced in giving, to my sister and me, a better childhood than they themselves had had. My memories of very early life are touching in that way." However, their origins were rather more benighted than perhaps she realized. Both Kit and Reg began their lives in circumstances of illegitimacy and considerable material deprivation. Reg's background remains obscure. Shirley claimed to have his birth certificate stating that he was born in Wales, but there is no such document among her papers; there is, however, a letter from Somerset House public records office in London from 1968, a response to her inquiry, advising that there was no record of his birth in Wales at that time. She may have been thinking of her parents' marriage certificate, which does indeed state his place of birth as Newport, Wales, and Newport is also recorded on his 1918 Australian Imperial Force enlistment papers, but neither of these documents carries the assurance of fact: the details on the marriage certificate were provided by Reg himself, and the enlistment form includes a declaration by his adoptive mother, Pauline A. Hazzard, that "to the best of my knowledge my adopted son, Reginald Hazzard, was born in Newport in Wales in the year 1899 on the 27 February." A handwritten note records that his baptismal name was "Reginald Crawford," and in response to the question "Are you a natural born British subject or a Naturalized British subject?" Reg, or perhaps Pauline, misunderstanding the import of the question, has at first written "British born," again asserting his Welsh birth, and has then crossed that out and written over it "natural born." (The question sought in fact to distinguish those born in Australia or Britain from those born elsewhere.) Despite these assertions, there is no record of the birth of a male child under the name of Reginald Crawford (or Crofford, Crosford, Crestford, or other possible variants) in the years around 1899 in the UK, or for that matter in Australia. Nor is there any record of his adoption, although this is not in itself unusual, as formal adoptions began in New South Wales only in 1923 and arrangements made before then were informal, private, and mostly undocumented. Shirley observed that her father's early life was "shrouded in unspeakability."

The AIF enlistment forms record Reg and his adoptive mother as living, in 1918, in East Sydney, then a poor inner-city area. They had moved there from Kempsey, in northern New South Wales, during the war, after Reg completed his NSW Qualifying Certificate, which enabled him to enter high school, in November 1913. In 1886 Pauline, then Pauline Amilee (elsewhere Amelie) Walsh, had married Charles John Hazzard, who died in Kempsey in 1905, leaving "no issue." Charles was the son of a baker and had been born into a middle-class family in Central London; the 1881 census records show two servants living with the family. How he came, in 1883, to leave London and travel to Kempsey is not known. Pauline was seven years older than Charles (she had taken ten years off her age on the marriage certificate). She and Charles were both significant figures in the community of West Kempsey at the turn of the century; they ran a successful bakery, and both were involved in civic and charitable events in the town. Charles was known locally as a breeder of prize poultry—his obituary in the Kempsey newspaper, *The Macleay Argus*, noted that he had "one of the best collections of pure-bred fowls outside Sydney"—and Pauline was a keen gardener and a regular winner of prizes at the local flower show. She was also a long-standing member of the Kempsey Ladies' Benevolent Society, and after Charles's death she became very involved in the local West Kempsey School, her "enthusiastic interest" commended by *The Macleay Argus*, which observed that "she may be termed the foster mother of the West scholars" for her support of local students to win bursaries and scholarships to attend high school. It is quite possible that Reg was an orphan attending the school, talented but otherwise without prospects, and that she took over his care as an extension of her other contributions to the school and community, or indeed that the adoption came about through the auspices of the Ladies' Benevolent Society. While Reg always referred to Charles Hazzard as his father, it does seem that Pauline Hazzard was a widow when she adopted him.

Colonial societies have always provided opportunities for reinvention and self-invention, and there are extraordinary stories from the Australian colonies in the half century before Reg Hazzard's birth—notably the Tichborne Claimant (a butcher from Wagga Wagga in New South Wales who travelled to England in the 1860s maintaining that he was Roger Tichborne, the heir to the Tichborne estate in Hampshire who had been presumed lost at sea and to whom he bore not the least resemblance) or, a couple of decades later, Herbert Dyce Murphy, who had lived much of his early life as a woman in England, then returned to Victoria, married a woman, and became one of the historical sources of Patrick White's late masterpiece, *The Twyborn Affair*. Although Reg Hazzard's more modest transformation seems to have happened mostly without his active involvement during childhood, it was facilitated, or necessitated, by the same social flexibility and dearth of formal documentation. It also led to some reworking of the official records in later years. Despite the repeated claims to Newport, Wales, Reg's entry in the 1950 *Who's Who in Australia* lists his birthplace as Kempsey, New South Wales, and gives his birth year as 1896, making him three years older than stated in his enlistment papers. This earlier date is also what is recorded on his death certificate, though this is unlikely to be correct, given that it would have made him nearly eighteen years of age when completing his NSW Qualifying Certificate, normally done around age fourteen.

It is possible that Reg altered his date of birth in official records after his marriage to Kit, who was born in 1897, to obscure the fact that she was older than he. His second wife, Mary, believed the earlier date. She also believed him to have been born in Kempsey and seems not to have known that he was adopted. Mary wrote to Shirley after Reg's death, in 1973, telling her that she had visited Kempsey to make connection with his family and background.

The Macleay, where your family stemmed from is a really beautiful area, lush and green and everywhere, wide waterways and incredible swamp bird life. I took many drives and found many folk who remembered your grandfather and his historic death in the then smaller community . . . There are still a few folk who went to school with your father and most of them have prospered in their own town and been content to never move on. They all had cuttings of your book reviews to show me and were very proud of "Reggie's daughter."

Reg made several trips back to Kempsey in the years before his death and indeed became quite the local celebrity. Interviewed by the local paper, he told lively stories about his childhood there and about his "father," Charles Hazzard, who had died after being struck in the head by a cricket ball when Reg was nine years old, a story local historians believe to be apocryphal. There is no mention of his having been born in Wales (nor any mention, anywhere, of a Welsh accent). Reg clearly wished to be seen in both his private and professional life as Australian-born, a "boy from the bush." Shirley on the other hand rejected these local beginnings. Her later insistence on a Welsh father and Scottish mother accorded better with her sense of who she more properly was—that is to say, not Australian—and who she would, or had, become.

To add to the mystery, the marriage certificate that records Reg Hazzard's birthplace as Newport, Wales, gives his father's name as Charles James Hazzard, "Deceased, Occupation: Engineer," and records his mother as "unknown." Nevertheless, Reg maintained a connection with Pauline Hazzard until she was quite elderly. Shirley recalled that "he was loyal to her, and he visited her," and she kept among her books a copy of *The Complete Works of Shakespeare* inscribed to her sister, "With best wishes to dear Valerie from Grandma Hazzard December 25 1939," suggesting some degree of connection and warmth, as well as cultural aspiration. Pauline is named as Reg's mother on his death certificate, although her maiden name is there given as "Pauline de Renard." On her own death certificate, she is said to have been born in France, and her father is recorded as a "Captain" by the name of "De Reynard"; yet her maiden name appears as "Walsh" elsewhere, including on her marriage certificate to Charles Hazzard, which records her as having been born in Ipswich, Queensland. She was married again shortly after moving to

Sydney, to an Englishman, Edwin Crescence Cook (that marriage certificate states that she had been born in Marseilles, France). Cook seems to have been a small-time no-good and was tried in 1917 for embezzlement from his employer, British Pianoforte Ltd. Pauline soon went back to calling herself Hazzard.

Pauline lived in East Sydney until her death, in 1948, and visited the Hazzards on the North Shore, as Shirley remembered: "She came three times a year to see us, and she wore long black clothes and was very old. She seemed to me terribly ancient, and she must have been terribly old." (She would have been in her early eighties.) Reg told his family that Pauline "'didn't spare the strap when I was a child,' and there had been a very harsh upbringing." It is tempting to see a representation of the severe and mysterious grandmother Hazzard in the strange woman who arrives at the family home in "Woollahra Road":

> A woman had come round the corner of the house and was walking very slowly toward the back door. She was dressed in black and carried a large, square hessian bag that flapped, almost empty, against her thigh. Her slow, slow walk carried her past the flowers and the vegetables and the barking dog, but she didn't look about her. By her face and her figure she was not old, but her walk was old. Her feet moved painfully on the smooth flagstone path. The uneven hem of her dress reached, in some places, almost to her ankles. She wore a round hat of black felt, crammed down on her head.

The terrible singularity of this figure, seen through the eyes of a young child, seems to carry some of the weight of her parents' harsh, dark past; her visit ruptures the surface of the family home and brings the deprivations of the distant slums of inner-city Sydney—the "sombre grime of terrace houses . . . a contagion from the British Isles, a Midlands darkness"—and the effects of the Depression tumbling into Ida's otherwise privileged and comfortable life.

Shirley certainly recalled secrecy and confusion about her father's origins, with the story about Reg having been born in Wales disclosed to the family "almost in tears," "one rather terrible night when my parents were pouring out woes, wrongs." Reg never told his family more: "He couldn't bear to talk about it." Shirley speculated that he had been sent to Australia as an unaccompanied child migrant—"he didn't know who his parents were, and I think there were many people who had come to Australia in that way, not only the Australians who were descendants of convicts, didn't want to acknowledge they had this family past." This seems unlikely. He is not listed among the child migrants arriving in Australia in 1911 and 1912, and also, if he had been one of their number, there would have been no need for his adoption, as child migrants were supervised, trained, and then sent out to work. After moving to Sydney with Pauline in early 1914, Reg attended Sydney Technical High School in inner-city Ultimo, but he left in mid-1916 before completing his School Certificate. His acceptance at this school indicates his academic aptitude, as well as Pauline's determination for him to realise his potential, as students needed to have achieved a good pass in the Qualifying Certificate and were required to pay fees of a guinea a term in advance before enrolling. His grades were respectable for the first two years, but by mid-1916 they'd begun to slip disastrously—he failed most subjects—providing a plausible reason for his early departure.

In January 1918 he enlisted in the Australian Imperial Forces, Sixth Brigade, as a gunner. He embarked for active service in June, sailing to England on the RMS *Orontes*, and arrived in Liverpool two months later, when he was taken to the Camp of the Reserve Brigade Australian Artillery at Heytesbury in Wiltshire. On December 3 he went with his unit to France, to the Département Somme, and he was admitted to hospital in Abbeville five days later. In February 1919 he was detailed for duty to the Australian Base Depot in Le Havre. By July 1919 he was readmitted to hospital back in the UK and treated for gonorrhoea, contracted, according to his record, from a prostitute in London. This was a common story, with Australian soldiers—"country lads, inexperienced in the ways of towns"—often the target of prostitutes when they arrived at Paddington or Victoria stations, but also with a reputation, shared with other colonial forces, as "drunken, rowdy, lustful and even dangerous." Reg was discharged after returning to Australia later that year. According to his *Who's Who* entry, he then studied industrial chemistry at East Sydney Technical College until 1921 and worked as a junior chemist at BHP steelworks in Newcastle, north of Sydney, the following year. In 1924 he was living in Rabaul, on the island of New Britain, in Papua New Guinea, a former German colony that had been declared a colonial territory of Australia by the League of Nations in 1919. The Australian government had established an Expropriation Board in Rabaul to administer the seizure of German assets in the wake of the League declaration, and positions there were made available to returning soldiers. The way of life was rough, as the historian Peter Cahill observes—"New Guinea had always attracted European drifters, but some of the Board's recruits were 'truly unspeakable.' They often coped well with isolated conditions, although many turned to alcohol"—and by 1924 efforts were being made to clean things up. Reg seems to have remained there until early 1927 before returning to Sydney to join Dorman Long at work on the Sydney Harbour Bridge.

Kit Hazzard's early life is a little less mysterious than her husband's, but no gentler. She was born Catherine Stein (pronounced "Steen") in Dunfermline, Scotland, and had travelled to Australia on the *Jervis Bay* in June 1925, following her parents, Janet (known as Jessie) and James Stein, who had made the journey some months earlier on the *Baradine*. It's not clear when Shirley learned that her mother had been born out of wedlock; it was something she never spoke about, but she kept the documentation among her papers. Catherine's birth record includes the names of her mother, Jessie McPherson, "weaver," and father, James Stein, "mechanic," both working in the damask factory in Dunfermline. Her birth is documented there as "Illegitimate," with a note appended that the birth was "re-registered on 15th June 1956," with the child "legitimated by the subsequent marriage of its parents." The formal change in the record was made at Kit's instigation. Kit's Scots background was important for Shirley, although the sense she had of it seems to have been embroidered, probably by Kit, giving a bourgeois gloss to what seems to have been a somewhat grimmer life. In her 2000 oral history interview Shirley gave a polished account:

> My mother's name was Stein, which . . . came over from Denmark and Norway and the East of Scotland. She was born in Dunfermline, the ancient capital of Scotland and kept some good memories . . . I don't know quite what her life was in Dunfermline. But she would sometimes talk of going to school and how sweet her grandmother was to her . . . Her mother was a Macpherson and . . . there were at least three brothers and one daughter who was my grandmother. And the three brothers, this was Scotland, the brothers must be educated. My grandmother had virtually no education, though naturally she read and so on. And my mother spoke very good English with a Scots accent that was quite pleasing. She had some Scots words that she used consciously, a little bit, to smile over: "Don't be such a bubblyjock." But Grandmother really spoke almost—dialect is too much a word—but she spoke a very thick kind of Scots, not quite Lallans. The three brothers all went to university and were marked out as follows: one should be an engineer, one a doctor, one a minister.

The details of Jessie McPherson's early life are sketchy, but what can be discerned from public records gives a rather different picture, with little formal education for any of the McPherson siblings, who mostly worked in the Dunfermline damask factories. The 1901 Scottish census shows Jessie's brothers Duncan and William, age twenty-nine and sixteen, to have been working as damask cloth finisher and apprentice plumber. The third brother, James, had left home, but he can be found in the 1891 census, age seventeen, working a power loom at the damask factory. Jessie's occupation is listed in 1901 as linen weaver, and the young Catherine Stein, age four, is also included in the McPherson family listing, bearing her father's name but living as "grandaur" with her mother and mother's family. The McPherson house, at 56 Grieves Street, was some twenty minutes' walk from where her paternal grandfather, James Stein, was living at Milton Green; however the younger James Stein does not appear in the 1901 census. By 1905 he was living in Glasgow and working as an engine fitter. In October that year he returned to Dunfermline and was married to Jessie by common law declaration, legal in Scotland, before the sheriff, with his father as one of the witnesses, returning sometime after that with his wife and daughter to Glasgow, to the working-class area around Govan. By 1911 Catherine, age fourteen, had left school and was working as a "Tailoress," in spite of having been, according to Shirley, "a clever girl, quick with arithmetic." Kit (then mostly called Kate) completed training in stenography sometime after that, working in Glasgow and also farther to the northwest in Oban as a secretary, and in 1925 she took up a position with Dorman Long on the Sydney Harbour Bridge.

Kit's father was a witness at her marriage to Reg Hazzard in 1927, but little is known of him after that. Shipping records show a James and Jessie Stein sailing to the UK on the *Hobsons Bay* in 1930, and Jessie Stein returning to Sydney on the *Largo Bay* in 1932 from a residence in the same Glasgow street where the Steins had earlier lived. Through the 1930s Jessie Stein lived with the Hazzard family in Willoughby and then for a time in Mosman. Shirley remembered her maternal grandmother as a source of rancour within the family; this led at one point to Reg moving away for some months when the battles grew too fraught. But while Jessie was difficult—there were reports of loud church music imposed on the household every Sunday morning—she was not the sole source of trouble. In fact, all members of the family were antipathetic, and all seemed to have crafted resentful or acrimonious space around themselves. Central to the discord was Kit, who clearly suffered some form of mental illness, not diagnosed or treated until much later. Her behaviour was erratic. "She could be so sensible, humorous, even delightful company," but never reliably so, to the enduring disquiet of her daughters. Shirley returned over and over in her writing and in interviews to her mother's condition and its effect on her childhood. She spoke of an incident when her mother asked her, at age six or seven, to come with her and put their heads into the gas oven and die together. Later, when Valerie mentioned this story during an argument, Kit claimed not to remember it. Shirley described Dora, from *The Transit of Venus*, as "a very mild dose of my mother—a destroyer who sees herself as a perpetual victim," and later described Kit's condition as "manic depressive," a condition now known as bipolar. She also tried to provide some context for her mother's behaviour: "My mother had grown up in a very dour atmosphere, although her grandparents apparently were kind to her, but she had a rather brutal father whom she hated, and that had really ruined her life. She never recovered from that. She was beautiful; she was melodramatic to the point really that became a kind of derangement. And as we grew up, very hard, as her condition intensified, to have around . . . She had a recurrent need for hysteria and would lash out, would sulk, and would let it be known through the house that she had been mortally wounded . . . She knew this about herself, but it took over and was dreadful." In *Transit*, Dora tells Grace and Caro, "I CAN ALWAYS DIE," a weapon that Kit would continue to hurl at her daughters long after they had left home.

An earlier version of Kit can be seen in "Woollahra Road," where Ida's mother is described as "dark and beautiful and very loving," with "strong, impatient opinions, and a quick temper that flared without warning and was felt through the house. Ida was both afraid to be out of her sight and afraid of making her angry." Kit was, moreover, homesick, and ill-adjusted to life in Sydney. In "Woollahra Road," Ida knows that her mother "hated the heat":

She couldn't breathe, she said, until the southerly started to blow in the evening—the cool south wind that reached Sydney from the sea. She couldn't bear to see the garden wither in the drought. One evening, she went out and watered the lawn, although that was prohibited because of the water shortage, and a passerby, seeing her with the hose, had shouted that he would report her to the City Council. Her mother threw down the hose in a fury, and came inside and said she was sick of the drought and the depression. When Marge told her it would get cooler soon, in May, she just shook her head and said she was homesick.

Kit also suffered from Reg's tightness with money; he restricted her access to funds for things like the "nice clothes" she coveted. In return, she shut down his pleasure in music, getting rid of the piano Shirley recalled him playing in her earliest years, and refusing to let Shirley take lessons, dismissing her interest as a childish whim. Nonetheless, Shirley remained sympathetic to her mother's vexations even while she suffered in their wake. She recalled that she was Kit's favourite: "I was very close to her when I was a child, and she loved me very much. More than my sister, which she showed." Kit's preference would continue to be a mixed blessing. Shirley was similarly aware of her father's good qualities, recalling that he was clever, with artistic capacities. She later described him as "a man of abilities, even some qualities, wounded by a forlorn childhood of which he almost never spoke . . . He was witty, articulate, but his grim marriage embittered him and he came to be something of a drinker, given to concealment and untruth. In earlier years, he could be fun to be with." She also recalled being anxious from an early age about his recklessness, his drinking and staying out late, worrying that he would have an accident driving home. "I think I lived on a knife-edge of anxiety, then and for quite a while, always expecting something to go wrong, and justly." She resented ever after not just the "monumental" selfishness of both parents, but also what she felt to be a lack of sympathy from Valerie. The sisters were never close, indeed were temperamentally opposed, and in their antipathies seem to have played out, in part, the tensions and discords of their parents.

Kit had left work at Dorman Long upon her marriage, in April 1927, and Valerie was born in September the following year. Reg remained with the company and prospered. He worked in procurement, sourcing and supplying goods and materials. He was also making professional contacts in the iron and steel industry that proved hugely beneficial to him in the years to come. Shirley recalled a brief period after he had left Dorman Long when things were difficult financially for the family, and her parents kept a shop, but it was not long before Reg took up a position with Australian Iron and Steel, moving quickly ahead in the firm, and soon he was able to improve his family's material circumstances. He had a house built in very desirable Mosman, and in 1937 the family moved to 30 Stanton Road, overlooking Balmoral Beach. The house extended over three floors, with large windows taking in the sweeping views of Middle

Head and North Head, down to where "in the slit of two headlands the Pacific rolled, a blue toy between paws." This house held Shirley's happiest early memories.

It was high, with more space and light than was usual in Sydney houses in those days. The living rooms were on the top floor, so that we could enjoy the sight of sea, sky, headlands. The light itself is a strong memory. From the long upper windows we watched the ocean liners depart for the great world; and not long before the outbreak of the Second World War, saw the flying boat Centaurus arrive from Britain bringing our first experience of "Air Mail". On summer nights we could sometimes see the flames of bushfires on the headland and ash would be carried to us on the wind.

As well as being compelled by the dramatically beautiful outlook of the Stanton Road house and its modern outward orientation, Shirley was also drawn to the local history it embodied. She recalled her parents poring over the deeds of the property and being herself struck by the fact that the previous owner had been a woman. Before Reg's modern construction, the Garden School had stood there. This was an experimental school in the Theosophist tradition, founded by two women and offering a "well-rounded if sometimes unusual education, including classes in Esperanto and eurhythmic dancing in the style of Isadora Duncan." Shirley was also struck by an adjacent property where a derelict house—"old, low-lying, weatherboard . . . countrified, with enfilade of rooms"—spoke to an earlier life of the area, when it had been "outlying and sparsely occupied." Again in this recollection can be heard that sense of distance and dejection she recalled from the Willoughby house, but also the sharpness of her observation of place and the lasting force of her recollection of her own by then far-off childhood. For the rest of her life she made a point of returning to see her old house whenever she was in Sydney.

The sisters now attended Queenwood School in nearby Mandolong Road. They made the short walk each morning from Stanton Road, "setting off down a long flight of cement steps . . . on mornings that were often brilliant but occasionally torrential . . . The steep walk home, in afternoon heat, was laborious." There is a sense of consequential isolation in her memories: "I recall the context as a silence: throughout the walk we rarely saw people or cars . . . I think it was not considered genteel, then, to show yourself on veranda or in garden, unless for some strict purpose—such as gardening itself, which was usually carried on at weekends by men. I don't recall, from my childhood, ever seeing people sitting out in their own garden simply for pleasure." Similarly, she recalled that visitors to the Stanton Road house would remark on the unusual placing of the living rooms upstairs to embrace the view—"rather censoriously, because innovations were a bit disturbing in a society where everything should by preference remain the same." The suffocating gentility of this world, the awkwardness around the sense of "showing oneself" in public, the resistance to change—all exemplified provinciality for her. Queenwood School on the other hand suggested older forms of refinement and sociality, gesturing back to colonial worlds. It had been established in 1925 by three women and named after an English school "situated on the heights of Brighton, overlooking the sea" that had been established by the mother of one of them. One of the Mosman school's founders, Violet Medway, wrote that her aim had been to offer her girls "beautiful surroundings" to promote "a love of the beautiful in nature." This was surely provided by the school's sweeping views, spacious grounds with shaded gardens, terraced, high stone walls at the back, and lawns sloping down at the front. The substantial house, built half a century earlier (Shirley remembered it as rather "shabby"), had balconies and a veranda facing north and east, allowing for both sunshine and tempering sea breezes. The girls wore grey box-pleated uniforms in summer and navy tunics in winter, and in the warmer months, due to wartime rationing, they wore socks, which required only two rather than the four coupons needed for stockings. She remembered a sheep, kept during the war years to keep the grass down "when there were no men to mow the lawns."

Shirley was mostly happy at school. She thought the teaching at Queenwood "enormously good," and had always been a precocious and avid reader, well before beginning formal schooling. She was clever and well liked, according to her old classmates, not athletic nor memorably pretty. She managed mostly to negotiate the social world well enough, although she recalled being lonely, living, as she put it, "much in books, and imagination, where one discovers affinities." There was a difficult period, around the age of eleven, when she became "quite nasty . . . a bully": "I looked around as bullies do for somebody weaker than myself . . . I picked on . . . one girl, which stays with me and from which one can never recover. This cruelty and the damage one can cause to someone else. I have no doubt she hated and feared me and dreaded seeing me and I really was very unpleasant." Looking back, she felt this was a reflection of the miserable situation at home: "I'm not excusing it by saying that I was unhappy, but it's that thing also of youth, which some people never lose, the sense that they're unhappy, they have no imagination for the unhappiness they may be causing other people." Some of the thinking through of such moments in her childhood was undertaken as she reworked memories into fiction. In the mid-1970s she wrote in her notebook:

> A child whose being protests against irrationality or injustice possesses an equilibrium that is more than self-protection. With no language but a cry. It was easier to lie—to Dora, to oneself, to God—than to face more (horror). As they would never give themselves up, however, they found instinctively the (excuse) for their integrity, which was a real if not full one: that Dora was not as other people were. Bring out Caro's growth—her awareness of deterioration in herself, her reflection on her own (cruelty at school) bad impulses, bearing these in mind later, wondering how they have remained, if at all. Bringing herself back—forward—into honesty.

An underlying unhappiness would persist, seeding difficulties in her later love affairs and agonies in her introspective moments. There is a deep vein of melancholy in her writing too, seen in the preponderance of orphans, or changelings, figures set staunchly alone or pairs of siblings preternaturally attentive to one another and ever protective (these idealised siblings provide an inverse footnote to her troubled relations with Valerie). But we might also think of moments of unanchored and irrefutable melancholy that define the isolation of her mature figures, as in this moment from *Transit*:

> Caro entered the house alone, and stood in the hall. There was a mirror on one wall, and she had lately taken to watching herself. Even when looking at a plain wall these days she might be picturing herself, if not with accuracy. Now her likeness was dark with the change from sunlight to shadow, or because her vision dimmed from momentary faintness. At a distance a door opened, and Professor Sefton Thrale called, "Charmian?" And Caroline Bell could not know why that simple fact should bring her close to tears.
>
> It was a state of mind. Or it was because she had stood long ago in a darkened room, a little girl of six years old, and looked in a long mirror cool as water. And, a door opening, had heard her father's voice call "Marian?"—which was her mother's name. That was all there was in it, that was the evocation: a small spasm of memory that could never elucidate itself.

The sense of loss here is defining, resonant, and utterly personal. Whatever consolations Shirley was able later to set in between the calmer, happier self of her maturity and her childhood memories would always, perhaps, be open to ruptures of this kind.

Within a couple of years, the Stanton Road house was sold, almost it seems on a whim, when a passerby admired it and made an offer to Reg, who happened to be in the garden. He immediately accepted, counting as nothing, it seems, that this distinctive house was his family's home, something he and Kit had built together, a measure of how far they had come from Glasgow and Kempsey. Kit was furious, and things between the parents "went downhill from there." The family moved to nearby Beauty Point, another scenic part of Mosman, looking across the bays and inlets of inner Middle Harbour from Fig Tree Point to Sailors Bay. The new house, on Bay Street, Shirley remembered as "also very nice, but it was never like the other." It was "smaller, with camelia trees on the lawn but too many hydrangeas. At the back it was buffalo grass and spiked shrubs, and a rockery hewn from the sandstone slope." From that rockery, as from the house just above, one looked directly down onto the water, with only a strip of bushland leading to the cliff and the walking tracks that wound down to Beauty Point and Quakers Hat Bay. Close by was one of the netted pools that scatter Sydney Harbour, offering swimmers a measure of protection from the sharks that are particularly numerous in Middle Harbour. Shirley developed a close friendship with Patricia Walmsley, then also at Queenwood and living around the corner, and the girls would swim at the Beauty Point pool or in another shark-netted pool at Balmoral Beach, or wander along and around Balmoral, where a little cricket ground was "an arcadian clearing among splendid trees. On the white beach of the adjoining yacht basin, roots of a great old Moreton Bay fig rose up in arcs from the sand." They went to birthday parties at Farmers department store in the city, where the birthday guest was presented with "a frangipani bouquet and a cake," or were taken to Bernard Heinze's youth concerts—"It was always the Overture to Rienzi"—or to the ballet: "I didn't know what to expect. When they didn't speak, I kept waiting for them to say something. Or to sing. It took me half an hour before I reconciled myself to the fact that it was 'a dumbshow' as I put it to myself . . . And something did register but I can't say I thought it was wonderful because of this absence of voices." She recalled these years as a time of "innocence, simplicity," despite the difficulties at home.

The outbreak of war brought changes. On hearing that Britain had declared war on Germany, the conservative Australian prime minister, Robert Menzies, "declared it his melancholy duty to announce that 'as a result, Australia is also at war.'" Shirley remembered the moment clearly—one Friday evening, "standing in the local tobacconist's with my father and sister, I heard over the wireless about Poland and Hitler, and learned that mankind was yet again going to war." At first Australia remained remote from the action, but with the fall of France in 1940, "the war began to have a more tangible impact on life in Sydney," with demonstration air-raid shelters set up in the Sydney Domain, a large, open recreational space on the eastern edge of the city, "as a guide to those who wished to make their own." The bombing of Pearl Harbor in late 1941 brought the immediate reality sharply home, and this was reinforced a few months later by the bombing of Port Moresby in Papua New Guinea in February 1942, and again, eleven days later, by the fall of Singapore, and four days after that by the bombing of Darwin, Australia's northernmost city. Shirley saw the newspaper posters announcing these events on "a blazing hot day" when she was nine years old, "riding on the top of a bus, home from a school outing." In May 1942 three Japanese submarines entered Sydney Harbour, and in June, Japanese submarines shelled both Sydney and the city of Newcastle, a hundred miles to the north. From July to November, the news in Sydney was dominated by accounts of Australian troops struggling to repel the Japanese who were advancing across Papua New Guinea on the Kokoda Trail. The war was very close now: less than a hundred miles separates the mainlands of Australia and Papua New Guinea, and Australia's northernmost inhabited point, Boigu Island, is only three miles (five kilometres) distant.

The sudden proximity of war had immediate consequences for Shirley and Valerie. Queenwood's large-windowed rooms looking down onto the harbour, an advantage in peacetime, meant that by 1942 the school had become particularly vulnerable—"a danger zone." Headmistress Violet Medway made the decision to evacuate the students whose parents wished them to be out of Sydney, and in early February some twenty girls were moved to Glenleigh—a two-story house in the Scottish baronial style near the then village of Penrith in the foothills of the Blue Mountains, an hour or two west of Sydney—for five months. The house sat on more than a hundred acres of land, on a ridge, its grounds sloping down to the Nepean River on one side, while on the other it looked down a wooded slope "across a flat paddock to the road back to Penrith." Lessons were held each day, but there were also domestic chores, sweeping, cooking, washing dishes. There were horses in the paddocks around the house, and the girls had a fair run of freedom catching and riding them, swimming in the river—Shirley "repelled by the saltless water and the ooze"—and rowing in hired boats. They slept in large bedrooms upstairs, with some scoring prized beds outdoors on the balconies.

While other classmates would recall the months at Glenleigh as a time of freedom and adventure, not so Shirley, nor indeed Valerie, who became so consumed by homesickness that she was taken back to Sydney. In *Transit*, Caro reflects on the new isolation brought home to her by the move in from the coast:

> The darkness deepened in silence more desolate for the squawk of a bird they had been shown in illustrations. Incredulous response cracked in Caroline Bell's own throat. Smells of dry ground, of eucalyptus and a small herd of cows gave the sense of time suspended, or slowed to a pace in which her own acceleration must absurdly spin to no purpose. The only tremor in dim foothills was the vapour of a train on its way up to Katoomba. It was insignificance that Dora had taught them to abhor, and if ever there was to be insignificance it was here. The measure of seclusion was that Penrith had become a goal. Caro took herself in her own tender embrace, enclosing all that was left of the known. Caro was inland. She had crouched into the angle formed by the balustrade and one of the high supports of the veranda. Bougainvillea was trained on the uprights; and a round plaque, cool as china, impressed her cheek. There were insects in the thorny vines, there was the scuttle of some animal in the garden below. Dora would have confirmed that death is not the worst.

This is a singular, existential moment: the adolescent Caro—the adolescent Shirley—face-to-face with a landscape at once hostile and inexplicable. Locked into a place and time where there can be no forward movement, no progression, she feels abandoned. If we take Dora in this passage as a placeholder for Kit, we can also see a recognition, even an understanding, of the dire banishment that life in Sydney seemed to have been for Shirley's mother. In an interview, Shirley would recall another similar moment, insisting on the sense of disidentification from provincial Australia, and also from the women's domain at Glenleigh: "Anywhere in the country then was desolate. There was a feeling you might be forgotten there, and at night the silence was the silence of a convent. There was a farm on the property, and I was sent down to get the milking can one evening. The sun was dying, there was the smell of cows, and I thought, Oh, to be more sad than this would be impossible. It was like a scene out of Thomas Hardy. It felt hopeless."

Glenleigh itself brought awareness of a larger world and history. Built in the 1880s for the Scottish shipping magnate and philanthropist James Ewan, who had emigrated to Sydney as a child with his family in 1849, the house and grounds had subsequently been leased to an ostrich farmer and a church mission. In 1940 it had been bought by Dr. Charles Monticone—"Italian, even if on our side"—who had worked as an interpreter for the New South Wales government during the war. The house was beautiful. "For its construction, coloured marbles and blond travertine had spent months at sea, fireplaces and ceilings had been dismantled outside Parma, where the ham and violets came from. And whole pavements of flowered tiles uprooted and rebedded." For Caro, "these rooms enclosed loveliness—something memorable, true as literature. Events might take place, occasions, though not during the blight of their own occupancy. At evening the rooms shone, knowing and tender." Here, finally, she had discovered substance, a transplanted beauty that could begin to inform the "glory" she might have apprehended in the world around her, an alternative to the misery of her life, and the life of her family, to date. The house spoke to her of a larger humanity, not only in its own graceful dimensions but also in the form of the Italian men who were interned as aliens on the property: "At dusk they led in the cows before being themselves led behind the wire." For the first time, it seems, Shirley discovered a world beyond the confines of Mosman and the British Empire: "In Australia, in wartime, Italy and Italians were a theme of derision to us—yet here were these prisoners, recognizable in simple human terms."

In September, the girls and teachers returned to Mandolong Road. War quickly became domestic, ordinary: "Buses were soon painted in swamp colours. Air-raid shelters were constructed, and a boom, useless, across the harbour mouth. You kept a bucket of sand in the kitchen with a view to incendiary bombs." In 1941 the new Labor prime minister, John Curtin, announced a "Turn to America": "Without any inhibitions of any kind, I make it quite clear that Australia looks to America, free of any pangs as to our traditional links or kinship with the United

Kingdom." With U.S. general Douglas MacArthur based in Melbourne from early 1942 as supreme commander of the South-West Pacific Area, including all Australian forces, Australia began the shift away from its British colonial past in recognition of the increasing significance of the United States in the region and the world: "One morning a girl whose father had been in America for Munitions came to school with nibless pens that wrote both red and blue, pencils with lights attached, a machine that would emboss a name—one's own for preference—and pencil sharpeners in clear celluloid . . . spread on the varnished table like flints of an age unborn, or evidence of life on Mars. A judgment on their attractiveness did not arise: their power was conclusive."

The war also brought opportunities for Reg, who was seconded from his position as general sales manager with Australian Iron and Steel to a senior post as comptroller of factory equipment at the Ministry of Munitions. Here too he was successful, providing technical advice on the supply of materials—fuel, ammunition, food—to the Australian forces and to the U.S. forces in Australia and making useful connections. While his career was advancing, Kit was bound to the labour of the home, making do in the face of war's privations, Shirley recalled, "like the other women absolutely ground down in the war. There was no service, no delivery. Huge weights they carried, long days making meals day after day." In this Kit exemplified for her younger daughter a larger complaint: "Oh the dreariness, and the sacrifice of women. How they stood for hours in the queues, everything being seized for the military of course. And my mother bore a lot in that. She was valiant, put up with a great deal because she came from a background of endurance, and nearly everybody in Australia came from a background of endurance then."

For Reg, there were also pleasures and indulgences. In the later stages of the war, when work pressures at the Department of Munitions began to lessen, he took up yachting, mooring his boat below the house in Beauty Point, joining the Middle Harbour Yacht Club, and racing competitively. Shirley recalled that he bought "an old boat with a very high mast, carried a lot of canvas and she was about 25 feet I suppose," which was later replaced by a larger boat, the *Coorayba*, "really quite an impressive yacht, not huge or luxurious, but she was beautiful. And he became Captain Bligh on board those boats; many yachtsmen are like this. This was a side of his personality that was even less attractive than some of the other sides that were then developing." While Valerie, always sportier and more interested in outdoor activities, often joined Reg on board, Shirley loathed it: "It was terrible. To be shouted at and I could never get the sheet on the cleat fast enough and I was always afraid of something going wrong . . . I was in a state of anxiety the whole time I was on board. Also, there's something terrible about these boats. You're out at sea, it's getting dark, and you know there is absolutely no way you can get off, and you won't be home for hours, and it's very uncomfortable, maybe it's raining or the sea is washing over you and cold."

Her inclinations were inward, her pleasures found indoors and away from her family. Reading had long been a source of solace—she had read well from the age of four. In *Greene on Capri* she recalls one of Graham Greene's childhood favourites, *The Viper of Milan*, which had been "on our shelves in my childhood. I have it still: a historical novel of the wars between the dukes of Verona and Milan ('Millun' as we then pronounced it) . . . A calm mingling of charm and horror sustains the reader's attention and dread: on a spring night in a moonlit garden, the fragrant wallflowers are 'the colour of blood just dry.'" There were also "huge old bound volumes of *Chums* that came from my father: issues from 1914 to 1917, their chivalrous and whimsical tone, and their jingoism, steadily challenged by the realities of the Great War." As she grew up, literature became a point of self-definition. Her mother remembered Shirley "very young, sitting on the bottom step reading poetry to me in the kitchen, asking me 'Don't you think that's beautiful?'" Her love of poetry and formidable recollection of it began almost as soon as she began reading and remained a stimulation and consolation throughout her life. She never laboured to memorise poems, feeling instead that she had been born already knowing them, and that they were "learned as if in a renewal rather than a discovery"; at times, she recalled, "I could hardly read the lines for excitement, ecstasy." At school they read "accessible poems by Browning by the time I was eight, and were reading wonderful stories by Conrad ("Youth"!) and novels of Dickens at nine or ten." For Christmas 1945 her friend Pat Walmsley gave her a copy of the *Po-*

*etical Works of Wordsworth*, a weighty gift between fourteen-year-olds. At fifteen she read Baudelaire, *"J'ai plus de souvenirs que si j'avais mille ans,"* and Auden and Byron, who would become lifelong passions. When she left Sydney in 1947, a group of her classmates pooled their pocket money to buy her John Masefield's *Salt-Water Poems and Ballads*. From her teenage years on, she was a committed buyer of books "whenever I got some pocket money . . . And the smell of them!"

In *Greene on Capri*, she also writes of her youthful excitement at reading an essay by Greene on Renaissance drama, an essay, she later learnt, that had been written "on board ship, in a wartime convoy circuitously moving, over weeks, towards West Africa—without reference books or light at night, and between turns at submarine and aircraft watch." She recalls buying the book, "in 1946—smuggling it home to avoid trouble, since it had cost thirty-two shillings of saved pocket money, and the flourish of independence was bound to cause a fuss," followed by "an ecstasy of reading that dazzled the eyes." Buying books involved a trip to the city. She would take the bus from Mosman to Neutral Bay and from there the ferry into Central Sydney, just as Caro does in *Transit*: "There was the gangplank, creak of hawsers, casting off, smell of throttling engines, and the sea slapping at green encrustations on wooden piles. She heard the hooting approach of the city, tram bells, the jarring of a great ignition." Like Caro, Shirley was acutely aware of the solitary agency these journeys lent her, "alone in the city . . . lifting a frayed book in a shop." Many of the books she bought at this stage were anthologies, including the *Best-Known Novels of George Eliot*, and commentaries such as *Impressions of English Literature* and *The Englishman's Country*, and Greene's *British Dramatists*. She bought them from the Grahame Book Company on the corner of Elizabeth Street and Martin Place, its Thoth logo inside the front cover of the books it sold, and from Swains in Pitt Street and the Roycroft Bookshop and Lending Library in Rowe Street, which advertised itself as "A Centre of Literature and Modern Art" and was run by Frances Zabel, who held "artistic Saturday afternoon parties there in the interwar years." Later, during the war and shortly after, when Shirley was visiting these bookstores, the area around Rowe Street was establishing itself as a bohemian destination, a possible source of the cultural and intellectual liveliness she sought. However, Shirley "distrusted" this bohemian world, thinking it was "pretending to be more louche or off-beat than it really was." She returned instead by ferry to the North Shore and the straitened cultural life of Mosman. Reading was also something shared—one of the very few things—with Valerie; Shirley held on to a copy of *Collected English Verse*, with its inscription, "To My Rival at Christmas, 1947, from Valerie."

The war provided inspiration and subject matter for early efforts at writing. Shirley and Valerie enjoyed producing, on an old typewriter, "romances from the war . . . usually about wounded RAF pilots"; "war-time heroes, stiff upper lip and a devoted, pretty girl." Her juvenilia tell of battle, survival, and heroes: straggling Australian soldiers, "red-eyed from want of sleep," "gaunt from foodless days," "tired but undefeated," making their way across "the Owen Stanley steeps" as part of the Kokoda Track Campaign in "The Track"; or of the "single Hurricane, flown by a Battle of Britain pilot" that "led the London Victory Air Parade, June 8th, 1946," one who will "know again this heaven that he flies, / And see these shining clouds, and realise / He was not there alone." There are also the heroic sailors who battle to save their torpedoed ship in "The Nelly Goes Down." In this story the writer's interest seems to be in the unfamiliarity as well as the fraught action of this nautical world, with its Conradian cast, much like the creak of hawsers and the sea slap-ping at green encrustations on Sydney Harbour ferries: "As the craft swung out from the davits, it was almost wrenched from the pulleys by the lashing turbulency of the water. Men jumped into the sea, far from the still-throbbing screws. The water received them and they sank into her salty greyness." Shirley's adolescent interest in war as a primary site of poetic commemoration is understandable, given the times, but there is in these early writings a striking alignment of masculinity with action in the world that seems suggestive, particularly if we compare it with the fraught, feminine isolation of Glenleigh, the sense of banishment and threat of "insignificance," intensified by the fact that it was a domain of women. Writing, even in these mannered if deftly crafted youthful poems (she noted that "compositions for school" were "shaped mostly to please the teacher"), seems from the start to be associated for her with action, agency, a place in the world. Occasionally, though, action might become womanly; in a class pageant around 1943, the girls in Shirley's class were each allocated a historical heroine and charged with composing a poem, to be recited in costume. The high drama of Shirley's poem (committed to memory by a classmate) leads one to wish that some record of her performance had also survived: "A pioneer of the skyways / A heroine of the blue / The stars alone her byways / Against the storms she flew."

From her earliest years, Shirley's deepest instincts had been oriented to the world of literature, and it was in this respect that life in Sydney seemed to her to be most lacking. While the decades she lived there saw much cultural experimentation and debate in Australia, that world was not really accessible or even visible to her. Through the 1930s and 1940s Australian writers were, like writers elsewhere, working through the dramatic ideological divides between right and left, as well as taking up the vexed questions of what a national literature might look like, but these were not questions that crossed over into the Hazzards' world. At school Shirley and Valerie and their classmates read "a handful of Australian poets—muscular (Banjo Paterson), or forlorn (Henry Kendall)"—and the work of Henry Lawson, but, it seems, no other Australians. Shirley would eventually meet the great Christina Stead in Sydney in the 1970s, but did not read, until well after she had left Australia, the extraordinary novels Stead was publishing through the 1930s and 1940s. One wonders what, as an adolescent, she would have made of these works, with their densely poetic accounts of the city of Sydney and the modern world unfolding and of young women and men like those she might observe around her, or, indeed, of Stead's utterly distinctive prose. Shirley's sense of literature at this stage, while passionately pursued, was highly conventional, understood as something produced elsewhere, and endorsed through the same colonial rubrics that had defined and limited the world for her from the beginning. In part this had to do with her family situation, which in many ways precluded access to a more spirited and contemporary cultural life. And up to a point she was aware of this: "In the circles where I was raised, I knew of no one knowledgeable in the visual arts, no one who regularly attended musical performances, and only two adults other than my teachers who spoke without embarrassment of poetry and literature—both of these being women. As far as I can recall, I never heard a man refer to a good or a great book. I knew no one who had mastered, or even studied, another language from choice."

The books she recalled her parents reading were popular and conventional rather than literary—Somerset Maugham, Howard Spring, A. J. Cronin, Warwick Deeping, Louis Bromfield—although Kit loved Kipling "and Swinburne, oddly enough"; these were the only poets "other than Shakespeare—oh yes, and Burns—whose volumes we had in the house." And for the most part, in the Hazzards' middle-class world, culture was a worthy duty rather than a pleasure. "Sundays in Australia were not lively. There was a terrible thing on Sunday afternoon when there was the Sunday dinner in the middle of the day and a terrible feeling after. And my parents . . . would take a little drive somewhere sometimes, and then we would go to the Art Gallery, which oppressed me terribly. It was so gloomy." She was confined, it seems, to the dullest and most constrained circles of her home city.

Shirley Hazzard left Australia in 1947. She would return on a handful of occasions, marvelling that the "elderly and careworn and at the same time unripe" country she remembered had "grown up," becoming at the same time "younger." She would become a champion of Australian writing and would write compellingly of the changes she witnessed in the country's cultural and imaginative capacities, the transformation of its society and politics after the election of the progressive Whitlam government in the early 1970s. She would refine her understanding and judgment of the country and its culture, wondering at its more recent currents while continuing, at times, to misread them. But in her fiction she would only ever return to the Australia of childhood memory, "the genteel suburb of a remote harbour at whose outer escarpments the Pacific surged and pounded," a world benighted and "provincialissimo," governed by "resentful obscurity," but a world, also, that offered memories of morning glory and gardenias, of light, and sea, and "nights of oceanic silence."

## 2.

# A FIRST GLIMPSE OF
# THE UNKNOWN

## 1947-1948

AT WAR'S END, Shirley was sixteen, still at Queenwood and Beauty Point. Her childhood sense of remoteness and isolation had not abated. Indeed, through the war years she had felt doubly confined by geography and by her sense that "this great conflict was taking place elsewhere and that our lives were somehow in a backwater, even in the Pacific War." On VE Day, May 1945, she went with her mother and Valerie into the city by bus to see the celebrations, in "the warm, drunken Australian night." Reg was not with them. He spent the evening celebrating in other company; as she later put it, "suiting himself." For the rest of her life she remembered this night with some bitterness, her father "coming back drunk near dawn. Leaving us with that prevailing memory of the victory, the occasion, his neglect. The pang, yes, for my mother, who had the spirit to take us to town that evening. Not mentioned among us, our father's usual desertion." A few months later, news of the bombing of Hiroshima and Nagasaki, which she caught by radio announcement while dressing for school, felt momentous, although here too was a sense of disconnection from the scale of violence and dislocation: "I hardly know why the moment was immediately understood to be important—anaesthetized as we were by six years of information on mass bombings throughout Europe and in Asia." Perhaps it was proximity added to scale—world war brought closer by this decimation than by the submarines in Sydney Harbour or the bombing of Darwin.

With peace came, finally, the "fortunate, formative" opportunity for escape. Reg was sent by the Australian government on a three-month trip north to Indonesia, which had recently gained independence from the Netherlands, and from there to Malaya and Hong Kong to look into opportunities for developing Australian trade. In 1946, on the back of his report, he was offered and accepted the post of Australian trade commissioner for Hong Kong and commercial counsellor for Canton (he had also been appointed acting Australian consul general in Manila, but this was trumped by the trade position). The Hong Kong posting was significant at this postwar juncture, not simply because of the increasing volume of Australian trade in the region but as a consequence of the colony's role as "an entrepôt for southern China," promising a channel through which access to China could develop. As Australia had no diplomatic representation in Hong Kong, the Office of the Trade Commissioner also provided consular services. This was a decisive step away from Reg's unpromising beginnings, marked by the arrival of diplomatic passports for himself and his family at the start of May. Shirley, still most of a year away from completing high school, had been offered the choice of continuing as a boarder at Queenwood, but she leapt instead at the opportunity to see the world, and the family prepared to move to Hong Kong, selling the Beauty Point house and moving temporarily to Marton Hall, an apartment-hotel close by Reginald's former office, in Margaret Street, Central Sydney. Shirley was greatly excited at having finally left the suburbs, and by this first experience of "city life!"

Towards the end of May 1947, after weeks at sea, they arrived in Japan, at Kure, the port of Hiroshima. They had travelled in a small steamship, the *Taiping*, one of the few vessels permitted to sail to southern Asia at that time, recently returned to its owners, the Australian Oriental Line, after wartime requisition. The *Taiping*, "little, old, durable ship," had departed Sydney Harbour on May 14, stopping only once on its way to Japan for a single afternoon "in a jungle cove of New Guinea" to get water, the passengers remaining on board. As well as the Hazzards, the *Taiping* was carrying wives of Australian officers in the occupation force in Japan, rejoining their husbands after war's separation. The journey, five weeks in all, was comfortable, even luxurious, "with at least two Chinese servants to every passenger." Shirley's first foreign arrival was prefigured by a long-imagined "great departure" from Australia: "The coast of my native land supplied . . . a first glimpse of the unknown: in the lights—seen from a deck on the first night of sailing to the Orient—of Australian seaboard towns that lay beyond the range of my landlocked childhood excursions. Those clustered lights gave the first sensation of passing a barrier; they were at once departure and discovery." The realisation that she was leaving a homeland of which she knew very little might indeed have struck her, but this comment reads more like a later reflection; so many seminal moments from her childhood and youth bear the polish of recollection and reworking. Nonetheless, it is a compelling image of a young woman making her way out into the currents of the world, "the thrill of arriving, in a red dawn, at the top of the world, having started from the bottom," with no sense of trepidation or even, really, of leave-taking. In their place, aspirations gleaned from books and the alacrity of her sixteen years propel her into the larger drama of travel through an awareness of the contemporary world and the ruination of war. This became dramatically apparent once they arrived in Japan: "This vast body of water, and the towns along the edges of the sea; we had never seen that architecture, the Asian masts in the harbours. And then we came into Kure, and it was just full of sunken ships, lopsided, capsized." The family would remain just over a week in Japan; from this fleeting but forceful detour, Hazzard would draw decisive scenes, images, and preoccupations for her two major novels, *The Transit of Venus* and *The Great Fire*.

The Hazzards were met at Kure by an army jeep and driver: "On an unrepaired road, where pedestrians wheeled bicycles in the dusk, they skirted large craters and dipped prudently into small ones. They were breathing dust and, through it, smells of the sea," and they were driven to a launch to cross to Eta Jima, an island in Hiroshima Bay some five miles to the west, just as Aldred Leith would do in *The Great Fire*:

> They were cast off, rocking on a swift sea, breeze rising and salt spray: a night sky starry above marching columns of cloud. The harbour lights drew away, and dim lights of the town. On hills and islands there was an ancient darkness, whose few lamps—of kerosene or tallow—were single, tremulous, yellow: frugal and needful . . . They were settling into the lee of the island, which was coming to meet them on a branch of white lights. At the mole, a uniformed sailor waited with a boat hook. The launch paused, plunged, sidled, drawing raucous breath. There was a paved quay dashed by foam and stained by tides—a stage from which a grandiose stair mounted to a portico of angled columns: a travesty of Venice, owing much to Musso. The naval academy of the defeated had become a hospital for victors.

Australian troops had begun arriving at Kure in early 1946 as part of the British Commonwealth Occupation Force (BCOF) and had primary responsibility for the military occupation of Hiroshima Prefecture until the early 1950s. By 1947 the troops were housed at the former Japanese Naval Academy at Eta Jima in a compound—alongside the living quarters were a hospital, a cafeteria, a library, a cinema—featuring gardens with trees and shrubs that had been carried from Hiroshima by barge, and it was here that the Hazzards were taken. The accommodation was perhaps unprepossessing: "a high narrow room with an army cot, a blanket, and one infirm chair. The little room had an unconvinced Westernism: dimensions, door, window taken on faith by untraveled Japanese draughtsmen." In fact the principal administration block of the compound had been styled after the Britannia Royal Naval College at Dartmouth and built of red bricks shipped from England. Beyond the compound could be seen the terraced hillsides, with tiny holdings tilled by local farmers, and the blue bay, with fishermen hauling nets around and alongside the capsized ships.

Although Shirley would draw much of the detail of the Japanese

setting for *The Great Fire* from the BCOF living quarters, it was the
devastation of the bombed city nearby that impressed her most force-
fully. Hiroshima was a scene to which she would return repeatedly in
her writing life, refining her thinking and her response to its enormity,
moral and material. She noted her family's reaction—"the conventional
one: that the bomb was an inevitable and justified—and even merciful—
outcome of the total war"—but observed that even among "these generally unreflective people there was some uneasiness in discussing it. No one
could explain why the bomb had not, in the first instance at least, been
dropped in an unpopulated place. That was the extent of objection." She
would later reflect, "I didn't even realize the impression it made till later
on when I began to write about those things and I realized that that had
been a crucial point of observation," and comment that this confronta-
tion with war's decimation from the perspective of the victor was for her
"the beginning of a more interesting imagination," of learning to think
"with compassion or imagination of the people who were our enemies,
who had gone to blazes in those two atomic droppings." Struck also by
her own privileged position within the schema of war, she later had *The
Great Fire*'s hero, Aldred Leith, observe the occupying personnel sharing
"intuitively . . . the unease of conquerors: the unseemliness of finding
themselves few miles from Hiroshima."

By 1947, Hiroshima was a destination for visiting Australian civilians,
who were there "in numbers, either individually and informally or on
group tours organized by the military, which advertised the opportunities
for taking pictures of the destruction." The Hazzard family was driven
to the site, again by army jeep—"like riding in state—the jeep being
open, and khaki with authority . . . The officer beside the driver was
pointing out, 'Here there was, apparently there used to be, you wouldn't
credit it now.'" Shirley was struck by the monumentality of the wreck-
age. In *Transit*, Ted Tice's experience of witnessing the scene invokes
an iconic image of the spectacle, captured in one of the most famous
photographs from the time: "In the past, the demolition of a city exposed
contours of the earth. Modern cities do not allow this. The land has been
levelled earlier, to make the city; then the city goes, leaving a blank. In
this case, a river amazed with irrelevant naturalness. A single monument,

defabricated girders of an abolished dome, presided like a vacant cranium or a hollowing out of the great globe itself: Saint Peter's, in some eternal city of nightmare . . . A catastrophe of which no one would ever say, the Will of God." *Transit*'s narrator goes on to observe, "It was now that Ted Tice's life began to alter aspect and direction."

The *Taiping* then sailed again, taking the Hazzards to Hong Kong, where the war, in its immediate aftermath, was "a lingering memory rather than a palpable presence" and the colony recovering from its onslaught. For Shirley, this was a significant and longed-for disembarkation, to have left behind both Sydney and a provincial childhood and arrived at a hub of the world: "At that time one could still travel in China, it was before the change of government but it was during the Civil War. That was an important experience for me. It changed many things in my life . . . The very dramatic, very worldly life there was what I had imagined real life to be. Also, it was going above the equator, now things came right, things like the seasons were in the proper order that was given in literature."

Striking and memorable in its topography, Hong Kong in 1947 was dominated by steep elevations, verdant green in the monsoon season, as described by the Australian expatriate Edward Stokes, who grew up there in the 1950s: "Hong Kong Island was only developed along its harbour front, with expansive hilly areas to the south. Kowloon, while well urbanized in places, straggled into semi-wilds towards a line of sheer peaks. Between them, the harbour was the focus of trade and, indeed, of the spirit of Hong Kong. Farther afield rural areas and an island archipelago were little populated and often superbly beautiful."

The colony of Hong Kong was at the centre of a newly forming world. Edward Stokes echoes Shirley's sentiments in his description of the postwar years as a time of massive transformation across the region:

In China, years of culmination for the civil war. For Hong Kong, a period of repair and resumption amid uncertainty, with the gathering sense of a future in which the Colony would no longer play second fiddle to Shanghai as the great cosmopolitan trading centre of the Far East. Meantime Hong Kong was licking its wounds of occupation and war, restoring its bombarded port and looted city, reconstituting its British institutions, and invigorating its established trading houses. The Chinese population, depleted during years of Pacific War, was engorged by a massive influx of returning "belongers" and refugees from the conflict within China. And the renewal of world travel was bringing, once more, the immemorial wanderers, the adventurers, the singular talents, and the loners to these coasts and cities.

Shirley was later to meet Stokes and to write a foreword to the book he compiled of photographs taken by the pioneering photographer Hedda Morrison during her brief visit to Hong Kong in 1946–1947.

Shirley's recollections of the colony spoke to the society she inhabited. Even from the perspective of a half century's retrospect, she saw the colony as defined by its past. In her essay on Morrison's photographs, she wrote that to arrive at Hong Kong in these years was to find "a colony retouching . . . its pre-war existence: the Royal Navy in the harbour, the garrison in the barracks, the pale shattered villas of the taipans rebuilding on the green and unencumbered Peak ('the Late Victorian hill,' as W. H. Auden characterized it on a visit in 1938)." The reality was of course more complex. The historian Steve Tsang notes that the local population was beginning to identify resolutely now with China rather than Britain, and that people were increasingly critical of the prewar British administration: "too much privilege, snobbery, discrimination, racial prejudice, corruption, and absentee exploitation against the local Chinese," seeing "not only the end of the war and misery but the beginning of a new era, one in which China had become one of the five great powers."

Nonetheless, in 1947, notwithstanding Hong Kong's growing importance as a political hub on the cusp of changes that would become global in subsequent decades, the central areas of the city spoke still to the robust stratification of its colonial past. Edward Stokes again:

The Second World War and the Japanese occupation had left Central District hollowed out, empty and shabby. Yet it was basically intact, its importance unquestioned. Indeed, as the colonial government sought to restore Hong Kong's order, life and economy, Central's governmental, commercial and symbolic purposes were doubly important. Strong contrasts, then as today, ran through the area: between the concerns of government and freewheeling commerce, between ornate buildings and the workaday foreshore, between European and Chinese areas. The physical layout of Central had been well established by the 1870s, reflecting the early division of land—as in many other colonies—into administrative, military and commercial precincts. The demarcation had survived. The European areas were more refined and far less densely occupied than the Chinese quarters such as Western District. Taller buildings, uncluttered streets and pleasing facades marked the European areas. Tenements, shophouses, streets crowded with people, hoardings, signs and festooned washing typified the Chinese ones.

It was to Central that Reg Hazzard moved his family, to a suite of rooms at the Gloucester Hotel, where they were to remain throughout their time in Hong Kong. Securing private accommodation proved in the end too difficult owing to the postwar shortage of housing. The Hazzards' suite gave on to "a wide, covered terrace that curved around two sides," overlooking "the busiest intersection in the city," a crossroads where "the trams of Des Voeux Road joined battle with the traffic of Pedder Street and Chater Road." There were glimpses of a landscape beyond the hotel and its streets: "One could not turn one's head without seeing either the harbour or the green mountain along whose foot the city lies." For the most part, the family's lives were confined to "a very tight-knit little" area "where there was the Hong Kong-Shanghai Bank, the Hong Kong club, the usual shops we went to, post office, the court; all that was crossed and recrossed all the time by the Chinese traffic, foot traffic, and rickshaws." Occasionally Shirley ventured farther afield, where she found the city itself:

Vegetation was as dense on slopes and heights as tenements were below, the tropics terraced around irruptions of pastel villas that climbed into humidity—pale houses ripped open by looters during the Japanese withdrawal, some scaffolded, others already restored.

In the city you might glance up any teeming street of stairs to find jungle at the top in a green overhang. The passageways of steps that led up from Queen's Road were stacked, like shelves, with merchandise—whole walls of print materials in bolts, looped-up cascades of plastic handbags, Niagaras of coloured belts, rafts and wheels of paper flowers for funerals, everything your heart could desire from UNRRA supplies to ivory penknives, table napkins from Swatow, and trays from Amoy stencilled with vermillion dragons. Ascending like an offering, all this branched at last into extravagant green leaf.

The life and liveliness of the scene contrasted with those empty gardens she had passed on the way to school in Sydney, and even the quality of her remembrance in these passages seems to have been animated by the life lived there.

She was at first largely an observer:

If you were sixteen . . . and living in an Eastern city with your parents, your main sensation would probably have been, as mine was, one of enforced detachment, for, while encouraged to observe, you were forbidden to participate. Though constantly enjoined to appreciate your opportunity, you were forbidden to seize it. I spent a great deal of time leaning on the rail of our hotel balcony. If I descended, it was en route to a tennis or tea party, or to decorous dances on board reassuringly British ships of war in the harbour where I learned the difference between a sloop and a destroyer. The Gloucester intersection was my first sight of what is called the real world (that is, the world you imagine to exist rather than the one you actually inhabit), and, having for many months no more profitable occupation, I was set beside it in a way that an invalid is put by a window—to enjoy a spectacle in which he may play no part.

Thus confined, Shirley lived what she called "a colonial life," joining her parents and sister for official functions at Government House and Admiralty House and Flagstaff House or visiting "the other consular people" and notable local families: "There was a man called Eu, who was immensely rich and had built houses around: Eu-cliffe, Eu-ston . . . Grey and immense citadels, English castles. Something that looked rather like Balmoral Castle. He would invite us. Very luxurious places; one was at Repulse Bay. The Kadoories, Armenian by origin, a very cultivated and interesting family, and they had a house out on the New Territories with fishponds and all sorts of marvellous things, and we would go there." It all appealed to Kit, who "loved going out and queening it over people and being rude to Chinese servants."

It was through her parents' social connections that Shirley found a job and a lifeline to the world beyond the Gloucester Hotel. A Royal Navy commander, Claud Barry, one of the many British officers they'd met at cocktail parties, offered her a junior position in a British interservices intelligence unit. The office she joined was tasked with, as one officer put it, "holding the fort until the more permanent and more secret bits and pieces of the intelligence service took their places and started operating." The staff worked closely with French and American units also in the colony to gather information about the progress of the civil war then playing out across the border in mainland China. At that point the unit was housed in the Hong Kong and Shanghai Bank, facing Hong Kong harbour (later the office would move into a military building near Flagstaff House). Built just before the war, the Bank, as it was known, was, at twelve storeys, the highest structure in the colony and the only one with air-conditioning. Shirley shared an office—which looked out to "the green rise immediately outside"—with Hilda Prata, "'Portuguese', as Eurasians often styled themselves then in the colony," with whom she was friendly, although not intimate. She also struck up a friendship with another woman from the office, Rita Xavier, who would later give her name to a compelling character in *The Great Fire*.

More interesting to Shirley were the young RAF officers who were also part of the unit, skilled linguists with expertise in Chinese languages, who worked alongside local Chinese teachers, translators, and administrators. She was struck by the knowledgeability and social ease of these officers, "people who had had what used to be called a classical education, and who displayed this knowledge in the most marvellous, natural way." One of these, not British but an officer in the British Army, was Alexis Vedeniapine, who would feature significantly in her life; two others, Christopher Cooper and Alan Green, also became important friends. Shirley was delighted at the willingness of Cooper and Vedeniapine in particular to recite and discuss poetry, as well as by her own ability to join them in this—"proof," as she reflected later, that she was "not alone in the world," that she was "not dreaming." It seems that Vedeniapine could match Shirley's extraordinary memory for poetry, and it is remarkable that almost as soon as she had left Australia, she had met others with whom she was so profoundly aligned. Chris Cooper later described Shirley as impressively cultivated and precociously well-read, and Alan Green recalled her sociability, lively manner, and "lovely face."

Cooper and Green shared a room in B Mess, the officers' quarters farther up the hill behind the Bank, on Macdonnell Road. These were the first significant friendships that Shirley names in her recollections, and both were sustained in the years after all three had left Hong Kong. She would later draw heavily on their stories in *The Great Fire*, from domestic details of living quarters to the involvement of their fellow officers in the Hong Kong war crimes trials; Alan Green recalled "death sentences being meted out and hangings in Stanley Jail, as well as long prison sentences, regularly reported in the local press." *The Great Fire*'s memorable account of the discovery of a wrecked RAF Halifax bomber is loosely based on Green's experience too. He had been, he would later recall, "interpreter to a three-man Hong Kong–based War Graves Recovery team . . . [who] recovered 31 bodies of British servicemen for re-interment (in British territory) in Sai Wan military cemetery in Hong Kong." The team was accompanied by "a unit of Chiang-Kai Shek's army, ostensibly for 'security'" on a round trip of five thousand miles, "mostly 5–6,000 feet above sea level." Green was just twenty-one at this point, on his first posting in Hong Kong, captivated by the beauty of the landscape and the scale of the experience; the event, when transposed in the novel to Aldred Leith, takes on a gravity that is, perhaps, Shirley's own.

She saw that period in Hong Kong with these "amusing, clever and literary" coworkers as itself an education, and every day "an adventure," even though the work was, for the most part, routine and not well paid. Her office duties involved using coloured flags and crayons to mark on maps first the changing positions of merchant ships in surrounding waters and subsequently the movements of the Chinese Civil War. Although references to her having been a spy seem to be exaggerated, there was nonetheless some aspect of rudimentary intelligence gathering involved. Alan Green recalled that much of her time was spent outside the office, "ostensibly keeping her ear to the ground and picking up gossip in Hong Kong's poshest hotel, the Peninsula," but he doubted that it could have had much real significance. This sense is certainly reflected in the account she provides in a piece she published in the 1970s, "Canton More Far," of being asked to unearth information about a member of the British expatriate community, known to her through her parents' social circles and living in what was then called Canton. After arranging an invitation from his wife to spend the weekend, securing a visa, and making the short and "unexciting" flight, she learnt that the target would not be there after all, and she spent the weekend lying around the house reading *Rebecca*.

The highlight of the excursion seems to have been a mild flirtation with the pilot on the flight out, and the spectacle of Canton as a city that "appeared to sway on its own silt," around it the Pearl River, its "colour closer to that of flowing land than of water." The Shanghai-based writer Paul French wrote after her death that Shirley had told him of another such mission to Shanghai, to deliver a parcel to an Englishman at the Cathay Hotel on the Bund and then collect one to bring back to Hong Kong by return flight, but this second mission seems likely to have been poetic fancy. Her 1948 diary records no mention (it does contain a reference to the Canton trip), and in 2005, when she returned to China for the first time, in a pencilled superscript over her entry for March 15, she has written, "Alec, I left Shanghai this day, 2005, for Hong Kong. In Shanghai, thought of your boyhood. The place is astounding," suggesting that this was in fact her first visit to the city. Alan Green commented that the story is implausible: "I myself was in Shanghai that year [1947] in February/March, and again later, and in a key position in my job at the

Joint Intelligence Bureau in Hong Kong not only to know which personnel visited mainland China and for what specific purpose. I have no recollection that Shirley figured in this or for what assignment." During her time in this office she also undertook her first professional writing assignment, "a two-page report on the Vietnamese emperor, Bao Dai."

These friendships and interests paved the way for Shirley's slow extrication of herself from family life; the family was, in any case, moving increasingly in different directions. Valerie was working as a journalist at the English-language Hong Kong newspaper, *The China Mail*, and throwing herself into social life, tennis parties, visiting nightclubs in Hong Kong and farther afield in Macau and even Shanghai, thrilled, like Shirley, that she was living at one of the great epicentres of the world, with the upheaval of the Chinese Civil War just across the border. This shared perception did not bring the sisters any closer; they were temperamentally divergent from childhood, and their interests were now leading them even further away from each other. In "Sir Cecil's Ride," a story based loosely on her experiences in Hong Kong, Hazzard's protagonist is energized with relief at leaving her family for an outing, particularly relishing escape from "the sister who said, 'You're daft,' sullenly, from bed, as she pulled on her sandals." Reg was creating his own diversions. He had, as yet unsuspected by his family, embarked on an affair with a woman he had met in Sydney, Mary Wycherley, and this would lead to an acrimonious divorce from Kit six years later. Kit, meanwhile, clung, in Shirley's eyes at least, to her younger daughter. She minded very much that Shirley was "onto something altogether else; she felt it and also that I kept quiet about it a lot of the time." Kit was, according to her daughter, "fiendishly jealous and possessive," and Shirley's new life "was taking me away from her. Once when I came back from Kelly and Walsh which was the bookshop in Hong Kong, where I got many books with my tiny salary . . . she said, 'Well I think you have enough books now.' I put that in *Transit*; Dora says it. Poetry was the enemy."

Shirley's surviving library from Hong Kong suggests that she was expanding her reading with a number of poetry anthologies; historical but also modern, poetry in French, and also the recently published translation of Chinese poetry, *Garden of Peonies*—an eclectic collection of personal favourites of the translator Henry H. Hart—along with collections by Rupert Brooke, Hilaire Belloc, and Robert Bridges, a wide-ranging assortment, but leaning toward the conventional. Nonetheless, she was developing and exercising tastes that went beyond those of her parents, turning towards "poetry which was, not exactly alien" to her mother, but the poets Kit admired "struck attitudes that I wasn't interested in. Kipling was patriotic, she liked him also for that, stirring ballads, but I wasn't the stirring ballads type." She was aware of contemporary poets; Auden was "already a rapturous enthusiasm." She also began reading the poetry of Thomas Hardy, galvanised by a shared sense of loss when she first read "After a Journey," in which the poet returns after the death of his wife to the place where they had met: "I understood absolutely what this man was feeling about the death of this love and that life. And how a child, or young adolescent does that . . . I knew what his age must mean to him and what this experience of living with the person he no longer loved and felt such remorse for. And the beauty of his youth gone . . ." Over the years of her life she would return to her early and instant affinity with this poem, struck by a kind of emotional precocity or prescience. Matthew Specktor, who knew her in her later years, recalled during a conversation about Hardy a charged moment when Shirley recited the poem from memory. The words brought her close to tears, and as she spoke, her face changed so completely that she suddenly seemed to become her younger self: "The distance between the poem and its meaning to her, whatever memories it carried, seemed to collapse altogether."

The Hong Kong office was under the charge of Major Richard Kindersley, whom Shirley found "pleasant, mannerly, but weak. He had served valiantly in the war and came from a mildly aristocratic family." In her eyes the real head of the office, "who did all the work and had the grasp of its possibilities," was Alexis Vedeniapine. Shirley wrote many years later to Vedeniapine's son, saying that Alec, as she called him, "was extraordinary, all our staff looked up to him and admired him; I would even say, loved him. He had no shade whatever of self-importance, his authority came from his evident knowledge and his capacity for action." Both Chris Cooper and Alan Green recalled Vedeniapine as principled and impressive, "a war hero, multi-lingual," but also "guide and friend" to them both "in the office, the Mess, and on evening and weekend long hikes round Hong Kong, especially Repulse Bay, Kowloon and the New Territories, and nearby islands." Charming and charismatic, Vedeniapine was also dashingly handsome, and an attraction developed very quickly between him and Shirley, although it was kept quiet from her family and the rest of the office. Although he is clearly the model for Aldred Leith, hero of *The Great Fire*, his background and character differed in substantial ways from the fictional figure.

Alexis Vedeniapine was a White Russian, born in St. Petersburg in 1916. His father, Piotr, was a colonel in the elite Preobrazhensky Regiment, and with the collapse of the Eastern Front in 1917, he returned to do battle against his fellow Russians during the Revolution, which he opposed. In the face of these upheavals, Alexis, then a baby of eighteen months, was taken by his mother, grandmother, and several other family and household members as they fled east. In an oral history recorded in the early 1980s, Vedeniapine recalled that they travelled for just over a year, a family group of some half a dozen, stopping at towns (including Ufa, where they bought property, expecting to stay longer), "hoping that the situation would restore itself and we would go back home and then when it was obvious that it wasn't resolving itself and the revolution was pressing on our heels, we would move a bit further, usually by rail, usually in cattle trucks," until they reached the end of the Trans-Siberian Railway at Vladivostok, where they recalled a family friend now based in Shanghai who was running a paper pulp import business. They exchanged telegrams and moved quickly to Shanghai, where Alexis spent his childhood years.

He grew up with enormous freedom, speaking what he described as a "local Chinese patois," learnt from the servants, which laid the ground for his later facility with several Chinese languages. A favourite pastime was travelling up the Huangpu River on the barges that carried night soil to farms north of the city and then cycling back. In the hot Shanghai summers the family would make their way to a friend's house in the mountains at Moganshan, three days by canal and donkey, and Alexis would go off walking in the mountains in the company of the gardener from the estate. His interest in and openness to local Chinese culture are

evident also in the stories he told later of being invited, as a child observing from the street, into family gatherings and celebrations:

> As a child you have a tremendous advantage, which you realise
> only much later in life, that a child has the entrée to almost any-
> thing . . . for instance a wedding feast going on, you happen to be
> passing by on your pushbike you stop and look, and somebody im-
> mediately comes out and drags you in and feasts you with tit bits
> and so on. Or somebody is working, building a coffin or carving an
> elephant's tusk, you stop and have a look, they will bring you out
> something to eat or invite you in to watch better. And I took full
> advantage of that.

Later, in Hong Kong, he would again display a readiness to connect with
local culture and people outside his official duties and the British colonial
presence, sailing and fishing with local fishermen as well as taking extensive walks around the region.

At thirteen, his parents now concerned that he was enjoying perhaps
too much freedom, Alexis was sent from Shanghai to Woodford, a boarding
school in Essex: "In my family there was tremendous English influence.
I think the English language was the dominant thing, not the English
people but the English language. The house always had the English classics, a great deal was read and talked about, in terms of English Literature. I was brought up with a great love of the English language and
poetry. So it was more or less natural for me to be sent to England." For
the duration of his schooling in England he did not visit his parents nor
they him. His affairs were handled by a guardian, and during the summer holidays he stayed at the Suffolk country house of Sir Newton Stabb,
a former manager of the Hong Kong and Shanghai Bank, a connection
made initially through shared friends of Alexis's parents but fostered over
the years by the warm friendships he developed with the Stabb family
and the large parties of guests they welcomed to the house. The youngest
daughter, Violet, recalled the warm bond that developed between Alexis
and her mother, and that the two would take off on jaunts together—
riding off on a motorbike one night—as well as the enormous freedom

that all the young people enjoyed during those visits. She remembered Alexis's competitive spirit and his kindness and good humour, and the two remained close friends until his death. Photographs from these holidays show Alexis among loose groupings of family and friends, standing casually around motorcars or posing with piano accordions or cameras, on deck chairs or sitting on the grass; a dark, good-looking young man completely at home in this very English world. His own family remained in China; his father had set up an organisation to assist Russian refugees in Shanghai and Peking, eventually separating from Alexis's mother and remarrying. His mother and aunt remained in Shanghai and, because they were stateless, avoided internment when the Japanese occupied the city during the war. They finally fled Shanghai just a few weeks before the city fell to Mao's forces in May 1949.

When Alexis finished school, he went to the Royal Agricultural College at Cirencester and then to work for a farmer at the edge of the Berkshire Downs. At the outbreak of war he applied to join up. That he was technically stateless posed in the end few difficulties—the story he told was that when signing up, he had been asked not his nationality but his religion. He replied, "Russian Orthodox," to which came the response, "I think we'll just put C of E"—and he was called up into the Duke of Cornwall's Light Infantry, training on the south coast of England "to repel an invasion that never came." He remained there some weeks, increasingly frustrated at the endless waiting to be deployed. Eventually he applied for and was accepted into the First Parachute Brigade, Third Battalion, to train as a paratrooper. This unit would take him to Tunisia, Sicily, and eventually the Battle of Arnhem. He received the Military Medal for his part in fighting in Tunisia, and in 1943, in Sicily, he was commissioned in the field. A year later, serving as lieutenant and as the Third Battalion's intelligence officer, he was parachuted into German-occupied Holland to secure bridges near Arnhem. During the terrible battle that ensued, his commanding officer, Lieutenant Colonel Fitch, who was standing next to him, was killed, and Vedeniapine, wounded by shrapnel, nonetheless assumed command of the group, organising the defence of a number of houses, for which he was later awarded the Dutch Bronze Lion medal. After being surrounded by German infantry with machine guns and mortars, he "repeatedly crossed and recrossed the street in spite of machine-gun fire and went from house to house encouraging the defenders," as his medal citation read: "He personally supervised the defence of every attack which was directed at the houses and often directed fire on the enemy as he stood in the open street."

Fighting alongside Vedeniapine and his battalion were numbers of free Dutch, members of the Dutch Resistance, wearing orange armbands. Once it became clear to Vedeniapine that the battle was lost, knowing that while he and his compatriots would be taken prisoner, the Resistance fighters would simply be shot, he urged them to remove their armbands and disappear. In his eyes, this was his great achievement in that battle, and what was recognised in its awarding was his service to the Dutch people. Eventually, owing to his injuries, he surrendered, after having been assisted by a family living nearby. Tragically, he believed for the rest of his life that the man who rescued him had been executed in reprisal. In fact, as his family learnt after his death, the man had escaped. Vedeniapine was sent to a prison hospital at Stalag IX-C. When he eventually returned to England, he underwent intelligence training and was assigned to Hong Kong after a brief appointment in India. Shirley knew the details of this story, and it was clearly part of the appeal of this charismatic man. She included some details in "Sir Cecil's Ride," where the young protagonist Elizabeth recalls in telling detail her lover's experience of war:

> A swatch of flesh was missing from his leg, leaving a purple cavity along the shinbone. Once he had drawn a map for her, like an old soldier, marking in the north bank of the Rhine, a bridge, the Polish brigade, the First Airborne Division. He had told her that the colonel's head was blown off while they stood together, and how he had lain for days untended in an upper bunk in a shed for captive wounded. All this was decently enclosed in war; it was like delivering a string of obscenities as polite conversation. The immense indecency of war he kept, a colossal secret, to himself.

Vedeniapine loved Hong Kong. He found it "fascinating, sad . . . Living at the tail end of an era, and very few felt like recognising

it." He became knowledgeable about its wider and more local
cultures:

> I got to know a great deal about China, the politics of China and
> about sailing and fishing, particularly with the Chinese fishermen
> in junks. That to me was an extremely interesting and fascinating
> thing because obviously I had done a bit of sailing but I knew
> nothing about junks, how they operated, the fact that the rud-
> der acted as a keel and you could wind it up, some of them had
> sideboards instead of a keel, watertight compartments long, long
> before the European ever thought of them. The fish themselves
> were exotic and odd and some of them monstrous. The whole
> thing was profoundly exciting and I loved every minute of it.

His work in the interservices unit was heavily reliant on the skills and
experience of local, "trusted, well-vetted" Cantonese/Hakka translators,
central among whom was Teik Yeo, local but with the rank of British
Army lieutenant, who had deep experience of postwar Hong Kong and
the New Territories, described by Vedeniapine as "a man of great courage who had worked underground and behind the lines, producing intelligence for our benefit."

Vedeniapine recalled with sadness an incident when a visiting British
Army brigadier from an intelligence unit at the War Office—"very knowledgeable, but not knowledgeable enough about the local situation"—
insisted on taking the team, including Vedeniapine and Yeo, to the Hong
Kong Club, where they were, inevitably, refused admittance owing to the
club's policy of not admitting Chinese guests. Vedeniapine was mortified
at this public slighting of his valued colleague. Chris Cooper recalled
Vedeniapine's principled stance on the open secret of gold smuggling in
the colony, and also his outrage at having his investigations shut down
because of the likely involvement of senior Hong Kong officials in the
operation. Cooper later wrote to Shirley that he admired Vedeniapine
"more than anyone else I have met" and outlined his remarkable character: "Vee has almost frighteningly high moral standards, but is more
impatient of stupidity than of moral weakness, which he pities without

really being able to understand it. People called him cynical because of
his fierce hatred of humbug and a certain disillusionment with a world
that fails to come up to his own moral code." Cooper also identified a
crucial point of shared experience between Vedeniapine and Shirley,
the fact that "like himself—you had acquired a high degree of English
(European?) culture in unfavourable surroundings (you in Australia, he
in Shanghai and the Army)," and he noted the way that Vedeniapine,
who sounded for all the world like an educated Englishman, was always
situated in a complex relation with Britain: "He loves England as only
the naturalized foreigner can, but with an East European hardness and
clarity of mind."

Vedeniapine's work was centrally concerned with reporting on the
progress of the civil war in China. His reports relied on a diverse group
of informants to provide an account that went beyond the U.S. and British focus on the Communist and Nationalist leaders Mao Tse-tung and
Chiang Kai-shek, and he argued on the basis of information from his
informants that alternative outcomes to the Chinese Civil War remained
possible. Many years later, Shirley provided a trenchant summary of this
in terms that demonstrate not just the quality of intelligence being gathered (and, it seems, disregarded) but also the intensity of her own engagement with the matter. She wrote to Vedeniapine's son, Peter:

> Crucial reports on conditions of the civil war in China went every
> two weeks to Whitehall—written by Alec and signed by Kinders-
> ley. What was "pitiful" was that—because the USA, in its total
> post-war power, was hell-bent on supporting Chiang-Kai Shek's
> derelict regime, and deluding itself that Mao would not prevail—
> "our" reports of the contrary reality were ignored. Alec's princi-
> pal contribution was to talk secretly with certain credible leaders
> of large factions in China that, if grouped even loosely together,
> would have acted as a brake on Mao's total power when the crunch
> finally came, at the end of 1948. Some of these factional leaders
> had been educated abroad, in Britain, France, or the USA: Li Tsi-
> shen, Tsai Ting-kai. A "faction" in China can be tens of millions
> of people, of whom Mao would have had to be aware. Whitehall

evidently sent our despatches on to Washington. As a result of that, our small office was "investigated" as possibly "Communistic." That APV was Russian would no doubt have been a red rag to their bull. Mao prevailed; and the US went on to pretend for a quarter-century that mainland China did not exist.

It was in this office and under Vedeniapine's influence that Shirley first began to develop the political insight and the doggedness that would in years to come characterize her criticism of, most particularly, the United Nations. Vedeniapine would later recall her impatience at incompetence or spinelessness shown by senior figures in the office: "You used to stamp your feet and swear obscenely about Dick [Kindersley] and Co." The admiration she displays for Vedeniapine's political judgment in her letter to his son indicates its influence on her own developing political views, her sense of the failures of world governments to grasp the reality of local political scenes, even though her own involvement in the intelligence gathering itself was minimal. While Shirley wrote this letter with hindsight and from a position of intellectual maturity, what she was writing was clearly based on her precociously informed understanding of the situation at the time. The views she developed here were informed not simply by Vedeniapine's intricate understanding of local politics but also by his staunchly anti-Communist views and his fierce defence of the importance of individuals and individual acts. In other instances when she responds to the often dramatic events around her, we can see more than residual traces of her early colonial identifications. For instance, in January 1948 she records protests against the British in response to an attempt by the Hong Kong government to evict residents and squatters from the then-infamous Kowloon Walled City, an enclave claimed by China: "Late afternoon news came that the Chinese took reprisals for Kowloon eviction by burning the Connaught in Canton. Tea with Rita. What on earth will the Br. Govt do?"

Shirley and Vedeniapine had first met in early September 1947, on a day marked by "clarity of sky and air," and soon were attached, if not publicly a couple. On New Year's Day 1948 Shirley recorded in her diary, "Half day at work. Alec took me for a walk before lunch . . . we climbed a hillside into a hollow and he took me in his arms and kissed me, differently than before. It was warm and green and blue and peaceful, and we stayed there until lunch time—Happy New Year!" This diary reveals a very different relationship from the grave passion shared by Helen Driscoll and Aldred Leith in *The Great Fire*. The attraction between the young woman and older man is clear, but so too are the vast differences in their experiences and interests. While they shared a passion for poetry, Alec was also deeply connected to the local world of Hong Kong, to active and solitary pursuits, and to his friendships with other men— sailing with Dick Kindersley, taking long walks around Hong Kong and surrounding islands, fishing. These were not worlds Shirley could or would share. At thirty-two, Alec was nearly twice her age, clearly charmed by her intellect and bright beauty but also reluctant to consolidate a flirtation into more public form, in part at least because of the impropriety of their age difference and, no doubt, also with an eye to his position in the office and in the British community in Hong Kong. He raised with Chris Cooper his concern at Shirley's "emotional instability and fretting," indicating his reservations about their compatibility despite being engaged by her "mental abilities." The romantic interludes recorded in her diary are not infrequent, but there was clearly some inconsistency in Alec's responses, some vacillation, and Shirley, consumed by anxiety, longing, and a confusion driven by inexperience with intimacy and affairs of the heart, was shaken by their fleeting nature. This was her first significant emotional connection outside her family, and it perhaps lent an intensity that in turn further constrained Alec's responses to her.

On January 18 she recorded her thrill at the suggestion from an older woman in the office that Alec might be "serious over me," and that he had "said to her I was 'very sweet' and 'thought a lot' . . ." On January 23 they spent the day together walking around Central—"along the waterfront past deserted godowns to a Chinese restaurant, low roofed, dirty, and extremely pleasant"—took a taxi to the Peak (Victoria Peak, or Mount Austin, at eighteen hundred feet the highest hill on Hong Kong Island), then walked back down together. The next day she was "happy past happiness, but with a certain afraid desperation. Oh Alec." After her father's Australia Day cocktail party on January 26, the pair slipped off together to one of the two offices at the Bank building that Alec had retained for interviews, to be "warm . . . and quiet and alone," but a few days later, consumed by desperation because he had forgotten her birthday, she "felt on the verge of tears all afternoon."

All this rings true enough as the feelings of a very young woman embarking on her first romance, but also of one who was, as she later put it, "inexperienced, ignorant, in these matters to a degree unimaginable today." Her behaviour was clearly distressing to Alec, who eventually took her to task: "Alec called me into his office today . . . He shut the door and proceeded to lecture me as though I were his youngest grandchild. Most of what he said was true of course, but some of it was unnecessarily brutal and unfair. He's right of course, and I am 'selfish and self-pitying and ungrateful' but who is the cause anyway? I promised to cheer up, but I was near to tears." Her perspective did not change in the days that followed: "I can't get over yesterday. I've never been as shamed and humiliated; I felt stripped in front of him and now I'm angry for being unable to take the truth, and with him for being so hard on me when he knew I wouldn't 'vindicate myself' without bringing him into it." The intensity—and the pleasure she takes in unfettered emotion in these entries—is adolescent; had been learnt, perhaps, at her mother's knee: "I was hateful today but I'll behave tomorrow. Let me have him to myself again soon, oh please."

It was not all misery. In later years she recalled "Alec and I on foot over the hills from Aberdeen to Hong Kong, a lovely deserted path and prospect, a bird alighted on the path, and we were still. He said, low-voiced, 'I think it's a plover.' Such pleasures were new to me. Respect and curiosity for Nature." At the time, she'd been caught up in feeling. Her diary entries see her circling back again and again to the same points of elation and despair. In February: "Alec was good to me again. Although I don't feel I can go on much more without something more definite. He is unfair. Why should he pick me up and toss me down like this? Please let it be different soon." In March: "(Please, God.) I wish it didn't look so appalling in black and white. I don't feel that he's obliged to return my feeling, but he has made the best of it as it suited him. This is awful. If he doesn't ring this weekend, it's all up, I think," and then three days later, "a lovely day" at the Bank. "He took me in his arms and was suddenly wild-eyed and passionate and 'wicked and loose' . . . I am happy and hopeful." Then in early April, "I'm struggling against this neglected feeling, knowing I have no right to be so, but oh Alec, am I not good enough?" Everything was intensified by the way the relationship was playing out in a very closed and constrained social world and across a very compressed stretch of time—by September, one short year after meeting Alec, she had left Hong Kong. While her inner world was being tormented by the peaks and troughs of adolescent romance, her social life in the privileged contours of colonial Hong Kong continued. It is notable that despite the intensity of her emotions, those around her appeared to have no idea of the romance, although there was some gentle ribbing from coworkers about "the eyes of Ahlex." Outside work hours, she was attending parties, sometimes with her family or with friends from the office, sometimes with Alec, or going to dinners at the Tientsin, or the Parisian Grill, or King Fu, and lunches at the Clubhouse at Deep Water Bay. On days off she would join outings to beaches around the island—spectacular locations, less than an hour's drive from Central, such as Shek O, Repulse Bay, Deep Water Bay, or Stanley—with Alan, Chris, Alec, and others from the office, sometimes conveyed by army jeep. Or she went walking.

Her diary records one memorable outing in August: "Alec rang at 9.30, came at 10.30 took me on an appalling walk to Repulse Bay and seemed irritated that I was worn out. Took me briefly in his arms and said he felt—'very guilty'." She returned to this walk in her story "Sir Cecil's Ride." Things are tense and difficult throughout, the youthful protagonist Elizabeth is poorly prepared—the wrong shoes, no hat or water—and her older lover impatient and unforgiving, impressing upon her the degree to which his excursions around the island were not something he was willing to share with her.

A dark-green Humber that came whirring sedately over the pass hesitated alongside them offering wordless rescue—the car itself raising eyebrows at two Europeans on the roadside in the heat. (This driver was white, coming up from the club at Deep Water Bay.) The second car slipped over the precipice with finality, like an emissary that has offered terms and been rejected: let battle commence.

"You wanted to walk," Constantin said. "And now we're going to walk."

It was not that she wanted to walk but that she wanted to be with him on the Sundays he spent walking. He knew this, and supposed he was challenging her to confess it like a fault. "It is here," he said, and they turned off the Magazine Gap Road onto a shoulder of gravel. There was an opening in scrub, then the path. There was even a lettered sign—three English words set on a tilted post, in soil so dry you might have lifted the pole out of the ground like a dead plant.

His finger prodded a skyline. "Our path goes right across that chain of hills." She could see it zigzag, disappear, flick out again. "And comes down at Repulse Bay." The names were often like this—combative, ballistic: Magazine, Repulse. It was a fact, universal, of colonial life.

This story, published in 1974, tells a rather different story about this relationship from the later, idealised version in *The Great Fire*. The man, Constantin, is, like Alec, a White Russian, a man who had been "stateless in Shanghai," but the focus is on a spiky incompatibility between the pair despite the high feeling between them. There is a harshness in the man's treatment of the young woman that borders on cruelty, and in response the young woman begins to acknowledge the possibility of his limitations of character: "But, now the enterprise was assessable, she did marvel that this had been done to her. If I had collapsed, if there had been an accident . . . With a taste of repugnance, she thought how he had said, 'You wanted to walk.' She hoped he was not going to give her grievances against him; she hoped, if so, she would not nurture them in the local tradition of the everlasting wrong." Nonetheless, it is love that propels the story's protagonist. Youthful Elizabeth marks the striking scenery while

returning, in her mind, to her feelings, unchanged regardless of the coldness being visited on her:

> The bay appeared on the left—or, it would be, west. Warships
> idled—a dove-grey carrier, a cruiser, sloops. All movement there
> came from merchantmen, ferries, junks, and from a Sunday line
> of little yachts racing out past Ly-ee-mun. Between island and
> mainland a concrete sea shone like an aerodrome on which the
> craft sped or stayed. For the yachtsmen it would be green water,
> ruffling the hull and cool-rushing through the fingers you trailed
> over the side. At Ly-ee-mun, where the girl once sailed with
> Freddy from the Secret Service, the water was deepest, and deeply
> blue. Freddy flung overboard the crusts of their sandwiches, say-
> ing, "Bong appitee, fish." She had watched the receding bread
> briefly inflate, almost expecting the snapper or garrupa to rise to
> it, like carp. Freddy was lovable. It was Constantin she loved.

Freddy appears in her diary as Freddy Williams, "a rather Oxfordian,
boring but sweet chap" who took her sailing, an excursion she recorded
as "Such nonsense. Quite sweet but nothing interesting at all. Tiresome."
On her own she seems to have been more predisposed just to walk—up
the Peak, or to Magazine Gap or Black's Link. On the Chinese New Year
holiday, she had made the two-hour trek alone, over to Repulse Bay on
the southern side of the island and back, reciting Keats's sonnet about
"lovely Laura" out loud as she went: "Made my mind a blank and just
walked and walked, mile after mile. My head felt much better and clear
for the first time in weeks." She later recorded in her diary a long walk
through Pok Fu Lam along Conduit Road to the west. And she recorded
more intellectual outings: "Went to lecture by Edmund Blunden at Government House, Light in Poetry; Three poets who died in the war: Keith
Douglas, Alun Lewis, Sidney Keyes (Chris knew about them)," and book
buying: "Alec had to have lunch in town and we walked down and had
an ice at Dairy Farm . . . Went to Kowloon and bought 'Fathers and Sons'
and Freud." She began reading Russian novels, drawn to them by their
association with Alec; her copy of *War and Peace* is inscribed "Bought

at Kelly & Walsh on Saturday 20 March 1948, Hong Kong. First Day of Spring."

Many years later she recalled meeting "at a gathering, a handsome, reserved, and pleasant person, still young, who was introduced as Miss Scott-Moncrieff," of whom "it was at once explained, in her presence, that she was—the niece, was it, or a cousin?—of the great translator" of Proust, adding, "She was one of the few women to hold, then, a distinguished, and beneficent, position in the colony: and it occurred to me that she possibly wearied of her reflected glory." Just as Shirley's political understanding was developing as a consequence of her proximity to intelligence work and by virtue of simply being present while an event of the magnitude of the Chinese Civil War proceeded across the border, so too the boundaries of her cultural world were being extended by these associations. Alec was central to this, with his affinity for poetry, but also important was her friendship with Chris Cooper. Their correspondence over the next few crucial years, he in England, she in New Zealand and then New York, would open up for her a world of contemporary high culture—music, ballet, art—that was as yet only nascent. And this would be crucial to her maturity, as important as the experience of romantic love: a way of defining herself, finding imaginative connection and solace beyond the remit of her family.

Her world was about to change again, dramatically. In late August, Valerie was diagnosed with tuberculosis, probably contracted at work, although it is just as likely that her daily life in the city would have been responsible. The disease was, as Shirley later put it, "rife" in Hong Kong at the time, with close to two thousand deaths that year alone. In the postwar years, it had become the highest cause of death in the colony, exacerbated by unstable living conditions, poor nutrition, and overcrowding. Ironically, in her capacity as a journalist, Valerie had written about the situation in *The China Mail*, criticizing the irresponsibility of the colonial government for the inadequacy of their response. Treatment options were limited—long periods of rest in a sanatorium and "collapse therapy" by removing ribs—and fatalities common. Streptomycin had just begun to be marketed in the United States, and Valerie's doctor advised Reg to send for it. The drug most likely saved Valerie's life and would certainly have accelerated her recovery, which nonetheless took a couple of years. The doctors were not yet familiar with administering such a new drug, though, and it seems she was given a much higher dose than needed, resulting in terrible side effects, including short-term loss of sight and hearing and long-term vertigo.

Plans were made for Shirley, Kit, and Valerie to return to Sydney immediately; Reg was to remain in Hong Kong a couple more months to await the arrival of his successor. Shirley was devastated at the prospect of leaving Alec, and her diary records a new anguish alongside the daily to-and-fro of elation and despair. She makes no mention of Valerie's condition or the family mood, which may indicate that she only became aware of the seriousness of the illness and the side effects of the medication later on, but even so, it speaks to the dire rifts now firmly established within the family. Shirley's attentions were hopelessly and exclusively attuned to the matter of love: "The last days in Hong Kong were scarcely credible to me. The day before our departure, the local press came to photograph us—parents, sister, myself . . . I look shell-shocked." The photograph, a formal record of an official moment, the family of the Australian trade commissioner departing, certainly speaks to a deep sense of disconnection. Each member of the family is looking in a different direction, with nothing drawing them together. Valerie looks a little older than her twenty years, but Shirley seems even younger than seventeen. Her hair is tied back simply, and her frock with matching cropped jacket is prim, its style suggesting an earlier era or a timeless immaturity. Most of all, she seems somehow disconnected from her body, unaware of or unconcerned about her physical being, anticipating perhaps Helen Driscoll from *The Great Fire*, who was, in the eyes of the Australian Brian Talbot, "the least physical woman he'd ever set eyes on. But he knew that such a girl harboured feelings, you had to stay clear."

The relationship with Alec was never consummated. On their last evening together Shirley offered to have sex, but he said no. She wrote to his son half a century later that the matter "trembled in the balance; but he—aware that I would do that mainly to please him, and that I was apprehensive—said, 'Let us go away from here' (where we were alone), 'Because otherwise I might do what I'd regret.' This was noble, truly." This account, from 2005, was written after she had covered the same material in *The Great Fire*. In the novel, Helen's offer—innocent, ignorant—also evokes the language and sexual ethos of an earlier time: "'Do you want me?' Words she'd read somewhere, with their outworn, sacrificial context. 'It would not be like that, it would be shared.'" There is no reference to such a conversation in her diary; only a series of chaste embraces across the course of the year: "We sat on the desk in the dark and made love to one another in a way that was at once childish and passionate, unpremeditated and imagined." At several junctures and in different registers, both in fiction and in letters or diaries, or recollected in interviews, she wrote of these events through the lens of her sense of the burdens of youthful isolation and the risks of moving into more adult worlds. In all these accounts, the sexual act remains outside the sweep of the story. In the leaps and gaps between them, we can begin to trace the lineation of a writer in the process of making herself.

# 3.

# SEA-GIRT, SOUTHERLY, SUNDERED

## 1948-1951

THE SENSE OF expectancy that had marked Shirley's departure from Australia in early 1947 was matched by the heavy gloom of her return late the following year. The protracted outward journey in the *Taipan* to Hong Kong via New Guinea and Japan was drastically counterweighted by the long flight back, in a converted wartime Dakota, leaving on the afternoon of September 18, with stops first in Manila, then Darwin, then Charleville in the remote Queensland outback, then flying on to Sydney across the "endless sorrow of the Australian desert." Shirley's diary does not record her feelings, but years later she wrote to Alec's son, Peter, of the "limbo of suffering" she endured alongside her mother, "in her self-directed drama," and sister, "stoical and silent." Helen Driscoll's letter to Aldred Leith gives a sense of the forlorn journey:

We reached Manila in the night, which was spent at an hotel—a good hotel that had a notice that "Firearms must be checked." My grief, numbness. Again, at morning, the interminable flight, the empty sky going on and on . . . Again, in darkness, reached Darwin—which, having been bombed in the war, would seem a shanty town were it not for the military installations. At the airport, people were kind, seeming to understand that some terrible experience was being endured. We were given a huge meal of steak and eggs, inedible.

Her early notes for this part of the novel, from 1987, are sharper, the experience more abject: "Dakota comes down at Darwin, at Charleville. Heat. Bunks with used, rough hot blankets in corrugated shed ('She's hot, she's made of galvo.') Fried eggs and hard steaks, fried bread. A whitish slicing of lettuce, browning from the knife. A ring of tomato like the washer from a drain (tap). The plane's loo ('dunny') like an outhouse in a back yard. In a scrap of mirror she sees herself, changed, a new face, stark, appalled, wretched." The onward journey, crossing the desert, took many hours. "One might have been crossing Mars. How to describe, except to say that an occasional sight, after endless uninhabited miles, of a solitary house there below tore more than ever at imagination. After the desert, there were more stops, more steaks, and the arrival."

The Hazzard women eventually touched down in Sydney on the evening of September 20, some fifty hours after their departure from Kai Tak. They returned to Marton Hall, where they had stayed prior to their departure from Sydney the previous year, but any earlier excitement was now extinguished by new unhappiness. The arrival itself on a cool and windy spring evening warrants no mention in Shirley's diary, just a terse note giving the landing time as six p.m. Helen Driscoll writes in a letter to Aldred Leith: "Today I walked out in the city, registering nothing, thinking about you. I have no tears, as if beyond them." Shirley's diary has no entry for the next two days; then, on September 23, we read that she "posted Alec a letter, oh Alec." Fifty years later, on September 18, the date she had departed Hong Kong, she added a gloss, a pencilled note: "This was the end of life for me," and then, on the entry for the arrival at Sydney two days later, "The terrible trip to Australia. All the emptiness. A dying, a death." On the empty date of September 21, she added, in this sorrowing glance back across the years, "Dreadful days. And the beginning of dreadful years," and at the diary reference to her letter to Alec, she quotes William Morris:

*Weep, O Love, the days that flit*
*Now while I can feel thy breath*
*Then may I remember it*
*Sad and old and near my death.*

The eloquence of remembrance, charged in 2005 with a new sense of mortality, invokes the sombre tone of *The Great Fire*. In 1948, however, Shirley was drastically more reticent. The reserve in her diary would likely have been matched by coolness in the company of her mother and sister. The mood at Marton Hall, with the three grieving, resentful, ill, or concerned women holed up together can be readily imagined. Shirley later claimed that her mother was "vigilant" in these days, "lest I should retain contact with Alec in Hong Kong." Yet there seems to have been some reworking of the facts after the event. Certainly there is no record of Kit's "vigilance" in Shirley's contemporary accounts in letters or diaries—in fact no mention at all of her parents' response to or knowledge of this as any kind of formal relationship. Valerie reportedly claimed not to know anything about it, and Alan Green and Chris Cooper were also in the dark until Shirley wrote them of her engagement to Alec in early 1950. Moreover, it is clear from Alec's letters to Shirley that as late as October 1949 she was yet to disclose the relationship to her parents.

More pressing for Kit than Shirley's involvement in a clandestine romance at this point would certainly have been her ongoing concerns around Valerie's health. Shortly after their arrival in Sydney, Valerie was taken to a sanatorium, the Lisieux Private Hospital at Wentworth Falls in the Blue Mountains, two hours west of Sydney, past Glenleigh, where the sisters had stayed in 1942, to complete her cure. The three women made the journey by train. The spectacular scenery of the train ride up to Wentworth Falls—with dramatic sheer sandstone drops, high ranges, and valleys forested with eucalypts, sassafras, tree ferns, and the spring flowering of wattle—went unheeded, the contrast of this wilderness with Hong Kong's urban liveliness no doubt overwhelming. And the parting, once Valerie was admitted at the Lisieux, was "desolate." Shirley recalled that Valerie, "who was always very stoical, very careful and guarding her emotions," and Kit, notably less stoical but more often than not completely self-absorbed, "wept in each other's arms when we left."

While Shirley acknowledged the weight of this parting for her mother and sister, and the medical concerns that occasioned it, nonetheless she remained preoccupied with her own sufferings: "I remember walking out of there, quite a walk to catch the train; [going] down the Blue Mountains bit by bit. And feeling, 'What desolation.' This road, this dirt road, this dust road, and nothing at the end of it. Terrible moments, really . . . My mother wept hysterically all the way down in the train, with my arms round her. Where, looking back, I should have had somebody's arms around me." The double movement of sympathy and withdrawal here speaks again to Shirley's youth and her emotional fragility. While she withholds sympathy, as a still-dependent younger daughter with no obvious alternative course of action, she continues to give in to her mother's emotional demands but resents the lack of consideration or support for her own secret loss. The blankness between the sisters, attested to in Shirley's silence at the time as well as in the cursory attention she gives to Valerie's condition in later accounts, is perhaps understandable in the context of this fractured family. It is also worth noting the similarity between this account of desolation in the mountains and Shirley's lament about the remoteness of Glenleigh a few years earlier. Her descriptions of both experiences ring true; what is striking, looking back, is the way that announcement of her despair swamps any recognition of the seriousness of her sister's illness or her mother's anxiety.

She strikes a very different tone in her single surviving letter from this period, written to Chris Cooper a few weeks before she left Hong Kong. Cooper had returned to England, and Shirley makes light of the family situation, the illness, the return to Sydney, explaining that Valerie has "very slight tuberculosis and has to go home for treatment. We were going back in five months anyway, and Dad thinks we would all be safer to go straight away." She presents the family as being of one mind about the return, and she is also sanguine about her prospects:

My mother and Valerie are going up to our place in the country and I'm going to . . . set about finding myself an occupation. You

see, I've besought my people to let me go straight to England—
said I'd go down the mines if necessary and so on—and they say
not for another eighteen months which is reasonable as I shan't be
eighteen for another four or five months. So the main thing is to
get myself training to fit me to go and earn my own living in England in eighteen months. I'm afraid it will have to be the usual
shorthand-'n-typing course, but there it is.

There is a substantial and revealing gulf between the versions she
provides of important events at different times in her life, from light
diffidence here to the anguish that would come increasingly to flood this
story. There was of course no "place in the country," and Valerie was seriously ill. Shirley's tone in this letter suggests a desire to present a buoyant
face to her friends, and to propose connections, however fanciful, with
what she imagined of their English lives. Downplaying the significance
of Valerie's illness suggests a desire to seal herself off from her family, to
limit her exposure to their misfortunes and demands. And in her letters
she would continue to underplay her sister's condition over the coming
months, barely responding to repeated questions from her friends about
Valerie's recovery. She would, nonetheless, draw on that experience in
*The Great Fire*, where several of the characters contract tuberculosis and
one of them explains that he is being treated with "a new drug from
America, which plays merry hell. Side effects, they say."

Both Alan and Chris, now returned to England, were preparing for
Oxford and, later, for the UK Foreign Office examination, and Shirley
envisaged joining them as soon as she could. In early August, Chris wrote,
"So you are still hell-bent on reaching the Old Country? And Oxford too,
the Mother of Learning! Well, I may even nod to you if we meet in the
High." Alan was sending money and asking her to post him in return
"some tea and tinned butter . . . I hope . . . that you will be able to practice
a little of this much vaunted Anglo-Australian friendship and help bind
the ties of Empire. In short, save me from starvation," while Chris joked
about her misery at returning to Sydney: "How happy you must be to be
back in dear old Australia, the land of the 30-hour week! I wonder if the
reality is actually as bad as your imagination painted it; I doubt if it can

be." Both advised her to begin preparing in earnest if she was serious
about Oxford: "Between now and you leaving for England . . . you ought
to be working furiously and at an inspired rate, on book work in preparation for whatever course you intend to take," reminding her "you had
better apply early, because [the universities] are terribly full."

Shirley had assumed that on returning to Sydney, she would be able
to resume her education, her enthusiasm no doubt piqued by new friendships and experiences in Hong Kong. However, in Australia in 1949 it was
still not common for young women, no matter how capable or qualified,
to attend university, and she was not qualified, having left school before
completing her final year. Instead of encouraging any intellectual ambi-
tions, Kit and Reg, who had made their way in the world without formal
study or qualifications, wanted to set their daughters up, as Shirley put
it, to "get a trade and earn our living." Next door to the Marton Hall
apartments, in the Kembla Building, was Miss Hale's Secretarial College,
and it was decided that this rather than university would do for Shirley.
Despite her apparent acquiescence in letters to Chris and Alan, Shirley
later claimed to have been devastated at the suggestion, setting it down
to parental malice: it was "the last straw" and "the Blacking Factory." It
is likely, however, that more practical considerations were in play, as Reg
Hazzard's next posting, as trade commissioner to New Zealand, was to
commence six months later, in March 1949, just as the new Australian
university year would be starting. Miss Hale's made sense in terms of
timing and accessibility, and it would also equip Shirley with the capacity
to earn her living, something she had already indicated would be useful.
In retrospect, however, like so much that took place at this time, it came
to seem the consequence of malign forces, compounding the crushing
sadness of separation from Alec.

Half a century later, Shirley wrote of this period: "Misery, foreboding, a life sentence . . . In this cruel time I wanted to die. Looking back,
I wonder that I didn't. The worst, beyond worst, of all was of course the
lack of letters." Again, there is some extravagance in the recollection.
She had in fact received two letters from Alec that first month in Sydney,
the first arriving only a week after she did. In the letters Alec is pragmatic and makes light of her trials: "As for the shorthand—it's your own

fault. However, if it gets you a job in the Australian Legation in London, it's worth it." Just as Shirley adopted a flip and ironic tone writing to Alan and Chris, so too Alec, while fond, was also laconic and humorous: "Dear Shirley, I got your letter yesterday and was, strangely enough, delighted. I need not tell you but will, as I know how young you are, that since you went away I have had moments of sadness that annoyed me very much. However I expect I shall be able to push this sort of weakness down into the less frequented byways of my soul." While Shirley's letters to him have not survived, it appears she had adopted a similar tone. Alec continued: "You make little of what must have been the most frightening few days in your life. Your poor mum must have been in a helluva state, particularly in Charlieville [*sic*]."

Shirley kept Alec's letters to her from this time; they mark the gulfs that were opening between them. In November 1948, two months after her departure for Australia, he also left Hong Kong, returning to England for a month of leave, which he spent in the country—"doing what comes naturally, at least to me. I amused children, annoyed cows and trod the air"—before being posted in February 1949 to Germany, to the British Army of the Rhine (BAOR). His role there was to interrogate and debrief Russian defectors apprehended while trying to cross into the NATO zone, work he found dispiriting, "dull and very disappointing. Most came over to our side because they were desperate, not ideological. Four years after the war, they hadn't been home." He found the larger BAOR project "futile" and "aimless" in the face of the larger, still intractable political situation: "I live in considerable comfort and hate it. I have developed a passionate longing for civilian life but regret to say that I can't do much towards achieving my ambition." In May, Alan Green wrote Shirley that he had heard from Alec "from an army of occupation in Germany, complaining bitterly how 'the role of conqueror sits heavily upon him.'" Alec's despair was more substantial than a simple response to the circumstances of those displaced soldiers. It was part of a larger anxiety that preoccupied him in the face of what he saw to be the inadequate NATO response to the USSR—more substantially, to the increasing threat of further war. This Cold War anxiety would continue to build in the course of the year that followed, with significant consequences not only for his own health and spirits but also, inevitably, for his relationship with Shirley.

Alec's letters over the next months of 1949, as the northern spring moved into summer, saw his thoughts turn increasingly to farming. In April he reflected on the "villages and country lanes" of Germany, where he felt "for a time . . . that the whole world was at peace and that cherry trees blossomed not only in every cottage garden but even in the hearts of men. If for nothing else, I shall be always grateful to the Germans for lining their lanes with fruit trees and for living in half-timbered red-roofed houses with snowy lace curtains and flowers in every window." He was considering taking an Intelligence position in Canada, which he thought offered "a slightly better opportunity for the aspiring peasant" than England. A month later he was still thinking through possibilities: "Nothing is settled about anything. I am casting about for ways and means of getting out of the Army and for something to get into once I am out. My main objective is still the land but hope in that direction is very small." By June, he had committed: "I have been offered a job as farm-manager and partner of a very good farm and on the strength of this have handed in my resignation . . . This decision took some taking as it means that for the first time in ten years I am to stand on my own feet and earn my bread. The job is a good one in that I shall be in charge of the place without restrictions." The partnership was with an old friend whose farm he had worked before the war. Alec was planning to move in September to Hemel Hempstead, about forty miles from London, in Hertfordshire, under an arrangement that would see him run the farm, with a house provided, a salary of eight pounds a week, and, once he was able to raise funds to buy a share in the property, a percentage of the profits. This did not happen for some time. What money he had from his family was committed to his mother and aunt, who were waiting in the Philippines for U.S. visas, having had to abandon most of their remaining capital on fleeing Shanghai earlier in 1949, ahead of the city's falling to Mao's forces. Their application to come to the UK as refugees had been rejected, despite Alec's wartime service, and this rankled. His concern about their welfare, compounded by the grinding daily toil on the farm as he tried to accrue funds to buy a part-share in it, would take a heavy toll on him in the months that followed. He was aware from the start that the enterprise would take some years to secure, and he made sure that Shirley understood this too, whatever her reluctance to take on board the practical considerations.

By now Shirley had completed her time at Miss Hale's and moved with her parents to New Zealand, where her father had taken up his trade commissioner posting. She felt this to be yet another "last straw," "a few inches further on the map from where I longed to be." Valerie remained at the Lisieux, with plans for her to join them once the cure had been completed. Shirley, Reg, and Kit sailed in early March 1949 on the *Wanganella*, a "handsome" ship, its luxurious appointments no doubt allowing the Hazzards to reimagine themselves, for the few days it took to cross the Tasman Sea, to be back in the confined privilege of their Hong Kong lives. Their arrival on March 14 in "farthest," far-flung Wellington would likely have confirmed Shirley's dire preconceptions about further banishment, despite the striking scenery of the Cook Strait, which separates New Zealand's two main islands. The cliffs on both sides of the strait, where the Tasman Sea meets the southern Pacific Ocean, hold a dramatic but also somewhat forbidding beauty, and Shirley, still aggrieved and self-absorbed, was in no mood to respond to its unlearned aesthetic. Passage through the strait is often rough, with numerous small offshore islands and submerged rocks creating turbulence, and tricky wind patterns and tidal flows making for choppy seas more often than not. As the *Wanganella* made its way through in the final approach to Wellington, the irregular and sparsely populated coastline would have seemed desolate to a young woman familiar with intensely urban Hong Kong and hankering for a gentler England familiar from literature. In Wellington, she was struck by "the brilliant airy cleanliness," an "immediate provincialism in the streets. Intense innocent blueness and whiteness of light," and the scent from the hills. Later, she would develop a sense of the particular beauty of these islands, describing in *The Great Fire* the weather and topography of Wellington with startling precision:

Air of an uninhabited freshness rushed at crescents and inclines with its southern chill. There was, too, a southward vision of grey sea, and of the distant gorse-grown hills that shaped the bay. Across the strait, and beyond the flung skein of farther land, the matter of consequence was the South Pole, to whose white magnet the nation was irresistibly drawn, even while directing its yearnings elsewhere.

The Hazzards moved first to the St. George Hotel in downtown Wellington, close to Reg's office at the Australian Trade Commission and close also to the British High Commission, where Shirley found work as a stenographer. "And everything was quiet. I remember once . . . in the St George Hotel, we had a living room on the corner, a sort of bay window, probably the fourth floor, about as high as you got in Wellington, and my mother said to me, Come to the window. This is the main crossroads of the capital of New Zealand at 6pm. Do you see one person? And it was true, not a car, not a nothing." Later, when the Hazzards had moved into their own house, Shirley missed life at the St. George, as Helen Driscoll does, while still disparaging the provincial silence: "In a way I regret the hotel—having got used to it, and having had my own isolated room there rather than being exposed to a household. I got used to its curry-coloured curtains, I suppose, and its mustard carpets, and to the kindly help who brought mutton and potatoes and blancmange, in the dining room, and extra blankets to one's bed. To the trams rattling past the central crossroad, and the total silence that fell at 6pm each evening, except Fridays, when shops are open late . . ."

Shirley's social world was very much trammelled by the social position of her parents and her father's professional appointment, even more than in Sydney or Hong Kong. When she commented decades later that Wellington "just was as dull as it possibly could be," she was really making the point that "I was so far from everything I wanted to be close to . . . I was just immured there." As in Hong Kong, her social life largely consisted of accompanying her parents to formal events written up in the local social pages.

There was such gentility, there was such propriety, and not that I wanted to fling over any traces, and there weren't places to fling over the traces, but there was no expansion at all . . . Again there were parties . . . and the Prime Minister and this and that . . . Everything was extremely proper . . . And they were nice. As long as people absolutely toed the line, they were nice, and I learned there that this also is a drawback because you can't really dislike them. You have no outlet, no real grounds for complaint except that you shouldn't be there.

A week or so after they arrived, Shirley accompanied her parents to a reception at the Australian high commissioner's residence in Khandallah; her costume—"a pale blue frock with silver platform sandals and pink and blue flowers in her hair"—and those of her mother and of the wife of the high commissioner were detailed in a piece in the women's pages of the Wellington press, signalling the kind of decorous and constraining sociality she lamented. While there were more cosmopolitan possibilities in Wellington at the time, just as there had been in Sydney, Shirley did not have the means, nor perhaps the inclination, to pursue them.

In mid-1949 the family moved to 29 Thompson Street, in the suburb of Mount Cook, close to the centre of Wellington and on the slopes of a hill called Pukeahu. The streets here rise sharply upward, giving the Hazzards' new house views out over the compact city and picturesque harbour. Reg arranged the purchase of the house for the Australian government and oversaw its renovation. It had been built in the 1920s, of wood—"nearly every house then in Wellington was, because of earthquakes which were shimmering always. Some tremors every few days." In *The Great Fire*, Helen Driscoll describes a house that sounds like the one in Thompson Street:

> . . . on a height, with mist in the mornings. I cannot say that anything is like Japan, though it may sound so. The rooms are fairly large, fairly sunless; elderly. A garden is shaded by trees, chiefly beech, and enclosed against the incessant wind by a hedge of yews. No flowerbeds, but many plants and bushes of the cool-flowering kind—fuchsia, hydrangea. Camellias have bloomed

since we came, in streaks of colours such as I never saw. There are
ferns and bunchy groves where violets and lily of the valley will
appear when September comes round . . . On the sheltered north,
where some sun arrives, a wisteria, bare except for greenery, is
strangling a derelict arbour.

Suburban garden beds and the listing of plants recall "Woollahra Road";
the recollection of topography and microclimate, the smell and feel of
the air, is remarkable. Even beyond this house and garden, the city of
Wellington is immediately present in *The Great Fire*'s descriptions. Hazzard wrote these scenes entirely from memory, a dense folding of this
unhappy time into lyrical prose: "Weatherboard houses stood back from
footpaths, insubstantial. Roofs of corrugated iron had been painted dark
red. Behind low palings or a hedge of box, gardens laid out like military
grids were unlikely to grow riotous with the seasons."

The novel is also eloquent about Wellington's provinciality, or about
Shirley's experience of provinciality, which is not to suggest that it provides a factual or accurate portrait of the city. Rather, this depiction of a
devastating and wounding sense of isolation, even abandonment, makes
sense above all internally. As she reworked her memories for *The Great
Fire*, she wrote of "an adult sadness, the sense of all things passing away,"
and drafted lines where Helen Driscoll takes photographs of the city with
her Brownie box camera, "Her attempt to make the place transitory."
We can hear the deep loneliness—and not just of the young woman—
behind these perspectives on the city, as when Elinor Fry observes to
Helen Driscoll that "this is not a venturesome society," or when an old
man on the bus to Lowry Bay—through hills that "bristled with thick
gorse, with which the founders had reconjured Scotland"—announces,
"quite loudly, 'It was the longing . . . They were longing for their home,'"
and the narrator appends, from Helen's perspective, that "All high-flown
utterance was to be deplored, alarming as nakedness." Later, the young
Englishman Sidney Fairfax tells Helen, "I was never so consistently
aware of my position on the face of the earth . . . Sea-girt, southerly,
sundered." Here, perhaps unconsciously, Hazzard fuses her New Zealand
imaginary with that of Australia, half quoting "Our home is girt by sea,"

the second line of the patriotic song "Advance Australia Fair" that in 1984 replaced "God Save the Queen" as the Australian national anthem. She aligns New Zealand closely with Australia, most dramatically in *The Great Fire* with the Driscoll parents, who represent a grotesque marriage of the two nations. She also makes use of a remarkably similar tropology of dereliction, "the antipodean touch of desolation: the path indistinguishable from all others, the wayside leaves flannelled with dust, the net bag. The walking into oblivion," in a moment that returns us, yet again, to the dusty road leading out of Glenleigh, or the Lisieux. Her imaginative map of Australia and New Zealand is circumscribed to the point of inaccuracy, but the sense of Sydney and Wellington as lived locations is at the same time almost unbearably accurate. Above all, she simply refused to become provincial again after Hong Kong had connected her to the significant action of the world: "One thing I had felt in the East was the consciousness of being in a great land, this vast place that was China, in a great land that wasn't looking to anywhere else. They didn't feel the tyranny of distance—they wondered why anybody else should be alive. That was the centre of the earth. That I had felt very much when I was there. They weren't wanting to be somewhere else; they were at the centre."

Valerie arrived in Wellington shortly after the move to Thompson Street, into a home riven as before with acrimony. In October, Shirley wrote to Alec saying that the battles between Kit and Reg seemed to have reached a crisis point, and that the situation was irreparable. However, the separation she expected did not eventuate, and things continued as before. Again, Shirley took refuge in books. "The redeeming thing for me was there were two or three very good bookshops, small, in Wellington." She would certainly have visited Parsons Bookshop at Lambton Quay in central Wellington, designed by the émigré architect Ernst Plischke and described by Igor Stravinsky as "the most beautiful bookshop in the world," with Wellington's first European-style café, Seresin's, on the balcony upstairs. As in Sydney, these bookshops were the outward signs of a richer, more thoughtful and aesthetic life of the city, threads of cosmopolitan connection to a larger world that remained just beyond her reach. "I never found the other clients, but I did find books there. I was buying . . . lots of Faber poets in broadcloth. Those slim volumes, how wonderful they were. New collections of Auden poems, MacNeice, Spender, Day Lewis, George Barker . . . Among these books I bought a non-Faber book of the same dimensions, poems of Leopardi translated by John Heath-Stubbs."

Beyond the fictionalised account of Wellington in *The Great Fire*, a picture of Shirley's life there can be gleaned from the correspondence of her friends Chris Cooper and Alan Green. She kept their letters, partly, it would seem, because of the substance of the friendships themselves, but likely they were important to her because these two friends were witnesses to her love affair with Alec, even if they were unaware of this at the time, and also, in a sense, witnesses to the transformation her life had undergone in Hong Kong, which her banishment to New Zealand was threatening to reverse. Because of this, her connection to them kept alive for her the possibility of a further reverse, where her life could be set once again according to its rightful coordinates, oriented toward the world of action, authority, significance. And, closer to her heart, the connection with them helped support the forlorn connection to Alec, and to the promise of love itself. In March, shortly after arriving in Wellington, Shirley had learned that Alan had also contracted tuberculosis in Hong Kong; his Oxford studies were put on hold while he began what ended up being a six-month cure in a local sanatorium. His inquiries about Valerie's condition continued, and continued unanswered. Chris was meanwhile writing to her of his travels in Italy over the long vacation and of the Ballet Rambert at Brighton. There was a continuing political conversation between the three. Both Alan and Chris responded at length to news about the December 1949 reelection in Australia of the conservative government of Robert Menzies, with Chris exuberantly condemning, "Fie on you miserable antipodean electors betraying the people's revolution! I hope you did your unavailing best to stem the reactionary tide?" while Alan wrote, "Chris tells me that you are further postponing your trip to England. What's up? Have you got cold feet? Or are you waiting for the Tories to make up a trio with Menzies and Mr Holland next spring? If that is what you are waiting for, take a tip and come right away. There's one place in this stupid world where the Socialists have come to stay. What's more I would hate the thought of not seeing you for perhaps five or ten years."

As well as enlivening and animating her take on local politics, these exchanges also recalled to Shirley the circles in which substantial conversations could take place. She had managed to form only fleeting connections in Wellington, one "an older woman who was the secretary of the High Commissioner, Norah . . . a very good person," of whom she wrote to Alec, eliciting the response, "Norah sounds just the sort I would fall for if you were not about. Tell her to remember your years and to restrain her uninhibitedness." And Helen Driscoll's bus trip to Lowry Bay, an hour outside Wellington, to visit her friend from French class, Barbara Baillie, was perhaps based on another friendship from the office: "There was no one to see how pleasant these two looked in their coloured clothes, or how, in passing there, they enhanced the scene. They felt it themselves: the waste." But these friendships were no replacement for those she had left behind: "This thing I had had in Hong Kong, this was like a death to me losing that. Any possibility of sharing, talking with a kindred spirit."

In Shirley's correspondence with Alec, their plans to marry were taking shape. In October he wrote, "I am in our new home and at least the first step in our great adventure has been taken. I get an idiotic feeling every now and again that you are already here, somewhere in another room." Shirley's response, far from embracing this artless affection, attends only to the fact that it marks her separation from him, in 2002 noting in pencilled superscript on the letter, "He could not know how terrible and cruel, to me, all this was in NZ." Her letters asked for declarations, to which Alec responded with practical details about farmwork, stressing always and with gentle irony the homely scale of his endeavour: "now tearing about doing such things as buying cattle, machines and looking through agreements which give me, among other things a guarantee of 'peaceful enjoyment' of certain lands." Attached to the farm was a small but attractive Georgian farmhouse, which he described as "middling but adequate."

It's got three bedrooms, dining room, sitting room, kitchen, tap water, flush lavatory but no electric light. The garden is a wilderness
but has possibilities. I am getting the furniture together and have
collected enough to furnish one bedroom, the sitting room and
kitchen . . . I think you ought to know and be prepared. One other
thing you ought to know is that servants in England are for the
very rich—I am only a short head in front of the church mouse.

He described in detail the repairs being made to the house—patching
plaster, repairing window sashes, painting—and the process of furnish-
ing it for her: "Everything looks fairly clean and cheerful and the furniture is all good stuff that fits in with a farm-house atmosphere. I am
still buying small bits and pieces second hand. I have planted some more
pears and plums and am waiting for two cherry trees. I believe bottling
fruit is quite simple and the jars look nice and cosy in the larder. You
will be just in time for that—which is just as well as I would be too ham-
handed for bottling." Again his tone is gently mocking, but there is also
a sharp concern that she should understand the kind of life he is offering
her: "The first livestock will arrive in a few days. This will be sixteen in-
pig gilts which means sixteen pregnant young sows that are breeding for
the first time. They will start producing in about two weeks and I shall
have to act as midwife to any sow in trouble. Sows sometimes eat their
young which is of course most unprofitable and probably immoral." Shirley's response to these details has not survived, but it seems unlikely that
she would have relished them, and somewhat unthinkable that she could
have imagined herself sharing his interest in farm livestock, let alone a
life built around them. Alan and Chris, on hearing some months later of
her engagement, wrote expressing their sense of the deep comedy in-
herent in the very thought of her on a farm. As Alan put it, "I can fair
picture you already, sitting cross-legged, up to your knees in cow muck,
milking 't'awd coos' (if tha' knows what that means!)"

Her plans to travel to England were meanwhile repeatedly being put
off, and it may well have been the case that she was feeling some trepidation at the thought of all those in-pig gilts. In May, Alec had written, "If
you could put your sailing date forward to, say, October—I would be the

happiest of men," to which she responded with the news that she would not be able to sail before the following February. In August, he was trying to humour her through desperation and keep her spirits high:

> In order to stave off the decline that you threaten to go into I am writing to tell you that all is well with me except that you are not here. Please do not go into a decline. I want you strong, lusty and breathing fire. Apart from purely aesthetic considerations you will need all your youth and strength when you take on the management of Gadesbridge Home Farm and all that goes with it . . . Write at some length, I beseech you and tell me what you think and also about your plans immediately on arrival in this country. The long-term plans we can settle when you are here. Eat plenty of fruit, relax and grow beautiful.

In October, she wrote that due to difficulties at home she would not be able to leave until April, and Alec responded again with encouragement and practical support: "I got your letter this morning and am at the moment a sackful of tenderness, longing, anger and impatience. I feel particularly vexed at not being able to do anything concrete about getting you away from the worry and bitterness that surround you at the moment." He offered to cable her money for her fare so she could "get the hell out of Australia," but he was concerned that she avoid a terminal break with her parents. Within a week she had written again, with news that she could not sail until May, to which he responded that perhaps this was for the best, as "by then I should have things a bit straight for you to take over and that you will be arriving in the best time of the year." In November, Shirley, finally and after much urging from Alec, told Kit about the relationship, sparking the furious response she had anticipated.

The disclosure shifted the discussion significantly, away from Shirley's larger anxieties and her desire to hear the language of devotion toward Alec's more pragmatic focus. He was concerned that his financial circumstances were not strong, writing in December that he felt "selfish and inconsiderate at having asked you to share so little," and he suggested that it might be wiser for them to wait until he had had a chance to establish himself on a surer financial footing. He was also concerned that farming might not be Shirley's ideal life:

> If you are prepared, I am fairly confident that we shall make out, albeit probably never to the extent of attending cocktail parties regularly twice a week . . . We have a house to live in and even now I have gathered together more than the minimum in the way of furniture, linen and all the other oddses that a house has to have. The future prospects are that unless a major disaster occurs to me or the farm, I should be in a position to set up on my own in about six years' time. The main snags are not that we shall starve but that the life of a farmer's wife may strike you as being too dull and lacking in scope. This is a serious and vital aspect of the thing and you will have to judge for yourself when you arrive in this country. I am peculiar in that I like this sort of life and would have no other. You probably do not know whether you like it or not being guided for the moment by your whatsit. I could not blame you if having seen the set-up you told me to go to hell. That would be a pity as you are the only girl I have ever wanted to marry but don't let that influence you too much.

Shirley, responding in January, was furious, affronted at what felt like a lack of passion and, more particularly, at what she saw as an overly casual response to the possibility of the marriage not eventuating. She was possibly also upset at the practical, domestic, and unglamorous picture Alec was painting and at his stark insistence that he "would have no other" life than on a farm. He hastened to reassure her that his tone had been "dictated by the feeling that my prospects when analysed coldly look pretty poor and that should you think so, then an off-hand attitude on my part would make it easier for you. I gather from your last letter that you are not daunted by the littleness of what I have to offer." Shirley had again delayed her sailing date, this time until the northern autumn. In January 1950 she wrote Chris and Alan of the pending nuptials. Chris was gracious and comic: "Am I surprised? J'en suis foudroyé! Pas d'histoires, ma belle, que tu as le diable au corps, en effet! (French seems the only language suitable for the occasion)," while Alan was a little more sharply mocking: "You certainly put your time in Hong Kong to good use! Miss Hazzard, the 'Compleat Angler' lands the largest fish seen in these parts for many a long year." Chris also counselled Shirley to be pragmatic: "Of course your family must be fought tooth and nail in the best romantic tradition—make sure your father doesn't cut you off with less than your fare to England, though! The world-forgetting are by the world forgot, and many a promising elopement has been ruined by lack of change for the train."

That same month, Alec wrote formally to Reg: "Although I might conceivably prosper, if all goes well, it is unlikely that I shall ever become anything else but a farmer of modest means. I earnestly hope that you and Mrs Hazzard will not deny your blessing." In their responses both parents advised delaying the marriage until Shirley was of age. Alec found both letters "understandable, sympathetic and reasonable," and wrote to Shirley that he would comply with her parents' wishes.

> Their main objection is that you are very young, a fact though known to me is one which I perhaps tend to ignore. They say that you have as yet had little opportunity of forming any clear idea of the sort of life you want to live and of the type of person you want to share it with. This may be a line of argument that you will scorn. It is however very true . . . Please don't go off the deep end but I think your mother and father are right. I have a feeling that you may still marry me even after a year or so in London but you will then be marrying me with both of us knowing what we are doing. At the moment only I know.

Alec's letter, written in early March 1950, is cautious, and makes every effort to preempt the kind of anguished response he had received two months earlier. Shirley was devastated, as she explained to his son fifty-five years later: "He never really knew what the scene, the scenes, were for me at Wellington. I couldn't write to him constantly of that, and it would also have hurt me to expose the situation in all its drastic drama. Only when he had been completely taken in by the 'reasonable' letter he received from my parents, did I write fully of their cruelty and my isolation within it. And he almost dismissed this, disbelieving, I suppose, that they could be so duplicitous."

This pattern of response is telling; the to-and-fro of calm reassurance and pragmatism from Alec and increasing desperation from Shirley. She does not entertain the possibility that Alec's judgment was based on his own assessment of the situation, seeing it rather as proof that he had been duped by her parents. There is also an implicit contradiction, albeit one that is understandable given what was at stake, between her anxiety at the delaying of the marriage and her own repeated postponement of her departure from New Zealand. There remains the possibility that there was more to the delays than simple compliance with her parents, as the delays began well before the engagement had been announced. Even given the difficulties at home, and even though she was gripped by a desire to be with her lover again, there is a growing sense of reluctance on Shirley's part to make the journey to Hemel Hempstead. Alec's constant admonishments to her to "relax and don't fret and worry" had no effect on her—in another of her later pencilled glosses, she underlined the words and then wrote "(My God)." The couple's emotional tenors were utterly at odds. At the same time, they were sustaining a tender dialogue around wedding plans—"Your ring is blue with the usual metal band. It is old and has been in our family for quite a few years. Forget it till you get here"—and exchanging photographs. Shirley had a very lovely portrait taken in Wellington, writing on her own copy that she had had it done clandestinely, at Alec's request, embroidering the story of love's concealment. For Alec, this was another opportunity for lighthearted banter: "In order to get you a presentable photo I shall have to dig up something taken ten years ago. The present-day editions too plainly show an ageing man dressed in faded overalls, sucking a whisp of hay."

Reading Shirley's situation through Alec's letters is difficult, but one thing that is certain is the stark absolutism of her response. That she was intensely and overwhelmingly unhappy and consumed with the irrefutable knowledge of her own powerlessness is unquestionable, but it is unclear whether something more was taking place in Wellington than just her parents demanding that she delay marriage for a couple of years.

It does seem that her later experiences of both parents, the increasing difficulties of her relations particularly with Kit, came increasingly to bear on her memories and push her toward ever more disastrous retrospective versions of events. An instance of this can be seen in her changed interpretation over the years of an event from that time: the non-arrival of one of Alec's early letters. The letter had been written on board ship as he returned to England from Hong Kong in November 1948 and posted from Aden. Years later, and in the wake of her reworking of this love affair in *The Great Fire*, Shirley decided that her mother must have intervened, maliciously, and disposed of the letter before it reached her. In a letter to Peter Vedeniapine she provided a detailed reconstruction of this possible but by no means likely event (given that Kit was not aware of the seriousness of the relationship until late 1949 and that letters from Chris and Alan around the same time were unaffected):

When we left Sydney, I had given the reception desk of the serviced apartments in which we'd stayed a forwarding address at Wellington, of my father's office. One noon, as I sat down to lunch with my parents in the NZ hotel, my father handed me a letter sent on to me from Sydney. I saw that it was from APV. I took it, put it in my handbag; ate my lunch, knowing that this treasure was in store for me when I went to my room . . . unutterable relief. Joy . . . His previous letter giving an address in Britain never reached me. He assumed that it was confiscated in Aden, and I supposed that was the case. Only of recent years has it occurred to me that my mother, taking it with our other mail at the reception desk in Sydney, seeing from whom it was, and opening it, had taken the opportunity to suppress both letter and crucial address. Even now, it is frightful for me to think of her doing this, plunging me into a despair thus complete. Yet it seems likely, and in character. She would have told herself that she was saving me—and she was entirely un-self-questioning, always convinced of her own right. If this was in fact the case, as I come to believe, how enraged she must have been, that day at table, to see me put the beloved letter into my bag; realizing she had been outwitted.

Alec's concerns were larger than Shirley's anxieties. He was working increasingly long days on the farm—"I started writing this last night after hay making and am continuing it the following morning before starting work. My life is completely surrounded by either hay or silage and we work well over twelve hours a day"—and overseeing ongoing repairs to the old farmhouse in order to make it acceptable for Shirley's arrival. His son, Peter, felt that extreme labour might have had a thera-peutic dimension for his father, a way of managing the lingering trauma of his wartime experiences. Alec was also still waiting for his mother and aunt to arrive from the Philippines, and he was concerned about how Shirley would react to them, noting that they were "far more foreign than I am": "I am a bit afraid of your reaction to them, but as long as you are prepared to meet two old, kind, foreign and to you very strange women, I think that everything will be all right." He was concerned at what he saw as the growing likelihood of further war and the question of whether or not he should join up if it did eventuate, on the one hand "determined to keep out" of it but with the feeling that "I shall have to go and spend the rest of myself in futility and fear." Further, the prospect of war opened the question of restrictions on travel; he urged Shirley, if war should come, "to do all you can to get over here as in spite of the added danger of bombing, I think you will be better off here than in New Zealand." He was wearied by the failures of world leaders to avert the crisis but also embattled by the growing authority of polarized ideologies: "I should probably be much happier in the midst of active fighting than watching disaster overwhelm a peaceful country on my doorstep. I also have no objection to fighting communism but I would much rather fight for something that I believe in."

Alec's letters strike a very different tone from those of Chris and Alan, who debate with Shirley the daily business of politics and the management of postwar economies and social transformations in Aus-tralia and the UK. Alec's letters are expressive rather of his growing anxiety at the unsettled state of the world; they reveal the fragility of a man who had endured extraordinary hardship in the still very recent conflagration. Above all there is fear: "I am afraid of another war—I am afraid the war might mess things up for you and me . . . How I wish you were here with me now." He had first mentioned his anxiety back in March, when his letters were consumed by Shirley's anguish at the delay of the marriage. He wrote then that he had "discovered something about myself that is rather frightening. I think it is due to my being away from real life for so long. This something is that I worry a hell of a lot about almost everything and most of it does not happen. Was I like that in Hong Kong?" There is growing introspection, and weariness. And he is becoming more and more aware of the distance between them: "I only wish you could come over a bit sooner. Everything would be so much easier and simpler if you were here." He describes "a complete spiritual vacuum" determining his thoughts and views, his despair about the world.

I suppose I oughtn't to mind being in this vacuum for I have the greatest part of the world for company. I do mind and feel unhappy. You and I were not born just to squeeze a living and hope that our old age is not penniless. Life on that pedestrian level is just as bloody in England as it was in Hong Kong. You are still sustained by hope, having read much and being a romantic with imagination. I also hope but unless a sign is vouchsafed me very soon I shall mock my hope. Forgive me if I frighten you but you may as well know what you are in for. There is a restlessness in me that is getting worse instead of better and this life that I lead on the farm only gives temporary relief by making me too tired to think.

After this, two months with no letter. On the other side of the world, in the face of this silence, Shirley was distraught, consumed by fears and "premonition." In October she cabled, "entreating" news of him. Alec's cabled response, "Reserve judgment writing Alec," was followed by the letter Shirley had been dreading. During the intervening months he had been bedridden with rheumatic fever, but more than this, he'd also suffered a kind of depression, an emotional collapse.

I have been trying to write to you times without number but have failed because you are too far away and because we have not seen each other for such a long time. I feel and have felt for a long time that I have made a mess of things in thinking I could shape this life into something that I could ask you to share with me. I realize that you will dismiss material considerations, but I also know that a minimum must be there for us to make a success of it. The minimum does not look like materializing for a long time to come. The enterprise is up to now a success but to get it that way meant unremitting hard work and will continue to mean that for another two years or possibly more. By this I mean that I get up at half past four and work till dark. I never go out for pleasure and am too tired to live and think as a human being. In addition to all this I find myself increasingly frustrated at the thought of doing nothing more, but just living. While I was laid up I was pressed down by the blackness of the prospect and of the horror of your disillusionment after you had seen for yourself. Don't for God's sake think I am saying all this to cover up anything else. There is nothing and nobody—it's just that the life I had visualized is not coming out as planned and I see no light in the distance. Please forgive me for hurting you and remember it is I not you that have been found wanting. Alec.

In the silence that followed this letter, she could feel "the unravelling of the whole." For Shirley, focused as she was on the extremities of romance, this letter would have been devastating—her word was "excruciating"—in its blank inventory of failure and dejection and in Alec's refusal to address her in anything other than his own terms. While he was overwhelmed with the demands made on him by the farm, the letter nonetheless reiterated implicitly his earlier assertion that he "would have no other" life. And despite the assurances she had given previously, Alec was convinced that this was not a life for her, not "something that I could ask you to share with me"; he was "pressed down by . . . the horror of your disillusionment after you had seen for yourself." It is the letter of a man at the limit of his emotional resources. Perhaps the most difficult part of it is the thread of submerged pain, the lingering trauma of his war experiences, undisclosed, possibly unacknowledged. We cannot know how much of that legacy of war and its effects on her lover were grasped by Shirley, then still not twenty years old. It is perhaps telling that in her characterisation of Aldred Leith in *The Great Fire*, she drew on details from Alec's letters, in particular his conflicted feelings on the possibility of renewed war. Still, the cast she gives them in the novel is not wearied despair nor fear in the face of further battle, but rather a continuing resolution, hopeful and directed to the future. In order to have the story continue to romance's conclusion, perhaps, the fragility of the returned soldier must give way to authority, even heroism.

Alec remained in her eyes "an extraordinary man of action . . . but of intellect also that informed whatever he undertook. Everyone felt it. There was an expectation that his life would exert a wide influence—whether on public affairs or in some other undefined purpose. He was a presence, with his unassailable integrity, his principles." She could not reconcile this image of him with the man who wrote to her of planting roses and bottling fruit and of the weakling piglet restored to health. Importantly, in the many accounts she gave over the years about this relationship, she does not mention the fact of his having broken with her, nor that she had delayed their reunion many times. Both truths are buried under the clamour of the story of her mother's obsessive intrusions and cruel prohibitions, a story not really supported by evidence, and which seems to have taken form only much later.

When Shirley travelled to England less than a year later, she made no effort to get in touch with Alec. He had continued to work and develop the farm at Hemel Hempstead, and she could easily have made contact, but did not. When Peter Vedeniapine asked her, many years later, why she had not, she explained that she felt that had they met again, Alec's strong sense of personal honour would have compelled him to marry her, out of respect for the fact that there had been an engagement. This is a complicated matter. It goes to the push and pull of who withdrew, who broke with whom. It suggests that Shirley had come to a more nuanced understanding of the difficulties between them, most particularly Alec's love for and commitment to the land, and realized that his life was not something she could share. Although she would come to blame her mother for the collapse of the relationship, it seems clear that at the time, at some level, she acknowledged that there was a more substantial cause, and perhaps even that she had come to recognise a core of incompatibility between herself and Alec.

Others were alert to this. Chris Cooper thought their similarity of temperaments might create difficulties in a shared life, and he had written on the news of her engagement: "You will have to guard, I suspect, against the ink of friction between two such mentally positive and 'nerveuse' people, but of course a mutual respect of differences is essential to any marriage." Alec's longtime friend Violet Highton, who had known of the relationship at the time, also thought them incompatible, not simply from temperament—she knew Shirley only by report and later by her public reputation—but because of their divergent interests:

I saw this lovely photograph he had of her . . . I was intrigued as to why they had not got together and had a future. But . . . I don't think farming would have been her métier at all. Whether they would have had a marriage, a life together, I don't know. Thinking about what I know and read about her intellect and character, I've thought to myself since that they would not have had a happy life together. They were incompatible long term. She was on a different path to him . . . He was highly intelligent . . . a wonderful man. But his life was not what she wanted.

The starkest account of just how substantial was that divergence of interests and concerns, what she and he each wanted, can be seen in a story told by Alec's wife, Cynthia, of a visit Shirley made to the Vedenia-pine farm with Chris Cooper in 1979, shortly before Alec's retirement from active farming. Alec was in the process of selling off his cows ahead of retirement and was finding the experience traumatic due to the close bond he had forged with the animals. Cynthia observed wryly that "the farm was not Shirley's natural habitat" and recalled that Shirley simply "didn't understand . . . She was oblivious to how important and difficult" this sale was to Alec. The two women walked together in the fields, and Cynthia tried to explain: "It's very distressing for him because he's bred these cows and he's having to sell them." Cynthia felt that Shirley never grasped this. "He didn't want his cows prodded about in the market. He would take them into the pens, he just used to talk to them, and they would follow him. Shirley didn't understand why he should be so upset at selling his cows."

In Shirley's inability to see, let alone share, those things that Alec cherished most, and in his awareness of that inability, can perhaps be found the real cause of the breakdown of their relationship. And if she had had some inkling of this, consciously or not, it would also explain what had led her to postpone, over and over again, her journey to join him. If she had also herself been withdrawing from the relationship—again, consciously or not—then the break made by Alec was itself an expression of, and not just a response to, her own reluctance to become a farmer's wife and the culmination of delays and barriers she had thrown in the way of the relationship. An emotional withdrawal from the scene, and perhaps from the man, can be read in the first version she wrote of the affair in "Sir Cecil's Ride," and in her reflections, noted in her diary, after visiting Alec's farm years later. However, this thread of possibility had disappeared from her understanding of the scene by the time she returned to it in writing *The Great Fire* half a century later, as her pencilled notes and tags on the letters and in her diaries make plain. Failing to make contact with Alec when she had finally closed the geographical distance between them, and then, years later, being unable to understand his pain at losing the livestock that were so deeply part of his chosen life as a farmer, suggest a more profound reluctance that she was, in turn, reluctant to avow. In her heart the affair remained as it had been in her imagination, encrypted, untouched by the passing of time. As she wrote across her old diary in 1990 on hearing from Alec's wife of his death: "A story from Thomas Hardy. A poem of Hardy: his poem and mine."

———■———

At the end of January 1951, with the conclusion of Reg's tenure in New Zealand, the Hazzards returned to Sydney ahead of his next appointment: the plum position of Australian trade commissioner in New York, which would commence at the end of the year. They were pleased to be leaving Wellington, but Sydney was not a wished-for destination. They stayed a third time at Marton Hall—Shirley must have felt keenly the sense of a cycle of disappointment—and then moved to a rented house in Waverton just north of the bridge. Shirley found secretarial work in the city and crossed the harbour by ferry each morning and evening. And she began studying Italian, prompted by the sense of recognition she had experienced on reading poems by Leopardi in translation the year before. She found a small private college in Castlereagh Street, central Sydney, that offered individual tuition, and she enrolled in evening classes taught by an elderly Italian, "probably an anti-fascist émigré." She found the lessons "cheering, learning something"; she also discovered an aptitude. When a group of Italian engineers visited her office, she was pleased to be able to converse with them, and even more pleased at the temper of their company and manner: "They found I could 'say something' in Italian, and they were terribly sweet. Of course, it was this gentlemanly thing which in Australia didn't exist." This charm of the Italian visitors, infinitely more appealing to her than the familiar Australian manner, marked out a social world worth pursuing. She compared the visitors with her employer, who was, she explained, more educated, "as you would use the word in Italian, *educato*, but he did not have the charm for me of these exotic people." She was also responsive to the change that was beginning to take place in Sydney and across Australia in the postwar years, with the arrival for the first time, in some numbers, of non-British immigrants, refugees from the European displaced persons camps through the postwar years. The first of these docked in 1948: "I had noticed the immigrants, when we came back from the East; this change, that there were what we called 'foreigners' in the streets . . . they seemed more interesting, more alive, less resentful." Finally there was a tangible connection to the larger world, to vistas of speech, taste, and comportment beyond the closed world of her family and class, an apprehension of that larger world she had glimpsed in Hong Kong.

The family remained in Sydney half a year, treading water, and then sailed in September for London. They had first-class berths on the *Strathaird*, which stopped first at Fremantle on the Australian west coast, where Shirley went ashore and bought Stephen Spender's autobiography, then again at Bombay and Aden, where she photographed a dhow gliding past the ship, and then on through the Red Sea and the Suez Canal. On board, Shirley once again found "people, interesting to me," both English and Australian; "things were brightening up." Her first glimpse of Europe was the volcanic island of Stromboli, in the Tyrrhenian Sea. Benedict's account in *The Great Fire* mirrors that first Mediterranean arrival:

> [We] sat up on deck all night in moonlight to see the coasts of Crete, to pass Messina, sight Stromboli at dawn. The ship's engines went on the blink, and we lolled awhile in the Strait of Bonifacio, within ecstatic sight of Corsica and Sardinia . . . [And] remembered that John Henry Newman had composed his hymn there in similar circumstances, and [we] furtively sang 'Lead, Kindly Light,' and cried. At Marseilles, the port had been destroyed in the war. We walked from the dock straight into the heart of the city . . . Along the Canebière.

It seems that Shirley made that stroll into Marseilles with one of her fellow passengers from the *Strathaird*, Justin Rickard, whose photograph appears in her album of the trip; slim, handsome, he leans on the ship's railing, half turning back towards Shirley's camera. Justin Rickard makes no further appearance in her letters or diaries, but he possibly gave his first name to one of the central characters in *The Bay of Noon*, an ironic and ultimately elusive character suggesting passage, transition, and possibility; a figure for the next stage of her life.

II

# 4.

## NEW YORK

### 1951–1957

THE *STRATHAIRD* DOCKED at the Port of Tilbury in late October 1951, and the Hazzards were driven the twenty-five miles to London, where they stayed at the Park Lane Hotel on Piccadilly. Shirley was charmed by the vistas; despite the "noble scars" borne of bombings, the city still "looked old and civilized and familiar from literature." There was a sense of colonial homecoming, certainly, but also a feeling that the cultural equilibrium she had felt in Hong Kong had finally been restored, that she had "come through the East which was another ancient civilization" to this one. She embraced London and spent long, wet afternoons wandering the British Museum, "that great plunder-house of Empire," still threadbare after the war. In some galleries she was the sole visitor, walking in the near dark, the lights off owing to "the great austerity, Britain on the rocks." She visited as well the bookshops in Charing Cross Road—bought copies of Henry Green's *Back* and *Nothing*—and made the long, sweeping walk eastward from Green Park to Saint Paul's, relishing scenes recognised from the books she had been consuming all her life. Reg took the family to the popular drawing-room drama *Waters of the Moon* at the Haymarket theatre, which Shirley always remembered: "Wendy Hiller, Edith Evans, Sybil Thorndike, an almost unbelievable cast. All wonderful. One was served tea in one's seat in the interval."

In her fond recollections of these experiences there is a sense of a new prosperity, of a level of gentility acquired, of moving, finally, in the right circles. "People were terribly polite and helpful. And there was gentleness. You didn't have to be matey. And of course, people were extremely spinsterish and reserved. Mostly this kindliness." She kept a photograph album from this time, in which she had pasted her snapshots; small, square black-and-white images of the usual sights and royal residences.

A more formal portrait of the family from this visit reveals a dramatic change of demeanour from the troubled group that had been photographed leaving Hong Kong. Stepping out into Green Park in smart coats and hats, with Wellington Arch behind them, the Hazzards look everything like prosperous Londoners, professional, solid. They have been drawn together, if only briefly, through Reg's success, and through that to what Shirley would later refer, more sardonically, as the "achievement" of London. The Australian press reported that as trade commissioner in New York, Reg Hazzard was about to become Australia's highest-paid public servant, and the family's elevated status is evident in their dress and bearing. Shirley in particular has undergone a dramatic change; the girlish ensemble chosen for the Hong Kong photo has been swapped for a tailored wool suit, her hair now stylishly short under a hat, her face discreetly made up. She looks toward the photographer, confidently aware of her good looks and also apparently happy to share the frame with her parents and equally striking sister. It is difficult to reconcile the image of this assured young woman, relishing the momentum and solidity generated by her father's professional success, with the awkward and distracted figure in the Hong Kong departure photograph, or indeed with the anguished recipient of Alec's letters the previous year, confined by youth and parental resistance. She was now far from the provinces, no longer insignificant or overlooked, and far also from the life of a farmer's wife.

Before leaving Australia, Shirley had been in contact with Alan and Chris, arranging to meet them when she arrived. The previous November she had written that her engagement to Alec was off, and Chris had responded with sympathy and concern for them both: "It is so difficult to know how to approach him in the state you describe—he is not exactly forthcoming at the best of times on what concerns himself . . . I'm not sure what to do now. If I write that I have heard from you that he has been ill, even omitting mention of breaking off the engagement, he may guess that I am 'meddling.'" Shirley evidently counselled discretion; she had undertaken to weather things in solitary silence. In February, Alan had written that he found it "heartening to hear you are in good morale and not letting the events beyond your control get topside of you." Several months later he noted that she had not written much about her "private disappointments," and he asked if Time was "doing its stuff as the Great Healer or have you no faith in these last resorts of the moralizers?" Once Shirley arrived in London, Alan invited her up to Oxford, also including Valerie in the invitation: "We can compare tubercular notes!" The day was cold and drizzly. Shirley arrived alone by bus from Victoria Station and Alan took her to visit the Fellows' Garden at Wadham, his college. There is no record of how she felt about finally getting to Oxford, until recently a wished-for destination.

After two brief weeks the Hazzards sailed again, on November 7, from Southampton for New York. Like the *Taiping*, the *Queen Elizabeth* had been returned from wartime requisition and restored to earlier luxury. The four-day journey across the Atlantic in first class marked the family's newly elevated status. Kit relished the formality, dressing for dinner, being waited on, and Shirley kept a photograph of the two of them in their evening dresses. The excitement of arriving at New York was tempered by the dramatic change of pace from London and Wellington: the "immense change of the modern world descended on me, the anonymity, the facelessness . . . a blast of very cold air." The city offered a less readily legible social hierarchy that took time to broach:

> When we arrived in New York I felt immediately the impersonality of the city, the fact that you didn't exist unless you had money. I didn't even reason what it was, but that was at the root of it. I felt immediately: Where is the centre? Where are the nice parks, squares, the buildings that seem somehow noble and comforting at the same time? I don't mean I hated the city on first sight. I thought it was interesting. But I was completely excluded,

although we had again this diplomatic life, but much less, because it didn't count much . . . We lived on Fifth Avenue and we had a comfortable life but it didn't count in the hierarchy of New York. It was being rich that counted . . . I felt that in the streets you didn't exist for yourself alone, people sized you up and thought, "Well here's just anybody." And I hadn't lived anywhere, even New Zealand, where that was the case.

It would take her some time to begin to get the measure of New York's social rhythms and its very particular cultural depth, to feel at home there. She would eventually make that connection, not so much through "being rich," although her material circumstances certainly improved once she married, and not just through her later renown, but rather through the circles of writers and intellectuals she came to join and the friendships she forged there.

Almost immediately she applied for a job at the United Nations, an institution about which she was "idealistic, like many people at that time." In these earliest days of its establishment the UN was in some ways identified with the city of its location, forming part of New York's defining postwar modernity. In 1949, E. B. White had written of the city's embrace of the new institution that it took "in its stride . . . one more interior city, to shelter, this time, all governments, and to clear the slum called war." The UN was really the first portal through which Shirley entered New York, and the alignment of the two remained strong in her thinking. For all her looking to the past for human continuity and achievement, she also possessed a defining current of idealism, particularly in her political thinking, and this was one of the ways she connected most strongly with the contemporary world. Mostly the present day fell short of her expectations, but her idealism persisted. Later, one of her Italian characters would reflect that monuments in the United States often depicted national heroes "in armchairs," an observation that speaks to the assured and informed thoughtfulness that was, in a way, encapsulated for her in the idea, the ideal, of the United Nations.

Her UN application was successful, and she began work that winter in the new offices at Turtle Bay, in the office of Technical Assistance

Administration. The TAA had been established in 1950 and was concerned with what was then seen as the "modish" area of the provision of technical assistance to developing countries. The director general of the TAA, the Canadian diplomat Hugh Keenleyside, saw international technical assistance in the postwar world as a new form of diplomacy, engendering new kinds of development in the wake of colonialism "on the basis of cooperation rather than exploitation." Like the rest of the UN, the TAA attracted large numbers of talented, often remarkable people from a range of professional backgrounds. Shirley found the office stimulating and her coworkers distinctive and interesting, and she would go on to develop attachments with many of them. Just as in Hong Kong, the friendships she established were mainly with her more senior male colleagues. She did socialise with other women from the office, most of them like her in junior roles, but they rarely provided her with the kind of stimulation she was looking for. She was frustrated by what she saw as their conventionality and the smallness of their vision. A year into the job, she wrote despairingly in her diary of an evening out spent watching "a poorish Italian film 'Two Cents Worth of Hope,'" bored and annoyed with her companions' "long and irritating session about Europe in the typical American manner 'the romance of it all—so quaint.' Ugh." She was also dismissive of advice offered by these female colleagues that she should develop other interests outside the office, noting in her diary that "I tried to say it was something more than interests; it was belief I needed, and affection, and security and confidence and someone or something to trust and love—and all the rest of it."

More interesting to her were the erudite, progressive, and connected figures among the UN staff, such as the British writer, editor, and translator Anne Fremantle, who had moved to the United States and become an American citizen in 1947. Although her family background was elevated—her father, Frederick Huth Jackson, had been a member of the Privy Council, sheriff of London, and director of the Bank of London, and her mother's father, Mountstuart Grant Duff, had been undersecretary for India, governor of Madras, and also a privy councillor—Anne was a Fabian Socialist and had converted to Catholicism in the early 1940s. Her husband, Christopher Fremantle, son of Lord Cottesloe, was

a painter and follower of the Russian mystic Gurdjieff. During the war
Anne had worked in London as an ambulance driver and as a broadcaster at the BBC, then moved with Christopher and their three children to Washington, where she worked at the British embassy, but she
resigned in 1945, critical of the requirement, as she saw it, that she "tell
lies about Mr Gandhi." After moving to New York, she worked on the
Catholic magazine *The Commonweal* before joining the UN as an editor and translator during the General Assembly sessions, working across
French, German, and English. She held gatherings of intellectuals and
writers—drawing on family connections and old Oxford friends, including Isaiah Berlin, Harold Acton, W. H. Auden, Leonora Carrington (who
later painted Anne's portrait), and Evelyn Waugh, and new New York
connections like Ivan Illich, Norman Mailer, and writers from *The New
Yorker*—at her cramped apartment on East Seventy-Eighth Street, which
became legendary. At the UN, Shirley quickly made Anne's acquaintance
and joined these parties. They remained friends; Shirley described Anne
as having "a generous heart, eccentric without the slightest pose," and told
the story that after she met Francis Steegmuller, she took Anne with her
to meet his father, a devout Catholic, to vouch for her Catholic credentials.
She later recalled first meeting W. H. Auden at Anne's: "When I was first
asked to come to dinner, was told, Wystan will be there. I was I suppose in
my 20s still, and whatever age I'd have been, had I been in my 90s, I'd still
have felt thrilled . . . It was exciting to me to, as it were, see Shelley plain.
It was meeting somebody who had influenced my life. His poetry I came
to very early in my life, and I don't even remember a time when his name
wasn't known to me . . . It remained thrilling to me that I had met him."

Another important friend in Shirley's earliest years at the UN was
Dimitry Varley, a senior economist for the UN Department of Economic
Affairs, another White Russian like Alec, cosmopolitan, politically engaged, and highly cultured. He was Shirley's regular companion for outings, to hear Dylan Thomas read and see Martha Graham dance. Shirley
also quickly became friendly with her immediate superior at the TAA,
Norman Luker, although she was regularly in despair over his failure
to promote her interests within the office. In a way the friendship was
a continuation of the sociability she had shared with Chris and Alan in

Hong Kong, a daily exchange of wit and wry amusement at the bureaucratic dance around them. Luker was Welsh, had won a scholarship to
Cambridge, then ran the Talks Department of the BBC before moving
to New York in 1949 as the BBC's North American representative. He
had been friends with Guy Burgess after working with him at the BBC
(and was responsible for one of only two known recordings of Burgess
talking, rather drunk, late one night after a dinner party in Luker's New
York apartment in 1951, just before Burgess returned to England) and a
number of writers including Leonard Woolf, George Bernard Shaw, and
Bertrand Russell. While Shirley often found Luker exasperating, she valued the breadth of his thought and connections, his deft, ironic responses
to the intrinsic comedy of the world, and found his arcane knowledge of
Victorian painted biscuit cases and music boxes diverting. The friendship
resembled that between the translators Lidia Korabetski and Algie Wyatt
in Shirley's 1967 UN collection, *People in Glass Houses*: "In the several
years during which Lidia and Algie had shared an office at the Organization, it had often been remarked that they made an odd pair. This
is frequently said of two people whose personalities are ideally comple-
mentary, as was the case in this instance. It was also commonly agreed
that there was no romance between them—as is often said where there
is nothing but romance, pure romance, romance only, with no distracting
facts of any kind." Although Shirley enjoyed baiting Luker's wife, whom
she found patronising, by flirting with him at office parties, what she
shared with him was not sexual; it was, rather, a love of words and insights. At their farewell meeting, just before Shirley left New York in
1956, Luker told her, "I keep thinking of things I'll tell you and then I
realise that you won't be there."

Despite or perhaps because of her initial idealism about the UN, Shirley very quickly developed a more sceptical perspective. She witnessed at
close hand the eddies of drama whirling around the institution in these
Cold War years. Her workplace became a target of McCarthyite hysteria.
Her denunciations of the UN as these developed over the next decades were
not aligned with those of the UN's conservative critics; rather she was concerned about the influence of U.S. domestic politics on the institution and
about what she came to view as its failed internationalism. Her perspective

was informed by her friends and coworkers, some of whom were directly caught up in the drama, and by witnessing at first hand the fallout of the initial breach of the UN's Charter. While the earlier and more fundamental contravention was as yet largely unknown by the wider public—indeed she would be the first writer to air these claims publicly—there was in 1952 and 1953 a significant public skirmish over claims of spying at the UN, and more substantially about "a Communist-dominated UN Secretariat hiding hundreds of agents engaged in subversive activities." In the end, espionage charges were proven against only one staff member, and even those were highly coloured by the McCarthyite context. They resulted in a voluntary resignation by the staff member concerned, David Zablodowsky, director of the publications division of the Department of Conferences and General Services and a former employee of the Office of Strategic Services (forerunner to the CIA). In 1952, in Shirley's first months at the UN, a grand jury found that there had been "infiltration into the UN of an overwhelmingly large group of disloyal U.S. citizens." Secretary-General Trygve Lie dismissed the claims; nonetheless, he later "cooperated" with the U.S. government, permitting the investigation of U.S. employees of the UN and dismissing the twenty staff members who invoked the Fifth Amendment as well as refusing to testify before the Senate Internal Security Subcommittee in October 1952. In 1953, the UN Administrative Tribunal overturned eleven of the twenty dismissals, forcing the new secretary-general, Dag Hammarskjöld, to offer to reinstate those dismissed and pay compensation to any who did not wish to return.

Shirley, not yet twenty-two, was very much swept up in the drama of it all, following events at close quarters in the office and through newspaper and radio accounts. Here again, she had the kind of insider perspective on the unfolding political story that she'd had in her engagement with the progress of the Chinese Civil War. Her response was not yet the formal outrage of her published UN writings; what had developed was a sense of the intensely human significance of these events. She was consumed by anxiety for her friends and colleagues, writing in her diary at the start of 1953, "Such a dreadful newspaper this morning—full of filth about the UN and with a list of names of 'undesirables' still employed—

including Dimitri [Varley] and Rhoda [Rastoff] . . . I feel this is the worst so far—blameless people listed with the implication that they are criminals; poor little people like Rhoda ruined. I can't bear it; I can't bear to be living in such a world as this where the only certainty is cruelty, injustice, heartbreak; and yet for most of us there is no alternative." She also made a point of going to see other colleagues who were on the list to express her distress at events, and she lamented, "I felt so terribly sorry and affectionate to Dimitry—all these poor sweet people with so much trouble and worry." She noted daily developments: "Oh Christ, the radio just said Weintraub resigned—poor devil, oh poor poor devil. Who can blame him? It's impossible even for the rest of us to go on much longer this way"; "Zablodowsky resigned today; Weintraub was called before the Grand Jury again. It goes on and on, blacker and blacker"; "Walter Winchell . . . announced tonight that a UN staff member 'will be bounced this week—initials DV.' It's not just poor Dimitry, the whole thing is finished and done with. It's been too late to do anything for two years now." In *Defeat of an Ideal* in 1973, she developed these early insights through extensive—even obsessive—research, to make substantial claims about the consequences of the McCarthyite persecutions at the UN.

Chris Cooper had cautioned her about taking her professional self too seriously: "So the prospect of an Active Life opens before you? Don't become a Career Woman, with black tailored suit and horn-rimmed glasses!" He suggested that her new interest in politics "might fill the gap caused by the absence of a sentimental side." In fact Shirley's sentimental side was not neglected for long; her time at the UN would be dominated not only by her ready engagement in its internal politics but also, and more intensely, with affairs of the heart. The most significant of these was a clandestine relationship lasting nearly three years with the director of Technical Assistance special fund operations, Arthur (known as Tex) Goldschmidt, but there were other flirtations, moody, unfulfilled. They troubled not so much her heart as her sense of social ease and confidence; sometimes friendly and pleasurable, often less than that. The men with whom she was involved through these years were significantly older, and most were married, which of course did not make for straightforward relations. More important, there was a sense across these experiences of

an inclination for complication—of access, of security, of desire itself—
that almost always precluded any chance of a happy conclusion. And this,
even while she was inexperienced in the world of sex and matters of the
heart to a degree that created no little anguish.

It is not surprising that the office was a place of romance and sexual discovery for her, as it was for many young women in these postwar
years. On the evidence of her diaries, her experiences were not so far
from those explored in popular culture of the period—the young women
living in a Manhattan apartment in Rona Jaffe's 1958 bestseller *The Best
of Everything*, or more closely, Shirley MacLaine's heartbroken elevator
operator, hopelessly in love with one of the company executives who will
never leave his wife and family for her, in Billy Wilder's 1960 film *The
Apartment*. Shirley was twenty-one, and the men she met were educated,
cosmopolitan, cultured, and in her eyes at least they had substance and
authority. In these ways they resembled Alec, who still came into her
thoughts, albeit more fleetingly as the years passed. She believed that
the world she was entering at the UN was a world that mattered; she
believed that love, sexual and romantic love, mattered as much as politics did. For her there was always a highly charged alignment between
these two domains; it informed her writing, but it also drove and determined her life. The close association of her personal life and the institution of the United Nations was significant for her experience of both
love and politics, and the one would always be charged with the other for
her. The fraught connection was, moreover, apparent to her even while
she was in the midst of it. In early 1955 she received a review of her
work performance that was "less than lukewarm," and she responded
with great distress, reflecting in her diary, "It is exactly like a personal
relationship—one puts a lot of love and faith and energy into someone
(in this case, into the UN) and cannot go on indefinitely doing so and
being rejected. I know I have only a dreary and limited future at the UN,
but I love the organization; I have suffered with it, for it, defended it,
loved it, missed it—and it won't even allow me to identify myself with
it. And, as with human relationships, after one is grown up one cannot go
on giving without at least recognition."

Her work at the TAA was low-level and routine: recording minutes of meetings, typing, filing, all of it less than stimulating. She seems to have approached it with some disdain, and her efforts were rewarded with similar lack of approval and little advancement. For intellectual enrichment she turned to her new colleagues, her own extensive reading, and the cultural energy to be found everywhere in mid-century Manhattan. She later recalled her first summer in New York, going with friends from the office to see Geraldine Page's legendary performance in Tennessee Williams's *Summer and Smoke* at the Circle in the Square Theatre in the Village; she was, she felt, "in New York at last . . . No air-conditioning then. The heat was inhuman, and suited the atmosphere of authenticity." She went on buying books. As ever, she was consumed with poetry: always Auden, collections by Pound, Joyce, MacNeice, Robert Graves, Roy Campbell. And prose. Graham Greene was a perennial, but also Denton Welch's coming-of-age novella *In Youth Is Pleasure* and, rapturously, Simone de Beauvoir's *The Second Sex* ("I am almost incoherent with admiration for her"). In the spring she took a short holiday alone to a resort in Bermuda. She lay in the sun and read Sade's *Justine* and Balzac's *Cousin Pons*, resisted advances from men, and made friends with two women from her hotel, a Mrs. Friedland and her mother, Mrs. Katzmann, both "so outspoken and intelligent and pleasant and we discussed civil liberties."

Music was increasingly a pleasure. As well as concert performances, she noted in her diaries details of what she was listening to on LP records, then something of a recent phenomenon. She visited her colleague Rajasooria, who had "a magnificent collection of records and a High-Fidelity phonograph and I had a simply wonderful time, choosing armfuls of Beethoven, hardly knowing what to take next. We played the five Piano Concerti, the Second Symphony, some sonate and trios—six hours, in fact." She saw *Coriolanus* at the Phoenix Theatre on Second Avenue, with Robert Ryan, "splendid—simple, faithful production and the wonderful acting." In March 1953 at the 92nd Street Y she saw Louis MacNeice, reading his own work and some Auden and Yeats, and his wife, Hedli Anderson, who sang—"simply wonderful—all vibrant and expressive and passionately interested"—then, a few weeks later, Edith and Osbert Sitwell, "all very cosy but not really impressive," and in May, "Auden and Marianne Moore introducing four young deadbeats." She found the younger poets "awful," but of Auden himself, shuffling onto the stage in carpet slippers, there was "nothing disillusioning at all."

There was little enjoyment to be found on the home front. The Hazzards were still living together through 1952, at first north of the city in Bronxville, and by midyear in an apartment overlooking Central Park on Fifth Avenue at Ninety-Eighth Street. Despite the apparently less unhappy interlude in London, there were signs everywhere that the long-anticipated breakdown of Reg and Kit's marriage was imminent. For Shirley it merely added to her own everyday heartbreak, as she wrote at the start of 1953: "Oh dear, oh dear, oh dear, oh dear, oh dear: This is another one of those evenings when everything and everyone is ringing with hate and resentment and bitterness and misery and rage and pomposity—and all so, so, so unnecessary . . . Oh, tonight after I came home and realised what was going on I came into the bedroom and sat down and just felt tired and lost." The cause, beyond Reg and Kit's lifelong incompatibility, was the affair Reg had been conducting with Mary Wycherley, who had been travelling secretly alongside the Hazzards from one posting to the next for some years. Originally from New Zealand, Mary had lived in Sydney until her divorce from Paul Wycherley in 1950. She had sailed to the United States from Sydney a few months after the Hazzards crossed the Atlantic, arriving in Boston in mid-1952 (her absence during the preceding months had possibly contributed to the temporary lifting of spirits in the family), and she took up a position in the office of the Australian Trade Commission in New York shortly thereafter. One evening in January 1953 Mary phoned Reg at home. Kit took the call and then listened in on the conversation, which confirmed her worst suspicions. Amidst the ensuing "mess and wretchedness," Reg walked out, and the formal dismantling of the marriage began: "At last, at last we are rid of his presence and have some hope of living a peaceful life—and Mommy may get for the first time some proper financial treatment."

Valerie had meanwhile found employment in the New York office of Paramount Pictures, where she had met a talented and ambitious lawyer, Robert (Bob) Barnes, some twenty years older than she. They began seeing each other, and Barnes often visited the Hazzards' apartment. He was able to offer initial legal advice to Kit: "Mommy depressed about trying to get a proper settlement. The wretch is trying to cheat her. Barnes called—very nice of him—and cheered her up a bit." While Shirley would quickly come to loathe her brother-in-law, she was initially happy that he was around: "Everything has been so messy and unpleasant. Last night dear Barnes, the lawyer, came to talk, had supper, stayed till two. So nice and kind and sensible." Very quickly the complexities of Kit's situation became evident: "Barnes came for dinner, stayed till midnight talking—oh so messy and depressing." By March it became clear that Reg was doing all he could to avoid paying any money at all to Kit: "Mommy terribly upset. The outlook is black and bitter but oh, how does this help? And it's so much better this way than it was having him around"; "Mommy so upset and wild and hysterical. We agreed to take what we could now and keep trying." There was no escape: "I had a lovely, sunny, solitary afternoon and went to sleep at 8.30. Woke to hear Valerie and Mom discussing (in screams) the day's catastrophes. I do understand. I do, I do—but couldn't it be done a little more easily for all of our sakes? And Valerie is so hard and selfish and brutal. I wonder how she would take it. After they were in bed I lay awake crying . . ." There were also, she later recalled, Kit's "various 'false' attempts at suicide, necessitating being taken to hospital but always performed in presence of either of daughters and therefore scarcely likely to succeed."

By May 1953 things had not progressed: "Tonight is terrible—she makes herself suffer and suffer and everyone else has to too. The usual talk of suicide and poverty and madness." The Australian government had allowed Kit to stay on in the Fifth Avenue apartment for some months after the break, but there was increasing pressure to find somewhere new to live. Valerie had told Shirley in March that Bob had proposed, and in June they announced their engagement. Shirley's response was downbeat: "I suppose it's not so bad as it seems and that they have as much chance as anyone to be happy—two guesses how much that is!" She had by now taken very much against Bob and would never change her view. She seems to have assumed that because she did not like or value him, no one else did either. From this stemmed her conviction, otherwise unsupported, that Valerie was marrying for money. Bob and

Valerie married that August and moved to an apartment in a new building near the East River at Fifty-Fourth Street while Shirley took Kit with
her to a small apartment in "squalid" East Eighty-Ninth. Shirley was
now almost solely responsible for her mother, who had no income, no
occupation, and no capacity to manage her emotions. In the evenings,
Shirley came home from her UN job to Kit, hysterical, "a tear-struck
mess." Shirley was supporting herself and her mother on her UN salary,
and she never forgave Valerie and Bob for not helping. "This was a stage
in which $5 a week would have made a difference," she later wrote to a
friend. Things improved a little over the winter after Kit found a job as
a typist at the UK delegation to the UN, and she began again to accom-
pany Shirley to the theatre, or to concerts and exhibitions or for drinks
after work, the lively life of Manhattan providing an intermittent easing
of the strain, although never enough for Shirley to relax. In the end, in
a kind of terrible culmination of Reg's restriction of funds throughout
their marriage, Kit realised she would have to return to Australia to sue
for divorce in order to extract any kind of settlement. She also learned,
more happily, that she was entitled to have the Australian government
pay for her to travel back to Sydney.

At the end of April 1954 Shirley took her mother to the *Queen Elizabeth* to sail to London. On boarding, they were invited to a lively party
in the cabin of the English actor Cedric Hardwicke, where Kit sprang
instantly back to animated life. Her dramatic change of mood, while
welcome, particularly in the wake of the long months of loud grievance,
was beyond capricious, and also something of a harbinger for the wild
inconsistencies that would characterise her behaviour for the rest of her
life. For Shirley just then, though, the unexpected deliverance marked
the beginning of a return from despair to grace:

> I took my mother to the ship. I had my glass of champers at the
> party and went ashore. I came back to that apartment, and I went
> down on my knees by the bed and said Thank God She Has Gone.
> And that was the beginning of freedom, and never since did I
> ever feel that oppression, that sense that I'm just trapped with this
> Incubus. Bad things have happened to me, grief has happened to

me, unhappy love affairs, all these things that happen to everybody, but never that again; being in the clutches of a person who
had really become deranged.

The Hazzard divorce was, inevitably, a scandal. Reg and Mary had
returned together to Sydney, arriving in early January 1954, and moved
into a house in Newport on Sydney's northern beaches. Kit arrived in
early May and immediately hired a divorce agent who staked out Reg and
Mary at their home and photographed them together in their bedroom.
The tabloid press relished the scandalous fall of the formerly fêted public
servant—"Commissioner Nabbed in Nude"—and Kit was granted her
*decree nisi* at the end of December. Shirley herself refused to follow the
coverage, "putting my hands over my eyes and ears." There is no mention of the divorce, nor indeed any mention at all of either parent in her
diaries for more than a year.

Shirley's attention was now wholly focused on her own affairs, which
were complicated. During her first summer in New York, in late July
1952, she had begun a flirtation, a romance, with fellow Australian Howard Daniel, then head of the Economic Development and Public Administration Section within the TAA. She had been instantly drawn to his
charm and polymath worldliness, attracted to a background that spoke to
a rather more adventurous ambition than the United Nations. Daniel was
twenty years older than she, born in Melbourne into a well-to-do family
who had made money in the North Queensland salt industry. He had
published a book on Hieronymus Bosch and later became an art collector
and philanthropist, and he published articles on topics in trade, economics, development studies, climate studies, and politics. His energetic and
somewhat eclectic presence in the world of letters might be indicated
by the story of the central role he played in the 1948 U.S. publication of
the Australian literary classic *Such Is Life*: he had pressed the University
of Chicago Press editor John Scoon to include it in a series of "'classics' from lesser known countries about whose literature even educated
Americans were ignorant." He had completed degrees in liberal arts and
law in the 1930s at Sydney University, where he was known as a stylish
and iconoclastic writer of "modernistic verse," a founding member and

first president of the Socialist Club, and editor of the university's literary magazine, *Hermes*. His tenure as editor was marked by some notoriety, particularly over his promotion of contemporary poetry—his final two issues of *Hermes* contained no prose; they were filled instead with "'*vers libre*,' of which Mr Daniel is a prolific writer and have been strongly criticised by students." He had also generated notoriety with his published criticisms of the contemporary student body as "erotically undernourished, politically non-existent and mentally bankrupt." He later wrote that while a student, he had "become obsessed by the economic and social injustices of the world," and went on to represent the Australian Communist Party and the Friends of the Soviet Union in a High Court case against the Australian government, which was trying to have the organisations declared unlawful.

There is some suggestion that Howard Daniel was a spy; in 1937, having left Australia for Europe, he fell foul of the local authorities in Sicily, where he was ostensibly viewing Greek temples. Just ahead of a visit by Mussolini to the island, he was arrested in a Syracuse café by plainclothes police and detained until Mussolini had departed; his camera was seized and its film exposed. His wartime exploits—shortly after the Sicily adventure, he joined an organisation helping to evacuate Jewish refugees from Europe—led to a somewhat wry description in the Australian tabloid *Smith's Weekly* as "real Scarlet Pimpernel stuff." The column added that as "one of the best swordsmen in Sydney," Daniel "fitted this role almost too well. Just before the war began, he had run a most attractive Austrian Countess out of Vienna . . . daughter of a hundred Viennese noblemen etc." In 1939, with the invasion of Poland, Daniel and his wife of four months, Judith Wolff, were in Bucharest, where they forged a friendship with the American writer Murray Morgan, another left-leaning adventurer. Finding it impossible to get to Port Said to take a boat to Australia, the Daniels travelled instead through the Netherlands to the United States, where Howard worked in various capacities, including in Australian government procurement in Washington. He returned to Europe for the last years of the war to work for UNRRA (UN Relief and Rehabilitation Administration), then returned to the United States. Murray Morgan's daughter Lane remembered him as "a fascinating, erudite, hilarious person with a great gift for friendship and a tremendous love of literature."

The flirtation, unconsummated but, on Shirley's part at least, fervid, was kept secret from their coworkers, and from Howard's wife. It is not clear how important the relationship was for Howard—Shirley would remain good friends with him and with Judith after her romantic affections had moved on—but for Shirley it was, for a time, everything. The only record is her diary, which begins in January 1953, when it appears that the relationship was close to running its course; there is an edge of anxious desperation, a ripple of despair across her entries, sparked by Howard's increasingly distant attitude and occasional outbursts of irritation at her manner and comportment. On New Year's Day 1953 she wrote of "a frantic, feverish, interrupted moment" the previous evening, followed by "later talk of 'exploitation' and the disadvantages of 'morbid dependency.'" She cast a nostalgic eye back to the previous summer, recalling "a rainy Saturday . . . in the Metropolitan when I stepped into this with that same utter trust." Much of her energy through the first half of 1953 was trying to recapture that earlier happiness. Most days she found reasons to go and see Howard in his office and was almost always disappointed: "I took The Economist down at 12:30 . . . I went because I longed to see him, because I wanted kindness and comfort, and because I have nothing and no one. He was <u>so</u> distant and apart; and bored." Part of the difficulty was her desire for tangible demonstrations of affection, wanting to be acknowledged. In late February she wrote of a dinner with Howard and Judith:

Went quite well except Howard simply won't take a word of criticism against Australia. I am really afraid of him and all tense and nervous in his company; when we got out of the car I closed the door and <u>brushed</u> his fingers and he made a terrible fuss (it couldn't possibly have been much) and swore and was cross and I nearly burst into tears—which was absurd but I just hate to have him speak so nastily to me. Later there were a few moments and "I still like you"—a long sad distance from "I love you madly."

In many ways she seems little changed from her younger, emotionally labile Hong Kong self, torn by unconfident desire.

The friendship with Howard was significant beyond its romantic dimension. Through him Shirley began developing social connections outside the UN, for instance with the photographer Jon Naar and his wife, Ruth, and their circles in Greenwich Village. Naar was English, from a London working-class Jewish background. He had worked for British Intelligence during the war (possibly where he had met Daniel), then moved to live in the United States. This was a substantial connection for Shirley; she would continue to see the Naars for some years, and Jon took a number of striking portraits of her. She was not a neat fit with their social world; in 1954 she reflected, after a party, that their "Bohemian guests" made her feel that she was "older than any of them; they talk such over-precious nonsense. No honesty about themselves at all." She would go and stay with the Daniels in their Yorkville home for the weekend, snatching moments alone with Howard whenever she could but also helping in the garden and spending time with Judith, who was, she reflected, "terribly good to me, I think I love her," adding, "I suppose most people could do without that kind of love."

In November the following year Howard was posted to Geneva; by then their flirtation had long since dwindled away, and Shirley was reconciled to the "true friendship with no anxiety" they now shared. And she was already deeply immersed in another affair. Years later, when her subsequent lover Tex Goldschmidt visited Howard and Judith Daniel in Geneva at Shirley's introduction, they spoke to him animatedly about their affection and admiration for her. Tex wrote to Shirley: "The Daniels were very nice to me, even to spending most of the time talking about you. Obsessive? Compulsive? Excessive? Maybe—general agreement on the broad issues—intelligence, wit, etc—some minor divergence. Judy wants to get a man in your life. Howard wants you to write write write. Let me read your last letter. Everybody beams with pride. Possessive? Anyway, you'd have thought each had invented you, and maybe they did."

There were flirtations and advances from men in the office, and Shirley's diary entries show her annoyed or touched by these. Dimitry Varley she found sweet; others were less welcome, and her own inexperience, sexual and social, a further trial: "Oh, why can't I handle this sort of situation by now? I panic and yet I feel quite dead inside. I can't bear it. I didn't want to hurt his feelings but I don't see why I should be pawed about to please someone when I hate it so." In July 1953 she was sent to work in Tex Goldschmidt's office while his secretary was on holiday. Tex was drawn to her intellect as well as her winsomeness, and she, as always, to his authority, charm, and sharp conversation. On July 15 they worked late, had dinner together, then took a drive through Central Park and went back to his house (his family were out of town), late, for a drink. Tex's advances were welcome but rebuffed. He was candid with her, and she was attracted, appeased, enjoying the flattery: "When we got to 96th and 5th he said, would we just drive through the Park. So we drove round and round and he did kiss me and I let him and I liked it. He was really very attractive and nice, and he said it was so nice for him because he was forty-three and I was twenty-two etc, and he was afraid of seeming foolish." The routine office flirtation quickly progressed to more intense exchanges: "He made love to me—just a little at first, just lightly—and then he got impatient and paced around the room and said it was all wrong and he didn't want a dam' virgin anyway and to hurry up and drink up and let's go." Their repartee came increasingly to circle around knowing references to *The Seven-Year Itch*, which had been playing for the past year on Broadway ("He said when was I going to drop another flowerpot and where was Gerry and why didn't I get that over with . . ."). By the summer of 1954 he had become Shirley's first lover.

Tex Goldschmidt was a significant figure, not only at the United Nations but in U.S. government circles more broadly. Before they moved back to New York, he and his wife, Elizabeth Wickenden, known as "Wicky," were one of the influential "power couples in Washington's left-liberal circles," where both had held high-level appointments since the 1930s. Tex was the son of "freethinking German immigrants to San Antonio, Texas." He had worked his way through college by means of "a combination of scholarships, loans, and part-time jobs." Before that he had worked as a runner on Wall Street, then talked his way into the economics program at Columbia University. He had been immersed in progressive politics there, a leader of student support for striking Kentucky miners in 1932 and protests against the university's expulsion of the student newspaper editor Reed Harris. He was mentored by Ernest Angell, a New York lawyer who had helped found the American Civil Liberties Union. Angell hired him as tutor to his son, Roger (later to become fiction editor at *The New Yorker*). Tex then volunteered for a time at the New York–based Emergency Exchange Association, established by Angell, where he met his future wife. Elizabeth Wickenden was a kind of progressive professional woman Shirley had not really encountered before, and relations between them would never be easy, even allowing for the affair. She had graduated from Vassar in 1931, also majoring in economics, and had travelled to Europe and the Soviet Union after college, before moving to New York, where she met Tex when she was also volunteering at the Emergency Exchange. The couple moved in together soon after they met, then married.

In 1933 Tex was offered a senior post in Roosevelt's Federal Emergency Relief Administration and he and Wicky moved to Washington, where they remained until 1951, "when it became obvious that the New and Fair Deal years were drawing to a close." They returned to New York, and Tex took up the UN position while Wicky continued to work as a welfare consultant. The Wickenden-Goldschmidts were feminists "in practice as well as in principle," and progressive, as Tex observed in his memoirs: "Neither my wife nor I were motivated by planned goals for ourselves but kept restlessly seeking for ways to nudge for changes that might yield progress in the evolution of our society. My own work was rarely boring. My role was almost always a yeasty one—critical, doubtful, experimental; on the cutting edge—or the left fringe, if you prefer." Their son Arthur Junior (Art) and daughter Ann both felt that Wicky was a reluctant parent, in contrast to Tex, who they felt adored them. Ann found her mother difficult, not really motherly. Art recalled Wicky saying that Tex "had promised her to raise any of the children they might produce." He was involved in the children's lives to a degree unusual for a father in that era.

When Shirley was detailed to work with him through the early summer of 1953, at the end of the emotionally taxing year of her liaison with Howard, she was ready to fall in love again. Tex, as he would later disclose to her, had had affairs before, approaching them as something extraneous to his family life: "I've been unfaithful to my wife but I don't make a practice of it and I don't carry a load of guilt: it's just as though I danced with someone." This could not have been more different from Shirley's approach to the affair, laden not just with her own sexual innocence but with an intensity and a vulnerability more in keeping with an even younger woman. She knew nothing about contraception, and Tex took responsibility for this. Their affair progressed through snatched hours here and there, at her apartment or his if the family was away, maintaining lighthearted and friendly relations at the office as a cover. The rushed nature of these encounters took their toll on Shirley. She was insecure, demanding of reassurance, and again her behaviour and insecurity provoked irritation and frustration in herself as well as her lover.

Increasingly, she came into the life of Tex's family, joining them for dinner, outings to the theatre or concerts, and on weekend visits to their country house in the Catskills, much as she had with the Daniels. Ann, then in her early teens, remembered Shirley as a rather prim young woman from the office whom her father thought promising and whom he had wanted to help. Arthur Junior, a little older, had a crush on Shirley, whom he thought beautiful, an older woman. Shirley took him to concerts and shared recorded music with him. He once tried to take her hand during a recital and she calmly withdrew hers, "as if she were an older sister." Shirley never developed a friendship with Wicky, although she wrote in her diary that she tried to like her, as she had, more successfully, Judith Daniel. She remained resistant to the feminist principles that governed Wicky's personal and professional life, preferring the more conventional hostilities prefigured by adultery. In mid-1955, writing in her diary about a telephone call from the Catskills house, ostensibly about a work matter, she noted that she could hear Wicky and the children in the background, and reflected that she was having, in Donne's phrase, "correspondence while the foe stood by." She immediately caught herself: "'Foe' is too much of a word; 'foe' would be a salve to my conscience. It is the trust I can't bear, and the friendliness—and my treachery." In early 1955, after an outing with the Goldschmidts, Shirley reflected that

Wicky seemed—perhaps it is my guilty imagination—a little short. When Tex asked if she wanted to go straight home she said, "unless you and Shirley want to elope." He said to me "How would you like that?" "That would be wonderful, but do we take Wicky and [their third child] Jeannie along for ballast?" So it goes on and I loathe myself. Shakespeare had a few words to say about this sort of thing in the "Let Me Confess" sonnet:

"I may not evermore acknowledge thee
Lest my bewailed guilt should do thee shame;
Nor thou with public kindness honour me.
Unless thou take that honour from thy name."

Mostly Shirley was distant and judgmental of Wicky, like the protagonist in her story "A Place in the Country," who observes of her cousin, with whose husband she is having an affair, "She had a slow, deliberate way of walking . . . It was the walk of a woman who dealt with men in a straightforward way and must suffer the consequences."

In the spring of 1955 she took a monthlong overseas trip, first to visit the Daniels at their home in Coppet on the shores of Lake Geneva and then, more grimly, to respond to a call for help from her mother, who was now living in London. Kit had received a small settlement on her divorce, had returned to London, where she found an office job at Australia House, and continued to send Shirley increasingly fraught and suicidal letters. Shirley took out a bank loan to cover her airfare, which compounded her anxiety about her lack of advancement in her professional life as well as her resentment of her sister, who it seems did not offer to help out financially. On April 7 Valerie drove her to Idlewild to catch the plane; Shirley was "inwardly distraught," apprehensive about Kit, about the expense of the trip, and about leaving Tex. In Geneva, the Daniels took her on glorious spring outings along the lake to Montreux and Lausanne, and into Burgundy, to Cluny and Pont de Vaux. After a brief interlude in Paris, London was even worse than she had anticipated. In what would become an endlessly repeated pattern of calling for help from her daughters only to visit upon them the full fury of her sense of the world's injustice, Kit turned on "scenes, hysterics, violence, screaming, icy resentment—the works," so that Shirley, already overwrought, felt herself "like a caterpillar at the mercy of a nasty child with a pin—she knows just where to prod to produce the agonised reactions, to subject me to the same old indignities."

Back in New York, the Goldschmidts invited Shirley to the Catskills for the Memorial Day weekend, with Tex, the children, and several of the children's friends. Wicky was to be in California; she had tried to arrange a chaperone for Shirley, but plans fell through. There were awkward moments with neighbours, at dinner—an incident revisited memorably in "A Place in the Country," where the adulterous couple must fend off well-meaning neighbours concerned about the propriety of the young protagonist staying there unchaperoned—but Shirley stood her ground, telling them she thought leaving with them would be discourteous to Tex, who was her host. Her happiness at the amount of time she was able to spend with her lover was qualified by the unexpected and unfamiliar labour and responsibility of a houseful of teenagers. She was embarrassed at not knowing how to cook (another neighbour had to come over and turn the oven on for the roast), reduced to tears by Tex's teasing, and then mortified when he rejected her advances on a walk in the forest. The deepest pleasure of the weekend seems to have been a childlike delight at playacting the role of wife with visiting friends: "After dinner, Helen and I washed up and Tex and Earl sat at the table and talked to us. I felt so—grown up." Later, "it was very nice—it was so pleasant to be there in his bed, in his house, as though (and this is what all this is about)—as though we were married. But afterwards he was tired and anxious to be rid of me, as usual."

Even while she was living through it, Shirley's sense of her affair with Tex was quite self-consciously caught up in a kind of family drama. While as his lover she resented the fact of his responsibilities to his family and the constraints on her own access to him, she also saw his family as a kind of substitute for her own, or as an ideal that had been withheld from her. When she first visited the Catskills house, on a weekend visit in the summer of 1954 with George ffennell and Dick Boke from the office, she was moved by the family scene she witnessed, and candid about the envy it aroused:

> It was dark when we got there, a lovely white Greek Revival house in a wooded valley among hills of corn and wildflowers, with the woods beyond. The Catskills are beautiful. We got out and from the cold dark suddenly came into a glowing, firelit room, peach-coloured walls, cocoa carpet, green cushions, with the logs sparking in the grate. The children ran into his arms and there was talk and kisses and laughter. I was touched to the heart. It was all at once so many things I've never had; he comes home to this warm, loving room, these eyes and lips and arms—my mouth trembled with the envy and appreciation of it. I thought suddenly how I might have been if this had been my home when I was a child and I know that I am starved for affection and love and security and this makes me what I am.

On one of the rare occasions she was able to spend the night with Tex, she was "deliriously happy. It was like being a child at a very special party—I was excited and proud and on the surge of a great crest of joy and tenderness."

Everything continued to refer her back to her own unhappy childhood. In July 1955 Valerie phoned to say that she was pregnant. "This surprised a lot of feelings in me—I felt tender and sad towards her—it seemed suddenly such a moment since we were children in the house at Balmoral. And I was jealous—I wished it were my baby. I want to have a baby so. I want Tex's baby. But nothing in the world terrifies me as much as the possibility of having one in these circumstances." And she reflected a little later, after spending the night at Tex's apartment, on "those two little girls in the house at Balmoral; one of them married for money to a man she does not love and now pregnant; the other leaving a man's apartment by the back stairs after spending the night with him adulterously." While Shirley's claim about Valerie's marriage was based on nothing more than her own conjecture, it is telling that she found a rare point of intimate connection to her sister in such moments of shared departure from marital propriety or convention, and in envy over a pregnancy. When Valerie's husband phoned Shirley the following month, "terribly distressed, to tell me that Valerie lost her baby," she was hardly moved. She visited Valerie in hospital the following day, dutifully: "She was all right and left that evening."

Inevitably, but not until the summer of 1956, Wicky learned of the affair. Tex phoned Shirley midweek and then went to Wicky in the Catskills, not returning until the following Sunday. The separation of the adulterous lovers Nettie and Clem in "A Place in the Country" echoes Shirley's diary entry, at key points almost verbatim:

> "Remember . . ." she began.
> "What?"
> "About my love."
> "Yes."
> "No one will ever love you so much."
> "No, I know," he said with slight impatience, as if this were irrelevant. After a moment he added: "Yes, it has been worth it."
> His tone was historic, she thought, like a farewell.

Then Nettie wonders, "What has it been worth? What is to happen to me? What am I to suffer? Calamity has a generalizing effect, and as yet she could foresee her suffering only in a monumental way and not in its inexorable, annihilating detail." For the first days, Shirley was consumed first with "just terror and nausea and anxiety," and then "the same, but for a sense of relief, in a strange way, that now there would be decision, finality, an end of concealment." When Tex came to her apartment, at noon on the Sunday, "I knew it was all over."

Wicky had offered a divorce, which Tex rejected. Shirley was overwhelmed by her sense of isolation, "floating on a great sea of unreality." When Caro Bell, in *Transit*, is cast off by Paul Ivory, her ordeal is also passed in a nightmarish otherworld of solitude: "Love had not been innocent. It was strange that suffering should seem so." Through the next weeks, Shirley contemplated suicide, but "I didn't want to die here in a hot little room, alone and afraid. And then, when I leant against the wall, exhausted and sick, I didn't want to live with the anguish in my heart either." Wicky wrote, acknowledging that she was "scarcely the ideal one" for Shirley to talk to, but noting also, "I probably understand your total problem better than anyone else—I feel it in my being and it is a strange form of retributive justice indeed," and adding, "we must forgive—even in oneself—mistakes made in this great human confusion. Self-forgiveness is the hardest—I think it can only come through the evaporation of past experience in the process of growth." Wicky's sentiments were apposite, but also, in pragmatic terms and from Shirley's perspective, somewhat cruelly premature. Immersed in her loss, Shirley was unable to see the larger canvas of sympathy and recovery, and the prospect of suicide stayed with her. By October, still bereft, she sought refuge with the Daniels again in Coppet. Flying first to London, she was shocked to find Kit attentive, concerned for her, maternal: "And this weighed heavily on my decision. As we sat together in a bar in Piccadilly that Saturday night, I wanted to say, 'Don't be nice, be cruel, be wretched, be as you were; don't make it hard for me. Don't make me feel responsibility towards you. Let me die.' But she was sweet to me, she loved me." The Daniels, too, were full of care. Some of the atmosphere of this visit is captured in the title story of *Cliffs of Fall*, where the protagonist Elizabeth, who has recently lost her husband in a plane crash, is staying with friends above Lake Geneva, numbed by grief, until her anguish is finally released when she suffers altitude sickness on a drive up into the mountains.

On her return to New York, Shirley made plans to leave the city altogether. She and Tex said goodbye in the UN gardens just before she left: "We walked down in the garden—now so bare and wintry and when we last walked there it was all daffodils and cherry blossoms." A year later, from Naples, she wrote again about her heartbreak. The entry, dated August 25, 1957, sits at the back of her 1956 diary, where it reads as a leap back into the past, into the ongoing present of the loss of love, asserting the pain of love's enduring, which would go on to sit at the heart of her writing:

Lately it has come so close to me, so unbearably close; were you to come to me now and ask me to go away with you, I would do it tomorrow. I love you, Tex, in spite of everything that happened. You hurt me bitterly; I don't believe that I will ever forgive you. But the sweetest thing in my life is the dream I have so often, that you love me again. There is a Neapolitan song—let me dream that you love me again, and let me die in my dream. Nun mi scetà [Don't wake me up]. If there were only some way to say to you "I love you still."

# 5

# A LARGER LIFE

## 1957-1958

WHENEVER SHIRLEY HAZZARD was asked about the definitive moments of her life, she spoke of going to Italy: "From the first day, everything changed. I was restored to life and power and thought." Being in Italy returned her to a prior and loftier order of being, anterior to Australia and her unhappy family; with it "a whole part of my life that had been suppressed came back." The significance was clear even at the time.

> 22 December 1956 Saturday, Naples
>
> I am in Italy.
>
> It is simply that one Friday, three weeks ago, I walked into Max Doerner's office and asked if, because of the UN emergency missions in Naples and Cairo, they were looking for applicants. On Monday I was called, interviewed, accepted, and on Friday I left New York for Naples.

Her sense of the moment—the occasion—of Italy is plain in the rhythm of the sentences that follow the stark declaration of time and place: plain monosyllables give way to a sequence of dependent clauses and descriptive phrases separated by a string of commas, drawing us into the story. Also striking here is the locution she would later deploy in the opening paragraph of *The Transit of Venus*— "It was simply that . . ."—heralding the arrival of an apparently unimportant figure, an arrival that will set in play events of high drama: a novel. As she later observed of the opening of *The Bay of Noon*, set in Naples in the late 1950s, "There has been a break with previous experience; something new is beginning."

In later accounts of this posting, highlighting its fortuitousness, she often spoke of herself as merely the beneficiary of decisions made elsewhere: "Entirely thanks to having studied Italian, I was precipitately sent on a year's mission to Naples . . . This was a time of crisis in my private as well as my working life, and the assignment came as if by divine intervention—the first of a series of miraculous reprieves that transformed my life." Yet her diary entry, the last for 1956, makes clear that it was she who requested the posting in order to leave the TAA office, which had become unbearable to her after the break with Tex Goldschmidt. While this doesn't play as nicely into the story of miraculous rescue, it does signal a shift in the story of her own self. From the tearstained, passive despair of the preceding months, immobilised by Tex's rejection, she responded with action, making a move, taking charge—taking care—of herself. She would find that much was difficult, but as time went on, her sense of the rightness of this move, to leave New York and embrace the unknownness of Italy, only became more evident. In part this was a function or consequence of Italy itself; she came to look back on those early winter months there as "realistic and clear and somehow enclosed." But more than that, she began to be aware of the importance of moving away from known worlds, the importance of movement itself. This would later become a touchstone for her larger thinking about life, her mobile protagonists and their shifting worlds. The other defining coordinate was loneliness, a quality to which she returned when thinking back over these years:

> The traveller equipped with even one introduction arrives with a card to play, a possible clue to the mystery. Yet those who have never experienced solitude in a strange and complex place— never arrived in the unknown without credentials, without introductions to the right people, or the wrong ones—have missed

an exigent luxury. Never to have made the lonely walk along the Seine or Lungarno, or passed those austere evenings on which all the world but oneself has destination and companion, is perhaps never to have felt the full presence of the unfamiliar. It is thus one achieves a slow, indelible intimacy with place, learning to match its moods with one's own. At such times it is as if a destination had awaited us with nearly human expectation and with an exquisite blend of receptivity and detachment. The moment comes: we intersect a history, a long existence, offering our fresh discovery as regeneration.

In these lines there is a sense of wonder at her own great good fortune. There is humility and also a grasp of the immensity of experience to which she had access, the privilege of travel, particularly in those postwar years. Perhaps she is paying tribute to those occasions when she speaks of them as having arisen through miraculous intervention rather than her own agency. She was still caught up in the long process of severing relations with her family and her place of birth and had not yet made a home for herself anywhere else. But the profound connection felt with Italy, the intimacy developed with its "long existence," provided a starting point for cure.

She left New York on December 7, 1956, "a frigid night," on a Pan Am flight from Idlewild. She was twenty-five years old. Her arrival in Naples on a bright winter morning was solitary, and this solitude largely defined the months she spent there. She was often resentful at Tex's abandonment: "I came here alone, knowing no one—he let me go to the other side of the world to be alone, with no word, no message, and I have had a hard, hard nine months." Her appointment was for a year, working for the United Nations Emergency Force (UNEF) in an office that had been established at Naples airport to assemble and fly supplies to the peacekeeping forces at Suez. She was lodged at first with senior colleagues in central Naples, in the Hotel Vesuvio, "one of the good hotels on the seafront," on Via Partenope, looking out on the bay. She marked the window of her room in the Vesuvio in a postcard to Valerie, noting that across the street were "restaurants, and a pier leading out to an ancient fortress on a tiny island—the picture doesn't do anything like justice." The fortress was the twelfth-century Castel dell'Ovo, "a medieval construction in blonde stone rising on a fragmentary villa of Lucullus," where, according to legend, the siren Partenope washed ashore after failing to seduce Ulysses with her song, and where later the poet Virgil buried an egg, warning that should the egg break, the castle and city would also fall.

If her location was mythic, her daily life was rather less so. Six, sometimes seven, mornings a week she and her colleagues were collected by the office "vehicle" and driven an hour or so to the UNEF at the "shattered" airport and then returned to their hotels in the evening. In the office she was again assigned routine secretarial work, mainly typing, work enlivened only by the fact of being transacted partly in Italian. Despite her—at that stage—rudimentary grasp of the language, she had the responsibility of dealing with visitors and phone calls in Italian, as the military officers could not speak the language at all. She shared the office with two young women, one of them Suzanne Puffet from Brussels, with whom she quickly became friendly. She also established a lasting friendship with Lily Aprile (later Gravino), a Neapolitan local who was also working there as a typist. Lily recalled Shirley as overwhelmingly sad that year, consumed by her recent heartbreak. Shirley's boss was a New Zealander, Major A. W. Cooper, whom Lily remembered as a "typical military man"; perhaps he was one of the unappealing types Jenny encounters at the NATO office in *The Bay of Noon*—"perpetually seething—with fury, with fear, and with the daily necessity of striking out before they could be felled by inapprehensible foes."

There was no consolation to be found in congenial colleagues. Apart from Lily and Suzy, Shirley found herself isolated.

Trapped with a handful of stupid, grudging, coarse people in a wretched, time-consuming office that has a nightmare quality about it. I have longed, longed for the companionship of my office in New York . . . I've spoken of my interests to no one all this long time—on one or two occasions at the beginning I tried and was put in my place as someone who wanted to impress their intellectual superiority on others. Oh dear dear God, how I have hungered for one of those dear conversations with Luker, for a talk with someone whose knowledge and understanding and humour is responsive to my own. Trapped between the 8–5pm, seven or at least six days a week at the office, and the inadequate knowledge of the language, I have known real loneliness.

In New York, she was missed, too, as Norman Luker wrote her just before the end of the year:

Your absence is palpable—I always seem to be hearing something in the elevator or reading something or occasionally even thinking something that it would have been pleasant to mention to you (had you been here I might have commented on getting the mimeographed paper on the Christmas party announcing that "invitations were to be on a restricted basis" that it appeared to be an occasion when we were letting joy be confined). I can of course pay the tribute of a sigh to my contributions to such unheld conversations but yours are a total loss.

Howard and Judith came to Naples in early 1957, but visits could be no substitute for more local and daily friendships. Howard later wrote her an enraging letter that she likened to Alec d'Urberville's preaching to Tess, noting it as a possible scene for a novel: "She held a letter and reflected that she was not the first woman to receive a homily from/by her seducer."

Her fellow workers at the UNEF were not only not *simpatici*, they also failed to embrace the life of the city around them. There were the English girls—"Angelas and Hilarys and Rosemarys who had wanted to get away from Reading or Ruislup or Holland Park," over whom "hung an immanence, a pale expectancy, as if their youth had not yet come to them." And the other expats, who were living out "their term of exile, requiring nothing of Italy or its language, passing among themselves stale, trumpery talismans of home, recreating a former existence from the shelves of the PX until such time as they should—on other, equally alien shores—speak with nostalgia and authority of the Bay of Naples."

But she was not just critical of the expats, or of her colleagues, the military men "who lived among men" and were "afraid of women." In an early fictional account of expat life, "A Sense of Mission," she would find comedy in the hapless romanticism of her protagonist's response to the city, most likely informed by her own. Clelia Kingslake thrills to have arrived in Rhodes and is "revisited by ecstasy" at the "glimpse of golden walls, of white shipping, of a tower, a fortress." On her first morning there, when Miss Kingslake hears on waking "the rhythmic crunching of waves up the pebbled shore," she murmurs to herself lines she had memorised, "Sophocles long ago heard it on the Aegean," and feels herself to be "in however modest a degree, the instrument of a great cause: in this setting redolent of antiquity she even risked to herself the word 'handmaiden.'" But this light mockery is counterweighted by the baser failures of Miss Kingslake's colleagues, who substitute their own interests for those of the organization they represent and for whom the only "Mysteries" to be found in the ancient city are heard in the aggressive Signor Grilli's rapid and sycophantic pronunciation of the name of the head of the local logistics division, "Mr Rees."

That year, she lived with an awareness of the weight and significance Naples would come to have for her life. The city was unlike any place she had encountered, "a blitzed town of large-eyed, overburdened, resilient people. Many of its great churches and palaces lay open to the elements; its waterfront was a shambles." As well as the massive bombardment of war, itself compounded by the eruption of Vesuvius in 1944, Naples had continued to suffer from "recent ravages of dictatorship and conquest," and consequently failed to attract foreigners. She felt herself to be one of a privileged few who were there then, one of "those who came to know Naples in that era" and "would feel attachment to it all their lives." Looking back, she had no doubt of its promise: "The city was the thing that was important to me and the region and being in Italy. Like going to the East it was a tremendous change in my life." She also found, retrospectively, premonitions of its significance, fancying Vesuvius, the "great dictatorial god" of the city, as having been prefigured in her first sighting on sailing into the Mediterranean half a decade earlier, of the volcano Stromboli, the "first outcropping of Europe." Although she left little tangible record of this time—no diary, just a handful of notes and few surviving letters—she did provide extended descriptions of the city for many years afterward, most of all in her 1970 novel *The Bay of Noon*, which she described as "a love letter to Naples." Like her protagonist Jenny, in those first weeks she was herself waiting "for the city and its intervention," waiting to step out from the office into life. As Jenny's friend Gianni (himself another outsider, from Rome) tells her, "'It's the city, the phenomenon of Naples itself, that knows something. It's like an important picture, or a book—once you've taken it in, you can't believe there was a time when you didn't know it.' He turned to me. 'This will change everything for you, being here. Naples is a leap. It's through the looking-glass.' And I looked out at the oval mirror of the bay." The promise here is for insight, but it is a perspective to be acquired only gradually: "It was necessary to live there rather than visit it to have a feeling of this great quality." That "feeling" for Naples would cohere in the shock of the city's embrace. For a young woman who had felt unhoused in the city of her birth, this was "a revelation . . . like going to heaven." Naples was "desperately poor," and yet:

> When I entered that city I knew that it was a *coup de foudre*. I knew that this was where I wanted to be. Bit by bit I began to have this great companion, the city of Naples, and of course to learn all sorts of things there—to change my way of looking at things, to enlarge my way of looking at things. The year passed with as much interior development in me as the previous four or five years and perhaps even more. For one thing, I became joyful . . . really for the first time I knew what joy was. It became a part of my life, I understood at last what that was. I saw life even in the midst of so much difficulty and suffering. It had vitality, there was blood in the veins and it was quite a different life from the life I'd been accepting and had even begun teaching myself to accept as a necessary and rightful thing.

The walk taken by Jenny early in *The Bay of Noon* carries the imprint of Shirley's own passage through the city; it is a walk she commends to her

readers in a 1982 essay on Naples—from the waterfront hotels to Spaccanapoli, "where the city 'splits' along its Greco-Roman axis, to the Gesù
Nuovo." Jenny walks up "a ramp of a street that rises to a corner where
Degas once lived with his Neapolitan relatives. The ascent, oblique, suggests the piazza above it by giving, as if through a door ajar on a high
landing, a glimpse of the exorbitant, gem-cut façade of a church, with to
the left a flash of red stucco, to the right an ornate obelisk." She crosses the
piazza to "the faceted stones of the church. From there one looked, then,
across at the bombed shell of Santa Chiara, half-reconstructed, and at a
derelict campanile on the one hand and a massive palace on the other;
and this I did for some moments, only showing it was new to me by en-
quiring, of the priest who came to close the church, the way to San Biagio
dei Librai." Striking in these passages is the sense of arrival, of encounter. If the evocations of Middle Harbour at Sydney conjured a nascent
sense of literature, the possibility of being a poet, and if the vistas of
Hong Kong opened out the topography of the global world, then Naples
was a site of self-discovery, "through the looking-glass," offering inward
as well as outward prospect. There is also the animation of the scene,
the liveliness that sits in sharp contrast to Jenny's own quiet isolation, a
liveliness that yet welcomes her. Shirley, too, was welcomed into friendship there, the acquaintance with Lily Aprile developing in the months
and years that followed to become one of the great constants of her life.
Perhaps it was with Lily that she had coffee that winter, "standing up at a
counter . . . fierce black coffee, a spoonful apiece, served in tiny cold cups
that were always wet from the draining board," or shopping for a Christmas tree for her boss, "giggling all the way like schoolgirls and wiping
away tears of joy."

What Shirley saw in the city's vistas encapsulated and defined her
own experience, her sensations and her emotions, becoming a kind of
visual shorthand:

When I think of that time, the thoughts and feelings we all had, I
feel—oh, as one does when one sees on the slopes of the Vesuvius
or up above Sorrento one of those old-fashioned, cream-coloured
hotels standing almost empty with all their old furniture that no

one values, their décor that only depresses, the two or three elderly guests, speaking low so as not to disturb by giving a sign of life.

She reflected often on the city's qualities of ancientness: "There are accretions, layerings like seabeds. One enters strangeness . . . If you come to live there, come to know it, you will live in other times." As she began drafting *The Bay of Noon*, she reflected on the complex sense of time that the city engendered for her:

> It is the oddest thing to me as I write this story, to remind myself of my present age which though mature, is by no means advanced, and of the actual distance between me and the events I am now recalling, which is only eleven years. The expression "That seems like another existence" would not do to describe the distinctiveness of that time from my present life, for it is the present life that seems like another existence . . .

This passage from her notebook is more than likely a draft for one of Jenny's reflections than a diary entry (it is not always possible to distinguish between the two) and speaks to the complex and layered reflexivity that would come to be one of her defining writerly traits. In this it suggests how central was the experience of Naples to her coming to writing.

The animation of Naples recalled that of Hong Kong in the vitality of its visual display, with Spaccanapoli its epicentre:

> A hundred shops and stalls that sold, as they are selling still, song records, coloured nylon sponges, the gauze and sugar paraphernalia of christenings and first communions, plastic Bambis, bolts of print material, gold jewellery and silver representations of arms and legs to be offered up to departmental saints . . . open sacks of coffee beans, stacks of books, new and seventh-hand, and barrows piled with hand-tools.

The apartment—Gioconda's—in San Biagio Dei Librai that galvanizes Jenny's entry into the city in the novel—"a deep square of a building, hers; pale stucco, divided into a dozen apartments, or a hundred . . . There were several flights of deep stone steps, unlit, uncarpeted"—was based in part on the Palazzo Marigliano in that same street. Shirley later wrote that Maria Marigliano, whom she and Francis had by then come to know, had lent, unknowingly, "a few details of her setting" to the novel, "not all of them complimentary, such as a Christmas card from King Umberto prominently displayed on the mantelpiece in July." The view from Gioconda's terrace—"From here you can see everything"—was modelled on that from Palazzo Marigliano:

> The arches and towers and polychrome domes were stacked there beside and behind each other like so much scenery backstage at a theatre . . . "That red curve of houses follows the wall of the theatre where Nero sang." The big thing below the cathedral had been a paleo-Christian temple. Those columns came from a temple of the Dioscuri, that church was the site of the Roman basilica. The question, "What is it?" took on, here, an aspect of impertinence; one might only learn what it had successively been.

This particularised looking, so central to the novel's voice, was based on Shirley's later years in Naples—this scene and other detailed renderings of the city draw on intensive notes: "Taxi driver said—'We (Catholics) will go to Paradise, e vui (Protestants) will come here.' Tiny ragged children with fierce faces, utterly adult. One furiously accosts Francis for money, when he says No, replies 'Allora, vai.'" But the joy that impels the looking surely began with that first visit. In an undated entry in one of her 1960s notebooks, clearly referring back to her early Naples days and to the mode of observation opened up for her then, she wrote: "There were many times, of which this winter day was the first, that I walked in Naples in a kind of delight of observation and strangeness, the desire to observe and the happiness of having all this to lavish it on." That capacity for intense and passionate observation, that minute attention and acute sensibility would come to be distinctive features of her prose, and her character, and are seen, already, in the record she kept of the city, cherishing her daily life in a place where, perhaps, she could begin to imagine feeling at home.

After some weeks at the Hotel Vesuvio she moved out to the western arc of the city, to an apartment—"high, humid rooms and a view that swept the bay, city and volcano, the long Sorrentine cape, and the island of Capri, which floated far or near according to the light"—in the Villa Mazziotti on Via Posillipo, "a red, romantic house that rises from the sea on Roman foundations." The fictional incarnation of the Villa Mazziotti in *The Bay of Noon* offers more detail:

> In order to reach the apartment one entered quite a different build-ing, that stood higher on the hillside, above and behind. From this one went down, in a tiny bathysphere of an elevator, through rock, and arrived at one end of a long corridor roughly tunnelled from solid stone, painted and tiled dark red. The corridor could be lit by a series of electric buttons whose sequence, timed for a loping run, provided a certain claustrophobic excitement. This deep crossing passed under Via Posillipo and through the tiny promontory of which my villa formed the prow. It ended in a flight of steep steps and a grilled door, beyond which were light, sky, and the sea. A glassed-in catwalk had been attached to the villa's side, leading past the doors of the many apartments into which the house had been divided.
>
> Nothing could have been more canny, more uncanny, more Neapolitan, than this means of access . . . There was another ap-proach, by water, disembarking at a landing stage of stone steps glossy with moss, being admitted to the house through another green-grilled door. The building itself was red stucco, lifted clear of the water on foundations of grey stone; seen from a distance it floated forward in air like a rusty boat in the slips.

Here again, prospect is everything: "My rooms gave on to a narrow ter-race that, in turn, looked directly across the sea to the volcano: the rooms, the terrace, were like antechambers to the spectacle, their purpose was to disclose it." After a visit from her new friends, Gianni and Gioconda, Jenny stands in her darkened apartment, looking "through the flawed, icy glass of the terrace doors at the lighted city to the left." It is not hard to hear a recollection, a celebration of Shirley's own solitary but purposeful arrival, in Jenny's assertion of joy: "The window returned my breath, slightly steamy with PX whisky and merged with the smell of narcissus and of the charred fire that Gianni could not light. It was in this confusion of the ignominious and grandiose that I experienced the first moments of pure happiness."

Beyond the spectacle of the bay, Posillipo gave a sense of history, "still recognizably close to the scene of past centuries—not only in appearance, but in its expansive relation to the intensity of the city." Posillipo also provided some relief from the wrecked and chaotic life of postwar Naples:

> To drive out from the shattered city after work to the colours and flowers . . . and old walls hung with plumbago, bougainvillea, and jasmine; to swim from inlets and grottoes of the blond tuff of which this cape is composed, to watch, from any balcony or shop front or curve of Via Posillipo, the unfolding light and adventure of the bay, was to achieve tranquillity without tedium—a life always animated by the energy and curiosity, the capacity for humanity and imbroglio, that pervade the Posillipo community no less than all the rest of this extraordinary metropolis.

She would return in later years, with Francis Steegmuller, to live, renting an apartment farther out, in the grounds of the Villa Emma. She would record, over and over, the view, the changing light, properties of the islands, boats passing. Looking down from her balcony to the sea, to the "seaweedy rocks" of Roman ruins just under or at lower tide rising just above the water, she would be reminded of Balmoral, the water views of her childhood. She traced the topography of the region through a line of poets: "Posillipo begins with poetry, at the Roman tumulus long venerated as the tomb of Virgil," in a park containing also "the austere tomb of the Romantic poet Giacomo Leopardi, who died in Naples in 1837," along with Jacopo Sannazaro, Salvatore Di Giacomo, and visitors Henry James, Norman Douglas, and Oscar Wilde, who, while "staying, impecunious and heartsick at Posillipo, completed 'The Ballad of Reading Gaol.'" The connection to Leopardi is utterly apt, given that it was his poetry that had brought her to Italy in the first place. And the density of the region's poetic heritage began to suggest to her new possible futures: "The ghosts of this region are too many—and too vital—to sadden us; rather, they create a company, ironic and benign, to which we ourselves may ultimately hope to belong." Posillipo was decisive in her writer's trajectory.

As pressure at the UNEF office eased, Shirley became more familiar with her surroundings, the continuing waves of change that Naples embodied. She drove south with office friends to Sorrento and Pompeii and Herculaneum. Entering Resina, just before Herculaneum, "with the Vesuvius rising over us, we came into a country market where a dozen stunted donkeys, each dragging its own teetering Vesuvius of ill-corded bales, applied their muzzles humidly to the Maserati as it inched among them. Not long afterwards this little town founded on the lava was submerged under the eruption of skyscrapers flung up by a housing project." During Christmas week she drove to Caserta with Suzy Puffet and Eddy Roscovitch from the office, and again to Herculaneum, where she was photographed sitting on a broken column, dangling feet in elegant shoes, wearing a good overcoat, light in colour, pleated skirt, and dark leather gloves. "And then there was Capri at the horizon. Having no free time, I could not reach the island for months, but there it was, afloat on the bay, and I knew that one day I would go." In the spring she made the crossing for the first time and then went back every weekend. "There were no hydrofoils then and the little steamer took two hours," but the journey, and the sea, were unforgettable: "Blue, brilliant, like an early morning of the world. A beginning, as it was for me . . . becoming, at 26, young." Returning to Naples, she bought a copy of Norman Douglas's *South Wind*, which she kept for the rest of her life. She later wrote about this period on the island:

Capri's modern prosperity was already astir, but there remained an old guard of those who worked the land and fished the surrounding sea; and even those by now owning, or employed in, hotels, restaurants, or shops could still turn their hand to earthy tasks. The Pucci-clad summer scene in the piazza was interspersed with the unselfconscious passage of purposeful women carrying baskets or demijohns on their heads, and of men pushing or hauling a laden cart.

It would always be to this older, more quotidian Capri, "the rural nature of the island's life," that she felt herself aligned.

Nonetheless, photographs from this time see her completely playing the tourist, above the Faraglioni, climbing up a cliff in her swimsuit, or posing, suntanned, smiling, with one of the donkeys that in those days carried tourists up Capri's steep streets. She would soon make friends on the island: with Anne Gargiulo, who had worked until that year in the NATO office in Pozzuoli and had then gone to live on Capri with her husband, Vittorio, and her mother, Lady Elizabeth Archibald, who was described by the Capri chronicler James Money as "one of the last outposts of Empire," a keen gardener who "stumped about the island in tweeds and sensible shoes." And Capri was likely where Shirley met the legendary author Sibilla Aléramo, at that time mostly resident there, "a great beauty," then "in her vigorous last years." Aléramo's name appears in Shirley's address book and also in planning notes for *The Bay of Noon* as "among friends of Gioconda at Rome." Shirley was transfixed by the island, captivated by topography and spectacle. On that first April visit, sitting for lunch at the Canzone del Mare at Marina Piccola, the scene—"the mountain-face . . . the painted sea, the motionless trees in relief under the rock face"—took her breath away, and she wrote in one fleeting diary entry from that year, "I am obsessed by Capri. I came here, miserable to the point of derangement . . . Capri saved me—dear lovely, loved place."

Certainly she was free, for the time being, of her family and, if not cured of, distracted from her broken heart. But even so, daily life was laced with anxiety. While she continued to attract admirers among the expat bureaucrats, she was not interested in romance. She wrote that she pursued, that year, "a collection of silly, pointless affaires," including, it seems, a dalliance with the American journalist Harold H. Martin, who told her in a letter from early 1957, shortly after leaving Naples, of "memories that were burning more brightly than I could wish," and wishing that he could "strike that perfect plateau of impersonality which you so happily reached in your first communication." None of these "affaires" were sustaining or salutary. Shirley hoped "each time" to find "some final diversion of my affections"; however "being with such relentless people I too have learned to be hard, to be selfish."

She was also despairing about her future. Her lack of national connection was not yet the imaginative boon it would become in later life, when she could pronounce that it was "a privilege to be at home in more than one place." For now she was unsettled, the pragmatics of living in Italy looking as if they might prove too much for her despite the tangible life to which they gave access. Her insecurity was no doubt fed by her sense of her flimsy status at the UN:

> Now it grows near the end of the year of my assignment, I know that I must try the FAO [the Food and Agriculture Organization, a UN agency] in Rome, that my hopeless future—or lack of future—in NY cannot be re-accepted without an attempt elsewhere. Even loving Italy as I do, even so, I'm afraid: I'm afraid to live in a foreign non-Anglo-Saxon country always, to be cut off from my own background irrevocably and forever. But I have had so much need of solitary courage this past year that I believe I'm equal to anything, even to the more and more likely prospect of a barren, single life, working as a secretary or at most a clerk—well, I suppose that's my fault and one should be glad to have had so much of the things that others covet.

Her year in Naples had not seen improvement in her secretarial or bureaucratic capabilities, and she would have to return to New York with little in the way of further professional prospects.

In mid-August, the holiday of Ferragosto, she and Lily went again to Herculaneum. At nearby Resina, they visited Lily's family home and lay in the heat "in the garden under the (rare, black) ilexes." Shirley was feeling light-headed, odd, disconnected. She had, it soon transpired, contracted hepatitis, not uncommon in Naples in those years, and she quickly became seriously ill. For eight feverish and debilitating weeks she lay in her rooms at Posillipo, as Jenny does in *The Bay of Noon*: "Even in the worst of the illness I would think of Bagnoli and the PX and the report and the Colonel, and be glad to be free of them and at home, nauseated, feverish, and turning deep yellow. When you are ill you can only be yourself—whereas in an office one is required always to be somewhat false, at least when one is subordinate. The preference for a serious disease over office life struck me, even at the time. Mostly my thoughts were not so coherent, and once or twice visited by passages of delirium."

Like Jenny, she spent the weeks gazing out at the bay, deepening her connection to its rhythms:

Below the windows there was always something going on. In the earliest mornings there were boats below, on a sea at that hour indistinguishable from inflamed sky; one lone boat, or a pair, or a group of them drawing up nets or lobster pots. No sound ever came landward from these boats except sounds of the sea—soft plashings of their work, or the mild collisions of hull and tide. If the fishermen spoke to one another, it was in voices too low to reach the shore. The men, like the boats, were weathered, single-purposed, uncolourful. In each of their practised movements there was the intentness, the restraint, that suggest not an industry but an existence.

The illness and convalescence brought her to the end of her contracted period at UNEF, but before returning to New York, she took a holiday, using leave she had accrued over the past several years and funds from her mission allowance. She went north in mid-October, first to visit Howard and Judith in Coppet—"weather unexpectedly warm, and Geneva and the Daniels in good form." She stayed a week, then travelled to Milan, finding joy in the museums: "Seeing that small Guardi for the first time would be enough to make anyone happy, I should think—the 'Laguna Grigia.'" From Milan she went on to "beautiful Verona, Vicenza," spending the shortening days walking and the evenings faced with "an excruciating loneliness." Then to Venice, "just too lovely, I can't bear to go," and on by train through Chianti, amid the last gatherings of the grape and olive harvests and the full loads of the almond trees. She was struck then and ever after by the changing quality of light in the northern Italian autumn, where "October is one of the most abundant months; and even November is often golden. What changes is the light, and the atmosphere of the days." In what was perhaps his most significant and fortunate bequest, Howard Daniel had provided an introduction to the Vivante family, who took paying guests in their home, "a rather dilapidated lovely old house, with a beautiful garden, an hour's walk from Siena." Shirley had written to Elena Vivante from Coppet, and the reply reached her in Venice, this letter "the second miracle," after the fact of Italy itself, in her return to health and life. Years later, on hearing of Elena's death, Shirley thought of her friend's handwriting, "bold, elegant, Giotto designs," and recalled first seeing it "standing one winter's day in the Piazza San Marco holding her envelope, addressed to me at Cook's in Venice; I had written to ask if I might stay at the mysterious villa and she had written back agreeing."

The Villa Solaia sits on a small hill, as the Sienese historian Roberto Barzanti puts it, "*come a godersi beatamente il sole*"—as if enjoying the sun's blessing—four kilometres from Siena, between the hamlets of Malafrasca and Ponte a Bozzone. Originally a farmhouse, built around 1600, it was renovated in the neoclassical style in the early nineteenth century for the Piccolomini-Bellanti family by the celebrated Sienese architect Agostino Fantastici. The house is large and, in those days, in the words of Arturo Vivante, "sand-coloured, the colour of the sun," with "an open and spacious atmosphere." Fantastici had added windows to the smaller and darker original dwelling, and a façade of elegant symmetry, with loggias to the right and left formed by Doric columns under classical pediments. These embellishments were modelled from cement, a trompe l'oeil in imitation of the travertine and limestone found in the area. At the front of the house, Fantastici constructed a double staircase, connecting the villa to the driveway, bordered by ilex, and to the gardens, planted with palm trees, oleanders, magnolias, and pines. There was a fountain and a fishpond, and ancient lemon trees; farther off an eleventh-century monastery, still in ruins in the 1950s; and, on all sides, views across fields and hills.

Shirley arrived that first time in the late afternoon, her taxi from Siena driving up to the villa along the avenue of ilex. She was met by Elena Vivante, who called her eldest son, Paolo, to join them. Shirley later recalled that meeting in a letter to Paolo's widow: "He came with his characteristic expression, slightly amused, civilised manner, his shambling, almost drifting walk. He would have been then in his late thirties. He was very much as he was throughout his life, and already engrossed in Homer." Elena then summoned her husband, Leone, and the household helpers, Ginetta and Emilia, "and thus I met the entire household in those moments, and knew the importance to me of this new beginning. Elena, Paolo. The house— the perfection, contentment, happiness." The family were likewise taken with their new guest, hailing her as "the girl with eyes like jewels." Later she would meet the other members of the family—Paolo's younger brothers, Arturo, who worked in Rome as a doctor but was often at Solaia, and Cesare. The youngest sibling, Charis, was then living in Africa, shortly to have a child with her Ghanaian lover. There were few other guests so late in the season, and Shirley was often alone with the family.

She recalled with great clarity her first excursions and discoveries: "The group of trees and small church just above Solaia—Monasterino. Walking up the chill main street of Siena to have my hair done at 'Le Tout Paris.' Seeing the Campo. Nannini near the Post Office, sitting out at lunch in the garden with Elena, Paolo, Arturo," and visiting the as-yet unrestored Pinacoteca Nazionale in the "freezing gloom." She returned to Solaia the following summer and on a short excursion to neighbouring towns wrote to her mother that despite Assisi being "perfectly beautiful," she would "be glad to get home to Solaia tomorrow, back to my chair on the terrace." Solaia was already, in her thoughts, home. And for the rest of her life she looked back on the fullness of her visits to the villa through the lens of its impossible, vanished perfection: "There could not now in this world exist any similar place. Free of pettiness, filled with poetry. It was Solaia that moved me to begin to write, and in this way delivered me into a happy life. Solaia was above all suffused with . . . sensibility and humane intelligence . . . Elena was the imperishable spirit and gives a spirit and genius of the place," and the family "principled people, incapable of inauthenticity or shabbiness or underhandedness."

The Vivantes were substantial and significant figures in the Italian cultural scene in the pre- and postwar years, immersed in Italian but also English literature. Arturo wrote of his family, "If my family had a hero, it was Shelley." Elena Vivante was an accomplished amateur painter, also a translator; in the immediate postwar years she had translated the novels of the popular early-twentieth-century American writer Thomas Wolfe. Shirley remained aggrieved on Elena's behalf that her work was not acknowledged in the published volumes, nor were royalties paid, even though hers remained the principal Italian versions for many decades. She was the daughter of Adolfo de Bosis, a poet and translator of Homer, Shelley, and Whitman and founder of the magazine *Il Convito*. Her mother was Lillian Vernon, an American who had come as a child to Rome with her father, who founded a Methodist-Episcopalian church there. Elena was also the sister of Lauro de Bosis, a classical scholar who, before he turned twenty, had translated three Greek tragedies into Italian, after which he composed a verse drama, *Icaro*. Lauro became the lover of the American theatrical monologist Ruth Draper, seventeen years his senior. In 1930, with fascism on the rise in Italy, Lauro had, with others, established the "Alleanza nazionale" to produce antifascist material and distribute it clandestinely. His mother assisted in the enterprise, and in 1930 she was arrested, together with other friends working on the pamphlets. The biographer Iris Origo records that Lillian Vernon declared at her trial that she had become involved "because I am not a sheep," an implicit response to Mussolini's famous declaration that "the Italian people are forty million sheep ready to give their wool to their régime."

The following year, Lauro staged a dramatic political performance that echoed the mythic heroic imaginary of Icarus, fulfilling, as the critic Gilbert Murray has observed, "the destiny of his own hero." Lauro's plan was to acquire and learn to fly a small aircraft, which he did in the summer of 1931, then to fly low over Rome scattering antifascist pamphlets and return afterwards to the nearby French territory of Corsica. In October he set off and released the pamphlets as planned, but he seems to have run out of fuel before he reached the island. He disappeared without a trace. To his mother, before the flight, he wrote, "I am not counting on failing. Whatever happens I shall have won. It is better to fall in the attempt of flying over Rome than to live for another thirty years as a peaceful bourgeois with utilitarian ideals . . . These letters will make an impression. Will they prick the conscience of my fellow citizens? Will they constitute a lesson in civic spirit? This is hardly my concern. I do my part. The others will do what they can." The day after his disappearance, a friend published "The Story of My Death," a six-page manifesto Lauro had written, in French, and entrusted to him before boarding the flight. The manifesto begins:

> Tomorrow, at three o'clock, on a meadow of the Côte d'Azur, I have an appointment with Pegasus. Pegasus—it is the name of my airplane—has a russet body and white wings. Though he's as strong as eighty horses, he's as nimble as a swallow. Drunk on gasoline, he bounds through the skies like his brother of old, but if he wants to, at night, he can glide in the air like a phantom . . . We are not going to hunt chimeras, but to bring a message of freedom to an enslaved people across the sea . . . We are going to Rome to scatter in the open air these words of freedom which for seven years have been forbidden like a crime . . .

Lauro's heroics would seep into his family's consciousness. Arturo recalled that he knew parts of "The Story of My Death" by heart, "for me the words were a purification from the sodden propaganda" plastered on walls around the town and at his school.

Elena's husband, Leone Vivante, from a secular Jewish family in Rome, was a philosopher of aesthetics. His writing on English poetics, particularly on the work of Shelley, had been admired by T. S. Eliot, who wrote a preface for Vivante's 1950 book *English Poetry*. Eliot had been directed to Vivante's work by the English art critic Herbert Read, who was one of the first English guests to come to stay at the Villa Solaia and later became Leone's friend. Leone was a somewhat otherworldly figure; while he continued to write and publish throughout his life, he never held, or sought, an academic position. Arturo wrote that his father was "a solitary thinker," with "no close friends among philosophers." While "to the end of his life [Leone] thought he would make a living from his books," his father, Cesare Vivante, an eminent jurist in Rome, was less confident that this would happen, and in the mid-1930s, "in the hope that his son would become self-supporting, bought him the Villa Solaia, a few miles outside Siena," then a somewhat gloomy and inward-looking town, afflicted by "fascism and the Depression" and lacking the economic vitality that would come after the war through tourism. To generate some of the liveliness—social, intellectual, aesthetic—to which they were accustomed in their Roman lives, Leone and Elena "invited friends, old and new, usually painters and writers, to come and stay," often for months at a time. The arrangements were casual, with people arriving often at short notice to spend time in the company of the Vivantes and one another. According to Roberto Barzanti, there was a flow of guests and visits between Solaia and other nearby houses: Villa Brandi in nearby Vignano, Villa Il Vallone dei Sadun, and Villa Geggiano (whose rooms painted with fruits and gardens were a model for Tancredi's bedroom in *The Evening of the Holiday*), forming a kind of network that brought together artists and other figures at odds with the fascist regime. Among the earliest visitors were the poets Camillo Sbarbaro and Eugenio Montale; Montale was accompanied in the early 1930s by the American Dante scholar Irma Brandeis. Barzanti adds to these a list that includes the poet Gianna Manzini and artists Filippo De Pisis, Marino Marini, Onofrio Martinelli, and Corrado Cagli, together forming a "Parnassus" that remained sheltered at least partially from the increasing fascist surveillance. Sbarbaro remained Elena's intimate friend (it was rumoured they were lovers) and would publish at her death selections from her letters to him in a volume titled *Autoritratto (involontario)*.

Ezra Pound was also there, in the early autumn of 1937. The teenage Vivante sons thought that Pound looked, with "his red beard and long hair," like Garibaldi. Pound came with his mistress, Olga Rudge, who was a friend of Elena's, and also staying at the time was Leone's father. The elder Cesare was approached one day by a local farmer whose son had inadvertently signed up to fight the fascist cause in Spain and wished now to withdraw. While Cesare, sympathetic to the fascists, declined to help, the farmer's story led the antifascist Leone to observe, in sympathy, that "plutocracies were less violent." Elena recounted the scene in a letter to Sbarbaro, highlighting the shared political identifications of her father-in-law and Pound:

> How lovely the world in this bright month, and the houses with the corn and the pumpkins and everything lovely and clear . . .
>     Ezra Pound asks the Prof [Cesare Vivante]: "Have you ever heard the Genoese dialect?"
>     Prof: "Oh yes! Much to my misfortune! But I hope that Mussolini will succeed in suppressing all the dialects!"
>     Ezra Pound: "I agree!"

Pound would later reproduce Leone's remark in his Canto 52, underscoring the divergent views between the two men:

> . . . *And Vivante was there in his paradise, the mild air*
> *the fields rolling eastward, and the tower half ruin'd*
> *with a peasant complaining that her son was taken for war*
> *and he said "plutocracies were less violent."*

Arturo, then thirteen but, like his brothers, "sharply aware of politics" and in the shadow of the death only a few years earlier of Lauro de Bosis in antifascist protest, recalled his father "telling us with a frown" sometime later that Pound had told him that "he mentioned me in one of his Cantos—said it as though I should feel honoured. The man is so vain, vanitoso."

The Vivantes' antifascist convictions and Jewish heritage meant that they became a particular target of fascist attention and were subject to increasing constraints on property and privileges through the 1930s. Arturo later explained, "No books by Jews were to be published; Jews were not to employ non-Jews, or hold property, or go to public schools. Since my mother wasn't Jewish, my brothers and I were considered only half-Jewish," and so Leone transferred the title of the Villa Solaia to the four children to avoid its expropriation by the state. But for Leone the situation was clear: "My father said we shouldn't live in a country where we didn't have equal rights. For us it was time to leave." In 1938 the family moved to England, travelling separately over several trips, with one or two children, meeting in Paris and then going on to England. The younger brothers, Arturo and Cesare, stayed with a family in Wales, while Paolo, who had won a scholarship to Pembroke College, was at Oxford, and Charis remained with her parents in Surrey, at "Joy Cottage," which had been found for them by Ruth Draper. When Italy entered the war, in 1940, Paolo and Leone were interned on the Isle of Man, and Arturo, by then at the King's School, which had been evacuated to Criccieth in North Wales, was held outside Liverpool, then shipped two weeks later with other internees to Canada. He was eventually released due to approaches made by Ruth Draper to the Canadian prime minister, Mackenzie King, and he finished his schooling in Canada before returning to his family in England in 1945. Paolo and Leone had been released earlier, and Paolo promptly volunteered for the British Army's Pioneer Corps, where he worked primarily as an interpreter (and slept in a bunk next to Arthur Koestler).

Leone worked in an intelligence office, and Elena found a position first as a cook at a British government-run kitchen, then as a translator and interpreter at the BBC, and later as an artist at Harrods. On the tenth anniversary of her brother's death, while at the BBC, she broadcast a memorial honouring his poetic act of protest:

> So in the secrecy of the soul's solitude, when one becomes the master of one's own life, and then gives it up, one must surely draw great joy. They must be happy to know that from the misery of everyday life they could attain such a poor moment of liberty. They must be sustained by the lightness of spirit, similar to that which gladdened the hearts of the saints. My brother must have died with this supreme lightness of spirit. And he was more fortunate than his companions, who were backstabbed by the murderous fascists.

Elena's words here draw audibly on the futurist-tinged heroics of Lauro de Bosis's writing, and like his, they also strike a distinctive tone of public responsibility and perhaps provided models for the forceful tone of Shirley's writings about the United Nations.

In 1946 the Vivantes left England and returned to Italy. "It was a time of hope," Shirley explained in a tribute she wrote after Elena's death:

But Italy was spiritually and physically a wounded land. Arriving at the shattered port of Naples, the Vivantes had made their way north through the ruins of bombarded towns. Not many months earlier, the front of war had passed along the same route. At Siena, in a summer dawn of 1944, the great bell of the Mangia tower had tolled as the German garrison silently withdrew towards Florence and the Allied troops entered, together with the partisans, on the opposite side of the city. In the post-war years, while the painted exhortations of Mussolini, still legible, haunted the walls of country villages, simple monuments were raised—in a Siena street, in the woods of nearby Monte Maggio, and throughout all Tuscany—recording the executions of partisans and hostages.

Shirley clearly felt the crossing of paths at Naples: her own postwar arrival in the city that had survived—was still surviving—the scenes witnessed by Elena and her family on their return.

Solaia had been used as a barracks by German and then Allied troops, but the family's possessions had mostly been protected by neighbouring farmers, who had "hidden the silver, buried a statue, put antiques and books in their own houses," although the retreating Germans had taken the car and horses. Leone's father, Cesare, had remained at Solaia through the war and had died there peacefully. The occupying Germans had known he was Jewish but had not harmed him, and the German doctor who treated him in his final illness attended his funeral. In the wake of the war, with the farmlands of Solaia neglected for the decade of their absence, the family was facing straitened circumstances. They sold off some of the land around the villa, and Elena went to work as a teacher in nearby Asciano, walking an hour into Siena each day to take the train to work and another hour back again. And they opened the villa to paying guests, "usually friends, or friends of friends from England and America." The exercise was a success; from the early 1950s until the late

1960s Solaia was filled through the summer, and often at other times, with guests; as before, mostly writers, artists, intellectuals—or those aspiring to be—in a more international mirroring of the prewar salon, paying 2,500 lire per day, with a little more for excursions or classes in art history or Italian.

That first visit of Shirley's in 1957 was out of season, at the end of autumn; the company was smaller, but the experience nonetheless galvanizing, and she quickly became a regular visitor. She described the scene to Chris Cooper a few years later: "It is an indescribably beautiful place where one pays little and lives well, and where the company is always excellent (also in the respect that you don't have to have it if you don't want it)." The *Partisan Review* editor Dwight Macdonald, whom Shirley met and befriended there in the summer of 1958, described Solaia in a letter to Mary McCarthy:

> This is paradise—a large country house . . . in midst of the Tuscan landscape which I think most beautiful anywhere, run by Elena Vivante, as great a woman in her way as Hannah [Arendt] who she resembles in vitality and gaiety, and her husband, a dim, odd aesthetic philosopher and gentleman farmer; 15 to 20 boarders, English or USA, all people like oneself (intellectuals of one kind or another); like a house party; good feeling prevails, we sit around 45 minutes after lunch, 2 hours after dinner and often rise slightly above small talk.

Shirley later drew directly on the Solaia scene for one of her earliest stories:

> Every evening of the summer, lanterns were hung from the oleanders and they had dinner in the garden. The table was a long and rickety affair on trestles, and there were always insects because of the lights, but on balance it was worth it. The evenings were cool even after the August days, which recorded heat, long after dark, in the villa's outer walls . . . The scene, too, was worth the discomfort: the white table, three flasks of wine, pale dishes of bread, red

dishes of meat, green bowls of salad; the summer dresses of the women, and a crimson shawl hung on a chair; everything scented by the flower beds, in eclipse beyond the lanterns, and by lemon trees, which stood about in great stone urns. Above the line of hills facing across a valley, the sky glowed from the lights of Siena, but the house at night rode its hilltop in rolling, dark countryside with the purposeful isolation of a ship at sea, and people around the table, too, assumed something of the serene animation of voyagers.

The central attraction for Shirley, as for others, was Elena, whose temperament Dwight Macdonald described as "large and free and courageous—maybe 'heroic' would be better." Arturo later reflected that his mother's magnetism flowed from a "fervour in the way she talked . . . Fanned by her, the conversation flew, took unexpected turns, met never a dead end. The subject might be anything—politics, the Pope, Piero della Francesca, a guest who had just left. Anything." Roberto Barzanti strikes a similar note in quoting the impression of one of the earlier prewar visitors, Fausto Saccarotti, of Elena presiding over a table that was furnished with fruits, herbs from the garden, wine and oil from the surrounding hills, and all around the flowing and spontaneous conversation: *"si parlava in libertà: sull'onda di Elena, fittamente, spontaneamente. Lo slancio e la naturalezza: queste le qualità che la facevano unica."*

After Elena's death, Shirley kept a picture of her on her desk in Manhattan. The photograph, taken at Lake Albano, near Castel Gandolfo, shortly after her marriage to Leone, is of a young woman in profile, but turning farther away from the viewer and the sunlight, looking out over a balustrade to distant hills. She clasps a long shawl about her shoulders. The photograph was possibly a prompt for the detail in Shirley's later tribute for her friend: "She was tall, slender but strong. The fine form and carriage of her head was enhanced by smooth hair, coiled behind. Her clothes were simple, unstudied and pleasing. In earliest morning, in a faded blue gown, she tended flowerpots in the garden, on the terrace that was a great flowering ledge over the valley. She disliked the ritual and rupture of dressing, girding oneself for the world and the day: 'Noiosissimo vestirsi.'" Shirley was not alone to write of Elena in elemental terms. Robert Sonkin, another regular guest and later Shirley's close friend, wrote of Elena as "all life," a creature from myth; "different from anything I had imagined or known. Tall, severe, vigorous," an "archaic [goddess]" in human form. For Sonkin, Elena bore a deep authority coupled with humility—"like a timid girl, she would ask 'Non ti pare?' after some splendid sentence"—and this bound the Solaia guests together in some larger company, each of whom "looked to her, relied on her insight and judgment, relished her outbursts of satire and passion, feared her disapproval, counted on the incredible breadth of her compassion and understanding." Elena became for her family and guests "in herself ... a perfection of life . . . Her utter nobility was always something that measured life and each of us squarely and surely, however much she herself respected completely the individuality and distinctiveness of everyone else, as something sacred, for herself she had no desire to judge or measure anyone but to be left alone."

The friendship Shirley forged with Elena across these visits was intimate, personal, while always haunted by the sombre history of the house and the family:

> One moonlit night of the late nineteen-fifties, we sat at the front of the house, on a stone bench still warm from that day's sun. Within expressive silence we heard the owl, and all the whirring, murmuring world of crickets, frogs, small insects. On such summer evenings there could be nightingales. In front of us, at the top of the driveway, the cypresses stood in pairs, black and mighty—so deep and dense, she said, as to offer a hiding-place if "'they' should come for you."

Here was the weight of momentous event and of individual self-realisation that had not, Shirley felt, been possible in the country or the family of her birth, nor in the independent adult life she had until then been able to fashion for herself. Elena embodied philosophical and aesthetic principles to which Shirley cleaved: "To have known her was to understand that the human ideal is not a striving for perfection but for wholeness: she was true, vital and entirely human, not a paragon but a criterion. She would have disliked such words, for she repudiated praise with real impatience, not weighing our human need to pay her tribute. More than thirty years after her death, her daughter-in-law Mirella said, of the years at Solaia, 'We knew then that it was a miracle.'" On the thirtieth anniversary of Elena's death, Shirley wrote in her diary that her greatest influence was "to make a principled life believable . . . She had lived it, she was it."

Elena was inseparable from the organisation and daily rhythms of the villa. Shirley recalled her sitting, in the mornings, in a quiet room at the front of the house writing letters:

A distinctive hand, dark ink on short blue stationery from Pineider in Florence. Throughout the day, she was at other work, in kitchen or dining room, or in an up-stairs hall of wardrobes and ironing-table, moving with the light step and immediacy she brought to every action: rapid, direct, without bustle. One would see her, too, in the late afternoons, seated in salotto or lemon-garden, sewing and mending; or in the old rustic wing of the villa, roofed with whitewashed beams and tiles, where on a worn sofa one might read or write undisturbed beneath the speckled engraving of the Fiera dell'Impruneta.

The quality of recollection here, Shirley's startlingly visual apperception, is as striking as the acts and objects observed. Much as she had been drawn over recent months to the exuberance, the material incommensurability of Naples' streets, houses, and ruins, at Solaia she came to attend with a like intensity to these gentler rhythms, marking the smallest events that signalled the passing day:

The light was the easier light of late afternoon. Farther along the wall, between the columns of the loggia, geraniums were flut-tered by a faint breeze. On a nearby hill, a bell was rung—an unmelodious, useful country bell. Two little barefoot girls in faded pink dresses and straw hats were carrying to the kitchen a basket of zucchini for the evening meal. Each held a handle, and the tilting basket was covered by the golden flowers of the plant; these would be fried tomorrow for the lunch table.

This attentiveness was another point of connection with Elena. In her 1983 notebook Shirley recalled Elena from that first visit—"paying tribute to the beauty around her, the blessed face of Mount Amiata: 'Non finiamo di rallegrarsi di essere qui. Che bel luogo! E il profile del monte Amiata? O caro e benedetto! Per quale motive un profilo di montagna fa tanto bene all'anima?'" This was clearly the matter of much of their conversation; even in letters simply confirming Shirley's summer arrangements, Elena included such moments: "The most beautiful change is in the light which is now September-like: pure, transparent, lemon-yellow and clear and the sun leaves before departing those beautiful slanting apparitions of orange on the walls indoors."

Shirley also developed friendships with other members of the Vivante family in the years that followed. Leone would ask for her thoughts on his philosophical writings, and she maintained a shared fondness with Paolo: "Dear Shirley, Thank you again for your letter and all your advice—it is all so well written and precise: like a map or a sketch where I can find my way without stumbling. So I shall gently start exploring the higher regions to which you give me the key." On the other hand, she always struggled to find common or temperate ground with the youngest Vivante, Charis, a strikingly beautiful, free-living artist with radical politics, who returned from Ghana with her baby daughter, Alba, not long after Shirley's first visit. The English writer Piers Paul Read, another Solaia guest through these years, wrote to his mother that Shirley "leads the anti-Charis group—the quiet sensitive types who cannot take the violence of [Charis's] personality." Shirley's friendship with Arturo centred on writerly matters. On her first visit he gave her a collection of poetry he had published in 1951, and she promised to bring her own poems next time. Their discussions were often practical—how to develop a story she was working on, Arturo suggesting that she "recopy" it—"recopying is like a new wave, I find often"—and she sent him her thoughts on his.

"Dearest Shirley, thank you so much for your letter and for everything you say. You say it so well I don't doubt you are a writer . . . It will be wonderful to see you when you come, I hope you'll still want to read me your poems, I very much still want to hear them." Arturo was himself just beginning to be published. Dwight Macdonald had spent time at Solaia in the summer of 1957, just before Shirley's first visit. He had liked Arturo's writing and had taken one of his stories to the fiction editor William Maxwell at *The New Yorker*. The story was accepted, and other acceptances followed.

Shirley left Siena in early December 1957, travelled south by train to Naples, and then sailed to New York on the *Cristoforo Colombo*. Leaving Italy, she may have reflected, like Jenny, that "there now existed at last a place that could be missed. Arriving in America, I was coming from this. Some part of me would always be coming, now, from this. Like the dye they had injected into my veins, the country coloured my essence, illuminated the reaction to everything else. Here, literally, I had come to my senses." She returned to the familiar darkness of Kit, who had returned to New York the previous year—having "loathed London beyond imagining"—just as Shirley was leaving for Italy. Shirley mused that while she was crossing the Atlantic en route to Rome, her flight had in all likelihood passed over her mother's ship "resolutely heading for New York." But she returned also to friends and the stimulating social and intellectual circles she was beginning to establish there. And she was back at the United Nations, moving offices and taking up a position as professional assistant to her former boss, Hugh Keenleyside, with a higher grade, but still offering, as far as she could see, few options for advancement. She knew she had to remain there at least in the short term, "because I hadn't a penny in the world except the tiny UN salary" and because she was on a UN visa, and as an Australian, she had little hope of obtaining any other kind. Returning to Australia was not something she countenanced, and even trying for a position in England would have involved beginning again in a new office at the lowest rung. "I had progressed at the UN although that's hardly the verb. I progressed to the stage of being a sort of assistant and having a little office of my own. I had such a miserable salary, I don't know how I got through those years."

Perhaps her claims to penury were exaggerated; there was, after all, enough money to travel to Italy for the next several summers, as well as time to spend there, thanks to the UN's generous allowance of six weeks annual leave: "I went to Italy on the charter flight and came back with $10 which I always reserved. I came back usually on the Friday so that I'd have the weekend to recover from the flight before beginning work and getting my pent-up salary and I got a salary advance to go away too. And I would come back with this $10." When she finally gathered the courage to leave the UN, she felt that it was a liberation: "I'd been trying to cope with this completely disillusioning bureaucratic life and pretending that it mattered in a way I didn't believe." Ever after she would say that "the real risk was to stay." Her capacity to imagine a departure from, an alternative to, working at the UN had been formed by her experiences in this past year, in Italy, in the values and the joy she had learnt in Naples and in the north. Solaia embodied principles she had tried to accommodate in her life: "It is difficult to convey without solemnity the homage paid in that house to civilised greatness; and the presence, whether invoked or latent, of art and poetry." The Vivantes made tangible to her not only these values but also something of her own worth: "It was there, and through them, that I was released into a larger life; restored to the measure of belief in myself that the United Nations had eroded." She would look back to this time and its significance within the story of her life: "My idyllic 'childhood,' 'lost domaine,' or what takes its place was Solaia. Moments of realised perfection, dreamlike suspension of time and 'complicity' of Nature. Perhaps not comparable, because heightened by consciousness; as childhood might instead be boundless with innocence." She was able, finally now, to inhabit the childhood she had always imagined for herself, to join, imaginatively at least, a family with elevated principles and sensibilities, to be recognised and welcomed by them, and to return from them to the larger world.

# 6.

## *SÌ, SCRIVO!*

### 1958-1963

IN EARLY JUNE 1958 Shirley flew out of New York on the charter flight. She went first to Geneva to Howard and Judith, then overnight by train to Florence, arriving just before dawn. "Sat down in the Gran Caffè Italia across from the station to have my breakfast out of doors. Pavements being hosed, sun shining. Ecstasy." She travelled on to Siena, where she was joined the following month by her new lover. Jan Ligthart was in his early forties and recently estranged from his wife. He had been born in Surabaya, on the island of Java in what was then the Dutch East Indies, later Indonesia, his mother of partly Javanese background and his father Dutch. He had moved to the Netherlands in 1929 and in 1952 joined the UN in the Statistical Office. Much of his time was spent outside the United States, in Haiti through 1956 and from mid-1958 in Africa— Addis Ababa and Mogadishu—but he was in New York in early 1958 long enough to meet and fall in love with Shirley, just back from Italy. They saw each other while he was in New York, wrote letters through the following months, and then had two weeks together that July, first at Solaia, then in Florence and Rome. Throughout the holiday there was some awkwardness, some misalignment of mood and tempo. Shirley was minutely attentive to a mismatch of taste and sensibility between them, which she would later capture with great precision in her fiction: "One can't ask to be left alone, she thought, or not to be touched, even once in a great while, without creating a scene—without changing everything. Do we have anything in common at all, she wondered—almost idly, because the sun had drained her. Will we manage it? Sometimes it is all right. But not today." A decade later, arriving again at Solaia, she thought back to her state of mind at the end of that visit, recognising a moment of rare inner calm and solitary self-purpose, already moving off into her own orbit:

Solaia July 1958. Lemon trees beneath my window, night before I set out for New York. Great night, though nothing to remark except moonlight and force of sharply defined trees. End of first summer of total happiness—as one might start calendar years (like the Napoleonic or the fascist eras) anew. Life begins there. Joy, the power of joy—I felt fearless, attracted Jan and others by untouchableness of my happiness. Birth, re-entry into this world. Me, secret, not spilling the beans inanely on every private moment, but with much inwardness.

Another decade on, in 1980, she recognised that earlier self again seeing two young Englishwomen on Capri. They were "lunching in a veritable bower of ivy and flowers, one got up to photograph the other. Souvenir d'Italie—it was a moment from my summer of 1958. The scene, the capturing, the evidence to take back to one's otherness: beauty, volupté, nature, ease."

Mostly she and Jan were on different continents and in different time zones, their correspondence impeded by postal delays. Jan wrote in early 1959, "In your letter of the 6th and 7th you say: 'I am lonely and letterless'. I read it the 14th and I know that you are going to be letterless at least three more days. I would like to send a cable now saying don't worry there will be one on Saturday, but that cable will arrive only today which is a week later again." Their planned holidays together were often thwarted by late changes to Jan's work schedule, creating a sense of disconnection that fed into Shirley's continuing insecurity. Her letters to Jan have not survived, so there is no immediate record of her feelings, but there is an almost constant throb of self-doubt in his letters to her, as well as his confusion over her feelings and frequent reference to her diffidence and her emotional demands. The relationship never really found stability; throughout, things were attenuated, difficult, unresolved. Shirley was still seeing other men in New York, and her life continued to be thwarted by difficulties with her family and at work. She was trying to secure a promotion at the TAA and also casting about for a posting in Italy at the FAO. Her application for a British passport was successful, which improved her chances, but a new position did not eventuate.

She was also very much caught up in new and expanding social circles, mostly through Solaia, which she visited every summer for the next five years, staying for two months or so each time. She would work, occasionally, while there, sitting in the loggia at her typewriter, but more often she toured around and spent time with the other guests. The English writer Piers Paul Read admired her but wrote to his parents that he came to find somewhat unappealing how she would collect people "in an irritating way." They went on to correspond intermittently, had friends in common in New York, and he later asked for her advice on his writing. She also met the poet John Hall Wheelock and his wife, Phyllis. They went on to form a warm friendship and often invited her for tea on Sundays with the literary critic Van Wyck Brooks. "It was the last of nineteenth-century literary America," Shirley recalled. She would continue to visit and exchange books with Wheelock until his death, in 1978. Hugh Brogan, who would go on to become a celebrated historian of America, was at Solaia regularly on holiday from Cambridge and would become a long-lasting friend; the philanthropist (at that time, also Cambridge student) David Sainsbury too. There was also Sophie Lester, who was close to the Vivantes and whose husband, George, ran an art gallery in Rome. Shirley's friendship with the Lesters was warm and continued in Rome and New York for some years. She also regularly saw John and Ginny Becker, whom she met through the Chigi Music Academy Foundation in Siena. Ginny had been an actress, Virginia Campbell, and John was a writer who had also run an art gallery in New York. Some years earlier, the Beckers had moved to Rome, where they lived an edgy, glamorous life, staging marionette shows for writers and artists, including Alice B. Toklas, Ingrid Bergman, Iris Tree, Bill Weaver, Aaron Copland, and Federico Fellini, who used them as models for Mr. and Mrs. Steiner, the hosts of the stylish party with a marionette performance in *La Dolce Vita*.

Shirley had met Dwight Macdonald during her first summer visit to Solaia, in 1958, and then met his wife Gloria, and they in turn introduced her to their New York circles at the *Partisan Review* and *The New Yorker*; these connections would shape the next decades of her life in Manhattan. One of her most significant friendships of these years was with Robert Sonkin, a philologist, and her neighbour at the East Fiftieth Street apartment block where she lived for four years from 1958. Sometime in 1959 she recognised the name on his doorbell as one she had heard at Solaia, mentioned affectionately by the Vivantes and the Macdonalds. She left him a note: "If you're the Robert Sonkin who was at Villa Solaia and even if you're not, would you like to come to a party." He came, and they became friends. Sonkin taught at City College. He was funny, sardonic; "a man of great learning and great intelligence . . . an inward and thoughtful person . . . a bit reclusive, a scholar." Twenty years older than Shirley, and gay, he was a good friend of the Victorian literary scholar and biographer of Lewis Carroll, Mort Cohen, and his partner, Dick Swift, a professor of politics who had an interest in the United Nations, and Shirley established a lifelong friendship with them too (despite their very different views of the UN). She and Robert became very close. They went to dinner and to concerts—the Budapest String Quartet "every second Friday in late autumn and winter at the Metropolitan Museum in the Grace Rainey Rogers auditorium, beautiful." Because they lived in the same apartment block, they paired up to host dinners and parties, for all the world like a couple. Elena Vivante wrote to Shirley that she would "try to tell people about [Robert] but of course there are no words—only his rare presence can in part explain or rather illustrate his unique individuality and singular value." This was a substantial attachment for Shirley, the first of a number of friendships with gay men who would increasingly shape her intellectual and emotional worlds.

Another great friendship from these Solaia years was with Archibald—Archie—Lyall, an obscure but legendary figure who, when Shirley met him, was close to the end of a colourful, maverick life. Archie was to have been a barrister, but he directed his attentions to more entertaining pursuits. He had been at Oxford with the novelist Anthony Powell, and the two travelled together through Central Europe in the summer of 1924. During and after the war Archie had worked for British Intelligence, Special Operations Executive, in Cairo, the Middle East, and the Balkans, as a judge for war crimes trials in Vienna, and then in various information services roles in Italy and Central Europe. He had published several travel books, a comic work of mock-anthropology on British customs, and a multi-language phrase book, *A Guide to the Languages of Europe*. In the mid-1950s, when he was living mostly in Italy, he had a brief career as a film actor and made some half dozen films. Remembered by friends as both Falstaffian and Rabelaisian, he had described himself to Shirley as "by nature both excessively indolent and extremely fastidious," and she recalled that even when sad, "as he occasionally was, was yet more lively than the rest of us in the best of spirits." She was drawn to this liveliness, to Archie's eccentricity and his capacity for pleasure: "One was never surprised at the interest shown in him as he walked the streets of Italian hill-towns, for Italians know a good thing when they see it—although Archie was pleased to attribute this interest to the fame of his film career ('I made a film with Sophia Loren once. I had to kiss her forty times and tell her I was glad she'd come to my party.')." He was, Shirley wrote to Dwight Macdonald, "an inspired figure of a type fast being extinguished, the arch (sic) enemy of organization life and of all abstractions: he even looked like the incarnation of humanism, with a walrus moustache stuck on as a disguise."

Shirley accompanied Archie on outings through the countryside around Siena as he gathered material for his final guidebook on Tuscany and Umbria. She recalled his reckless driving and the pleasure she took in his "back-handed" manner of speech: "('Got to go to the Monte Oliveto: the monks've just put in a bar. Some frescoes there too'), interspersed with deft quotations ('Hello, I'm on the wrong side of the road. Ah well, home thoughts from abroad')." She memorialised him in the figure of Algie Wyatt, the shambling translator who works, grudgingly, for the Organization in *People in Glass Houses*, a man in every important way in excess of his employers. She wrote in her memorial tribute: "After Archie's death, I borrowed some of his characteristics . . . for a piece of fictional writing, and I quoted verbatim from Archie's last lines to me, the concluding lines of the last letter I had from him." Those lines appear in "Nothing in Excess":

> Algie's last letter to Lidia was written only a few days before he died, but reached her some weeks later, as he had neglected to mark it 'Correo Aéreo.' In this letter he reported the discovery of several new contradictions in terms and mentioned, among other things, that Piero Della Francesca died on the same day that Columbus discovered America, and that there is in Mexico a rat poison called The Last Supper. Such information is hard to come by these days; now that Algie was gone, Lidia could not readily think of another source.

At Archie's death, in 1964, Shirley made the acquaintance of his great friend Patricia Clarke. Patricia had worked with Archie in Cairo, where she held famed parties (after one of them, Theodore Roosevelt's son Kermit gave her a flying lesson over the pyramids). Patricia and Shirley went on to forge a warm friendship, which lasted until Patricia's death, in 2007. Shirley saw her whenever she was in London, and Patricia would come to play a central role in the ongoing burden of taking care of Shirley's mother on her regular doomed trips to England.

Shirley had begun writing in earnest, concentrating, through 1959, on what she described to Jan Ligthart as "bad poems." In October she sent him one, which he found "lovely even though it sounds like a fairy tale to be heureux jusqu'à la fin du monde." Years before, Tex had encouraged her to take writing seriously, convinced, after reading her letters, of her talent: "I would now, more than ever, have you write. Before, when I only got a sort of second-hand look at your letter to Howard, I was already convinced. Now that I have received the appropriate (if not full) measure directly I know this is what you must do with your perceptive mind. You communicate with such charm and wit and apparent ease and you have so much to say." The aesthetic feast of her year in Italy—coupled with its loneliness—seemed to bring this prospect closer, to make it seem thinkable. Solaia provided her with subject matter—scenes, characters, events—and propelled her from poetry to fiction. Back in her office at Turtle Bay, during her lunch breaks she would walk back to her apartment to write, and she also gave over her evenings and weekends. She began sending stories to *The New Yorker*. In November 1959 she received her first rejection, but with a letter encouraging her to write more. The following April a second story was turned down, but her spirits were quickly buoyed as she felt the writing was going well. In mid-July she was off again to Solaia. Jan had hoped to join her there or in Rome, but his uncertain schedule interfered with their planning, and arrangements were left hanging. He found the extended separation difficult, and in August he wrote to her at Solaia, proposing that they end things.

Shirley was furious, but the disappointment had been overshadowed even before it happened by a letter from *The New Yorker*, this time an acceptance. It is not clear whether she had revised those first rejected stories or if this was new work. Either way, she now knew someone on the inside, which changed everything. The previous month, just as he had done the year before with Arturo Vivante, Dwight Macdonald had offered to take one of her stories to the magazine, which meant that it would circumvent the slush pile and go straight to William Maxwell. Maxwell was legendary, by many accounts the most significant editor of short fiction in the United States through the postwar decades; he had worked with J. D. Salinger, Vladimir Nabokov, John Cheever, Mavis Gallant, and Eudora Welty. In a memoir of his friendship with Maxwell, Alec Wilkinson wrote that Maxwell brought to the work of editing "a selfless interest in encouraging talent, and an intimacy with the catalog of technical possibility" and that he simply took pleasure in good writing. The writers Maxwell worked with were "on the whole so accomplished that his position also involved taking delight in what they brought into being." He was "extremely receptive to women writers," and his relationship with Shirley in the years that followed was "golden," a "meeting of minds." With a devotion—what Wilkinson described as "a near spiritual hunger"—for literature that echoed her own, William Maxwell was surely Shirley's ideal first reader.

Although the beginning of Shirley Hazzard's writing career was not quite as instantaneous as she later gave to believe, it was swift enough,

and the achievement of the stories so beyond question as to appear, in retrospect, inevitable. And she did indeed receive her first acceptance as she
stood in the kitchen at Solaia, a joyous intervention. She later described
in a story the scene in the kitchen each morning when the letters came,
and the protagonist, Harriet, went to check them: "It was the butcher
who brought the mail from Florence once a day; his small grey delivery
car trundled up the drive about eleven o'clock. Occasionally he was late.
There was talk with the maids before the bundle was laid down, with the
day's meat, on the kitchen table, and there were papers, circulars, letters
to be turned over before Harriet could be sure that there was nothing for
her." And in her notebook, she recorded the arrival of William Maxwell's
letter:

Went to the kitchen on Wednesday morning 3 August 1960, to
see if there were letters for me—expecting only the usual disappointment of Jan. Elena, sorting the mail, handed me two letters. When I saw one was from *New Yorker* I tore it open, saw a
check ... "I am very happy to tell you ... Very happy ..." Handed
it to Elena, who embraced me, was pleased as if it were her own.
Went upstairs, suffocated with pleasure and excitement and have
been so ever since—a sort of nausea and unrealisation of all this
means. So happy. Everything else diminishes—all the loneliness,
pain, helplessness, self-doubting. At least for the present. And the
liberation, in another sense, by the check for $300, with $200 to
follow. Yesterday at Bionciardi to have my hair done, Charisina
had told them—extravagantly—what I do: "Signorina, Lei è
scrittrice?" What an absurd pleasure to say Sì, scrivo!

And so it began. "That afternoon I walked across the fields into Siena
and bought a notebook so I could write those stories." She began writing
on the last page of the notebook, not confident that her thoughts were
"important enough to write from the front." She wrote immediately to
Dwight Macdonald: "A note to thank you for your kindness in exposing
Mr William Maxwell to my communications ... This morning I received
the most welcome news that the New Yorker finds my most recent effort

acceptable. It is, incidentally, another story using Solaia as a background (though indeed only the second Italian one I have written)." While it was not her first story, nor indeed her first submission, there was from the start a clear recognition that this was an extraordinary debut. Maxwell later recalled that it was "an astonishment to the *New Yorker* editors because it was the work of a finished literary artist about whom they knew nothing whatever." He felt that she had nurtured her own talent without advice or tutoring; she does not appear to have shown her work to anyone else, apart perhaps from Arturo Vivante. Maxwell commented that he had "never asked her how she began writing. She must have gone through a period of apprenticeship of one kind or another, but under whose eyes? Her own, I would think."

On September 6, Maxwell wrote again, enclosing the balance of the writer's fee and expressing his hope that "you will have another story for us soon. Also, perhaps you might like to drop in to the office some day and talk about possible work. In all events I would be delighted to meet you." When they met in November at his *New Yorker* office, Maxwell encouraged her to take the "little time it may all take" to develop her work. That month she received another rejection. She had sent a draft of a story, "Mount Victoria," to Henry Robbins at Knopf in the hope that they might take it as an outline for a novel. Robbins wrote back that while there were strengths in the piece, he "thought that the whole lacked depth and substantiality" and that it wanted "the complications and conflicts needed in a novel." He encouraged her, nonetheless, "to use this intriguing setting of Hong Kong just after the war, with everyone apparently so anxious to resume pre-war society as usual, for a story with a much broader cast of characters and a richer texture than you've chosen for <u>Mount Victoria</u>," advice she would follow, although not for many years.

Things moved more quickly at *The New Yorker*. She signed a first reading agreement in February 1961, just half a year after that first acceptance, and was assigned to the editor Rachel MacKenzie, as Maxwell was reducing his hours at the magazine to pursue his own writing. Shirley initially formed a warm friendship with MacKenzie, although their relations would later sour. Their correspondence indicates how little editorial work was required even on these first stories, rarely more than "a few small questions, mostly punctuation," bearing out Maxwell's sense that she was a self-directed writer with a deep intuition. It speaks also to the apprenticeship she had undertaken, not only the years of writing "bad poetry" but, before everything, the years of reading poetry and committing it to memory. Four months later, she was described in *The Sydney Morning Herald* as "one of the newest stars on the New York literary scene," with five stories sold to *The New Yorker*, an impressive debut that she was happy to emphasise, with just a slight turning of the facts: "And I only started writing a year ago!" The *New Yorker* atmosphere was conducive. She later wrote of the magazine's editor William Shawn as "a rare bird, an unprecedented and unreproducible, and irreducible figure," and of his partnership with William Maxwell through those mid-century years as "a period of literary achievement that, I imagine, no prominent magazine will ever enjoy again." In July, Dwight Macdonald wrote to Mary McCarthy that over the previous year, the "English writer" he had met at Solaia, Shirley Hazzard, had sold several stories with a Solaia setting and was "thinking of giving up being a bureaucrat."

"Harold," the story accepted by *The New Yorker* that August morning, was not published for another two years, by which time the magazine had published several others. It is a luminous story: an evening at a pensione outside Siena, an awkward young poet who reads his work to a group of guests in gentle defiance of his impossible, harrying mother; the principle of poetry's authority is reasserted:

> When he had read aloud for a few minutes, the boy looked up, not for commendation, but simply to rest his eyes. Charles said quickly: "Go on." The inclined young face had grown, in the most literal sense, self-possessed ... He spoke as though for himself, distinctly but without emotion, hesitating in order to decipher corrections, scattering his crumpled papers on the table as he discarded them. It seemed that no one moved.

"Harold" was built around an incident from the summer of 1959, and it was important to Shirley. The delays in its publication continued throughout her otherwise sunny correspondence with Rachel MacKenzie.

Shirley wrote in July 1961, "It is nice to think ['Villa Adriana'] may be published this summer. What will become of poor Harold??" to which Rachel replied with the news that "Villa Adriana" had now been published and that "the new schedule, just delivered, has 'The Worst Moment of the Day' down for September 3. Isn't that happy news? No signs of 'Harold' as yet; I hope you can bear it." After "Harold" finally appeared the following year, Shirley wrote of it to Piers Paul Read: "There was by the way a very early story of mine (New Yorker had kept it for ages) about Solaia in the magazine on 13 October. It might amuse you for the setting." Harold was, she told Dwight Macdonald, "from life—real name Patrick. Patrick has since had some poems published, but I haven't heard of him for a year or more." It seems the young man's experience with an impossible mother resonated with her. The immediacy and audacity of Harold's achievement as a writer announced, in a way, her own, and she continued to accord it primacy as her first story.

Her second was "Vittorio," the writing of which had preoccupied her through 1960; she found it difficult to write from the perspective of an older man surprised by love. The upturning of Vittorio's life comes about when he invites an English couple into his family home—in a town resembling Siena—as paying guests and unexpectedly falls in love with the young wife. The story turns on Vittorio's realisation that the young woman, too, has fallen in love—with him.

> It was with astonishment, more than anything else, that he saw her eyes enlarge with tears before she turned from him toward the house—an unbearable astonishment that called upon all his capacities for comprehension. He followed her in silence. They entered the house together and began to climb the stairs. He was profoundly aware of her, moving slowly and sadly at his side, but it did not occur to him to speak. He felt that he must be alone to think about it, that there must be some rational, disappointing explanation.

She sent "Vittorio" late in the year, and it was quickly accepted but then overtaken for publication by the third story sent, "Woollahra Road," based on scenes from her Sydney childhood and published, in the end, first. In fact, she was less than confident of the appeal of "Woollahra Road." She sent it to Rachel MacKenzie in January 1961 "for your opinion rather than submitting it finally for consideration . . . It will be such a help to know what you feel about it." The story was accepted "in a whiz," as Rachel put it, and the acceptance was followed just as quickly by the offer of the first reading agreement in February. In March she sent Rachel a revised version of "The Worst Moment of the Day" (she later referred to this as "the second story, really, that I ever wrote"), another Solaia story about the awkward complications of love's decline against a backdrop of searing summer, "a high pagan explosion of a sky." She received a response less than a week later. Rachel wrote that "Of course" they wanted it, "It's such a beauty—insights, atmosphere, immaculate writing." William Shawn had described it as "Just about flawless."

These later stories fleshed out the world of those Solaia summers, the guests at the villa, and the rhythms of their days. They also recorded, after the event, the decline of Shirley's affair with Jan. "Villa Adriana" follows a couple who are visiting the Villa Adriana outside Rome. Their blunt, truncated conversation flickers dismally through the patter from tour guides in multiple languages:

"So you see . . . there wouldn't be much point . . . I'm sure you agree . . ."

"I'm not quite sure what we're talking about . . ."

"Simply that it wouldn't work . . . We would make one another unhappy—we do already—and it's as well that we found out in time. That's all. It's quite impossible."

"I don't understand."

"And that," she returned, "is precisely why."

Shirley later, perhaps ill-advisedly, sent the story to Francis Steegmuller, in the early months of knowing him. He read the story, somewhat critically, as a kind of code for Shirley's own critical and hypersensitive response to a lover.

She quickly fell back into her old routine of choosing older, married—

Shirley and Valerie, 1930s. The sisters were never close and came to regard each other with increasing hostility through their adult lives.

Shirley recalled her early years as having been rather lonely, living, as she put it, "much in books, and imagination, where one discovers affinities."

Queenwood School, 1920s. The house had balconies and a veranda facing north and east, allowing for sunshine and tempering sea breezes.

Alexis Vedeniapine was born in St. Petersburg, grew up in Shanghai, and went to school in England. He was the first great love of Shirley's life. They both worked in the British Combined Services office in Hong Kong in 1947 and 1948. Vedeniapine was a decorated war hero, fluent in several Chinese languages as well as Russian, English, and German, and, like Shirley, was a great reciter of poetry.

As the Hazzards prepared to return to Australia in September 1948 after a year and a half in Hong Kong, they were photographed by the local press. Shirley was desperately unhappy to be leaving, because of her love affair with Alexis Vedeniapine.

Shirley had this portrait taken in 1949 or 1950 in Wellington during her enforced separation from Vedeniapine, who was establishing himself as a farmer in Hertfordshire, England. She was nineteen years old, unable to travel to him without her parents' approval.

Green Park, London, 1951. In late October, the Hazzards arrived in London on their way to New York, where Shirley's father, Reg, had been appointed Australian Trade Commissioner. They stayed only a few short weeks, but Shirley remembered it as a defining visit; she had at last left the provinces behind.

November 1951. Shirley and Catherine (Kit) Hazzard. Shirley remembered how much her mother relished the formality and luxuriousness on board the RMS *Queen Elizabeth*, sailing from London to New York.

Catherine Hazzard, 1950s. Kit was a perennial concern for both her daughters. Through her later years she drew unstintingly on their affections and energies. She moved restlessly from city to city around the world, unable to settle anywhere for long. She was, Shirley remembered, "strikingly beautiful, even into later life, and had fine taste in clothes."

Howard Daniel, early 1950s. Daniel was the first of Shirley's senior UN colleagues to attract her romantic interest. Their flirtation lasted from 1952 through 1953, and they remained friends for some years.

Arthur (Tex) Goldschmidt, early 1950s. Like Howard Daniel, Tex Goldschmidt was articulate, charming, politically progressive, and flirtatious. Shirley's affair with him lasted nearly three years. It ended unhappily in mid-1956 and she requested a transfer to Naples.

Robert Sonkin, 1950s. Sonkin was the other kind of man who attracted Shirley. Like Daniel and Goldschmidt, he was articulate, well-read, and charming. He was the first of a number of gay male friends across her life.

Shirley, late 1950s

Outside the Villa Cimbrone, Ravello, 1957

Capri, 1957. Shirley made the crossing from Naples to Capri nearly every week-end from April to August that year. Visiting the island lifted her out of the misery and despair of her broken love affair with Tex Goldschmidt.

Villa Solaia, 1950s. Howard Daniel provided Shirley with an introduction to the Vivante family, who lived at the Villa Solaia, outside Siena. Solaia had been a kind of salon for anti-fascist writers and artists before the war; later, the Vivantes began taking paying guests, mainly writers and artists, from abroad. Shirley first visited in late 1957, then returned every summer until 1963.

The company at Solaia was important for Shirley, and at its heart was Elena Vivante, a woman of great character and intellect, described by guests as "heroic" and "a figure from myth." Shirley wrote that Elena's great gift was "to make a princi-pled life believable."

ABOVE LEFT Dinner at Villa Solaia, 1960s. Leone Vivante is at the head of the table, with Shirley at his left, and Paolo Vivante to her left. Further down the left side of the table, his face half obscured, is Roger Pryor Dodge, a dancer, choreographer, and jazz writer. To Leone's right is Frances McClernan, a writer, with her husband, Maurice Hindus, also a writer, on her right. Further to his right, again with face partly obscured, is Hannah Loewy, a friend of Albert Einstein's. Charis Vivante is seated at the far head of the table. (© Pryor Dodge)

ABOVE RIGHT Dinner at Villa Solaia, 1960s. Arturo and Nancy Vivante are seated in the middle of the table. (© Pryor Dodge)

Italy, early 1960s

At the United Nations, 1961

Author photo, circa 1963
(Blackstone-Shelburne, NY)

Muriel Spark photographed by
her editor, Harding Lemay, in
Knopf's offices. Muriel sent the
photograph to Shirley in February 1963, early in their friendship, and a few weeks after she
had introduced Shirley to Francis
Steegmuller.

Shirley had first met Jon and Ruth Naar through Howard and Judith Daniel during her early years at the UN. They introduced her to a more bohemian world. Jon Naar took up photography in the early 1960s, later becoming an acclaimed street photographer and portraitist, and photographed Shirley a number of times during the early part of his career. (© Jon Naar, www.jonnaar.com)

Jon Naar took a series of photographs of Shirley outside the United Nations building in Turtle Bay. The UN remained for her a site of relentless contestation for the rest of her life. (© Jon Naar, www.jonnaar.com)

hence unavailable—men as her partners and found no more comfort than she had with Howard or Tex, or Jan. Her diaries tell of flirtations during this period with two colleagues from *The New Yorker*, staff writers Barney Lefferts and Brendan Gill. The two men regularly worked together on the Talk of the Town column; it appears that neither knew about the other in Shirley's private life. She seems not to have disclosed either affair to anyone, but she kept an envelope with notes and cartoon sketches from Lefferts, with whom she had had a brief fling in 1960. She met Gill in early 1962, just days before she left the UN, at a party at the apartment of another *New Yorker* writer, Ved Mehta. She found Gill "Irish, tall, lean, funny and clever in a wiry, energetic way." After the party they had dinner, then went back to her apartment so she could pick up the proofs of her new story (ironically enough, the story was "A Place in the Country," based on the weekend she had spent at the Goldschmidts' Catskills house back in 1955). The evening was pleasant: "I was pleased and amused—it was so all-at-once and sweet like the evening I met Barney." It led to a second date a few days later and then, after a few awkward weeks when Gill failed to call, to another brief and dispiriting affair. She found that isolation and a sense of abandonment were no easier to manage at thirty than they had been at twenty, and she wrote in her diary of "an endless pattern" of disappointment and humiliation: "It is the pattern of abandonment that kills, slowly kills. Only—only it is so shaming. I wait. Telephone bells burst in my heart. I wait. Ruth Naar telephones. My sister. Robert. I wait. I begin to accept but still I wait. Now I know, but there is still the possibility for a day or two—till Monday. Then I can start to heal again." In the middle of all this, one evening when she was miserable, "sick with despair from BG's indifference," she ran into Lefferts: "We spent an hour together, talked like lovers, I forgave everything the instant he took my hand and said, after a silence of two years—'I love you'—That night he came and made love . . ." Some difficult knottings and repetitions were being played out in these fleeting affairs, which brought only the briefest pleasure. Yet something had changed; the failures of love now seemed to matter less, and the heartbreak was short-lived. In the wake of these dalliances Shirley would go on to forge a warm professional relationship with Gill—they had what they referred to as "spiritual lunches" together—and she seems quickly to have shaken off any lingering awkwardness.

In February, Chris Cooper wrote asking for news: "Talking of writing, did you ever get that book published? . . . And what about that 'threat' of matrimony (I think that was the word)? Are you in fact married?" Settling down with Jan was no longer, if it ever had been, a possibility; nonetheless, Shirley's desire for conventionality, for marriage, children, domesticity, a desire that had formed the substance of many, many laments in her diaries over the past decade, endured. This led in turn to difficulties with those less serious lovers and also to complications in her friendship with Robert Sonkin, which had come to resemble the kind of intimate partnership she desired and had so far been unable to establish with her lovers. Her diaries show her still often deeply unhappy, overwhelmed by a sense that she was alone in the world, and the enormous shifts in her life over the past half decade, when a world of animation and beauty and affection and professional achievement had opened up for her, were still not enough to assuage her melancholy. She wanted to be in love and to have her love returned, and Robert was, for a time, the object of her desire:

> R came today. He was cruel, unaccommodating, reducing me to nonsense with unresponsiveness. I had asked him to come to Claude's lecture with me on Monday and as he was leaving, he said "I don't want to sit through some miserable French lecture." "Don't come then." "I don't think I will." I had tears in my eyes from the rudeness, but from little else. In a way a relief, because it makes what is so improbable impossible when he does these things. But at its (for me) crudest and (for him) cruellest, he is a substitute for a man in my life.

She struggled with Robert's often distant manner, which seemed to be at odds with his larger qualities: "The illusion I cannot overcome is that, because of his particular sensibilities . . . I think, keep thinking, that he must be sensitive to my pain. With all my intellect, I know this to be

false. I cannot transmit that knowledge to my heart. And why? <u>Why?</u>
Sometimes in his presence I think my heart will burst from my breast
with the need to give him my love. I <u>know</u> that he does not want it. Yet
I cannot make myself behave accordingly." She had just returned from a
Christmas party:

> We are asked constantly together, as though we were lovers, which
> could hardly be further from the truth, could it? All the time I was
> trembling, at the edge of tears, distraught. Men made love to me,
> when their wives were in another room . . . I kept wanting Robert
> across the room, like a woman in love—Once I thought, Now I am
> going to cry. I feel the isolation, the pathos, at my heart. I try to
> think No, one can't give way, self-pity etc, but then all the rest of
> my life is made up of trying so hard, making it fit, all by myself.
> This burden I bear alone, at least. Appallingly alone.

Her comment "like a woman in love" indicates the awkward nature of
this intimate relationship with a gay man. It is possible that she had not
yet grasped the fact of Robert's sexuality and was responding to rejec-
tions both overt and subtler on his part, rather than a simpler or more
pathological cruelty in itself.

The stories she was writing through 1961 and 1962 reflected these
complications and sufferings. The young woman in "The Party" endures
an evening of her lover's cold and dismissive manner. As she is leaving his
apartment, he comments on her "mournful face. Not tragic, of course—
just *mournful*." She responds, tearfully, "You should be trying to build
up my confidence . . . instead of doing everything to demolish it." And
he: "'Confidence is one of those things we try to instill into others and
then hasten to dispel as soon as it puts in an appearance.' 'Like love,' she
observed, turning to the door. 'Like love,' he said. "Exactly.'" She wrote
even more directly from life in the twinned stories "A Place in the Country" and "The Picnic," which tell of a young woman's affair with her
cousin's husband, the discovery of the affair, and its consequences. These
fictional characters are starkly different from the protagonists in Shirley's

real-life drama with Tex and Wicky Goldschmidt. Nonetheless, parts of
"A Place in the Country" retrace events described in her diaries. And the
story's climax, the scene where Clem tells Nettie that they must part, is
drawn almost verbatim:

> "I think I told you I no longer loved my wife."
>
> "Yes," she said.
>
> "I only said that once, didn't I?"
>
> "Several times," she answered, unaccommodatingly.
>
> "Several times, then," he agreed, with a touch of impatience.
> "In any case—I see now that I shouldn't have said that. I mean,
> that it wasn't true."

In both diary and published story there is a marked absence of sympathy for the other woman in the adulterous triangle. May, the conventional
mid-century wife and mother, and Wicky the purposeful professional
woman bear no resemblance to each other, but it is telling that they are
equally unvalued by narrator and diarist. The first story treats the affair between Nettie and Clem with light irony and earnest gravity, but
there remains no question about the unshakable importance of love. In
the second story, when the three protagonists meet up again for a picnic, something has shifted. The narrative now shuttles between Clem
and Nettie, both a little taken aback by the fading of sympathy between
them. May is given no interior voice, no perspective. She bustles on the
sidelines, looking after the children, leaving the former lovers to themselves. In the final paragraph, in a moment quite outside Clem and Nettie's affair, which has limped to its inevitable, unsatisfactory conclusion,
May is suddenly brought right into the centre of the frame:

> Upright on her rock, May gave a short, exhausted sigh. She closed
> her eyes for a moment, to clear them, and Ivor called out that she
> must watch him, watch the game. She looked back at him without
> smiling. On either side, her palms were pressed hard against the
> stone.

May's singular presence here derives not only from the contrast with her earlier reticence through both stories but also from the splitting of the narrative into two stories, which has the effect of separating out the beginning and end of Clem and Nettie's affair, setting it into the larger context, the fragile, continuous thread of May's married life. The ironies provided by the contrary movements of love, its capricious genesis and its fading, are compounded by the shifting of narrative point of view and eclipsed by the image of the monumental endurance of this secondary character.

"The Picnic" moves in the direction of May's grave and unironic perspective through a flickering of awareness from the other protagonists and, most particularly, through Clem's faltering grasp of his wife's substance. Just before the final scene, he reflects:

> In all events, his marriage had survived Nettie's attractions, whatever they were. It was not easy, of course. In contrast to Nettie, May assumed too many burdens. Where Nettie was impetuous and inconsiderate, May was scrupulous and methodical. He was often concerned about May. She worried, almost with passion (he surprised himself with the word), over human untidiness, civic affairs, the international situation . . . May had a horror of disorder—"Let's get organized," she would say, faced with a picnic, a dinner party; faced with life itself. If his marriage lacked romance, which would scarcely be astonishing after twenty years, it was more securely established on respect and affection. There were times, he knew, when May still needed him intensely, but their relations were so carefully balanced that he was finding it more and more difficult to detect the moment of appeal.

Clem's insight hovers somewhere between grasping and overlooking things. His observation begins with the psychological commonplace that a long-standing marriage might lose romance but then moves to something sharper. The complexity that opens up at this point is built on the ironies flagged at the start of the passage ("whatever they were"; "of course") and signalled here again by the interposed "he knew." It is what he knew that is being questioned or troubled here. It has to do with his wife's agency and her desire, which, he is learning, do not coincide with his. He understands that May's desire for him is definitive rather than the other way around, and he is, moreover, aware that he is increasingly unable to read that desire with any precision. This is the moment that prepares us for the story's conclusion, the leap away from the back-and-forth of the lovers' conflicting viewpoints to the figure of May alone on the rock, grimly aware of her isolation.

There is nothing in Shirley's youthful diaries, despite the overlap between the two accounts, to prepare us for this moment of writerly sympathy. Nor is there any sense that her own views about her affair with Tex, his breaking with her, and Wicky's part in that had changed at all by the time she wrote this story; it is more than likely that she clung, with her customary tenacity, to her initial, unfavourable judgment of Wicky. In early 1962 she had been planning for these two stories to form the nucleus of a novel, but by September that year she had set them aside in favour of the stories that would become *The Evening of the Holiday*. Perhaps it was the image of May, alone on her rock, that indicated that there wasn't really, after all, a novel to be written about these characters, or, perhaps, that the story that might be told would not be focused on the adulterous couple—that in the end the most interesting and substantial character might be the jilted and resilient wife. As a story, "The Picnic" shines a little less brightly than her other early efforts, including "A Place in the Country." But the distance effected in it between the remembered and recorded matter of Shirley's own life and the larger understanding and sympathy found in the fictional version is striking. In it we see the moral vision that would go on to become one of the distinctive features of her mature work. Perhaps it was with "The Picnic" that Shirley Hazzard became, incontrovertibly, a writer.

For the rest of her life she would say that *The New Yorker* first reading agreement saved her life; with the accrued bonuses and cost-of-living-allowance payments that made up the magazine's complex but generous payment arrangements with its writers, she was soon financially stable in a way she had never been before. In January 1962 she handed in her resignation to the United Nations. She had hoped, briefly, that becoming a published writer might propel her career at the UN in more congenial directions, but this was not to be. Before she left, a friend and senior colleague, Edmund Jansen, took her case to the UN personnel office, describing the situation of her continuing lowly and undemanding employment as "absurd" and arguing that she should be moved to the more highly paid professional category and given writing and editorial work. The response from the personnel official was, Shirley recalled, "'Talk about distant prospects.' Hearty laughter. That decided it for me."

Shortly before leaving the UN, she had met the writer Ved Mehta, who interviewed her for an article on international technical assistance that he was writing for *The New Yorker*. Mehta, blind since a bout of childhood meningitis, had only recently joined the magazine staff and would go on to become for many years, in the words of William Shawn, one of its "most imposing figures." He published histories of India, and reportage, and a multivolume memoir of his life and family. The article for which he interviewed Shirley was not in the end published, but a friendship came of it. She was fond of Ved, although she later felt that he had at times been manipulative: "Ved would collect information and lead you to make indiscreet comments, then repeat it." The Macdonalds were also friends with Ved, as was Anne Fremantle.

Sometime in 1961, most likely through Anne Fremantle, Shirley had met the British editor and literary bon vivant Alan Pryce-Jones, a colourful figure whose career reached back to London's Bright Young Things of the 1920s. Since the end of the war, Pryce-Jones had been editor of *The Times Literary Supplement*, turning it, in the words of V. S. Pritchett, into "by far the best literary periodical in England," extending the magazine's reach and scope and embracing diverse literary talent while maintaining its highbrow reputation. Pryce-Jones, who was gay and extravagantly well-connected, had been married to Poppy Fould-Springer, from a wealthy Viennese Jewish background. Patrick Leigh Fermor wrote that "Alan knew everyone in the world and his stories were hilarious and leavened throughout with his sense of the absurd." He had moved to the United States in about 1960 to take up a position as advisor to the Ford Foundation, and, Fermor continued, "for a time it looked as if he had abandoned Britannia to elope with the shade of Edith Wharton." Pryce-Jones was in every sense Shirley's kind of man, and the two quickly became friendly. He, in turn, introduced Shirley to Rache (Horatio) Lovat Dickson, who had been born in Australia and had attended school in Rhodesia (Zimbabwe) and university in Canada. He had run his own publishing house before the war and then joined Macmillan as an editor.

In January 1962 Lovat Dickson was in New York to find new authors, and Pryce-Jones told him that he thought Shirley Hazzard "quite the best of the newer short story writers who had emerged in the last year or two." Lovat Dickson agreed, writing to Pryce-Jones after his meeting with her that "of the genuineness of Shirley Hazzard's talent even if it only appears at the moment in glints, I haven't any doubt." Macmillan's advisory reader was less impressed, describing her as "an almost unbelievably clever writer within a limited range," with "a single mood" prevailing, which weakened the "electrifying and sometimes profound" achievement of individual stories. This reader advised against contracting with her for a novel: "My guess would be that while she is an accurate (though morose and mildly obsessed) observer and a needle-sharp negative commentator, she is not by temperament a creator of large positive things. I would not bet much on any sustained fertility of her creative imagination—not, that is, on the evidence here offered." Macmillan opted not to follow this advice and signed a contract for a collection of short stories and a novel. Shirley signed with Knopf for U.S. publication at the same time, and her first collection, provisionally titled "A Place in the Country" after what was felt to be the strongest of the stories, began to take shape. Her new life was about to begin.

Another new and glittering friendship was with the celebrated Scottish author Muriel Spark, who was also in New York in January 1962. The previous October, largely at the urging of Rachel MacKenzie, *The New Yorker* had devoted an entire issue to a condensed version of Spark's latest novel, *The Prime of Miss Jean Brodie*, and in January, she arrived for the launch of the U.S. edition. Spark's biographer, Martin Stannard, wrote that New York was "ready for [Muriel] in a way that London was not. [Her U.S. publisher] Lippincott had booked her into the Algonquin, arranged parties, press interviews, dinners and a trip to their Philadelphia Headquarters. *Brodie* was published on the 17th . . . Lippincott threw a cocktail party at the St Regis hotel, where Updike, W. H. Auden and Lionel Trilling paid homage . . . The next day she was lunching at Le Pavilion with . . . William Maxwell and Rachel MacKenzie." Shortly after, Rachel invited Muriel and Shirley and the *New Yorker* poetry editor Howard Moss to her apartment for dinner; Shirley walked Muriel home, went up for a drink, and the two became friends.

The Beaux Arts hotel, where Muriel was staying—"more arts than beaux" she would quip—was on East Forty-Fourth Street, just a few blocks from Shirley's apartment, and through that January and again when Muriel returned to New York in October, the two saw each other almost daily, went to the cinema, concerts, dinner, "all drifted on a stream of talk and laughter." They called each other Shirlers and Mu. Shirley wrote to Chris Cooper, "Muriel Spark is here for the winter. She is a Great Dear. She has a horrifying habit of telling everyone the truth, and things have been lively during her stay. Be interesting to see what she produces on the American way of Life." Muriel gave Shirley the number to her bedside telephone, a number, Martin Stannard observed, "withheld from almost everyone else." That closeness was important to both, but it also took its toll, with Shirley increasingly distracted by Muriel's "two-hour calls." While she found Muriel "so interesting to talk to," she knew that after the calls she would be "not much fit to work." Muriel, she said, "needed *benzina* to get going. One was the fodder for this. One tended to give in because of the mastery of the thing. Not because one was weaker but because it wasn't one's way of doing things."

It was Muriel who was behind Shirley's break with Rachel MacKenzie. After the first months, Shirley had begun to find Rachel's attentions a little oppressive; solicitous consideration led to intrusive questions about where she had been if she missed one of Rachel's evening phone calls, and finally Rachel announced that she was moving to East Forty-Eighth Street "to be closer to you." She invited Shirley and Muriel for dinner several times, Shirley finding the atmosphere more and more "claustrophobic." Finally, Muriel broached the subject to Shirley: "How long have you been putting up with this?" Shirley felt as if a light had been turned on. Rachel had, she realised, "a crush." She discussed the situation with Robert Sonkin, who said, "I foresee nothing but disaster." After she spoke to William Shawn, Maxwell was reinstated as her editor. Shirley also felt that Muriel was possessed of a kind of second sight; she called her "Muriel with the x-ray eyes" and believed, she later told Martin Stannard, that "somehow things happened, odd things, when she was around." Later Shirley and Muriel, too, would fall out:

> She was a very good friend to me in those times, and I would have marvellous times with her but there was always a feeling: What on earth is coming next? The abyss was yawning there. And she would have, especially when she was working very hard on a book, she would have real tantrums, not at me, but at the world, or felt absolutely persecuted by people who took her time. And one did wonder when this would come round to oneself.

It did of course come round; Howard Moss took her aside in later years to tell her that she was not exempt from the catty remarks Muriel often made about people. It was, she recalled, "a shock. Stays with me."

Shirley and Muriel had a number of friends in common: Howard Moss, Brendan Gill, Anne Fremantle, and Ned O'Gorman, from Muriel's Catholic circles (Muriel had converted to Catholicism in the early 1950s), Mort Cohen and Dick Swift, Robert Sonkin. Anne had introduced Shirley to W. H. Auden, and to Elizabeth Bowen, whom she continued to see in New York, England, and Italy over the next decade, a low-key friendship based on mutual admiration. In the early autumn of 1962 Shirley held a lunch in her apartment for Bowen, with Muriel and Alan Pryce-Jones, and wrote afterwards in her notebook, "Women got more good-looking in her presence, or put on their individuality." Whenever Shirley was in London, Muriel would throw parties for her, with guests including Doris Lessing and Christine Brooke-Rose, whom Shirley found rather "a sour-puss." More usefully, Muriel would ask Kit, now mostly living in London, out to lunch in order to give Shirley more freedom. "Muriel was very nice to my mother. They got together as two Scots. Muriel understood that there was a lot to put up with. But they got along well, and she would ask my mother round." Years later, on hearing of Rache Lovat Dickson's death, Shirley looked back to this period as "that rather brief, ecstatic early time of my writing."

In 1962 Shirley also met the poet James Merrill, at the home of her friend Mary Williams Cortesi in Stonington, and there began another long and substantial friendship, grounded in deep affinity, with a gay man. There remains little by way of formal record of their friendship: a note from Merrill in June 1963 asking Shirley to a party, saying he'd been trying to reach her by phone for weeks (she'd been in Spain with Francis Steegmuller), a card from 1979 in which he writes of his memory of her "reciting poems on Mary Cortesi's carpet," a few later notes. But it was important to them both. Robert Pounder, who later met Shirley through Merrill, recalled that the two were very close. Steven Aronson knew them both and thought of them as being "on the same plane. He had the same manner that she did. He was arch in the same way and he was putting on the same airs. What lay behind it with both was a genius. Insight after insight. Inimitably, unforgettably expressed." There was also, in consequence of that affinity and that shared genius, warmth and delight in each other's company, extending to Merrill's death in 1995.

Shirley spent the summer of 1962 at Solaia, and wrote to Ved Mehta:

> It is a perfect delight and leaves nothing to wish for. I have had thoughts of coming back to New York at the end of August, as planned, and collecting a few winter clothes and coming straight back here. I daresay this won't come to anything, but I do feel so free here . . . I do very little, though I have a whole story worked out in my head and have done some work on it. The days pass in disporting myself, talking and giggling, lying in the sun, going for walks, reading etc. I'm having long train rides with Stendhal, who is ideally suited to reading on journeys.

From Solaia she went to Rome, where she stayed with Sophie and George Lester, and then to Naples and, for the first time since 1957, to Capri: "Arriving last night in the boat from Naples, we could smell the flowers while we were still at sea—all of Capri seems heaped with bougainvillea and oleanders." It was possibly on Capri on this visit that she met Sebastian de Grazia, an American political philosopher who would become another longtime friend, both in Capri, where he had a house, and in the United States. In September, "even more distraite than usual about the return to New York," she moved into an apartment on East Fifty-First Street, a new building, "in the part of Manhattan I like best." It had "a skyscraper-y view of the city and at night is rather nice, like a little box hung above the nearest buildings. Also, it is near the river, which one can see if one plasters one's face against the window and squints." It was, as she would always remember, "my first home, earned and achieved by myself, never marred or tainted, or spoiled."

The most important of all the consequences of Shirley's friendship with Muriel was the introduction to Francis Steegmuller, which Muriel described, memorably, as her own "best novel ever." In late January 1963 Muriel gave a party in her Beaux Arts rooms—"a tiny suite, tiny, tiny . . . a little party, about a dozen people." Before the party, Muriel had told Shirley, "There's a man coming I think you ought to marry." While Shirley, now in her early thirties, was somewhat accustomed to people making such comments, she was surprised to hear "this banal thing" from Muriel. Muriel mentioned that she had met Francis Steegmuller at Dwight Macdonald's. Shirley recognised the name—she had "read a million things of his"—and then promptly forgot Muriel's words, "or mostly forgot." The evening came, it was cold and beginning to snow, there was a bitter wind. Shirley wasn't feeling well. She had a sore throat and thought, "Am I really going to this?" but then she did. She put on "a nice black velvet dress" and walked, with her mother, who was in town, and Robert, around the corner to the Beaux Arts, where guests who had been invited for an earlier time, including Auden and Stephen Spender, were preparing to leave. Shirley saw her friends Ved Mehta, the artist Saul Steinberg, and Howard Moss talking with Muriel's Jesuit friend, Father Vincent Blehl, and went to join them. Kit left shortly afterward to go to the Australia Day party at the consulate. ("Thank God," Shirley added in her diary.) The door opened, and a man entered—"very tall, with a very austere face," wearing "a fawn-coloured greatcoat. A sort of British Warm." Steegmuller joined Shirley's group; he already knew the others.

Shirley knew that this was the man Muriel had said she should come to meet. They went and sat together on the "one good armchair," Shirley on the seat and Francis on one of the "puffy, big, rounded arms . . . and then we talked. And we knew it wasn't the last time we were going to talk." She would return to this scene in interview after interview, noting the same details, Francis's austere appearance, his beautiful coat, the chair, the *coup de foudre, colpo di fulmine,* and the shared conviction that there was "something destined about it" and that they would talk again. She would insist on the centrality of accident, "an accidental quality" to the meeting, as well as a sense of inevitability: "We sat down in a corner together and stayed there. When we came out of that corner, you might say, we went and got married."

Of course it wasn't quite like that. Francis, too, had nearly not come to the party; he had been dropped off by the woman he was seeing at the time, Margaret Watherston, an art conservator, who continued on, as Shirley later put it, to "wherever she was going, home. And perhaps he was expected to dinner, I don't remember if that was the case. But he said, I should stop off at this party and that was on the way, and she was in the cab and dropped him off. Supposing she had said, 'Well I'll come up with you, I'd like to meet Muriel Spark'? All these things, imponderable." But there were also more practical consequences. Perhaps Francis did miss dinner that evening while he was caught up so deeply in conversation with Shirley. Nonetheless, he would continue to see Margaret for many more months, creating no little distress for Shirley and possibly also for Margaret, and it was not until rather later in the year that he and Shirley reached any equilibrium or sense of shared commitment to each other.

After that evening, they were quickly in touch. In early February, again at Muriel's urging, Francis sent a note:

Dear Shirley—Not knowing whether you are the 'S. Hazzard, 400 E50' in the phone book [Shirley had recently moved to Fifty-First Street; the telephone directory took time to catch up], I make no inquiries and just write you thus c/o Our Club, to suggest the following: If it's true that we're to be both of us at the Maxwells on Friday the 15th, wouldn't you stop off here for a drink on the way and we could go on together? That is, if this is on your way and if it's convenient. Or I could pick you up if you preferred. Anyway I'm happy at the thought of perhaps seeing you again. Till the 15th I trust, Francis Steegmuller.

Shirley had often walked past Manhattan House on East Sixty-Sixth Street and was familiar with its stylish modernist lines. She later claimed to have had a Muriel-esque premonition that she might live there one day. "I just had a feeling it had something in store for me." Entering Francis's apartment, she noticed the impressive artworks he had collected with his first wife, Beatrice Stein, over the past several decades: "What a beautiful Redon." A week later, Muriel wrote from London, asking for news: "How is the affair* with Francis* (no innuendos intended) getting on? Tell me how the dinner party went, please do." She received in reply not the happy response she might have been expecting, given how sure she had been of their compatibility, but a letter telling of complications that had arisen, complications that gave rise to a period of significant disconnection and confusion on both sides.

The mismatches, not-quite-conflicts, both slight and substantial, over the coming months were perhaps inevitable in the face of their very different backgrounds. The age gap of twenty-five years was heightened by the disparity in their professional standing: Shirley's writing life was just beginning—her first stories had only recently been published—whereas Francis had fourteen books, with another due later that year. And though neither had come from an especially privileged background, Francis had certainly had the kind of formal education that allowed him to move seamlessly into the elevated cultural circles that had opened up to him through his first marriage, while Shirley's early life had been sorely lacking in such qualities and opportunities, and she had acquired whatever she had much more recently and solely through her own efforts. And yet they were both struck by the connection that sparked between them that first evening; their shared tastes—with Taste itself, honed through assiduous application, so essential to both—and interests, energies, and capacities. They would be married at the end of the year; the complications between them were also perhaps the basis of what would go on to become the only mature and sustained love affair in Shirley's life. It was, in a sense, what she had always dreamed of.

She would later describe the early years of her marriage as "the happiest she ever knew," in part perhaps from sheer relief that the lonely years looked to be over. Along with those affinities, there was the simple fact of Francis's material circumstances—his good overcoat, his paintings, his Rolls-Royce—which would have suggested to her what marriage with him might mean in terms of her own still somewhat precarious circumstances. It is telling how quickly, once the marriage had been agreed upon and the wedding invitations sent out, Shirley rose to the occasion. Her change of tone and demeanour is clear in a letter she wrote to Chris Cooper later that year:

He is Francis Steegmuller, an American writer who has spent much of his life in France and has written biographies of Flaubert, Maupassant and recently Apollinaire. (Strange details to be giving you—I should perhaps just say that he is tall, dark and So On, and that we are terribly happy.) We are being married on 22 December, at Sharon Connecticut where F. has a country house. Then we shall be living in Francis's apartment . . . We fly to London right after the wedding, shall be there from 25 Dec to New Year's Day, staying at the Connaught where we hope and pray that you will come and visit us—please. We then go to Paris or Rome for a little while and return to NY on 13 January; we shall come back to Europe to spend the summer.

She delights in the new "we" and sounds as if she had been born to this life—a far cry from her stalled UN career, the $10 brought back from her annual trip to Italy, the misery of her family life, and her subsequent difficult single years. Marriage to Francis Steegmuller did indeed change her life; it was the final dramatic transformation confirming that she had left behind her obscure background. It gave her grounds and wherewithal to fashion her life and herself around the coordinates of literature, integrity, and love. Much of her attention in the years to come would be turned to obscuring, refashioning, and forgetting where she had come from. But before that could happen, there were important obstacles to overcome, not in her past life but in the new circumstances of her present.

III

# 7

# FRANCIS

## 1906–1963

FRANCIS STEEGMULLER WAS twenty-five years older than Shirley. He had been born in New Haven, Connecticut, and grew up in nearby Greenwich. His mother's father, Jeremiah Tierney, had come to the United States as a child in 1851 from Ballylooby, Ireland, then worked as a hatter in Danbury, Connecticut. In 1862 he enlisted in the New York State Militia, and at the end of the Civil War he went on to study law, later becoming judge of probate in Greenwich. Francis's mother, Bertha Tierney, was born in 1879, one of six children; her mother died later the same year. Her uncle was the Catholic bishop of Hartford, and two of her sisters became nuns—a path Bertha resisted, choosing instead to study at Columbia University Teachers College. Both Judge Tierney, whom Francis described as "a very, very fervent—I must say bigoted—Catholic," and his brother the bishop were steeped in Democratic Party politics in Greenwich. In an oral history interview Francis gave in 1978 he described how Greenwich changed while Bertha was growing up, from being a sleepy rural town into "a kind of bedroom for New Yorkers, especially for wealthy people." Judge Tierney was, according to Francis, "crotchety, and disagreeable to live with." Because he had "worked hard to 'make something' of himself," he disapproved of Bertha's decision to become a teacher rather than a nun. He also disapproved of her engagement to

Joseph Steegmuller, but all the same came in his later years to live with him and Bertha.

Joseph's father had also been an immigrant. Matthew Steegmüller had travelled to the United States from Bremen, Germany, as a young man, and worked as a baker first in New York and then in Branford, Connecticut, where Joseph was born in 1877, one of thirteen. Joseph was also a devout Catholic. He worked as a bookkeeper, commuting to New York throughout Francis's childhood. Francis was born in 1906, his brother Lawrence in 1911, and a third brother, who died at just a year old, in 1918. They lived first in Greenwich, in a house near a woodland "full of dogwood and other trees, flowers, birds," through which Francis walked to school, and later in Cos Cob, "a nice old place, a pre–Civil War house, a great big house, much too big for my mother to take care of," with a large vegetable garden and chickens and pigs, which Joseph looked after on weekends. The family had a rowboat and another small boat with a motor: "We used to go out on the Sound. We would chug over to the various small, uninhabited islands in the Sound and swim from there." The family's relative lack of wealth in the community of Greenwich was formative for Francis, who was always conscious, he said, "of the difference between the rich and the not so rich." And he recalled "great divisions of society" newly opening up in the town. "It was a kind of social division that existed in many places, but it had not existed in Greenwich before . . . The trains my father commuted on to New York, the morning trains, had club cars on them which wealthy men would travel in and play cards in."

Mostly, Francis went to public schools: "My family couldn't afford to send me to one of the private schools and I don't know that they would have anyway. I'm not a bit sorry at having gone to the public schools. I had excellent teachers." When he was in fifth grade, Judge Tierney insisted that he needed a more formal Catholic education, so Bertha agreed to send him to "the parochial school in Greenwich." It was not a success. Francis recalled nuns with whips, "little rattans . . . and they used those rattans on the hands of the students quite often." He was unhappy and after one term returned to the public system. His mother had been concerned by the amount of time devoted to catechism and by the stories

Francis brought home—"tales of superstition and gory tales of people being converted on their deathbeds, told by the nuns." He was a good student, absorbed in his studies, particularly French. In high school, he and his neighbourhood friend Stanley Martin "zoomed way ahead of the rest of the French class because we enjoyed it," conversing together and at home in French whenever they could. Francis joined the college stream, although his father had wanted him to take the commercial path: "My mother had always expected that my brother and I would go to college, and there seemed no doubt that we would go. My father, I think, was not so keen on the idea. He hadn't gone to college himself. He was one of thirteen children, only one of whom, the youngest, had gone to college; went to Columbia. The rest of the family had all chipped in to help him go."

Francis was young, only fifteen, when he finished high school, so he followed his father's wishes and took a year's break, studying shorthand and typing at Merrill Business College in Stamford from September until year's end, travelling back and forth from Greenwich by trolley, and then working in an office until the following summer. This meant that he was able to take on secretarial work during his college years to help cover his fees and expenses. Before going off to college, he made his first overseas trip. He had begun visiting a neighbour, Muriel Steele, an English actress who had recently moved to Cos Cob while her husband, Vernon Steele, a Chilean-born actor, was in Hollywood seeking work. Francis was intrigued by Muriel, the photographs of her as Rosalind in the living room and "her beautiful English voice! She was very kind and nice; faded-looking, her small, quite fine features sharpened." They talked of the theatre, and travelling, and Francis's future. In 1923, realising that her husband was not coming back, Muriel returned to England on the SS *Canopic* and promised to put in a good word with the ship's captain for Francis and his friend Stanley Martin to secure positions as summer crew. Some years later, Francis began working this material into a story: "Miracle! Sudden telegram from SS Canopic, at dock in NY, to Cos Cob ordering both FS and SM to report (July). Exaltation, fear & trembling! (FS had never been away from home except for one summer camping trip with uncle and cousin in Catskills during which he annoyed everybody by displaying intense homesickness ... )" Francis and Stanley sailed to Southampton as assistants to "Pants," the pantryman. They had left without passports and were consequently allowed only a few days in England, until the arrival of the next westbound-sailing White Star. They stayed in Weymouth, in Dorsetshire, in the "custody," as the immigration officer put it, of Muriel. They hired a car and drove about: "Hardy country; enchanting villages, churches. Walked in fields, stiles—clotted cream with raspberries . . . all heaven. White horse cut in green turf on seaside cliff visible from Weymouth. Rain on St Swithin's Day." In Southampton, "the bookshops! Incredible!" Francis picked up a "nice early edition of Shelley (c1830)." On their return sailing, this time aboard the SS *Homeric*, they stopped at Cherbourg, "looked longingly at France, and enjoyed hearing French chatter aboard the tender." Francis and Stanley both stayed in touch with Muriel over the years, and in his unpublished story Francis recalled a fleeting encounter with her husband: "Years later, one view of Vernon Steele, who remained in Hollywood . . . the profile of a priest in the last scene of the . . . film of *Madame Bovary* with Jennifer Jones. Only the profile shown, like a shadow. And only when names of actors appeared on screen at end was the priest's shadow identified as Vernon Steele's. A bit part if ever there was one."

In 1923 Francis began at Dartmouth, transferring after a year to Columbia, where he completed a BA in 1926, Phi Beta Kappa, and an MA in 1927. He took a course in biography with Professor Henry K. Dick, and also a special honours course with only a handful of students. Henry Dick was something of a legendary figure at Columbia, recalled by his colleague Irwin Edman as "an arresting and contagious example of the old-fashioned scholar, gentleman, and, in the best sense, an amateur . . . the teacher as artist." The art historian Winslow Ames recalled Dick's idiosyncratic teaching. In his classes, students would read from their work each week and then write critiques of others' work. Professor Dick then critiqued the critiques, in "an endless chain . . . an extraordinary, extraordinary procedure." Francis composed his first book this way, bringing it to class each week, "chapter by chapter," revising as he went. The book, *O Rare Ben Jonson*, in the then popular genre of fictionalized biography, was published in 1927 by Knopf when Francis was just twenty-one. He told the story that on signing the contract, Blanche and

Alfred Knopf invited him to dinner. They had planned to take him to a restaurant, but when he arrived and they saw how young he was, they just took something out of the refrigerator. The book was published under a pen name "because I thought my name Steegmuller was ugly. And I thought it would be nice to have this rather romantic name of Byron Steel." His classmate at Columbia, the historian Jacques Barzun, with whom Francis would maintain a long friendship, later observed that "Columbia College in the Twenties was a place peculiarly favourable to young talent in literature," fostering in the second half of the decade "Clifton Fadiman, Lionel Trilling, Meyer Schapiro, Cornell Woolrich, Edgar Johnson, and Francis himself." Barzun added, "No doubt the watchful presence of Mark Van Doren, Raymond Weaver and John Erskine—themselves frequently in print—aroused emulation in the gifted, whom these benevolent elders then nurtured into the profession." Shirley recalled a conversation between the two men about their time at Columbia, with Francis remembering Jacques as "remote and infinitely beyond his daily considerations" because of his scholarly accomplishments, while Jacques responded that he and others had assumed that Francis's aloofness through those years was grounded in conceit because he had already published a book, only realising later that he was "merely shy."

Francis also credited Henry Dick's classes for sparking his interest in modern art. "The first week of the fall semester his walls were bare. The second week, two or three paintings, one of them a landscape with poplars by Claude Monet, a name I'd heard. The next week, some pictures that were to me very strange: several were signed 'Degas'—large drawings and pastels very free in manner! Also 'Utrillo' and 'Matisse.' These names were all new to me." Eventually Francis overcame his shyness to ask about the paintings, and "before long I was visiting Durand-Ruel and other galleries and reading *The Art in Painting* by Albert Barnes." All this fed into Francis's enduring interest in France and French culture, and he continued to travel there whenever he could. The first few years after college he wrote articles for the publicity magazine of the White Star shipping line and was paid in passage credits, securing him trips to France. In another unpublished account of these years, he wrote of the deep sense of recognition he experienced on first arriving in France, an "overwhelm-ing" sense of déjà vu "and the first taxi ride across Paris—from the boat train at the Gare St Lazare, under the arches of the Louvre, across the Carrousel, over the Seine bridges, to the Left Bank," which struck deep and was "never forgotten."

Even in these early travels Francis was making connections. He didn't join the already defined circles of American expatriate writers in Paris but did make friends among them and more widely. In 1928 a translation into French of his Ben Jonson book was published by Firmin-Didot un-der the title *L'aventureuse existence de Ben Jonson, Poète de la Cour des Tavernes*, and Francis sent a copy to the Viennese author Stefan Zweig. It's not clear why; although Zweig was an acclaimed author in the United States as well as Europe, his popular biographies of Marie Antoinette and Balzac would not appear for nearly a decade. In any event, Francis received a gracious reply, expressing disappointment that their paths had not crossed in Paris and thanking him for "your excellent book which I know already in English, but which I will read again now in French—and let us hope: soon also in German. I will immediately indicate it to a Ger-man publisher that we have no Biografie of rare Ben." Francis continued writing, and publishing, if somewhat eclectically: in 1928, with Knopf, *Java-Java*, a camp fantasy, which Francis described as having been influ-enced by Paul Morand, that appears to have sunk without a trace. Francis later commented that no one much liked it, but it was "published just the same," and in 1930 another fictionalised biography, this time of Francis Bacon, with Doubleday. He had also begun publishing short, slight comic pieces in *The New Yorker* in 1927. From the start he was writing across the—in those years—still relatively permeable divide between academic and popular literary worlds.

In autumn 1928 Francis returned from Paris to take up a position at the Experimental College at the University of Wisconsin-Madison, where he taught a course on "American Civilization," in addition to some classes in freshman English at the main university. His contract ran until 1930, but he took a semester's leave the following autumn and travelled again to France. The Experimental College was a short-lived venture founded by the educational theorist Alexander Meiklejohn. It aimed to provide students with a broad grounding in critical thought, without the constraints of formal academic disciplines. Steegmuller did not find teaching congenial, even in an unconventional environment such as this one—"I'm not a teacher. I don't like to teach. The students and I got along very nicely, I liked them, we liked each other, I think." But he preferred to focus on his own work. He did remain friendly with Meiklejohn, whom he described as "my first and much beloved boss," and his wife, Helen. The most important friendship he forged at the university was with Harold Stein, who joined the English faculty at the same time and remained a couple of years longer, before leaving to work for the Roosevelt administration and later becoming a political scientist. At Wisconsin, Harold cut a dashing figure in his fur coat; he held parties where he served bathtub gin. His older sister, Beatrice, came to visit in the spring of 1929, and they drove out in Harold's car into the country-side around Madison, enjoying the scenery, which for Harold and Beatrice recalled Germany, where they had travelled with their parents during childhood. Later that year, Francis travelled to Paris to spend more time with Beatrice.

Beatrice Stein was a young woman of considerable qualities. A talented amateur painter, she had worked in her early years as a storyteller, taken on by welfare organizations "to tell stories in settlement houses; chiefly to groups of children then known as court cases." The settlement houses were established in poor areas, with wealthy volunteers providing education and other support for mainly immigrant women and children. Beatrice would continue to be an admired teller of stories. She had contracted polio at the age of ten, and for the rest of her life was unable to walk unaided. She was some seven years older than Francis; like him, she had spent the previous decade travelling often to France in the company of her mother, pursuing her interest in art. Her father, Leo Stein, had died in the influenza epidemic of 1918. Her mother, Gerda Goldfrank Stein, was herself a somewhat formidable woman. After the death of her more conservative husband, she began to explore left-wing politics, and in 1921 she had her chauffeur take her to the Sacco and Vanzetti trial so she could picket in support. There was, her granddaughter Helen Stein recalled, pride in the Stein family for Gerda's radical connections.

Both of Beatrice's grandfathers had been successful merchants—
Solomon Stein in Chicago and Max Goldfrank in San Antonio, Texas,
and later New York, and Leo Stein had made a significant amount of
money, also as a merchant. Leo and Gerda Stein and their family lived
very well in New York. They first bought a brownstone in East Eighty-
Fourth Street between Park and Madison Avenues and then moved, after
Beatrice contracted polio, to an apartment in the El Dorado, a luxury
eight-storey elevator building on Central Park West between Ninetieth
and Ninety-First (forerunner to the iconic El Dorado now occupying this
site, which was built in 1931); the elevator was important for Beatrice's
mobility. After her husband's death, Gerda took particular care to make
provision so that her daughter would have the financial means to live an
adventurous and independent life, even at the expense of her brothers.
She established a trust fund, managed by her sons, to provide an income
for Beatrice; and her will, prepared in 1947, directed them to manage the
fund so that Beatrice "may at all times have sufficient to live in comfort
and ease." Beatrice devoted her life to painting, and to the larger life of
the arts, in which she was sustained as much by her strength of character
as by her means. Francis later spoke admiringly of how, when he first
met her at a party in Harold's rooms in Madison, Beatrice had had no
hesitation in climbing down from her chair and pulling herself across the
floor, not bothering with her stick or other support. Her family remembered her as a person of consequence, "somehow larger than life" in her
bearing and the way she took things on. A photograph from around 1920
of Beatrice with her friends Clara Guggenheimer and Helen Rosenthal
in the Connecticut woods shows a striking young woman, walking stick
tucked under one arm—the three are posing on a rustic bench with pipes
in their mouths; perhaps the stick is working as another prop. They are
all wearing bulky knits and long woollen skirts, and a dark felt hat frames
Beatrice's strong features. The photograph captures a lighthearted pose.
Beatrice is certainly playing along with the others, but there is also gravitas, directness, and sureness in her demeanour that, along with her handsome face, draw the eye.

Clara was Beatrice's lifelong friend, and Gerda Stein was also friendly with Clara's mother, Ida Guggenheimer, another wealthy widow living on the Upper West Side of Manhattan. Both Ida and Gerda were involved in progressive circles, and both devoted their time and considerable resources to the arts and to civil rights activities. Ida, who was a member of the American Labor Party and the American League for Peace and Democracy, was perhaps more involved than Gerda, and her connections would be important for both her daughter and for Clara in later years. Although Beatrice did not go to college, she was particularly engaged in the intellectual and cultural milieu in which she grew up and came quickly to share her mother's convictions and political involvements, including her patronage of artists and writers. A key connection was the art critic Walter Pach, friend of both Ida and Gerda. Pach played an important role in the development of modern art in the United States; he was central to the establishment of the Society of Independent Artists in 1916, based on the French Société des Artistes Indépendants, and had also been centrally involved in the earlier Exhibitions of Independent Artists, which were aimed at providing a space for American artists experimenting with new styles. Most important, Pach had been involved in setting up the 1913 Armory Show, which introduced modern European art, and Cubism in particular, to American audiences.

Pach was Beatrice's first art teacher, and he helped her make connections with artists in Paris. In 1927 she wrote asking him for advice as to where she should study. He replied, giving her addresses of schools and galleries in Paris. He had first thought of the artist André Lhote for her teacher, but then he learned that there were stairs to get to Lhote's studio, making this impossible for her. Instead, Pach proposed that Beatrice contact his "good friend" Jacques Villon, whom he thought "one of the best painters living," adding that Beatrice might enjoy visiting Villon and his wife. "Write in French in advance and ask when he'll be home, as he has no phone. I suppose you'll go by cab: his house is perhaps three miles beyond the Porte Maillot, just near the Place de la Défense." Pach had met Villon and his brothers some years earlier while gathering works for the Armory Show. Beatrice would become Villon's student for many years and, from early on, his friend and patron. Villon was the brother of Marcel Duchamp and of Raymond Duchamp-Villon; the three brothers had moved to Paris from Rouen at the start of the century, first to Montmartre and then in 1906 to Puteaux, where Villon would remain. In 1912 Villon gave the name "Section d'Or" to the group of artists who had consolidated around the studio, including himself, Duchamp, Duchamp-Villon, Roger de La Fresnaye, Francis Picabia, Albert Gleizes, Jean Metzinger, Robert Delaunay, and the poet Guillaume Apollinaire.

In the summer of 1929 Francis met up with Beatrice in Vienna. They went on to Paris, where he was, he wrote, "one of the many young Americans writing novels" and she "one of the many young Americans studying painting." He stayed in the Seventh Arrondissement, where he and Stanley had stayed on their earlier trips together, and Beatrice took him to meet Villon and his circle. Francis met Pach in Paris that year and was given one of Pach's etchings. He also met Beatrice's mother, Gerda, who arrived mid-autumn and travelled back to New York with them both before Christmas "on the Bremen—one was still willing to travel on a German ship in 1929; they hadn't put up the pictures of Hitler yet . . . Things changed radically after we were home. The Great Depression set in." The Depression saw a shift in the philanthropy practised by Gerda Stein and her sister, Edna Goldfrank, who now lived with her. They left their large apartment at the El Dorado and moved to more modest quarters at 75 Central Park West, where they remained for the rest of their lives. Francis later wrote in his memoir of Gerda that "by most standards, these were still luxurious, though certain outlying relatives and friends, living in greater grandeur, pronounced them unduly modest." He added, "Perhaps they didn't know that what was saved on rent, and more besides, was increasingly going, both in direct remittances, and in the expenses entailed in giving affidavits, to bring from Germany people in danger of their lives. This activity brought its unending rewards. Many of those who arrived, both old intellectuals, and very young men and women, became Edna and Gerda's friends; and there were a few of them who we all came to think of as part of the family circle."

Beatrice and Francis continued to see each other and to travel together. In 1930 Francis began work as a copy editor at the newly founded

*Encyclopedia of the Social Sciences*, run by the New School in New York. Alvin Johnson, the director of the New School, wrote later that Francis had impressed them all as "a man of some literary promise." That same year Francis published his second novel, *The Musicale*, a light, satirical treatment—whimsically (and somewhat ambitiously) echoing *Mrs. Dalloway* in structure—of a musical performance that takes place over an evening in a midwestern university town. The novel was read as a roman à clef by some of Francis's former colleagues at the University of Wisconsin-Madison, who mailed him, anonymously, clippings from local newspapers featuring interviews with those who claimed, with some chagrin, to recognise themselves in his account. In the face of this he decided to abandon writing novels. In 1934 he began writing for *The New Yorker*, mainly "casuals" and Talk of the Town pieces. Soon this undemanding writing also palled; he felt it did not provide him with the opportunity for "accomplishment" that fiction had offered. He later reflected that he "missed the struggle that had accompanied [novel writing]—the hope, as long as I had it—the possibility—that the accomplishment might be large. In my *New Yorker* work I saw no such possibility. Others in the offices around me, were writing masterpieces—Thurber and Perelman were comic geniuses. I knew that my writing for the magazine was not up to theirs," and he added disarmingly that "easily though it came it didn't improve when I tried harder."

In February 1935, after Beatrice announced plans to travel to Egypt, Francis decided to go too: "It seemed to me that for the sake of my future—our future, as I hoped—I had better follow her without delay." They spent several weeks in Cairo and Upper Egypt and in June travelled to Vienna, where they were married on July 1— "The wedding in the Vienna Rathaus was short and snappy," Francis wrote to Stanley Martin— and then to Paris, where they stayed until late September. That year, and for many years afterward, from July through September they were at the hotel Palais d'Orsay, attached to the Gare d'Orsay. They had two or, when Francis needed a separate study, three rooms on an upper floor, "a sunny pleasant apartment looking south over the rue de Lille. In the larger room, furnished informally as salon-atelier, Beatrice . . . worked at her easel." In the evenings, after Villon and Beatrice had discussed what she had produced that day, they would be joined by Villon's wife, Gaby, and the four went to dine in the "handsome" restaurant of the hotel, or Francis and Beatrice would go by taxi to the Villons' at Puteaux. Francis recalled that other guests in those prewar years might be the sculptor Marcel Gimond or Robert and Sonia Delaunay or Albert and Juliette Gleizes. "When Marcel Duchamp was there the conversation could become hilarious . . . One season, I think in the late 1930s, Marcel rented a stand at the Concours Lepine, the inventors' fair at the Porte de Versailles, to market his 'Rotoreliefs,' color discs revolving simultaneously on a gramophone. He would return each evening, announcing with sarcastic pleasure that not a single person had stopped at his booth; until, finally, triumph!—one was sold, for thirty francs."

Villon made etchings of both Steegmullers and a painting of Beatrice, now in the collection of the Metropolitan Museum of Art. The Steegmullers bought Villon's work: *La Table Servie, Instruments de Musique* (now at the Art Institute of Chicago), *Soldats en Marche* (now at the Centre Pompidou), and others, which were returned to Villon's birthplace of Rouen after Shirley's death. In 1937 Francis and Beatrice went to the Exposition Internationale des Arts et Techniques dans la Vie Moderne: "A landscape hanging in the big show of modern French painting at the Petit Palais that summer was the first Dufy that had interested us. It was one of his views of the bay of Nice, with intense blue water and sky, violet mountains, a colorful crescent of shore-front buildings, and beaches dotted with figures." They were not successful, but they bought another, smaller, Dufy a week or two later from a gallery in the Boulevard Montparnasse, hung it up in their hotel room, and then took it back to New York. These works formed the foundation of their collection, which they continued to build slowly over subsequent years.

Throughout his years doing research in France, Francis was alert to the complications of working as an outsider, particularly within the strict formality of French institutions. What was already distinctive in his writing, and would continue to be honed in the work he would go on to do on French subjects, was his deep familiarity with the language, but also with the life behind and within the language: customs, practices, objects, a familiarity gleaned over many decades. A story he told about Villon exemplifies the qualities of aesthetic attention, animation, and delicacy that defined Francis's own approach:

> As a lover of poetry, especially the poems of Mallarmé, Villon enjoyed pondering the meaning of words. When I was writing a book about Flaubert and experiencing difficulty in finding equivalents for French terms, I sometimes sought Villon's help. One of the words I asked him to speak about was "volupté." We were sitting at a café in the Gare St-Lazare, and I remember watching the streams of commuters passing before us on their way to suburban trains as he reflected. "Eh bien," he replied, "d'abord, la volupté, c'est un don"—La volupté . . . is a gift—and he went on from there, pointing to some of the most drab of the commuters as possible possessors of that gift in one form or another. That Villon himself possessed the gift of volupté is evident in the very blacks and the gradations of his etchings, no less than in the most richly chromatic of his canvases. Volupté: also delicacy, finesse—and gaiety.

In Paris the Steegmullers' circles widened to include writers as well as artists, and Francis developed a lifelong friendship with the scholar and translator Norbert Guterman. Guterman was a close friend of the philosopher Henri Lefebvre; both had been members of a group of left-wing students at the Sorbonne in the early 1920s, and both were also associated with the surrealists, particularly Tristan Tzara and André Breton. Guterman was a refugee from Warsaw, living in Paris without official sanction. In 1929, under the pseudonym of Alfred Mesnil, he published in *La revue marxiste* the first translation of fragments from Marx's *Economic and Philosophic Manuscripts of 1844*, which had appeared in German only two years previously. A few years later he was obliged to leave Paris, having lost the support of the French Communist Party in "extraordinary and much debated" circumstances in 1929. Francis had met Guterman in New York through his Columbia circles, and the two would go on in later decades to collaborate on translating and editing a collection of essays by the nineteenth-century literary critic Sainte-Beuve, as well as *Papillot, Clignot et Dodo* (1964), a working into French of the nineteenth-century children's poem "Wynken, Blynken and Nod." In 1937 Guterman introduced the Steegmullers to some of his Paris circles, including Henri Lefebvre, whom they liked and continued to see when they were in Paris. Beatrice was keen to support Guterman's work: "For years Mother has felt that criticism of novels has been written in superficial, over-personal fashion. When I told her of your new book and your attitude she immediately felt that it would give her pleasure to help you write in a less hurried fashion—if possible." She offered to support his writing for four to six months at $50 per month: "You can accept this perfectly easily as it is offered with pleasure as a gift, not a loan, and write with no strings attached. My practical Ma encloses a check on the hunch that the arrangement will be agreeable to you both." Beatrice's philanthropic actions worked always alongside friendship and her particular intellectual interests.

Before leaving New York for Egypt in 1935, Francis had been reading the letters of Gustave Flaubert:

In letters to his friends, collected in other volumes that I was soon reading, I found Flaubert referring to an early illness that changed his life overnight, describing scenes from a long tour of Egypt, the Near East and Greece, and breathing lamentation or ecstasy or both over his pages as he stumbled to write *Madame Bovary* . . . My Egyptian journey was the richer for my knowledge of Flaubert's—I had his letters and travel notes with me as we explored Cairo and travelled up and down the Nile—and in fact so fascinating was everything that for a time I saw the most congenial challenge not in the writing of a good book but in the mastery of hieroglyphs and Egyptological studies.

In Paris, Francis began studying Egyptian. He consulted with an Egyptologist at the École Nationale des Langues Orientales "and was soon deciphering some of the inscriptions on the obelisk in the Place de la Concorde." He abandoned this plan on arriving in London: "Speaking my own language, hearing English voices, and with literary associations on all sides, I knew that what I wanted to do was to write in that language, make it my life." The book he then wrote was his first important and enduring publication, *Flaubert and Madame Bovary*, published by Viking in 1939.

It was an immediate success. Steegmuller's old classmate Lionel Trilling, who had recently been appointed assistant professor of English at Columbia, wrote in no little excitement:

> I'm so full of enthusiasm that I scarcely know where to begin . . .
> I suppose that the best and truest praise I can give it is to say that
> Flaubert would be proud of it. For in many ways it is Flaubertian. You've kept yourself out of it and have been objective but
> not falsely objective: I mean you haven't tried to keep out love of
> your subject. You never make the mistake of trying to "interpret"
> Flaubert and you know that the only understanding comes from
> presentation . . . You've made a noble spectacle very exciting. For
> the first time I think, you have made a literary labour have the
> dramatic heroism of a labour of science: nowadays people find
> it easy to represent the latter but they can scarcely even conceive
> the former. I find it gratifying to see a literary hero for a change.
> I mean that very seriously: I was moved and I was "inspired" by
> the story . . . The lightness of the narrative touch never gives one
> any sense of insecurity about the scholarship, which I can see is
> enormous.

The book was well and widely reviewed—the "cultivated elevator men" at the Steegmullers' Fifty-Seventh Street apartment building congratulated him on the "generosity" of the published responses. F. Scott Fitzgerald included it in a list of the books that had been most important to him. When Francis learnt of this decades later, when Fitzgerald's letters were published, he responded, "Oh if I'd only known of this at the time, what it would have meant to me."

By now Francis and Beatrice were well established in Paris, where they spent several months each summer, returning in September to winter in New York. They travelled more widely as well, to Bermuda in 1936 and regularly to Italy, all of this supported by Beatrice's trust and, more modestly, by Francis's paid writing jobs. They were in Milan during Mussolini's Ethiopian war, cutting their visit short after finding the atmosphere unbearable. In the spring of 1936 Villon spent a few weeks in the United States visiting Katherine Dreier (cofounder with Duchamp and Man Ray of the Société Anonyme), and Walter Pach, who was teaching at Bowdoin College in Maine, and the Steegmullers. Villon stayed with Gerda Stein on Central Park West and from her apartment "made the drawings for what would become his pair of lithographs of New York skylines." In 1939, with war imminent, the Steegmullers urged Villon to come back, with Gaby, to the United States; Villon declined: *"Il faut rester avec son tribe."* He continued to paint despite the intractable conditions. Through the war and after, the Steegmullers sent the Villons money, and later food parcels and packages of warm clothes. Duchamp, who made his way to the United States in 1942 via Lisbon, had helped to pass on funds from the Steegmullers to his brother, and he brought paintings with him to give to Beatrice and Francis in return.

In 1942 Francis began working with the U.S. Office of War Information, which had been established to provide the public with news about the war. He was an editor in the Bureau of Overseas Publications, on West Fifty-Seventh Street. In 1944 he was transferred to the Office of Strategic Services, the intelligence agency formed in 1942, precursor to the CIA. His role at the OSS seems at first to have involved mainly writing and editing, although the letter detailing his secondment notes that he had been "recruited against the requirements set forth in cable 61211 from London," which requested men:

> to be used for authorized missions to the Maquis and lodgement areas, for recruiting and infiltrating native agents to be attached to field armies, and men to be used for post-armistice work with the allied forces in Germany. Men in either job should not have their connection with OSS a matter of public knowledge. We are not certain exactly what type of work this man will be doing but he has been recruited against the requirements of this cable and presumably will be used for the work described above.

There are no accounts of Francis being involved with secret information gathering, nor of recruiting or infiltrating. More significantly, this appointment saw him working outside the world of letters for the first time.

On joining the OSS, he moved to Washington, while Beatrice remained in Manhattan, at the Hotel Meurice on West Fifty-Eighth Street. Francis was angling for a posting to Paris, although he wrote Beatrice that he feared his chances were slim, as priority was being given to "the far East—China, Burma, India and the southwest Pacific—and several times it has been stated that European operations are being greatly curtailed. Natural enough." He was also concerned about his earning capacities in the current climate: "It goes against my nature to say so, but I wonder whether we should buy another picture, even a $400 one? Think it over. I consider my future decidedly in doubt and if I'm to write a novel we may have to be careful for a while. It would be lovely to have it. No New Yorker check yet—I wonder if the story appeared in today's issue." According to a piece he published in *The New Yorker*, he and Beatrice sold their Dufy around this time for a slight profit in a transaction that saw them the prey of unscrupulous dealers in both Paris and New York. There was more success with other purchases, but mostly they kept what they bought: a Degas pastel, *Après le bain*, in 1943; a Renoir oil, *La Femme aux Cardes*, in 1941; a Pissarro oil, *La sente des Pouilleux, Pontoise*; several Picasso etchings; along with earlier purchases from before the war: a fourteenth-century polychromed head of "a Queen or Virgin" in limestone in 1938, a fourth-century BC Greek marble bas-relief the year before, and a third-century Greek marble bust of a child the year before that. Money was not a serious concern, given Beatrice's generous trust fund. But Francis's note urging restraint indicates his wish to contribute to their joint finances and signals also perhaps some sensitivity about his life as a private scholar supported by his wife's income. Some members of the Stein family felt that Francis behaved at times in an entitled manner, and he may have been aware of this.

Francis did eventually get back to Paris at the end of the war. In May 1945 he joined the staff of Jean Monnet, the French diplomat and political economist who would go on to become a key founder of the European Common Market. Monnet was then based in Washington, working to establish economic supports between France and the United States. Francis was sent, according to briefing letters from Monnet's office to the U.S. Embassy in Paris, "to review the subject of Reverse Lend-Lease aid given by the French to the U.S. and the other United Nations for the purpose of disseminating the facts in such a way as to improve the relations between France and the rest of the World." Francis flew out from Washington, D.C., the flight taking nearly two days, stopping at Labrador and near Glasgow en route to Beauvais airfield, then still being run by the U.S. Air Force, and on by "Air Transport Command bus (one of the old Paris buses) to the ATC" on the Place Vendôme. "Quelle émotion to see shell-marks on France, Beauvais looming up out of ruins, and then Paris!" He was given "a room in a queer little hotel—Hotel de Perey in the Cité Retiro, which goes off the Faubourg St Honoré near Hermès. It is requisitioned by the army, which has turned over a block of rooms to the Embassy, which has given me one. I can stay indefinitely—no charge except tips (about 20 francs a day). But it's a leave hostel for enlisted men who naturally aren't sober or quiet and there's no telephone in the room." Nonetheless he quickly became "rather fond of this funny little hotel . . . where I'm living free at the expense of the State Department or the army, I don't know which. A hotel of fourteenth class but I have bath and hot water. No telephone or bells—wrecked by former occupants—Germans or war correspondents, I forget which. I'm seeing both U.S. army people and French officials, most of story will probably come from former."

He stayed in Paris about a month. He made a short trip to Normandy: the specific nature of his business undisclosed, but he published a story about the U.S. army clearing the beaches of unexploded mines, with himself wandering, comically unobserving, through the operation, narrowly escaping injury. His letters to Beatrice through this time provide a gripping window onto postwar Paris, familiar but also utterly changed: "City absolutely extraordinary . . . The inflation! The hats! It's a frightfully shabby city full of people who look like summer vacationers in strange clothes. Cherries and strawberries being sold on carts. Bullet marks on buildings, whole facades being repaired, plaques along the rue de Rivoli saying 'Ici est tombé, le 25 août 1945 X-X-, mort pour la France.' Flood-lighting, beautiful." The mood was overwhelmingly sombre:

> At the Gare d'Orsay, a constant stream of returning prisoners. Most of them have worked on German farms and are OK. These are not the political deportees—a different story. At all hours of day or night a double line of trucks extends up the Quai d'Orsay to the Chambre des Députés, waiting to take prisoners to other stations or to their homes. Some families spend all day there waiting for their men to show up. There's a bakery shop, money hand-out window, our station buffet restaurant is their restaurant. What a variety of costumes! Some in rags, some with words "French soldier" on their arm, some with German loot, all tanned and dirty and bearded and exhausted and excited. Some fall fast asleep on the floor.

The larger significance overwhelmed him somewhat: "Impossible to describe to you the psychological atmosphere of Paris till I see you; one alternates between pity and utter hatred. The casual treatment of returned prisoners is enough to turn the stomach." He visited the Palais d'Orsay, with food parcels for the staff: "Our furniture is intact . . . I finally saw M. Millet who has aged a lot. They pretended it was the housekeeper's personal furniture, so it was not used or taken by Germans. They look forward to having us next summer. Most effervescent was your favourite baggagiste, who almost wrung my hand off and said you were the nicest person in the world to think of them all." Other visits to old friends were distressing: "Visited Simonne [Maubert] again the other night—she loved her ceramics work and is asked to return to it at good pay but won't because it's in the quarter where Roger was taken—she can't bear to go there or to lots of other places in Paris where she pleaded with Germans for his release. One day she went to the prison bringing him food and was handed his clothes and fainted. She says she just 'exists'—has no interest except to keep busy."

Francis had made contact with his brother Lawrence, then stationed with U.S. Forces in Germany. They hoped to meet, but didn't manage to. He saw the Villons often, taking food and clothing, and Beatrice was meanwhile sending parcels of both to their French friends. Requests for, above all, "matière grasse" spoke to the war years of near starvation, and there was joy at the stylish woollens Beatrice packed to supplement more meagre wardrobes. The appearance of these packages was, "despite heroic attempts at self-control, frequently the cause of such emotion in my hosts that everyone present became shaken and red-eyed." Francis wrote a piece for *The New Yorker* noting changes from prewar visits, the conspicuous absence of "the dogs that patrons used to bring with them and that often ate out of their plates. In all my stay in Paris I saw only one dog in a restaurant. He was given lettuce leaves to eat, and he ate them." He offered to a French friend who visited him one evening an orange he had brought back from the U.S. officers and embassy staff mess, "apologizing for having no other refreshments. 'Excuse me for laughing at your apology,' he said. 'This will be my first orange in five years. May I really eat it?' He ate half of it and took the other half home to his wife."

These meetings were important, to sustain their prewar life and the connection with Paris that had been significant to both. Francis went to art shows with Villon and Cleve Gray, a young American soldier who had befriended the Villons and would later become a friend of the Steegmullers in New York: "Stopped in at a show of young painters. Nothing particularly noteworthy seems to have happened in painting—nobody young that's very wonderful . . ." He was more interested in an exhibition of Villon's and in other cubist shows. He and Beatrice continued to buy art: Picasso etchings and a third-century Greco-Buddhist head from Gandhara that had formerly belonged to the writer André Malraux. He loved to tell how he had bought the Redon pastel *Fécondité: Femme Dans Les Fleurs*—which had drawn Shirley's attention on her first visit to his apartment and would later grace the cover of *The Bay of Noon*—for $600 at the Art Institute of Chicago fire sale of artworks in New York in 1948. The coda to this story was that two decades later he would be contacted, somewhat impertinently he felt, by the curator of paintings at the Metropolitan Museum, inviting him to donate the Redon to them.

After the war, Francis and Beatrice continued to work and to travel—to Vermont, where Beatrice's brother Edwin Stein had a cottage in the village of South Londonderry that the Steegmullers had adapted to accommodate Beatrice's wheelchair; to New Mexico, where Beatrice liked to paint and draw; and to the Caribbean, as well as Paris. In 1946 they went to Cuba and then to Europe. In Paris that summer they saw the Villons at Puteaux, with new visitors joining the group—the art dealer Louis Carré, and the art historians Lionello Venturi and Jerome Mellquist, both of whom would later write on Villon. Francis was working on a biography of Guy de Maupassant and planning a new book about James Jackson Jarves, an American journalist who had been one of the first collectors of Italian Primitives during his tenure as vice-consul of Florence in the mid-nineteenth century. Francis also began photographing the wrecked and recovering city of Paris, recording views from "the rue de l'Université and the rue de Bellechasse to the dark arcades of the Place des Vosges," the skyline from the upper levels of the d'Orsay, and outside Paris as well: "His travels led him on to Mont St. Victoire, to the Palais des Papes in Avignon, to Aix on market day in front of the cathedral, and to Étretat, where fisherman's nets were strung up along the esplanade."

Francis's new interest in photography had developed out of his friendship with the writer Ralph Ellison, who had worked for some years as a professional photographer. Francis hired Ellison to take the author photos for his Maupassant book and also to print up the photographs Francis had taken of Maupassant's childhood home, Les Verguies. They had met through shared *New Yorker* connections, the editor Stanley Edgar Hyman a close friend of both. Beatrice's association with Ellison was more substantial, made through Ida Guggenheimer, who had become Ellison's supporter and patron, and Ida's daughter, Beatrice's longtime close friend, now Clara Binswanger. Ellison had met Ida through Angelo Herndon, an African American activist deeply involved in labor politics and the Communist Party. Ellison's biographer Arnold Rampersad writes that the bond between "this hungry young black writer and this aged Jewish woman activist was a twin love of literature and the left."

Although Ida Guggenheimer is generally understood to have been the dedicatee of *Invisible Man*, there is also the suggestion, in an undated letter from Ellison to Steegmuller, that his mother Ida Ellison had also been "on my mind when I dedicated the book to Ida G." Ellison wrote that he had "thought of this as a private matter—a joke, if you will—and of no particular [*sic*] to the reading public," but that it had "upset" Ida Guggenheimer and had "led, I'm sorry to recall, to the end of a friendship which I valued more than I think she understood." He felt that the breach with Ida had occurred because the implicit ideological stance of the novel was "simply too much for her and thus she probably felt that I had betrayed her trust." Ida's politics had continued to shift to the left and were, by the early 1950s when the book was published, "pro-Stalinist," and thus at odds with Ellison's less doctrinaire views.

Ellison met Beatrice at Ida's apartment in 1944 and after that was a frequent guest at the Steegmullers' through the mid- to late 1940s. He met Truman Capote there and often saw other mutual friends, such as Alfred Kazin, John Cheever, Stanley Hyman, and Lewis Mumford. Over the years of their friendship with Ralph and his wife, Fanny, Beatrice and Francis provided loans, including for medical procedures, all assiduously repaid. More important was their offer of a place for Ralph to work on what would become his masterpiece, the novel *Invisible Man*. In July 1947 the Steegmullers were in Santa Fe, Francis working on Maupassant and Beatrice too overcome with the heat to be able to paint outdoors. They wrote to Ralph and Fanny suggesting that the Ellisons might want to take a short vacation in Edwin Stein's cottage in Vermont: "I put the 'our' in quotation marks because we don't really own it although we remodelled it and used to go there a lot. We'd be awfully happy if you could use it for a while." Three weeks later, Ralph wrote joyously of "the wonderful vacation you've made so unexpectedly possible." Staying in the cottage had provided him and Fanny with some easeful weeks together swimming, hiking, taking photographs. Most of all, being at the cottage was enormously conducive to writing. He was producing "five pages a day," and felt that "a shackle had been removed from imagination. For now the stuff flows; I'm no longer elaborating a conceptual frame, but inventing," and was no longer anxious at the end of each writing day that inspiration would be lost when he returned next morning. It was not just the seclusion of the cottage that was proving so productive for him, but also the beauty of the place:

> In musing over the difference between my ability to work here and my floundering at home, I've concluded that since I'm concerned a great deal with cloacal and subterranean imagery and symbolism, working in our little apartment (with its long, narrow entrance, into a small, low-ceilinged room, dark and warm) is too close to what the imagination is struggling to transform. While here in a valley among mountains looking out upon a flowery hillside complete with spiders sinister, butterflies and hummingbirds, things don't seem nearly so desperate. Imagination is imagination again and I've regained some of the pleasure of writing.

So productive was his time there that Ralph returned alone in the autumn. This time the isolation, along with the cold, was more challenging, but he continued to make progress.

The following spring, when the Steegmullers left for Paris, Francis gave Ralph the keys to the office he kept in a building at 608 Fifth Avenue so he would have a quiet place to work. The office was on the eighth floor in a suite of rooms belonging to the jewellers Samuel and Augusta Mann, who guarded Ralph's privacy, took him to lunch, and encouraged him to write. It was his until the Steegmullers returned in mid-October. Ralph wrote Francis in late June, "Until today, which is doing its best to smother me, my work has moved ahead with a kind of magic. I have been putting in a fairly full day of writing here at the office then leaving my ms until the next day and if I can continue this way I won't mind how hot it gets and by October I can present the boys with a big thick headache of a novel." Fanny too was pleased with the arrangement, writing in August, "Can I tell you what the use of the office has meant to Ralph? No better thing could have happened for him. Last week he had written 50 new pages since he went there the Monday after you'd gone, new pages, not rewritten ones. All of which makes me know that the book might have been finished by now had he had all along a suitable place to work." Rampersad

notes that Ellison's presence there was unexpected in that white neighbourhood: "To catch the sunlight, Steegmuller had set up his typewriter
next to a window that looked across to the roof of Radio City Music Hall.
When white people there saw a black man sitting at a typewriter, they
sometimes could not hide their curiosity or their alarm." This might have
proved to be a problem, Ellison observed, "had I not been consciously concerned with a fictional character who was bent upon finding his way in
areas of society whose manners, motives and rituals were baffling."

In Paris in the summer of 1950, Francis and Beatrice met the writer
Richard Wright, along with Albert Murray, who would later become an influential music writer, novelist, and intellectual in Harlem and was then
on leave from the U.S. Air Force. Beatrice liked Murray. She took him on
short trips outside Paris with their Paris driver, her mother Gerda, and
their friend Simonne Maubert: "Our trips were strictly bi-lingual. Al is
studying the language now and is moving in esoteric circles." Al and Francis also spent time together, taking long walks around the city. Villon took
Francis to meet Picasso, "a most attractive (I mean forcibly so) personality and at present doing some splendid sculpture. Very proud of his two
recent children—one and three, I think, or two and four." Their circles
continued to grow, particularly among the large cohort of American writers either living or working in Paris in the postwar decades. The *New
Yorker* Paris correspondent Janet Flanner, "Genêt," was a friend, as was
Jenny Bradley, the Belgian-French literary agent responsible for much of
the then extensive cross-Atlantic literary traffic; in Francis's description,
Bradley was "the handsome, imposing, always impeccably turned-out em-
inence grise of the Franco-American literary market."

Francis also travelled by himself. In January 1951 Beatrice remained
in New York while he took off on an extended Italian trip. He had spent
time there the previous spring and summer, completing research on
Jarves. Beatrice had accompanied him for some of the earlier trip, travelling from Paris by train with her mother, her aunt, Edna Goldfrank, and
André "(the unemployed youngster who drives me). He is coming to help
Francis haul me up and down the flights of Italian stairs awaiting us."
(The Steegmullers found travelling in Italy together particularly difficult
given the scarcity of elevators and the apparent reluctance of hoteliers to

offer assistance.) During that 1950 visit Francis had also met Alberto Moravia. At Moravia's house he met the American William Weaver, who had
been living in Italy since the war, first in Naples—where he was friendly
with the local writer Raffaele La Capria, renting a room with his family
in the Palazzo Donn'Anna in Posillipo—and then in Rome. Weaver would
go on to become an acclaimed translator and music writer, and a good
friend of the Steegmullers. Remembering those years in Rome, Weaver
recalled, "We ate in the same restaurant every night, and it was like a
club. Visconti would drop in and eat with us and Alberto Moravia and Elsa
Morante. I met people I didn't even know I wanted to meet until after I
met them." Soon after, he went on, "other young Americans arrived, and
you met everyone who came to Rome because the American colony was so
small." He and Francis took long walks together around the city.

Returning to Europe in 1951, Francis flew first to Paris to collect the
car, drove back to Rome "for a 'long' stay," but then took off for a week
in Greece "with appropriate emotions, and after it Rome seems crass and
vulgar and modern." He wrote Stanley Hyman that he was finding it
difficult to settle down to writing: "After a spurt of work (due I think
to bad weather) I have relaxed again and seem to get through the days
without thinking"; writing fiction seemed "so sticky after two big biographies that I bid fair to become a second Ralph as far as agony is
concerned." He was lonely, writing to Gerda, "Everyone who writes com-
mending Beatrice for her determination not to come to Europe this year
seems blithely unaware that I miss her." He went to Florence, where he
found "a most delightful room which I'll have to economize next month
somehow to pay for; utterly comfortable with a big terrace," and he visited Bill Weaver, who was renting a villa nearby and invited Francis to
come and stay there through the summer. He went to Ravenna with
Edna Goldfrank, where he met up with Lionello Venturi, who was there
to give a series of lectures on Byzantine art. Francis had "the momentary idea of passing the summer in Ravenna . . . But if I'm lonesome
in places like Rome and Florence, how would I feel there!" His biography of Jarves had just been published in the United States, and on
the strength of it, Venturi was encouraging him to devote himself to art
history. Francis wrote to Beatrice, "He thinks I could become America's

best art writer, having great sensibility and being now in the process of rapidly learning much about art and seeing so much of it. He thinks it might be a great advantage to such a career if I were to live in Rome permanently—thinks it would give publicity and prestige value as well as being more pleasant in so many ways than New York which is certainly true." The previous summer, Francis had visited Bernard Berenson at I Tatti, the villa above Florence that Berenson had bought in 1900. With no formal art history training—he had studied literature and languages at Harvard—Berenson had become a celebrated European art historian and was renowned also as a serious collector. He perhaps provided another model for Francis of a serious amateur scholar of art. After the visit they exchanged brief letters, Berenson hoping that Francis would return: "You interest me, and I believe in you."

Francis wrote Beatrice that at the opera in Florence he "ran into [English novelist] Angus Wilson, who at once asked for you. He's in Italy on a brief holiday, with the same pretty blond (no 'e' on the end of that word) that we saw in Paris," and that he had had dinner with Somerset Maugham and his secretary, where they discussed Francis's *Maupassant*. He was invited to meet Frank Wooster and his wife, Mary, the mother-in-law of Alan Pryce-Jones, who would later befriend Shirley in New York. Mary had been a Viennese Jewish heiress, Mitzi Springer, and her first husband, Eugène Fould, had been Frank Wooster's lover; "Homosexuals make the best husbands," she declared. She had married Wooster after Fould's untimely death, remaking herself in the process as "Protestant" Mary Wooster. She was, Francis wrote, "a great favourite of Berenson's," and Francis also found her engaging. She was

about 65, knew Mme Straus, Proust, Anatole France (is a niece of Mme de Caillavet's) . . . I signed my Maupassant; she showed me where I had mis-spelled the name of one of her friends. I pointed out that the mis-spelling was in a document supplied me by a relative of that friend. She informed me that said relative 'is now ga-ga' as I would discover were I to visit him in his apartment, no, house, on the Place d'Iéna. Her son-in-law of the *TLS* [Alan Pryce-Jones] admires my books . . . and I am invited to come again.

Frank Wooster, Francis wrote, was "full of talk, reminiscences, about their flight from France in 1940, with 'Elsa Schiaparelli sleeping on the stairs of Lisbon's smartest hotel and Elsie Mendl sleeping in the lift' etc. They themselves found rooms in a brothel." After a month in Florence, Clara Binswanger arrived, and Francis travelled to Venice with her, then both returned to New York in the summer. In Francis's peregrinations and his speculations about writing through this time, there is a combination of aimless wandering and passionate interest that seems to belong to an earlier time. As with his short-lived plan of pursuing Egyptology in the 1930s, his interest in art history was surely prompted by genuine and discerning interest; at the same time there is something of a dilettantish cast to the prospects he outlines in these letters, something to do with his continuing status as private scholar, freed of the need to earn a living. Nonetheless, he was pursuing his writing with daily seriousness and attention. As soon as one book was completed, he began casting about for the next. He sold stories to a huge range of magazines—and in these golden mid-century years of magazine publishing there were plenty of opportunities.

On his return to New York at the end of the summer in 1951, the Steegmullers moved apartments, this time to a newly completed apartment complex, on East Sixty-Sixth Street. Manhattan House was stylish, sleek, and modern, constructed of gleaming white brick, with a garden and lobby stretching its full length from Second Avenue to Third. It had been designed by Gordon Bunshaft, a prominent exponent of the International Style, who also lived there and became a friend. They filled the apartment with modernist furniture and art, entertained friends, wrote, drew, and painted. They maintained warm relations with Beatrice's family. Her niece Helen Stein remembered the quality of attention the couple paid to all their nieces and nephews, inviting them one by one to the apartment, taking them out to lunch, attending to particular interests or achievements. Lucia Stein's talent for painting was praised and nurtured, and Francis read and commented on the stories Helen was writing. When they learnt of Helen's growing interest in civil rights matters, they made her a gift of a Lead Belly record. And when Adam Stein was in Frankfurt in the late 1950s, they arranged for him to visit Ralph Ellison, who was there in the summer of 1959 as the chief American delegate to the PEN Congress.

In Rome that summer, Francis had heard mention of the writer Eleanor Clark, from Laurance Roberts, the director of the American Academy in Rome, and from Bill Weaver. The following year, he read Clark's new book, *Rome and a Villa* (which would go on to win the National Book Award for nonfiction), admired it, and wrote inviting her to visit. She came by Manhattan House, and from this visit developed a warm friendship that expanded to include the novelist, poet, and critic Robert Penn (Red) Warren, who would become Eleanor's second husband. Francis was particularly struck by Red Warren's attentiveness to Beatrice, and a close bond formed between the two. Francis had always admired Beatrice's refusal to be confined by her disability, and he was minutely attentive to the response of others to her. When the Steegmullers visited at the Warrens' Vermont house, Red helped Bea with her wheelchair down the sloping path to where they were having a picnic lunch. Francis observed:

> Most people were courteous and helpful with her, but Red remarkably so and in a very understated way. One day he told us— but particularly telling *her*—about how he came to lose an eye, when he was accidentally shot by his brother. There seemed to be some connection there between his physical impairment and his particularly thoughtful manner with Beatrice. No one else would notice, except me, because it was just as it should be. I of course had a very keen feeling about various people's reactions to her condition. Red's was particularly exquisite.

The friendship between Bea and Red was also grounded in a shared love of traditional stories and ballads and African American spirituals. Bea's interest in these was itself anchored in her early years as storyteller to children in disadvantaged urban communities, and she had honed her performance over the years, making use of an extensive repertoire of material. She had been friendly with John Jacob Niles, who had collected traditional songs, stories, and music from rural America. There was something striking about her telling of tales. While some derived from her own German-Jewish family background, stories she had grown up with, her repertoire was capacious. In 1958 Francis published a piece about her in *The New Yorker*, "Another Storyteller's Story," which describes her arresting presence and suggests how steeped this was in the forms and practices of courtesy and respect that were possibly not always found in the elevated social worlds in which they mixed:

> Last year, my wife and I went to a cocktail party where we met a handsome, black-haired young man, introduced by our host as being from Oklahoma. "Are you a Chippewa?" my wife asked him, sociably. He nodded. "Then you must know my favorite Indian forest story," she said, 'The Man Who Married the Moon.'" "Not by that title, but tell it to me, and I'll tell you if it's one of ours," he said. It was. My wife faltered a few times in the telling, being rusty, but the young man put her right each time. It was a curiously primeval antiphony to listen to, up there above Park Avenue. They finished in triumphant unison: "Then he found the girl whose face he had watched so many nights in the moon, and he never came back to earth." Quite a few of the other cocktail guests had gathered round to listen, and they seemed to find that ending delightfully happy and satisfactory. At another party—a dinner, this time—there was a young woman who said proudly that her father had been a mighty teller of Irish tales. When my wife said that she, too, had told Irish stories, the young woman looked at her with mistrust. "Did you tell 'The Bee, the Harp, the Mouse, and the Bumclock'?" she demanded. "I did," my wife said. "Well, when you got to the part about the pans and the pails, what did you do with your hands?" "I did this with them," said my wife, making a crisscross gesture. "Bless you!" said the young woman. "There are those who always do this"—she made a different gesture—"and that's dead wrong, as you well know."

Another important friendship forged in the postwar years, one that would continue after Bea's death, was with the *New Yorker* fiction editor

William Maxwell. In Maxwell's memorial tribute to Francis for the American Academy of Arts and Letters, he recalled that he and Francis had first met in the 1930s when he was asked to edit one of Francis's stories. "Since it needed editing the way a cat needs two tails, my connection remained slight." After the war, the Maxwells and Steegmullers met up again at a party, "and the four-way friendship that instantly sprang into being turned out to be life-long." In 1960, when Maxwell was struggling to finish *The Château*, a novel about Americans in France, he called on Francis to "tidy up" the French, and he incorporated in the novel some of the dialogue he and Francis had had about it. The Steegmullers were also good friends in these years with the writers Alfred Kazin and his wife, Ann Birstein, and intersected with their lives among the New York intellectual circles of the Upper West Side of Manhattan. Birstein felt that Francis was someone who helped to "leaven" the "New York Jewish intellectual loaf for them." Francis always had something of the air of an outsider from established circles. Lewis Galantière, who translated Antoine de Saint-Exupéry's *The Little Prince*, first met Francis while both were working at the Office of War Information. He was asked to write in support of Francis's candidacy for membership in New York's Century Club:

> [Francis Steegmuller] looks a little like General de Gaulle and is about as tall. He never speaks out of turn, not from shyness so much as out of respect for other people's right to be heard. There is also in him an impatience with silliness which makes it hard for him to make small talk in company where he finds men airing second-hand views or the unlovelier kinds of prejudices . . . If I were asked what was his outstanding characteristic, I would say it was integrity. This does not mean that he is not amusing and ready for amusement in the right place and at the right time; but he is no hail fellow well met.

Similar notes were struck later by Francis's friend the French scholar Victor Brombert, who made much of the connection with Flaubert: "Francis Steegmuller and Gustave Flaubert were surely meant to be friends.

Steegmuller's sense of style, for one, would have pleased Flaubert, as would his dedication to literary excellence and to art in general . . . Those who had dealings with Francis Steegmuller over the course of his long career will recall his discretion, his refinement, his elegance in everything he did."

In writing terms, these were prolific years. Since the acclaim of *Flaubert and Madame Bovary* in 1939, Francis had published four novels, a collection of his *New Yorker* pieces, and the Maupassant and Jarves biographies in 1949 and 1951. The novels were light confections: three detective stories under the pseudonym of David Keith—the first of which, *A Matter of Iodine*, was awarded the 1940 Red Badge Mystery Prize—and *States of Grace*, a satirical romp—one reviewer suggested it had "a kind of goat-like exuberance"—about a battle over relics found in a Catholic church in Cairo. The biographies were more substantial, although lacking the weight of his *Flaubert*; while working on Jarves, Steegmuller himself declared his subject to be merely "an interesting blind alley." Its lightness notwithstanding, the Jarves drew Francis's work to the attention of art historians, including Douglas Cooper, one of the earliest authorities on cubism. Cooper had studied at Cambridge, Freiburg, and the Sorbonne, had worked briefly as an art dealer in London, and had then become the first serious international collector of cubist art. He had devoted a substantial portion of his substantial inheritance (derived, as it happened, from the New South Wales real estate holdings of his great-grandfather) to acquiring works by Picasso, Braque, Gris, and Léger, published influential commentaries on their work, and later curated major exhibitions in the UK and the United States. He had bought the Château de Castille near Uzès in Provence and restored it, and from 1950 it housed his collection. Picasso was, according to John Richardson, Cooper's lover at the time, "his most assiduous guest," and he produced "a series of maquettes for the great murals . . . in the former *magnanerie* at Castille." Cooper went on to be a significant friend to the Steegmullers over the next several decades.

In the years after *Jarves*, Francis vacillated over whether to concentrate on literary or art history projects. In the first instance he had returned to Flaubert, producing in 1953 a volume of translations of his

letters. *La Grande Mademoiselle*, his biography of Anne Marie Louise
d'Orléans, heiress and niece of Louis XIII, was published in 1955 in
the UK and the following year in the U.S. by Farrar, Straus and Cudahy,
with whom Francis had signed a multi-book contract. André Maurois,
whom Francis met in Paris through Jenny Bradley, wrote that he "liked
it immensely. It is a biography after my own heart, true, scholarly, and
yet never pedantic. You have done justice to one of the more dramatic
subjects in French history of the XVII Century and your knowledge of
French things is such that at no moment had I the impression the author
wasn't a Frenchman." But Francis was still tempted by art history. In late
1954 he had been approached to write a history of the Art Institute of
Chicago, a project he considered for some months and then declined. At
the same time, he was exploring the possibility of a book on Cézanne,
and one on Gauguin (although he described himself as "no great lover
of Gauguin's work"). He was also considering other artists. He wrote to
Douglas Cooper, "Géricault has tempted me for years. Those manias—all
the corpses and horses' asses. (His mother died young; his uncle owned a
harras—do you like to speculate on such causations? I do.) . . . I love Géricault's painting; we have a little one; this I'd certainly do if there were
facts available . . . Delacroix, on the other hand, I like almost as much and
there's a lot more material . . ." In spite of these attractions Francis felt
all along that his truest alignment was with the literary, telling Cooper
that "writing about artists and their work seems to result in about 99%
failure—much greater lack of success than writing about writers . . . Last
night I found I literally couldn't see that one Villon in front of me was
necessarily a lithograph and the other a pencil drawing."

In summer 1956 Bea's nephew Adam Stein, then at college in the
United States, came to Paris for a few months while André Philippon, the
Steegmullers' regular driver, was not available. Francis and Beatrice stayed
as usual at the d'Orsay. They kept a prewar Ford, larger than most other
Parisian cars, which Adam manoeuvred through the streets. He looked after parking while Francis and Bea visited galleries and museums, making
use of service elevators to provide access for her wheelchair. Adam drove
them outside Paris too, on a trip to Belgium to visit friends, and to Chartres.
Francis was working on a new Flaubert project: translating *Madame*

*Bovary* for the Modern Library. There was great interest around this book: 1957 was the centenary year of the novel's original publication in French, and Roger Straus noted in a letter to Alfred Knopf that "there is going to be much hoopla about it." Francis revised *Flaubert and Madame Bovary*, which was republished by Vintage to coincide with the new translation. Both books were successful; both have remained defining works, and just as the substance of the earlier book had been apparent from first publication, so the reception of *Madame Bovary* was overwhelmingly positive. In September, John Cheever wrote to Francis:

> I'm not quite finished with Bovary but . . . I want to say how wonderful I think it is. I haven't checked it against the other translations, or against the French and I see no reason to—it seems much more than a translation. You don't seem to have rendered it from one language into another—you seem to have brought it from one kind of light into another. You've done the lady a great service and no one deserves it more than she. The simple excitement with which I could read this book as a young man is long gone. It seems now—page after page—to be in its penetration and accuracy downright terrifying. There is no place, no scene or paragraph, where I've missed the French.

Bill Maxwell also wrote with enthusiasm:

> Dear Francis, it's absolutely marvelous . . . The effect is of a layer of callous peeled off, leaving something luminous and alive. You can, for the first time, eat the food and touch the people and smell and see everything. And reading it, I am continually reminded that Flaubert was an aesthete, and continually driven to reflect, as Mrs. Woolf was in her novels, "Human life, human life!" It goes on like a refrain behind whatever is happening. It is not like a translation but like a redoing of it in English. The cadences, the diction, the shifting naturalness of the style are all incomparable. And all those glittering effects, as when M. Rouault remembering how his bride rode pillion behind him, looks back and sees that there is nothing

on the road. I don't know why I think Flaubert meant this to mean the total emptying of the past, any more than I know why I think he meant to convey, when Emma is making conversation with Charles and says that she doesn't enjoy country life, that her destiny is already final and that it is only a matter of a little while and she will have the taste of poison in her mouth. At every point there are these effects, these double-takes, which are new to me, and ravishing. [Harold] Brodkey was so excited he kept groaning for pleasure, and he had read the book twice before and never cared for it. I could paper a room with my favorite passages.

The translation was, moreover, a commercial success: on the popular radio program *The World of Books*, the host, William Kennedy, commented that it was "competing in sales volume with contemporary bestsellers" because this new translation made it "more readable in English than ever before."

*Madame Bovary* was hugely important to Francis. It would continue to define him publicly, primarily as a scholar of Flaubert, but it also carried a distinctive personal charge, as indicated by a story often told by the Steegmullers and recounted by the translator Richard Howard. "One June day in 1956 (at the age of forty-nine), upon completing his years of work on *Madame Bovary*, Francis found himself typing the title page of the translation of that novel to be sent to the copy editor: '*Madame Bovary* by Francis Steegmuller.'" This was not just the biographer's overidentification; Shirley recalled that Francis had always "felt close to [Flaubert's] presence, and felt passionately about *Madame Bovary*." He had told her that when he was young, Flaubert's personality "attracted me very much. It was as if I were reading about myself." His achievement was recognised in France with the award of Chevalier of the Légion d'Honneur in August that year, indicating how substantial his reputation outside the United States had become. His *La Grande Mademoiselle* was being translated into French and would be published in Paris by Éditions Denoël. Roger Straus observed that "this is most unusual for a French publisher to translate back from English the work of an American writer on a French historical character." Francis decided, a little surprisingly, to follow the success of *Madame Bovary* with *Le Hibou et La Poussiquette*, a working into French of Edward Lear's long poem "The Owl and the Pussycat." The translation took him just a couple of hours, and the book went on to commercial success. While Francis was credited with the title's neologism, in fact he had taken it from life. "La Poussiquette" was the name of the cat belonging to the cubist painter and printmaker Marie Laurençin, friend of Jacques Villon.

Francis's other projects did not always proceed on the same basis of familiarity. Some would take time to reveal themselves to him. He recorded his thoughts on this in the notes he made of an interview made during lunch at the Café d'Orsay in late 1957 with the poet Pierre Reverdy, whom he had approached in relation to his planned next project on Apollinaire:

> I told him how I regard my writing. Like all writers I have things to say, and sometimes these things take the form of a novel, sometimes the form of a biography, or what people call a biography. But I don't consider myself a biographer de métier. For some reason I find it hard to speak directly, as do writers of novels; perhaps it's timidy [*sic*]—I hide behind other people and speak through their mouths. These have to be people capable of expressing my thoughts, preferences, ideals, etc. they are people I come across in my reading—usually by chance. (During this he kept nodding sympathetically, patting my arm—he interrupted only to object to my statement that I "hid" behind other people: "No, he said, you simply express yourself through them.") At present I don't know whether Apollinaire is one of those people or not. If I don't know that he is, I will write nothing about him.
>
> He said, "You are capable of knowing who and what you are—most people are not capable of this—so your decision will be the right one. Your book will probably take a form that you have no idea of in advance, and you will not understand what is happening or why it is happening. That is the only true artistic creation."
>
> Never in the world, he said, would he have spoken with me this

way—"as if we had been friends for twenty years"—if he hadn't felt about me in a certain way . . .

I thanked him, told him he'd given me courage, his talk had been precious to me, and had been utterly different from anything I'd imagined in advance. He told me that was the greatest compliment I could pay him.

In spite of his success, and the longevity and range of his literary output, Francis nonetheless remained unsure of his worth as a writer. Bill Maxwell wrote Eudora Welty that "Beatrice Steegmuller says that all Francis needs is for somebody to tell him each morning that he is a good writer, but it has to be a different person each morning; she isn't enough, and so she has given it up, except that she understands how he feels when somebody does." The art historian Sidney Geist, friendly with both Francis and Beatrice, recalled that Francis seemed to friends and acquaintances to have depressive qualities and a deep insecurity about his writing. In his diary early in 1959, Francis noted, next to his regular appointment with the psychoanalyst Martin H. Stein, whom he had been seeing for some years, "General confusion. Great inadequacy—as common with every other man. Castrated. Age. No use to write anything else. NO IDEAS." Beatrice too was in analysis, with the charismatic and fashionable psychoanalyst and art collector Werner Muensterberger (whose patients in the 1950s also included Laurence Olivier, James Dean, and Marlon Brando). She was so fond of Muensterberger that she left him a Villon etching after her death, not, as she put it, "for professional services but because I laughted [sic] so often and enjoyed such beautiful art there."

In April 1959 Francis and Beatrice flew to Paris, where she remained while he travelled south to Greece and Turkey. He had begun working seriously on Apollinaire, assisted by Liliane Ziegel, a researcher who often worked with American scholars in Paris. They would continue to work together, and Liliane would become a close friend. He wrote to Freya Stark, the explorer and travel writer whom he had met through Florence art historian circles, telling her he would be taking her book on Greece with him, and she replied, from Treviso, thanking him for his: "nice letter." She mentioned a mutual friend, the writer Alan Moorehead, and said that she was "glad to think of <u>Ionia</u> being taken to its native haunts, and if you bring it to the land of Mytilene sometime in the second half of August, you will probably find me gathering about there."

In Athens, Francis visited the Acropolis:

> Best visit . . . George Dontas, Conservateur du Musée de l'Acropole let me go up to see the KORAI. All in cellophane bags! The guard takes off the bags one by one—the beauties appear. Will soon be open to public. Almost alone on Acropolis. Sky blue between columns. Sitting at top of staircase leading down to museum. Salamis, sea and distant mountains all blue—like best Côte d'Azur light. Too much for me. One Kora was, too.

He flew to Istanbul "over Marathon, Euboea, Mytilene. Arrive to find Istanbul full of rams smeared with red and yellow dye for Bairam. Hilton Hotel. Taxi to Blue Mosque. Walk to Saints Sergius and Bacchus . . ." He was away a month, sailing from Piraeus to Venice and then flying back to Paris. Beatrice was planning a small exhibition of her paintings in New York, for which Villon would compose a catalogue introduction. She wrote to the Kazins, "Not a picture painted. So none for sale. Nothing written. So no criticism possible. Together and apart (Francis in Near East) we've had a wonderful time."

On their return to New York in the late summer of 1959, Beatrice was diagnosed with breast cancer. She underwent a mastectomy and continued daily radiation treatment at Mount Sinai Hospital through the end of the year—Francis wrote to Robert Giroux, "She rests when she can. Her spirits are good." The following year Francis's novel/loose family memoir, *The Christening Party*, was published. But most of their energies were directed to arrangements around Beatrice's care and to weathering losses in both their families. Francis explained to Lionello Venturi, "As you know we've had a miserable winter, with Beatrice seriously sick and operated, not to speak of the deaths of her brother Edwin and of my only brother. But Beatrice is stronger now, and things are more peaceful." They spent time that summer in Connecticut, Beatrice "triumphant at making the journey without fatigue." In December, when it became clear that the cancer was progressing, Beatrice composed a note to Francis, including a list of bequests for friends after her death, including "any drawing to my nephews and nieces whom I consistently doted on." She said that she would ask Muensterberger "as a friend—if you should want to talk about me occasionally, if he will see you. I know he will because he knows I love you," adding what survives as her only written comment on her marriage, a final note: "Our different backgrounds made the going rough sometimes, but your love comforts me today as my love and belief in you must comfort you. Uncounted kisses, Bea." The following April, the exhibition of her drawings was held at Carstairs Gallery on East Fifty-Seventh Street: *Drawings by Beatrice Stein (Mrs. Francis Steegmuller)*. Jacques Villon sent Francis notes to be used for the exhibition catalogue, highlighting Beatrice's integrity as an artist, the quality of emotion as tangible presence in her work—"COEUR and DESSIN aligned"—and her receptiveness to the physical world. The drawings were "a distillation of Beatrice Stein's life—of landscapes she has loved in France and else-where, of everyday details that she has jotted down, recorded, written in shorthand—a shorthand of the heart, as it were."

In early June 1960 they made one last trip to Paris, where they saw the Villons. Francis interviewed Braque about Apollinaire and planned a side trip to Italy to stay with their friend the artist Randolph Morgan, then living at Positano, in order to give Beatrice "the 'independence' my temporary absence will afford," but it all proved too much for her. Francis wrote to Douglas Cooper,

Bea's strength did not hold out and we returned by air to New York where she can receive more rational and familiar care. I never did leave Paris, except to take the airplane home with her. At least she was able to have her much desired reunion with the Villons a couple of times and to see the big Villon show. Those, after all, were the things she greatly desired to do. She is comfortable here . . . She speaks of beginning to draw soon again, and I hope she may be able to . . . If you write to Bea, I know you will make it casual, as we are playing the whole thing down and merely sharing her regret that this temporary weakness prevented her from staying in France as long as planned.

Two days later he wrote again: "Bea . . . spends most of her time resting and dozing these days, which she thinks will make her stronger. Once in a while she sparks up and does a bit of drawing. Her courage remains formidable, but she's tired of being told so. She says she'd rather be well than have a good character."

Over her last weeks, Francis sat up with Beatrice at night, filling the hours as she slept watching televised Russian-language classes on the nurse's television set. She died at the end of June at the age of sixty-one. She and Francis had been married just a few days short of twenty-six years. Francis's father wrote to her lifelong friend Clara Binswanger in early July:

> Beatrice was an inspiration to all of us and her memory will be revered all the more as time goes on. What a help and encourage-ment she was to Francis—in fact she was all this to everyone who came within reach of her smile. Francis spent the Fourth . . . here in Sharon and I had a happy hour with him there. I was proud to see how well he is facing the situation. Even though the most difficult time is yet to come I know he will measure up to our ex-pectations, yours and mine.

Francis also wrote to Clara, letting her know that he had taken on a housekeeper, "to occupy maid's room for I don't know how long." He reassured her that he was coping, and that André, their Paris driver, was also in New York with him. His statements about his grief, even to close friends, were characteristically reserved: "You can imagine the outpour-ings in the letters I receive." He went to Europe at the end of summer; "stayed in Italy seven weeks and felt much the better for it. Then two rather trying weeks in Paris liquidating a few matters, seeing old friends and almost drowning in associations. A week here has helped even things out again and I'll be glad to be home and at work, I think." As usual, work meant more than one project. Apollinaire continued to preoccupy him, and alongside this, he and Norbert Guterman were working on *Papillot, Clignot et Dodo*, which Roger Straus had accepted with enthusiasm: "I speed to write you that Bob Giroux and I think Wynken, Blynken and Nod is beguiling, delicious and highly saleable." No doubt Francis was prompted to take this on in the wake of the unexpected good news of the extraordinary sales of his earlier children's book translation. The following spring, with the royalties from *Le Hibou et La Poussiquette*, he bought a Rolls-Royce Silver Cloud II. He described it as unostentatious, "the old model," costing the same as a Buick. It was a gold colour, and Francis chose canary yellow for the highlight strip that ran along the side at hip height. He hired a man from Rolls-Royce to drive the car from Crewe to Paris, to give him time to learn to manage it himself. From Paris he wrote to Robert Giroux that Rupert Hart-Davis was going to contract for the Apollinaire in the UK and that he would be glad to head south to Italy, "out of the cold," adding that he had driven the Rolls-Royce at a hundred miles per hour "and think that you would enjoy its steadiness at that speed." The next months were consumed with trying to recalibrate his life around the loss of Beatrice and the solidity of their shared lives, to take up alone those pursuits that marriage to her had made possible.

Francis Steegmuller would go on to be admired as a great biographer, not only of Flaubert and Maupassant but also of Cocteau and Apollinaire, and a major translator of Flaubert. He would write a book on Isadora Duncan, as well as shorter pieces on related topics, spin-offs from the biographies, on the drag aerialist Barbette, on Queen Christina, on Stravinsky. This list includes several gay-coded figures, traces of another facet of Francis's public self, reputedly something that "everybody knew" about him. It was something assumed, if not exactly known, by members of Beatrice's family, and it was certainly spoken of in New York literary worlds, in *New Yorker* circles, where it was noised about by Brendan Gill and Ved Mehta, while Robert Pounder and Vincent Giroud, who knew Shirley through her friendship with James Merrill, confirmed that stories of Francis's sexuality circulated in gay literary circles and more widely. The art historians Hugh Honour and John Fleming, whom Francis and Shirley would come to know during their years in Tuscany, were another source of these stories. They were "amused that Shirley seemed to be completely unaware . . . or rather had reinvented Francis as this perfect role model of a husband, whereas he'd been, in their views, a very, very sort of, active homosexual." Possibly their view of this had come from Muriel Spark, who was, certainly in her later years, convinced that Francis had been the lover of Leo Coleman, a dancer and photographic model whom Francis met while researching Cocteau—Coleman had appeared in Cocteau's film *Blood of a Poet*. The two men remained friends for many years, Leo writing to Francis occasionally and Francis visiting him when he and Shirley were in Rome. Muriel's views are summarised by her friend Penelope Jardine in a note archived with Shirley's letters to Muriel. Jardine quotes from a late, cross letter in which Shirley writes of her affection and Francis's for Leo, noting that "Francis, like others, undertook to subsidise some of Leo's small, crucial debts of rent arrears or telephone." For Jardine this supported Muriel's view that the two men had been lovers, as, she commented, "Francis was notoriously stingy." The surviving letters from Leo to Francis do not indicate that the men were lovers. They are friendly, giving details of an uneventful, everyday kind, with no suggestion of any particular intimacy. Beyond this, there seem not to have been any specific lovers named. The art historian John Pope-Hennessy, who came later to be a good friend of the Steegmullers, was dismissive of suggestions that Francis was closeted. Pope-Hennessy's partner, Michael Mallon, recalled, when Honour and Fleming "brought up, once again, the subject of his supposed repressed homosexuality: 'That is an interesting subject, but not, I think, one that applies to Francis.'" Other friends had similar doubts; John Richardson, the former partner of Douglas Cooper, said he had initially assumed Francis to be homosexual but later decided that he was not.

As a writer, Shirley Hazzard was in no sense innocent or unaware of the complicated routes that sexual desire takes, as is everywhere to be seen in her fiction. In *The Great Fire*, Aldred Leith observes, "The experiment of love is itself aberrant, more often than not, and doesn't lend itself to classification." Shirley was aware of such complexities in the lives of her friends too. She spoke to John Cheever's biographer on this in relation to Cheever and also noted of the writer and editor William Maxwell, "Bill never made a secret of the fact that he'd had a brief homosexual life before his marriage . . . He felt he was so sensitive that he could never have friends or a normal life." Francis's analyst, Martin H. Stein, whom he saw from the early 1950s until 1964, was for some years president of the New York Psychoanalytic Society, an institution that at that time pursued conversion therapy. From all this, not much can really be deduced with any certainty, and certainly nothing that would challenge or disrupt recognition of Francis and Shirley's devotion to each other. What remains, and remains important for Shirley Hazzard's life and work, is that she found happiness in marriage to a man with inclinations toward literary and artistic figures and subjects marked by complexity rather than transparency, with a preference for the undisclosed rather than the vaunted truth, interests that drew her to him, which she shared.

# 8.

## *AMITIÉ LITTÉRAIRE*

### 1963-1966

IN JANUARY 1963 Francis Steegmuller's diary recorded a busy social whirl. Along with two short visits to his father in Connecticut and regular sessions with his analyst, he went to dinner with friends—Apollinaire scholar LeRoy Breunig, medieval historian Giles Constable, publisher Bob Giroux, poet William Meredith, Ralph and Fanny Ellison—and on outings with Margaret Watherston, a conservator at the Whitney Museum. On January 26 he had a lunch date with Harold Nicolson, husband of Vita Sackville-West, and was expected, after Muriel Spark's party at 5:30, to dinner with the journalist Irving Kristol on Riverside Drive, but he elected instead to stay at the Beaux Arts hotel talking to Shirley Hazzard. He had further sessions with his analyst on January 29, January 30, and February 1, a little more frequently than usual, suggesting some need to talk through a new relationship that had quickly announced itself to be important. He and Shirley exchanged notes and sent each other books and stories, their dialogue writerly from the start. On February 15, as arranged, Francis drove Shirley to dinner at the Maxwells' and then saw Margaret the next day. On February 20 he had a lunch date with Margaret followed by dinner with Shirley, and the following Tuesday he went with Margaret to an event at the Whitney. In early March he recorded fragments from a dream in his diary, notes no doubt to help him recall key details to discuss later with his analyst: "Dream marvellous [illegible] with Bea. No grief on waking; later dream . . . we go off hand in hand . . . I tell them (or want to) that it's not what it seems, and I say (to whom? Myself?) 'I don't like that hand-in-hand business anyway.'" The apparent resolution here—absence of grief, rejection of intimacy, assertion of preference—may well have been occasioned simply by the fact that he was, briefly, away on a two-week trip to Rome with his father. It certainly suggests that his present relations with the two women were shadowed in some way by his only recently ended marriage.

By the time they left New York on March 14, Francis and Joseph Steegmuller's trip to attend the beatification of Mother Elizabeth Ann Seton (who would go on to become the first American saint) had produced no little difficulty for Shirley. She had been planning to go to Italy around the same time, as Elena Vivante had been recently diagnosed with terminal pancreatic cancer, so Francis suggested that he and she might fly together to Rome and then travel on to Spain afterwards. Shirley loved the idea, then cooled on it, partly because the dates clashed with a party she had agreed to host with Alan Pryce-Jones, at Muriel's request, for Maurice, son of Harold Macmillan. (Francis dismissed this as "a party for Names.") She vacillated. Muriel was all for it:

> My Girl, I can't make head or tail of your reasons for not going to Rome if you are attracted by an attractive man who asks you to go with him and his Pa. It's the most romantic notion I've ever heard of in my life, so if you don't go, it must be that the heart has its reasons that reason doesn't know. As for being afraid of being hurt, don't think I don't know what you mean, goodness I ought to. But one is hurt anyway, every way, and one has joy unforeseen as well. Maybe he's afraid of getting hurt too. (Christ, I sound like Aunt Ellen's column in the Wigan Star.) Anyway, it may be that Francis is a Pedestal-woman man, and would be attracted by your sweet nature as much as your handsome mug and form. Do let me know developers, and if serious in outcome don't forget to start off on the right foot and make it plain you've got a vocation as a writer first and a cook second.

In her reply, Shirley set out her concerns at some length. Francis's behaviour had been, from the start, confusing; there was "a sort of detachment that did not fit at all with the fact that he wanted to see me constantly." The invitation to travel to Spain had been made at a dinner party, "obviously feeling that this had no implications that might prevent its being said before other people." She added that "in all these weeks of being with me Francis has never so much as held my hand." A few days before he flew out, Francis sent her a coyly "anonymous" letter, advising "that FS had been involved with another woman when he met me, felt he had committed himself to her, did not know how he could extricate himself—the point being that he would rather have SH. Could I advise?" A correspondence continued in this stylised vein, between "Lo Scrittore" and "La Scrittrice." Francis began, "A writing friend tells us of meeting a seemingly marvellous writing girl by chance (as much chance as can be present at such moments) at a party given by a far from usual mutual friend," but he owned that it all now seemed to have been "too good to be true!" and that he felt it might be best "to try to salvage an 'amitié littéraire'" from it all. Shirley responded:

Lady authoress has statement to make . . . For her part she may say that she does not believe in Chance. That she has no accompaniment and is in fact sola solissima. That the quasi-accompaniment to the party, while congenial, is of quite other inclinations . . . She must impress upon her readers . . . that she is of serious nature in such matters, that her experience in this direction has been of a kind that has tended to keep her sola solissima, always allowing for rare possibilities occurring at parties given by common friends . . . Scrittrice is trying to think of examples of amitié littéraire . . .

Their letters continued as Francis's departure approached. Shirley was concerned that he was less serious than she: "I cannot set out on venture with built-in obsolescence. Tried to say before—these things matter deeply . . . If you ask me to come, I will come. I feel that that is saying a great deal. Otherwise will stay home and write sad stories." Her sad stories were part of the problem. They suggested to Francis, as she later explained to

Muriel, "Deep Feelings." They exchanged books and compliments. Francis had early in their friendship paid tribute to her accomplishment: "You may be on the brink, but I'm the one that's open-mouthed, a pathetic look of puzzlement o'erspreading classic features." Shirley wrote that on reading his *States of Grace*, she had been "much impressed by the Real Writer dazzle" and "reminded . . . sometimes of Muriel's books, the same unimpeded flow of sharp observation." In return, she had sent him her "Villa Adriana," which he remembered "from a time when I didn't know your name." She had based the mismatched couple in the story on her tetchy experiences with Jan Ligthart, but tellingly, Francis saw something of himself in the story too: "You'll probably smile when I say I like it less well than the others. Special pleading for the female. Much to be said for your pedant. In his minutiae he finds——? No sympathy for one so reduced?" Immediately Shirley regretted having sent it, but she argued for it nonetheless: "Don't know why there shouldn't be special pleading for the female though; circumstances are specially against her. Unjust to say she didn't show sympathy for the pedant—to have written it at all shows sympathy for him. The unsympathetic side is really only my envy—would love to do instant syntactical translations of inscriptions etc. also—I did make her out to be rather tiresome too."

In the spring of 1963 Shirley was working on her first novel, set in Italy, a tale of romantic love eclipsed by its own waning. *The Evening of the Holiday* was contracted to Macmillan and Knopf after publication in full in *The New Yorker*: "On Monday I took my piece of writing to Bill [Maxwell] . . . and was no sooner home than he telephoned to say he Loves It . . . Having the thing finished is a tremendous weight off me—it was one of the hardest things I ever had to write . . . partly because it is a piece about happiness, deliverance etc, and it is harder to elaborate happiness than grief—happiness speaks for itself." The middle section of the novel, when Sophie and Tancredi reach an equilibrium and accept the chance to love, is the first such moment in her writing. Her earlier stories had chronicled the inevitable pain and the perplexities of love; now she was finding herself confronted with the possibility of reciprocity, lives and hearts coinciding, and had begun to write of that. Over the coming months, in the shadow of ever-shifting relations with Francis, she would compose the later sections of the novel, tracing love's almost inexplicable decline, itself overtaken by the death of Sophie's aged aunt.

Meanwhile, both Paolo and Sophie Lester had written advising that Elena's condition was worsening and urging her to come immediately. Shirley wrote to Francis in Rome to tell him she was going. While they were still, she wrote, "a little at cross purposes," she felt that things were "getting better," and on that basis she proposed that their Spain plans might be revived: "Will you make some suggestion of how we might meet? I would like to come to Paris—have never done that trip from Siena, but assume one goes to Paris via Florence and Milan?" Francis's response was not what she had hoped. He replied from Rome, declining the offer to meet in Paris and proposing, again, that they pursue an *amitié littéraire*. He explained that the "thoughts that led to this . . . are all bound up with your writing, which is so much more part of you than in the case of most writers I know. That your development as a writer looms tremendous, I prophesy."

As well as indicating future fame, Shirley's writing suggested to Francis a difficult emotional lability. He wrote that he had been overwhelmed by her "sad stories," but also by "the silences on the telephone: for me, just emerging from a vale of tears, that was not at all what I wanted." He felt that had she joined him on the trip to Spain, "you would have entered the shoes of your lady at the villa or the one at the party, but in real life with the ghastly pedant—selfish brute feeling himself just those things and a heel besides." He appealed to her sense of a truth between them: "Too much has happened too fast, things have become too thick. I dislike the word 'casual' in these matters, and my original implications were not that; but they were cheerful, light in what I think a good sense. But things went so quickly beyond that . . . Perhaps 'cheerful' seems a cheap word to you. Not to me: it's one I've paid a high price to be able to use again." Shirley had by now, in late March, arrived at Solaia, making her last visit to Elena, whom she found "emaciated" but "aware of everything, herself." Elena told Shirley that she believed she would be married within the year. Just as the complications of Sophie's love affair in *The Evening of the Holiday* are subsumed by the larger loss of the death of her aunt, so for Shirley, Elena's decline was all important: "The visit to

Solaia has been right. It is important to have come, even perhaps of a little help to them. It is all pain. Pale delicate Spring in the countryside; the
grass is filled with flowers." She flew back to New York from Rome. Her
flight went via Paris, and while she was sitting on the tarmac, Francis
and his father boarded the plane. She would later speak of this as a kind
of fated accident. "It seemed to me to mean something," but it had in fact
all been arranged. She had written Francis advising her flight details. All
three flew to New York, with Shirley in the seat between Francis and his
father. Francis spent the flight explaining that inviting her to come to
Spain with him had been his way of trying to resolve the situation with
Margaret Watherston: "He said he 'could not sleep with two women at
once' and that was why he had asked me to go to Spain, since that would
have eliminated the simultaneous nature of the affair." Shirley wasn't
particularly impressed, finding his account "a bit academic," and she
wondered aloud, "What would have happened after we left Spain? Well,
we would see."

Back in New York that April, the *amitié littéraire* continued: Shirley
sent Francis a clipping from Housman about the bodily ground of poetry,
"a shiver down the spine . . . constriction of the throat and a precipitation
of water to the eyes"; they went to dinner and to the theatre; and Francis
continued to see Margaret. In April he drove Shirley to Ossining, where
they had lunch with the Cheevers. Muriel continued to be full of hope
about their prospects, but she also raised questions:

> Surely, dear Shirlers, there is a very deep feeling floating around
> between you and Francis and that is something indestructible—
> that is, if the feelings are loving ones, as they are. I don't know
> what or how to think of all you tell me, and perhaps by now devel-
> opments have happened. You know, I can't help feeling (but I have
> a personal bias in this respect) that you might consider asking him
> whether the "other girl" is male or female. Perhaps this is an ab-
> surd idea—forgive it, if so. I can only judge by my poor wee self—
> how I go falling for that type, time and again, and never, really,
> for the wholehearted male! If this is too far-fetched and you are
> sufficiently in love to cope with the conflict, there's nothing like

a real love affair to resolve the problem—any problem—tho' it gives rise to others. My heart and thoughts are with you, Shirlers dear. All that matters is that you are full of possibilities in life and work. I'm enormously pleased to hear that the novel's going well, it will be a famous one, born of suffering as the best are—but not too much pain—that's fatal.

Shirley replied, dismissing Muriel's suggestion about Francis: "He is, though very determined in some ways, extremely shy in others and doesn't have an over-supply of intuition in dealing with women. All this rather naive and refreshing after the hermaphrodite group one has become so accustomed to (I too had thought of your suggestion that he might be ambiguous, but no, it isn't at all like that.)." By the end of April, things were back where they had been in February. Francis was having lunch with Margaret, dinner with Shirley, and seeing his analyst the day after. Nonetheless, Shirley reported that things were, in Muriel's word, "improvers," and Muriel reported herself pleased "that you're a little bit in love and that my first hunch was more or less on the right lines tra-la . . . I've been thinking of you constantly—and now that I'm officially 'told' you must convey my love and sweet smiles to Francis." She also advised her friend to "plan your summer on existential lines . . . move with the hares at the moment." Shirley welcomed this advice; she was spending more time with Francis, staying with him at his father's house at Sharon, Connecticut, where she gathered flowers and recited Apollinaire: "'Il aurait voulu ce bouquet comme la gloire / Jouer dans d'autres mers parmi tous les dauphins.' Green fields, trees barely out, cardinals, wrens, blue jays, soft rain. Put on parka, walked in garden."

Elena died at the start of May, Shirley's first bereavement, distant, but keenly felt. Paolo wrote, "My mother died yesterday—there was a crisis a week ago, affecting the brain—in a state of coma, half-delirium, a few moments of clarity, perhaps she did not suffer too much. Her presence was so splendid that everything now seems senseless. What can I say or do? No consolation is possible, but our love for her shall always be a bond between us." Sophie Lester described Elena's last days: "Paolo spent the nights on the little sofa at the foot of her bed. Her sister Virginia

came from Rome to help Ginetta nurse her. The poet Sbarbaro came
to stay a few days with her. She heard the nightingales return to the
spring garden. One day Paolo began to read [Leopardi's] 'La Sera del Dì
di Festa,' and when he stopped, thinking that she did not hear him, she
went on reciting the poem, softly but accurately." And the trip to Spain
was on again, scheduled for the end of May. Francis left first for a week
in Paris to see Jacques Villon, who was dying, and a large Delacroix exhibition that he was writing up for the glossy magazine *Show*. He wrote
Shirley from the plane, his tone fond and light. He reflected on a new energy and direction between them: "Speaking of conversation, don't you
think there is something almost humorous about our switch from talk
to action? So complete, so drastic, so instantaneous after-long-hesitation-
and-then-conviction-that-the-old-way-was-preposterous? (I'd like to coin
that Adjective in German!) Other adjectives: 'remarkable,' successful,'
'divine'! Perhaps: 'to-have-been-foreseen'?" In Paris, after seeing Villon
and the exhibition, Francis spoke at length to Liliane Ziegel, seeking her
counsel on whether he should marry Shirley. Liliane told him he would
be crazy not to.

In New York, Shirley was deep in writing. She spent the weeks before
leaving for Spain working frantically on *The Evening of the Holiday*, the
first instalment of which had been scheduled for publication in *The New
Yorker* the following month. At that stage it was still called "The Fountain"; it is possible that the change of title was a response to the report
Shirley had read of Elena's last days, the reading of the Leopardi poem
that had struck her so tellingly when she'd first read it fifteen years earlier. Shirley was also enjoying the fact as well as the prospect of closer
intimacy with Francis and reflecting on the abandoned visit to Rome:
"I still feel slightly odd but less so than before; no doubt getting accustomed." In requesting delay, he was perhaps setting out just the kind of
complication—of sensibility, and seriousness—that her earlier relationships had lacked, suggesting grounds on which marriage might start to
become thinkable.

In Seville, ten days into the trip, Shirley wrote the first of a series of
despairing diary entries. The difficulties now seemed graver than the earlier misalignments of mood and expectation, with notes even of cruelty

in Francis's insistence on an anticipated end to their affair. She recorded fragments: "'When we part, you'll be upset . . .' 'What about you?' 'Less.'" And: "In the lovely garden at the Ritz in Madrid, when something said about possible pregnancy (mine)—as a joke—and he said abortion; I No; then—'I accept no other solution.' 'I might, though.' 'I doubt it.'" She later reflected bitterly on the trip in her diary:

> From the second day—the first was lovely—it was a constant nagging about the lack of my prospects, that this was a passing thing . . . Because it only showed in me as tears and entreaty, he thought there was no judgment involved. Instead every one of those remarks was a nail in the coffin of my affection and esteem for him. He must have made up his mind within the first few days that he was coming back to MW—and I had better get the idea. In case I didn't get it the first sixty times, it was finally spelt out in words of one syllable.

But she was attentive too to the complications of his position, his confusion and apprehension, which answered her own. When Francis mentioned in Seville that on return to New York he planned to spend time with Margaret, Shirley observed, "If this (with me) could intervene, the association must have certain limitations," to which he responded, 'Maybe it's the limitations I like.'"

Overall the trip was unhappy and lonely. They were in Seville when news came of the death of the old pope, John XXIII; walking in the city, they found it "swathed in black, draped, wreathed, shuttered, depopulated." Shirley would later recall Spain as a grim and mordant place, "overhung" with the residues of Franco, "a pall of authoritarianism . . . and a sense of provincialism." William Maxwell wrote that in her letters she sounded "very alone among all those polite, reserved, sad, pale Spaniards." Perhaps, like Caro Bell in *The Transit of Venus*, she had been confronted there with the threat of "dedicated spinsterhood" in the figure of a female cellist, dressed like a nun, whom Caro faces each evening in the dining room of her hotel in Granada: "Once in a while her dark eyes would meet Caro's with melancholy, recognizing tenderness, as if to affirm a bond. As if to state: You and I will make no part of that enervating and degrading struggle." And Caro wonders if the future held for her only "solitary, chaste, ineffectual decades."

Francis was at pains to explain his situation to her. Shirley summarised this later to Muriel:

> A lot of remarks about not getting serious, I mustn't think of this as love, etc. interspersed with displays of emotion, and passionate attention. I not knowing where I was in all this. Constant talk about wife, constant . . . Then . . . in tears, said he could not get used to difference in our ages (25 years); that he had had a Personality for a wife before and did not think he wanted it again . . . Didn't really know what he wanted, future a great blank. He said he felt towards me as he felt when he was a child at school and someone offered him a prize: he went to pieces because he didn't know how to handle it. That he had got into such a habit of calculating the future that he didn't know how things would be if he didn't work them out in advance.

It all felt like "something in a Goya nightmare painting." The only point of amity and pleasure seems to have been reading one of Muriel's novels aloud together on the flight home: "The Bachelors (of all things!) Penguin copy bought in Madrid. Made us shriek with delight even in our woe-begone state."

The uncertainty continued after they returned to New York. "He leaves books, letters, a lock of hair, an Augustus John reproduction that looks like me—phone calls . . . He doesn't know what he wants." Shirley joined him in Connecticut on the first day of summer, they had lunch with his old high school teacher Catherine Wood, and slowly she began to reflect on the appeal of "the ambiguity of F," having wondered earlier "if the depth, the wish for meaning is only in myself and wished on him in my mind." She wrote often to Muriel, airing her frustration. "Sometimes he is v sweet and all goes well. Then he goes home and wonders whether he has committed himself to anything, and next time Acts Remote, though he is not much good at that. All very well but I'm getting tired of waiting round for the fcking Judgement of Paris; the Judgement of Shirlers is going to assert itself one of these days . . ." In mid-July he called at her apartment and they went walking "in the deserted UN garden and saw the espaliered pears . . . Perfect moment," a scene she would recall each spring, over and over, through her life, looking back on this as the time "when we began to believe in marrying." Through these months, Francis was selling some of the artworks he and Beatrice had bought: the Renoir oil, two Picasso etchings, and the Degas pastel (this last for $80,000; his dealer wrote, "it's a wrench but think of all that pretty money invested in General Motors"). Muriel was convinced that Shirley would soon be "a married lady . . . and feel sure it will come to pass in the way that's right for you both. You must hire a housekeeper the very first thing and have plenty of room in the house." She also advised a more assertive demeanour: "Why don't you swear at your lover? You're too ladylike with him by half." There was to be one last misstep—a wounded outburst from Shirley in early August, after which Francis sent a card, breaking things off once more.

This time Shirley responded with greater understanding, apologising. She also acknowledged the significance and substance of his grief for Beatrice: "A great sorrow like yours is an awesome thing, to be given the time and space it requires. Perhaps too, since these things cut one off in some ways you have not quite <u>known</u> how unnatural and distressing to me that situation of ours was, and the demands it has made all these months." She did not mention, but might have, that he had suffered a further blow with the death of Jacques Villon while they were in Spain, a loss that mirrored her own with Elena. In any event, she was shortly to leave for London and Italy—"It seemed the best thing to be Up and Go"—which offered a temporary absence to see what could be salvaged from the affair: "I think it is the best thing, and will give you space to consider. The truth is great and shall prevail and I think it will rear its battered head for us, distance or no."

She flew to London in mid-August. The city was "magnificent as always—stately and beautiful . . . Can't help missing the more voluptuous joys of a city where on Sunday afternoon the barrel organs are played beneath plane trees, pink boats glide up-river, the peacocks wheel their tails on verdi prati surrounded by rose gardens and pear-trees . . ." She spent time with Muriel and with Kit, finding them both, as ever, a little overwhelming, and with her New York friends Dick Swift and Mort Cohen, as well as "old China friends, ex-Italy friends, ordinary domestic friends." The main object of her visit was to meet with her Macmillan editors, Alan Maclean and Rache Lovat Dickson, who treated her "regally." *Cliffs of Fall*, a collection of her *New Yorker* stories, was scheduled for publication in mid-October. She left a week later—"it is quite hard being here, mostly because my mother is so implacably sad"—for Rome, then Solaia.

The Vivantes were all there, along with old friends the Lesters, and Archie Lyall. Shirley showed Archie her Macmillan cover, with its author photo of her reading a copy of *Flaubert and Madame Bovary*; Archie "immediately turned it upside down and asked 'What's the significance of the Flaubert? And don't tell me there isn't any.' I smiled enigmatically . . ." She drove with Archie to Montalcino—

A lovely drive, a high, isolated, ravishing spot . . . and in a valley a few miles further on a marvellous twelfth-century church, St Antimo, which looks as if it had been dropped there by mistake and should really be in the South of France . . . At the church, which is quite by itself in the valley, with a village on the hill above—there was an alabaster wall in the garden with a graceful tree laden with pomegranates, all ripe and glowing, ready to be hung over someone's bed . . .

She walked in the hills around Solaia—"I am nearly staggered by this countryside, whose attractions I thought I had become accustomed to"—and went with Paolo to Elena's grave, "a lovely spot with a view of the city on one side and towards Chianti on the other—in a rather crude modern cemetery." On a day trip to Florence she ran into her Capri friend Sebastian de Grazia. "I said he must come to dinner in NY and meet some nice people who liked his book—almost identified These Nice People, just for the sake of saying their name."

Returning to Rome, she was pressed by John and Ginny Becker to go and stay with them at their converted fisherman's house in Sperlonga, a cluster of old houses high above a cliff an hour or so away on the coast, a destination for artists, writers, and the 1960s jet set. She drove down with them in mid-September. Also sharing the guesthouse was Francis's friend from Rome, Bill Weaver. Francis wrote, "Bill can be great fun. Use your own preferences whether or not to tell him you're hearing from me. If you do, of course give him and his friend (Pippo, is it?) my best, but think twice about deciding." Sperlonga was perfect, granting space and time for reflection and recovery, and for imagining, once again, a shared future:

> Why aren't you here? I am sitting on a balcony with a lamp and the roar of the breakers below and nothing visible except the fishermen's lamps out to sea (v nostalgic to someone with an oriental plus a Neapolitan past). This divine place. Ginny showed me everything today, then said, "We'll see you at the beach tomorrow and we hope you'll come to dinner tomorrow night"—one could hardly ask for more respect for one's solitary tendencies. So I went and bought wine, bread, cheese, coffee, acqua minerale, jam and the best prosciutto I've ever tasted, and picked figs in my little terrace garden; and posted a letter to Francis. And then I walked in the little town, and finally right along the beach (as far as the Grotta). Painted blue and yellow and red fishing boats pulled up, marvellous clear water, two women walking with baskets on their heads, vast sea, golden light, hills behind; thought very much of Francis . . . I'm on my way to bed . . . You should hear the sound of the sea—Sophocles long ago heard it on the Aegean . . .

Distance was allowing space for reflection. "It is lovely that the letters are spiralling to their pathological conclusion . . . What a long time it has been since I left you dodging about Grand Central Station. It must have been useful, this separation, since it has been so hard—and especially here, when everything indicates combined presence of F & S . . ."

She returned to New York to a new equilibrium. The last reference to "MW" in Francis's diaries is September 4, after a session with his analyst. On September 7 he had written, "I am much alone—seem to want this, apparently, in order to spend a few minutes, whenever I feel up to it, at the typewriter." In mid-October, Shirley joined him in Sharon for his father's birthday; there were still anxious and hurt moments, but no drama. She recorded in muted tones the changing season: "Long dry autumn. No autumnal mellowness—weather so dry, that the leaves, when they did at last fall, lay around the trees in circular patterns like broken glass." She began drafting her story "Le Nozze," scenes of a couple preparing to move in together, choosing and measuring places for the woman's books and furniture, sorting objects from their past lives. The woman picks up an intricately patterned plate from a service that "Nina" had helped the man choose. She finds a crack in the plate, "not that you'd notice, with that design," and he responds, "You never understood about Nina . . . I needed time to work that out." The story concludes with the man reflecting on his having chosen, in the end, "Love." Francis took Shirley to meet Clara Binswanger, another final note, making ready for remarriage. On October 17 *Cliffs of Fall* was published in London, its U.S. release scheduled for the following month, with a book party held by Mort and Dick. Bill Maxwell wrote, "What a fine book it is! The stories look (and read) even better than when I read them first—and you won't, like John O'Hara to Benchley, say, 'What was the matter with them the first time?' I am so proud of you. I couldn't be prouder if I'd invented you. There's love!" Francis wrote a card accompanying flowers: "My word is as good as anybody's—the book is lovely. No false commotion about it, nor about SH, nor, I hope, about her loving FS." In a final alignment, his own *Apollinaire, Poet Among the Painters* was published that month too, to a warm reception, and it would be nominated for the National Book Award for biography the following year.

After their books, the wedding. Shirley was thirty-two years old, Francis fifty-seven. Kit wrote to Francis, "Shirley and you seem to share

a very particular happiness, which is a rare commodity and is to be treasured. I am so proud of her for the person she is as well as for what she
has accomplished, apart from loving her more than anyone else in the
world," and Paolo Vivante, joyously, to Shirley, "This is wonderful, shat-
tering news! I did think that there was something going on, but not that
it was gelling so far; so far indeed, that in a moment you have passed, as it
were, from one cycle to another, suddenly disappearing round the corner
of our perspective, no doubt to reappear again in a new, even more splendid form. And it was so very good that there was not a long boring period
of betrothal, so it is quick, glamorous, serious, grave all in one." Muriel
rang from London and then wrote, "I keep thinking of things I meant to
tell you yesterdy to make you laff, as the time lag has left so many hap-
penings of mutual concern in the air, but I feel we got a lot in yesterday
all the same, it was great. You are looking luvly these days, like a girl with
a glowing future, and as I'm psychic it will surely be as I say. See you on
Choosdy at Hotel Volney with Francers—Looking Forward—Love, M."
In mid-December, Shirley wrote to Chris Cooper:

> My book appeared this autumn and was received in a generally
> pleasing way. Here we are still shaky from the terrible happenings
> of November [the assassination of President John F. Kennedy]—no
> one can quite realise it, and there is a sense of a sort of public
> aghastness. It is strange to be getting married after All These Years
> of an independent life, a sort of terrifying delightfulness about it
> all. I have of course just got my new apartment into shape and am
> saying little private goodbyes to it all the time. But Francis is so
> good, for me and to me, that I don't really expect to miss a thing.

Later, days before the wedding, looking out at the city from the windows
of her apartment, she thought, "How fast it all is going."

They drove up to Sharon in the gold Rolls-Royce, taking Clara Binswanger with them. The scene was quiet, domestic—years later Shirley
recalled, "We washed up!" The wedding was in the afternoon, a party
for friends, and then they drove back to Manhattan through the snow,
the flags at all the post offices along the way flying at half-mast to mark

the last day of official mourning for President Kennedy. A few days later, on to London, where they saw the Macleans, Rache Lovat Dickson, and Muriel; they drove to Essex to see Chris Cooper and his family, then to Cambridge to Hugh Brogan, Shirley's friend from Solaia. They spent Christmas with Kit, who "sobbed throughout"; one of Kit's friends, whom Shirley noted was "(hated)" by her mother, telephoned to say that Kit had been talking of suicide. They left in haste for Morocco "pour patauger en plein Delacroix" (to wallow in Delacroix), as Francis put it to the Kazins. It was Shirley's first time in Morocco, and she was struck by the familiarity of the ancient landscape, its contours, "European rather than African," giving her to "imagine how France or Italy might have looked before spaciousness was diminished by overpopulation." The scene is captured in a photograph described in her story "The Meeting," which she began drafting in the wake of this visit: "The hills were sometimes covered by green grasses so short that after heavy rain the soil showed through in violet streaks." They flew to Tangier, were driven to Fez, and then on over the Atlas Mountains to Volubilis, where, Shirley recalled, "the ruins were almost covered with narcissus (the smell, unromantically, made me sick, eventually, it was so overpowering), the light glorious, the countryside going on forever, so it seemed," and on to Ouarzazate. In "The Sack of Silence," she recalled the sequence of towns: "Bassae, Volubilis, Tarquinia . . . Ruins mostly. Places where the noise has had time to die down. The tumult and the shouting dies; if you live long enough." Returning to Tangier, she noted the constant wind blowing off the Mediterranean; she could see Gibraltar in the distance. Her note-book has fragments of scenes, possibly for stories that remained unwrit-ten: "Beach on Atlantic side—endless gold sand, great breakers (little rose-painted blistered hotel restaurant called Rolinson, green doors for beach lockers with numerals in both Arabic and Roman). Vine-covered roof terrace. On sand, one or two peasants on horseback. Ships going towards Gibraltar or coming out from the straits. Nearby, Roman ruins (and Phoenician) of seaside town of Cotta." And in the markets, "things of use and beauty," stalls of fruit and vegetables, "peppers, eggplant, to-matoes. Mint."

They were back in New York at the end of January, and Francis decided, "even after Fez and Meknes," not to proceed with Delacroix. Shirley moved into Manhattan House and, as spring approached, sat through the day in the building's elegant garden, working on her novel. In February she heard of the death of Archie Lyall, alone at a clinic in Zurich, and wrote a tribute for a memorial collection that Archie's friend Patricia Clarke was putting together, one friendship leading to another; another Solaia connection expanding her world. Francis continued to see his analyst, to Shirley's consternation. His diary in March records the single word "Pressure." Shirley remained through her life hostile to psychoanalysis. She set down her thoughts on the subject in her notebook, singling out for rebuke its "lure of authority" and the fact that interpretations were "at expense sometimes of sense of humour or proportion." Other criticisms were more particular:

> Analysis, curiously, does not seem to enlarge subject's tolerance for frailties of others. Encourages engrossing self-examination of own intricacies, allows subject to imagine these of singular interest to others but does not widen compassion or sense of general requirements. For example, F distressed because of guilt towards first wife due to greater pleasure with me. I, seeing him distressed, ask "Is it because you feel guilty?" Doesn't feel able to contend, goes to psychiatrist. Back an hour later, much relieved: "It's just because I feel guilty." . . . Absorbed in own irrational distress; oblivious to effect on new wife of pronouncement of this kind combined with trip to psychiatrist one month after wedding.

In their arguments, she was distressed to find her behaviour echoing her mother's:

> Lean on sink, after days of feigning unawareness or of showing concern; think "I could always die." Comes, is furious to find tears. We sit down, on floor and sofa. "I asked you if you would look after me" (Harshly). "I think this is one of those times when I

need looking after." (As though there were other times). Utter oblivion to comparable sentiments, requirements. Self-pity, lack of connection . . . His grief is sacred (But so is everyone's.) Only true grief is loss of loved one by cancer. Nothing else weighs.—Oh what sorrows everyone experiences, even in their dark imaginings.

When they travelled to Rome that spring of 1964, she found Francis introspective and self-absorbed. On May 30, recalling how she had the previous year so much imagined their "combined presence" there, she recorded her disappointment, her sense of prospects thwarted:

> Borghese Gardens. Here I sit where I sat five years ago, in tutti sensi. Paradoxically, this city never seemed more beautiful, this morning with the slightly uncertain sun, light breeze—oh the trees are marvellous, not yet harmed by the summer. It is—God—some joke so stale, so predictable that it would hardly be worth playing on someone. The whole city cries out with life—pleasure, romance, serenity. This journey—how many years imagined—touches all the nerves, of memory, disappointment, of the worst kind. Touches, alas, that nerve full of tears, that particular hurt, so I sit here . . .

The following day, they visited Villa Adriana, after Francis recorded in his diary a dream "of two women who resent me. One is—? Who? The other, MW, whom I catch sight of on her sidewalk, in burlesque and her big scoop hat and cape—a silhouette—but she stops immediately as she sees me approaching from the street, and I immediately tell the people I'm with she doesn't want to see me, and walk rapidly in the other direction." The next day, Shirley wrote bitterly in her diary, "To be married—is to be in Rome for the first time with someone, staying at a lovely place, and to be standing at the window one fine Monday morning wondering how one will spend the day alone." (Was she perhaps thinking of Dorothea Brooke?) Francis was also noting his anxieties: "The feeling that unfinished business was interfering with his present happiness. He had been supposing that the unfinished business was BSS, but could he perhaps be attributing to her what really had to do with MW? Too sensitive to be happy with one when that meant hurting the other; solution not to marry the wrong one, but to live alone and miserable!"

Despite these moments of hurt and chagrin, they were happy to be there and to be together. On June 3 they flew to Greece: "After Italy it is like going off the high diving-board—completely different, in appearance, light, contours, vegetation, personalities and colours, everything—except of course that it is still the Mediterranean and that so much of their history has coincided." Athens was dominated by the Acropolis, "hard to believe that anything so spectacular can be so beautiful—its beauty is so haunting that it seems to come into your room at night (after the evening floodlighting has been turned off). You walk up there over a steep rocky path . . . and there it sits . . . buildings all in creamy-gold marble . . . on a white-stone hilltop." After a visit to the Archaeological Museum, Francis noted in his diary: "Masochist uses analyst as audience for his woes and self-denigrations. To grovel and abase himself in front of someone new. Self-sabotage in all fields. Masochist is non-aggressive—timid, passive, whining. Homo. Longing for father. Homo at base of male masochism." They travelled on to Delphi, passing by "the foot of Mount Parnassus, then the crossroads where Oedipus slew his father." The ruins at Delphi, "immense," a strenuous afternoon's climbing, and then driving up the slope to the Castalian Spring. A night there—"in the morning sat down to breakfast with eagles flying overhead"—then they were driven down through olive groves "drenched with their pale, prolific flowering" to the harbour of Itea, "a cluster of sun-coloured, flat-roofed cubes . . . as busy as its temperament will permit it to become," to take the boat south to the Peloponnese. The ferry trip to Patras appears in "Out of Itea": "The sea, on all sides, reflects capes and mountains, rocky or grassed, wild or cultivated, all with that legendary significance that in Greece seems to be not merely in the eye of the beholder but some knowledge possessed by the landscape itself." The travellers in the story pass the "sloping headland" where Byron landed, then "Missolonghi. Where Byron died," and learn that their destination, Olympia, was "on the border of the district of Arcadia." In Mycenae, they had a guide, Mr. Aristotle, "who had known

Schliemann when he was a boy." From the Peloponnese they went on to Mykonos to spend time with LeRoy Breunig and his wife, Ersi. The Breunigs would remain lifelong close friends; at Roy's death, Shirley remembered him as "the first friend of Francis' I met and loved truly, and at once."

This was, as Francis later wrote to Red Warren, "a summer of glorious loafing." They had "lovely swimming" at Capri and caught up with Alberto Moravia and Bill Weaver in Rome. Shirley was eager to share with Francis not only the beauty of Siena but also, at Solaia, what had become for her "home," infused with memory:

> The sense of home. What others have returning to parent's house or town where they grew up. Everything natural, comfortable. Myself too, feeling purified, at ease, more real, easier to be natural, easier to be good . . . Going upstairs alone to wash my hands— every step more familiar than anything else ever will be—stairs, undulations or corridor, furniture of bathroom, oval window. It is, quite literally, where I grew up.

It was all, perhaps, bound to collapse under the weight of expectations. She felt keenly that Francis was unimpressed by Solaia. After one teary episode he responded, "Why don't we split up?" This was not the first time he had made the suggestion, and Shirley reflected, "It is the kind of threat people make assuming it will not come to that, and it sows the idea in all its consequences." She reminded herself that "he is dear and good to me" and that he was preoccupied with his past and his loss: "One cannot compete with the dead . . . The dead are safely dead . . . They cannot reappear to remind you of their imperfections, of the times they were coarse or boring or bossy." Thinking through her dilemmas in the woods nearby, "a beautiful place, cool and green," she resolved to leave off lamenting and to begin "reassuming my identity." She looked back to previous happinesses and to her achievement over recent years of "balance in my life," a way of managing what she felt to be the constant demand that she compromise her wishes, desires, and tastes—a way of being married. Against this, she set her own memories and priorities, the well of past Solaia happiness:

> It is silent except for birds, as beyond the trees a wood and the cream villa. I think of Archie. I think of having <u>fun</u>—fun that was none the less concerned with sensibility but did not sow runners of difficulty, of dis-ease. And resentment. I have loved, always, being in Italy but I wonder if I will have the courage to come again for a very long time. This has not been right. If I was too set on it, I could not be more sorry—I feel I have been in a state of apology throughout our time in Italy.

Her first resolve in the matter of "reassuming my identity" was "simply to do so." She also decided that she should try to have a child, thinking that this would provide for her "a position other than a sort of guest-on-sufferance" in her marriage. Finally, "to do my work and make it go" with "less apology, less abdication from what is suitable to me, less guilt . . . ; more fun and more work. Less dwelling on oneself." Many of these thoughts and the difficulties that led to them were also, it seems, being pursued in the novel on which she was continuing to work through these months. When *The Evening of the Holiday* was published in 1966, she was asked in an interview, "Why did Sophie walk away from love?" She responded with more candour than would become usual: "It was a futureless love in the sense of being able to have a life within society, and children. She was also limited within her own self. I tried to suggest she was a person with not infinite capacities for passion as it were; she had protected herself. As many sensitive people are, she is perhaps over aware of her susceptibilities and protects herself too much." The novel that emerged was of course far more than simply the product of these fraught contemplations around the difficulties of her own sensitivity and the fading chances of conventional happiness, just as its pervading melancholy did not depend only on the grief at Elena's death; all these qualities can be found to differing degrees in the earlier stories, and all would continue to develop in her later writing. But her comments in this interview suggest a particular confluence of factors, concerns, pressures, gravities bearing on her through the period during which this first longer work was developing, which the writing also allowed her to pursue.

When they returned to New York in September, she and Francis prepared to move from the fourth floor of Manhattan House upstairs to a larger apartment, where they would remain for the rest of their lives. Shirley found it difficult to pack up her furniture from her East Fifty-First Street apartment so soon after moving in:

> The sadness of losing things. Losing them in more than the sense of having to get rid of them, also in having to feel all their imperfections. These things I acquired with such effort—no one knows what effort. Being made to apologise for them instead of being proud—the complete disregard of what it is to make one's way without a penny other than what one earns, without training, without help of any kind. Will there ever be pleasure to me again like looking round the room in the evening? If I had to let these things go for some reason, it would be all right for me—but without the slightest comprehension and with ridicule or disapproval. No possessions will ever matter to me so much—perhaps, even: no possessions will matter again.

Meanwhile, they were considering a house in Italy. It seems that Francis had been less unimpressed by Solaia than he had seemed, for when Shirley learnt that the Vivantes were looking to sell two old houses in need of repair at Monteliscai—a twenty-minute walk from Solaia—and proposed that they consider buying, he agreed. The property was to be in Shirley's name. She wrote to Cesare Vivante, "I can't tell you how delighted I am that we are going to be part-time Senesi and inquiline di Barbarossa." In the end, however, it all proved too difficult. A year later, after much correspondence, deposits paid, lawyers hired, and restoration work planned, the proposed purchase was dropped. Negotiations had broken down irreparably due to obstacles raised by the youngest Vivante, Charis, with whom Shirley's relations had always been difficult. Cesare told Shirley that Charis's obduracy was wholly due to the fact that Shirley was the would-be purchaser.

Shirley's family members were also presenting intractable difficulties. She was in touch again with her father, who had written in early 1964 asking her to "bury the hatchet and write to me occasionally," which she did, although they never became close. (A couple of years later, Reg wrote, after seeing recent photographs of her, "It is a peculiar feeling to look at a picture of your own daughter and realise that with the lapse of time, I could have passed you in the street and not have recognized.") Meanwhile, Kit's misery in London had reached another endgame. She sailed to New York in late 1964, spent the holidays with Shirley and Francis, and then set off again, flying to the West Coast and sailing on to Sydney from Vancouver. Valerie, Bob, and their three children had been living in Sydney since October 1962, the move prompted by Bob's concern at the social unrest that he felt to be a consequence of the civil rights movement in the United States. Shirley's view was that Bob had been attracted by the "White Australia Policy"; Valerie's son Hamlin understood his father's view as having been more that the unrest in the United States was not going to be quelled "quickly or easily or peacefully," and that this was not the place he wanted to bring up his family. The Barneses had quickly settled down in Sydney, moving to Vaucluse in the city's moneyed eastern suburbs, and the children attended exclusive private schools.

Valerie and Bob wanted to help Kit through the difficulties that faced her on her arrival in February 1965, most particularly the need to find somewhere to live but also her ongoing money problems. Bob offered to help manage her finances, but the arrangement angered Shirley and was quickly discontinued. There was also the issue of Kit's things, possessions she had been carrying around with her since her divorce a decade earlier. Valerie was a little overwhelmed when she confronted it all. There were, she wrote Shirley, five trunks full of ratty old blankets, "a dirty old matted quilt . . . the two green bedspreads from our beds as children in Beauty Point." Kit had protested to her, "If I get a place of my own I will need them, and they were hardly used, they are practically brand new." It wasn't just household effects, Valerie continued, hoping to strike a comic note:

> Eight coats—not including a fur one. I persuaded her to throw one horror out but she argued about another one, very old. She was keeping that to make into a winter dressing gown. I couldn't budge her on that one. She seemed to think I didn't care if a poor old lady froze to death. The button jar—a bag of old rags "very handy for patching"—dregs of underwear—completely useless coats and jackets "to be made over"—pieces of fur "that might make up into a collar"—some remnants of material that "might come in handy." That old pink hostess gown which she bought when I was about 8, when I thought it was LOVELY and which she has LITERALLY never worn. A dress from New York in 1952 which a drycleaner ruined and which she has never worn since—"perhaps something could be done with it . . ."

Shirley didn't see the funny side. She responded, accusing Valerie of interference and coldness toward Kit. Valerie countered swiftly, reproving Shirley for "personal abuse because my way of offering help differs from that which you believe to be correct":

> Despite the attraction of your easy formula of signing a check to dismiss difficulties, I still think it more kind to take some trouble trying to arrive at a common-sense solution of very common difficulties . . . Your "advice" to us was a unilateral action and in my mind a rude and unwarranted interference with my relationships and with Mother's. Please do not hide behind a noble idea to "help Mother"—depicting me as some kind of overbearing ogre from whose influence you must rescue her can hardly be of comfort to her, any more than I find it attractive.

The sisters seem to have reserved their greatest animosity, always, for each other. For all their differences of taste and inclination, and politics, there is a remarkable similarity in the alacrity with which they went into battle with each other. Shirley penned long, furious letters to Valerie, setting out her views, and Valerie, just as forthright and accusatory, responded in kind. Shirley warned Kit to stay clear of Valerie, and Kit wrote regularly to both that she would prefer just to "disappear." It went on for twenty years, unresolvable, some kind of primal battle. A week or so after the above exchange, at Shirley's urging, Francis wrote to Kit, proposing that she return to New York to escape the influence of Valerie and Bob and advising that she keep any such arrangements "confidential." On this occasion Kit did not see the urgency, and she remained in Sydney, but not for very long. She was lonely; her only friends were those she had made on the voyage out, and she took on occasional volunteer office work at Sydney Hospital to pass the days.

In New York, the Steegmullers' move to a larger apartment in 1964 was in part a response to Shirley's wish to have a child. That wish was not fulfilled; she had a miscarriage at some point in the first decade of her marriage, an event that went unrecorded in her diaries but left a trace in the fiction—"It wasn't this I meant to share"—and sometime in the 1970s, she underwent a hysterectomy, again not recorded. In time, she would come to draw on the larger consolations, often recalling the observation Francis made, one evening they had spent reading together after a day of writing, that children would have made such days impossible.

In the weeks after returning from their four-month European sojourn in 1964, Francis's diaries show the Steegmullers seeing a number of friends—writers, editors, publishers: Ved Mehta, Robert Sonkin, Jon and Ruth Naar, Sebastian de Grazia, Mary Cortesi, and James Merrill from Shirley's old circles; Francis's friends the Kazins, the Breunigs, the French scholar Mina Curtiss, Knopf poetry editor Harry Ford, writer Renata Adler, the poet Richard Howard, and Giles Constable, along with the Maxwells, Dwight and Gloria Macdonald, Howard Moss. Many were closer to Francis in age than Shirley was; there is a sense that with her marriage she slipped quickly into an older world. Most remained friends, although not all. Francis had long been friends with Mina Curtiss, but she and Shirley did not get along. John Pope-Hennessy recalled that Francis had said to Mina, "If you cannot be polite to my wife, then we can no longer see each other." After a few years, Francis made contact with Mina again, but was told, "It's no use. I will be civil for a few months, and then I will just lapse into my old ways." The names of other writers appear fleetingly among their diaries and correspondence, sometimes just a fragment of gossip or social chat, like the story about Robert Lowell that Shirley told, years later, to Anthony Hecht: "Did I tell you how once he spoke to me about an incident he had learnt of from Francis' life of Maupassant?—Maupassant's having swum out to rescue a swimmer in trouble, who turned out to be Swinburne. Lowell said: 'After all—you can't blame him—He couldn't know it was Swinburne.'"

At dinner at the home of Jack Leggett, the novelist and later director of the Iowa Writers' Workshop, they met Mary Ellin Barrett, a journalist at *Time* and *Vogue*, the daughter of Irving Berlin, and her husband, Marvin Barrett, a journalist and editor at *Time* and *Newsweek*. Mary Ellin, who would become an intimate and lifelong friend, recalled how intertwined were the spheres of work and pleasure and influence in the lives of the Steegmullers and their friends: "Shirley's New York was a very particular one. First of all, there was hard work at the center. You worked on a magazine, or you wrote books, you were a musician or a lawyer. You went to the theatre, you went to the opera, you went to the movies, you read the books as they came out, you went to dinner in people's apartments." At the Knopf fiftieth anniversary dinner in 1968, the Steegmullers were among a crowd of literary luminaries: Elizabeth Bowen, Clifton Fadiman, John Hersey, Carl Van Vechten, Muriel Spark, John Updike, Lillian Hellman, William Maxwell, Janet Flanner's partner Natalia Danesi Murray, Langston Hughes, William Meredith, Alan Pryce-Jones. Shirley would later remember Elizabeth Bowen saying of the event, "Civilization is in this room." Shirley's interest was not restricted to these elevated circles; Mary Ellin's daughter, the poet Katherine Swett, remembered Shirley as always completely "celebratory" about all her friends and their work.

Within the large and loose circles of literary Manhattan, there were also more defined groupings, and the Steegmullers connected lightly with several of these. As well as Francis's Columbia connections and the *New Yorker* crowd, they mixed with writers and editors from the *Partisan Review*, *Commentary*, and *Dissent*, the New York Intellectuals. They remained aloof from the ideological debates that characterised these circles and in particular were unmoved by the battles still playing out around anticommunism and anti-anticommunism, finding no urgency in them. The writer Benjamin Taylor, who knew Shirley in her later years, observed that she "didn't care about this argument . . . She didn't think that was real; it didn't come from the deep soul." In a 1981 letter Shirley spoke critically of those from these circles who had "mostly been 'left'— sometimes communists, sometimes less doctrinaire—in their youth, having been madly naïve about Soviets; and having no capacity for ever being wrong in their own eyes. It is their own errors they hate. They have been taking this out on 'leftists' ever since." In a similar vein, that same year, in an oral history interview about Robert Penn Warren, Francis described himself as one of those who "had not been communists, not been Stalinists, and hadn't become Trotskyites either, but we were what you might call New Deal Americans" who tended to "take this whole thing more kindly than they do." He recalled being in a taxi with Red Warren and Eleanor Clark, going to dinner at Lillian Hellman's, when Eleanor had made a passionate denunciation of Hellman. Francis observed, "Lillian takes those kinds of things very easily. She's quite hard-boiled, and quite a sophisticated person. And has changed her ideas about those kinds of things considerably. A fact that ex-Trotskyites like . . . Eleanor don't seem to realise."

Within these circles the Steegmullers were distinctive figures. Alfred Kazin's biographer wrote that Alfred and his then wife, Ann Birstein, had always found Francis charming, "a figure of intellectual grace out of a different era who had survived into 'overheated New York,' quietly coexisting with 'Norman Mailer and other public declaimers who dominated the literary scene at the moment.'" Kazin noted in his journal that "the Steegmullers had this gift of turning their dinner guests into replicas of *their* social graces." He was entranced, in the early years of their friendship at least, by Shirley's social energy, and after one dinner he wrote in his diary of "the magic of Shirley the Hazzard. When will we learn from a woman like this—with her incredible gentleness, the light that fills where she is, that love is a form of intelligence—a way of listening to the world, of taking it in, of rising above one's angry heart . . ." He later changed his tune, enraged by the Steegmullers' withdrawal in the face

of the terrible rows they witnessed between him and Ann during the acrimonious breakdown of their marriage, and hating what he called "F's
snubs and little faggy airs of distaste." The writer Steven M. L. Aronson
recalled meeting Shirley and Francis for the first time in 1969 at a small
dinner hosted by the poet William Meredith at his sister's Manhattan
home. Also at dinner were Lionel and Diana Trilling, Norman Podhoretz, editor of *Commentary*, and his wife, Midge Decter. It was a literary
gathering at which, Aronson observed, the Steegmullers stood out, not because they were less famous than the others, although that was true. But
where the other guests, even in conversation, were somehow "out to gain
advantage" over each other, like "literary politicians," the Steegmullers
exemplified a "gentler sensibility," content to let their work speak for
itself. There was a combination of connectedness—mixing with the most
exclusive literary circles of New York—and reserve, a detachment, even
aloofness, a decision, or choice, not to belong, and this combination would
come, over the years, to define their social lives.

The Steegmullers cleaved to people practising a similar discretion
to their own, whether within or outside well-known circles. They were
good friends until the ends of their lives with the novelist Paula Fox and
her husband, the writer and translator Martin Greenberg. Another warm
and long-standing friendship was with Dorle and Dario Soria. Francis
had known Dorle Jarmel since his college days, when they had been introduced by Irwin Edman, a Columbia philosophy professor. Dorle had
gone on to become a music journalist and then publicist for the New York
Philharmonic. She had been Toscanini's secretary and had been involved
in Leonard Bernstein's legendary 1943 Carnegie Hall debut. Dario Soria
had, as Shirley put it, removed himself "from the fascist incubus of prewar Italy" and had come to New York for the 1939 World's Fair, where he
met Dorle. The couple managed several significant music recording la-
bels, and Dario later became managing director of the Metropolitan Opera Guild. Over the years, their friendship with the Steegmullers would
interlace with other friendships and Italian associations, and through the
Sorias, Shirley and Francis came to meet and mix with New York's music
circles, becoming friendly with the great bass Boris Christoff, the cellist
Raya Garbousova, and the former ballerina Vera Zorina (Eva Brigitta

Hartwig); they (with Kit in tow) shared a box with Danny Kaye at the Metropolitan Opera for Joan Sutherland's New Year's Eve performance at the end of 1973, and attended a party for the Boston Ballet during Rudolf Nureyev's 1983 tour. What mattered always was the friendship itself. Shirley admired the way Dorle's professional life was grounded in love: "Her love for music and its practitioners drew up all her initiative in the shared life with Dario." In her eulogy for her friend, Shirley noted all the "benefactions" of the Sorias and their "furtherings of great and good events," but these were, for her, secondary to the "precious friendships . . . formed under their auspices."

Their friendship with Robert Penn Warren and Eleanor Clark was "long and precious." It reached back to Francis's first marriage, was reanimated with Shirley's arrival and marked by long arcs of shared reading and serious writing. In an early letter to the Steegmullers Red Warren set out his sense of the quality of their friendship: "You all have great gifts, publicly visible, but you also have a great gift, only available to the more private view—the gift for making friends happy. You have made this friend happy before, and now your letter(s) puts me deeper in your debt. I felt good for days after it came." Over the decades, the four read and discussed one another's books with great seriousness; Warren's poem "Flaubert in Egypt" was inspired by Steegmuller's work on Flaubert, and in 1967, when Warren won the Bollingen Prize for his *Selected Poems*, he wrote Francis and Shirley, "I liked getting the prize but I wouldn't have liked it nearly so well if I hadn't had your telegram too. Your telegram was like your giving me another prize. Truly, I value it." There was much discussion of poetry, particularly between Shirley and Red, and a shared love of Thomas Hardy—"I should have known, too, that Hardy was for you," Red wrote—and of France and Italy. Shirley included in *Greene on Capri* a mention of Red's visit to the island in the autumn of 1939 after the outbreak of war in Europe. Standing at the parapet of Villa Jovis, he "looked out helplessly at history—'There once, on that goat island, I, / As dark fell, stood and stared where Europe stank'—and threw a small stone, his protest, down to the sea: 'I could do that much, after all.'" Shirley and Francis would visit the Warrens' hexagonal wooden house in Vermont, with its view of the nearby brook and mountain, for

Christmas parties and other, quieter gatherings. Shirley recalled staying overnight in one of the small bunk rooms—the house had been built as a ski house, meant to accommodate numbers of visiting children—rather cramped, with Francis unable to stretch to his full length in the tiny bunks and Eleanor pounding on the door early the next morning because she needed to strip the sheets for the laundry. "This was not," Shirley pointed out drily some years later to Rosanna, the Warrens' daughter, "the Hassler Hotel."

Rosanna felt that her parents and the Steegmullers "connected imaginatively at an essential level" and that it was important "that in each couple, both partners were acknowledged as powerful writers, so it was a true artistic foursome of equals." She recalled that Francis's and Shirley's books became "part of our family conversation." There was a larger principle at play here, a belief in the importance of the expression of shared writerly experience. Shirley wrote of this later to another writer friend who had admired one of her books: "I am delighted my book gave you, of all readers, pleasure . . . Because, as Auden says in his delightful Letter to Lord Byron, 'Art, if it doesn't start there, at least ends, / Whether aesthetics like the thought or not, / In an attempt to entertain our friends.' Meaning, as Proust (this time) put it, 'some friend of my thoughts.'" Rosanna, herself a poet and scholar, would go on to develop a significant friendship of her own with both Shirley and Francis, a friendship grounded, as her parents' friendship with them was, in literary affinities, through French as well as Italian literature. Over the years, she had intense discussions with them both about their work and, in time, about hers. High feeling flowed both ways; Shirley came to regard Rosanna as her *fille manquée*. On the birth of Rosanna's first child, Shirley gave her a toy—a stuffed pink lamb with a music box inside—and confided that it had been bought for the child she had expected, hoped, herself to have.

Also substantial, formative, was their friendship with Bill Maxwell and his wife, Emily, which had begun with Shirley and Francis's first outing together in February 1963; the shared connection was, Shirley later wrote, "an immediate talismanic bond." Literary affinity and shared sensibility and taste were all paramount. Emmy was an amateur painter with literary interests—she had studied poetry at Smith and wrote reviews of children's literature for *The New Yorker*—but had chosen, as the Maxwells' friend Harriet O'Donovan Sheehy wrote in her obituary, "to put the nurturing of Bill's talent ahead of her own." There was, according to their friends, in the relationship between these four "a kind of radiance," rarefied, erudite, receptive, generous. Paula Fox recalled an evening she spent with the Maxwells at Shirley and Francis's apartment: "It was an intense, concentrated, and effortless gathering. When we all stood at the door to say good night, it seemed as if no time had passed since our arrival."

Maxwell was, Edward Hirsch observed, "the most present of anyone I've ever known as a person. He immediately, if he liked you, started talking to you about your childhood. It sort of dismantled everything else. For me with him it was love at first sight. Friendship was immediate. When he spoke to you it was as if you were the only person." Benjamin Taylor recalled, "With Bill Maxwell there was no small talk. You just sat down and started talking about books." Shirley would have prized that complication of sensibility and comportment, that presence, and presence of mind, and presentness, and all the talking about books. She admired Maxwell's writing, particularly *The Folded Leaf*, although she was less impressed by *The Château*, ironically enough the book Francis had helped with. In 1961, early in their friendship, Bill had presented her with a copy, inscribed, "For Shirley Hazzard, whose beautiful and firm beginning it has been my great pleasure to watch." She wrote the following year to Rache Lovat Dickson that she found *The Château* "heavy going—it has rather an air of All Done By Hand, it is completely lacking in passion of any kind, or spiritual adventure; this may be a result of his having gone through a profound psychoanalysis between this and his previous books. At any rate, he is an extremely nice person, with a very delicate intuition." The connection between Shirley and Bill over their longer friendship was intense. Alec Wilkinson described seeing the two of them together as "just sublime. Two gigantic sensibilities that were utterly enfolded with one another." Maxwell and Francis were also close, but Shirley and Bill were "two people clearly capable of appreciating each other fully. To love each other without having any emotional or erotic complication to it. Just pure love. For the artist, for the character, for the person." The friendship was a central force in Shirley's mature life.

# IV

# 9.

## SMALL MASTERPIECES

### 1966-1970

IN JANUARY 1966 the Steegmullers made a second trip to Morocco, returning to New York mid-month, a few days after the publication of *The Evening of the Holiday*. This, Shirley Hazzard's first novel, is an exemplary pastoral, the initiation of a young woman into a world of love and pleasure. It is also an elegy, with the story of the love affair between Sophie and Tancredi tightly counterpointed with the story of the death of Sophie's aunt, Luisa. The interest is less with plot than with the atmosphere of anticlimax, of "the evening after the celebration," drawn from the Leopardi poem that also gave it its title. Shirley had first read the poem in a Wellington street, aching with the separation from Alec, and it seemed clear to her then not only that poetry could express the whole of feeling but that in this expression was profound consolation. She felt that her novel had its beginning in that recognition.

Complication is evident throughout, the stately advent and decline of love marked by a kind of comedy of irony, with mismatches—between characters, between surfaces and depths, what is said, what is felt—abounding. Love itself continues precisely because the lovers part, and their parting is necessary because of the nature of love. We cannot know, the narrative tells us over and over, and it is all inevitable. Luisa spends the days of the novel and the love affair observing, mainly in silence, the events unfolding around her. The reticence and introspection of her story work to still the progress of love and to inflect with melancholy the certainty of its passing. Luisa's death, like much of the romance between Sophie and Tancredi, takes place in a narrative ellipsis; what we witness is the anticipation of the event and its consequences. In the final chapter, when Sophie returns to Italy after Luisa has died, some months after the end of the love affair, Tancredi is only a trace of loss, his gloves glimpsed through the window of his parked car. The elegiac final scene of a train leaving the station provides an allegory of perennial, repeated loss in the stop-start interruption of the carriage full of soldiers and their bugler's "wistful music" played over and over—"always the same air, an antiquated sentimental tune that belonged, perhaps, to a regional song."

Throughout the novel, time is upended, complicated, its passage thwarted—the past is never past. At one point Sophie remembers a failed love affair, remembers listening to the man's "complicated exposition of the reasons why he could not love her in return," and she is "glad now to be reminded of the intricate, lasting nature of any form of love." Tancredi, sitting with Luisa and Sophie in the garden one evening, waiting for the nightingales, remembers having heard them at his family's seaside summerhouse some thirty years before. He reflects that Luisa would then have been a young woman: "I would have been in love with her, he realized—and the absolute certainty of this touched him deeply. It struck him like a loss actually suffered, impoverishing his experience, diminishing all his prospects." This imagining of an impossible and wholly speculative romance as something that has actually taken place, and that has consequences extending into the future, suggests an understanding of love that is in defiance of chronology and the world, something wholly interior, without external reference points. It also speaks to love's overwhelming consequence.

Alan Maclean had sent congratulations when the story appeared in *The New Yorker*: "You have told the story quite beautifully so that every word counts and it is . . . an almost perfect example of what can and should be done with a modern pastoral." Reviewers now echoed that view, describing it as "one of the most beautiful short novels ever written," one

with "an almost miraculous ability" to give "living balance and proportion" to "the great moral design" of human fate. There was praise for the
novel's combination of restraint and passion, its emotion "often as urgent
as a hurrying heartbeat." Its real-world reference points were noted, the
heroine described as "half English, half Italian, and wholly antipodean."
*Time* magazine observed that while *Cliffs of Fall* had seen the author
likened to Katherine Mansfield, Elizabeth Bowen, and Rosamund Leh-
mann, "in this near-perfect first novel . . . Shirley Hazzard proves that
she writes like no one except herself." She was the first to acknowledge
the slightness of the plot. Asked in a radio interview to outline the story,
she said, "It is a love story. The story of a woman who comes to Italy and
meets a married man. They have a summer romance. She leaves him—or
rather, they leave one another." For Bernard Bergonzi, while the plot was
"of a wearily familiar kind . . . when we read what Miss Hazzard has actually made of this unpromising material we are usefully reminded that
the right treatment can perform miracles." Others agreed: "Much of the
book's charm arises from the fact that the reader never quite discovers
how Hazzard makes a small masterpiece out of such unlikely material.
Partly it is because her prose is so understated that it forces the reader to
become uncommonly attentive."

The UK publication followed in the spring; Shirley wrote to Howard
Moss, "My book came out just now in England and is well-ish reviewed
(at somewhat economical length) in various papers. One (New Statesman,
I think) said there was not much more to say about it than that it was
very good and very well written; and, being like Greek temples, belonged
to Classicism . . . I think this last may have been intended as a slight." *The
Spectator* described it as "an object lesson in how little a novel needs to go
on about; beautifully poised, meticulously selective, the technique almost
amounts to a con-game where our imaginations do the author's work for
her." Australian critics pronounced themselves less impressed by the novel's restraint. L. V. Kepert noted the comparisons with Forster and James
made by American reviewers and cautioned that "one would not want to
lift her quite so high." Neil Jillett felt that the novel relied "too heavily
on implication" and that the author, while showing promise, still needed
to develop her craft: "If she learns to distinguish between nuances and

saying nothing, she could become a novelist of great delicacy and authority." And Suzanne Edgar felt that the author had "neglected character
development" and provided only "fairy floss: a delightful exterior with
a disappointing nothingness inside. A love story without real flesh and
blood lovers to elicit sympathy."

The same year, Shirley was awarded one of the American Institute
(later Academy) of Arts and Letters annual literary grants. The citation,
by institute president George Kennan, described her as "a writer whose
fictions are marked by signal penetration, wit, and grace, and who remarkably contrives to unite a sophisticated approach to the scene she displays with a disarming tenderness for those characters who have a claim
upon it." Its flat generalities notwithstanding, this was her first significant public affirmation. Shirley Hazzard the writer had come into view,
moving beyond the orbit of *The New Yorker*, with a writerly ethos, a place
in the imagination of the reading public, and the respect of other writers. Through these years she had also been writing the "Organization"
stories—oblique, wryly satirical studies of the perpetual mismatch of
glum bureaucracy and individual aspiration, desire, and imagination—
that would later be published as *People in Glass Houses*. And she'd been
travelling. Three or four trips a year back and forth across the Atlantic
came to make the pattern of the Steegmullers' lives a mirror of the life
Francis had led with Beatrice, made possible by the money she had left
him from her considerable inheritance in the form of artworks and a
significant portfolio of shares. When funds were low, he sold a painting.

Francis began work on a biography of Cocteau, proposed to him by
his friend William Abrahams, an editor at Atlantic–Little, Brown. Francis
had secured a release from Farrar, Straus—Roger Straus had been willing to agree to it because, he told Francis, "The Cocteau story is pretty
much common knowledge, and not very exciting"—although this arrangement would later sour. Francis had taken some time to decide to
do the biography, initially rejecting Abrahams's suggestion out of hand
because he had no liking for Cocteau's work, but then, as he began to
read more, he "found some of the poetry finer than I had known, and the
novels strangely attractive, and the films fascinating." He came to feel
that Cocteau "played up his own trivial side" and that there was much of

interest and worth in the oeuvre. His mind was eventually made up after a visit in April 1966 to Los Angeles, where Igor Stravinsky had invited him to look at Cocteau material among his papers. Shirley went too and was captivated by both Stravinsky and his wife, Vera, whom they met over several evenings. She made a detailed record of the conversation, the green and ivory living room, and revelled in a recitation of Pushkin. Years later, she recalled with great clarity a moment during dinner when Stravinsky suddenly peered intently into a bowl of flowers that was beside him on the table. "An insect was prowling among the flowers, and he remarked on its perfect happiness at that instant. The moment is vivid to me now, his voice, his bent head beside me and his enormous ears, the smell of the stock, the late light pouring into the small pretty dining room from the garden."

They went every year to Rome. In July 1966 they spent time there with the Kazins and visited Alberto Moravia, whom Shirley regarded with some bemusement, finding in him a "dated type of despair: idealistic, despondent, sombre, melancholy (antithesis of Mailerism) . . . Sunk in thoughts too deep for tears." Moravia drove them all to his country house on the shore at Fregene. Shirley enjoyed Moravia's liveliness and his inconsistencies and his sharp commentary on contemporary American letters even though she felt he embodied a contemporary Italy that did not accord with her own somewhat idealised image:

Fine windy day, sea rough after night's storm. Roads at Fregene full of lakes. Moravia drove in fits and starts, jumpily as his nature, turned down wrong road just near home even though he comes there almost every day at this time of year. Deaf on right side. Hard to converse with unless one makes some impact. Kind, nice, inconsiderate [sic]. Speaks good of almost everyone ("He's a nice man"—Of Blanche Knopf: "She was very nice") except Capote: "A snob and his book's a fake." Talks always intelligently, wants to get opinions on, above all, writing, criticism, ideas, but has no idea of allowing one to develop one's opinion, show one's personality in a cumulative way. Restless, peremptory, genuine—he cares only for truth, makes no poses, has no pretensions. Lives in modern

box apartment in Rome, modern shack at Fregene (where the
one beauty, the pines, is being despoiled by a disease), yet when
we saw a beautiful villa (Torlonia) near Fregene, said "That's the
sort of house I would like to have." (Why not, then?) and spoke
of modern Rome as utter ugliness—"Italians don't like beautiful
things." Drives crazily but says "Look at the way people drive,
crazy, no wonder so many accidents."

A few years later she ran into Moravia again on Madison Avenue—
"in ugly dark blue summer suit, tieless, with dark blue shirt buttoned to
neck in Italian way"—on his way to watch the launch of Apollo 11 on
television.

That summer Shirley and Francis drove from Rome to France to stay
with Red Warren, Eleanor Clark, and their children Rosanna and Gabriel
on the island of Port-Cros, just off Toulon. On the way, "on an empty
curve of beach near San Raphael," they happened upon Raymond Duncan, brother of the legendary dancer Isadora Duncan. Raymond, also a
dancer, was on the beach with his Greek wife, Penelope, engaged in a
private performance, "like driftwood spars upright, in shredding robes
and sandals, supporting one another, upright, but only just. And Francis
exclaimed, 'My God! The Duncans!'" Raymond Duncan died shortly after, and Francis's next project would be centred on Isadora.

Port-Cros was a nature reserve, with no cars, a tiny population, and
just two hotels, one in a converted former TB hospital. Eleanor had written to them of the island's attractions: "Oleanders, that clear, blue-green
water, little beaches with scrubby hills rising behind . . . I don't know
if radios etc are forbidden or if it is just a spell that falls on everyone."
They observed strict writing hours until two p.m., Red under a fig tree
and Eleanor in a "hot and pungent" donkey shed. When the Steegmullers arrived, they followed suit, working through the morning and then
walking to the beach to swim in the afternoons. "La mer ne bouge pas
ici," Shirley wrote. They then drove on to Provence, to stay with Douglas
Cooper at the Château de Castille near Uzès. Cooper had a reputation
for being difficult. Shirley recalled him as "not necessarily honorable or
kind; he was known for betraying people," but "always fun to be around."

One of the highlights of her stay there was "the revelation of Leger which was one of the many pleasures of the room we had. I realised I had never seen—or looked at—Leger properly before." Cooper owned several Légers; he had been a good friend of the artist. In addition to the one in the Steegmullers' room, he commissioned the large canvas *Les Trapézistes* to hang on a tall bare wall at the first-floor landing. (*Les Trapézistes* was later purchased by the National Gallery of Australia, whose early acquisitions became the subject of much impassioned discussion between Shirley and some of her Australian friends.) In early August they were in Venice, where they called on Peggy Guggenheim at the Palazzo Venier dei Leoni to talk about Cocteau, and then they flew to London.

In England they pursued the trail of Cocteau to Pinner, an outer suburb of London. While Francis was interviewing Reginald Bridgeman, who had been secretary to the British ambassador to Paris in the early decades of the century, friendly with Cocteau and a frequenter of avant-garde circles, Shirley walked around Pinner. Sitting in a tearoom, she overheard and noted down a conversation she would later use in *The Bay of Noon* to stage the scene of Jenny's search for the enigmatic Justin Tulloch, which culminates in news of his death, glimpsed in a newspaper in the tearoom—"Will you be mother?" At dinner with the Trillings in London, discussion turned to the Nobel Prize for Literature, which had recently been awarded to Nelly Sachs and Shmuel Yosef Agnon. Shirley asked, "'But why not Auden?' Then realise I have offended no less than three people there: (Mrs) Lowell, Sir Isaiah Berlin, Lionel himself . . . Berlin says, first Nobel Prize for Literature was in 1901 to Sully Prou-dhon, who said, 'Si Victor Hugo savait.'"

Their time in London was cut short by a brief detour to Stockholm. There was a drought, which Shirley would later recapture in *The Transit of Venus*: "The Swedish earth was blowing like fine sand: a world passing on the wind, seeping away, pulverizing. In the countryside, birches were leaning to the ground, dying in shallow soil. Only the sea stayed sceptical, an arctic blue: the same salt and tarry smells, the scavenging gulls." They were there for the Queen Christina exhibition at the Nationalmuseum, which Francis was reviewing for *The New Yorker*. They met with officials from the Swedish Ministry of Foreign Affairs, then took a boat across Lake Mälaren to Drottningholm Palace. The boat also found its way into her novel: "open with rows of wooden seats, like a small bus. All varnished inside, and the varnish sticky with salt and sun. Scarcely a dozen passengers, but twice that number of circular lifebelts painted with the name of the boat, the umlaut picked out in red."

At the end of August they returned to New York, to Kit, who had turned up a few weeks earlier, determined to try again in the city that had been the site of so much unhappiness. Trying again included, she insisted, "paying my way." She had transferred funds from Australia—Francis and Shirley had their accountant set up a family trust to manage the money—and was determined to find a job, although her plans were a little vague: "I've often thought I could have enjoyed a very small but select library in a small community, running a good cup of coffee on the side, with comfortable seats and free magazines. Probably only a dream . . . But if I can't find a job in New York then I've been thinking the foregoing in a small town or large village in England or even Scotland, could work." She had set herself up in a small hotel near Grand Central, her domestic needs addressed by the purchase of "an enamel dish, useless specifically but adaptable as a tea boiler, frypan and stew pan. I'd guess it would last the difference. I had a spoon, fork and knife, so Robinson Crusoe had nothing on me." By October, Shirley had decided that "all problems are Relative . . . —or at least parental."

At the start of December, Francis returned alone to Paris, where he stayed at the Ritz, conducting interviews and visiting the Villon retrospective at the Grand Palais. He wrote that he had "finally bearded Doudou [Édouard Dermit—Cocteau's adopted son and heir] . . . and I have a date with Jean Marais for next week. On the phone the latter sounds more like a Belle than a Bête." He dined with the writer André Maurois and his wife: "Mme Maurois, speaking of my Shirl: 'Mr Steegmuller a une ravissante femme, une romancière, sous le nom de Shirley Hazzard . . .' M. Maurois (interrupting and addressing me): 'Your wife's book is very good, you know.' FS: 'I know!'" He was also invited by the Goudekets—Maurice Goudeket had been the third husband of the writer Colette—to meet "people who Know All and will tell all." Shirley remained in New

York to keep Kit company. She worked on proofs of *People in Glass Houses* and began drafting another novel. On December 7 she commemorated alone her first arrival in Italy: "Ten years ago tonight. Then—oh, Italy, Solaia, freedom, everything . . . How happy I was arriving in Rome just ten years ago—it was my first real sensation of happiness, much tasted since. Everything changed. All as if a moment ago, fresh, marvellous." She joined Francis at the Ritz just before Christmas; they were given the room they had had the previous year, "ordinarily that of the Comtesse de la Rochefoucauld, absent in winter," and spent Christmas "eating chevreuil in the sun at Chambord—heaven—what an escape from the family Xmas tree."

Francis had been commissioned to write about the recent devastating floods in Florence for *The New Yorker*. In late December they went on to Florence by train. "For a last freezing hour the train laboured through the mud-laden flood . . . Florence lay as if stranded along the Arno." In the ruined city, "everywhere, indoors and out, the ghastly line was streaked along saturated walls." Later, Shirley wrote, "in streets and shops, the tears and courage, and the Florentine durability—the Florentine toughness. I saw the great Cimabue laid like a living casualty on a trestle table, and the books heaped up like pulp at the Certosa di Galluzzo. I saw a cat called Gianna who saved herself by clinging for a week to a ham suspended from the ceiling of a salumeria in Borgo Ognissanti." They stayed at I Tatti, the villa bequeathed by art collector Bernard Berenson to Harvard University, with their friends Myron Gilmore, the I Tatti director, and his wife, Sheila. In their small dining room one evening Francis commented, "How could I know, when I dined in this room with Berenson in 1950 that you and I would dine here alone, years later?" On the feast of La Befana (Epiphany) they lunched with the Gilmores at Castellina in Chianti: "much amity, good will, sensibility, civilization." This was another moment Shirley would commemorate each year at the season, marking signal moments of her life, recording also the act itself of recollection and acknowledgement, with a kind of formality, in her notebooks. She found I Tatti beautiful if a little gloomy, preoccupied with its own past and Berenson's life there: "All shrouded, shuttered; old man's comfort, other generations. Sunless, beautiful silent alley of cypress; no large windows . . . somewhat dark. But great comfort, even cosiness. Books inscribed, others—Trollope—with frontispiece of comments by Mary Berenson."

In January 1967 they were back in Paris, at the Ritz for several months. This was Shirley's first immersion in the deep literary life of the city: "Proust had often visited the hotel to see his friends, and all those years later it had retained the memory and the atmosphere of such a clientele. It had preserved its appearance, its feeling, its distinction." The Ritz staff were discreet about the "recognizable" friends of Cocteau who came to the hotel to speak with Francis; only with "the film stars" did their discretion drop: "They were captivated by Jean Marais." Francis went to Coco Chanel's apartment on rue Cambon to meet her. "She was frail, yes. But not one of those persons [whom Francis interviewed] was dull or forgetful. They were aware that they were near the end of their lives, at the end of what had been, among the elders, a sometimes vicious camaraderie. It was a singular era, and it's true they could on occasion be pretty merciless with each other. Theirs was a kind of science of knowing how to say incisive things." Occasionally Francis was himself the receiver of such sharpness. Initially he got along well with the vicomtesse de Noailles, but then he displeased her by interviewing someone she had told him to avoid. "The next time he called her, she picked up the phone—she recognized his voice—and said, 'Je suis sortie.'" Others of Cocteau's friends were more difficult still. Francis had had, he told Douglas Cooper, "no luck with Picasso—no reply whatever: I know they're bombarded, but couldn't they be a little less grossier considering that I did come nicely recommended by you and Francine? Charlie Chaplin just as uncouth, the two of them a great contrast to the otherwise universal courtesy."

In Paris they saw mainly Francis's friends: Liliane Ziegel, Jenny Bradley, the Goudekets, Janet Flanner, who had been loosely connected to Francis's prewar circles, the Apollinaire scholar Marcel Adéma, and Julien Cain, a former administrator of the Bibliothèque nationale, who had been imprisoned by the Vichy government at Buchenwald and, since his retirement, had become a scholar of Cocteau. They had the English diplomat Christopher Burney, another Buchenwald survivor, and his companion Françoise Green to drinks and dinner at the Ritz. Shirley had known Burney previously through UN circles. She was shocked by his decline—"thin, drawn, pessimistic, not even very kind"—but found him also "civilised, humane, truthful, still attractive, but like a dying man in every way and clutching at straws of self-esteem." Burney "spoke of Julien Cain, whose talk 'kept me sane in Buchenwald'—now patronises Burney, it seems." Later they dined "chez Jenny Bradley" with Jacques Porel, whose mother had been the Parisian comedienne Réjane, immortalised by Proust in the character of Berma, and himself a youthful friend of the author's. In her notebook Shirley observed, "French people—talk of the past in a way that invests it with monumental, historic quality, with infinite nostalgia and a sense of having all fitted into some almost heart-breaking depth."

In the spring, briefly again in Rome, they met Mario Praz, who gave Shirley an inscribed copy of his 1929 *Unromantic Spain*, a bleak commentary on the culture of Spain—clearly, he and Shirley had exchanged views on the subject—"a souvenir of my first making her acquaintance." She later described him as "a figure from another century, such as one comes across in Italy still—very odd indeed, obsessed with objects and tastes" and wrote that his autobiography contained "many unlikable things . . . but almost nothing uninteresting." The fragments in the diaries Shirley kept through these years give a sense of the seriousness with which she approached the social life that had come to her with this marriage. While in part she was recording significant if at times obscure names, there is also, always, a concern with reflection, learning, and taste. She was embarked upon the delicate process of crafting herself as a person of significance, of carrying herself in these circles.

There were, always, family difficulties. Kit was increasingly unsettled in Manhattan and in the spring determined to return to London. She wrote to a friend, "I decided I couldn't just go on indefinitely accepting such big help from S and F, who offered it so generously and lovingly, and that I must go on where I can stand on my own financial feet. So, though I don't respect England any more, lost all my old patriotic fantasy, I'm on my way back to see how I can manage." At the same time, Francis's father, now advanced in years, had been suffering increasing ill health, and Francis moved him to a nursing home. Francis wrote to Ved Mehta, "Family matters are always a bore, but this crisis, combined with the illness and death of my brother's widow, whose only prop I seemed in certain ways to be, has been like a bomb under the working and social life of Shirley and me." They spent July in Capri, one of the first of what would become regular visits. Francis had made arrangements to interview Léonide Massine at his home on Isola Lunga, an island off the Amalfi Coast, about his collaboration with Cocteau on the ballet *Parade*. They made the "hour's serpentine drive" from Ravello to Positano, then hired a *motoscafo* to Capri, stopping at Massine's island on the way (a difficult visit, captured in wry detail in *Greene on Capri*). The following month they went on to Florence. They had taken a two-year lease on Il Pozzino, "a farmhouse" in the hamlet of La Romola near San Casciano in Val di Pesa, "a morning's walk" from Florence, in "an undulating ocean of vines, olive trees and woods of umbrella pines." Francis wrote to Douglas Cooper, "Divine here. Hot and lovely—the grapes purple—the white cows plowing the olive groves—from our upper terrace we see the Cupolone . . ."

*People in Glass Houses* was published in the autumn, again by Knopf and Macmillan. The publishers set the book somewhere between a collection of stories and a novel, numbering the story titles like chapters. Most readers approached it as a collection of interconnected stories about the people who work in the offices of a large international organization called, simply, the Organization. Bureaucracy, with its deadening impact on individual life and on the life of language and its capacity to represent human truth, is the collection's main subject. The repetitive tedium of daily work fills its pages. The Organization's employees are occupied throughout with endless labour: filing, typing, translating, hunting for pencils, waiting for the lift, standing in the lunch queue; their efforts largely unacknowledged or invisible, supplementary to bureaucratic business. Two decades later, looking back on the collection, Shirley reflected on the subject of work in fiction:

Characters rarely have professions in modern novels. When they do, it is often an "interesting" one, being an architect, for instance, or a surgeon. You see them going out to work, and you see them coming home, but you seldom see them actually toiling. One would scarcely think, from reading contemporary fiction, that for hundreds of millions of people on this earth the working hours are the largest part of waking life. The greater part of their lives is spent in an office or factory, which admittedly is difficult ground for fiction, but nevertheless a human place, made up of human beings as well as machines.

Work brings humanity into the bleak world of bureaucracy: "You remain always conscious that a system isn't just an abstraction, it is made up of individual human beings who are responsible for themselves and the rest of us. We can see at this moment in history . . . the difference one determined person can make."

Macmillan promoted *People in Glass Houses* in bookstores near UN European offices: "I think we have now covered Geneva, Rome and Paris and other places where they speak UNESCO." Early responses were caught up by the book's UN references, and some were negative. The first criticism came before the book appeared; Shirley recorded in her notebook an encounter with UN under-secretary-general Brian Urquhart at a party: "'Why are you so bitter about the UN, Shirley?' (said bitterly) then I should 'stop this romanticising about the UN.' Subsequently said he had recommended that twenty floors of staff be eliminated years ago; that there were 'thousands of errors'; that they (UN staff) were unbearably smug, insulated like a small city.'" *The New York Times* ran an acerbic review by Frederic Raphael, who dismissed the book as satire that simply reinforced "the comfortable despair of the conservative who believes in the folly of aspiration, in the irremediable frailty of man" and presenting "the viewpoint of world-weariness as opposed to that of impatient or revolutionary rage." Such criticisms of her criticisms of the UN would continue throughout her writing life, leading perhaps to the prevailing but mistaken sense of her as a conservative critic of the institution. Francis wrote in some anger an unpublished letter to the *Times*: "The 'review' of Shirley's book by Raphael yesterday was in no sense a review of a work of literature; it was an attack on Shirley's character. I am really ashamed that the 'Book Review,' with which I have been happily associated, should have printed it."

For Shirley, the subject of the UN itself was less important than the portrayal of bureaucracy, the study of office life. When "Swoboda's Tragedy" was published that summer in *The New Yorker*, she had already heard from Ved Mehta that a friend who worked in the Justice Department's Office of Public Affairs liked it so much "he made everyone in his section read it and he says he's going to have passages of it included in his letter of resignation." The *Times* followed Raphael's review with an admiring response from Charles Poore that applauded the book's satire, noting that its target was little different "from any other buzzing lair full of organization men" and delighting in Hazzard's "joyful lampooning of pomposities, her solemn owls who shuffle multilingual papers, her vivid foreign scenes, her tenderness toward the few who are truly dedicated and ask no fanfare for devotion." He argued that this "places her on a high ground between Katherine Mansfield and Evelyn Waugh." Other reviewers shared that delight, finding the satire "analogous to and . . . every bit as good as Mary McCarthy's *The Oasis*." There was praise for "the demure humour" that concealed "a formidable satiric punch," and for the writing itself: "Her turns of phrase are exquisite." For her part, Shirley was delighted by the response from those working in the Secretariat, telling one interviewer, "Some UNO people can't believe you're not writing it at them—that you're trying to do something more than provide a roman à clef. I'm frequently told I've described characters who in fact joined after I was there. People fall formidably into type."

She was already at work on her next novel but cast down in the face of increasingly difficult news of her mother, now, inevitably, unhappy in London. As Valerie had reminded Shirley earlier that year, these constant uprootings had become "a repetitive pattern" that would "go on being repeated wherever she may go . . . Mother has now been travelling from place to place (fleeing from place to place?) since 1953." Kit had moved into a flat in Chelsea, "a bedsitter with small stove and use of bathroom, but handy to Kings Road and buses etc . . . It is taken by the month for £30." She saw almost no one, just those of Shirley's friends who were still in London—Patricia Clarke, Mort and Dick: "I talk to few . . . which leaves a lot of time to think of me, which is an unprofitable pastime and dangerous." By the winter she was writing to Shirley again about ending it all: "I've always considered there comes a time when one is redundant, in my case early . . . and don't say I haven't tried . . ." These letters left Shirley "full of woe . . . ability to work utterly drained, good cheer utterly drained. I try to fight it, must not let her get at Francis too, through me. The selfishness, the total unawareness of anything but self . . ." In February, Francis wrote sternly, pleading with Kit to consider the effect her "recurring threats to 'disappear'" were having on Shirley:

> Isn't this the kind of abandonment that you yourself suffered from your husband? Why inflict it on your daughter who loves you? Of course she worries about your situation anyway, but you are threatening the ultimate cruelty. We have been unable to plan, waiting for information from you . . . Please be in touch with us in a normal way, and let there be an end to this business of your "disappearing."

Kit replied, a note marked "Personal": "We're not on the same wavelength. Both have things to say, which mean nothing to the other, so writing on and on is useless." She booked her passage back to Australia—planning this time to visit another of her shipboard friends in Tasmania, and the crisis, for the time being, yet again, passed.

In the spring Shirley and Francis were on the *Cristoforo Colombo*, taking the Rolls-Royce back to Europe. They docked first at Lisbon, went to the Gulbenkian Foundation, located then in a beautiful villa outside the city, then drove to Sintra. Shirley remembered this trip as "something celestial. The uncrowded world, then." They sailed on to Naples, still with the car, and drove north to Il Pozzino. That spring, they "roamed among the iris and ate our lunch under the wisteria," and they returned in the summer and again in September to work and escape the busyness of Manhattan, a schedule they followed loosely over the next few years. At the end of their visits they would drive the car to Geneva, where it was garaged during their absence. Ahead of one of these trips, they were dining in Florence with a wealthy group, and a woman asked Francis if he would take a package to Geneva for her. When he realised that the package was an artwork that she wished to spirit out of the country, Francis bristled. The woman rushed to reassure—"Of course I wouldn't ask you to do anything illegal," and he responded, quietly, "Madam, I thought you were."

Life at Il Pozzino was conducive to writing, and Shirley embraced the local ethos as an ideal model. She wrote later to Alfred Kazin, "Your book makes me think of something our baker's wife said once, in our Tuscan village—as she emerged from her hot lifetime's work one blazing noon: 'Il lavoro si deve fare con un pò di passione.' [Work must be done with a little passion.] Right on." They had recently made the acquaintance of Harold Acton, historian, private scholar, and self-described aesthete, reputedly the model for his friend Evelyn Waugh's character Anthony Blanche in *Brideshead Revisited* (Acton discounted this claim) and renowned for reciting T. S. Eliot's *The Waste Land* through a megaphone from the window of his Oxford college rooms. He was described by Anthony Powell, another of his contemporaries, as having "no great individual talent save that of representing his generation—and that was wonderful." Acton, "half-American yet Anglo-Florentine," lived at La Pietra, his family's Renaissance villa on the outskirts of Florence. He was also a legendary— "weapons-grade" in one account—snob. His elitism was part of his appeal to Shirley, whose snobbery was of a different, more inclusive, kind (although she was, one friend observed, herself "a fabulous name dropper"). Acton had known Cocteau—his memoir recounts how Cocteau responded when asked what he would save if his house were burning: "I'd take the fire"—and he responded to Francis's biographer's letter professing enthusiasm for Francis's recent *New Yorker* essay on the Florentine floods. He also praised Shirley's tribute to Archie Lyall, whom he had known at Oxford, claiming that he was himself "too 'Latin' to appreciate [Lyall] and his works," but that he had found him "strangely pathetic." Shirley sent him a copy of *People in Glass Houses*, which he admired, telling her that she had "shaken my belief, never strong, in the value of UNO."

They joined other circles in and around Florence, were friendly with Nicky Mariano, Bernard Berenson's former companion at I Tatti, now living at Vallombrosa, as well as Bill Weaver, and his friend, neighbour, and fellow music writer, *New Yorker* correspondent Andrew Porter, in their compound at Monte San Savino. They drove the Rolls-Royce into Florence or to other local sites such as L'Albergaccio, the stone house that was occupied by Machiavelli during his exile from Florence, or farther afield to the Villa Marchio in the hills outside Lucca to visit Hugh Honour and John Fleming. Honour and Fleming were celebrated art historians, working as private scholars, like the Steegmullers, and both, like Shirley, with no formal university study. Shirley remembered their first visit, when they were served coffee in the garden "from a Pisan coffee-set and were nuzzled by a little dog called Tory." She looked back on this as a "precious" and joyful friendship, its pleasures arising, as she wrote Hugh years later on John's death, "from harmonies that we all, I think, enjoyed singly and together; yours and John's, Francis' and mine: the immense good luck."

In the spring of 1968, in Florence, they were at dinner with Alfred Knopf and his new wife, Helen, and their guests, the American political commentator Walter Lippmann and the celebrated Renaissance art historian Nicolai Rubinstein. Shirley found Lippman "boring, impervious to possibilities outside <u>his</u> world of politics, absorbed nicely the compliments I paid him (I seated on his right) on his resistance to LBJ over Viet Nam war." She was irritated at his lack of interest in her: "looked vaguely surprised when someone asked if I were 'writing another book,' as if just possibly he might have missed someone that mattered. Not a single question in <u>my</u> direction—all the other way, he must be the centre of things." She compared Lippmann unfavourably with Rubinstein, seated on her other side, who talked with her "about things beyond ourselves—matters of language etc." They dined with Nicky Mariano and her sister Alda Anrep at Alda's home, San Martino a Mensola, with the English art historian Philip Pouncey, and visited the reclusive English poet and art collector Osbert Sitwell at nearby Montegufoni. Shirley admired Sitwell—particularly the way he "takes his time, is almost silent, although in perfectly kind and reassuring way, waits for one's personality to manifest itself"—and found his home "a representation of experience, of personal taste, of authenticity, of the passions." And they regularly visited Acton at La Pietra: "Harold's garden—as if designed by moonlight. Vast enclosures of clipped ilex, box, yew, cypress; umbrella pines. Deep green deepening to black. Terraces of green descending, it seems, infinitely. Chalky shapes of stone statues set into walk of green. Slight wildness of grass, no flowers there, only in garden of Villa above— surrounding house itself, where there are roses, tagete, tubs of gardenia, fuchsia."

She was drawn to figures like Acton and Sitwell, who exemplified a long alignment of English and Italian culture. Another was Uberto Strozzi, descendant of a noble Florentine Renaissance family of art collectors and patrons, whom she visited with Francis that summer and again in later years. In her notes on first meeting him, she wrote that he was "1/8th Italian!" and recorded his "careful anglicisms . . . such as 'belfry' for campanile; 'carabineers,'" a feature she would give to Gianni in *The Bay of Noon*. She was delighted with him and with her visit:

> Beautiful English, beautiful manners. Hair almost shaved, speckled with flaking scalp disease. Terrible dark brown teeth. Soft English flannels and jacket, gentle way of behaving. Civilised, eccentric as perhaps Cowper might have been. Keeps Florence telephone in name of mother (English "Gwendolina") whose lovely little girlish photograph he showed us at the end. Bits of burnt toast in fireplace of (1820) pale blue and gold room. Hat device by Collini—mentioned in his memoir, never paid for. Pearls, gold lapis lazuli, Leda & Swan—flat, exquisite. On pictures, large ugly numbers pasted, on canvas itself, for an exhibition a few years ago in Venice. He said he keeps them there because the catalogue of the exhibition is the only list he has, and so he uses it to identify them. I said the numbers were so large, so ugly. He said, delightedly, "Aren't they awful? Quite like a lottery."

That July, Lionel and Diana Trilling visited Il Pozzino with their adult son, James. The friendship between the Steegmullers and the Trillings was grounded in the years Lionel and Francis had spent together at

Columbia and in the Upper West Side intellectual circles where the Trillings were central and the Steegmullers occasional participants. Lionel and Francis maintained a warm and mutual professional respect. Shirley and Diana were not favourably disposed towards each other, and Shirley was also disparaging, albeit more mutedly, of Lionel. She regarded them, above all, as parochial and disregarding of the larger currents of art and culture to which she and Francis committed themselves. Her diary records boredom at Diana's conversation at Il Pozzino, "subjecting us to an hour of discussion" about the fate of her contentious piece on the 1968 Columbia student riots, which had "no doubt wisely—been rejected by Atlantic," using "preposterous jargon" and exposing "her stupidity (From Piazzale Michelangelo: 'I really don't think much of that dome')" at every turn. Lionel she found "wilted . . . yes-yes-ing at everything and above all at the obsequious praising of English aristocrats—'if you'll excuse the word' as he calls them." The Trillings had come to Florence from Solaia, where they had stayed, presumably at Shirley's recommendation. Shirley had been there the previous month and had recorded her continued devotion: "Moonlight, Italy, countryside. Momentary glimpse of past solitude, aridity, singleness, enforced silence, reflection. Missed, always." The Trillings made critical comments about Solaia, prompting Shirley to private fury. After outings to Montegufoni and La Pietra, Shirley was unimpressed by her guests' failure to appreciate the "heavenly countryside," and recorded all their lapses of taste in her diary: "Comment on leaving [Montegufoni] 'Do you know that his father bought this, land and all, for only 3000 pounds?'"

After *People in Glass Houses*, Shirley changed publishers to Atlantic–Little, Brown. The editor Billy Abrahams, a friend, "a most delightful person, he loved writers, loved books," suggested that she move when Francis did with Cocteau. Shirley felt little loyalty to her first publisher once Henry Robbins, her principal editor, had left in unhappy circumstances. She felt that Knopf had "not been at all expansive with me," giving only "a tiny advance," and she had been frustrated by much of the editing, which she found intrusive. Through the first half of 1969, with Francis "in full Cocteau," Shirley completed her second novel, *The Bay of Noon*. Francis spent several weeks in Paris, watching Cocteau's films,

then met Shirley in Geneva, where they picked up the car and drove
to Il Pozzino. Elizabeth Bowen wrote to Shirley, sorry that their visits
would not coincide——"It was unbearably tantalising to arrive back from
Italy yesterday evening and find your letter saying you were about to be
there"——and adding that the previous week, in Italy, "I found myself
continually thinking of you and the Italy of your stories." William Meredith visited them later that spring. Shirley invited him to dinner, with
Harold Acton the other guest. "We'll go to the length of putting ties on,
but all else will be of an almost inconceivable informality."

Shirley worked on proofs of her novel through the summer, and in
July she and Francis were in France again. Cocteau had also taken Francis
to America. Early in the research, he had written to Gloria Swanson, who
responded that "she likes my work but barely knew Cocteau; when I think
how I adored her at 15!" And he had, with the help of Paolo Vivante,
who was then teaching classics at the University of Texas, tracked down
the drag aerialist Barbette——born Vander Clyde in Round Rock, a few
miles out of Austin——and flew west to meet him. Barbette had had a glorious career in Europe through the 1920s and 1930s——"The French paid
me the supreme compliment of thinking I was somehow too good to be
true"——and Cocteau, who described him as "an angel, a flower, a bird,"
wrote that he had seen "no comparable display of artistry on the stage
since Nijinsky." Barbette had appeared in *Blood of a Poet*, in a Chanel
gown, as a substitute for the vicomtesse de Noailles, whose husband had
funded the film and who had withdrawn from it having been scandalised
by some of its content. Barbette was charmed by Paolo——"What a particularly elegant ambassador you sent me!"——and provided Francis, along
with his recollections, with names and details of Cocteau associates still
living in Paris. In 1969 Francis published in *The New Yorker* an account
of his meeting with Barbette, the first of his Cocteau writings.

They returned to New York at the end of summer to find Francis's
father "quickly failing." They went to Sharon, "to spend the day with
him . . . a peaceful and affectionate time . . . the last time we saw him——a
few days later he died . . . Since then——an infinity of the sad detail that
comes with these events, and many stirrings of ancient connections that
F had been out of touch with for many years." Shirley was worried——

still, again—about her mother. Having had a marvellous time on the voyage to Australia from cold and friendless London the year before—"the ship so comfortable, passengers pleasant, weather good etc; this uncommitted life with daily company laid on is ideal for her (would it could last forever . . . )"—Kit was once again unhappy. She had gone to live, at the urging of a friend, in Hobart, Tasmania, sending "a torment of letters which had included such encouraging observations as that it was as much of a mistake to have come to Tasmania as 'going to New York had been.'" For some years Shirley had tried to convince her to stay in New York, but Kit refused, "saying that it would make her materially too dependent on us." By 1970, however, Shirley had had a change of heart, due, she wrote Patricia Clarke, to "the really horrendous developments here and the rocketing expenses and difficulties of New York life," but also no doubt in an attempt at self-preservation. She had offered to come and visit Kit in Sydney (she and Francis had thought they might travel by way of Japan and Cambodia, to see Angkor Wat, on the way out). Kit's response, "Don't bother—the hello is not worth the goodbye," was, as Shirley observed, "neither encouraging nor gracious." Shirley and Kit continued to exchange letters, weekly or more often. Shirley regularly sent her last season's outfits, which Kit altered to fit, and Kit responded by sending slips and roots of native Australian plants for Shirley to grow in pots in her apartment, along with, every Christmas, iced fruitcakes. In her letters and phone calls, Kit managed to keep her two daughters at odds with each other, fanning their differences, it seems quite deliberately. Valerie had for some time grasped this, realising that Kit reported on her own circumstances quite differently to each of them, and she crisply pointed this out to Shirley:

> The last time she was in NY, for instance, you were writing how she should stay in NY because she was so "Happy and busy", and she was writing to me that she had never been so lonely or miserable, even in London. All that you said about her in Hobart was quite wrong, according to what she told me at Xmas . . . The "kind and understanding landlady, concerned and helpful" is (according to Grandma) a dreadful old cheat who shouldn't have rented

her such a room in the first place, although Mother's "friend"
Brenda arranged it all . . . The kind landlady also cheats on the
household bills, and the only reason they can live together is that
Bessie is never at home. I called a few times after the operation,
and none of Mother's "nice acquaintances who are helping to dispel the loneliness there", according to your letter, came to see her
in the hospital or after, even Brenda. Her big friend is Brenda's
mother, who is 92.

The simmering drama of Kit diminished in importance, for a time at
least, in the face of the publication of her second novel. *The Bay of Noon*
displays a kind of sureness and seriousness—of style, story, subject—that
does not perhaps reveal itself readily to readers expecting the straight
Anglo-Italian romance it appears, at first glance, to be. Romance is even
more elusive here than in *The Evening of the Holiday*, and there is even
less of a conventional plot. Our attention is taken up primarily by the layered detail and textures of the city of Naples, but also with the crossings
and recrossings of desire, rather than romance, between the four protagonists. There are two couples: one apparently unable to achieve erotic or
domestic equilibrium (Gioconda refuses to move to Rome to live with
Gianni, who is married, and he continues to be diverted by other women)
while for Jenny and Justin a connection never quite begins; they remain
fixed in the opening stages of a romance, unable to proceed: "Asyngamy,"
Justin declares. "The inability of two plants to achieve cross-pollination,
owing to their unsynchronized development." There is more sex in the
metaphor than in the rest of the novel. There are thwarted fumblings:
Gianni tries to kiss Jenny on a visit to Herculaneum and they eventually
have a brief and unencumbered affair near the end of the novel, after
Gioconda runs off to Spain with Justin and before Gianni himself leaves
to bring Gioconda back. But none of this is really the point.

We are told early on that Jenny has come to Naples "because I was in
love with my brother," an assertion that colours everything that follows
with a faint impropriety. Jenny tells Gioconda that Justin reminds her
of her brother, extending the impropriety to this relationship, closing
it off. Within the romantic tradition, Peter Brooks tells us, the threat of

brother-sister incest is precisely the threat of death, the literal end of the story. Jenny has come to Naples to move away from that situation, away from the mute perfection, the short circuit it offers, "into detour, into the cure that prolongs the narrative." So the story, insofar as it is a story, is about delay, and about deferment, or digression, or misdirection. The outcome of journeys, we are told at the end of the novel, "is immaterial. One can only discover what has already come into existence," and in searching, "we are like those early explorers of Australia who died of thirst on expeditions to the dead centre of a continent, always thinking they must come ultimately to water—to an inland sea, to a lake, a river, a cascade."

If *The Evening of the Holiday* set romance alongside pastoral and elegy, *The Bay of Noon* works the experience of love through myth—an engagement with archetypes and with the deep past, the stones and ruins of Naples—but also through comedy. We might think of that great work of fraternal cross-dressing and displaced desire, *Twelfth Night*; Jenny's assertion of too great a love for her brother perhaps recalling Olivia's unseemly and excessive mourning of hers. The world of Shakespeare's play is a domain in which the to-and-fro of proxy courting, love marked by mistakenness, and the weariness, feints, and unexpected intensities of desire play out unfettered by any real sense of propriety. The restoration of order at the end of the play is only partial. There is much that is similar in *The Bay of Noon*, particularly in the strange affair of Jenny and Justin. Initially Justin pursues Jenny, or appears to, quoting "Lochinvar" to mock his own mock-heroic status as he drives her to the office. Despite his apparent candour, he remains illegible, enigmatic; as a Scot, he is both English and not (no more English than Jenny, whose childhood was spent in Africa), both familiar and unknowable, both lover and betrayer, and, by the end of the novel, both found and lost. He tells Jenny that he is bored by love: "At this moment, as one might say, women delight not me," at which Jenny wonders "was he passionless, perhaps, or effeminate," and he responds, "Nor men either, though by your smiling you seem to say so." His inversion of Hamlet's lines generates a sense of unstable gender that ripples through the novel: when Jenny observes of Gioconda, "Like Othello . . . only the other way round," or when Justin sings, "*Why am I always the bridesmaid / Never the blushing bride.*" In this way Justin's role is something like that of the transvestic figure in romantic comedy, "there and gone at once," as Marjorie Garber puts it: "Nobody gets 'Cesario' (or 'Ganymede'), but 'Cesario' (or 'Ganymede') is necessary to falling in love."

But falling in love is not, it seems, the point either. Jenny's ultimate journey in the novel is to seek out Gioconda; but this too is displaced. The meeting, if it happens at all, is not described. The narrative dissolves, and dissolves again, first into the physical experience of crossing the Bay of Naples—"The engine subsiding, we re-enter the elements. It is dark, the boat comes splashing quite tamely into port and the journey recedes, throbbing, like a toothache. There are lights, colours, large-eyed faces of pale people on the breakwater and the soundless up and down movements of their feet stamping with cold"—and then into a series of false starts and reflections on non-arrival. In the end, the interest of the novel is not with the events it describes, nor with the characters. Even the city of Naples, whose presence animates everything that happens and which Hazzard herself felt to be a character, a participant in the novel, is, by the end, out of the picture, left behind as Jenny boards the *aliscafo* for Capri.

As she sets out to find Gioconda, Jenny looks back on the events of the novel: "That epoch, our time at Naples, seems historic now. It doesn't seem like modern life. But it didn't seem like modern life then either, it was more like life than modern life, more lifelike, livelier, likelier." This is writing that works, as one reviewer put it, "on the nerve endings, not the cerebrum." The play of sound in these sentences—rococo, insistent—connects "like" to "life" in all their permutations; connects the work of figuration, writing, poetry, to the question of living. Words enliven and endure; they allow for human expression, which is ever Hazzard's primary concern. Jenny continues: "Relics are not the less obsolete for their superior vitality—like the vineyard that has been left to flourish intact on the Vomero, among the deadly apartment buildings, not so much showing how it was as what has happened to it." Alongside its devotion to the work of language and expression, this novel turns on the matter of time. It redirects us over and over to the question of "how we came," the meaning and continuity of the past and its persistence in our lives. The question of time, along with the large matter of love, would continue to preoccupy her for the rest of her writing life.

*The Bay of Noon* was released in the United States in April to "a truly heavenly reception"; a review in *The New York Times* by Christopher Lehmann-Haupt, Shirley felt, displayed an "almost total sense of what the book was about, what the author's intention was." Lehmann-Haupt wrote that he had approached the novel "with the misgiving that Miss Hazzard's sort of writing—Anglo-Saxon fiction of sensibility, let's call it—simply wouldn't do for these thunderous times . . . Now that I've read *The Bay of Noon*, my faith in sensitive narrative prose is restored." The UK release followed the next month, with a more muted reception. Claire Tomalin found the book somewhat passionless: "The slight plot resembles a Jamesian parable of the intersection of Anglo-Saxons and Latins, but since Jenny's talent seems to be mostly for vicarious emotion, her story resembles a fine, faded tapestry, the colour drained away from the subtle arrangement of stitches." *The Bay of Noon* was nominated for the National Book Award, but "scratched," as Francis put it, "at the last minute" when it was learnt that Shirley was not a U.S. citizen. Forty years later, it would be nominated for the Lost Man Booker Prize (a special award for books published in 1970, when they had not been eligible for the prize due to a change in the rules for submission) in the UK. Bill Maxwell wrote to Francis:

Delectable is surely one of the words you could apply to Shirley's novel. Also Beautiful. Moving. And Not Like Other People's Novels. It has stayed with me like an experience. I didn't see where she could go in writing about love after *The Evening of the Holiday*. But of course she did. It's a sort of post graduate course. For readers with mended hearts. And who would know, reading it, how hard it was to do. There it is, like something out of nature, the only way it could be.

The year 1970 was to be the Steegmullers' last summer in Florence. On the way there they were briefly in Rome for dinner with Muriel Spark. Things were not easy between Shirley and Muriel these days. Their relationship continued at a formal level, and in 1968 Shirley wrote an admiring review of her work, but there were difficulties. When

Muriel moved to Rome in 1966, she had established herself there, underhandedly Shirley felt, with the help of Shirley's friend Ginny Becker, something Muriel had "distastefully" kept from Shirley. Later, Shirley felt, Ginny had been "'dismissed,' when her usefulness was exhausted." Muriel had since surrounded herself with what her biographer Martin Stannard called "a crowd of Mussolini-fanciers" and "elegant right-wing footlers." A happier occasion for Shirley was a visit to Lake Nemi—"a crater lake of an extinct volcano . . . less than an hour from Rome, and a very ancient place where the Roman emperors used to have festivals, with decorated floats and pleasure-ships"—and the nearby ruins of Tuscolo before they headed north to Il Pozzino. At first both were mostly hard at work, the days too hot to go out. Alan and Robin Maclean came to visit— Shirley served them pigeon—then Billy Abrahams and his partner, Peter Stansky. They saw the Gilmores and Harold Acton, drove to meet Hugh Honour and John Fleming for lunch at Pescia, and dined with the Irish writer Seán Ó Faoláin at the Villa San Michele. They drove to Greve with the Gilmores—"There is a statue in the square to Verrazzano (the navigator who first discovered the harbour of New York)—he was born there, at Greve, where his family were lords of the local manor; their castle is still there, still owned by them 400 years later . . . It is strange to think of a navigator being born and bred in such a land-locked little hill town—but perhaps that's why he wanted to navigate"—and to Siena. Outside Siena, they climbed up the hillside to Lecceto, "an abandoned monastery whose already arduous little road was flooded out a few years ago, making the walk up almost impossible . . . We were up there alone with beautiful paintings and frescoed cloisters, standing in the middle of woods that are encroaching now on the building—grass growing into the arcades, birds nesting in the chapel."

The extent of the Lecceto abandonment, beautiful though it was, alarmed them, and they took photographs that Shirley sent to John Pope-Hennessy, then director of the Victoria and Albert Museum in London (and a friend of Bill Weaver's), to request his intervention. Pope-Hennessy took up the cause and approached the former director of the Siena Pinacoteca, Enzo Carli. Restorations were made, and a new and significant friendship with Pope-Hennessy ensued, linking with the Steegmullers' other Anglo-Florentine connections (Pope-Hennessy would move to live permanently in Florence in 1986). At the end of August, they packed up the house, arranged for their belongings to be shipped back to New York and for the Rolls-Royce to go England (where they would have it garaged in Hampstead for the next few years), bid goodbye to Tiger, the Il Pozzino cat, and left for the last time. They detoured for a week in Venice at the Gritti hotel. Shirley recorded impressions of a child's funeral she saw on an outing to the Chiesa di San Zaccaria: "Sea almost level with design of paving in front, as if one flooring were exchanged for another"; "Three men in black overalls detached yet complicit, like accomplices . . . Then—a child's coffin, tiny, white, quickly covered by black acolytes, with black cloths as if it were obscene. Party of baffled, silent mourners."

From Venice, they returned to New York for the publication of *Cocteau*. The proofs had arrived in April with the release of *The Bay of Noon*. The months before publication had been marred by a disagreement between Francis and Roger Straus. Francis was incensed that after granting him a release to publish his *Cocteau* with Little, Brown, Straus had commissioned another Cocteau book, Robert Phelps's *Professional Secrets*— which Shirley described as "a wretched little anthology of supposedly 'autobiographical' writings in Cocteau's works"—and arranged for it to be published the same month. After a terse exchange of letters, Francis terminated his publishing agreement with Farrar, Straus and Giroux in July, ending many years of friendship with Roger. The topic remained sensitive. In June, Francis wrote angrily to Robert Giroux that Roger was circulating "a mythological version" of the dispute and accusing Francis of having been "unfaithful." Later that year, Ved Mehta mentioned to Shirley that "at the Straus's, Steegmuller is the main topic of conversation." Francis wrote quickly back to Ved, offering to show him "my complete file of Roger's and my exchange or correspondence—which without comment from me would tell the story. (It is a story which, rather than having 'sides,' is a 'whole' in its revelation of his duplicity and immaturity.) . . . In over forty years of dealing with publishers—whose vagaries you yourself well know—I have never encountered anything remotely resembling his destructive, and self-destructive, folly in connection with my Cocteau." The two books were often reviewed together, with Phelps suffering from the comparison in some, such as Mark Schorer's *New York Times* piece, which suggested that "Francis Steegmuller, even while correcting or questioning it, uses a good deal of the material that Mr. Phelps uses, and the need for Mr. Phelps's book, therefore, ceases to be exactly pressing." There was further vindication when Francis won the National Book Award for biography the following year. He took pleasure on learning that one judge, Erich Segal, a Yale classics professor (and author of the bestselling *Love Story*), voted for *Cocteau*, even though, Francis observed, "the one Greek word in the text of my book is wrong." Shirley wrote Patricia Clarke that *Cocteau*'s "immortality has been instantly recognised, which is only right and proper, but nevertheless gives me great joy."

In the wake of the award, Francis reflected on his biographical subjects in an exchange with Jacques Barzun. Flaubert, he avowed, "remains the literary hero," while Maupassant he "scarcely succeeded in 'feeling,' either as man or artist," finding the most moving part of his story "his desperate struggle to get out of bureaucracy, and the gradual evidence of talent—then genius. The last is of course my reason for the involvement." With Apollinaire, it was the enchantment of the poetry, which overcame Francis's dislike of "coteries and café sittings and bohemians." Cocteau allowed him to write more about the "modern world," and the appeal was built on immersion in that world and on his own changed perspective. As the research progressed, he found himself "growing engrossed in Cocteau—fond of some of his selves despite the others—and I ended being his defender against all kinds of people, especially the multitudes of the solemn and the crass, not to mention his special partisans . . . I suspect that the particular appeal of Cocteau has to do with my being older. Years ago I needed Flaubert the hero, and probably couldn't have put up with Cocteau's contradictions, which fascinate me now."

In 2000, reviewing a new biography of Proust, Edmund White was critical of Steegmuller's treatment of Cocteau's sexuality in the biography, writing that he "pretends that the great love of Cocteau's life was the Princess Natalie Paley." Shirley leapt to Francis's defence in a letter to the editor, and White responded, saying that he stood corrected "about the details of Steegmuller's account" but insisting more broadly on what he called the "underreporting" of the homosexuality of such figures as Proust, Gide, and Cocteau, and citing another point in the book where Steegmuller had relegated important details of Cocteau's lovers Jean Marais, Édouard Dermit, and Paul Morihien to an oblique footnote. White concedes that those people Steegmuller interviewed "might not have been so open in an interview in the 1960s as . . . in the 1980s," maintaining that his point held in relation to a "salutary change in the cultural climate" since the book was first published. In fact the contemporary reviews praised Steegmuller's treatment of these aspects of Cocteau's life, with *The Times Literary Supplement* noting that "the lapse of seven years since Cocteau's death has permitted him to deal with greater frankness than would have been possible in his subject's lifetime with the question of his 'homosexuality at once overt and discreet,'" and also that "except, understandably, for Édouard Dermit, Cocteau's latest 'adopted son' and heir, all Cocteau's associates are commented on freely, sometimes amiably, sometimes mordantly."

Francis had already begun work on what he hoped would be his next project. After he had interviewed Stravinsky about Cocteau, he was approached by Vera Stravinsky and Robert Craft, Stravinsky's longtime friend and associate—and eventual biographer—with the suggestion that Francis might write the authorized biography. He was given access to archives "that the Stravinskys have so far kept under lock and key," working through them at the Stravinsky home in New York, where he would see the composer, as Shirley wrote to Kit, "now unreachable—he is so frail, won't see anyone, doesn't like to talk . . . in the afternoons, being wheeled out to the piano in the living room, where he sits and plays Bach for hours by himself." Kit always enjoyed the proximity to famous people that Shirley's life provided. On hearing about Francis's latest project, she wrote suggesting that the Christmas cake she had just posted to Shirley was "a biggish one so perhaps you can halve it for Mrs Stravinsky. Or I'll send another?"

The following April, Francis returned to Venice to attend Stravinsky's funeral, at the invitation of his children, and later published a *New Yorker* "Letter from Venice" about the occasion. This was the first of his Italian essays. As much as his current research on Stravinsky, it drew on

his growing familiarity with Italian culture and his continuing inter-
est in spectacle and the world of performance. The scene he describes
is primarily visual but also hangs on a moment of profound and moving connection found in posters displayed around the city offering "an
Italianate proclamation printed in black and purple on a white ground,
of [Stravinsky's] carefully considered wish: THE CITY OF VENICE
DOES HOMAGE TO THE REMAINS OF THE GREAT MUSI-
CIAN IGOR STRAVINSKY, WHO IN A GESTURE OF EXQUISITE
FRIENDSHIP ASKED TO BE BURIED IN THE CITY WHICH HE
LOVED ABOVE ALL OTHERS." He describes the Orthodox service
held in Santi Giovanni e Paolo, "a towering Gothic church . . . scarcely
less than a museum of paintings, by Giovanni Bellini, Lorenzo Lotto,
and Paolo Veronese. The several Veroneses are on the ceiling of the
church, and it was here that Stravinsky's coffin was brought on the fourteenth, after being transported from New York to Fiumicino Airport in
Rome and thence by hearse and ferry to Venice." The drama of the event
is established through a sequence of details: the "theatrically handsome
ecclesiastic: young, olive-skinned, black-bearded, with finely cut features,
almond eyes, and an expression of scarcely credible serenity, wearing a
tall black headdress and brilliant gold vestments," the archimandrite of
Venice, who had been invited to officiate by the cardinal patriarch of St.
Mark's, "one of whose auxiliaries, a Roman Catholic bishop, with a violet
zucchetto on his head, sat near the altar as host"; the acoustic difficulties
of performing Stravinsky's *Requiem Canticles* in this setting, with or-
chestra and choir in the deep apse of the church, from whence "sounds
emerged thinly"; the procession of bishop, coffin, flowers, and family "up
the centre aisle and out to the waiting gondolas," resembling "one of
Carpaccio's pageants, with accents of today"; and the flowers themselves
bearing inscriptions "ranging from a red-ribboned salute from the artists
of the Soviet Union to the Stravinsky grandchildren's '*À Grandpère bien
aimé.*'" And he notes, among the mourners at a brief prayer session the
day before, "a gray-haired ancient who, sitting with a woman companion, did not leave at the end but remained, almost motionless, in his seat
throughout the morning," adding, "Not everyone recognized him as Ezra
Pound." Francis spent some ten months on Stravinsky's papers, but in the

end the project was abandoned. He believed that Craft had planned all along to thwart the project. He turned back to Flaubert and began work on the Egyptian travels, a project suggested to him by Graham Greene, whom he and Shirley had begun seeing on visits they had lately been making, with increasing regularity, to Capri.

For most of their years together thus far, the rhythm of the Steegmullers' lives had been driven by Francis's research, which involved archives and interviews in Paris and Southern France. The conclusion of *Cocteau* meant a change of habitation as well as of focus. Francis had extensive connections and friendships in Paris, and Shirley had also come to feel at home in the city. But with *Cocteau* published, that life, with its roots in the prewar, was drawing to a close: "His friends in Paris from the 1930s, all older than he, were disappearing one by one; and the new friends made through Cocteau were also for the most part elderly and starting to drop away. He felt that the city for him would be a haunted place; and the modern changes dismayed him—skyscrapers, a new hardness . . ." The Steegmullers would revisit the city regularly, but they never lived there again. The following year they returned, for one last summer, to Tuscany, after which they would turn south, to make a longer and more lasting association with Shirley's first Italian footfall, Naples, and with Capri.

# 10

# THE TRANSIT OF VENUS

## 1970-1980

AFTER *THE BAY OF NOON*, Shirley turned for a time to nonfiction, mostly highly critical pieces about the United Nations for American magazines. This new focus on what she called "public themes" may have reflected something of the broader post-1960s climate of public agitation, but she was never involved in the larger antiestablishment protests that came to characterise those years. Her resistance was not to the act of protest itself, more to the tenor of organised dissent, and it was grounded in an antipathy to political allegiance, to what she called "the 'party' mentality," which she found "dishonest because never candidly declared." This individualism was informed by its Cold War context, gleaned through personal connections, but also by a sense of larger history. Years later she explained her views to a friend: "When I was first in America, I had friends who were passionate Democrats, some of them having gone from university straight into New Deal. I used to wonder that they would not hear of expelling the southern Democrats—whom they nevertheless utterly condemned—because they were 'essential' to the Party and to the immediate holding of power, or so it then seemed. It's no illusion that history punishes such apostasies." These were long-held convictions about the importance of independent thought and individual positions in politics, and they led her to stand aloof from the sharp ideological battles that continued to play out within the left-leaning circles within which she and Francis moved.

Her perspective had been forged first through her conversations with Alec Vedeniapine about the micropolitics of the Chinese Civil War and later in discussions with Chris Cooper, particularly during the year he spent at the École Normale Supérieure in Paris, from where he wrote criticising "so much facile and uninformed anti-Americanism" among students, "in the land of 'en principe.'" (Shirley drew at times verbatim from Cooper's correspondence for parts of Ted Tice's Paris letters in *The Transit of Venus*.) She explained her views to Alfred Kazin: "I feel as you do about protests etc—that they are a dreary and thankless business for artists to have to involve themselves in and that the maximum influence still rests in one's work, however far it may seem from the context at that particular mo. However, an occasional lifting of the head seems necessary, just to show it is not bowed on these matters." In January 1968 she and Francis had a letter published in *The New York Times*, written in support of the singer Eartha Kitt, who had criticised, during a White House reception, the U.S. response to civil rights protests and the pursuit of the Vietnam War, for which she was attacked in the press. The Steegmullers supported Kitt's outburst as an expression of frustration such as that felt by "the many thousands of Americans who have for years attempted by more conventional methods—with no success whatever, and often to the tune of expressions of official displeasure—to obtain Presidential recognition of United States policy in Vietnam [and who] may well feel that such unbecoming behaviour as Miss Kitt's is a last resort for those who have exhausted other avenues." Here again is her concern with the individual protest, the bootless yet necessary criticism of the powerful, whatever the odds. That spring, when Columbia students protested the war and the university's hitherto concealed connections to the Institute for Defense Analyses—causes that in themselves might normally have prompted her support—she rejected a request from Dwight Macdonald for donations to the students with a terse letter, arguing that the students and protesters constituted an "Establishment" of their own. This was the event about which Diana Trilling had written, drawing scathing private commentary from Shirley during the Il Pozzino visit that summer; quite possibly it was the Trillings' enthusiastic support for the protest that prompted her coolness.

In October 1970 Shirley published "A Call for UN Reform" in *The New York Times*, the publication marking the twenty-fifth anniversary of the founding of the United Nations. This, the first of many essays she produced on the organisation, lamented the UN's introspection and ineffectuality and called for "informed, public indignation" in response. She thought the *Times*'s editors had "expurgated" her essay, so that it "appeared with the most painful passages excised," but she hoped nonetheless that "it may do some good—so far the reaction has been extremely sensible and sympathetic with lots of UN people writing to say they felt 'relieved to see something real about the UN in print for once' etc." Her criticisms dwelled on what she felt to be points of original error: the separation of the General Assembly and Secretariat into two "demi-spheres of an enclosed world" and the UN's larger failure to be a properly accountable and above all international institution. It is interesting, and perhaps surprising, given the extent of her engagement with daily politics in the United States, Britain, Australia, and Italy—her letters through the 1970s are full of the oil crisis, the recession, strikes, terrorist events, elections, and above all the perfidy of Richard Nixon—that in her political writing she would turn almost exclusively to an institution with which she had been closely associated only in her youthful years, with which she now had little connection.

This first publication led to a further invitation to write "a long article on the UN and the UN state of mind." She felt "somewhat passionate towards doing it; only, it will use me up in the fires of indignation, and take weeks away from writing my novel which I care much more about and which is demonstrably more useful . . . and certainly less harmful than the UN." In the spring of 1971 she spent two weeks in Siena working on it. This long piece would preoccupy her for the next two years. She realised that convincing Little, Brown and Macmillan to do it as a book was "the only way it will be published, as it is too long for magazine publication and in any case—even in these times—too controversial. I have had a long talk with The New Yorker about it: they have been very nice about its nature but don't want to get into publishing something so polemical, for the views of which they would be seen to be responsible." From the start she found writing on "public themes" to be a disruption: "Not getting on with my novel worries me all the time . . ." Nonetheless, she would continue for years to commit herself to writing about the UN.

Another major distraction from her novel was her mother, still living in Sydney but keen to be on the move again. Shirley tried reasoning with her: "Darling if you are intent on returning to England nothing I can say will stop you. The pretty little town is a myth—Hobart is a pretty little town. You know all that. The English manner and way of doing things, which you've tried various times, you violently hated." It had been a difficult year for all the Hazzards. In March, Kit had written in some agitation in response to a stern letter from Shirley that she felt "like the gnat on a pin before your discerning analytical mind (the little there is to be analysed being the self-revealing fulcrum)." In May, Valerie wrote Shirley that Reg had asked her for money, and when she declined, had told her, "in one of the nastiest bits of writing I have ever read," that he would not speak to her again. For some time, Valerie's husband, Bob, had been unwell, in and out of hospital, and he died suddenly that September. In the wake of all this, Valerie was finding Kit more difficult than ever. After being diagnosed with retinal vein thrombosis (a minor condition causing only some loss of vision) Kit convinced herself that she was close to death. She gave Valerie "details of the disposal of her body . . . and her goods," which was, for Valerie, "The end. I have been dealing with those problems far too close to home, and very distressing, to take kindly to her discussing them for no good reason." From the safety of New York, Shirley scarcely responded to Valerie's distress beyond courteous expression of sympathy at Bob's death. Her attention was on the larger melancholy that seemed to drive her mother's moods and actions: "The only place she believes in as being satisfactory is the place she is not in . . . As she gets older, this immaturity breaks my heart for her, as its consequences are infinite loneliness and her own lapsing into despair." It took her some time to grasp that her mother's difficult behaviour was a consequence not simply of a difficult personality but of mental illness, and that what was needed was regular and sustained medical attention. Valerie came to the conclusion around this time that Kit required more substantial care, and that she should be moved to a nursing home; this would become a point of antagonistic dispute between the sisters for the next decade and a half.

A new figure on Kit's scene was the Australian novelist Elizabeth Harrower. Harrower had grown up in and around Sydney, had travelled to the UK in 1951, when she was in her early twenties, and had settled, for a time, in London. Her first novel had been published by Macmillan in 1957, her second the following year, and her third in 1960. She had returned to Sydney in 1959 and worked first for the Australian Broadcasting Commission, then as a book reviewer, then in the Macmillan offices, and had continued to write. In 1966, when she first met Kit, she was about to publish her fourth novel—her masterpiece, *The Watch Tower*. Kit was then living at "The Chimes" apartments in Macleay Street in inner-city Potts Point. There was something erratic about Kit's bearing as she walked around the neighbourhood—"like Blanche Dubois," Elizabeth used to say—that brought her to the attention of Norma Chapman, proprietor of the legendary Macleay Bookshop. Kit introduced herself as Shirley Hazzard's mother to Norma, who admired Shirley's work. Norma phoned Elizabeth and, on the strength of Elizabeth and Shirley both being Macmillan authors, suggested that they might meet. Elizabeth invited Kit for a coffee at the Macmillan offices in the city, where they talked about writing and about Shirley and themselves. Elizabeth took to Kit, who, despite her difficult behaviour, was clearly possessed of some personal charm and a lively manner. Kit wrote to Shirley about that first meeting with Elizabeth, about her kindness and her admiration for Shirley's work, and Shirley wrote back her thanks, saying that she was looking forward to reading Elizabeth's novels.

Thus began a long, important, and complex friendship between the two writers, a friendship with the intractable Kit—referred to in their letters as YM and MM (Your Mother, My Mother)—at its heart, but one concerned also, from the start, with reading, writing, and world affairs, including, most particularly, the cultural and political transformations unfolding in Australia from the early 1970s. Though they met only a handful of times, they corresponded regularly for half a century. Shirley admired Elizabeth's writing and described her as possessing "a calm and witty humanity and strength, a most unusual emanation of authenticity and sensitivity." Francis too was a great admirer of both Elizabeth and her work. He called her "Saint Elizabeth" in his letters (possibly not the best idea, given the patterns and expectations and resentments that quickly began building up) and sent *The Watch Tower* to his agent, Cyrilly Abels, in the hope that she might interest U.S. publishers. (He later told Elizabeth that the problem Abels had found was the Australian setting, and he confessed himself ashamed at this cultural chauvinism.) Elizabeth was more circumspect, at least in her later years, in her account of Shirley. Clearly there was some admiration for Shirley's work, but she came to insist that she liked only the early novels. And over the years of their friendship, as she weathered Shirley's escalating demands and witnessed her continuing criticisms of Australia, Elizabeth came to feel hostility as much as friendship.

In early 1971 Kit began making agitated arrangements to return, again, to England. Elizabeth meanwhile had finally persuaded her to see a doctor. Elizabeth would later tell of meeting Kit in Martin Place in downtown Sydney, and of Kit's behaviour being so concerning that she called a psychiatric hospital from a nearby phone box. She wrote Shirley regularly of her concerns about Kit's mental state and also her relief that they had found doctors who prescribed antidepressants—the "yellow pills," which seemed to help—rather than the methedrine Kit wanted. Kit had been prescribed methedrine after her divorce—at that time it was often given for lethargy or depression, or weight management—and she wrote Shirley of her hope that she'd be able to 'trick' a young doctor into giving her 'cheeruppers' in place of the 'yellows.'" She also wrote, more alarmingly, to Francis in 1976, just a few months short of her eightieth birthday, with a request that he find her some:

> The other day when I was examining old bottles of pills etc, I
> found the one you gave me years and years ago, with a little note

inside that "These will perk you up till you've been here long enough." There were four left, and I took one, and even at their ripe old age they still had enough pep to make me feel human, and I walked back from the shops walking on my toes!! So if you remember what they were and can get some WITHOUT TROU-BLE, I'd be deeply grateful. No hope of getting anything useful to me here. BUT NO TIME OR TROUBLE. I tried to auto-suggest to my local doctor here that "I didn't suppose there was any hope of getting the Methedrine, dear doctor. Mike S gave me some for fun when I was here in 1953, and I foolishly threw away when I left." An ominous lack of humour. He tells me that caused the trouble in Dec . . .

Taking Kit to the mental health service in 1971 seems to have been the point at which Elizabeth began taking an active role in her care. Shirley was of course relieved that there was someone nearby to keep an eye on her mother and to help her attend her medical appointments. She wrote to Patricia Clarke that Kit's "having two or three friends such as this sensitive and intelligent Elizabeth Harrower, who understands her most wonderfully (but don't we all?) is in itself a terrific alleviation." Alan Maclean was in Sydney that March and called on Kit in order to report back to Shirley. He had, he wrote, "a v nice evening," and felt that Kit seemed "to have quite a grip on herself and her situation and apart from her expressed wish not to be a nuisance to you or anyone, she appears bent on trying to have a nice, rather than nice-martyred, time and prepared to have human relations with both humans and relations. She said she had only come eyeball-to-eyeball with herself in the last four months and Elizabeth Harrower who likes her and likes you too confirms that things have improved vastly." Alan also offered to meet Kit on her arrival in Southampton: "She promises to contact me earliest and we will keep an eye. Shirley, the Mum-front is obviously not too bad. I like her and would genuinely be glad to see her in the UK (as we say here)."

Kit sailed a few weeks later, another journey with little object other than leaving wherever she happened to be. Once again, the voyage itself went well: "Bulletins from Tahiti are that my dear Mum is enjoying herself heartily, was seasick, lost a suitcase (found off Raratonga), is 'terrified' of the Purser, and in all ways having a good time . . . I feel great relief at her decision (as I feel it probably is) not to try settling again in England (imagine!), especially as she gave terrific description of farewell party at the ship in Sydney, even my sister showed signs of wishing her return."

Her arrival in England was, however, a disaster. Just before the ship docked at Southampton, Kit slipped on the companionway and hit her head, suffering a broken arm and neck injuries. Shirley and Francis, who had driven down from London, waited four hours on the dock, watching a thousand passengers disembark, then "forced our way on board and found her prostrate in her cabin, in a pitiful state." They took her to a hospital and reorganised their plans in order to spend the next six weeks taking her sightseeing, driving to Winchester and Glastonbury, and to Wilton House in Wiltshire. And Kit enjoyed herself, although there was a thread of defiance in the account she gave of her holiday to Elizabeth Harrower: "They've taken me to Haymarket to see Gladys Cooper in Chalk Garden, to the Covent Garden to Boris Godunov with Boris Christoff in the lead. He is an old friend of theirs and I met him and his wife . . . behind scenes after I'd seen him die out front . . . Lovely bland, kindly days. With a Rolls and nice driver too. Shirley maintains she will stay here till she puts me on a ship. Sorry. But there it is and my fault." Kit's return voyage to Sydney was mercifully uneventful. She made friends on board (in a manner that would become a trademark of her fictional avatar, Dora: "It's funny how I always manage to attract the one or two. Who take to me. I don't know why,") with a Mrs. Parsonage, who had, Shirley observed, "the right name," and who looked after her and made sure she took her tablets. Elizabeth wrote Shirley that "the trip Has Done A World of Good."

In the spring of 1972 Shirley and Francis were again in Capri. In these first years of long stays on the island they stayed at the Hotel San Felice, where they spent their days walking well beyond the usual trails of visitors, gathering wildflowers, which they dried in their room, and writing. Capri never provided the setting for Shirley's fiction, as Naples and Siena had done, beyond a fleeting visit in *The Bay of Noon*, but she found poetry there and for the rest of her life chronicled its changing scenes and figures:

> Navy-blue sky, hot sunny days, cool nights. Early, unblemished green, vines coming into leaf, lemon coloured; lemons in profusion on trees, like grapes. The man who gives donkey rides is dead, after an operation; the donkeys are in a field at the other end of the island, living the life of Riley, for no one wants such work. Mechanised carts . . . Judas trees, portulaca. The coast less often visible—refineries etc. Three statues have been dredged up at Pozzuoli. Meanwhile divers and helicopters rake the gulf for three bodies, shot in a scuffle with an American marine over contraband jurisdiction. (A villa is unearthed in Pompeii.) The relatives line the shore at the strategic point, a crowd in black . . . the sound of the sea rising through the pines. Descending to the Faraglioni, the yacht burning bright on a sheet of sea.

Through these months, in Capri and then back in New York, Shirley felt she was facing "a crisis" in her work, a "sort of depression" at the slow progress of her novel and the overwhelming labour of writing about the UN. By early July she was close to the end of her UN book, "bankrupting myself by altering it (adding to it, that is) in galleys. It REALLY is almost done, and I'm far more satisfied with it and so glad that I went through the agony of postponing etc. but the great apparatus of annotation at the back of the vol has nearly killed me." They were back in Tuscany, renting a small house on the grounds of I Tatti, "in amazing tranquillity— . . . the loggia giving on to the garden and the terrace giving on to the countryside, where in fact we spend all our time in this marvellous weather, are peaceful and beautiful; angelic Maria comes every day to clean us up and feed us, but not one other soul ever approaches and the serenity is practically subversive in this world of 1972." Later in July they were in London briefly; she and Elizabeth Harrower finally met in person after half a decade corresponding. And her novel inched ahead in images and fragments:

England late July 1972. Visit to Wilton. A little curly mound of a dog, like a chrysanthemum. A little chrysanthemum of a dog . . .

Apartments in NY Building like cabins on great stationary ocean liners docked along the piers of streets.

"Incurable optimist"—as though one had not responded to treatment.

Francis's celebrated *Flaubert in Egypt* was published, and he set to work translating and editing the first volume of Flaubert's letters. They returned to I Tatti for August and then again to Naples and Capri for September, establishing a pattern they would follow for the rest of their lives.

Back in New York for the winter, Shirley arranged for Kit to spend Christmas with them. The visit went well; Kit was thrilled to share what she had in more miserable and begrudging moods come to refer to, rather bitterly, as Shirley's "Lovely Life." Shirley found her mother "frailer and . . . aged," and began to feel apprehensive about her future. For Kit's routine care, she would continue to rely on Elizabeth and continue to lament that her sister would not take on more responsibility. (In fact, it is clear that since Kit's return to Australia, Valerie had shouldered a far greater burden than had Shirley.) In early 1973 she heard from Margaret, her father's second wife, that Reg had been diagnosed with cancer of the bladder. He underwent surgery, "spent his last six weeks totally paralysed, though conscious," and died just before Easter. Shirley and he had been somewhat in touch, exchanging occasional letters in which he wrote about his vegetable garden and long drives with Margaret around New South Wales towing a caravan, and she sent him her books. Things were easier between them outwardly, although she never saw him again after he left New York to be with Margaret, and she never forgave what she saw as his betrayal of her mother, her sister, and herself.

It was left to Elizabeth to make sure that Kit was "not left alone with her thoughts" at Reg's death; she invited her to stay for the Easter weekend. "Thus ends," Shirley wrote Patricia Clarke, "part of a saga: I wish that for my mother there could now be, simply, a sense of the preciousness of life." This was, of course, not to be. Kit remained resolutely—and, it seems, desperately—focused on the minute here and now of her own anxiety, discomfort, and resentments. Shirley drew on her mother's antics over the years as she drafted the character of Dora:

> Dora would begin to talk (on shipboard, or at a hotel etc). She would be at her best, Dora acting out with considerable skill the lonely but plucky little woman, something of an original. Like all good performances it gained from her belief in the role. The unwary, or bored, responded—"I had an interesting chat in the lounge today—a woman who's been everywhere." She sets her snares in this way, building up confidence and credit for the moment when she could seize her prey: when she could tell her troubles, or even, better still, go to pieces in tearful outpouring.

Kit would continue to generate both dark comedy and anxiety: "My mater writes me that she has a bad foot and (oh how characteristic) is 'walking extra hard on it as that is usually the best cure.'"

In the spring, *Defeat of an Ideal: The Self-Destruction of the United Nations* was published to "good and prominent" reviews, "rockets and bombshells," but also "extraordinary silences in certain parts of the press," due, Shirley felt, to "suppression coming from the UN exertions." The book argued that from its inception the United Nations had capitulated to U.S. domestic policy by agreeing to the surveillance of UN employees who were U.S. citizens, in contravention of the UN Charter. Christopher Lehmann-Haupt described the book as "a tumultuous lovers' quarrel" and a "polemic" that "is finally about the most interesting, encouraging, and hopeful thing to be said about the United Nations in a dozen years or so." Alongside its main concern, the book created a significant local stir, described by a *New York Times* columnist as "a literary feud, peppered with charges of censorship, cowardice, hypocrisy, male chauvinism and sloppy writing" that had "boiled over in New York's literary community." Midge Decter, the literary editor of *World* magazine, had commissioned a review of the book from Shirley's longtime friend Anne Fremantle. Decter was married to Norman Podhoretz, from *Partisan Review* circles, whom the Steegmullers also knew. Decter was, it seems, unaware that

Anne and Shirley were friends. She rejected Anne's positive review, advising her that "the problem is political" and that it would be "extremely sticky" for Norman Cousins, prominent liberal and the editor of *World*, which was always very supportive of the UN, "to publish this kind of unsparing, unequivocal attack." Anne was outraged and told Shirley, who was furious, and wrote to *World* and to *The New York Times*. The *Times* set out the details of the spat and quoted Norman Cousins, saying he "backed Miss Decter 100%." Shirley and Francis both wrote to Cousins, whom Francis knew, taking issue and pointing out Decter's duplicity, and Cousins eventually responded with a brusque apology.

Shirley was affronted not to have more public support from friends for the book:

Alfred Kazin—having my book three months in silence, then telephoned day after Midge episode breaks: how brave book is etc. "As the greatest American poet who happened to be a woman named Em Dickinson, said, 'The truth is so rare it's delightful to tell it.'" (Did, and does, NOTHING for the book.) "How nice." . . . Tells me, "No other book I've read on public affairs had so much that I didn't know. I didn't know 90% of the facts in your book." Incredulous . . . Likewise, Lillian Hellman, who writes me a nice note ("a shocker") after two months, and does NOTHING but "hope the book rewards me." . . . However, she is old and sick. But might that not be a reason for doing, rather than doing nothing? . . . Ah well. Something good in NOT having anything done—the book living on its own, owing nothing.

The *TLS* published a review, "laudatory, front-page etc, but . . . excluded or distorted the entire message." Believing the misrepresentation to be deliberate, Shirley wrote to the editor: "It is a too-oft repeated experience (to be reviewed without mention of the US-UN conspiracy) for me to believe it an accident." In June she was invited to address the British Parliamentary Group for World Government in London. The talk went, she wrote Elizabeth Harrower, "very well. I was quite prepared for three cats in a basement room—but no, an excellent and attentive audience in a solemn chamber with long windows on the Thames (the room itself was in the House of Lords), and there were members of Commons and Lords present, as well as all the rest." She had flown in from Italy—she and Francis had spent June on Capri, absorbed as much in the Watergate revelations as in the sea and the light—to do it, along with a series of talks about the UN for the BBC: "I think all the London thing has been useful. Alan has already reprinted, and that is cheering."

She flew back to New York, where she was quickly overwhelmed again by family troubles. Kit had stopped taking her yellow pills and started penning wild letters. Shirley telephoned her mother's psychiatric nurse and Elizabeth, who both went round to Kit's flat, where they spent hours "hearing her woes, soothing and befriending her, and finally getting her back on to the pills and an incipient even keel." By the end of the day, Kit had begun to cheer up, as Shirley recounted to Patricia: "Nips of brandy were downed by the trio, dusk was now arriving after the long hours of tribulation. (Elizabeth and the doctor . . . must have felt they attended a particularly arduous birth, although Elizabeth did not say so.) Elizabeth remarks: 'Kit told us that she had been unlucky and had never found anyone to listen to her troubles—it was then that we all had the third brandy.'" Shirley was particularly concerned that Kit's drama should not interrupt Francis's work. After hearing of her mother's new plans to travel yet again to England, she wrote to Elizabeth:

Neither F nor S is immortal. Despite a Mum-myth that we are both 21 and indestructible, we may not be on hand for emergencies, even if we were willing to be, under such self-inflicted circumstances. Above all, I cannot drag F around to interminable crises of Mum-in-England. He has been looking after others all his life and now it is time for someone else (me) to think about him. He still has books to write, even if I were to give up all and simply worry about MM—which I sometimes feel is happening.

Elizabeth was carrying the increasing burden of Kit's needs, including applying for an Australian government pension. Shirley sent through the financial documents from New York, but it was Elizabeth who wrote the letters and managed the meetings. Elizabeth also arranged for Kit to get a hearing aid. Shirley wrote regularly, apologising for the interruption, urging Elizabeth to get back to writing her novel, and then piling on the requests for help: "It is enough imposition that you should have had to hear the foregoing, but I have another thing to ask. Which I beg, you will sign off from if it looms as a bore and a trouble beyond even what I imagine." The blame rested, in Shirley's view, with Valerie: "As ever, I'm struck by the weirdness of even asking you such things when I have a sister in Sydney. Even if V did not give my mother any affection or companionship, she could perhaps have done a few practical things for her. But never." There was some understanding, from her own perspective, of the intrusion of all this into a writer's life: "A bombshell into work—I stare for hours at a page, with nothing but rooming houses in Devon passing through my head . . . Which makes me think how this may reach you when you are also staring at a page—more productively—and in no mood whatever for the dreary foregoing. Please forgive it! . . . Elizabeth, let me know candidly what you think. I can't say 'if it's too much to ask' because I always know it's too much . . ." The requests continued: "As we seem determined to try your goodness and patience down to the last syllable, could you let me know if you'd really be willing to march MM to the hearing-aid centre and hand over the lolly? If so, how much should said lolly be?—It MUST be the best hearing-aid . . ."

On Capri, Shirley marvelled at her great good fortune, "enjoying what seems to be the last of so many intricately woven pleasures of nature and civilisation . . . remote from the sorts of electric currents that produce New York and make one work there." One later year she wrote in her diary of the courtesy of a Capri local who had stopped to speak to her and Francis as they sat in one of their regular restaurants, Le Grottelle, near the Arco Naturale, admiring "the ghostly glory" of the view: "'Godete l'incanto [Enjoy the enchantment], e scusatemi.' (for conversing and 'interrupting' us) What one loves most of all is that it is representative, as such a remark would not be elsewhere." In September 1973, still on the island, she noted W. H. Auden's death, in his sleep in Vienna. She wrote to William Meredith: "It tolls a mighty bell. His life unresolved. He seems simultaneously a Younger Poet and a G.O.M. of English Letters—both roles he cultivated too . . . A good death, though . . ."

Auden had been, from very early on, a defining poet for her, central to her understanding of the modern world. She had met him occasionally in New York through Anne Fremantle, and she always enjoyed speaking about these meetings, but she rarely mentioned that on the occasion when she tried to take up with him his line "Poetry makes nothing happen," and to say to him that poetry had certainly changed *her* life, he dismissed her words and "brushed her aside." Back in New York for the winter, she attended a memorial event for him at the Academy of Arts and Letters. Hannah Arendt, one of the speakers, chatted with Shirley beforehand: "Arendt said Auden had youthful, boyish, English look into 1950s—then over a few years, something happened. I: 'You mean something spiritual.' She: 'No, physical.' I: 'I thought you might have meant, a love affair.' She: 'Yes, exactly, a love affair.' I: 'That's what I meant by something spiritual.'" They also discussed Auden's late renunciation of some of his poems, Shirley insisting on the rights of the reader: "These were poems some of us had grown up with," to which Arendt responded, "It remains to be seen whether words so inspired could be insincere." Earlier that year, at the news of Elizabeth Bowen's death, Shirley had gone back through the notes and letters she had kept from Bowen, the photographs taken of the two women together in Shirley's apartment: "Found myself thinking of her bracelet, earrings (that poisoned her flesh), her cigarette case (always tarnished and needing re-silvering), presents from the beloved."

Francis was now working on Isadora Duncan, editing a volume of her correspondence with her manager and lover, Gordon Craig. Shirley thought it all "marvellous, and marvellously moving. Craig is a monster, a monster, but oh, they are all electric, Ellen Terry, Isadora, Craig; it was easier to be electric in those times, before mass-ness descended on us like the night. I don't mean that existence was pleasant or social conditions were other than hell: I mean that personality and temperament were in great and spontaneous variety, breaking out all over and even in barren places." Francis was also caught up in publicity ahead of the publication of the French translation of *Cocteau*, scheduled for the tenth anniversary

of Cocteau's death. "A trail of French broadcasters" came to Capri to
interview him, after which he went to Paris for "a marathon week of
Parisian attentions." Shirley went with him and was "so glad to have
seen F in all his glory." In November she was invited to address the UN
Staff Association in New York. All this cut into "what is more important
to me, writing my novel—the present one said (by me) to be half done
but probably still at the beginning." She had written another story for
*The New Yorker*, "Sir Cecil's Ride," based on her Hong Kong memories,
published that March. Bill Maxwell wrote, "Thank you for that beautiful
story, which stays so firm in my mind, and please write another."

Every spring and autumn, she and Francis went to Capri, returning to
New York through the summer to avoid the crowds that were beginning to
visit the island during these years. What was important above all to Shirley
was the sense of community she found there—"having the acquaintance
of . . . shop-people, people encountered repeatedly on walks, occasional
coffee-person in café in piazza; no large-scale social obligations or necessity
to reconcile affinities or views, but pleasant continual casual exchange."
It was due to the very local nature of relations, "gently paced encounters
during one's necessary or unnecessary outings . . . the regular encounter
with the whole community." She contributed to this spirit of shared fortunes, and her connections were forged through small, private moments
and gestures. In late 1978 she wrote to John Saumarez Smith, proprietor
of Heywood Hill, the London bookshop where she and Francis regularly
bought obscure and out-of-print titles, to thank him for the arrival of a
copy of Compton Mackenzie's *Gallipoli Memories*. She added a gloss:

> The present owner of the plant nursery on Capri is the son of Mimi
> Ruggiero . . . who was Mackenzie's great friend and is written of
> with great affection in *Gallipoli Memories*. "Our" Ruggiero, who
> is well in his seventies, had a precious copy of the book, inscribed
> by Mackenzie to his father. As this was displayed sometimes to vis-
> itors, the inevitable happened; and last year a tourist carried it
> off. When Ruggiero told us of this, we wrote to you—with usual
> happy result. It was the same edition—the only thing we couldn't
> replace was the "dedica". On the morning of the book's arrival on

Capri I took it to the Ruggieros, who received it in most solemn manner. Next morning my doorbell rang—there was their beautiful daughter-in-law with arms full of roses from their garden. Ruggiero, who is a reserved, rather taciturn man, has since told me stories at length about Mackenzie and others of the vintage then living on the island—an extraordinary period, more so than I think anyone has brought out.

Through their visits to the Heywood Hill bookshop they met Elizabeth Archibald, who worked there, and who in turn introduced them to her family friends Isabella and Vittorio Ripa di Meana, from Rome. The Ripa di Meanas, who owned a villa on Capri, La Schiava, were cultivated and erudite, with friends in the worlds of music and politics; they would remain close to Shirley for the rest of her life. Elizabeth Archibald too remained close, seeing Shirley regularly in Capri and in New York; she recalled the atmosphere of the island in those years, the impression it gave of a kind of village, because there were no cars through most of the island: "Everybody walked, you constantly ran into people you knew in the streets." She also remarked on the extraordinary attentiveness of Shirley's response to the smallest events and features of life on the island—her "heightened sensitivity to absolutely everything around her, whatever it was . . . taking in the details . . . the personal or the local . . . Above all she was interested in people: the shopkeepers, her cleaner, the taxi-driver."

Another friend during these Capri years was Laetitia Cerio, whose late father, Shirley noted, "a rather awful man as I privately deduce, was a great figure on Capri, a sort of Grand Seigneur of the island during the Norman Douglas-Compton Mackenzie decades (he is pilloried in Mackenzie's novel *Vestal Fire*)." An accomplished designer (she had worked for Pucci) and linguist, Laetitia had grown up in North and South America as well as in Italy. At a dinner at Laetitia's in the mid-1970s Shirley met the disgraced former British Conservative politician John Profumo and his wife, Valerie Hobson. She was underwhelmed and enjoyed relaying her thoughts: "We found him ok, I suppose, but weirdly unreconstructed by his experiences—lots of name-dropping . . . impressed on us that the name Profumo dated far back (of course to good family) and that the clan had been long since anglicised (—perhaps that's what went wrong?) Weak face, though weirdly recognisable in spite of having no telling features . . . Must be awful to have a scandal in your name – even Watergate had an impersonal title." However, she enjoyed talking to his wife, another enthusiastic reader of Patrick White. Shirley would remain friendly with Laetitia but was often disaffected by her manner. Laetitia became, Shirley later wrote, "with age, a doyenne of Capri personalities, a stylish and fastidious grande dame, at the centre of the island's occasions and institutions."

These were the years of her friendship with Graham Greene, elegised in her Capri memoir, which traces the long lines of literary companionship, terse and argumentative more often than not. Shirley kept a detailed record of her meetings and conversations with Greene from the late 1960s, as if she'd planned all along to write about it. But she was also astonished by the mere fact of having befriended him—her notebook records details of a meeting in late 1970, a comment: "GG-SH—Is this not one of the strangest things?" Greene's books had been among her earliest favourites, her enthusiasm for his work passionate. Nonetheless their friendship was combative, and Greene was clearly irritated by Shirley's verbosity and her willingness to argue a point. For her part, she felt that he sought out friction and found equanimity dull. She pencilled his initials in her copy of Marvell's "Dialogue Between the Soul and Body" next to the lines "Joy's cheerful madness does perplex: / Or sorrow's other madness vex."

There were also easier moments between her and Greene, mostly tied to their deep connections with the island. Both were involved, through the mid-1970s, in a contretemps that unfolded between the local Capresi and a new parish priest who was loathed for having suppressed ancient festivals, including the celebrations for San Costanzo, patron saint of the island. The priest was felt by the Capresi to have "'Protestant' views— that is, contempt for saints, martyrs, and probably Madonna as well." It was also suggested that consequences of some of his actions were already being seen, as Shirley explained to Graham: "There was a fire last year in the church, not of human or other determinable origins; a painter's ladder started to collapse for no reason when the parocco walked under it . . . and so on." The priest's final offence was to have installed "nightmarish electronic chimes at the Duomo which brayed forth pop songs." After complaints went unheeded, Shirley asked Graham if he could "intervene with a word in the right place, if he knew someone at the Vatican. He said, 'The only person I know at the Vatican is the Pope. If you do me a letter in Italian to the Pope, I'll send it.' Letter composed (complete with proper papal usages! How much we learnt . . . ) and sent, with no charge, from the local post office; under the Concordat with the Vatican, Italian posts are free to holders of high papal officers and their correspondents." Miraculously, the letter was heeded, and the chimes ceased.

She had applied, the previous year, for a Guggenheim Fellowship to work on her novel, and she learned in late March that she had been successful, receiving an award of $10,000. That month she published another piece about the United Nations in *The New York Times*, "800 biting words," criticising the UN withdrawal of support for an Amnesty International conference on torture and its broader failure to acknowledge dissidence and public protest. The article drew the desired response:

> The UN is beside itself with rage—the "orientation" courses for new recruits last week included injunctions not to read my works. This was reported to me by one of my stalwarts, and I wrote the Sec-Gen asking that these practices, which violate the provisions for freedom of expression and free circulation of information set forth in the Universal Declaration of Human Rights etc should immediately cease. As I added, in the interests of coordination, they should be aware that the orientation courses for <u>senior</u> appointees have recently been in touch with me asking my advice on how those particular activities could be improved . . . It has many amusing aspects.

The article was quickly followed by another. She had been outraged to learn that the recently published *Gulag Archipelago*, by the Soviet dissident Aleksandr Solzhenitsyn—the publication of which exposed conditions inside the Soviet prison system and then led to Solzhenitsyn's arrest by Soviet police and his deportation into exile—had been removed from the shelves of a bookstore on UN property in Geneva at the apparent behest of the Soviet government. Her article criticised the UN for its failure to uphold its own charter, under which staff "are sworn not to 'seek or receive instructions from any government'; to uphold the free circulation of ideas and information 'through any media and regardless of frontiers.'" This piece also prompted outrage, with one UN official complaining that she had accused Secretary-General Kurt Waldheim of having "censored" Solzhenitsyn, to which Hazzard responded, "I do not accuse the United Nations of censoring Aleksandr Solzhenitsyn's works at bookshops under its influence: I state it as an incontrovertible fact."

The volume of material generated around these labours is astonishing—weeks and months of work. She did not publicise her efforts, but her vast archive of UN-related material gives some insight into her tendency to obsessive rage on the subject. Her concern was with the importance of public disclosure and accountability, and her tenacity was grounded in her conviction of the necessity of individual acts of critique and protest. All this can be seen in a letter, not for publication, that she wrote to Philip Jessup, formerly a U.S. representative at the UN and a prominent defender of the institution. She and Jessup had exchanged sharp disagreements in letters to *The New York Times*. She then wrote to him privately: "Even I, who am long aware of the conditions that have nourished this present case, read the enclosed press release grieving. Scrutinize as one will, one will find no utterance regarding Solzhenitsyn's rights or those of any other author. No word of praise or in defence of this great and brave man, or homage to his life and art; nor of human pity for the vast suffering recorded in his works." There is some mismatch between the resonant force of her language and the smallness of the event being tackled. Her righteous fury at the UN's actions or its inaction lapses into self-righteousness; it can seem solipsistic, self-generated, and itself inured to criticism. The UN remained something of a disavowed battleground for her. In her notebook in 1977 she recorded in some irritation an exchange with a friend in response to one of her UN anecdotes: "SH tells of incident, running into UN females on bus. Friend: 'So you can't escape them.' SH: 'It's they who can't escape me.' Assumption that I am on the run quite contrary to all evidence—I in fact hound them down the nights and days . . ."

Public themes were becoming a significant part of her profile; in 1975 she was awarded a Poynter Fellowship, normally given to journalists, at Yale. Through her UN agitations she had become friendly with Ivan Morris, professor of Japanese language and literature at Columbia, internationalist, and founder and chair of the American section of Amnesty International. Morris had been born in England, moving later to the United States, where he studied Japanese and worked in intelligence for the U.S. Navy during the war. He had been one of the first interpreters to go to Hiroshima after the bombing, and he was an important translator of the work of Yukio Mishima, one of the most internationally significant modern Japanese writers, as well as being Mishima's friend and correspondent. Morris was thought by some of Shirley's friends to be one of her models for Adam Vail in *The Transit of Venus*, and certainly their close friendship deepened her familiarity with formal activism around political causes. In an early letter, Morris wrote of rediscovering after an evening in her company "the precious art of laughter which I thought had deserted me during the last few weeks"; on another occasion he wrote inviting her and Francis for "a quiet weekend" at his house at Sachem's Head on the Connecticut shore: "Please let me know so I can start looking forward to it." Morris's scholarly writing—particularly his study of the nature of heroism in Japan, the idea of "a special nobility in the sincere, unsuccessful sacrifice"—would later inform her treatment, certainly, of Japanese characters and subjects but also of the character of Ted Tice, "honouring the faith, not the failure." But his most profound influence was the kind of political involvement he practised: informed, committed, restrained. Like Shirley, he had eschewed direct involvement in supporting the student protests at Columbia in 1968. She attended a conference on torture organised by Amnesty in April 1973 at CUNY and drew on the detailed information presented there in her continuing critical responses to the UN. These political connections and involvements also made their way into her fiction. In 1973 she recorded in her notebook that a publisher had declined a book on torture prepared by Amnesty, saying, "The feeling here is that we've done our pro bono publico stint for this year," a line she would give, in *Transit*, to a publisher rejecting a volume of dissident poetry.

Shirley was always concerned with the detail as well as the larger dramas of politics. She was endlessly eloquent on the subject of Nixon, whose name appears often in the margins of her books of poetry next to key lines, for instance from Byron's *Don Juan*: "The vulgarest tool that tyranny could want, / With just enough of talent, and no more, / To lengthen fetters by another fixed / And offer poison long already mixed. / An orator of such set trash of phrase, / Ineffably, legitimately vile, / That even its grossest flatterers dare not praise, / Nor foes—all nations—condescend to smile." She was riveted by the Watergate hearings, "a strange dichotomy of horror and hearteningness," following them energetically (asked if she had seen *Last Tango in Paris*, in cinemas that year, she responded, "We'll get to it when Watergate closes"). She told Muriel that while they didn't have "a telly, our wireless has just about had the casing burnt off it this summer."

> As to Watergate, one can hardly believe it is happening, as these supreme pests who persecuted us for years are one by one led forward to their Nuremberg. Mitchell . . . Ehrlichman and Haldeman . . . Yes it is awful of course, but at the same time it is immense relief and health and justice. Even for worst criminals on trial I usually feel the awfulness of it, and just see human wreckage; and am rather enjoying the new experience of hearty pleasure as these gauleiters are brought down, who did so much damage to every one of our liberties and to so many persons . . .

It was only on the resignation of Nixon that she took up U.S. citizenship; she explained that she always felt she could not have done this during the Vietnam War and that Francis proposed it as an act of "solidarity" with a country that would "get rid of Nixon." When Nixon resigned, "I applied the next week." Her rage was not confined to Nixon; she later wrote that she could not think "that anyone, Reagan or not, is worse than Nixon. Rather each one makes the next possible—as Johnson made Nixon possible. Nixon is satanic. Something that came in with Reagan is a new dimension of blatancy in evil—whereas Nixon's speciality was diabolical hypocrisy." Twenty years later she reflected, in some despair, on the continuing political devilry: "Bush, Cheney, Rumsfeld—Not just the classic thugs of political history, but—as with McCarthy—with a new inauthenticity, the absence of a dimension, almost a physical vacuum. America committing intellectual suicide."

Lengthy political discussions were a feature of her correspondence with Elizabeth Harrower. In 1972, the first Labor government in nearly a quarter century, led by the charismatic Gough Whitlam, was elected in Australia. Elizabeth Harrower wrote often of her excitement and of the transformation of the country that followed. Tom Keneally recalled the significance of those years for writers: "With Whitlam, half the country was suddenly writing novels"—a transformation from those earlier decades during which he—and Shirley—had grown up, when "what had been absent in Australia was the possibility of a career in letters." Francis remarked that this election "recalled for him the days of the New Deal and the sense of relief and invigoration." Shirley was full of praise for Whitlam, who did "hugely civilized things for the arts." She now felt that Australia compared more than favourably with the United States: "Whereas the public library, the Metropolitan Museum and the Met Opera in New York are all facing closing through lack of funds, scarcely a month passes in Aust without new arts centres opening to do important things." In November 1975 Whitlam was dismissed by the governor-general, the (unelected) representative of Australia's head of state, Queen Elizabeth, prompting deep and furious responses from Labor voters; and in the subsequent election, the conservatives, led by Malcolm Fraser, came emphatically to power. Writing to commiserate with Elizabeth, Shirley drew parallels with the U.S. experience:

The election result vividly recalled Nixon's 1972 landslide . . . by which I mean, a deliberate, self-destructive selection by a population of the group that will bring out the worst in them . . . Something that has been v hard for me to realise, brought home to me by Viet Nam, is the colossal indifference of people generally to evil. I do not want to suggest that other eras were better in this way . . . I used to think, if you could bring the truth home to people, they would mostly care. I'm afraid I don't think that any longer. The truth of Viet Nam was brought home day after day, year after year, to Americans, and they did not care. They don't care now, either, and have simply expunged it from their minds. Some of this seems to be in the Fraser-Whitlam result.

Through these years she had continued to receive from Kit "occasional grisly threats of the cottage in Devon," her mother's dream of moving to a "lovely little town," which Shirley continued to ignore, while acknowledging that at some stage they would need "to go out there and fix things somewhat, but we cannot get up the stamina as yet—it requires the courage of ancient heroes." In 1976 she accepted an invitation to appear at the Adelaide Festival Writers' Week, and in late February she flew with Francis to Australia, her first return since 1951. The trip was filled with unexpected delight: "The country, people, and cultural activity are an utter revelation, and we had an absolutely splendid unforgettable time." Francis wrote to Jacques Barzun: "Australia is a revelation—Adelaide something like a modern version of one of the more enlightened ancient Greek city-states." Their experience at the festival "reminded us that there actually can be a beautiful city where people live well and happily today."

Before Adelaide, they went to Sydney, where, inevitably, things were difficult. Kit had announced before they left New York that she was planning to leave "so that we could be 'free to enjoy ourselves without her.' This set the scene for grisly dramas on arrival . . . scarcely an affectionate word, dogged refusal to admit we'd come ten thousand miles to see her, and when I reminded her that we had done so she icily replied, 'Very kind of you.'" After Shirley had returned to New York, Kit was rushed to the hospital for an untreated dental abscess. Shirley wrote, "I truly believe I will not feel guilt, at least not of any irrational kind, if MM predeceases me (which I sometimes doubt)—partly because of having the perspective of F, who has been so good to her and who yet sees it all and confirms that I am not dreaming some of this weirdness." In Sydney,

Elizabeth Harrower had thrown a party, where Shirley met the ageing Christina Stead, recently returned to Australia after half a century in the United States and England. The two later exchanged admiring letters; in hers Shirley copied out the text of "To Ned" by Herman Melville, whom Stead described in her reply as "my old friend (and yours)." Elizabeth introduced Shirley to her extensive circles of writers, artists, and Sydney's left-wing political elite. Patrick White had them to dinner, writing to a friend that he and his partner Manoly Lascaris "like the Steegmullers very much." (This would change.) Shirley drew extensively on Elizabeth's connections, as well as her insights, in her research for the long "Letter from Australia" she published in *The New Yorker* in December 1976 detailing the dramatic changes observed in Australia since the dark years of her departure. Although her delight at the cultural energy she witnessed on this visit would take on a more critical edge over the next few years, she certainly devoted considerable time and energy through the 1970s to celebrating and promoting Australian writing through her circles and connections in New York.

She was excited above all by the work of Patrick White, Australia's first literary Nobel laureate. Her piece on his 1973 *The Eye of the Storm* had made the front page of *The New York Times Book Review*. In it, she had added to her glowing account of the novel some forthright criticism of the New York literary world's parochialism:

All Patrick White's books have been published here by the Viking Press; but have had the minimum of attention in this land whose own fiction is increasingly oppressed by ethnocentricity of reference, range, content and criticisms. White's reputation in the United States has been created in the most durable form: almost exclusively between himself and readers . . . Novels or poems in translation—from Russian, French, Spanish or Japanese—may more easily find a publisher in America than any new work of quality from Australia . . . W. J. Weatherby recently described in the *Times Literary Supplement* his fruitless pilgrimage through New York bookshops on the day the Nobel award was announced for Patrick White. None of White's books was in stock. The grotesque riposte of the book business to this situation would of course have been, "We didn't know he was going to win the Nobel Prize."

In the wake of her "Letter from Australia," Shirley advised *New Yorker* editors Frances Kiernan and Howard Moss on interesting Australian writers, as the magazine wanted to publish an issue focusing on Australian material. Kiernan wrote that "without your suggestions and advice, I doubt that the project would have been possible." The project never came to fruition, but over the years, Shirley continued to make introductions and offer advice to Australian authors wanting to be published in the United States.

She continued, too, sporadically, to publish short pieces about writers she admired, prompted by new publications: the reissue of Jean Rhys's 1928 novel *Quartet* in 1971; Neapolitan writer Matilde Serao's 1884 *Il ventre di Napoli*, republished in the wake of the 1973 cholera outbreak in Naples; and in 1978 a piece on Barbara Pym. With all these, her impulse was to pay tribute to neglected greatness, to continuance of admiration. At home in New York, her days were a mix of pleasure, stimulation, distraction: "We hear music, go to ballet, in the winter mostly. Francis goes to films, I almost never (frightened of being frightened to death or bored to death which is worse). How can one describe one's days?—they are usually filled up with people, incidents, episodes, stuck into wads of work and thoughts and silence and talk like currants in cake." They continued to see old friends—the Warrens, Maxwells, Breunigs, Kazins, Barzuns, Barretts. Everett Fahy, director of the Frick Collection and later curator of Renaissance art at the Metropolitan Museum of Art, had become a close friend, visiting often at their apartment and going with them to exhibitions. Shirley valued, along with his erudition, his "great love for" art, his capacity for friendship, and his "generous heart." Through Everett, they knew Alison West, then a curatorial assistant at the Frick, who had long been "in their ambient" through her stepmother, Mary McCarthy. Shirley knew McCarthy, but not closely: Both women, West commented, "had powerful intellects and were probably rivalrous." They met only occasionally, despite spending so much time in the same cities.

"Of course, Mary and Elizabeth Hardwick were great friends, and Shirley and Lizzie did not get along, giving one an idea of tastes in friendship and perhaps of intellectual camps." Francis had also had somewhat prickly relations with McCarthy after he wrote correcting several points in an essay she had written on *Madame Bovary*. (McCarthy wrote back at length and somewhat testily, "Dear Francis: What are the inaccuracies in my Madame Bovary essay?" and then by way of answer to her own question, "What I say in the essay is offered as a guess—my own. Hence it can't be called an inaccuracy.") Although less connected to *The New Yorker* through these years, Shirley nonetheless maintained warm relationships there with writers and editors, many of them younger than she, such as Frances Kiernan, who had been Bill Maxwell's assistant during the days when he was Shirley's editor and later herself moved into editing. The Steegmullers developed a substantial friendship with Evan Cornog, who had been Shirley's fact-checker on the Australian piece. Cornog's wife, the translator Ann Goldstein, observed, "They loved Evan, he was like their son. They accepted me because I came with him."

Art and the art world were mainstays. There was, as Alison West put it, "a sense of knowing cities, knowing museums, having a certain way of life, approaching things in the same way, knowing the same people." They were part of an informal group, "Il Circolo Tessitore"—the name a fond tribute to Bill Weaver—which included Dorle and Dario Soria, Harold Acton, John Pope-Hennessy, and others. Along with their connections to Italy, there was a shared erudition, privately acquired and sustained outside the academy. Shirley had long been at home in such company; the commitment to acquire knowledge of and develop familiarity with high culture that drove her early years in New York was now more assured but no less avid. And in her notebooks and diaries she continued to record snippets of conversation from events she attended, her often critical take on the world she now inhabited. After a dinner in New York in 1972 for the artist Jean Dubuffet, which she and Francis attended with Douglas Cooper, Shirley wrote in her diary that she had heard a man saying, across the table to Francis, "I'm damn rich." She added, "What he has really said is 'I'm Dan Rich.' [Dan Rich had been chief curator at the Chicago Art Institute at the time when Francis bought his Redon.] But the other meaning would have been quite in keeping with the audience." She described an evening, a few years later, with "a charming friend from England," Lawrence Gowing, a celebrated art historian. Gowing was another who exemplified the dedication Shirley so admired, of one working outside art institutions: "Eccentric man, troubled by a singular stammer, who has written on a remarkable diversity of painters. He is lovable and intelligent. He told us he had just turned down a knighthood; he said, 'I know the graceful thing to do would be to turn it down and not speak of it, but I'm not up to that.' He then quoted Cocteau on honours: that the important thing was not to turn an honour down, but not to have deserved it." (Gowing nonetheless accepted a knighthood in 1982.)

The United Nations continued to preoccupy and distract and to keep her from her novel. She had a very particular and tenacious adversary in Under-Secretary-General Brian Urquhart, who had been involved in the establishment of the UN in 1945. A great supporter of the organization, Urquhart was frequently pitted against her in public debates, and their private paths crossed frequently as they had a number of friends in common. The *TLS* had reviewed *Defeat of an Ideal* alongside Urquhart's biography of former UN secretary-general Dag Hammarskjöld, which Shirley described as "dreary, and dishonest," and in 1990 they would exchange fiery letters in *The New York Review of Books* over claims made in her second UN book, *Countenance of Truth*. The writer Steven Aronson recalled, "I had the Urquharts and the Steegmullers to a party at my apartment and the next day Brian and Shirley each called to complain that I'd invited the other." In her diary, Shirley quoted a wartime poem by Robert Conquest to describe Urquhart: "Like those who now in greater luck and liberty / Are professionally pitiful or heroic," and Urquhart was equally dismissive: "She thinks she writes about the UN; knows nothing. She was in clerical."

In 1977 Shirley was invited to speak on a panel for UN Women's Day, with the anthropologist Margaret Mead and the activist Bella Abzug. This was Shirley's first encounter with Mead, an outspoken supporter of the UN, and she was appalled, a feeling confirmed the following year when Mead invited her to lunch at the Cosmopolitan Club and then railed about the damage she felt Shirley was doing to the UN. In a long

piece she drafted about the meeting, possibly with a view to publication, Shirley detailed Mead's lack of courtesy, including "parking her
chewing gum on the rostrum" before giving her speech at the Women's
Day panel, arriving nearly an hour late to the lunch, and delivering
"apoplectic" tirades during it. As with her run-ins with those who opposed her views—Midge Decter and Philip Jessup, but also Valerie—
there is clear delight in Shirley's mobilising of the forces of righteous
outrage:

MM: Listen, I've never spoken against anything. You just mobilise
hostility. I never spoke against fascism; I never spoke against
communism.

SH: Do you call that a proud record?

MM: I'm telling you I never spoke against anything. That's why
I never had any trouble with the Attorney-General's list. I always speak positively.

SH: You felt no obligation to object, then, when the UN suppressed
news of famine in Africa, and nearly half a million people died?

MM: I certainly did not. People have to operate through channels.
Sometimes they go right, sometimes they go wrong. T'aint that
it's wicked, just the way the world is, after all. (Affected a folk-
siness in talk, sometimes talked in telegraphese.) . . . After a bit
of angry munching, MM got up . . . and said, "I'm leaving at
once because I have a lot of important things to do." When she
showed heightened impatience at the elevator, I said, "I waited
forty-five minutes for you. And I'm here at your request." MM
again turned on [her assistant] Helen Reurs, "That's your
fault." That was the last I saw of her. Helen Reurs telephoned
me that afternoon: "It was better than television."

When Shirley recounted the afternoon at dinner that evening, Dwight
Macdonald delighted her by declaring his view that Margaret Mead was
the "greatest philistine. The greatest, unsurpassed!'"

All this was distraction; her real work continued, slowly, behind the
scenes. In May 1979 the *New York Times* poetry editor Thomas Lask

reported in his column that "a major novel by Shirley Hazzard . . . longer and more complex than anything this writer has done previously" would be published the following spring. Prepublication marketing affirmed the event and the achievement: "Shirley Hazzard's first novel in many years is already being hailed as a literary masterpiece." With publication came reports of the extraordinary labour of the novel's construction—that it had taken a decade to write, with "as many as 20–30 drafts per page"—feeding into the sense of its consequence. *The Transit of Venus* is undeniably a masterpiece, one of the great novels of the century. Its complex, densely wrought plot traces the lives of two Australian sisters, Caroline and Grace Bell, across the globe, through lives, marriages, and love affairs. The sisters take up with public figures—writer, scientist, doctor, bureaucrat, activist—while around them unfold the dramas of the globalising postwar world: "In America, a white man had been shot dead in a car, and a black man on a veranda. In Russia, a novelist had emerged from hell to announce that beauty would save the world. Russian tanks rolled through Prague while America made war in Asia. In Greece the plays of Aristophanes were forbidden, in China the writings of Confucius." There is an insistence on the weight and substance of human words and lives, a sense of expectation and portentousness that comes straight from melodrama. The novel begins with the arrival of a marked figure, a stranger, at "the farthest and largest house" in the middle of a storm wreaking devastation at once ordinary and mythic: "Housewives were rushing, and crying out, 'My washing.' And a sudden stripe of light split earth from sky." The action, largely visual, sweeps from the elemental world of vale, hill, castle, and deluge to a richly domestic interior, a circular hallway, a bowl of roses, a newspaper, "a dark picture framed in gold." A little later, the melodrama is made explicit: "A little curled chrysanthemum of a dog was in heaven at her approach. 'Grasper. Grasper.' The dog jumped up and down, speechless. Someone was shaking a bell. Grace was opening a door. And the lights went up by themselves as on a stage."

The novel's melodramatic cast is part of its stern moral project, its concern with questions of truth and goodness, which, along with its commitment to the matter of love, set it somewhat outside the concerns of the late-twentieth-century novel. Central to melodrama and its drive to truth is a preoccupation with disclosure or revelation, what in the novel Paul Ivory calls "the compulsion to tell." There is a kind of mercilessness in the novel's telling; knowledge itself becomes "a fearful current in which a man might drown." In a memorial Shirley gave many years later for the poet Anthony Hecht, she spoke of how, "in certain music of Schubert . . . the composer seems to be asking: 'How much can I hurt you?'" There is something of this ethos in the novel; Matthew Specktor observed a kind of violence in its "willingness to destroy its own hope." Throughout, the steadfastness of love is counterweighted with dramatic reversals and contradictions, themselves generated by errors of ignorance; the costs of not knowing. At the heart of the narrative is an audacious and wholly melodramatic prolepsis: in the early pages we are told that the protagonist, Ted Tice, renowned scientist and devoted suitor of Caro Bell, "would take his own life before attaining the peak of his achievement. But that would occur in a northern city, and not for many years." That revelation is, by the novel's end, buried in the mass of narrative detail and accreted clues. The event itself, Ted's suicide, having acquired its full weight and significance only in the final pages with Caro's long-delayed returning of his love, is not told—rather, is not retold—but instead is left hanging just outside the scope of the novel's events, a matter for the reader's imagination. Arriving at the last page, we cannot be confident of the status of what we have read, because the significance of key events—murder, betrayal, disaster—has been obscured, disclosed out of sequence and through apparently inconsequential details. The question of the moral importance of truth, of knowing and understanding, is everywhere evident. And yet the movement towards truth that sits so dramatically at the novel's heart—Caro's too-late realisation of Paul Ivory's crimes and of Ted's great and complex goodness, the movement of fate itself—is complicated and troubled by questions of chronology and sequence, catching the reader up in the novel's webs of knowing and not-knowing, of missed clues and signs, of being wrong. All this is perhaps summed up best in Francis's comment on the manuscript: "No one should have to read it for the first time."

There is something untimely about this novel, above all stylistically.

In 2010, Michael Gorra wrote that it "would have seemed old-fashioned in 1980," when it was published, a view echoed by other readers who, in the decades that followed its publication, seem often to have been delaying, holding off, even resisting its appeal. Geoff Dyer wrote that he had finally turned to read *Transit* twenty years after buying a copy and was struck then by the sense that he was reading it "at the perfect moment," that he had been in fact "destined to read the book at this moment," his experience chiming with the novel's deep investment in destiny. David Miller, a few years later, wrote of his irritation at how long it had taken him to read the novel and that having begun, "I was ensnared, like having been bitten by a puppy or kitten that wouldn't let go until it tasted blood." Another decade on, Michelle de Kretser remembered that in 1980 she had wondered, "Why the fuss?" She had read the novel and "forgot about it for twenty years"; then, opening it again, "the sensation came, like a blow to the breastbone," from the first page, "the shock of the great."

There is also *Transit*'s untimely relation to feminism. The second wave that was exploding all around through the years of its writing is barely evident in its pages, despite its interest in women's lives. Shirley was not, then or ever, drawn to feminism; her concern with women's authority and agency in the world was expressed through other modes. The philosopher Akeel Bilgrami, a friend of her later years, describes *Transit*'s Caro Bell as "one of the great women characters of the modern novel—someone we recognize for a kind of strength at a time when feminism was not in the air, and so women possessed of such strength had no peg of doctrine to hang it on." Bilgrami proposes that Caro's situation is particularly poignant because, unlike her great antecedents—Emma Bovary, Anna Karenina, Dorothea Brooke—she "lives and loves in the decade just before the turn to feminism, and so all the reader's urges on her behalf are of the sort we feel when we think of a 'close miss'; and yet Shirley is confident in her resolve that these qualities of character and temperament in Caro might well be the more interesting for *having missed*." There is in this view a richness in the combination of feminism's proximity and its absence.

The genesis of *The Transit of Venus* across the decade of its writing can be traced across Shirley's notebooks, literally in longhand. In those notes, the novel's narrative density is there right from the start, also the moral coordinates of the central lovers, the global scope of their story, the occulted prose, the core symbolism of light, and the elements. In 1969, while she was still working on *The Bay of Noon* proofs and before she had developed very much of the next novel at all, she had decided its conclusion: "Ending of book—Years later they meet in a foreign place, each taking planes to different places. Has been said throughout the book that he will die in a plane crash (before reaching fifty etc). He persuades her to come with him at the last." The novel's final note, "the great gasp of ocean when a ship goes down," took shape later—it appears in her notebooks some time in 1973—but still well before much of the story had been laid down. She initially planned for it to begin with what became almost its final moment: the coming together of the lovers. Her notebook from 1973 records "Stockholm: He dressed as if from an office (some meeting of statistics etc); she as if she had simply been waiting his emergence. The sun on their faces, on his balding, solar forehead, as if in their condition it could not burn them. Not subject to elements, to dailiness." She had then thought to move back to the start of the narrative: "(After Stockholm, retrospective to begin). It was a storm of national dimensions. By nightfall billboards in London would be reporting devastation . . . On a shadeless morning the sky had turned purple, had lowered itself like an awning petrifying the branches . . ." She also decided early, after working with a number of different names, on calling her protagonist Caro and noted two possible titles in her notebook: "Title: (The) Transit of Venus; Title? Dark She, Fair She," and a year later, "Title: Time Exposure / Transit of Venus."

On its publication in the spring of 1980, reviews, laudatory, were also personal, even intimate; readers were drawn fast into the novel, experiencing shocks and revelations along with the characters. In *The New York Times*, John Leonard wrote that *Transit*'s "business is to break the heart" and confessed that "although I suppose that such emotions are inappropriate to criticism, I finished the book angry and in tears." The affect was itself a function of the writing: "No matter the object—a feeling, a face, a room, the weather—it is stripped of its layers of paint, its clots of words, down to the original wood; oil is applied; grain appears, and a glow. Every epigram and apostrophe is earned. A powerful intelligence is playing with a knife. It is an intelligence that refuses to be deflected by ironies; irony isn't good enough." The allusive prose that had beguiled readers of the early novels was now fully formed, strikingly not of its time, but drawing, somehow, on the long traditions of literature. Anthony Hecht spelled this out in his formal introduction to her in a 1983 Library of Congress series of public talks on poetry. Shirley Hazzard was, he said,

> A writer of fiction in a series of programs usually devoted to poets. But by dint of the craft of her work, the lyric movement, the volu-minous literary resonance of her beautiful and meticulous prose, she very evidently elects to keep such company. For she brings to her writing that wealth of literary tradition that poets have al-ways conceived to be their special heritage, but which only a very few novelists have tried to make use of . . . What distinguishes her writing above all is that she takes her words seriously, as very few novelists do these days. Her words recur within her text like lyric refrains, each repetition bearing a new increment of meaning. Yeats could do that sort of thing, and Shakespeare, and Joyce. It is more than mere technique; it is knowing the reach and dimen-sion, the metric weight of each simple, innocent word, and using that knowledge to advantage.

In the *TLS*, Valentine Cunningham asserted *Transit*'s achievement: "Great big novels aren't necessarily great novels. But when, like 'A phrase' in that phrase of Auden's, they go 'packed with meaning like a van' they stand some chance of greatness. *The Transit of Venus*, coming as richly freighted as it does with multi-layered meanings for the unpacking . . . has the weighty feel of great fiction." There were meanings to be un-packed in the dense and allusive prose, something about which Shirley herself was happy to comment. She wrote, in response to questions from the literary critic John Beston,

> The many allusions of mythical and literary kind throughout the book are intended always to serve the meaning and the plot,

though to give pleasure in a way as well. It is not necessary to recognise or be aware of them—for instance, when on p323 there is "always something new from Africa," a reader need not recognise this as Pliny's proverb: "Ex Africa semper aliquid novi"— although some will. But it has in itself, I think, a long echo of recorded time, and gives a momentary feeling of "men of affairs" in their temporal little dealings with huge phenomena of history.

The poet John Malcolm Brinnin wrote that on finishing the novel, he had immediately picked it up again and reread it: "The didactic side of me wants to treat it in the way art historians take paintings and reduce them to geometry, just to show that, behind all the shapes and colours there is that reticulum of ideas, that controlling hand," adding that he was "in a sort of enchanted jeopardy: I swear you write just for me."

When Billy Abrahams moved to the West Coast, Shirley had left Little, Brown and moved to Viking for this novel. Her new editor was Alan Williams, whom she described as "a princely man, very very knowledgeable, a great love of the arts, of music, of painting." With the publication of *The Transit of Venus*, Shirley wrote, "Dear Alan, make the most of this letter, you'll never have another like it. I want to say I've been entirely happy with everything that happened between me and the publisher. It's thanks to you." She was, she said, "happy with the advance . . . happy with the lack of editing (he said I don't want to change a thing—this was very important to me) and even happy with the advertising." *Transit* went straight onto the bestseller lists; Viking's marketing, grounded in a conviction that "a great book could sell in great numbers," was validated. Shirley was both gratified and perplexed by its success: "It says something about how things come around in literature—how things that seem to feed the public taste are not all there is." She proposed that the fact that "my book is a real story" was perhaps at the heart of its popularity. She spoke also, somewhat elliptically, of the weight of tragedy: "The lives of people you see looking out the window seem happy, but often they're floating on the top of terrible things. I don't mean to sound fatalistic—I have a happy life—but so many things are left to chance."

*The Transit of Venus* won the National Book Critics Circle Award for best novel of 1980; Francis noted to a friend that this was "in some ways the most esteemed of the prizes, even though there's no cash." In her acceptance speech Shirley observed that the award marked the acceptance of her, "as someone born far from this country" into "the writing life of this land" and commented that she doubted "that this could occur in quite the present form anywhere but in America." She spoke about the importance of art as a form of human continuity, signing her novel and its achievement into the longer past, and she acknowledged the contribution of William Maxwell, who had also been nominated for the award for *So Long, See You Tomorrow*, as her earliest supporter and guide, paying tribute to "his genius and his generosity." Maxwell, who was present at the ceremony, wrote afterwards to Francis:

> When Shirley began to speak I thought of the gloves on the back seat of the car and the bugler on the train. All those beautiful books and not a lame sentence in any of them. As she went on talking my sense for what is in wrapped packages told me that she was going to mention my book, and I thought no, she couldn't possibly do that; the occasion is against it. The occasion was swept aside. I felt as if I were sitting under a waterfall. But the whole speech is a marvel, and it took Shirley to say it. I don't think it will end there. She has a way of changing the world.

Maxwell had been contacting members of the American Academy of Arts and Letters, seeking nominations for Shirley for the Harold Vursell Award, given each year for recently published prose notable for the quality of its style. She did not win (the award went that year to Tom Wolfe), but her nomination was endorsed by Bernard Malamud and Arthur Miller. Miller wrote Maxwell, "I am in the middle of 'Venus' and have not been so enthralled by a book in many years [. . .] I think she merits everything anybody can give her."

This was, according to Jonathan Galassi, who met her around this time and would become her friend and later her publisher, a moment of triumph that brought "a new degree of international fame and acknowledgment of her individuality and power as a writer." As well as marking a shining present, the novel cast a sombre glance back to Shirley's past. In 1978, deep in the writing, she had heard from Chris Cooper that he had seen Alec Vedeniapine's name in a newspaper, and from this, with the help of the London Macmillan office, she tracked down an address for him in Wales. Her diary records in fleeting terms her intense response: lines from *Middlemarch*, some ambiguity creeping in through the trammels of citation: "APV—Thirty years . . . believed me better than I am in everything but one—I mean in my truth to you." A few days later: "The idea that she could go, in a day. And that she would not," and again, "Alone to Tiberio. Glorious day. APV. Oh God. The pain, after so many many years, years. Walked down in tears."

She wrote him a letter, and in July 1979 they met in London, where he was attending a meeting and she was seeing Alan Maclean. In addition to running his farm, Alec had taken on a role within the UK Milk Marketing Board, representing dairy farmers, and was involved at that time in negotiations with the European Common Market. In her diary Shirley noted, "Good grey suit, pin-striped 'Milk Board tie.' Affecting. He had not enough money to pay. I paid." After this entry, she wrote lines from Auden, flagging them "from Hong Kong, 1948, walking on grassy path beyond office":

> *Look Stranger . . . Far off like floating seeds the ships*
> *Diverge on urgent voluntary errands;*
> *And the full view*
> *Indeed may enter*
> *And more in memory as now these clouds do,*
> *That pass the harbour mirror*
> *And all the summer through the water saunter.*

This is followed by a draft of a poem, unfinished, "Long Division (Arrival) Wellington Harbour 1949," that begins, "Without you, gorse, firs, ten thousand houses unaware of you . . ."

She was with this fragment clearly returning—imaginatively, emotionally—to the Hong Kong novel she had long struggled to write, which, over time, would become *The Great Fire*. At the same time, the irreducibility of loss, renewed all over again, also steeped the novel she was then in the process of completing with pervasive melancholy. While *The Transit of Venus* is dedicated "Once more, for Francis," the epigraph, from Robert Desnos's "Le Dernier Poème," with its traces of the sufferings of World War Two, binds the novel also to that earlier, first, love:

> *J'ai rêvé tellement fort de toi,*
> *J'ai tellement marché, tellement parlé,*
> *Tellement aimé ton ombre,*
> *Qu'il ne me reste plus rien de toi.*

Years later, in a poignant parallel, the enduring grief of Francis's death would inflect the writing of *The Great Fire* with a like loss.

# A FATED CONNECTION

## 1980-1985

WHEN *THE TRANSIT OF VENUS* was published, Patricia Clarke wrote asking if the characters of Grace and Dora had been based on Valerie and Kit, and Shirley responded at some length:

> Grace has nothing to do with any relative of mine. She is a mere Figment. Dora, now. I have been waiting for the blow to fall, the penny to drop, the hell to break loose. It may at any moment, but so far there has been no reaction, although MM wrote a (nice) letter about receiving the book and loving the first thirty pages . . . It is possible as you say that she will not bear to recognise—but that would mean giving up a chance for outrage; unlikely. Another poss is that she simply won't be able to concentrate enough to get on with the book—this has been suggested by a friend at Sydney, since MM is now so truly addled, poor thing; her last travels were a crescendo of disorganization. Never will I forget helping her take off her hat and finding it stuffed with travellers' cheques.

Kit's disorganization now clearly indicated more than just eccentricity or being difficult. She had for some time been writing "ghastly letters (Dear Shirley . . . with best regards . . . )" to which Shirley responded "normally, affecting not to notice." She then began complaining to friends in Sydney and writing to the New York–based trustee of her finances, "accusing F and S of embezzling not only her funds but her U.S. pension as well. The trustee tried to reassure her this was not legally or practically possible, but the accusations continued." Shirley wrote to Kit "as if we did not know of the rancorous aspect of the affair, explaining for the millionth time that it is a family trust etc etc but also saying NICELY that she is welcome to withdraw anything and everything. As we have spent thirteen years vainly urging her to spend her money instead of living like a church mouse, it does seem hard lines." (They would discover after Kit's death that she had squirreled away close to thirty thousand dollars from her income through this period.)

In the spring of 1977 Kit had taken herself off on a sea voyage to London, via Honolulu, where Valerie was now living (Kit was there, as Shirley put it, as "a barely invited house-guest"), the trip unannounced except to the New York trustee. She did not stay long. Shirley and Francis wired her money at Southampton, where they learned from the trustee that she was to dock, only to find that she had sailed back to Sydney almost immediately after arriving and had failed to claim the funds. Two years later, back in the UK after yet another frenzied voyage, Kit was rescued by one of her few remaining English friends, a Mrs. Tanner, "who had humanely gone to Southampton to prevent MM from ending it all. She succeeded." Shirley mused that "the world where MM partly dwells" was the world of Angela Carter, "or at least that Angela Carter has a wave-length into some of that contorted fairy tale." The dark comedy with which she invested her mother functioned as a form of protection, walling off the chaos. Nonetheless, the guard was easily breached, as when, hearing Shirley tell one of her terrible Kit anecdotes, a friend commented, "So you're still fighting with your mother." Shirley responded, in deep umbrage, "It's many years since I fought with my mother—in fact, never fought with her; and for long now negotiate-from-a-position-of-strength."

In August 1980, in Sydney, Kit collapsed and was taken to hospital. She had suffered a stroke, was "sometimes quite lucid, making arrangements for cheques and key etc, at others very wandering in her mind." She was increasingly rageful, and her psychiatric nurse urged Shirley not to contact her or to fly out to see her "as she is in no shape to cope with surprises. However something may alter v quickly. It is all uncertain, and I am (more or less) prepared to take off to Sydney at any moment if necessary." It fell, again, to Elizabeth Harrower to look after things. Among Elizabeth's papers is a list of tasks to be undertaken, along with costs incurred during this hospital admission—taxis, trunk calls to New York, rent arrears to "rent man—Wayne or Lane?" The list includes a note to "Burn S's letters . . ." It is not clear if this was Kit's injunction, but only a handful of Shirley's letters to her mother survive, in contrast to the overwhelming volume flowing the other way. There is no discussion of the matter in Elizabeth's correspondence with Shirley; it remained another unspoken act. The following year, Kit was moved to a nursing home, from where she wrote Shirley "appalling letters—'I am in prison, wish to die, misery etc' and I have to remind myself they are truly no worse than in her previous solitude, of which she wrote me 'No one would let a dog live this way,' and of which she now writes: 'How happy I was—if only I could be back in that lovely flat.'" Yet again, it was Elizabeth who, with her cousin Margaret Dick, took on the "monstrous task" of clearing and closing up Kit's flat, as Shirley put it, "a sort of last straw of ultimate largeness of heart. I don't wonder that it shattered you both. As you say, no matter how much horror one has allowed for in this case, there are always revelations—or, rather, another degree of revelation. A worst one hadn't wanted to know."

Through these years, death seemed to be all around. Many of their friends were older, and frail. Ivan Morris had died suddenly and prematurely in Bologna in 1978. Shirley wrote to his mother, "It is almost the greatest loss I have ever had." Dario Soria died in 1980, and a month later, on Capri, Shirley had a phone call telling her that Robert Sonkin had died that morning; in her diary she wrote lines from Shelley: "'Thou who didst waken from his summer dreams . . . so sweet, the sense faints with picturing them.'" In 1983 it was Dwight Macdonald. Shirley remembered him as both "impossible" and "a friend of 25 years—Francis knew him a lifetime; but it was Dwight and I who were closer." Dwight was, Shirley felt, "peculiarly a New York person (and I hear him pronouncing that word person in his old-fashioned New York accent, a vanishing phenomenon of the city, like so much else—an educated and, even, in a kind sense, genteel inflection for which it was necessary for him to have been born and raised in the city)." She had admired his "high refined absence of rancour and personal savagery," and she missed him "in the way you miss something that is never going to be even approximated again":

> He was an inveterate arguer, loved to argue, was disappointed to find anyone agreeing with him; yet, because he was a gent in a deep way, he never "argued for victory" or got personally abusive. He was, if anything, over-receptive to points made against his own view—would swing around and reverse himself when convinced he was wrong. That could madden you—"What, Dwight, do you have no consistency at all?"

The following year, it was Lillian Hellman; Shirley and Francis toasted her memory on Capri. This was another long friendship, and they had continued to spend time with Lillian intermittently in recent years. Shirley made notes of one meeting from 1979, when Lillian was still mobile:

> Calls me to take her for a walk. (She almost blind, after operation, overkill of médecins). Fine, mild day. Down Madison to 59th, where we sit at counter in a Japanese restaurant. She says, "Let's get this straight. This is my lunch." I protest. She says: "Shirley, don't cross me. I'm a dying woman." And so she is. Courage, the laughter. "Those who would hide you"—ie when on the run . . . This is a test, pre-eminently, of independence of character. There is no telling in advance, from any "rule" who would be brave. But one does know who goes with the pack—even if it is their own little pack—and who stands alone. Rare, the latter.

Months before her death Lillian came for dinner: "What spirit can still invest a shred of suffering humanity. Now entirely blind, a scrap, a bone; scarcely able to walk—comes with friends in taxi two blocks, met by wheel-chair, carried into our flat; carried to bathroom, food chopped

for her at table, hand guided to glass, and to the fatal and inevitable cigarette. Why is she nevertheless so much more real and life like than many
many others? Still, this round has taken it out of her—she is a wraith of
what was." She likened the aged Lillian to

> what one might imagine—I mean, truly and deeply imagine—
> Queen Eliz (the first I mean . . . ) to have been in age; an un-
> subdued spirit but tremendous canniness about experience; much
> self-dramatisation, and much astonishing direct insight and, per-
> haps oddly, courtesy, consideration, at times. Steel as well as fire.
> I felt last night—as we are near departure—I might not see her
> again. However, she has amazed us before on this theme. She told
> me she feels terribly reduced in mind as well as body: "I always
> had an idea of who I was. Now I lie awake in the night wondering
> who I am, what I seem to people now." I told her that most people
> never even get round to wondering who they are. That produced
> her pleased and husky laugh—voice still deep in the frame of a
> little bird.

Shirley had begun work on another novel, but she was also preoccupied and distracted by other, mostly public, concerns. In early 1980, with
Francis, she had composed "a stern letter" to President Carter and Sen-
ator Moynihan to protest their Intelligence Reform Act, describing it as
a "plan for unleashing anew the CIA," and she encouraged friends to
follow suit. This was by no means an isolated protest. At the start of 1981
she wrote Elizabeth Harrower that in the course of the previous year she
and Francis had "literally written thousands of letters between us."

> We have no help, must beat them out ourselves; civil rights, hu-
> man rights, congressmen, UN reformers, decent citizens, account
> for more than half; real work for the rest. The writing of such
> letters has become an immense burden to me, and I fear this year
> the world will somehow have to do without me as a public-spirited
> missive-mailer. The writing of UN articles also has just about
> killed me, and has a lethal effect on real work . . . But no one else

will do these particular things. However, no one else will write my novel either.

Alan Maclean and Francis asked Elizabeth Harrower to try to convince Shirley to concentrate on writing her novel rather than all these public letters and articles, but this was something Elizabeth felt she could not do. In a pattern that would endure, and to Shirley's increasing chagrin, Francis was able to continue working solidly despite such disruptions and was now close to finishing the second volume of Flaubert letters (the first was being reprinted, having sold out before its official release) while she remained distracted by her other commitments. Francis's projects still largely determined their travel, in ways that brought, also, enchantment. In June 1981 they flew from Rome to Tunis to view the ruins of Carthage. They stayed at Sidi Bou Said with a friend whose house had appeared in the opening scene of Flaubert's *Salammbô*, returning to Naples on the weekly overnight boat. Shirley recorded the scene in her notebook: "Vast beauty of bay encircled by small mountains," with historical details: "Scipio took the Punic forces by surprise by going behind Zaghouan, which was to have been their last retreat, instead of attacking only from the coast"; flora: "Oleanders, cypress, eucalypts, figtrees in abundance, bougainvillea, jasmine, geraniums, palms, pines"; also people: "stalls of nougat and nuts. Man carrying tray of jasmine wrought on stem (men wear behind ear) and wreaths for women's necks." And, always, "the light, an event in itself."

News came that film rights to *The Transit of Venus* had been sold to United American and Australasian Productions. It was to be directed by Gillian Armstrong, whose landmark 1979 film, *My Brilliant Career*, Shirley had admired. She and Armstrong met in Rome that summer, and Armstrong remembered her as "warm and gentle and very enthused . . . that a young Australian woman had done so well," pleased in particular at "the possibility of the film of her book." She was struck by Shirley's intellect and the "inner steel" she detected beneath her warmth and gentleness. Armstrong, however, quit the project early after it became clear that UAA had rather different ideas from hers about the film. Later, Patricia Lovell was signed as producer; again, Shirley was pleased: "She is a very nice person—gifted, lively, straightforward, and interested in many things which her earlier, conventional life as a housewife, mother etc had kept her apart from. I like her v much." However, even though the production company had put "quite a lot of money into Viking's advertising of the book in order to get up public interest supposedly," progress on the film stalled, then halted altogether. Shortly after, Shirley began discussions with Pat Lovell over a film of *The Evening of the Holiday*. This too floundered, although a screenplay was produced—there had been a suggestion, sternly rejected by the author, that the heroine might be Australian—and the proposal revised several times over the next decade, but this project did not eventuate either.

The draft of "Mount Victoria" that she had sent to Knopf back in 1960 had long since been discarded, but she was pursuing Henry Robbins's suggestion that she make use of the postwar Hong Kong setting for a novel. In May 1984 she wrote in her notebook: "Title: The Great Fire (cover: Turner painting of Houses of Parliament burning.)" She had most likely decided on its central story as she was finishing *Transit*, compelled by the reconnection with Alec in 1979. Three years after that, she and Chris Cooper visited their old friend together. In September 1982 Shirley flew from Italy to London, and then she and Chris drove to Wales, stopping first at Chris's "(shattered!) old stone house in poetic countryside—fells, woods, streams, all stone buildings," past Tintern Abbey, "glory," winding on to the Vedeniapines' farm outside Whitland. The welcome was warm and affectionate. Shirley took immediately to the Vedeniapines' son, Peter, "very nice, grown, quiet, witty. I say, stroking Feetham the cat at breakfast with the back of my hand: 'I can't use my hand because there's honey on it and she'd be washing herself all day long.' Peter: 'She's got no other plans.'"—an exchange she later used in *The Great Fire*. Shirley was anxious throughout the visit, had not slept well, felt she talked too much: "I feel I should be quieter—one performs."

Shirley and Chris were shown around, met neighbours, admired cats and garden. She felt how much more anxious she would have been had Francis been with her but wished he could have seen the countryside. She was unconcerned about any awkwardness that might have been experienced by Alec's wife, Cynthia, who continued to be "extremely hospitable." In the evening, there was "much talk of the East, photographs. Always, the fact. Also, a consciousness of what he has renounced. I 'renounced'—failed life with him, and went on, miraculously, to life. He renounced his larger life." On this she was adamant, unforgiving. The sorrow of that first, devastating romance had not left her; she measured her own achievements against Alec's and found *him*, above all, wanting. She felt vindicated and was struck above all by "this theme—this transcendent theme—of fulfilment and non-fulfilment; and those who bind themselves to limitations . . ." There is a coldness in her assessment of the situation, the scene, suggesting that the matter was not closed for her. Her friend Alison Parente, to whom she spoke years later of this visit, felt there was on Shirley's part a rather brutal refusal to countenance the significance of Alec's marriage and present life. Questions about the enduring meaning of that early love, and of their lives since parting, would continue to preoccupy her as the writing of her fourth novel proceeded with agonising slowness over the years that followed.

In the spring of 1982 Shirley had been invited to deliver a series of three lectures for the Gauss Seminars at Princeton. These lectures, to which she gave the title "The Lonely Word," provided an occasion to set out formally her sense of the larger significance of literature: from the public role of the poet to the close relationship between poetry and truth, the nature of literary fame and longevity and of poetic remembrance. For the first lecture she drew on her experience in Naples the previous year, of attending the commemorations of the *bimillenario*—the two-thousand-year celebration—of the death of Virgil, which included weekly readings of the *Aeneid* in Latin, at various historic sites, including Lucullus's castle. She had found it all "thrilling" and "Tennysonian." In a way these lectures were a culmination of her lifelong project of passionate self-education, her encyclopaedic curiosity and preternatural memory for poetry, and her desire to pay tribute to the past. The Steegmullers' friend the Princeton French scholar Victor Brombert recalled that the talks were beautiful but somewhat overladen—"studded"—with quotations. Joyce Carol Oates was also there and described the lectures as "impressionistic, marvellously informed, inimitable," and Shirley herself as "infinitely gracious, serene, attractive, beautifully informed."

The Steegmullers had a complex relation to the academy. Many of their friends held academic positions, and they were regularly invited to speak to academic audiences. At the same time, both remained defiantly outside academic life and were hostile to the formal practice of literary criticism, particularly as it had developed in the postwar decades. Shirley set out her objections at some length in a 1976 essay, "A Jaded Muse." Apart from his brief time at the University of Wisconsin-Madison in the 1920s, Francis had always worked as a private scholar, a category that in itself harked back to earlier times and was already a rarity in the mid-century. He was rather sensitive to his position outside the formal academy; his friend the medieval historian Giles Constable felt that Francis saw himself as not properly appreciated and his work not really accepted by academic scholars, although there is plenty to suggest that the reverse was true. Edward Said was an admirer of *Flaubert in Egypt*, which he taught in his Columbia Orientalism seminar. And Francis had been a regular guest speaker at Bill Weaver's translation classes at Columbia through the 1970s. On occasion there were points of difference and complication in the reception of his work, some of which rankled. For instance, the *New York Times* review by the Oxford French scholar Enid Starkie of his 1963 *Apollinaire: Poet Among the Painters* had led to a sharp exchange of letters, which the *Times* also published. Starkie praised the book but noted some slips in the scholarly citations. Francis took umbrage: "Must it be assumed that one is ignorant of every publication one does not mention?" The exchange illustrates the kind of negotiation made necessary by working as a belletristic scholar outside the academy, unconfined by its protocols. He and Enid Starkie went on to establish warm relations.

Shirley had rather less direct contact with the academy, but those associations were also often vexed. In the late 1970s she had had a rather brusque exchange with William Scheick of the University of Texas, Austin, who had asked her to contribute a piece to a special issue of *Texas Studies in Literature and Language* that he was compiling on Patrick White. He asked if she might waive payment for the piece, a suggestion she found "discouraging." She wrote that "not only do all writers I know 'sometimes do things for the love of them alone,' but indeed rarely have an alternative," and that she never ceased to wonder "at the expectation that writers, alone of working persons, should receive no remuneration for their labours." This was, she felt, a reflection of "the attitude of society towards creative persons." A few years later, when Scheick contacted her again, this time to arrange an interview to be included in another special issue of the journal, on contemporary women writers, she apologised. "You are very large-hearted to write to me after my irascible letters, some years ago, on the theme of the unpaid author," adding that she would be "honoured to be included."

It was through private friendships rather than formal institutions that the Steegmullers maintained their connection to scholars and scholarship. One such was with Donald Keene, another Columbia professor of Japanese literature, whom Shirley met at Ivan Morris's funeral. A few years older than Morris, Keene was also a friend, translator, and correspondent of Yukio Mishima and had served as an intelligence officer in the U.S. Navy during the Second World War. While interrogating Japanese prisoners of war, Keene had discovered their diaries, had written about them, and had gone on to forge an especially intimate connection with Japan. Near the end of his long and distinguished life, much of it spent living there, he was granted Japanese citizenship, a rare honour. Shirley's friendship with Keene was one of the most vital of her later life. Their shared reading and conversation were important for her, and he described her as "one of the most extraordinary people" he had ever met. Other significant friendships were forged through such institutions as the American Academy of Arts and Letters. Francis had been elected a member in 1966, with William Styron and Edward Albee. In 1982 he received the Academy's award for biography, and Shirley was elected an academy member; both, as Donald Keene wrote to Elizabeth Harrower, "signal honors in a country which does not often pay homage to writers." Francis's citation was given by the Henry James biographer Leon Edel. Other organisations, such as the New York Society Library, of which both she and Francis were members—Shirley a trustee from 1974 until her late years—and the Century Association, a private New York club for writers and artists, were also important in their social lives.

In summer 1982 they were both invited to speak at a congress of translators in Rome, attended by the novelist Anthony Burgess, whom Shirley found "a very entertaining and clever speaker, but an ego of truly preposterous dimensions; accompanied and abetted by wife, Italian, swathed in black burnous and affecting a bohemianism I'd have thought about 50 years out of date." The following year, in Naples, she attended a conference of papyrologists. This was a kind of consolidation of her immersion in the city of Naples, its streets and buildings, but also its deep history. A few years previously she had been introduced to the Naples historian Carlo Knight (whose name derived from "English ancestors who came to Naples to be court jewellers to Maria Carolina and other Bourbons"). Knight in turn brought the Steegmullers into his Neapolitan circles, introducing Shirley to "the sort of people she wanted to know," including Barone Maurizio Barracco and his wife, Mirella, who owned the Villa Emma on Posillipo, where the Steegmullers would later rent a small apartment. The house and grounds of the villa were a source of joy, as Shirley wrote after her first visit: "Magnificent house and grounds, splendidly kept. Pompeiian red. Neapolitan hounds, sand-coloured, lie lion-like in grass. Enfilade of high rooms filled with light. Lunch in long room, series of windows on bay. A vast terrace over the sea. A paradise." In 1984 the Barraccos set up Fondazione Napoli Novantanove (Naples 99), aimed at drawing the attention of Naples's citizens to the wealth of art in their city, through the "Porte Aperte" program, which opened, on scheduled days, hundreds of historic buildings that had been closed to the public for many years, some for so long that no locals could remember their interiors. The program had a dramatic and revitalising effect on the city, drawing visitors from the rest of Italy and abroad, and Shirley was animated by it all. The Barraccos were impressed, too, by the Steegmullers' deep engagement with and love of Naples, "not only the Gulf, which is beautiful, but the historic heart of the city," a long familiarity that reached back to a time when visitors to the city "did not dare" to walk about. At the Barraccos' invitation, Shirley spoke, in Italian (by all accounts her Italian was impeccable), at a Fondazione event in the ballroom of Villa Pignatelli, in Chiaia. She had been invited, she explained to Elizabeth Harrower, "as foreigners' words count somewhat in embarrassing officialdom; but never so nervous . . . Lovely, kind audience; I had made notes but deplore speeches that are just read off, so it ended up conversational."

Carlo Knight provided two further important introductions, the first to Roberto Pane, historian of art and architecture at the University Naples Federico II. Shirley wrote of him to Chris Cooper in 1983: "Roberto Pane, polymath of 87 years, historian of Naples, artist, architect, classicist, legend, scourge, omnivorous reader . . . Energies exhausting to those half his age. Fearless in exposing incompetence and corruption, tireless in challenging officialdom. Often arrogant in manner; but such faults are used as an excuse for ignoring the mighty truths on which his arguments repose—although repose is not a word otherwise associated with him." Pane was very much Shirley's kind of man. And the feeling was reciprocated. Knight said that in a way Pane "fell in love with her." Pane also took memorable photographic portraits of her, celebrating the refined beauty of her middle age. Shirley described a conversation with him to Donald Keene:

> Roberto Pane was inveighing the other day to us against some massive work on Bernini produced by a Princeton Prof . . . which apparently reproduces every last detail of every minute evidence of Bernini's life without distinction etc. Pane, leaping from his chair with outrage, burst out against this author's insensibility towards historical experience: "He mentions the Counter-Reformation in passing—in passing! As if it were no more than a road accident. To us!—who have it still (drawing fingers down his arm) on our very skin!" ("La Controriforma!—che noi abbiamo sempre sulla pelle!")

She recorded a visit by Pane to Capri one autumn day when a tremendous storm broke as they sat on the terrace after lunch. She was as thrilled by Pane's excitement as by the spectacle:

> A Capri storm—all forces, Nature, unleashed. When I said that storms were a greater drama on Capri, he said it was in part the

reverberations from the rock face, from the amphitheatrical con-
figurations and recesses: "With certain thunders, the very grottoes
resound." So many observations—such erudition—he consumes
one with one's effort to sustain his energy, let alone meet it. Epi-
curus, Lucretius, Petrarch (dialogue with Saint Augustine), Fried-
lander, Edgar Wind, Gaudi, above all Virgil; Proust, Baudelaire . . .
He says Virgil probably came to Capri—accompanying Augustus,
to read to the Emperor here. Very probable. (To think of Virgil, at
Palazzo a Mare . . . )

Pane was one of Shirley's models for exemplary comportment, for
huge enthusiasm, high feeling, excitement at the world and at what it
was possible to know, and for art and intellect and understanding. She
aspired to the quality that Pane himself most valued, that of "Coerenza,"
which, she explained to Donald Keene, "in the Italian sense, means con-
sistency and a sort of integrity of persistence (as well as having our own
sense, clarity)." She quoted Pane saying that he would "defend with my
last breath the memory of the human past." These values were central to
her life; learning ingrained with lived experience, with feeling, "sempre
sulla pelle."

Carlo Knight also introduced her to Marcello Gigante, a philologist,
papyrologist, and scholar of Greek. Knight and Gigante had been responsible, in 1980, for discovering the location of the Villa dei Papiri near
Naples; they "identified the lost entrance to the eighteenth-century dig
at the Villa dei Papiri—hidden in a well in the 'modern' town of Herculaneum; and thus established the 'ubicazione' of the villa itself, which
had been lost." Shirley was completely caught up in the excitement,
the "wonderful adventure" of the discovery. "She felt in the middle of
this. When she met Gigante, she practically became one of the papyrologists." What excited her most of all, Knight recalled, was the idea
that unknown writings by Virgil might be discovered in the library. She
accompanied Knight and Gigante first to the International Congress of
Papyrology, held in Naples in 1983, about which she wrote for *The New
Yorker*, and, some years later, on a special tour of the Pozzo Veneruso, the
just-opened central shaft of the Villa dei Papiri. She was delighted by

A FATED CONNECTION   359

the congress—"Formidable erudition was imparted with an amiability whose very disclaimers were stylish ('I am not myself a demoticist')"— particularly at finding her own principles and concerns echoed there by others: "The concept of written language was not common to all ancient cultures, and trends of our own era indicate how it might die out or revert, as in past ages, to a skill practiced by an accomplished few. In such a context, every gesture of civilized meaning gives courage. As the Naples congress closed, its organizing spirit, Professor Marcello Gigante, director of the Institute of Classical Philology at the University of Naples, described it as '*un atto di amore*' on the part of Naples toward culture." In her extended account, brimming over with technical detail, and her own animation, of descending into the villa, she set the moment into the context of the anglophone rediscovery of Italy: "To have entered the Villa dei Papiri on a recent spring morning is to invoke Horace Walpole, who, describing in 1740 the first revelations at Herculaneum, wrote home to England: 'We have seen something today that I am sure you never read of, and perhaps never heard of . . . there might certainly be collected great light from this reservoir of antiquities if a man of learning had the inspection of it.'"

From 1979, the Steegmullers rented an apartment on Capri in the Via Sopramonte, with a terrace looking out across the gulf towards Naples, and from 1984, in Naples, an apartment off the Barraccos' Villa Emma in Posillipo, its terrace covered in bougainvillea, looking out on the bay and in the distance to the islands and, closer in, around the bay to Vesuvius. Continuity in their lives was created by the rhythm of moving between these apartments and Manhattan according to the seasons, two or three trips each year, back and forth, restorative. In Rome they stayed always at the Hassler hotel, at the top of the Spanish Steps (reputedly at reduced rates), dined at Otello, a short walk away, and they had regular drivers, the Casillo brothers, to take them to and from Naples. There was also their Naples driver, Salvatore Marigliano, who would be with them for the rest of their Italian lives.

Shirley's embrace of Italy was always with an eye to the past; her friend of later years Robert Harrison recalled that what she loved about Naples was the sense that the city had not altered, essentially, for centuries. She felt that "if Virgil were to sail one day into the Bay of Naples, he would recognise it, it would be an unchanged landscape. What she loved was the tenacity with which Naples has remained constant and unchanged." There was also, always, in her response, a sense of the vitality of her own associations, and she recorded these too, binding her own life and experience into the changing scene as she observed it. In late 1980, returning to Rome, she noted that it was twenty-four years, "almost to the day," since she had first arrived there:

> Yesterday evening, driving from Naples, we entered by Porta San Giovanni in Laterano, having passed the same Ciampino. Then, I was going to Naples for the first time. The story since, my life. The change of the city—ambiente as it was then close to the past, even with traces of the rural and much of the provincial. Now—the screaming materialism of the Condotti-Frattina strip, armed guards, police in armoured vest . . . Money, anger, crime, indecency in all forms, while also physical health, relative material gains, less humiliation of the helpless poor.

And alongside her delight at the remembrance and the longevity of her association sat the melancholy of past journeys, of first arrivals and, always, departures: "Byron to TG [Teresa, Contessa Guiccioli, Byron's last lover] from Ravenna, Autumn 1820: 'Each year this season kills me with sadness.' Leaving Italy.'"

She recorded the changing views from her Naples and Capri homes almost daily in her notebooks, detailed scenes that brought together momentous and unremarkable events and the stages of her life in a new and significant coherence:

> An hour's heavy rain in the night. Second brief rain in three months. Clearer, cooler, but still humid morning . . . Before going to piazza I saw a stroke of white at sea—a sail, two sails, but far out and blurred. A large yacht, possibly. Took alterations to Signora Romana. Chicca has four kittens, tiny, still blind, in a box. Came home; to lunch at Arco. On arrival, saw nearby at sea, headed for Salerno, a four-masted barque, white, white sails. Had forgot-

ten her earlier appearance. A beautiful, dreamlike sight—one could only think how many such passed these waters. She came on, alone—nothing near her at sea. A fair wind, and she moved steadily; stately but with an effect of floating in air as much as on sea. Strange even to think there were men aboard her. After a while, small, fast boats streaked out to look at her, a tanker appeared and crossed her course, she grew fainter. However her slight cloud of white was visible a long time. (Perfectly described in Praz, "House of Life.") In 1957, recovering from hepatitis, I saw a great barque put out under sail from my balcony at Posillipo. One afternoon, a Saturday or rather a Sunday. Her sails not white but tawny, lacquered with use and brine. As a child I used to see the Pamir at Circular Quay, at the same pier—now a group of modern flats—where the Taiping was docked. Tonight a high wind came up, shaking the doors and windows, prelude to much-awaited storm perhaps. Ship safely at Salerno, in port . . .

These writings are not simply a diary record of events, nor merely fragments that might later generate scenes or characters or story lines. Her daily observations, the mapping of light and water, of island or city lives, of ships and cats and lizards and birds, are a testament to her days. Through them she forged an intricate, intimate connection to place, to the places that became over the years her home.

In Rome, the Steegmullers regularly saw their Capri friends Vittorio and Isabella Ripa di Meana, who lived near the Hassler. They also saw Giulio Colavolpe Severi, a political analyst at the Italian public broadcaster RAI, whom Shirley had befriended on a Rome–to–New York flight. Giulio and Francis became particularly close. Shirley reflected, later, of the two men, "What an unexpected friendship, theirs." They saw Giulio whenever they were in Rome, and he and his family visited them on Capri. They went with him to Oriolo Romano, north of Rome, to the home of his parents-in-law, driving, as Shirley wrote,

by back roads and about a century . . . out of step with current affairs. What serenity, what simplicity—a stone town, little more than a village where almost everything is seventeenth or eighteenth century, where great avenues of elms radiate from the piazza ("le olmate" which I learn are celebrated) where no tourist could be seen, there was nothing chic, no boutiques, no shops other than household kind, and the small stone houses are without exception . . . of fine proportions and in fine condition . . .

A few years later they visited Giulio's family house at Fano on the Adriatic, "to spend some summer days; beautiful and unforgettable." They engaged one of their drivers and made, in "hot summer, dry white light, a magnificent diagonal drive through Abruzzo to the Adriatic and then into the Marche. Not another car on the road until we came to the sea at Vasto. Marvellous ledge-like 'scenic' road until, after Ancona, we drove briefly inland to visit Recanati." Recanati, the "native 'paese' of Leopardi," was itself a site of pilgrimage. The town remained, Shirley wrote, as Leopardi had immortalised it, "fairly breathing out his suffering there, his ecstasy over the surrounding countryside and the sea, in short, his genius."

On Capri she celebrated the embeddedness of time and habit and ritual. She wrote one October to Patricia Clarke:

Here—it is summer still, after some colossal equinoctial storms. Tonight a full moon—and a small wavering light on top of the mountain at the little church of Cetrella; a long steep walk up to it; one goes rarely. Once there, on a fine day, it is paradise, with a great view of what seems to be most of Italy. At this time of year a young Anacaprese goes up regularly for a day or two, sometimes with companions, to paint and restore the very damp interior of the church. Once a year, a mass is still held there for mariners. (Most Capri mariners now make their fortunes taking tourists to the Grotta Azzurra but doubtless they still deserve our prayers.) Such silence . . . such velvety nights and soft air . . . all hotels closed but one, most restaurants, all fancy shops. I wish we could have stayed all November . . . We spent a day at Ninfa last week, south of Rome—incredible beauty, streams, flowers, ruins, a Corot light.

Naples continued to entrance; her fascination and deep familiarity was with the life of the streets as well as the art treasures. She wrote over and over of this to friends:

A week ago we were sitting in church in Naples looking at a great altar-picture—where "gloomy Caravaggio's gloomier stain / Bronz'd o'er some lean and stoic anchorite." The really tremendous Caravaggio in the Misericordia is only accessible at Sunday morning Mass. Also, numerous other works in churches can only be seen on mornings of feast-days . . . We decided to spend Saturday night in Naples, go to these monuments on Sunday morning and head home on Sunday afternoon. We were thus at Mass four entire times on the Day of the Dead—plus some fragments. Saw also the Donatello tomb in Sant'Angelo a Nilo and various other splendours. The church where the Caravaggio is, within the great palazzo of the Misericordia is itself a terrific sight, extraordinarily narrow, high and very beautiful interior. Between these holy undertakings I was "mugged," harmlessly, by a youth (burly) who struck me—presumably to command my attention—while with his other hand snatching my (trash only) purse. He reckoned without my vice-like grip on the purse, and my returning his blow not by presenting another cheek but by giving him a hearty slap (cheered by crowd of bystanders). He ran off and we went into Scaturchio, which was crammed with worshippers and had cappuccino and cornetti with the preserved L2000.

She loved to recount the story of their visit to the pet cemetery early in their Naples years. The concierge of the Excelsior Hotel where they stayed gave them directions to the cemetery, somewhere near Virgil's tomb, at Mergellina. "Anybody can go," he told them, "And you can take your pet, whatever it is, to be buried. There are only two rules: it must be in a box, and the box must be open. *Perché l'uomo è capace di tutto.* [Because man is capable of anything.]"

In the spring of 1983 they were joined by Everett Fahy. Everett had

not been to Capri before and "only rarely and sporadically in this region."
There were "revelations for him, much enjoyed by us. He produced just
the right sharp intake of breath on being 'taken' into certain cortili and
chiostri of Naples." Their friendship was of long standing, nearly twenty
years, but Shirley felt that they "entered another dimension" on this trip,
"partly from sharing so many joys—some of them new for all three of
us; many of them enhanced for us by sharing them with Everett for the
first time." They went south to Reggio Calabria, to see *I Bronzi*, two fifth-
century BC bronze statues that had been brought from the sea at Riace a
decade before and been recently, finally, installed in the Museo Nazionale
della Magna Grecia at Reggio: "Stupendous, Homeric; something 'new'
to absorb." They drove from Sorrento, stopping along the way at Padula
"to see the stupendous certosa," and stayed overnight at Cosenza, "an
ancient town clustered around hilltop, now being gradually abandoned
because of discomfort while a big, characterless agglomeration of modern blocks takes over on the plain below." She remarked everywhere the
changes in the ancient landscape: "The relative prosperity and modern
convenience of the plaster barracks of a new town, encircling and strangling the old one recurs; one sees the orchards (whole countrysides of
peach and cherry blossom, of vast olive groves and lemon and orange
trees) still flowering for a last time among the blocks of flats where their
companions have been uprooted." Back in Naples, she went with Everett
to Virgil's tomb, and to Leopardi's "in the same beautiful solitary place"
on the morning of his departure. She wrote to Elizabeth Harrower, "The
fortnight here was characterised by Everett as a revelation. Well, it always is revelation here, I find. We went to San Carlo to hear Moussorg-
sky's opera of Flaubert's 'Salammbô'—magnificent music, well sung, but
doleful and unsuitable mis-en-scène I thought. Thus Uncle Gustave is
still with is."

In the summer of 1983, in what might later have come to be seen as
a harbinger of falls and frailty to come, Francis was knocked down in a
Naples street by two men on a motorcycle. As he wrote in a memorable
essay, the scene and event were familiar enough: "The victim carrying,
most indiscreetly, a bag; the assailants—the *scippatori* as they are called
in Naples—motorized, swift, skilled at snatching, careless of maiming.

The victim, from instinct or defiance, attempts to retain the bag, is in consequence thrown to the ground by the velocity of the motorcycle and dragged some distance—feet or yards—until the bag has conclusively changed hands." The vivid impersonality of the writing, its suggestion of generalised experience, gives some sense of the violence of the event, and its terror. Later in the essay he revisits the moment of impact, providing all the detail that might be wanted, but that detail is itself set in the context of the larger drama, of the Naples streets, both before and after the theft. He gives a brief history and topography of the area where they had been strolling, the Porta Capuana, one of the ancient city gates of Naples: "Outside the gate, a dry moat, then a busy open ground, site in past centuries of gardens and of a celebrated outdoor theatre; now traffic-ridden, populous, poor, and unresolved; exposed, in high summer, to a grimy sun: Piazza San Francesco." He observes, "These summer evenings in Naples belong to the poor," as everyone who can afford to leave for the coast, or the countryside or abroad, has gone.

> All afternoon, the city languishes in the long siesta, reviving only with the approach of night. At dusk, in the ancient central quarters, shutters are flung back, Neapolitans appear at doors and windows and on the innumerable small balconies that project from upper floors. Men and women and whole families saunter into the cooling streets to take up their parts in the vast theater of city life—a performance in which tourists rarely appear and few outsiders can even claim a walk-on role.

Implicit in the scene, in the story, is the couple's deep and local familiarity. They walked down Spaccanapoli, greeted a family celebrating around a wooden table that was "crowded with dishes, bowls of fruit, bottles," the table set up in "a dusty crevice between palazzi, beneath a tiny pergola of grapevines." The family returned their greeting—"But watch out for the bag." Around the corner, the same warning, with the offer of some grilled sweet corn. When the *scippatori* struck, Francis was dragged some yards along the pavement; then he blacked out.

Next, the frantic drive by two "Samaritans" who had been passing, white handkerchief held out the car window, to one hospital then an-other, a sequence, a rush, of generosity, care, civility. Recalling that the hospital orderly had addressed him as "*Professore*," Francis commented: "I am not a professor, but in Naples, where designations are inspired by appearance, one perforce acquires an idea of one's type." Carlo Knight arrived to help, donated pyjamas; then his wife, Ella, joined Shirley in the corridor outside: "their lovely faces, their contrasting beauties—dark and fair—and their pretty clothes (Ella an angel in blue and white linen, S a Modigliani), their air of summer health and well-being." His spirits lifted, Francis was greeted by hospital workers: "How do I feel? Better? I already look better! All will be well, *Professore*; everything passes away. Such is life; such is fate, our destiny." The following day, with Francis dis-charged, amid preparations for departure to Rome and New York, Shirley went to the Naples Questura to make the report required for the insurance claim. After recording her profession as "writer," the police officer "laid down his pen to ask, earnestly, 'And what future, Signora, do you see for the arts in such an epoch as our own?'—a question that occupied them for some time." And when Shirley left, the same officer insisted on calling her a taxi despite her saying that she wanted to go by foot. "I'll telephone for a taxi—if only because, after such an experience as yours, my dear Signora, one may feel too solitary. Let us spare you at least that lonely walk."

In September 1984 Saul Bellow came to Capri to receive the Premio Malaparte. Shirley was on the island alone; Francis, who knew Bellow slightly, was due to arrive in a few days. The evening before the ceremony Shirley had run into Alberto Moravia on her way to dine with friends. Moravia seemed to her "more compact" than before, and well dressed in "Capri clothes." She greeted him tentatively, and he responded with enthusiasm, asking after Francis: "I would like so much to see him. We know each other so long . . . You come often to Rome, but you never get in touch. You must let me know." After speaking with Moravia about the ceremony that was to take place the next day, Shirley wrote a note to Bellow, introducing herself and giving her phone number in case Bellow might "care to see a different Capri." The next morning, she attended the ceremony at the Certosa di San Giacomo, a fourteenth-century for-

mer monastery. She was consulted on pronunciation of some names—
Isaac B. Singer and Augie March—for the citation and at the lunch was
seated at Bellow's side. Later, in her diary, she wondered, "He possibly
asked this?—was it to speak English? In any case, then began a delightful hour." Shirley was delighted at being able "to speak from the great
underswell of poetry and literature, and art, without pretension, without
literariness or artiness—or artfulness, or artifice. Tried not to monopolise . . . We spoke about 'enemies we would not forgive,'" and about
"Hamlet, Shakespeare," and laughed a lot. "Nice face in laughter—very
fine skin, wrinkled, like silk over the refined features. Around us, above
us, the pines—fragrant, sighing in the wind . . . Check shirt, lightweight
dark suit. Well-dressed, good face." Bellow mentioned Lillian Hellman,
and Shirley responded that they "remained friendly." He continued: "'It
didn't bother you that she lied?' 'Yes of course. But there was more to
her than that and we didn't like those who were profiting from the attack.' . . . (Esprit de l'escalier: I should have said 'She did tell lies but she
could also tell the truth. The others rightly envied her that capacity.')"
After lunch they walked together up the steep path to the Villa Jovis,
trailed by a crowd of journalists.

———■———

Through the first half of 1984, Shirley had been preoccupied with
writing a series of lectures for the Australian Broadcasting Corporation.
The annual Boyer Lectures, broadcast on ABC radio, are given by prominent Australians from a range of backgrounds with the aim of stimulating debate. She found the writing challenging—"These lectures are
killing me," she wrote Donald Keene in June—not simply the formal
demands of public address but the larger question of how to speak in and
about the country of her birth, so long held in conflicted relation. Her
lectures were brave. They presented a strong criticism of "long traditions
of nationalism . . . a nationalism which at present runs high in Australia,
and which, in my view at least, might prove detrimental to ideas and
standards if it is not reconsidered." She went further:

Australians themselves are impatient with complacency when they find it elsewhere. To the civilising current—to what the philosopher William James called "the appreciative chronicle of human master strokes"—Australia's contribution is distinguished, but as yet small. It might even be thought disproportionately small, given the relative ease and liberty, the endless opportunities which many Australians enjoy. But master-strokes are mysterious in origin, and not always lured by opportunity.

And more sharply: "Australia is not an innocent country. This nation's short recorded history is shadowed, into the present day, by the fate of its native peoples, by forms of unyielding prejudice, by a strain of derision and unexamined violence, and by a persistent current of misogyny." Her comments provoked, in some quarters, fury, mostly at the fact that she was making these claims having long since left Australia; it was perhaps felt that this in itself should have disqualified her from speaking so trenchantly. Many years later, reflecting on this reception, the novelist Michelle de Kretser observed, also sharply, that the nationalism that had been the object of Hazzard's criticisms was itself instrumental in the public repudiation of her lectures, disqualifying her from "offering any opinion about the country that wasn't wholly complimentary." There was also, in some quarters, a sense of something like betrayal, given the sharp difference of tone and mood in these lectures from the celebratory account she had provided eight years earlier, in her *New Yorker* "Letter from Australia." The Boyer invitation had presumably been extended in part on the basis of that earlier piece; if so, the organisers had possibly overlooked her deep and often stated conviction to "bring the truth home to people."

She had established some substantial connections to Australia in recent years. In addition to Elizabeth Harrower, she had developed friendships with a number of prominent Australians: the poet and editor Geoffrey Dutton and his then wife, Ninette; the former premier of South Australia Don Dunstan; Edmund Capon, director of the Art Gallery of New South Wales, and his wife, Joanna; and the art patron Ann Lewis; as well as with the writers Patrick White, David Malouf, and Murray Bail, and, in New York, Sumner Locke Elliott. She corresponded with Geoffrey Dutton and

Murray Bail for some years and remained friendly with Ninette Dutton and the Capons. Some, like Don Dunstan, were initially welcomed but would come to frustrate and irritate; on the other hand, David Malouf, "an exceptional person: a generous mind," remained an important if rather distant association. Sumner Locke Elliott, more than all the rest, became close. He was rather older than Shirley and had been living in the United States since 1948, first in Los Angeles, then in New York, writing for theatre and later for television. He was the long-term partner of the screenwriter Whitfield Cook, and was closeted until his 1990 coming-out novel, *Fairyland.* Clever and hilarious, Sumner was known as one of the television producer Fred Coe's "Golden Seven" screenwriters, along with Paddy Chayefsky, Tad Mosel, and, later, Gore Vidal. Whitfield Cook told Sumner's biographer that Sumner had been asked to write the screenplay for *Breakfast at Tiffany's* but was replaced when he refused to change the sexuality of the protagonist (there seems to be no other record of this). Gore Vidal described him as "A great wit. Very charming," although that friendship was often vexed. Evan Cornog met him often at Shirley's and said that "in an ideal mass entertainment world, Sumner Locke Elliott would be a perennial guest on every talk show. He was a fascinating talker, a wonderfully large-scale personality." Sumner shared with Shirley an ambivalence toward Australia, a sense of being unappreciated there because their success had been achieved overseas.

Shirley described Sumner as "a current in my life . . . He was funny and generous with his wit, as with everything else . . . His sensibilities were, like his animation, a way of bringing life. His vitality was never wearing; it was delightful." The pair shared memories of the Sydney of their childhood, Sumner providing a relentlessly comic take that helped Shirley maintain a liveable distance. In their lengthy "Australian conversations" on the telephone, Sumner deployed a fanciful version of the spoken vernacular of that time, which habitually left Shirley "speechless and wiping away tears of laughter," as did his letters:

Dear Shirl and Frank, It was bosker to get your card, cobber, and know youse are never out of your cozzies, half your luck mate and that you are feeling better, look a real relief to my mind, like

I didn't want to write and arsk so thanks for the info. Oh dear old Shirl, you are going to live to be eighty five and become tiresome . . . I am pleased you and Frank are happy and you must enjoy yourself to the full and don't give us a thought though how you can stand those Eyetalians is beyond me and so risky eating that foreign food and being so near a Volcano . . .

Shirley drew a certain comic licence from Sumner's comedy, that offered protection from Kit's chaos as it edged closer to what she referred to as Shirley's "lovely life." Traces of his voice might also be heard in the comic-grotesque tones of the Australian characters in her two later novels.

With other Australians there were significant disagreements. Shirley was dismayed by a common Australian response to Bruce Beresford's 1980 film *Breaker Morant*, which told the story of the prosecution for war crimes of Australian officers serving in the British Army during the Boer War. The film was popularly seen in Australia as defending a heroic stance by the Australians against the British. Shirley was incensed by these claims because she felt there were no grounds here for Australian chagrin at the hands of the English. She set out her objections at some length in a letter to Geoffrey Dutton, who had praised the film. She argued that the British, whose "own sins . . . are gross enough," were not to blame for the involvement of Australians in the Boer War. "Is not the 'fury and dismay' you write of, in Australia, about the sufferings of Australians in 'British' wars coloured by self-dramatization and an evasion of self-knowledge?" And "What the devil were Australians doing in Viet Nam?" It was not just Australia's view of the past that offended. In 1985 she wrote a formal letter to the prime minister of New Zealand, David Lange, congratulating him on "the historic stand that you and your government and the people of New Zealand are taking on the issue of nuclear arms. I am Australian-born, and only wish that [the Australian prime minister] Mr Hawke would follow your fine example." She liked to side against prominent and self-aggrandising Australians, writing to Elizabeth Harrower of the art historian Robert Hughes: "When I wrote on Australia in the New Yorker, he wrote me an ineffable letter saying he liked the article so much he 'wished he had written it' (assumption that he could) and had noted that I had said the great book on Australian origins had yet to be produced. He then said, 'I am writing it.'" A few years later she commented with some glee in her diary that when she told John Pope-Hennessy that Hughes had written of Naples as being "poor in mementoes of the Renaissance," he had responded, "Now doesn't that just give the whole game away."

A friendly correspondence Shirley had developed with the Australian writer Murray Bail through the 1970s became a site of some terse differences of opinion. Bail was a trustee of the National Gallery of Australia in Canberra and had been involved in deliberations and decisions on the gallery's acquisitions. Shirley was fascinated by this involvement, her interest prompted in part by her memories of the penury of Australia's art collections during her childhood. She was particularly exercised by the controversial 1973 purchase by the gallery of Jackson Pollock's *Blue Poles* for AU$1.3 million (around U.S. $1.8 million), at that time the most ever paid anywhere for an American painting, and she seems not to have been mollified by Gough Whitlam's resonant public defence of the purchase with reference to values aligned with her own: "No country has a greater need than Australia, remote as we are from the great galleries of the world, to acquire works of art from other nations and civilisations . . . Overseas galleries have always recognised that the function of any gallery other than the most provincial is to offer a comprehensive view of world culture."

Shirley's taste in art was conservative, as was Francis's; neither admired contemporary art nor indeed anything much from after the war. Seeing her first abstract expressionist show at MOMA in 1953, she had written in her diary, "Ghastly, ghastly. I can't bear to think there's anything in it; it's just the negation of everything I believe in for art and beauty and truth. Hateful nothing." And in the margin of one of Murray Bail's letters to her, where he had observed that with the exception of Fred Williams, whom Shirley also admired, Australian artists were "subservient to foreign styles, exactly as the Americans were to the French until c1950," she had commented, "Should have remained so." She wrote to Bail in 1977 that she and Francis "both thought that excellent Australian people connected with the Aust [National Gallery] acquisitions were

awfully naïve" and were being duped by unscrupulous New York dealers
and curators. Bail thought that her advice, "while given with the best of
intentions, was not really useful." He felt that she failed to acknowledge
the expertise of the NGA trustees, all of whom, he said, knew more than
Shirley did about art, "not just pre-1850 painting." The confidence with
which she asserted her views and enthusiasms could certainly seem patronising. But there was more to this disagreement.

In early 1980 she had an enraging letter from Bail. She had introduced him to Everett Fahy, whose advice on art acquisition she had
thought would be instructive, explaining that "Everett quietly 'finds'
paintings for museums and does a lot of institutional good by stealth,"
but Bail was unimpressed. She did not keep a copy of his letter, but its
tenor and import can be gleaned from her furious response, which quoted
particularly egregious phrases back to him. He had been dismissive of
Everett, of his love of opera and his high art principles, as well as of his
partner, Channing Blake ("bloody Channing"). He told her that he only
really valued modernist art—he didn't care, he wrote, for paintings "with
religion in them"—and said he wanted to institute a "halt to pre-1850"
works in the National Gallery's acquisitions. Shirley was possibly missing
a note of teasing flippancy in his letter; she was furious at the insult she
perceived to her friend, her taste, and herself. Most of all, she bristled
at the assertive nationalism that she felt underpinned the attitudes he
expressed. She responded, "Australians can't be fooled, can they. They
can be proud of having cut the masters down to size; at least within Australian waters . . . 'Christ we're rough,' you say. And proud of it." His
attitude, she told him, "made me feel what a narrow escape—from my
point of view—I had. Even that the narrowness of escape heightens the
gratitude for my pleasure in these things."

She took her anger further. She and Francis had planned to bequeath
their art collection to the Art Gallery of New South Wales. Bail's letter
changed their minds about the bequest:

> As I mentioned to you when you were here, we had left our own
> pictures to an Australian museum. It is you who have finally con-
> vinced us that they have no place there, and we are revoking the

bequest. I know this has no meaning for you; yet it does for us, and might have for others. It is likely there are Australians—ie among the public—who might enjoy [the pictures]. But the declared museum attitudes and self-evident policies make clear that pictures like ours—certainly the "outmoded" pre-1850 Delacroix, Parmigianino, Dutchmen-in-Italy, etc—would almost certainly be promptly sold by an Australian museum; or at least would remain unshown. In any case, they should go where there is receptivity and affinity. That is most particularly true of pictures that were acquired with much love, and little money. Even those after your cut-off date—Pissarro, Picasso, Braque, Villon and co—will fall foul of your successor with his "no pre-1950" proclamations. As you say, a busy man. Busyness is part of the trouble. Some of these matters have a claim on silence and reflection, and the struggle to acquire a right to judge. You proclaim yourself a "modernist in literature as well as in painting." "ist" is usually a pejorative suffix, I find. Modernism dates faster than anything. Whereas genius in a modern form always touches the eternal. (Loud Australian jeers here.) That is Flaubert, or Byron.

She sent a copy of her letter to Elizabeth Harrower, who was also friendly with Murray, and Elizabeth phoned him, "half indignant, half laughing." In the accompanying letter to Elizabeth, Shirley went further. Bail's rejection of her aesthetic principles was, in her eyes, a kind of moral failing. He showed, she wrote, "no curiosity, no humility, no love for pictures . . . terrible insecurity, envy, and the need for the unearned show of 'moral supremacy' in all this. Like jeering at Everett for loving opera. It is all so obvious, so crude, so minuscule, and so disheartening."

There had also been fractious exchanges with Patrick White, exacerbated by reports from Murray that at a dinner at Patrick's, Shirley had been "the subject of malevolent jeers," something she found wounding. She had not been the only target at the dinner, with other literary women, including Nancy Keesing, then head of the Literature Board of the Australia Council for the Arts, also subject to ridicule by Patrick and his guests. Shirley tackled Murray directly on this too: "Your rendering of the evening with Patrick gives an impression that Himmelfarb's factory-mates got together." (Himmelfarb, the protagonist of White's *Riders in the Chariot*, is persecuted, then grotesquely executed in the Australian suburbs.) "Does no one at Sydney ever get bored with taking easy shots at Woollahra matrons? Does no Australian man, for that matter, ever get bored with his own misogyny?"

After a year or so, Shirley wrote again, saying that "enough time had passed" and proposing that they continue their friendship. There remained persistent differences, particularly around questions of literary taste. Along with her hostility to nationalism, Shirley was irritated by the staged irreverence of much Australian writing of the 1970s and 1980s. After reading Clive James's *Unreliable Memoirs*, she wrote Murray, "My toes will never uncurl. If Australians think being sick into innumerable glove boxes shows virility, how can they object when they are taken up on it?" She returned to the subject in her next letter, and he responded with an appeal to realism—"If something exists we feel it should be examined and declared"—but wrote in his notebook a more acerbic response: "How S's prissy aversion to vomit, especially in literature, has produced the very opposite to what such 'refinement' intended—an over-bearing provincialism." He doesn't seem to have made this criticism to Shirley directly, but he did include the passage in the published version of his notebooks; it was a claim he wanted to be read and marked. For her part, Shirley returned to the theme in *The Great Fire*, lamenting "the Australian myths of desecration... tales of fabulous vomiting into glove compartments or punch bowls, of silence ruptured by obscene sound..."

A more significant battle for her was with Patrick White. In December 1979 she had received a letter from him about *The Transit of Venus*. Viking had sent him the galleys without informing her. White's biographer, David Marr, later wrote in sympathy:

> I had grown used to Patrick's tough, uninvited criticism of people's work but his letter to you about *The Transit of Venus* and your reply restore some sense of the pain that these exchanges must cause. I can only imagine what it must be like to open a letter from the man and find <u>that</u>. There are a couple of other letters in which

At her typewriter, mid-1960s

Francis Steegmuller, circa 1960

Beatrice Stein Steegmuller at the Vermont house of Robert Penn Warren and
Eleanor Clark, 1950s. Beatrice is in her wheelchair, with Robert Penn Warren to
her left (in a checkered shirt). The writer Jean Stafford is second from the left.

In January 1966, Shirley and Francis made a second trip to Morocco, returning for the publication of Shirley's first novel, *The Evening of the Holiday*.

Paestum, 1960s. The Steegmullers returned often to Paestum when they were in Italy. They would make the drive down the Amalfi coast from Sorrento to Ravello, then on to Paestum.

In 1961, Francis bought a gold-colored Rolls-Royce Silver Cloud II with the proceeds of his surprise bestseller, *Le Hibou et La Poussiquette*. Through the 1960s, the car was garaged in Switzerland, and they collected it whenever they were in Italy or France. They later took it to England.

In summer 1966, Shirley and Francis visited Robert Penn Warren, Eleanor Clark, and their children Rosanna and Gabriel on the island of Port Cros, just off Toulon, in the south of France.

Shirley with Douglas Cooper and his housekeeper Marie, Château de Castille, 1966. Francis was friends for many years with the controversial English art collector and writer. He and Shirley visited Cooper several times in Provence at his home, the Château de Castille, which housed an extraordinary collection of Cubist works.

With Elizabeth Bowen at Manhattan House, 1969. Shirley came to know Bowen in the early 1960s; they exchanged warm letters and saw each other occasionally over the next decade.

With Robert Penn Warren and Eleanor Clark at the American Academy of Arts and Letters, 1970s. Rosanna Warren remembered this as a friendship grounded in a sense of the seriousness of writing. It was, she felt, "a true artistic foursome of equals."

Shirley and Francis with their longtime friend and Shirley's first editor, William Maxwell, Christmas 1985

The Neapolitan historian, classicist, and polymath Roberto Pane was another of Shirley's exemplary men—erudite and passionate. Pane admired Shirley enormously in return and took a series of compelling photographs of her.

On the Capri-Salerno vaporetto, 1977 (Photograph taken by Evan Cornog)

With Elizabeth Harrower and Lily Gravino, Shirley's oldest Neapolitan friend, at Le Grottelle, Capri, 1984. Elizabeth's trip to Italy, long awaited, was acrimonious and fractious, a disaster on all sides.

In September 1984, Saul Bellow came to Capri to receive the Premio Malaparte. Shirley was seated next to him at the lunch, after which they walked together up to the Villa Jovis.

Shirley, Villa Emma, Posillipo, 1980s

In the late 1980s, Bill and Emmy Maxwell began inviting friends for a long lunch at their Yorktown Heights house to celebrate Bill's mid-August birthday.

Shirley and Bill Maxwell at his birthday lunch, Yorktown Heights, mid-1990s

On Capri, alone, 1995

With her friend the writer Paula Fox and the artist Yvonne Jacquette at the
2007 American Academy of Arts and Letters Members' Dinner (Photograph ©
2007 Benjamin Dimmitt)

Late, last portrait (© 2008 Alan Thomas)

he criticised the book; it says something for his fidelity, I suppose, that his lines to you are marginally tougher and a little more detailed than anything he wrote to anyone else.

Patrick's letter was certainly patronising: "Dear Shirley, I should have written you long ago, after reading The Transit of Venus, which was full of impressive insights and solid detail. Some of your other books I've found too dependent on atmospherics and décor. You are still inclined to strike attitudes and pirouette round yourself, but only here and there." A brusque exchange followed, Patrick apologising "if some of my remarks hurt . . . but to me you do lead an unusually charmed life writing away in the NY apartment and Capri villa while collecting your celebrities and charmers and pairing them off round the world." Shirley did not reply. In her letter to Murray Bail, she described Patrick's letter as "feline" and added, "Patrick knows nothing of our life." A few months later, Patrick wrote to Francis, praising his recently published Flaubert letters, and adding, somewhat disingenuously, "I hope Shirley's novel has been well received and that she's not too offended by some of my remarks." Francis responded, "I don't think Shirley was at all hurt by your words about her book. It was simply that we weren't sure if your letter was friendly, and wondered how you could have formed the impression of our 'charmed lives among celebrities,' complete with 'villa in Capri.' You are certainly the greatest 'celebrity' we know. And in Capri we have two rented rooms in an ex-pensione . . ." Shirley wrote to Elizabeth that she didn't believe Patrick had any goodwill toward her, and that "anything I wrote him seemed to provoke a cheap shot of a joke or an easy sneer. A lot of sneering these days. He writes quite differently to Francis. Falling into the common error that F has a different viewpoint from mine; whereas F is far more taken aback by P's tone to me than I am and far more turned off." When White's autobiography *Flaws in the Glass* was published in 1981, Shirley declined a request from the Australian *Bulletin* magazine to review it (she found the book "so—inadvert . . .") and was horrified to find that her demurring was then reported in the Australian press. It seemed to her "a violation" that they published the information, "giving it a significance it never had in the first place."

Along with her public praise of his work, Shirley would pay private tribute to White's achievement, after his death in 1990, in a dignified letter to his partner, Manoly Lascaris:

In this world without Patrick's Pantocrator presence, we've thought much of your own days, and the great change in them; and hope you will not mind the words of admiration and solidarity. Patrick so often spoke and wrote of the influence and consolation you brought into his life that one feels one may speak of that here and of the strain of all these last exigent months. So great a force emanated from Patrick—of personality, opinion and gift—that it was hard to bear in mind, in earlier years, that he had been in uncertain health nearly all his life. He achieved his huge intention, surely?—and determination always seems a current in his books, part of the implacable integrity. He was one of the very few writers—novelists, that is—born in this century who wrote great books and was not afraid of the deepest and largest themes, or of the complex poetry in which they must be expressed. His influence is always said to be immeasurable—well, of course it is. But perhaps particularly in giving courage to others to take on the world, as he did. Australia will never recover from him—which is to say it will never be able to slump back into the old torpor (and the newer forms of stupor will ever be subject to PW's "mineral stare"). The world is different because he lived and wrote; and the debased word "art" has a revived authenticity when one thinks of him, an artist.

She was dignified too, a few years later, in response to David Marr's sympathetic letter to her, but also unstinting in her condemnation of what she saw as Patrick's failings of character:

Patrick's affinity with Flaubert, mentioned often by him and I think referred to also in a letter . . . to Francis, often rings truly. However, in later years, Flaubert's misanthropy continued to be relieved by strokes of genuine appreciation, spontaneous affection, rational humanity; even, one might say, there was still a basis of civility. Whereas Patrick's reason, and imagination for the lives and sensibilities of others appeared to abandon him, and he took satisfaction in wounding those who wished him well. It is that satisfaction, more than the unprovoked wound, that dismays one, I think . . . Your own book on Patrick was heroic, if I may say so; herculean. Sometimes very painful to read, for the rudeness, the folly, and the sadness of waste. Also, for the submissiveness towards Patrick White of those who should have resisted—if not on their own accounts, then on behalf of others, or merely of the truth . . . Well, as he intended, Australia will be reeling from Patrick White for a long time.

Her visit to Sydney in August 1984 to record the Boyer Lectures went well: "the happiest days I ever spent there, and far too short." At the Mosman Nursing Home, when the carers told Kit that her daughter Shirley had come to see her, Kit was convinced she was someone else. "The strange thing," she said to Shirley, "is that you do look like her." Shirley was glad, later, that she had visited, "because something perhaps passed between us; or at least I felt that one could give a particle of comfort just by being there." Elizabeth Harrower threw another party, with Gough Whitlam among the guests—"an evening of great quality," Shirley wrote to Whitlam, "thanks to Elizabeth, her friends, and their friendliness. Moonlight on North Head did no harm either." She spent good days with Elizabeth and finally persuaded her to accept the invitation, repeated over many months, to visit, first in Italy and later in New York. The offer—Shirley and Francis wished to pay Elizabeth's costs—was intended as a gesture of appreciation for all that Elizabeth had done for Kit; this was possibly in itself a source of chagrin, prompting the unspoken response that such extraordinary assistance could not be recompensed so easily. If it was, it's not clear that Shirley ever grasped this.

While the prospect of Elizabeth coming to Italy and New York filled Shirley with delight—she wrote to Donald Keene, "Elizabeth is coming!—at last—to Italy"—for Elizabeth it had the reverse effect. She was anxious about the cost and, apparently, unconvinced by reassurances from

Francis and Shirley that this would be their pleasure. Francis wrote to her: "As to material questions: we both despond to think that the small and irrelevant sums of such a trip will be left to you in our wills, when they could be used now, in life, to give us joy. It is strange to have to exhort you, of all people, to 'have a heart'!" Elizabeth wanted to be away for only six weeks in all, and Francis possibly struck an unwise tone in his letter in exhorting her to reconsider this: "Alarm was caused here by your saying on the phone that you'd be skooting right back to Sydney after not much more than a month. Of course you must do what you feel like. But, Elizabeth, it does seem to me that you may not know in advance what you will feel like if you give yourself a chance."

Elizabeth was anxious about travelling altogether, as her cousin Margaret told Francis. Shirley knew that there were a number of factors distressing her friend; Elizabeth had been forthright about the difficulties she was facing: "One purpose of the whole trip, from our point of view, was to remove her from the pressures of friends' troubles at Sydney which, she told us, had put her under a doctor's care and created grave problems of blood pressure." For all her concern, Shirley failed to see that Elizabeth was finding her manner patronising, and Francis could well have compounded that sense. Through September, Francis wrote several times, urging Elizabeth to extend her trip and reporting discussions he and Shirley had had about her Australian circles. Some of this would certainly have offended. Francis weighed in on concerns Elizabeth had expressed about some of Patrick White's behaviour, quoting Shirley on the subject:

"One of the many monumental reasons to get Elizabeth away from Australia even for a while is the seismic measuring of repercussions that builds up in any ingrown circle." I think I quote almost verbatim. And she has lately been saying things like: "Patrick White seems to have gone off the rails into bitter megalomania; but would he be so far derailed if he weren't confident that every tremor would be measured, and would cause tremors among others? Time to stop the tremors; time to come away . . . Surely you would see Sidney Nolan [the Australian artist, formerly close to Patrick, but now estranged] in the UK? Surely you wouldn't fear to see him because PW might learn of it? That makes PW's 'friendship' into tyranny."

While Elizabeth was herself prepared to venture criticisms of her close friend Patrick, for Francis and, above all, for Shirley to criticise this behaviour clearly crossed a line. And just as Patrick had made "the common error" of assuming that Francis's views differed from Shirley's, thus exempting him from criticism, Elizabeth would continue to focus her resentment exclusively on Shirley.

A further complication in the relationship was surely bound up with Shirley's now elevated international reputation. After *The Watch Tower* in 1966, Elizabeth had completed but not published a fifth novel. The writing had been funded by an Australian Commonwealth Literary Fund fellowship, which enabled her to quit her job at Macmillan. In early 1971 she had written, in response to Shirley's enquiries about the manuscript, "Alan [Maclean] accepted it for Macmillan's in London, but we both know (though he is too compassionate to say so) that it is disappointing. Whether it will be more inhibiting in the long run to publish and face justified harshness from critics, or to write off two years' work and the CLF's $6000 is the choice. There was an interesting book to be written, but I blocked it for all sorts of reasons and my concentration disappeared. People." She continued "cutting and re-typing" but decided to withdraw the manuscript, and the book was not published for another forty years.

Elizabeth arrived in Rome in early October. Francis and Shirley met her at the airport and took her to the Hassler hotel for a night or two before going to Capri, where they had booked her into a pensione. From the start, the mood was brittle. Shirley wrote in her diary of her friend's prickliness: "the animosity in the taxi from Rome airport, good heavens, expressed against 'people from outside' (awful, at the time, and now); animosity to me; in never asking for a word in Italian; oddly, in never looking at our bookshelves, unwillingness for any independent gesture, let alone action; seething emotions of abysmal chauvinism; and above all in the constant mention (and nothing else was ever invoked) of the hotel room at the Hassler: a room without a view." Things did not improve on Capri, where Shirley felt Elizabeth "seething with an antagonism towards me." At dinner one night at the Capannina with Donald Keene, who was also visiting, "amid friendly talk and laughter," Elizabeth proposed a "sudden toast: 'To Francis, the kindest person at the table.'" Shirley responded tersely, "It isn't a competition." While she saw her own actions as simple generosity—"I am not only doing everything I can think of to appease and gratify, but working hard on it all, planning, arraying, escorting; giving up all my time"—for Elizabeth the whole experience was patronising and humiliating. But even with that, Elizabeth's hostility seems to have been excessive. Shirley's diary records her "saying—when I propose to 'take' Elizabeth and Donald to the Arco itself, before lunch—'There you go again; I don't accept orders' . . . At times, seems unhinged."

Elizabeth flew to London, earlier than planned, and off-loaded to Alan and Robin Maclean her deep frustration about the Italian trip. Shirley and Alan had had a terrible row a year or so beforehand, when Alan, "in a rage," had taken Shirley to task for having repeated something he had said out of turn. Their memories of the event differed, and he had shouted, "Admit you're wrong for once. JUST FOR ONCE. ADMIT YOU'RE WRONG." Shirley had resisted, feeling that Alan wished her to "say ('confess to') something I did not believe to be true." This incident, still simmering, no doubt coloured the Macleans' response, and they agreed with Elizabeth about the relentlessness of Shirley's behaviour and how difficult she was. Alan related to Elizabeth a story about sitting next to Shirley on a plane and feeling so trapped by her constant talk that he had to seek refuge in the airplane toilet: "She just would not stop!" Shirley and Alan would later repair their differences, maintaining a warm friendship for the rest of their lives. For the moment, though, things were testy. Alan encouraged Elizabeth to write to Shirley from England to say she would return directly to Sydney and not come first to New York as planned. In the event, Shirley was relieved:

> I was apprehensive, afraid, really, of her hostility, her resentment and flaring, uncontrolled barbs; so unexpected, all that. What came over her?—she was deranged. One could not respond, first because all embarrassing and dismaying and not a legitimate "contest"

and then because, as we were giving her the trip it would have been indelicate to "get the best of her" or tell her off. She so much invited it, that her unconscious may have hoped to provoke—thus facilitating her precipitate, longed-for return.

She wrote to Donald Keene of her sadness at the way things had fallen out, observing that in her view, the matter was, for Elizabeth, "far more complicated than she is able to admit to herself." Shirley's view was that the problems were all on Elizabeth's side: pressures of those Sydney friends and an "extreme apprehension with the unfamiliar" had meant that "the shock of direct experience" had been "perhaps too much for her after a long withdrawal," prompting the outbursts and the early return.

The event simmered for the rest of their lives. When Patrick White died, in 1990, Shirley and Francis telephoned Elizabeth from a phone box on Capri to express their condolences, and she wrote back, "Of course, [Patrick] was infuriating and hurtful and said many non-wonderful things about everyone, but equally, he was extremely lovable, kind and funny." In a clear reference to her own labours with Kit, she added, "He tried to rescue me from myself when no one else did. In the days when I had a strange obligation to save people's lives, he said, 'You're an artist, and you're acting like a social worker!' Another time, he said, 'I get depressed when I think you're not writing.' Not many deeply mind whether other people write." Next to this last comment, in the margin, Shirley drew a large red question mark. Elizabeth signed off with another barb: "This room where I'm typing is hideous with papers overflowing from filing cabinets. So those not destroyed will go to a library soon. When there is only one of you all these things seem tedious, not to say mountainous, but must be done . . . You'll be arriving home with work completed, proofs on the way, good events all over the place. Take care of yourselves. Thank you again for your call from the phone box. That was nice."

As Shirley continued, hurt and angry, to think through Elizabeth's visit, it became more and more representative of her larger relation to Australia, a sense that was reinforced after her Boyer Lectures were broadcast that November. She had remained in contact with the ABC's Peter Morton, who had looked after things during her visit, and he sent on to her letters of appreciation from the public, "most quite beautiful," including one from Bert Black, a retired school principal from Lismore on the North Coast of New South Wales, who had been "playing and replaying your first lecture" and reflecting on "the forward-looking contemplation of 'what might be,'" as he waited to have surgery to amputate his leg. Shirley wrote back to say that it was "for a listener such as yourself—thinking, feeling, attentive and intent on enlarging life—that my talks have been prepared; not because I expect instant or complete agreement with all I say, but because ideally one is speaking to a kindred spirit, and to someone who will revolve ideas in the mind." Published reviews of the lectures, however, were less engaged by her appeal to the continuities of poetry and less convinced that the criticisms of Australian nationalism were justified. Some were outright hostile.

The critic Don Anderson dismissed the lectures as "a speech-day address by the headmistress of a girls' private school, of, dare I say, Queenwood" (Shirley's old school) and criticised her "apparent ignorance of contemporary Australian thought and letters" and of "current social and political events." In this last point he was mostly correct, although her correspondence with Elizabeth Harrower reveals a sustained and detailed discussion of Australian political and cultural affairs, and her 1977 *New Yorker* essay about Australia is detailed and informed about the contemporary Australian scene. Beyond this, critics of her lectures also disregarded her belief that writers must challenge and criticise nationalistic assertions. These were matters already encountered in her battles with Murray Bail and others. In the moment, it was the ferocity of Anderson's comments, and their implicit misogyny, that hurt most. It is worth noting that this was not an isolated instance. In 1980, amid the glowing international reception and extraordinary success of *The Transit of Venus*, another Australian critic, Peter Pierce, had dismissed the novel as "the best-dressed women's magazine fiction of its year." Two decades later, another Australian critic, John Docker, wrote of *Greene on Capri*: "The book claws at its reader, calling admire me, admire me. Get away, I thought. I responded to the book's preciousness by (as it were) manhandling it; I underlined, wrote in the margins and notated 'fuck' next to particularly studied phrases (like 'cold evenings of Rilkean stars')."

For Shirley, it was all enormously distressing, driving her back to an ancient wound in the name of her country of birth. In her diary, she reflected,

What hatred; and self-hatred . . . what hatred in that paradoxical Australia. These "reviews" primitive, unleashed. This is what I wrote about in the talks—not only that aspect got these people on the raw, however . . . It is the appalling lust for "exposure" ("she gives the game away" says the wretched Anderson) . . . The playground bully blustering around in so many, many Australians, predominantly but not only men. The seizing, like a beast, on what they take for the sight of blood—the need to regard an utterance from the heart as an opportunity to stick the knife in.

She lay awake one night, consumed with it all. She felt unwelcome, unappreciated in Australia and by Australians, her earlier delight at new connections crushed by this hostile response. "What a dispiriting episode. What a wretched outcome to my long work and thought to do with those lectures and my beautiful visit to Australia." She was to deliver a lecture on Australian art at the Frick Collection the following February. "When the—rather dreaded now—Frick talk is over, let me 'close Australia down.' No more doomed attempts to help, no more than casual associations. How hard for me to learn such lessons—but Australia is a fated connection for me. Perhaps I'll go there again. And in a way, I hope I never will. The compulsion to alienate goodwill, and the hysteria. To exclude as 'unknowing' the insight of even an uninformed outsider who nevertheless has a developed eye and ear."

Kit died in May 1985 in her nursing home in Sydney. Shirley did not return for the funeral, instead making her way, alone, to Capri. Francis explained to Alfred Kazin that Kit had been "long in a world of her own," and thus it was "useless for Shirley to go to Australia now: when she saw her mother there last summer she wasn't recognized." At the funeral, Valerie and Elizabeth were Kit's sole mourners. Valerie wrote Shirley with details, after which they were only rarely in touch. The animosity between the sisters had by now dulled without receding. Shirley wrote bluntly of it to Elizabeth: "As to our 'estrangement'—hers and mine—it has never been anything I took satisfaction in or wanted to maintain, it was just inevitable given the circumstances and her implacable dumping of all on others. But it hasn't, from my point of view, been an 'estrangement' for years and years. Merely boredom. What would be the point of our getting together in any sustained way, I wonder—we have nothing to say to one another and no common interest." The absence of shared interests was demonstrably true, but Shirley's pose of bored resignation here does not quite gel with earlier moments of fraught, if somewhat frustrated and indignant (but also sentimental), identification from her diaries—the "tender and sad" feelings at the memory of "two little girls from Balmoral." Something of the unresolvable nature of this relationship might be seen in the repeated return in her novels to idealised pairs of siblings preternaturally bound together or cruelly kept apart: Caro and Grace, "dark she, fair she," in *The Transit of Venus*, and the perfect accord of Helen and Benedict, the desert-island castaways "my brother and me," and their anguished separation in *The Great Fire*. And Jenny in *The Bay of Noon*, moved "to desolate tears" at a letter from her brother, Edmund, "so separate did we seem from one another then, each in a place unimaginable to the other, each irrevocably set on his tangential course, the dividing ocean once more between us . . . *Seigneur, que tant de mers me séparent de vous*."

On Capri, Shirley grieved for her mother's life as much as for her death: "One of her tragedies—as I do believe she had tragedy—was the inability to believe that other people appreciated her best qualities and had goodwill towards her; that she did not need to keep testing affection till it collapsed under the strain." She wrote to Elizabeth—"You were so good—immeasurably good—to her. What was bearable in her latter life was in great part thanks to you"—and she thought long about her mother's life and qualities:

What almost no one could know was that her trouble was more than just an exaggeration of the unleashed Mother of her own balked generation; but a real instability that was sometimes madness. Yes, I'm relieved of course that the last prolonged twilight finally ended. Most of the strongest feelings I might experience have been used up, at least for the time being, and only come in twinges. I chiefly feel—"Rest, perturbed spirit"; and the waste; and sadness when I think of childhood times when MM was clearly, as I now see, more often than not a lively and practical woman, not yet tipping her imbalances in dread directions. Reading the letters about her, I'm reminded too of what so often appeared in her life—that she could not really believe in the goodwill of others, and in her process of testing used it up, wore it down, and scared it off.

In the end, "It is so sad that if one were to dwell on the whole of it one could not bear it." This was a last substantial break with Australia. While Shirley maintained some Australian friendships, and she and Elizabeth continued to correspond, civility masking resentment and hurt on both sides, there were fewer connections to be sustained, and more wounds to be protected.

V

# 12

# THE ROOM NOT AS
# I THOUGHT IT WAS

## 1981-1994

CAPRI HAD ALWAYS been a place to work. Increasingly, though, the quiet it offered was interrupted by what had come to be "a deluge of visitors," some of them "unknown to us or almost so, friends of friends, relatives of friends, acquaintances of acquaintances, etc. We swore that if it occurred again, we would just leave the island, rather than continue as the Capri Greeting Facility." There was something of an implicit contradiction. Shirley lamented the interruptions to work and at the same time continued to issue invitations. Her diaries are full of the names of visitors, friends and acquaintances close and distant. In 1981 the former South Australian premier Don Dunstan was in Italy making a television series (something Shirley would have found irritating in itself). She had earlier met Dunstan during her visit to Adelaide Writers' Week, and had found him congenial and engaging, and she had seen him several times since, but his visits didn't always go well. In late 1981 she wrote to Elizabeth Harrower:

> I have walked with Don along the flower-strewn paths of Capri in
> scenes of inexpressible beauty while he has given me a monologue

about his handling of the South Australian legislature, or the virtues of early Dobells or the cooking of yabbies; and wanted to shriek with pain. Silence, solitude, reticence, consideration for the interests of others, submission to new knowledge—all unknown to him . . . When we say we must work, or—having lunched together—tell him we'll not see him before dinner, he looks incredibly like My Mum: downcast, sadly smiling, rejected. For all of four hours!

Other visitors were more in tune. Since the 1970s they had been friendly with the writer Bruce Chatwin, "a delightful person, a man of great culture, intellect and charm," whom they had nominated for the E. M. Forster Award at the American Academy in 1979. They had stayed on occasion in his London flat, carried memories of "good times with him, unforgettable impressions from his talk," and had been glad to meet up with him again a few years previously at Dwight Macdonald's. Bruce arrived on Capri unannounced one June evening in 1983: "We were out on our terrace having dinner one night about nine. F had just come back from some library work in Rome, on late boat, we had just sat down. Gate bell rings. I call down from top of stairs 'Chi è?' Reply: 'Bruce Chatwin.' How nice it was to see him. 'Bruce, you look very brown, that must be Australia.' 'I rather think it's Everest.' He was here for a week, in tow to a Condé Nast group and somewhat tied to the vita-in-villa life from which we are quite detached. However we saw quite a bit of him and it was fun." Nonetheless, welcome interruptions were interruptions all the same, and Shirley's novel was not moving forward.

It was not just the visitors. She was finding Francis's behaviour at times demanding and intransigent. She wrote of "the crushing, the neurotic coldness and moodiness, the narcissism" and of incidents when her mood had been shattered by "gratuitous misery, anguish. Sick at heart. Waste, disappointment, deathliness. Lack of life." There were "Moments—bad hours—of dread, too, about inability to have solitude, silence, leisure to create a context of thought, and hence to work. And the—complete—impossibility of making this dread understood. No one to take my part. Always: 'But I do these things too' (ie domestic at

Posillipo) or 'You've complained ever since we arrived'; or turn away and walk out of the room." Some of this was her habitual response to feeling thwarted or unvalued, the intensity of which she had battled to contain from their earliest months and years together, and her tendency, as one great friend of her later years put it, to "take things personally." At the same time, there was clearly a heightened sense of vulnerability through these years. In 1983, despite her hostility to psychoanalysis, she began seeing Martin H. Stein, who had been Francis's analyst. Her diary records their first session: "exposed nerves, defences low, tears at surface. In part because first occasion in so long that my own feelings—inner feelings—were found wanting of being weighed. I had forgotten, as well as renounced, their importance to anyone else. (To him, of course, merely professional) But—this was only professional importance. Kind, professional, intelligent and handsomely paid for." She began drafting a scene from their encounter: "S with MS: He, mere flicker at watch, practised concealment of the action. She—incidentally—in her talking: 'You'll tell me when it's time?' He, taken aback—watching her, to find himself so closely observed. At same time, does not dislike it. Her (high strung apprehensions, intelligence, ability to surprise) appealing."

Along with her deepening concern about not writing and her sensitivity to criticism and to coldness, Shirley was concerned that Francis was becoming unable to share what she called "Tasks," the daily labour underpinning their lives: "If I could have at least read books in this month, done a few pages work . . ." She wrote of his "inconsistency sometimes like derangement. Inaccessibility to reason," driving her back to her own "frightened childhood where nothing made sense and one's attempts to placate were always exposed as desperation," invoking over and over the sense, paraphrasing *Middlemarch*, that her circumstances always set her "best self in prison." With hindsight, it seems likely that at least some of Francis's behaviour that Shirley found so difficult was a symptom of a larger problem involving cognitive decline, which was beginning to make itself apparent through these years.

On July 8, 1984, after a trip to Siena, Shirley's handwriting, in pencil, records the day's uneventful but precious events in Francis's Hermès diary, much as one or other of them would do almost every day: "Early walk to Campo. Hot sun. At 10 leave in car with driver. Drive to Rome, Hassler, lunch; Villa Medici, red sun going down, walk to Spanish Steps. Mild night, soft." This entry is written around the edges of something illegible in Francis's hand, also in pencil and subsequently erased, leaving a large, blurred section in the centre of the page. On their return to New York, they completed formal legal declarations "relating to possible senile illness in the future," lodged with their doctor, indicating, perhaps, some awareness of a problem. In his entry for September 24 that year, Francis wrote amid the daily record, "My confusion in subway. Horrified by what I wrote on July 8 about being in Italy—why do I forget feeling that way?" Several years later, in 1987, Francis requested and received material from a right-to-die organisation, the Hemlock Society, which he kept in his study alongside a paper bag containing two full bottles of Nembutal, the prescription specifying them as a sleep aid, and a crumpled note, in his hand, "40–50 Nembutal slowly." It is not clear when a formal diagnosis was made of his condition; it was not until August 1994, two months before he died, that there is any definite record in the diaries of medical consultation, with Shirley noting that he was scheduled for a CAT scan and adding, "Cognex is the drug for memory. New, dangerous to people for future years."

In any case, the onset of symptoms was slow, and Francis continued to write, see friends, and travel. It may well have been in the context of this decline that Shirley initiated what became a long-standing tradition of their reading aloud to each other morning and evening. The practice reached back to their earliest times together, reading *The Bachelors* on the flight home from their unhappy trip to Spain in 1963. They began with Gibbon's *History of the Decline and Fall of the Roman Empire*, and by July 1985 were "on the downward slope":

I already dread the closing of the last vol—but perhaps we'll just start again at the beginning. We have read every word, skipped nothing; have twin texts. I read text aloud, F reads the footnotes—it works out pretty much even as the notes are so extensive. What a gigantic task, what a giant. The chapters on the early Church do make it hard to have Christian thoughts towards the Fathers of same. Gibbon makes a sense of proportion possible towards every era except ours—that is to say, no sense of the relative can cope with the nuclear possibility; or probability, as it often seems.

The practice was restorative, reinstating intimacy threatened by Francis's condition. Shirley wrote years later to Chris Cooper, just months before Francis died,

> It was Francis who, on our evening return from Capri, read your letter aloud, as I was putting Rita's pasta into the oven. At such a moment, Francis is quite as he was—the immediacy of the well-written word restores him. It's the same when we read aloud together—with magnificent Coriolanus finished, we are for the umpteenth time re-reading Hamlet. When, at the outset, Francis (whose "turn" it was) read out: "'Tis bitter cold, and I am sick at heart," he put down the book and said, "Who will ever be able to say why such a line is Immortal. Mastery."

Her pursuit of the United Nations continued. In early 1983 she spoke to a New York group, the "Junior Fortnightly," which met several times a year to discuss matters of civic and public interest. It did not go well. In her diary she recorded her unhappiness:

> This was a ghastly evening. I was asked to speak on UN. Did so. Snow, few present. At first, tentative agreement; then contemptible stream of platitudes from G Sorensen, the city's UN "official," swung the women round like sheep, all congratulating themselves on warmth of sentiments towards UN. Every exhausted fallacy self-gratifyingly resumed. No call on their humanity, their imagination, decency, reason, met with receptivity of the slightest kind. I felt—this is what it has always been. They do not give a damn who goes to the wall as long as it isn't them. How indecent; how evil, really . . . Only Mrs Levin spoke—quietly—for me.

Phyllis Lee Levin wrote to Shirley after the meeting to thank her and express her agreement with Shirley's views; Shirley invited her to tea, learned that she was also a writer, and another long-standing friendship was forged.

Other such moments of sympathetic encounter were more fleeting, but nonetheless galvanising. In May 1984 Shirley had lunch with Leonard Boudin, the prominent civil liberties lawyer who had defended Paul Robeson, Daniel Ellsberg, and Benjamin Spock; he was the father of Kathy Boudin, who had recently been sentenced to twenty years in jail for her part, as a member of the radical Weather Underground group, in the murder of an armoured car driver. Boudin had asked Shirley to lunch to talk about her UN writing. As she walked up to the Harvard Club, where Boudin was waiting for her, she recalled that she had drawn on a previous meeting with him, years before, for a detail of the character of Adam Vail in *Transit*: "the sleeve and cuff, the impressive simplicity, intelligence, receptivity; assured, in good sense." Boudin had also contributed one of Vail's notable lines in the novel: "When someone was raising funds for the Socialist Workers Party case (in a Park Ave apartment!), his handling of the antagonistic questioner—a woman—'You are right to reprove me, and I am right to be angry.'" After asking Shirley to speak about the UN, Boudin remarked, "You are the only one who has written about it." She found this moving: "No one has said this. I tell him that perhaps five people have supported me in public—five. (I can't even count them, beyond Ivan, but want to err on the side of amplitude!—Oh yes, Morton Mintz, Dr Seidmann; Lowell Flanders of course.) I said— Sorrow. It has grieved me. Has taught me a lot. I tell him, at the beginning I thought questions would be asked, reforms might be set in motion. Then I learnt that one does it for other reason—to keep truth alive."

As they were leaving, Shirley asked Boudin about his daughter, "not wanting to intrude, to dramatize my 'interest'—He at once speaks openly of it, even (we are in the lobby) with special clarity. Has taught himself to do this?—Anyone could hear. So naturally does he do this, showing me photos of Kathy Boudin's lovely little child, that it is even unnatural—or superhuman." Boudin spoke about his hope that his daughter's parole-appeal time might be reduced. Shirley reflected, "Such reality. (Like Jean

Rhys: 'How many of you could stand this?')" Her detailed diary record of this meeting indicates how significant the encounter was for her, not just Boudin's support for her UN stance but more broadly, the human dimension of political acts. The moment as recorded suggests a kind of novelistic quality to her public engagement, a constant tying together of threads of observation and significance and moment to form a scene of integrity a private reference point. There is always a larger concern with truth underpinning her work, a point where the public and private meet in the experience of poetry, humanity, civility, even love.

These invitations, formal and informal, to speak about the UN had followed several recent publications. In January 1980 she had revealed in an essay in *The New Republic* that Secretary-General Kurt Waldheim had concealed his wartime association with the Nazi youth movement. She later wrote to *New Yorker* editor William Shawn: "I had also learned that Waldheim was falsifying his military record under Hitler, although I could do no more than allude, then, to his having served in more campaigns than the single one to which he admitted." Shortly after, in a profile in *The Washington Post*, Waldheim and his wife were quoted naming her and angrily refuting her claims, which they described as "unsubstantiated." The *New Republic* editor Martin Peretz contacted her to ask about her sources for the claims. She wrote later: "And, having heard—and met—some of the evidence, he too became convinced that the assertions about Waldheim could be made with entire confidence in their veracity." Peretz then wrote a follow-up piece, in the wake of which Congressman Stephen Solarz took up the matter. Solarz wrote to Waldheim and to the CIA, asking for "elucidation of Waldheim's Nazi past," receiving from both "a written denial." Shirley appeared on a panel alongside Solarz. When the story was picked up again six years later, in a long piece by the journalist Jane Kramer in *The New Yorker*, the facts as Shirley had flagged them were verified and the story became newsworthy. In response, Martin Peretz published a short account of the earlier pieces in *The New Republic*, adding that a lawyer had approached him after the 1980 publication advising that further commentary on these matters would result in a libel suit from Waldheim. Peretz wrote that he had replied, stating, "If Waldheim sued us he would find himself in discovery proceedings. That was the last we heard about a libel suit. Now we know why." Shirley, initially frustrated at having had her signal role in bringing the story to light overlooked, was somewhat mollified when Jane Kramer wrote to her: "You deserve enormous credit for being . . . as I now know, the only person to have persisted in publishing the truth about that odious man over all those years when it was convenient to pretend that he was decent."

In the late 1980s Shirley returned to the Waldheim material, fleshing out those initial claims in a series of essays published first in *The New York Review of Books* and in 1990 collected as *Countenance of Truth: The United Nations and the Waldheim Case*, with a dedication to Ivan Morris. This was to be her final public word on the matter; she had felt "some obligation." But there were limits:

> I can't go on with it. If this book doesn't make any immediate impression, at least it's on the record of history, and I suppose the ultimate reason for writing is to tell the truth. In the beginning I hoped to change things, but one loses that expectation. But I think that a truth set out takes on a life of its own. These aren't private truths, they belong to everybody, although they always come back to personal conduct. People talk in categories; even I have to use this phrase "the leadership of the UN," but these are single men—we can use the word "men" because there are so few women in the leadership—human beings who should be answerable for their actions.

The process of writing the book had been torturous, and with its completion she felt that she had finally "sprung from the Waldheim incubus."

New York remained a source of stimulation despite its demands and difficulties. If the city could not offer Neapolitan or Capri vistas, there was still poetry in the scene: "NY night sky 2am / The balconies of towers riding the sky / Glassy balconies of skyscrapers riding the night / Clouds at last visible, scalloped against the moonlight / Clouds like reflected fire. City, night of a holiday weekend—the avenue, red lights flicking on and off—Walk Don't Walk—the city playing to an empty house." The Steegmullers' lives were busiest there, their social circles most intricate, always expanding. Jonathan Galassi met them around this time at Janet Flanner and Natalia Danesi Murray's Park Avenue apartment, where Natalia and Shirley gossiped in Italian "with mild conspiratory irony about the domestic habits of I Capresi." Shirley had first met Janet Flanner in the early 1960s, describing her to Muriel Spark as "exceedingly enchanting . . . a brilliant little bird." One way of suggesting how the Steegmullers' social worlds worked might be to draw on a comment from their friend Jacques Barzun, who wrote to Shirley that he had been asked to describe the "literary circles" he frequented, and that he had responded, "I acknowledge no circles, only close friends." Evan Cornog was astonished at the company they kept: "So many people who were just the tiniest sliver of the population in terms of their knowledge of a particular area," such as Bram Pais, the physicist and science historian, or Harold Varmus, who won the Nobel Prize in Medicine in 1989—people Evan "knew from the bookshelves, but never expected to know in life." Learning was "baked into the conversation. Not learning, that's too instrumental. It was about the effervescence of the conversation." At the heart of their sociability was generosity and a love of erudition. Shirley herself was at the heart of all this. Katherine Swett recalled, from her youth, the spectacle of Shirley at a social gathering, sitting on the couch, "holding forth about Samuel Johnson," commanding the room. As a teenager, Swett had been struck not just by the erudition implicit in Johnson's name but also by Shirley's authority, her distinctive "female style." Evan Cornog also spoke of Shirley's ability to converse on a wealth of subjects, combined with "her respect for people of serious scholarly or artistic attainment, and she was herself just brilliant and so fascinating to be around and she attracted people and became part of all these circles."

Her attention and courtesy, moreover, were seen in any and all social situations, friends recalled. "Whether it involved a New York dinner party or thanking (and generously tipping) a custodian who had opened a locked church door so one could admire a neglected example of Neapolitan baroque architecture. She was tirelessly humane." She also befriended people from all walks, making friends while waiting in line at the bakery or for a bus, bringing people—as Phyllis Lee Levin put it, "a little girl or an old lady"—back to the apartment for a cup of tea, perhaps giving them copies of her books. Her diaries record some of these: "Half day at Naples . . . Bookshop (bought Somerville and Ross and early edition Golden Treasury). Took books to be rebound, Via del Grande Archivio, da Fiori, P. San Domenico, Libreria Guida, bought Salammbô. Coffee Scaturchio. Chiostro Santa Chiara; met Emanuela D'Orsi 11 years old (a Raphael) and her mother Lina D'Orsi. Got address. They kissed me when we parted." Francis, more reticent, and guarding his writing time more jealously, was less keen on surprise new friendships. These chance meetings did not necessarily continue, but some unplanned connections, like that with Giulio Colavolpe, or Will and Alison Parente, whom they later met on Capri, did. In the late 1990s Shirley wrote to Edward Mendelson because she admired a review he had published of Seamus Heaney. Shirley wanted to talk more about this and a friendship ensued. She took up opportunities for conversation and discussion and learning and friendship wherever they offered themselves; this was something that would not change, even as the circumstances of her life did.

In the late 1980s Bill and Emmy Maxwell began a tradition of celebrating Bill's birthday each August at their house in Yorktown Heights—"long festive lunches and summer afternoons out of doors or in Emmy's studio." Over the next few years a regular group of guests gathered: the Maxwells, Shirley and Francis, Edward Newhouse (a *New Yorker* writer from the postwar years), and a group of younger writers, the poet Michael Collier, Alec Wilkinson, and Annabel Davis-Goff. These gatherings were, Michael Collier remembered, "quietly joyous events. Bill was in his eighties, and he was at a point in his life when he just enjoyed being alive." It was also clear that everyone who came "wanted to be there. People felt genuine joy in each other's company, because of Bill." Shirley's long friendship with the Maxwells expanded with these new encounters. Alec Wilkinson did not take to Shirley at first: "I thought she talked too much." But over the years, he began, he said, "to pay attention to what she was saying, and then of course you couldn't hear her talk enough. You were in the presence of someone whose gift was so profound that you better just shut up and listen. The amount of poetry that she could quote . . . The appreciation of it, a great discernment."

Francis attended the birthday lunches most years; he and Shirley drove up the first few years with Annabel Davis-Goff, later with Alec Wilkinson and his wife, Sara Barrett. As Francis grew frailer, he would take himself off for a nap in the course of the afternoon. Michael Collier recalled as a kind of tableau a scene from one of Francis's last times: "Sitting on the deck of the Maxwells' house and having drinks and then dinner and the sun going down. Gently beautiful. This image of Francis and Shirley sitting together and the sun going down behind them." This was a scene and a moment, Collier felt, about friendship across age groups. "You never stop learning from people who are that much older than you and are kind of in love with each other. And who have endured so much. I think about that moment a lot—that particular image of Francis and Shirley together." The poet Edward Hirsch joined the birthday lunches later, after Francis's death. He was struck immediately by Shirley, "the sweep and range of her conversation," and after that always angled to be seated next to her. She was, he said, "the most cultivated person" he had ever met, and it was also immediately apparent that this was not by virtue of social class. "I knew even without her telling me that she did not come from a cultivated background. She had a kind of natural aristocratic manner. Also, she was not an academic. Her learning was completely a kind of felt learning. I felt she must have been self-educated." At the heart of this was her tremendous repertoire of poetry, beginning with Leopardi and Italian poetry, then French—"all these poems by Aragon, that she knew by heart"—and then moving on to English poets: Hardy, Milton. After listening for a while, Hirsch laughingly told her, "It's a good thing there's such an age difference because otherwise there'd be a problem." Shirley was far from offended. He went on, "It just sends me when you quote poetry." She put her hand on his arm and said, "There's a lot more where that came from." At the same time, she was, Hirsch felt, very much a "defended person." Conversations with her "were very attentive and very focused. Very compelling. The personal was a kind of backdrop, mostly through poetry. You felt a well of feeling behind this and behind these poems. More of a shadow sense of what you felt about her depth and her character."

Annabel Davis-Goff had started coming to the birthday lunches soon after meeting Bill Maxwell in 1989. Maxwell had written to her on the publication earlier that year of a memoir of her childhood and early youth in Ireland. He admired the book, and a friendship developed. And a friendship also developed between Shirley and Annabel, one of the most important of Shirley's later life. It was a friendship, like so many of Shirley's, across something of an age gap, grounded in a common sensibility and receptiveness to literature. There would also have been some shared sense of having come into Manhattan literary circles from outside. Although many of this group that formed around Maxwell had come from elsewhere—Edward Hirsch from Chicago, Michael Collier from Arizona, Bill himself from Illinois—Annabel and Shirley shared a quite specific colonial displacement, Anglo-Australian and Anglo-Irish, and while this was not in itself something they discussed, there were common perspectives. Annabel had come to the United States in 1969, had worked in film and television, had been married to and was now divorced from the film director Mike Nichols, and had published two novels as well as the memoir that brought her to Maxwell's attention. She also shared with Shirley a background of having had little in the way of formal education or money; as young women, both had had to make their way in a difficult and unfamiliar professional and social world abroad, and both, in a number of ways, had reinvented themselves. They shared a sense of literature providing, as Annabel put it, the chance to "escape upwards." The word that appears in Shirley's diaries about this friendship was "affinity," although Annabel insisted that the core of the friendship was Shirley's very particular generosity, her knowledge eloquently shared. Once when they were in Venice together, Shirley took Annabel to see the Carpaccios at San Giorgio degli Schiavoni and then transcribed Ruskin's dream of St. Ursula for her. On another occasion she sent Annabel Leopardi's "La Ginestra" with her own translation, and on another her copy of Dover Wilson on *Hamlet* after a discussion of the play.

Shirley's generosity was often remarked by her younger friends. Evan

Cornog was struck by the way that, from the start, Shirley and Francis included him as an unknown in their circles. He recalled that Shirley gave a dinner to celebrate his completing his doctorate, inviting her friends Elliott Carter the composer, and the artist Saul Steinberg. Jonathan Burnham became friendly with Shirley after he had edited the UK edition of *Countenance of Truth* for Chatto in 1990. "It was characteristic of Shirley that even over this minor essay, she invited me to meet her in New York, invited me to dinner, and we talked for about three hours about French literature and my life and her life and Francis's. I was a British editor of a minor piece. Looking back, I really didn't deserve that kind of attention. But it was totally characteristic of Shirley that she would do that . . . She had so much more to give to me than I had to give to her at many levels." Around the same time, the Australian writer Helen Garner met Shirley in New York. Garner was not an admirer of Shirley's writing, but she was charmed at her warm welcome and her elegance, and by the care Shirley later showed in writing a "comradely letter" of support in the face of the angry debates surrounding Garner's controversial 1995 book, *The First Stone*.

There was another side to this generosity. Shirley's sociability, the alacrity with which she shared her learning and her enthusiasms, could turn at times to intractability, particularly about the UN. And there was the matter of her tendency to monologue, noted by many, and even for good friends sometimes a problem. Annabel heard before she met Shirley of her capacity to monopolise and found that conversation generally involved "finding a moment when you could interrupt." Most people really did not mind. Benjamin Taylor memorably described her as "more cataract than woman once she got going, and everything she has to say is of interest." Ann Goldstein, impressed with Shirley's range of reference, also felt she had "this very hard intellect" that involved speaking her opinions but not listening. After attempting at first to present alternative views, "I realised there was no point. So I was content just to listen to her." Michael Mallon felt that "what she had to say was so much more interesting than what most other people have to say that I was happy to let her discourse." People felt that it wasn't about Shirley wanting to dominate. It had, Alison West said, "nothing to do with pride. Just the tidal waves of knowledge that she had stored up and that she was eager to share." And it was of a piece with the authority of her bearing. Evan Cornog made the point that Shirley "wouldn't let stuff pass if she thought it was intellectually or in character shoddy in some way. She would call people out on it. Not in a throw down the gauntlet way but you'd know it had been noticed." Alec Wilkinson felt that this quality made her something of "an assassin." She was "not judging so much as measuring, observing," and this was part of her sharp focus on the world: "She was paying attention. Ferociously. It was her habit of mind to pay attention." Francis carried similar authority, although he tended to defer socially to her. In company, many friends observed, "it would be Shirley being vivacious and lively, doing most of the talking, protecting Francis. He was always quieter, she much more the dazzling one." Akeel Bilgrami recalled one dinner at the Steegmullers' apartment with Edward Said, an occasion both guests felt to have been "marred" by Shirley dominating the conversation, talking endlessly about the UN. "She wouldn't give Francis a chance to talk because she was so incensed—about Waldheim, about bureaucracy, about everything to do with the UN." At the same time, Bilgrami found that one-on-one she was notably less garrulous, was indeed an attentive conversationalist, completely charming, "keen on probing what you thought."

On occasion, Francis too made it plain that he had had enough vivacity. For Shirley, such moments—when her spiritedness was rebuffed and she was left feeling misunderstood and unvalued—sat alongside her ongoing chagrin about not having time to write:

> I woke in the night thinking that I am getting old, with no new work accomplished, and no inward <u>increase</u>. So many good things—but on this—a blank. Not a shred of real understanding, nor wish to understand. Immediate rebuttal, egotism. Tonight, sweetly, to dinner at a new restaurant near us on Third Ave. Pleasant; we sat in window . . . Because of two glasses of wine, spoke about [World War II British civil servant Jock] Colville's diaries I'm reading . . . As I'm speaking, with (a little) animation, feel the lack of response, the boredom on the other side. Whenever I

show spontaneity there is this. Surely connected to a compulsion to make me feel that spontaneity is a show, unwelcome, of foolishness. Cannot be mere chance, so long, time after time. Yet it was that, perhaps, I had to offer. The best self in prison. On the other hand, my "compulsion" to go on having—showing—such a spontaneous self . . . When we got home, I came—yes, stupidly, incredibly—with the book in my hand. Before I said a word, there was this: "Another time . . ." Thus, no expression of the heart allowed me—neither the spontaneous sharing; nor the loneliness, the subsiding "with a shudder" . . . I feel within, often, like a bleached bone.

The Steegmullers maintained long friendships. Francis and Beatrice had known the artist Randall Morgan for many years, and the friendship continued with Shirley. Morgan had arrived in Naples during the war and stayed, living for long periods in and around Positano. He settled finally with his former lover Peppino, Peppino's wife, and their son— Randy's "familia"—at Torca, a "beautiful house and prospect—green, blue" which he painted over and over. Shirley and Francis made regular trips to Sorrento, where they would meet Randy and Peppino, visiting on one occasion the Villa Astor, which had been the home of the philosopher Benedetto Croce in the early 1900s: "Vast garden allowed to be a judicious 'wilderness'—palms, bamboos, cactus, ferns, agapanthus. Heavenly terrace on sea, nineteenth-century 'Roman' busts. Cats and dogs."

In 1986 Shirley's old friend James Merrill was in Italy with his partner, Peter Hooten. They made their way to Capri, then came to lunch at Posillipo with Shirley, Francis, and Randy Morgan, who was also visiting. Merrill wrote to the novelist Samuel Lock of the transformative, restorative quality of this day. It was, he wrote, like "inhabiting a postcard," a world of "'beauty' and 'civilization,'" and of "the beautiful manners of people." Later he wrote to thank Shirley: "I can see through shut eyes the magic driveway and the enchanted terrace, and feel the little blue waves of talk and silence, all of which made for such a perfect afternoon." Shirley had regaled her guests with the story of their cook, Rita, "a drama in herself," and of Rita's acerbic response to Shirley's request "please for a

quieter life": "Silenzio e solitudine sono le cose più brutte del mondo."
[Silence and solitude are the ugliest things in the world.] Merrill had
been taken by the story, and added in his note to Shirley that as he and
Hooten were leaving, they'd caught a glimpse of "Rita and her lover
from the taxi window, and gaped as if they were film stars." Years later
Merrill wrote a poem about Rita and presented it to Shirley at dinner, a
note folded by her plate:

> *Silenzio e Solitudine*
> *Neapolitan Cook*
> *On hearing the Signora needed these*
> *In order to write her book.*
> *Nothing in life's more offensive to You Know Whom!*
> *Rolling her eyes at the plaster skies*
> *And clattering out of the room.*

After Merrill's death, Sandy McClatchy sent Shirley Merrill's copy of
*The Princess Casamassima*, as "emblem of mutual feelings" and figure
for their late friend's "Jamesian brio before the pageant of life," and to
signal his admiration for her work: "Believe me, Transit of Venus was one
of his very favourite books; he was forever pressing copies on strangers."

In Capri in the mid-1980s Shirley met Will and Alison Parente, who
were regularly on the island for long periods at their Villa Monte San
Michele. Will was the son of Prince Gaetano Parente and Lady Margaret Anne Cavendish-Bentinck and had inherited Monte San Michele
in 1976 on the death of his father. The villa had descended from his
maternal great-grandparents, Lord Algernon and Lady Blanche Gordon-
Lennox, who had bought it in 1900. Alison was a child psychotherapist
in London. They had already noticed Shirley and Francis around Capri:
"They stood out in a particular way. Shirley because she was so smiley
and so distinguished and always immaculately dressed. And charming.
Francis was tall, thin, handsome and you could guess from his face that
he was an interesting person. This was a striking couple. They looked like
interesting, significant people." One June morning, walking to or from

the *piazzetta*, the Parentes' young children attracted Shirley's attention. There was a conversation, then an invitation to Monte San Michele for drinks, a short, steep walk up from the Steegmullers' Via Sopramonte apartment. It was a walk they would often retrace over the next twenty years. Shirley recorded in her diary how, on this first visit, they walked around the extensive villa grounds: "Stupendous. Will Parente takes us up through brambled path to, first, huge Roman construction, drowned in growth, one of a series circling the hill. Inner cisterns; a great trough, many unexplained inner details. Then in cima, more Roman 'cisterns' with a room, once frescoed, 'fitted' as a church then, beautiful circular walks." This was the kind of scene that entranced Shirley—local, almost inconsequential, and full of the past.

At the heart of this friendship, as so often, was literature. Will and Alison felt that for Shirley, poetry and novels were "probably clearer than her own everyday experience," offering an accessibility, "a way of talking about life." Literature itself constituted a language that was "more important than any other language," that "could reach the parts that other forms cannot reach." And through this interest in literature Shirley pursued questions of human psychology. Once, during a conversation with Will about *War and Peace*, Shirley recalled Denisov's response to the death of Petya in a skirmish: "He rode up to Petya, dismounted, and with trembling hands turned Petya's blood-stained, mud-bespattered face— which had already gone white—towards himself. 'I always like sweet things. Wonderful raisins, take them all,' he recalled Petya's words. And the Cossacks looked round in amazement at the sound, like the howl of a dog, which broke from Denisov as he quickly turned away, walked to the wattle fence and held on to it." Shirley commented that "Denisov's response—the last thing that would be expected of him, his character is tough, above all—was completely right." She believed, Will recalled, "that we saw more of Denisov at that moment than Freud would ever have been able to. She felt that the formal discipline of psychology would never give you that kind of insight, that focus on the unexpected and the often overlooked."

Another important friendship was with Salvatore Marigliano, their

Naples driver, who drove them and their friends and guests whenever they were in Naples. Salvatore called Francis "Don Ciccio" with great fondness and took care of him as Francis's capacities declined, waiting with him at Posillipo while Shirley was in the city or at Capri, then helping him dress, and driving him to meet Shirley on her return. In 1991 Shirley and Francis hosted a celebration to mark the graduation of Salvatore's daughter, "a large gathering of the Salvatore family before the fire in our middle room . . . How nice it was, how nice they were. One relative (a sort of auntie) pinched my cheek so hard I yelped." They went, a few years later, to Salvatore's son Pasquale's wedding, and Shirley wrote an account of it at some length, suggesting the significance of such events for her and registering her delight in the forms and formalities, the respect paid to guests, the deeper Neapolitan sociality:

> Pasquale's sister and her fiancé Claudio come in car to our place at Posillipo and drive us to Baia-Bacoli where reception is held . . . First, much kind greeting, much embracing of "Ciccio," and briefly we sit outdoors to wonderful oysters ("Lucrine" oysters). Then indoors—again, much introducing etc—we greet Pasquale and meet Monica, in charming white . . . Salvatore is "in giro," masterminding all . . . There are babies in arms and children running—all these later become of course over excited and desperate with fatigue; some fall asleep, head on table, others in parents' arms. All guests are well dressed, and, in Italian-Neapolitan way, both blithe and decorous. (Nobody gets drunk or querulous or shouts; blessedly, no one makes a speech) . . . A huge meal of many refined courses—all seafood . . . with fizzy white wine of the zone, also v good. Abbondanza. All fare of the ancients.

As in so many of these extended accounts in her notebooks, not novelistic in themselves but providing a mark, a trace, of novelistic attention, there is Shirley's excited attentiveness to detail and continuity: the rooms, the activity, the human life around her, bedded in the past. Salvatore remained a significant friend for the rest of their lives. Annabel remembered, on a Naples visit, as they prepared to set out somewhere, catching sight of Salvatore, far shorter than Francis, reaching up to re-arrange the scarf around Francis's neck.

The serious attention Shirley paid to custom and form is evident in her careful record of Salvatore's family events. On Capri too she was deeply versed in local gossip about businesses, families, individuals; she knew intimately the stories of cherished births or other achievements. She patronised the same small handful of trattorie: Le Grottelle near the Arco Naturale, where she ate almost every day, and the Ristorante da Gemma, always in the pizzeria where the locals ate, rather than the dining room favoured by tourists. She knew local customs, such as tipping the pizzaiolo. Other Caprese recalled, in admiration, that "she understood even the Neapolitan dialect." And she always attended events such as the Blessing of the Fleet and the Feast of San Costanzo, patron saint of the island. She described the procession in 1991:

> Saint's silver bust trotted round the island on a throne decked with flowers, followed by procession of hundreds. It is his "milennium" (how established, uncertain). Our Roccardo [Roccardo Ruocco, from da Gemma] is one of the four bearers of the supporting poles; and has shown us his raw shoulder. Delightful processions with bands (three, all simultaneously playing different airs), cascades of flung petals, children bearing garlands; an authentic remnant of uncommercial times on the island, all that Norman Douglas might have wished, including a rope of corals around the neck of a saint.

After a visit to Capri in the summer of 1987, Bill Maxwell wrote to say that he was thinking of Shirley and Francis "settling down in the corner table of the kitchen at Gemma's . . . I should return the funicular ticket but instead have pinned it to the wall above my desk, to remind me of the piazza and the two of you reading your mail and Il Mattino. It is such a pleasure to have an idea of your daily habits. When I can go in my imagination to where you are, where you are is not far away."

In Naples, there were also traces of Shirley's past in the city, such as a long-ago neighbour of the Villa Mazziotti in Via Posillipo who recalled to James Merrill in 1986 that "there had been a 'Shirley' while he was growing up"—a long arc of remembrance, a sustained inhabitation. Jonathan Burnham visited her in Naples in the early 1990s and was struck by the image of Shirley and Francis navigating the "dangerous, crazy, noisy streets . . . walking sturdily along, somehow both fragile and very strong at the same time." Burnham was particularly struck by "the contrast between these two enormously sophisticated, very delicate people and this rough and tumble city, where they were absolutely at home." Shirley would chat with waiters and shopkeepers: "I could tell the affection they all felt for Shirley and Francis. It was extraordinary. They were deeply well known. And loved. Recognised as these Anglo-Saxon eccentrics who loved Italy and Italy loved them back."

Shirley treasured those moments when her connection to Italy was acknowledged by locals.

> In Piazza dei Martiri, in bookshop when new salesgirl asked if I was an (old) client the remaining ancient retainer said: 'La Signora è cresciuta qui.' [The Signora grew up here.] Moments later, in Via Calabritto, a setter came out of a shop as I was looking in. The owner called the dog back—I said apologetically, 'Stavo ammirando il cane.' Instant reply: 'Lui stave ammirando Lei.' [I was admiring the dog / He was admiring you.] Da Marinella (tie-shop, old, delightful) owner genially greets us, presiding in his chair. Dedication of time, civility, humour.

Such courtesy was, for Shirley, of a piece with local respect for the arts. She recalled sending, in 1973, a congratulatory telegram from the Capri post office to Patrick White on hearing of his Nobel Prize: "The cable boys (far from the imposing stern professional ethics of indifference to message) were thrilled, having just read the news in the papers. 'Dev'esser bravissimo! Auguri!' Auguri indeed." In early 1984 Francis recorded in his diary an episode in Rome when their taxi driver began reciting poetry as he drove them back to the Hassler hotel one evening. Shirley of course joined him, and together they recited works by "Palazzeschi, Pascoli, Foscolo," and then, inevitably, Leopardi: "all of Silvia, much of

La Sera, L'Infinito, La Ginestra, Pastore Errante, Vaghe Stelle. Beautiful. His name Ernesto. (Spoke of Wilde). Refuses payment absolutely. Boy at Hassler door says, 'It is only among simple people that there is poetry now.' Both, all three, near tears." There were many such moments: "Lively, youngish taxi driver, finding we were writers: I write too, but with my mouth. And with my hands." They consulted a doctor in Naples about a sprained arm, "a charming elderly orthopaedist, man of culture, who has remained faithful to the Futurists and himself paints in that manner." They found that he had come to meet their ferry from Capri, and then refused payment. Francis observed, "These experiences make you feel you never want to leave this place."

Beyond and beneath the life of Capri and Naples was the topographical, the meteorological world, no less lively and intricate. Shirley was captivated by the scene around her and by the changing seasons, writing lengthy and detailed accounts in her notebooks and in letters to friends. November 1988:

> The vegetable stalls have persimmons, fruit of cactus, pomegranates, chestnuts, swags of garlic and pepperoncino, in addition to the usual cornucopia. Walking down our Posillipo viale in the dark, woodsmoke smells, jasmine and pine smells . . . We breakfast and lunch outdoors, sometimes too hot; then light a fire in the evening in our small fireplace. On Capri, visionary clarity. Today, lunch at Arco, three tables occupied, euphoria. One sees the mountains above Paestum. Soon they will have white tops. Island mornings are divinely beautiful now, one knows what it once meant to be here. Only the sound of shots profanes as hundreds of tiny birds are mown down. A tiny red-breast came to our door, a refugee, trembling. Early dark on Capri is austere, soundless, desolate. This evening, what a sunset, with the island etched on it quite black and seemingly without lights.

In April, the islands around looked "as if cut into gulf, stencilled. Clear, golden air, far visibility," and in June, "At this moment we're having our daily experience of what Neapolitans call 'la trubbeja de' cerase' (la tropea delle ciliege), a brief late storm that often appears from a clear sky at the season of ripe cherries—its proper time is somewhat past . . . On the Posillipo our nights are heavy with the scent of jasmine, just in time to replace the orange blossom."

They adopted local cats and fed them; Herodotus and Nelson and Miscia. "My one-eyed cat Nelson has been joined by Miscia, who wants to have her kittens among F's sweaters. Nelson's bad eye is in great trouble. But his good eye is very compelling—as must have been the case with his great namesake's." She recorded Nelson's comings and goings in her diaries and was worried about leaving him alone when they went back to New York in late 1988. "We've fixed him up with a bed in the little storeroom, and someone will feed him. But—that trusting little musino, and that now luxuriant coat; and that look of new health that brings a gleam even to his missing eye. He comes in our laps and is stroked and called Nelsoncino, and Nelsie, and even (Australian) Nelse. He squeaks when we arrive from an absence. More fondling, more hypocoristic endearments." When Nelson died after several years at their Via Sopramonte apartment, Francis observed with sadness, "What it means is that there's a little less affection in the world." In Naples, Shirley fed lizards on the terrace, remarking their quasi-domestication: "They usually arrive when we're eating outdoors, spurning the breadcrumbs they once eagerly munched in their odd little jaws, and chomping thoughtfully instead on chicken and sweet biscuits. Their method is to disintegrate the biscuit first, which leaves little crumbled heaps. I didn't expect to spend so much of my latter years cleaning up after a lizard." The *New Yorker* editor William Shawn once said that "his great treat to himself" was to telephone Shirley in Italy to hear her describe their "life and surroundings on the terrace— like a paragraph or passage in a book one wants to treasure."

It was being in a place, in Naples or Capri, or New York, that preoccupied her days; that, and care of Francis. Nonetheless, work did continue, slowly, on *The Great Fire*. Her unresolved, unresolvable relation to the fact of Alec Vedeniapine's later life—his marriage, children, the farm that had been his dream—made the shape and story of the novel based on that early love difficult to set down. She spoke candidly about this after the book was published, how long it had taken to get the tone right: "I had it always in mind, but it didn't please me . . . I wrote quite a bit and threw it out. I didn't like the tone, didn't think I was ready." She turned to other scenes and stories, several of which were published as stand-alone pieces over the next few years. The first of these, telling of Peter Exley's arrival in Hong Kong in 1947, was in *The New Yorker* in June 1987. Bill Maxwell wrote,

> What an extraordinary story. And if it is part of something longer, what an extraordinary novel we have to look forward to. How I love to see a really good writer proceeding confidently farther and farther out on the end of a limb. And it is not only where he ended up, it is where you have! I was lost in admiration of how securely you handled the masculine point of view, though you have demonstrated this talent before. Not only the point of view but the private masculine world. At times I could smell the sweaty socks.

Shirley sent copies to Chris Cooper and Alec, and Chris wrote back, "Alec was as impressed as I am by the Proustian power of recall you show in the Hong Kong story; in fact your mental abilities obviously inspire in him a marked sense of awe—a bit of a reversal of the situation of forty years ago, eh?" Important for Shirley at this point was the acknowledgment of that past time, of the self she had been, a self in the process of being reimagined in the novel she had been drafting, now already for so long. That past story itself constituted an insertion, an interruption, into her daily life. She copied Chris's letter into her notebook in full and added, "These last words, read silently in the street as we waited to cross Third Ave (to buy food etc for weekend) gave such pleasure, as testimony. Chris is the only witness now, the 'evidence' that it has not been mere fantasy. Otherwise, unshared, and infinitely solitary. Also, though sadness in themselves, the words refer to that disposition of 'roles'—authority on his side, adoration (and yet some personality too) on mine."

In 1990, alongside *Countenance of Truth*, she also published translations of two poems by Elena Vivante's friend, the poet Camillo Sbarbaro, "Even If You Weren't My Father" and "I Wake Alone," in *The New*

*Yorker.* She left no commentary on the process beyond passing references to the labours and delights of translation, but the poems themselves speak to the prevailing perceptions of her life: ". . . were it not / for Nature, . . . / all the speechless world of things / . . . I think that I would die of solitude."

In September she marked the deaths, three days apart, of Alberto Moravia in Rome and Patrick White in Sydney. The news, not unexpected in either case, was nonetheless "somehow shocking." Both were, she wrote Donald Keene, "difficult men, and both, I'd say, writers who had lost impetus in later years. But, in part because of formidability, they were the kind who don't die, don't appear subject to death." The following month, "Graham Greene, on phone, tells us he is living from constant transfusions. (He sounded very ill; but livened up as he developed antagonism.) This strange procession, as Barbara Pym calls it." Greene died six months later; Shirley remarked that after Moravia's death, the Italian newspaper *La Repubblica* had the headline "Senza Moravia," and added, "For Graham too, there were hardly any English-speaking people who had not grown up aware of him and somehow counting on him to be there always." A few months after Greene it was the turn of her old friend Sumner Locke Elliott, of cancer. Red Warren had died the previous year. Shirley and Francis had gone to Vermont for the usual Christmas visit in 1988; Warren's biographer, Joseph Blotner, writes that Shirley sat with Red looking out at the winter scene. "She thought of Hardy's 'The Darkling Thrush' and intoned the lines 'Winter's dregs made desolate / The weakening eye of day.' And he, without missing a beat, took up the next line: 'The tangled bine-stems scored the sky / Like strings from [*sic*] broken lyres . . .'"

In marking these deaths Shirley was acknowledging private, personal loss alongside the formal passage of time, and of an age; this would become one of the themes of the memoir of Graham Greene to which she would devote her time for the next several years. The public deaths also framed another loss, larger because there was no context in which she could speak of its significance. Alec Vedeniapine had long been in failing health. In February she telephoned, and they spoke, as always, of the past. When the news came some months later of his death, it was absurdly belated, the moment already lost in the time of their other, later lives, a scene from Hardy, or one of her own novels. She was on Capri. "Returning together from a velvety perfect night, dinner at Arco, lights of coast, far off fireworks for San Pietro e Paolo—some lightning—I called Chris. Speaking of APV—as we discovered, at cross purposes—Chris suddenly said: 'But you know he's dead?' Thus a break in the past forty-three years. This point of reference, this centre; gone. Nothing now can be added, or change."

Unacknowledged and unacknowledgeable, Alec's death, the persistent and reiterated loss prompted endless recollection, reflection: "As if one had swallowed a stone. The compulsive blighting." Inexpressible—not simply because the right to the expression of grief remained with his widow and family, but, this perhaps most of all, because grief's object was itself impossibly past. As well as the "centre, gone," there was also completeness, forestalling understanding. And once again she voiced a criticism, the sense of some falling short on Alec's part, some "incapacity—not for love, exactly, he was affectionate—but for passion, for great love, for intimacy sustained; for imaginative love. Compared with mine, what was his love? Strange but it was passive." Alongside this she felt, if not anger, then the burden of her husband's increasing frailty and her boundedness:

> The wish to be away, to regain my being, to matter, to give pleasure. To matter. What use to enumerate episodes, words? Nothing is but what those represent. And that is the world, in essence, for humans. For the present, no wish to live, that is to be lively. Yet, always the life struggling up, wanting to cast off the blight. Rebellious, the impulse to be alive, oddly different from "wish to live." Waste . . . The typewriter clicking, rattling, pounding on, the machine running ahead like a locomotive over every appeal for love, for company. The reciprocal time to do my own work, think my thoughts, live in my appropriate state (cannot express this—return to the realm of spontaneity, of poetry, to the centre). Clicking, clicking, rattling, pounding on.

These resentments were not voiced outside her diary, and she ever maintained, quite simply, the rightness of her decision through these years to prioritise Francis's work—the joint project with the translator Barbara Bray, correspondence of Flaubert and George Sand, and a study of the French-Neapolitan life of the Abbé Galiani—over her own. It seems likely that she contributed to the writing of these books, although this was never explicitly acknowledged beyond vague comments about his failing memory and his need of her help. Both projects treated the subject of correspondence, of relations between a man and a woman, while also depending themselves on collaboration, that is, on a woman's contribution. Shirley was a longtime admirer of George Sand, particularly in relation to Flaubert. What she admired, she wrote Murray Bail, was Sand's "life of sustained heroism—free love, anticlericism, liberty of conscience, a working independent life: all these now taken for granted, she wept and sweated blood for them: reviled, ridiculed, exploited. Once in a while she drives you bonkers with the Pollyanna approach to Flaubert—how could she suggest he get married, raise a child . . . and so on. But she is noble and, in a large and profound way, _true_. And sometimes Flaubert shrank by contrast, I felt." She felt that the project was itself important, but above all, it was important that Francis be working. She often tried to persuade him "to abandon Flaubert, or Galiani, for a few days" so that they could travel, for instance to Puglia, where she had not been for many years. But "it became too onerous to suggest to him, that is, that journey would have been too tiring for him. He had consecrated his energies to getting those last two books finished, realising that memory and concentration were beginning to fail him."

Beyond this, she found pleasure and connection in daily routine: "We generally have warm days; but often light the fire in the evening and have our dinner in front of it. After which, read our Thucydides, which we've now finished—one night, could not stop, went on to end of book by mutual agreement. That tragic work, whose tragedy is multiplied by the thousands of times it has been repeated and disregarded . . . So we return to NYC changed by the experience." They had bought a large painting by Randy Morgan, brought back to Posillipo from the United States. Randy and his familia came from Sorrento to oversee the hanging and to have lunch on the terrace. "Nice to see the artist greet his long-absent works and sit down in our entry to clean our new acquisition . . . It is a view of one of the Sorrentine mini-capes, Capo San Lorenzo, looking out to a dream-like Capri. Maurizio and Mirella [Barracco], who participated in the hanging, said, 'How can you leave when your place looks so lovely?' A question."

While Shirley's book inched ahead—two further extracts were published in 1990 and 1994—Francis completed both of his. The first was published in 1991, Francis "carried shoulder-high through the streets of Naples, metaphorically speaking, for his Galiani enterprise," and galleys for the Flaubert-Sand letters arrived shortly after. Leon Edel wrote to thank Francis "for sending me your little masterpiece—as I have already said, a jewel. It is good to have it from you and to think of the long years we have been friends on both sides of the world. You inscribed your Maupassant to me when we lunched once in Chinatown, in NY, in the late 1940s or early 50s [Francis has added in a pencilled margin note: 30 Jan 1950]." Among the reviews of both books, Francis was particularly touched by one from the English novelist Julian Barnes, who made mention of "the precise, elegant, and wise interpolations of Francis Steegmuller, our premier English-language Flaubertian." Barnes and Steegmuller had maintained a warm writerly friendship over the previous decade. Francis had admired Barnes's 1984 *Flaubert's Parrot* in typescript and in the years following their first exchange—"Dear Doctor Barnes . . ."; "Dear Mister Barnes: Please forgive the 'Doctor.' I wonder why I was taken in by that feature of the delightful performance. Its particular audacity, perhaps, in a Flaubert saga? In return, please skip the 'Professor': I'm an 'MA' but that's ancient history"—had occasionally sent brief details of Flaubert discoveries. In his obituary—one of few published in the UK, where Steegmuller's work was not so well-known—Barnes wrote: "In his later years, Francis Steegmuller had the bearing of an extremely wise and extremely benign Supreme Court judge. Even his socks, I couldn't help noticing the first time I met him, were judicial: very long, very black and very silky," adding that his work showed "how the mind should travel."

And as his accomplishments were honoured, Francis's decline

continued. One day in Posillipo, Shirley found that he had written on the wall beside his bed, "Dreamt that BTS [Bertha Tierney Steegmuller] liked this book." Shortly after, he collapsed onto the table in a restaurant in Rome. He revived quickly, but the doctors were concerned. Later, back in New York, he had a bad fall on the escalator in Bloomingdale's, was helped to safety with no major medical issues detected. Nonetheless, Shirley wrote Donald Keene, "It was one of those events where the abyss yawns—that abyss described in the Iliad, shortly before the encounter between Achilles and Hector that ends with Hector's death, where the fearful underworld threatens to break open, that underneath of things feared alike 'by mortals and the immortal gods.' I think of that passage in connection with the interior of the crater of Vesuvius . . ." There were additional chores now for her, such as ensuring that Francis had full notes—scripts, really—for interviews. He would write down in advance the things he wanted to say, and Shirley typed it all up, reordering things and adding key details: "My wife's name is Shirley Hazzard. All her novels in Penguin . . ."

Spring 1993. They were driven, as always, from Rome to Naples. "Great scene of flowering orchards, yellow mustard, white daisies— hemicircle of dark mountains snow-capped. The violets I planted among the geraniums last year are in bloom." Francis remained at Posillipo, resting, as Shirley wrote in his diary, "an interval to recover full powers of concentration and fortify memory," while she went to Capri to open the apartment. Salvatore came to collect Francis and take him to meet Shirley, who was returning later the next day on the Mergellina boat. They were reading *The Odyssey* together, then *Timon of Athens* at Posillipo and *Hamlet* on Capri. When they returned to Capri, Shirley encouraged Francis through notes in the diary: "F coraggio for climb to house and then the stairs. Bravo." Giles Constable and Pat Woolf visited, and Pat wrote later of the lingering traces of their time there:

> Your yesterday-today-tomorrow plant is much in our minds with its sweet fragrance. I remember your recital of poems, Shirley, and as we drove close to, but not through Verona, small fragments like bits of the wall came back to me, and thus, to us, as we discussed

our dinners and our walks, your attentiveness and your wisdom. It
was a pleasure, and a lesson to watch you both with your Neapolitan friends and helpers—transient blessings lightly conferred and
received amidst great beauty. And in the dailiness of life.

In June they telephoned Bill Weaver in Tuscany and spoke with Muriel, who was dining with him, "to congratulate on Dameship and to
exchange a word. Moving. 'Old times.'"

Managing three homes on two continents increasingly took its toll,
and Shirley's diaries recorded "the death of one thousand tasks." A pair of
notes from 1994 give a sense of how burdensome it all had become. The
first sets out her vexation, the second Francis's gentleness that allowed it
all to continue. "Dear Puss, Think about this. My little piece about Elena
Vivante, which you just read, is the first piece I have been able to write
in months—wrung out from my non-existent 'time.' You drew attention
to two possible errors, and that was that. Could you not say something favourable?" Francis's response, on identical paper, his handwriting jagged
and uneven, showing the effort that writing now took: "Dear Shirl—It
was inexcusable of me not to <u>say</u> what I thought, and what I assumed
you must have known I thought about this marvellous, and marvellously
beautiful, tribute. <u>Please</u>, forgive to the extent you can."

To lighten the daily burden of care, Shirley took on an occasional
companion-carer for Francis. They had met Bill Hall when he delivered
books to them from an Upper East Side rare book dealer. On Bill's first
visit, Francis greeted him, asking, "Is it all right that I'm in my pyjamas?" Bill was charmed by Francis's gentleness, his touching grasp of
his own condition, and by Shirley's care. He recalled her having Francis
talk his way through a pile of old photographs. She would sit with him
and ask him about the photographs, then, after they had looked at a few,
would say, "Francis, you keep going." And so he would, naming friends
and places, past travels, their life together, happily unaware that he was
now on his third or fourth time through the pile. Shirley arranged for Bill
to spend time with Francis so she could do errands or make visits. The
first time, she explained that she would settle Francis in the garden and
leave a note in his suit jacket to explain who Bill was. When Bill arrived,

Francis was sitting in the sun. Bill told him he was there to take him for a walk, and Francis responded, "You'll have to excuse me. I'm terribly absent-minded and I have no idea who you are." Bill explained about the note, Francis took it out and read it: "Oh. All right then, let's go."

There were many such moments. When Francis forgot the name of a friend, Shirley "came and put her hand on my shoulder and said, 'Francis, this is Bob Pounder. You know Bob.' 'Oh yes.' She was the most courteous person I ever knew." One night in New York, Jonathan Burnham was there for dinner. Francis showed Jonathan a photograph of his brother, who had died thirty years earlier, a young man in uniform. "You look exactly like my brother," Francis insisted, and then repeated it. Jonathan said later to Shirley, "I don't think I look anything like Francis's brother. She said, 'You don't look anything like him. But Francis loved his brother, and he loves you, so he's putting the two things together.' It was this extraordinary compassionate insight into his condition." During a visit in early 1994 from Martin Stannard, there to interview Shirley about Muriel Spark, she was trying to get Francis to recall his days in the OSS during the war. "'But you *must* remember that,' Shirley insisted, 'you *must*.' He didn't. And so she tenderly sketched out a few of his anecdotes for him." Francis told Stannard, "It's all kinda jumbled up, a terrible mess." Mary Ellin Barrett recalled, "Francis would say, 'Don't ask me about yesterday or last week.' And he made a gesture. 'You have to go *right back*.' I would think of something from far back and he was fine." At times he was able to participate more substantially. Shirley noted in her diary a visit from Bram Pais and Saul Steinberg in 1993, when Steinberg talked of his Rumanian childhood: "When I understood where I was, I decided to leave." "(Like Australia)," she added, and then wrote Francis's response to the visit: "How to write anything of this delightful—elegant—occasion? Lofty but never losing touch with laughter and simpatia."

Shirley had begun writing her memoir of Graham Greene, prompted by an exchange of letters with his friend, Michael Richey, "a writer, sculptor, graphic artist, lone long-distance sailor." Richey had been with Greene in the café on Capri in the late 1960s when Shirley walked past and provided the last line of the Browning poem Greene was struggling to remember, the meeting that sparked their friendship. He wrote after

Greene's death to ask the details: "It's a pretty story and I'd like to get it right. What was the poem and what the passage?" In her reply, Shirley began, in effect, writing the book: "The meeting in Capri, and the days that followed, are a very pleasant memory—which goes, for my part, as follows: I was sitting in the Gran Caffè on a day—it seems to me—just after Christmas, doing the crossword in the Times. The weather was awful, not really cold but inexorably wet. The piazza of Capri was pretty well empty, and the very few tables inside the caffè were mostly unoccupied. It was about 11:30 or noon . . ." Her account continues for several pages and includes many of the elements of the story of the friendship with Greene around which the memoir developed. Richey responded that hers had been "quite the nicest" letter he had ever had. They went on to become friends, and she worked on the memoir over those last years of Francis's life, when she had not the time or capacity to take on the more demanding work of her novel. After his death, the writing provided a frame and receptacle for the public expression of her grief.

The year 1994 began, as it would end, with death. In February they heard that Harold Acton, ill for some time, had died. Shirley later wrote of his significance in her life: "I can scarcely say that I 'think often' of Harold, because there is nothing intermittent about it: he is part of the consciousness, I think, of everyone who knew him well, and we know there will never be anyone remotely like him again. He belonged to an era (and to some extent a class) of high culture and wit and extraordinary articulateness; all this played with style and great good manners. I loved him." The spring saw her as ever with Francis in Italy, first in Rome with the Ripa di Meanas and Giulio; then they were driven to Naples: "Rain en route but ecstatic sense of spring countryside." They learnt there of Ralph Ellison's death, and Francis wrote to his widow, Fanny: "You will know how many many memories are stirred for me by this event, and images of years when we were all young, or younger . . . Ralph was blessed in his talent and in his use of it; and in his life companion." News came next of Randy Morgan's diagnosis of cancer and, shortly after, of his death. Shirley wrote an obituary for *Il Mattino*. She was unable to attend the funeral, as the Sorrento ferry schedule would have meant leaving Francis alone all day. Francis was, she wrote in her diary, now largely "unrealising of things around him." She snatched moments to work on her Greene memoir, with "infinite" interruptions. There were domestic demands, Francis's needs, but also the endless distraction of the beauty around her: "May 3—Bellissimo. To town for flowers, food—such a scene of the gulf from Via Petrarca . . . Lunch outdoors—flowers, birdsong, sea. Enchantment of the scene. Read *Antony and Cleopatra*—overwhelmed, both." Her oldest Naples friend, Lily Gravino, came, and Chris Cooper visited from England. As the days became warmer, Francis was more often unable to manage: "To Capri after long exhausting 'toil' for S at Posillipo—arrive to find wilting Capresi . . . F arrives exhausted. Dinner Gemma, in room adjoining pizzeria where air-conditioning strongest. F broken reed. S at end of tether—the inability to register and therefore to share. Preoccupied with survival. Late, S in despair. Sleep helps."

By late July they were back in New York: "Heaviness. Air and sky like mustard gas. S struggling with horror-mass of papers—bills, correspondence . . . F, today, frighteningly unable; out of things. No way to pass an hour—sleep, wander about, look at paintings, catalogues. S, despair. Tears at heart. Find F sitting in hot chair at dining table, incapable. At 6, attempt short walk. Return in great anxiety—F exhausted, scarcely conscious. Revives later. All dreadful." They had dinner with Bill Weaver, who had recently moved back to New York, and with Dorle Soria, Evan Cornog, and Ann Goldstein, and then Shirley went by herself to Bill Maxwell's birthday: "Beautiful day, place, friends." She later carried great remorse from this time, feeling that she had not been as patient with Francis as she might have been. In mid-September they set off again for Italy. Shirley was hoping to attend a conference on Capri about Tiberius: "New documents, in fact incised bronze tablets, have been discovered in Spain dramatically bearing on Tiberius' arranged murder of Germanicus and then of Gnaeus Piso, his instrument; these more than validate the drastic narrative in the Annals of Tacitus—an account long disputed as too condemnatory of Tiberius and now seen to be if anything over-lenient." However, her attention was wholly taken up with Francis. Returning home from the piazza one day in late September, she found him, with "no pants, sitting at top of steps with blood over face and arm, dazed. A fall into plants etc. Horror, also for what could have been."

Most days, they rode together to the Arco Naturale in one of the small motorised Capri chariots. After a meal at Le Grottelle, Francis would be driven back to their apartment by chariot while she walked back alone. These solitary walks were now, she wrote, "Essential." They provided a benign rhythm, a connection to "Capri com'era," counterweighting Francis's looming collapse and the intensive domestic arrangements needed to keep things going. On October 20, early in the evening, back at Posillipo, he took a sudden turn for the worse. Shirley phoned Salvatore, who came, drove them to the Ospedale Internazionale. Francis was very weak, but he "revived somewhat with treatment." He spoke to a male nurse: "You have beautiful hands." Lily arrived. As the hours wore on, "deterioration, incoherence"; then, just before midnight, "sudden change, unconsciousness—brief struggle for breath. Gone. My darling."

Salvatore and his wife drove Shirley home a few hours later, their joint presence a silent tribute to her loss and their own. She returned to the hospital next morning with Salvatore "to pay bill, to 'arrange.'" Lily was already there. "Inexpressibly good to me, she is perfect. Salvatore brings an undertaker 'cousin' to arrange F's cremation near Bologna. All terrible. But they comfort me. We see body again. Cannot write about this. To Municipio in Monte di Dio. (Lily left flowers on his body). At home— all good to me, helpful. Salvatore will go with F's body. Exhausted and trying to absorb. Make many calls." In the following days the calls continued, and Salvatore drove with Francis's body in an ambulance the nearly four hundred miles (600 km) to Bologna; there was no closer crematorium. A lonely journey for Salvatore, a final gesture of care, of love, for Don Ciccio. Shirley does not seem to have considered accompanying him; as at Kit's death, she saw no need for that kind of acknowledgment.

These were, Shirley's diary records, "strange days." She observed as always the light and the elements: "big storm, then fine, windy day. Splendid light. A huge old three-master passes, high sea." She wrote to Valerie, a rare event now, walked up the long driveway at Villa Emma to the gate to post the letter. Salvatore returned from Bologna with Francis's ashes. Friends visited, called, wrote obituaries. The London *Times* included a photo of Francis taken by Alan Maclean on his last visit, a few days before Francis died. There were private tributes that spoke to the intimacies Francis had established over his writing life. One came from Leon Edel:

> I read with distinct sorrow the news of Francis's death and want to send you this word of participation and sympathy. As you know, we were casual friends, "postcard" friends, but I knew him from the time of his life of Maupassant and we shared our Gallicisms and the Flaubertian-Jamesian history, as well as our biographical interests. He was kind and generous in his responses to my queries, and I enjoyed answering his—and then there remains our small time, yours and mine, in the UN, and I have warm memories of our various brief encounters at home and abroad . . . I have always cherished (and almost know by heart) Francis's remarkable translation into French of "The Owl and the Pussycat" (as well as that of Bovary and the splendid two volumes of Flaubert's letters).

George ffennell, whom Shirley had also known in her UN days, also wrote in admiration:

> I have been personally acquainted with three remarkable people: one was Churchill, whom I served as one of his Private Secretaries for a short time at the beginning of the war, another was philosopher Wittgenstein, whom I got to know as a student and then as a friend at Cambridge, and then Francis, whom I place in the same category of greatness, for his pure and elevated talent and enormous capacity for hard work, combined (this is a rarity) with natural goodness and warmheartedness.

Bill Maxwell recalled Francis's gentleness and of their devotion: "You were the climate he was meant to live in. How much love this took on your part these last difficult years we know only too well, who were witness to the accomplishment," and Emmy his devotion to Shirley: "What an extravagantly hors de siècle life you led together, and how happy you made him. It always seemed to me he could just barely believe his good fortune. He never stopped rejoicing in you."

At the end of October, Shirley made the delayed journey to Torca to pay late respects to Randy Morgan, a journey that must have felt also like a kind of tribute to Francis. She took the *aliscafo* to Sorrento, in "great beauty of the morning." This trip had long been a favourite excursion: "to see the (fine, small) museum, do a few errands, and lunch in a divine garden." At the hotel, where they had stayed many times, she was given their "'old' room, large, two beds under red striped coverlet, brass rails. Handsome. We have been pleasant together—as it is, fear of dreariness." The drive to Randy's house was "punctuated by awful constructions amid beauty—cyclamens under olives," and she arrived "in radiant heat." Randy's familia greeted her. "We speak of poetry—Leopardi (I quote). Then to cemetery at Marciano Santo Liberatore. Many visitors dressing graves for All Saints—View of Capri, silver)." She returned to Capri in the afternoon to a telephone call from John Pope-Hennessy's partner Michael Mallon to tell her that John had died. The call formed a sad pair with one she had made to Florence ten days before, and the two deaths bore the weight of shared lives. Michael had written to Shirley after that first call:

> I remember, shortly after we first met ten or twelve years ago, that I spotted you both at an exhibition of Holbein drawings at the Morgan library—your arms interlocked, moving slowly from one marvellous sheet to the next. I thought of going up to say hello, but you looked so happy together, so complete in yourselves, that I hesitated to intrude. Instead, I stood at the end of that long hall in the Morgan and watched from afar, with a mixture of awe and envy, what seemed to me a perfect communion of two united, but strongly individual souls.

She left the island early the next morning and travelled north by train to Florence to attend John's funeral. The journey drew memory after memory: "Vines in trees, cyclamens, buffaloes, Formia Gaeta. The scene of Ninfa, thoughts of Nemi, the aqueduct, Minerva Medica . . . E fieramente mi si stringe il core / A pensar come tutto al mondo passa [and fiercely my heart aches / Thinking how all this world passes away / And leaves no trace]—Dark then, and we pass Orvieto." Arriving in Florence, "Again, memories—of my 1950s arrivals, ours after the Flood of '66." At her hotel, "so much remembrance, remembrance." Everett came to collect her, he "at his briskest. What does he feel? Takes me to see John's body in fine coffin. Unlike F, he seems himself, not 'entirely' dead." The next morning, she went with Michael to Piazza Santissima Annunziata, and they walked, with Andrew Porter, the music writer Francis had first befriended forty years earlier with Bill Weaver in Monte San Savino, and Everett, to the tiny church in the corner of the square, San Girolamo e San Francesco Poverino. The Mass for the dead was in Latin, with "fine music from small group of five singers. <u>Dies irae</u>. Lively sermon by priest of striking build and appearance, in black and gold cape (Michael has given him a quotation from John's memoirs: 'I believe in many improbable things' and he develops that.)" After, she went with the others to the cemetery of Allori, "then to Omerio, beautiful scene, for lunch." In the formal observance of the rituals and customs of mourning with this group of men, friends from Francis's past, Shirley was honouring his distinct life. She wrote a few days later to Donald Keene: "Harold Acton, John, Francis—these three were long friends and all have departed within a year. Singular spirits, from a world where singularity was possible, and un-selfconscious."

Before leaving Florence, Shirley retraced past steps, "to Procacci, then to Santa Maria Novella, bought trifles, coffee at Giacosa." The morning, "radiant, warm," was her first time there without Francis since 1962. She went to the Chiostro Verde, first visited with him in 1964: "Thirty years, in a day, an afternoon passed. Everywhere the shared life, the nevermore." With memory after memory, she was, she later understood, "only just realising, then" the fact of his death. Back in Naples and on Capri, every act, every scene recalled earlier moments: "Terrific storm sky near sundown. Rain. Leaning outdoors near midnight. Remembered how thirty-one years ago I leant out my 51st St window, the last of my solitude then." On the boat to Capri: "Storm—sun—storm. The trip—how many times together. And once, perhaps ten years ago, when I thought—Oh, if I did not find him on return—" and, returning home in the early dark:

"No lights switched on for me on stairs, and he not there . . . And he not there, and never." In the mornings she woke to grief and recalled John Cornford: "The wind rises in the evening, reminds that autumn is near. I am afraid to lose you, I am afraid of my fear." She walked to the Arco. "Tonight, in sharp chill, the lamp at Cetrella . . ."

This daily record of her bereavement structured her life, most intensely for the first weeks, then months, of widowhood. Her diaries continue to note minute changes in the world around her; the least event was cause for remembrance. Her sense of loss would hardly lessen over the twenty remaining years of her life. Robert Harrison, who met her nearly a decade later, saw in her ongoing, monumental grief for Francis something of Virgil's Andromache, "pouring out libations / to the dead—the ritual floods, the gifts of grief." Matthew Specktor also saw Shirley often in those later years as he worked on a screenplay of *Transit*, finding in her constant reference to Francis deep affection and a shared language, but also "a story that she told herself about him, about the quality of their love and their relationship," a story that was "not so insistent that it was being over-claimed" but was nonetheless "so enveloping that there was no sense that she was ever outside it," in a way that half suggested Miss Havisham. "She was living within the shrine she had constructed to their marriage."

In Rome on the way back to New York, she grieved with old friends—Giulio, the Ripa di Meanas, and Michael Mallon, who had travelled from Florence to take a final leave of her. They had lunch, "intimate. His intelligence. Both wept at goodbye in Piazza di Spagna." Arriving at the Hassler, she was greeted by the staff. "I could not restrain tears—they, too, all moved. The arrival, when we had come for thirty years together. Housekeeper came to room—the same one, uncontrollable tears. At Otello, tears—kindness." And in New York, again, friends paying tribute, offering sympathy; Giles Constable and and Pat Woolf came when she arrived, the Maxwells, Annabel, Bill Weaver. James Merrill came for tea with his little dog, Cosmo, and afterwards they walked together down Third Avenue "in the mild evening, exchanging verses of Byron and recalling Wordsworth on the death of friends." Whitfield Cook, partner of

Sumner Locke Elliott, came to the city to see her. She was struck over and over by "incredulity that all that life is over, the life together," and at dinner with friends she felt "the lack of his coherence, stature he brought."

Everyday tasks such as having her hair done and passport photos taken were grim affairs, presenting her with an image of herself "elderly, a prim old harpy. Will I never again come home to someone who loves me?" There was terror, "fear of dark, even brief moment in unlit room," and a sense of profound dislocation, echoing Henry Reed: "As if I wake from the beautiful dreams of thirty years to find 'the room not as it I thought it was, But the window further away and the door in another direction.' Sometimes, alarm at intensifying depletion, dark state of mind when alone . . . Feeling of incoherence. Chaos. Dark caverns of feeling." Friends continued to provide solace, albeit briefly. She held a dinner for Jonathan Burnham, Ida and Bram Pais, Everett, Saul Steinberg, Evelyn Hofer: "The first time without him: worst was while preparing. When they came—kind, amusing, delightful." She passed on some of Francis's suits and ties to Evan and his pale blue pyjamas to Everett. With Paula Fox she spoke of feeling "near to death these days," to which Paula replied, "I know. I love much in my life, but—I can't wait for it." And when friends left in the afternoon or evening, grief returned, "a Richter scale, a geometrical progression, not numerical. It redoubles, extends, intensifies, augments, deepens." Grief had become a daily point of reference, providing a vocabulary and disposition that would never leave her: "It is the sadness, evoking all sadness, all our mortality, but sadness in the attested, agonising, intimate experience, the immense pain of sweet and cruel memory—it is that from which one wishes to be gone, needs a great forgetting. 'Il nostro tragico destino.'"

# 13.

## *SOLA SOLISSIMA*

### 1995-2016

IN FEBRUARY 1995 James Merrill died of complications from HIV-AIDS. Shirley spoke at his memorial. Allan Gurganus wrote to her afterwards, "Being at James' place was rendered so much easier and more significant by your being there. I was so aware of our having so recently lost so much. 'We shall never see their like again.' And yet, having known people like James, like Francis, justifies a lifetime of one's own attempts—at writing clearly and living one's ethics. I found your presence so beautiful and consoling." Shirley's memorial began with a quotation from Merrill's "164 East 72nd Street":

> "'Do you ever wonder where you'll—' Oh my dear,
> Asleep somewhere, or at the wheel. Not here..."

She went on: "How strange to know, now, the answer to that question: Tucson, Arizona. James has departed, with his quicksilver charm of speech and spirit, his face of a sagacious boy—a face, lately, like crinkled paper over fine bones, fanning into laughter." The quality of Merrill's friendship was her theme; she was honing, now, the language of loss and the sharp joy of remembrance: "James, kind and candid, amused and so amusing, and self-possessed as a cat; an unexcelled yet mannerly intelligence. One felt that he understood everything, even the future, and expressed the knowledge lightly so that we, and he, could bear it; that he remembered what was illuminating, lively, and beautiful, and all that he had read."

Her days were taken up with papers—"the wrong kind of papers," she wrote to Julian Barnes, "all the material and bureaucratic details apparently inevitable to a case such as mine—although we had the simplest Will in the world." In April there was a memorial for Francis at the American Academy, with Bill Maxwell one of the speakers. Bill had phoned Shirley the day before and read his piece to her. She was offended and hurt: "Much about Bea, her stew, her warm heart. Some good things about F. One waited for something to matter, to be real. I appeared pretty much inconsequential, our marriage an incident. Perhaps Bill's age—he'd expended himself on Beatrice. I said that I'd spoken French before we met, a connection or two. Then, 'You might say that we were happy.' . . . One thought, he would understand then; or that Emmy would." However, on the night, "the speech came out just the same, with the dutiful addition that one 'need only see them to understand they were happy.'" The following month, she was in Venice with Annabel and spoke at length about this hurt and about the "last awful years of F and Bea. I cried in restaurant. Helpless." The following January, at a dinner at the Academy, she spoke to Bill about Beatrice's last years, the difficulties Francis had endured. "He said, 'Noticeable.'" Her focus shifted between wanting acknowledgment of her place in Francis's life and wanting acknowledgment of the endurance required of Francis in his life before her. Her diary notes are not clear about what, exactly, it was he had been enduring, and Francis himself left no record of a particular burden beyond that of loss and grief. Perhaps the desired acknowledgment had come to stand in for her own endurance, the strains and responsibilities she had borne through the difficult years of Francis's decline.

In Rome that spring of 1995, at the Hassler, there were nightingales: "Things heard, scarcely credible: the water in the Barcaccia in Piazza di Spagna (3 am) and, same hour, a nightingale—which (whom?) I've traced into the tangle of wisteria and yellow roses beside an abandoned house between the Scalinata and the Rampe di San Sebastianello. There were two birds, calling each to each—perhaps another type of night bird, but I couldn't imagine that the song was other than a nightingale's." She thought of how Francis would have taken pleasure in the moment, "and within a pebble's throw of the house where the honorary nightingale [Keats's] died, in 1821." At Otello, dining alone, she took her copy of *Antony and Cleopatra*, which they had been reading together. She underlined Cleopatra's plea, for "such another sleep, that I might see / But such another man," and noted the date and place in the margin. She was on her way to Capri, "with my pages, there I trust to be augmented into a ms." The island's beauty was "deepened and fraught with the presence of Francis," and on her return to Naples, where she was met, as always, at Mergellina by Salvatore, "I <u>see</u> F walking towards me as he would do when I went over for the day—<u>See</u> him." In Naples, "atmosphere of Scirocco. As I waited in Riviera di Chiaia for bus—some desolation— then home. The unreality. The reality." She was struck, over and over, by her new isolation—"to see oneself sitting here at breakfast in the bright morning, the blue sky . . . as if alone on earth. Terrible to do the identical 'things' alone."

The lease on the Via Sopramonte apartment was up, and she decided it was time to leave, after twenty-five years. As she packed their things to go into storage at Posillipo and at the Parentes', she marked the finality of this last "divesting—of the flat, of our things . . . throwing away association—a preparation for death." The combination of demands on her was distressing: "On the one hand the boring awfulness of packing, dismantling. On the other, the plunging continually into the anguish of his absence, and presence—the two excruciatingly combined, the same." There were as always moments of beauty. "At this season about 3.30–4pm the white white light enters, on the white walls. Briefly only. Twenty-five years of seeing it on these curves and angles. Now, the last . . . A year ago we had gone to Naples, leaving here together for the last time. Last, last time, after all the others." After dinner at La Schiava with Elizabeth Archibald and Vittorio and Isabella Ripa di Meana, Elizabeth walked her home, "in moonlight. Night so soft, so perfumed." Amid all this change her work was now "essential to my survival," the "appalling sense . . . of life dragging me on and away" meant a "loss of appetite for new ventures except my book."

Back in New York, she struggled to write, distracted by negotiations to buy a small apartment on Capri, the only place she ever owned. She had sold the Pissarro to raise the funds: "Strange to have all that money now. It comes from Francis, like almost every good." Meetings with old friends were both comfort and reminder. She saw Bram Pais: "lovable, frailer; sweet to see him. We spoke of Francis. Last time we lunched there, à quatre, Spring 1994. It was March. On the path, the first crocuses were then, then, after a bitter winter, the last that he saw." LeRoy Breunig died in January; on the phone to his widow, Ersi, "We wept. Always the helplessness to alter. The impossibility, no appeal." She saw Jacques Barzun at the Society Library, finding him "exhausted and aged at last"; they exchanged "poignant written notes." And in the summer, visiting Paula Fox in Brooklyn, she was overwhelmed by bleakness: "Coming into dark house in Clinton Street, smell of cats, of mildew, of garbage, of decay. Paula and Martin OLD from their experience. As we talked, life began to flow back. But—at first—alarming, sad."

The following February, Rosanna Warren phoned to say that her mother, Eleanor Clark, had died: "Memories, now, continually. The memories of greater life." In early March, Shirley went with her to Boston for Eleanor's memorial. Rosanna had come to New York the day before to attend another memorial, at the Cathedral of St. John the Divine on the Upper West Side, for the poet Joseph Brodsky, who had died in January. Rosanna joined other poets—Czesław Miłosz, Derek Walcott, Adam Zagajewski—to read Brodsky's work. Rosanna's cousin Rebecca Jessup and Shirley attended the service with her; then all three took a taxi through a snowstorm to LaGuardia for the rocky flight to Boston. At Rosanna's house, Shirley camped "gallantly" on a foldout sofa in one of the children's bedrooms. The next morning, Rosanna recalled, "we gathered our wits and celebrated my mother's life in a spare, handsome Protestant church . . . where Shirley delivered a beautiful, heart-felt, elegant tribute." Shirley spoke of Eleanor's love of France and Italy, "not only for spectacle and language and otherness and for a different incorrigible vitality; but also for what Thomas Hardy called the 'tears that people old in tragedy have left upon the centuried years.'" And she remembered, later, the "intelligence, expressiveness, authenticity, affection" of the occasion.

In the spring she returned to Capri to make the final arrangements for the purchase of her new apartment in Via Sopramonte. The Parentes were still in England, and she stayed at Monte San Michele, "lovely house, real and good. The kindness. The plain, big, lovely room, with terrace on stupendous cypresses and the mountain." She sat in the loggia at her typewriter—"only work can touch the centre"—and observed that Francis "would want it, would be pleased." In May she broke, finally, with Muriel Spark, after some years of cooler relations. In 1993 she had been interviewed by Muriel's biographer, Martin Stannard, and had provided, among other details, a story about Francis's friend Leo Coleman, a model and dancer who had worked with Cocteau and had later, on Francis's recommendation, worked for Muriel in Rome. Coleman had some years before written Francis telling of how he had been summarily dismissed by Muriel "for chronic unpunctuality." Shirley told Stannard the story, and he mentioned it to Muriel. Muriel was furious. She wrote in December 1995, admonishing Shirley for what she saw as a betrayal. When Shirley saw Muriel's name on the envelope, she expected a letter of sympathy or condolence after so long a friendship. Instead she found, as Stannard put it, "a litany of irate questions," with no reference to Francis's death, and Shirley decided this had to be the end. She wrote to Muriel, setting out the story as she saw it, and concluding, "Francis never wronged you, it was not in his character. And I feel that you know that. Nor have I wronged you. It is this atmosphere of 'wrongs' that poisons things. Let's hope it can one day be exorcised."

Shortly after Francis's death, she had written to Evan Cornog and Ann Goldstein with "a suggestion":

Do you remember that you spoke to F and me about your trip to Paestum?—About wanting to see (without having to drive) the Amalfi coast etc. F later said to me that, when the time came, he thought we might like—if you agreed—to make you a present of the journey, and that you should do it rather at leisure and with a measure of style. His idea was that (if you began at Capri) you might spend a night at the good hotel (Excelsior Vittoria) at Sorrento, then a car (we had found a Sorrentine driver) to the San Pietro (hotel just beyond Positano); next day, with a San Pietro driver, to spend a day at Ravello; thence to Paestum in the morning. Something of the kind? If you were in favour of the plan, we might do the first night together at Sorrento, since, as he said, "The first time at Sorrento one needs help." . . . You may have quite other plans. However, do think about it? If you do decide in favour I might still come to meet you in Sorrento as you set out so that we could dine together at "Il Parucchiano" . . . No urgency. We'll think and talk.

To bring Francis's planned gift to fruition was a tribute to him. From the start of their friendship Evan had seemed a kind of son; this gift was perhaps a kind of inheritance. In late April, Shirley took the *aliscafo* from Capri, met Evan and Ann at Sorrento, and they had lunch as planned. "After they left I sat in 'lounge' by windows—splendid sight . . . Thought of how we came here that evening, in soft rain with Everett in March 1983. Perfection and one knew it." She returned to Sorrento and Il Parrucchiano again a few months later, "Alone . . . beautiful. Intense sadness, everything we did happening to me alone. At port, waiting for Capri boat, shed tears. Wrote a poem, sitting there on bench."

*At Sorrento*
*I think the world is full of women whispering to their lost loves,*
*Of men and women murmuring to their dead . . .*

The summer of 1996 was consumed with the new apartment: renovations, payments, complexities. In New York in August there began what would become increasingly frequent incidents of disorientation: "These days, their humidity—have been scarily irreal—as if some retreat from normality." Her body's response to meteorological shifts seemed a continuation of grief. "The light in late afternoon was the light of all our July and August afternoons in the city. Beautiful, excruciating, immobilising," shading slowly into a greater debility: "How strange, this summer, how detached, how sorrowful." She felt that she had had, with Francis's death, "a kind of 'stroke.' And how strange that 'stroke' is one of those equivocal words, like 'fast.'" Change was everywhere around her; Manhattan House had new management who were trying to buy out long-term tenants in rent-controlled apartments. Her agent, Julie Fallowfield, retired. She signed with Lynn Nesbit, and shortly after for a two-book deal with Farrar, Straus and Giroux, overcoming the long-standing antipathy that had remained from Francis's contretemps with Roger Straus. She was drawn through her friendship with Jonathan Galassi, her admiration for his work as poet and translator. She also had new publishers in the UK. Virago Press had been established by Carmen Callil in 1973 on the crest of the women's movement, to champion women's writing. In 1978 Callil began Virago Modern Classics, which published new and out-of-print books by women. They had been wanting to publish Shirley's backlist for some time, and in 1995, with Lennie Goodings as publisher, secured the rights to *Transit* and *The Bay of Noon*, which they went on to republish that year and then to reissue in 1997 and 1998. Shirley signed with Virago in 1999 for her memoir and new novel, and they went on to acquire her backlist. Committing to new publishers, she was granting herself stability, a context for completing her last works.

In November 1996 she returned to Capri to her new apartment. She had been determined to complete it with a floor of traditional Capri tiles such as she had admired in Graham Greene's Anacapri house, tiles "of such great quality and durability, with a depth of as much as two inches," their beauty "enhanced by the tactile purity of a glaze luminous yet liveable that . . . suggests, by some fugitive tinge of rose, the underlying terracotta." The tiles, locally known as *le riggiole*, "are individually fired and can be reproduced and laid, these days, only at high expense." And even in these practical arrangements there were reminders of loss: "Elderly man in ceramic shop who has just lost his wife said: 'Every so often I cry. And then I am again with her.' Just so." The following spring, renovations were completed, and she began to move her things. "All looms splendid . . . It is, will be beautiful." But the apartment was above all "a place you have not known." A decade later, it seemed, finally, to have become a culmination of her Capri associations, a story extending beyond Francis's presence there, but nonetheless a tribute to him: "This blue and white place, lovely, simple, that I've made out of my island's long dream. A place you would have loved because it is right and beautiful and like both of us. Appreciation of beauty is among your gifts to me."

There was still, always, much to lift her spirits. She spent time with old Capri friends, Anne Gargiulo, whom she had first known in the late 1950s: "Anne, such a dear, can be such a bore," and the increasingly frail Laetitia Cerio: "Some classic moments—boredom—but on the whole more touching than expected; we remembered." Hugh Honour and John Fleming came to lunch at Posillipo in early December. They talked and sat by the fire and then gazed, from the terrace, at "Fuji-like snow on Vesuvius, wonderful bronze sunset from Ischia. Gulf, 'a Lusieri' with delineated Vesuvius declivities." The following spring Donald Keene arrived: "What a good presence. Again, there is the stature." She went north to spend a few days with Mary Ellin and Marvin Barrett, who were staying on the lake at Bellagio. Shirley knew the area well and took them around, to the Villa Monastero at Varenna across the lake. Mary Ellin recalled that when Shirley left to go back to Naples, the hotel concierge was full of admiration; he had never seen her like for charm and elegance.

She maintained friendships with a number of Australians in New York. The writer Kate Jennings and her husband, designer Bob Cato, were good friends for many years. Susan Wyndham, a journalist based in New York through the 1990s, became friendly with Shirley after interviewing her for an Australian feature in early 1993. In August 1997 Shirley accepted an invitation to deliver a lecture at the Sydney Institute. This would be her first time in Australia for more than a decade, and she approached it in some trepidation through "the long, long flight in the dark, wondering why I had ever got into it all." She arrived at dawn on August 3, "a beautiful day coming up," and was met by her friend the art patron Ann Lewis. The lecture went ahead without incident. Once again, the Sydney days were full of charm, "every 'midwinter' day has been like early summer, and with an inexpressibly beautiful clear light . . . Sydney is full of memories for me while I'm here. I think little about these things while I'm in NY or Italy. The light here is itself poignant and evocative to me, recalling childhood mornings and afternoons." She saw Elizabeth Harrower, Edmund and Joanna Capon, the film producer Pat Lovell, the New South Wales premier Bob Carr, and Peter Morton from the ABC, whom she arranged to call for her so she could cut short a visit to Valerie, "dismaying, a person waiting to die." She had by now almost no connection with her remaining family. Valerie's elder son, Hamlin Barnes, had moved back to the United States in 1976 and had written several times over the years, hoping, as he told her, to be able one day to come to know his famous aunt. Shirley's responses were brief, brusque, discouraging, and they never met, although she did see Hamlin's twin sister, Cathy, occasionally. In December 1998 Valerie wrote Shirley to tell her that her younger son, Robbie, had committed suicide five months earlier. Valerie said she had not been in touch with him for years, "but I did hear of him, and knew that he was on a downhill slide—which started when he was 15." Cathy had come back to Sydney to help and had been "very kind and sweet, and dealt with his 'friends'— I have never wanted to see them. Anyway, between us we have got his messy affairs sorted out and everything is settling down for both of us." Shirley's letter in response spoke only briefly of Valerie's news and the larger estrangement: "Waste of being, of being young, waste of a future that closed down so early. Knowing nothing of his life, and now having to imagine his lonely and sad death, I think of the unknowable minutes and horrors that descended to that." She was saddened, she wrote, that Valerie had waited so long to send her the news. "We share little in the way of interests and opinions, but are bound by memories of which we're the two remaining 'repositories'; and can keep in touch about such ultimate things. How impenetrable and absolute, this mortality, the locked door." It's unclear if this impulse to connection with her sister was a change of view from her earlier sense that the gulf between them was, on her part, a matter of "boredom" rather than "estrangement." Either way, it did not bring any warmer or more frequent contact between them.

She did, however, maintain warm friendships with other families. Friends came to visit her in Italy, welcome incursions into her solitude, keeping her from the work she was inclined, anyway, to shirk. When Michael Collier arrived with his family from Rome, Shirley arranged for Salvatore to meet them at Mergellina and take them first to the path, just outside the station, leading past the Leopardi monument to Virgil's tomb, then to Pompeii, and back to Posillipo for a late Thanksgiving lunch with Shirley. From the terrace they looked down on the ruins below the waterline, and they phoned the Maxwells, reconjuring those connections. When Rosanna Warren and her family visited, Shirley walked for two days through the streets of Naples with them, "devotedly and with the mad generosity she had." She took them to churches, and they walked along streets built over Greek roads, making sure they and particularly the children understood that history. Talking endlessly about the life of Naples, she led them beyond the museums through the port area. Rosanna's children were appreciative, and Shirley "appreciative of that." This kind of welcome was extended to many friends: Shirley arranged for Salvatore to drive Edward Mendelson and his wife when they visited Naples in her absence; Katherine Swett came to Naples with her family, and Shirley took them around, less understanding of the needs of younger children, but always with energy and courtesy.

In New York, she was slowly settling to a new life alone. The city in late autumn was "like a poem. Hardy-like strangeness 'historic.'" In November 1997 she walked up to Eighty-Sixth Street to visit the Maxwells "on foot in rain, wind and odd high light. Felt on East End Avenue near the park that I was in an unknown city—undulant, hilly pavement, carpet of yellow leaves, fronds of raindrops. Generous, beautiful. Bill is more than ever his spiritual self. How brave, composed, beautiful always is Emmy . . . Felt lighter after this. Entirely natural to think of you having been with us." She took Annabel and Everett to dinner at Vico, then walked home with Everett, "30-odd blocks in crisp night, half moon, swift clouds, wet but dripping streets. Thought, and spoke, of Keats," then reflected, a few days later, "I have such truly lively and sweet times, am animated—or over-animated—with my friends, and come home, to thoughts of taking my own life, and sensations of inexpressible sadness." It was not simply the long grieving that consumed her; she was also beset, increasingly, with "Tasks": endless "appointments," bearing a sense of "urgency about menacing details that negate life." Even on Capri she felt "spiritually and physically exhausted. Sometimes, walking up from the piazza, I have had the sense that I'm dying. Life ebbing, the downwardness of things."

She felt newly old. Catching sight of her reflection, she saw an ageing face, "my feeling for my youthfulness dissolved." Her body and comportment had changed too: "I find I take longer steps—used to take two to Francis' one. He would laugh at it. Now, more 'independent' outright step, the step of a person alone. How the involuntary change affronts, alarms. All I want is what we had." And she calculated, again and again, the time of her loss and its relation to her larger story: on her sixty-eighth birthday, she was now "more than twice my age when we met. And you were 57 then and seemed so much older than I. But it didn't count, really." She wrote to Donald Keene that her life seemed now to stretch back into history:

> I saw Hiroshima in ruins, I knew a Hong Kong without skyscrapers, a Capri where the town, of domed roofs then, was a village; a Posillipo that was mostly countryside . . . Heard Eliot read <u>The Four Quartets</u>, saw Kristoff sing Boris, walked about a blitzed but marvellous London of staggering civility . . . Yet am always . . . wishing I could revoke the irrevocable . . . When I was young, before I started to write, I fairly often wished to die—and for quite "good" reasons. Then, like George Herbert, I "recovered greenness," and have felt my life to be so fortunate. Still do. But the sense of death has come back to me.

This grand backward view, guided first by the recollections around which she wrote *Greene on Capri*, now nearly completed, led her to return to her novel. Fragments began to appear in her diaries, notes and phrases on the calculations of youth and age and death, the negotiation of these through desire and love:

Image of Avernus—deathly, no birds etc—garden . . . Audrey (having a morning moment of "youth," as I in HK, '47, going to meet APV), says "once in a while, I feel what must be youth" . . . "My brother has never been young." . . . "You also have been definitive of youth." She: "once in a while" (from above). He: "It may catch up with you." She: "Do you think that can happen?" He: "Yes." He laughed. "If you live to a great age." He said, "Depends—on circumstances, accessibility, luck." "Have you been young?" "Not really. Some glimmerings, as you say. On a good day. But soldiers don't recover youth. Scorched."

In 1997 and again the following year she attended performances of a dramatization of *Chère Maître*, Francis and Barbara Bray's volume of the letters between Flaubert and George Sand, the two roles played by Peter Eyre and Irene Worth, and reflected that Francis "would have enjoyed it more than anyone." As her novel inched forward and the Greene memoir approached completion, she had also been writing short essays: a reflection on translations of Proust had been published in 1994, her tribute to Elena Vivante had been included in a small volume of Elena's paintings privately published by her family, and she had recently written introductions to Geoffrey Scott's *Portrait of Zélide*, a work Francis had admired, and to Iris Origo's biography of Leopardi, one of the coordinates of her life. She drew energy and focus from the writing. *Greene on Capri* was published in the spring of 2000. It reached back to Francis's illness and death, and Shirley was "glad to have done it," especially, she wrote Michael Richey, "as it enabled me in a way to relive our own Italian times together." While the memoir had begun in the pleasurable rekindling of friendship with Richey, its completion and publication were, despite the acclaim it mostly received, attended by rancour, a very public tussle with Greene's lover and final companion, Yvonne Cloetta. Greene was more the occasion for the book than its true centre; that was given over to Francis and their shared life on the island, while the account of Greene's character presents only a partial picture of the man. Even from this, it is clear that the friendship was not itself substantial and that acrimony rather than affinity often determined their time together. Shirley was perfectly aware that Graham Greene, any more than Patrick White, did not admire her outspokenness. Against that awareness she set her own sharp account of his character: "It's a book by a woman and no woman has written about Graham—women were a very great part of his life—and also a book by a remaining writer because he knew a great many writers but almost none are left to write about him." She would continue to insist that there was or should be space for dissenting and critical accounts of writers by writers, particularly those who had weathered disputes in their friendship: "'Scrutinizing,' or the attention thinking people give to their familiars, was certainly part of our exchange." This view was not shared by some of those close to Greene. First came a letter, bitter, from Yvonne Cloetta accusing Shirley of betrayal, hypocrisy, and untruth, closing with an accusation of cruelty: "Cruauté? <u>Vous</u> avez dit Cruauté?"

A review published in the Canadian *National Post* under the name "Judith Evans" seemed to be the work of Cloetta. It claimed that Shirley had "put herself on the wrong side of history. Didn't you ever ask yourself, Shirley, why he wasn't as fond of you as you would have liked him to be?" Cloetta then wrote a letter to *The New York Review of Books*, criticising the review they had published in June: "It is a pity that David Lodge, for whom Graham Greene had a great esteem, was taken in by all the wicked lies hidden behind the beautiful prose of Shirley Hazzard." This response was borne out by others close to Greene, including his niece Amanda Saunders, who wrote to the *New York Review* to protest both the book and Shirley's "vituperative" response to Cloetta's "thoughtful" letter. Saunders concluded, "I do know that Graham commented that Shirley Hazzard intruded herself too much, had a tendency to talk a great deal, and that as time went on he sometimes ended up discreetly trying to escape. Perhaps Ms Hazzard sensed this: her misrepresentation of him smacks of palpable resentment." Shirley responded, defending every point, as always, chapter and verse, and with her own sharp additions:

Greene's reiterated longing for peace, contrasted with a wilfully agitated existence that drew him to scenes of conflict and oppression, is a central dichotomy I need not re-examine here. Similarly, in a late letter, the "real, quiet love" for Yvonne that Graham indubitably felt, and of which he wrote to Catherine Walston, is illuminated, in the same letter, by his piercing comment on a lack of stimulus in that last attachment. (The letter has now been published by a biographer with whom Yvonne Cloetta incautiously cooperated.) It has never occurred to Yvonne that one had sought to spare her.

Through 2000, it was clear to their friends that Emmy and Bill Maxwell were both increasingly frail and, by the summer, that Emmy was close to death. Bill was reading *War and Peace* to her, and then to himself. Shirley later wrote that his "solace and pleasure in the book were an event in those rooms." When Bill grew too weak to hold the book, Annabel came each afternoon and read for him. Throughout these days Shirley also came often and, if the Maxwells weren't well enough to see her, sat in the living room. These long daily visits were important. Alec Wilkinson, who was also there each day, felt that "Shirley and Bill connected on some level that was beyond social. Shirley was *there* in a profound way, the way one person would be there for another, to ease the burden, drawing on all the capital of the years of friendship and regard . . . There was something fierce about it . . . She was seeing their friendship, their love, to the end. Attending it. The attention of love. It was in character of what she would do. It was duty in the best sense."

Emmy died in late July, and Bill eight days later. A memorial for them both was held at St. John the Divine that December. Shirley wrote to Donald Keene, "Magnificent day, slightly autumnal and there was a gathering afterwards in the church garden, where I had never been before and which has wonderful trees." Bram Pais died suddenly the same week in Copenhagen, and a few weeks after that, Ersi Breunig. For Shirley these were "not only regretted farewells, but there is the irrefutable sense of dwindling: humanism itself on the way out. What Yeats wrote in his late years: 'And I am in despair that Time may bring / Approved patterns of women or of men, / But not that selfsame excellence again.'" There had been an evening of celebration of Maxwell's life and work two years before, at the Century, on the fiftieth anniversary of his membership, and Shirley had been asked to speak. John Updike wrote her afterwards to ask for a copy of her speech, noting that he would, anyway, "remember the glow and precision" of her words. On reading Updike's obituary in *The New York Times*, Shirley wrote to Donald Keene that she thought it "quite good and with more heart than one might have expected." She also spoke at the Academy after Bill's death, of their "unclouded friendship of forty years" and his great and humane intelligence. When John Fleming died that June, Shirley wrote to Hugh Honour, a private eulogy: "Those pleasures arose from harmonies that we all, I think, enjoyed singly and together: yours and John's, Francis' and mine: the immense good luck, in each case, of two people having found one another and having passed much life lovingly and in closest companionship—sharing, as far as sharing can be, everything. To write that truly would be inexpressible."

While much of her life continued in New York, there was, with the new apartment on Capri, a fuller turning to Italy. Shirley thought more and more on her expatriatism, her embrace of Italy. To Donald Keene she observed that in her early years on Capri there had been foreigners, many, of diverse background and singular qualities, who made their home there. "These were reflective, civilised personalities, some of them writers or artists, no air of celebrity or exclusiveness, or even pronounced eccentricity; but distinctive, and often with an unostentatious 'style' of their own, an individual manner of speaking that might be outdated in a pleasant way and was always simple and appropriate." She had, she wrote, imagined that there would always be, on Capri, such figures, "elders," but now realised "that I am probably the last of the tribe. I felt at home with their existence and I suppose it's now the existence I perpetuate."

In 2000, as if in public confirmation of these sentiments, she was made an honorary citizen. Will Parente observed that this was uncommon, even unheard of, for someone who was not Caprese. It was, he said "a sign of how accepted she had been in Capri, people did feel she wasn't just a visitor. She was really interested in who you were, who your mother was, who'd had a baby and so on, and she was accepted. She was really an honorary Caprese, quite literally." Will and Mario Coppola prepared the testimonies and references. Shirley was delighted by the mixture of jollity and provincial gravitas of the citizenship ceremony that was held in early October, and she felt honoured by it, absorbed it as part of her own tribute to Capri. She knew everyone, was intricately interconnected with Caprese dignitaries and locals as well as with the visitors and expats. And she was remembered long after: her photograph and Greene's remained on the wall at da Gemma until it closed, in 2012, and for many years the waiters and the proprietor of Le Grottelle expressed their sorrow at her decline and death, pointing out "her" table and bringing out their copy of her book.

Alice Brinton and Cathie Healey met Shirley during these years. They knew her first by sight as a solitary figure walking about the island in espadrilles and blue and white shirts, carrying a shopping bag and wearing Francis's old straw hat. They were later introduced to her by Benjamin Taylor. Alice mentioned having seen Shirley on an earlier occasion, walking down from Tiberio, her arms full of flowers, and Shirley remembered that this had been when the Ripa di Meanas had sold their house, with its beautiful garden, a bank of mutabilis roses. "How could you leave a garden like that?" she wondered. Cathie and Alice invited her to lunch at the Villa Lidia, where they always stayed, high on the northeastern corner of the island. She walked up the long slope, they had lunch, Shirley mentioned that it was Graham Greene's birthday, they toasted him, then climbed farther up the incline on the property to the belvedere, which looked down on the Villa Malaparte off to the south. Shirley had thought she knew all the island and was delighted to discover a new view and prospect. In conversation over the years of friendship that followed, she invoked Francis's memory and their life together at every turn, not sentimentally but quite straight: Francis and I did this; Francis used to say. She was always lively—"With Shirley you were having fun"—but the solitariness that overwhelmed her in her diaries and private moments was also plain. Alice recalled leaving her after a visit to Posillipo. They had brought their border collie with them on the *aliscafo* to Mergellina, where Salvatore collected them and drove them to Villa Emma. There was an afternoon of conversation on the terrace, with the bougainvillea, the light and water. Shirley showed them the apartment, the rooms—

this is where Francis worked, this is where I work—the dog slept under Francis's desk. Leaving, they looked back as Salvatore drove them up the long oleander avenue and saw her standing there quite alone: "There was a gap, something missing. At a time of life when she should have had somebody. She with this tremendous gift for friendship."

By the summer of 2002 her novel was making solid progress. Chapters covering secondary narratives had been drafted, polished, and published years ago—the thwarted relationship between Peter Exley and Rita Xavier playing out in postwar Hong Kong, and the young protagonist, Helen, alone and beleaguered in New Zealand. She had taken longer to settle on Helen's name, kept changing her mind, until one day she heard someone call out to a young girl in a gallery at the Metropolitan Museum and said to herself, "That's it. Helen she is." Much of the Japanese material was also long since written; as far back as 1988 she had been asking Donald Keene for details about travel times and other practical matters of life in postwar Japan. In Capri, as she began work on the novel's central love story, she turned to her 1948 diary— and fell back into the past. She was overwhelmed, "filled with remembrance and love and sorrow . . . the sweet confiding intimacy of that love I'll never know again, but know in my being as the centre. The great great love I began in September 1947, a destiny." Her "work," now, was more than writing the novel; it was "reverie" and a revisiting of days, a "life 're-lived,' . . . Love, anguish, the long sorrow. My youth trapped in that private tragedy, cruel destiny." She was redrawing the longer story of her life as a line that connected Alec to Francis, "who completed the rescue." Her labour as writer was, now, to pay witness to that story: "The creation, re-creation," and "My homage— monument—tribute as it is to be." The emotion thrown up by the diary meant that "all is changed, until I can assimilate the revelation and learn to bear it." She annotated her 1948 diary, commenting, reflecting, correcting the record of half a century past, and erasing the distance between then and now. She turned to Alec's letters, which she had had copied. "They look estranged in their mechanical version—your hand, on the envelope, on the page, stops my heart and never ceases to do so. And never will."

The more sanguine and critical perspective on that love affair that had developed through the intervening years gave way to the anguish of first love all over again. Her reimmersion in the past seems to have determined, to an extent, the plot of the novel that she was writing. She said as much to Donald Keene:

> As to my work—you ask if it goes "smoothly". That is not the word, though I'm so happy doing it. It draws in part on experiences from my Eastern youth, which I revisit with enchantment and anguish; and has involved the re-reading, after many years, of diaries and letters that wring the heart. However such things are usually fertile in one's work, and I hope that will be the case. And in fiction one can correct an ultimate tragedy into a suggestion, at least, of a "happy ending". That is, set life right, as one can't manage to do it in reality.

She mused in her diary on the alignment of passion and morality shadowed by her own sense of fated misalignment—the coming-round of things and the too-late that are so completely expressed in *The Transit of Venus*—in her new novel. And she reflected on the timing of her own coming to love: "Reading these excruciating letters, our tragic story, I realise that one—and at any rate I—needed half a lifetime to prepare to deserve—or to be a person who might deserve—love; to subdue self and to comfort, nurture, inspire perhaps and share the life of such a man. We need what we can't have: the rehearsal for the rightful life. With . . . Francis it came right, as right as ever such a life can be. The strangeness of this dichotomy, the re-living of a great love." The coming "right" of her life with Francis now seemed to provide the "happy ending" of her past story with Alec, a happy ending that she sought to write into the book.

Through the next months there was a speed and energy to her writing that was quite new. The impediments that had drawn out the earlier chapters, and had seen *Greene on Capri* take eight years to complete— impediments of sociable interruptions, care, and tenacious grief— dropped away. With her earlier books she had left little record in her diaries or letters about the experience of writing, beyond lamenting the difficulties of finding time to work. That too changed; through late 2002 she recorded day after day the significance for her own life of this story and its writing down. And the world changed around her to reflect this; the Capri weather seemed to recall Hong Kong or New Zealand, and sitting in the Bar Tiberio, she thought, "How natural if you should have come—say, from the Bank, or other errand—to join me." She wrote hard, nearly every day, through the winter and early spring. On January 31, 2003, she wrote in her diary "My Manuscript," in large letters underlined, and at the end of April she sent it off. By mid-May she was editing and in June had the galleys.

The book was, however, not quite finished. In late July, after the galleys had gone out, she changed the ending. The changes were not dramatic; some phrases reworked, a handful of additions, including the final sentence, "Many had died. But not she, not he; not yet." Nonetheless she made much of them to friends and also later in interviews, drawing attention to the stronger sense of hope—the "happy ending"—that she had wanted to create. Anthony Hecht read both versions and described her "final touches" as "masterly." He added, "I remember reading an account somewhere of Constable remarking that when their paintings were exhibited together, Turner would show up at 'varnishing days,' which were open to the public, and, at the last moment, introduce a tiny dab of red paint at a point that reorganized the entire painting, and commanded attention. Constable acknowledged his jealousy."

Hecht's word "masterly" also applies to the novel as a whole. If its plotting is less adventurous than that of *The Transit of Venus* and its central characterisation, Helen Driscoll's somewhat flimsy goodness, ultimately less compelling than, say, Caro Bell's complex errors, *The Great Fire* still astonishes with the scope and weight and liveliness of its created worlds. It draws on the forms of epic, tracing exile and return home in the shadow of war and cataclysm. The hero, Aldred Leith, is a writer and a warrior; his challenge to the barbarism of the world takes the tangible form of a written record of the impact of war on its victims. The contemporary world of the novel—the aftermath of World War II—is rendered archaic, severed from the present day of its reading and writing through these epic dimensions. Indeed, it is drawn back into another present altogether through the sense of delay and, again, untimeliness, conjured by references to outmoded communications and attenuated human connections. All these temporal nuances are there, too, in the prose, from the opening sentence: "Now they were starting." The first word, a deixis, draws us into the shared time, the Now, of novel reading; which leads immediately to the past continuous, "they were starting." "Finality," meanwhile, runs on and on, "an exhalation." The sentence breathes; Hazzard-land. The imagined geography is Hiroshima, Hong Kong, and Chinese provinces—the colonial Far East now become the centre of the world. Place, as always, makes demands, determines perception, calls to account, as Peter Exley observes when the short winter first arrives: "The island itself was less fictitious now, newly populated, as it seemed, by quilted crowds, newly smelling at dusk of charcoal and wood smoke. You were no longer out from Europe or out from anywhere, but drawn inward to a continent. You approached the immense reality, or your own acceptance of it."

Against all this, the love affair between the young Australian Helen Driscoll and the British war hero Aldred Leith is at once impossible and inevitable. The lovers are kept apart, and the impediment to love, its complication and suspension, is figured in the largeness of the novel's world, "the distances that he, and she, must travel." The letters they write trawl slowly across the surface of the globe (even when their envelopes are marked "AIR, for freedom"), their passage compounding the time they take to write, and to read. This labour of writing and reading is important. Helen Driscoll, sitting at her desk in Wellington, New Zealand, is "repossessed of her powers," no longer insignificant: "If the incidents of her days were weighed for possible recounting in the letter, that was less for their interest than as an opportunity for expression, even for artistry." Here, domestic, provincial space is crossed over by projected desire, by flight and rescue—the rescue of writing—trajectories as material as fences or roads; and within this marked space, a young woman writing her way into the world. There is also Hazzard's intimacy with characters and sensibilities, the attention she devotes to inner and moral worlds. And there is the singularity of her prose, with its capacity to animate worlds wholly for their own sake. Here a character stands looking at a pile of firewood, drawn into its immensity as the novel's own time slows almost to a stop:

> The scrubby bark, coruscated, or the smooth angular pieces like bones. Forms arched and grooved like a lobster, or humped like a whale. Dark joints, to which foliage adhered like bay leaves in a stew. Pinecones, and a frond of pine needles still flourishing on the hacked branch. And the creatures that inched or sped or wriggled out, knowing the game was up: slugs, pale worms, tiny white grubs scurrying busily off as if to a destination. An undulant caterpillar, and an inexorable thing with pincers. Or the slow slide of an unhoused snail—the hodmedod, as they called him here—revisiting the lichens and pigmentations and fungoid flakes that had clung to his only home—freckled growths dusted, seemingly, with cocoa; red berries, globules of white wax. Wet earthy smell, forest smell.

The response was elated, the novel acclaimed. But there were also readers for whom *The Great Fire* was a disappointment, readers who found that, where previously every sentence had been a revelation, with this last, late novel, this had become merely a style. John Banville, whose novels Shirley admired, saw a decline from *Transit*'s "earned elevation of tone" to what was "here, all too often, merely a kind of mannered haughtiness." Others were unconvinced by the plotting, feeling that the novel left readers "with a rather gauzy sense of consequence, more contrived and thin than its larger subject requires." Some years after its publication, Michelle de Kretser suggested that the central Hong Kong story was "a kernel, bitter and exact," around which a novel had "ripened, excellent in parts, elsewhere gone soft." The novel's long-delayed culmination that had preoccupied its author for more than twenty years was a function of an extraordinary concentration of emotion and energy, but it had also been brought about by her wholehearted embrace of the story of a past made whole. And that process of making whole—of repairing somehow—past loss with a fiction of completeness allows a personal story of love finally and simply returned to engulf, or overshadow, the rest.

At the end of July, Bill Weaver turned eighty, and Shirley made the journey upstate to Bard College, where he had returned to live after a stroke the previous year. She found her old friend "reduced, small, thin, a boyish face on an old man." The gathering of his friends, "kind, lively . . . The summer countryside, lush and green from rains. Over and under all, the sadness. One is <u>made</u> to feel one's age." A little later she heard that her old—first—publisher, Alan Maclean, was "losing memory and ready speech down in Dorset. Mortality, sadness." Dorle Soria had died the previous year, just after Bill Weaver's stroke—"a new wave," Shirley wrote, "of infirmities, departures, mortality." Back in Italy in the autumn, she was again at I Tatti, at the invitation of her old friend Joseph Connors, whom she had met when he was director of the American Academy in Rome in the late 1980s. Joe, "a lovely man, affectionate, considerate, erudite," was now director of I Tatti. She stayed in Nicky Mariano's rooms: "Memories and also of Solaia, outside my windows—Perch'io nol spero." She took the long train ride to Pescia to have lunch with Hugh Honour. Back in New York, there was a buzz about *The Great Fire*. She signed books at Lenox Hill Bookstore: "All kind, delightful, time-consuming. Days full of my book: beautiful, this outcome." Then the touring began, to literary festivals in Toronto and Chicago. She did a reading at Georgetown University and one at Yale, where she saw again, after a gap of many years, Hugh Brogan, whom she had first known at Solaia. The meeting was "delightful—the real words, the true meaning." The following year, she would meet, again after a long absence, another old Solaia friend, David Sainsbury, and note in her diary, "These long long associations . . . ," and meeting Sainsbury again two years after that, she wrote, "An evening of memories. Solaia holds us: the last, the miraculous paradise."

The excitement about *The Great Fire* continued, and Shirley embraced the attention. In early November she did a master class at the 92nd Street Y (she told the assembled group that she couldn't teach them how to write). Then the National Book Award, the press, interviews, more book signings, more travel. Against all the public regard and attention were private celebrations; dinner at the Century with Victor and Beth Brombert was "lovely, le passé retrouvé." She went to London a couple of days later for the UK launch. She stayed with the Parentes, and Alison was surprised to see her in a completely new light, as the professional writer, keen to see that the book was being presented properly, keen to do the interviews. Old and newer friends came to the book launch. Michael Richey spoke about that first meeting, with Greene, on Capri. Shirley loved the busyness, the distraction, the celebration. The following year she was a finalist for the 2004 UK Orange Prize for Fiction (later the Women's Prize for Fiction), which had been established in 1991 in response to the dearth of women writers nominated for major prizes and was open to international writers. She returned to London that summer for the announcement and went with the other finalists to the Haye-on-Wye literary festival. The prize announcement was made in London on June 8; that evening the planet Venus passed directly before the sun, a transit Shirley might have thought auspicious, but the prize went to Andrea Levy's *Small Island*. The signal event of this visit for Shirley was the sixtieth anniversary of D-Day a few days before. She had watched the celebrations on television in her London hotel room: veterans gathering, uniformed and medalled; reenactments of the historic landings; thousands of poppies thrown into the sea from a plane. She was moved. For her, this was "the remnant of millions of people, most of them men, who died, who destroyed themselves, who destroyed the youth of other countries, and came out of it ruined."

In London she heard that *The Great Fire* had won Australia's most prestigious literary prize. The Miles Franklin Award is given each year to "a novel of the highest literary merit that presents Australian life in any of its phases." The stipulation about "Australian life" had recently been loosened, making *The Great Fire* eligible despite the relatively small number of its pages actually set in Australia. Shirley's publishers had not entered the book for the prize, but the judges had requested copies. She was moved by this long-awaited acknowledgement. The announcement was made at the State Library of New South Wales by Cate Blanchett, who emphasised connection across the arts: "The bequest from one artist to another is actually the highest of honours." Shirley spoke, from London, of "this filament of beauty which is art and life and consideration and civilised behaviour" that persists despite war and "all the contrary events and the difficulty of life in its circumstances." She thanked "beautiful Cate Blanchett," and she repudiated, again, the idea of nationality: "I have never felt particularly Australian or particularly anything. People do insist on roots, but I've never felt that way." Her comments brought to the fore her testy relationship with Australia, somewhat revived with this novel. Some Australian readers felt that the Australian characters in *The Great Fire* had been crudely drawn and that the depiction of the country and its culture was outdated. Indeed, one of the Miles Franklin judges was concerned that the portrayal of Australians was "so unflattering that people might criticise the judges for their choice." When the question came up in interviews, Hazzard responded that what she had written about Australia was true about the country she had observed in her youth: "I think people would be astonished if some of that were played back to them: the racism, the White Australia Policy, and for most people there was no doubt it should be like that." Her novel was historical, and she wasn't backing down.

She was juggling the demands of her revived literary renown, delighting in the attention and warmth but worried as ever about finding time to write. She spoke to Sandy McClatchy for a *Paris Review* profile of how her life had been for the past year, "in wonderful ways, out of my control—travels, appointments, talks, readings, readers, lovely times, lovely people." She was, she said, "very, very grateful," but still she missed the "reverie" needed for work on her next novel, which she could only "visit . . . under cover of darkness." In Rome in July 2004 she heard that Paolo Vivante had died. "Crucial event, a further departure from Solaia. Such memories—never again. Such a place, such immortal beings. My rescue into happiness." On a grey day in October she gathered wild cyclamen on Monte San Michele and remembered Siena, and Francis. "This was for you. How often—here, and in Anacapri, you would sit on a rock, a wall, patient, while I plucked hundreds of them. Above all, at San Leonardo al Lago. Immortal beauty. Our love of the place, sacrosanct."

In New York in December she saw her old friend the labor arbitrator Theodore Kheel: "Ted so reduced—has become a small man, but rising wonderfully to the occasion. Spoke with me in despair about the election, Bush, the diabolicalness." She spent Christmas and New Year's on the Venetian island of Torcello with Ned O'Gorman, whose friendship reached back to her early years in New York and Anne Fremantle's soirées. Torcello, in "light rain and acqua alta," was "a paradise." She carried with her photographs of Francis from their trips to Positano, Sorrento, Tuscany, Ninfa. She and Ned spun out their meals with talk and poetry; she took the ferry to Venice, thinking always of Francis—"fine wanderings and pauses, suffused with your presence, our dear companionship"— then returned to Rome. "A beautiful remote week this has been. Last sight of the spread lagoon and Lido, the long Adriatic, the Apennines in snow. Then the descent to Rome, like velvet, green, green." She dined with Enzo Crea, publisher of limited-edition literary, art, and architecture books, and talked about poetry "of Mariani, of Seferis, Cavafy, Palazzeschi. Delightful—we stayed late, all Rome below us, lights, domes, towers." Back in New York later that month, at a memorial for Anthony Hecht, who had died the previous October, she spoke, again, of poetry:

Tony heard voices. You won't misunderstand me in this. He listened to, and for, the crucial voices of our expressive past and of our flabbergasted present. He greeted his centuried familiars. Weighed the continuity, and the discontinuity, and visited the ancient world. His examinations—of Auden, of Keats—were not a dismantling but an act of affinity. Or, if there were dismantling, he had that rarest ability, to return the examined work to its mysterious wholeness.

She had been invited to the Sydney Writers' Festival in July 2005 to attend a formal event marking the previous year's Miles Franklin Award. Before that, she was to go to the Hong Kong Literary Festival. "Fearful of mortgaging so much time and energy when I want to get on with new work," she felt she should go nonetheless, aware that Hong Kong after sixty years would be "unrecognisable, perhaps mercifully" and that return would mean "scratching around among the skyscrapers to find some elusive shred of the past." Yet as the date approached, this came to seem a "sentimental journey." She left New York on March 5, "The coming round, at last." At the heart of the journey, there remained "Our parting that morning. A death. Heart break. Alone. The anguish of the years to come. How did one survive? Rather one died and had to reinvent a self . . . Now as if, years and years too late, I come to 'where we haunted here together'. Heart-shaking, the completion, the incompleteness."

Return, however, did not provide a neat parallel to her memories. Her plane landed not at Kai Tak, site of her earlier departure, but at the new airport on Lantau, "a mass of air terminals, flyovers, highways and concrete modernity. The future." And the days that followed were a time of "utter strangeness . . . Much sense of acting in a trance. Utter unfamiliarity. Our places extinguished. A scene from science fiction"; "I feel like—what?—a patient. Tabula rasa . . . I look as if anaesthetised, although we speak freely. I am full, full, of impressions, almost without emotions." She revisited her past sites: "Sir Cecil's Ride, the Star ferry, the Peninsula for tea"; the Helena May hostel where her female cowork- ers had lodged, "Entirely recognisable"; lunch at the restaurant near Magazine Gap, "The Bunker," which was itself "Memory—the room, the rock-and-earth drop immediately beyond the window, the sluicing rain, the green greenery 'silently' shaken by wind. The drive there and back, winding mountain road, inexpressibly familiar"; Shek-O "scarcely changed, the hills, the drive, Big Wave Bay. 'Labourers' removing slabs of turf, the women in the straw hats." Other locations, such as the Glouces- ter Hotel at the corner of Des Voeux Road and Pedder Street, "where one afternoon you, Alec, laughing, held out open arms to me," had been obliterated, only the "contours recognisable . . . the slight slope of Pedder Street." A flying visit to Shanghai was also all Alec: "The Bund . . . the long street called Mao Ming . . . courtyards, inner lanes, near the French and British erstwhile concessions . . . your familiar ground in youth." She carried with her Alec's childhood photograph; it was all a form of pil- grimage. The flight back to New York was long, stopping over at Tokyo, then "white Alaska . . . the unending tundra. Our rooms. A great journey, magnificent."

In June on Capri she thought miserably about the Sydney trip. Following so soon after Hong Kong, it seemed a further retreat to the cold arrival of 1948: "I felt my loneliness, dwelt on the terrible Oct 48 and onwards—the Blue Mountains. Desolation. The break in letters from APV. A drawn-out death . . ." Although she was making the journey to be fêted for the Miles Franklin Award, this last return to Australia seemed to promise only disappointment. She thought "miserably of Valerie's brutish letter" (which she did not keep) and of "Elizabeth H's provincial hysteria" and vowed, "No more long journeys." It was difficult too, to leave Capri, the beauty: "On the hills above and behind me, the convolvulus—colour and season always bringing to mind the morning glory at the port of Amalfi, our times there—en route to Salerno, to Paestum, and the early mornings of return . . . I suppose I'll never go there again—the boat, the coast, the convolvulus. The glory of the morning." In Sydney, she was disoriented from jet lag, also perhaps from anxiety and the absence of familiar people and places. Friends who had not seen her for some years marked a decline. David Malouf noticed her focus drifting in and out during conversation. At the Miles Franklin dinner, she mistook Susan Wyndham for Gillian Armstrong. Her speech went on and on, coherent but rambling, as if she wasn't sure how to brings things back on course. At a book signing the next day, David Malouf recalled, she stayed for hours, chatting ten or more minutes with each person in the line. Malouf was standing off to the side, waiting to take her back to his house for dinner as they had arranged and as she seemed to have forgotten. He didn't mind at all: "They loved it and she clearly loved it. It was clearly something she couldn't do without. It was kind of amazing . . . I could see how much energy she was getting out of it and pleasure. She loved that thing of being able to share interests and stories and talk with people, even if they were strangers."

The many points of contradiction and rupture that had always characterised Shirley's relations with Australia were evident in this last visit, tempering the pleasure and celebration of the award. Having announced herself "Australian for life" for having spent her first sixteen years in Sydney, she also insisted she had "never felt particularly Australian." Claimed as an Australian writer, she was at the same time often carefully reminded of how little she really knew about the place. Her own responses fed into those complications. David Malouf felt that she never really grasped the extent of the changes that had taken place in Australia in the half century since she left, and that this left a gap between her and her readers there. Mark Rubbo, one of the Miles Franklin judges, thought that the fact that her books were published overseas carried both practical and symbolic complications for her Australian reception, marking the distance. Contradictions also play out in her ongoing reputation in Australia: there was certainly always admiration and acclaim, and in 2011 she was elected an Honorary Fellow of the Australian Academy of Arts and Letters, but from the start there had also been criticisms of a perceived "elitism" and, at times, overt hostility that never quite went away. In 2019 Michelle de Kretser published a sumptuous tribute, lauding Shirley Hazzard as the first Australian writer she had encountered "who looked outwards, away from Australia," writing books that were enlarging, "expansive," and compellingly at odds with much Australian writing.

As well as its dislocation from Australia, the defining untimeliness—of form, style, subject matter—of her work also feeds into the ongoing mismatch with Australian readers. In 2019, Susan Wyndham wrote that she too had been unresponsive to *The Transit of Venus* in 1980 because it seemed to be at odds with most of the important Australian writing of the time: "In the wake of books such as Helen Garner's *Monkey Grip* it seemed to belong to an earlier, more decorous era." This sense of Hazzard's disconnection from Australian literature because of the refinement of her writing has persisted, but it has also been reworked in later years; has been itself refined. Wyndham later, like de Kretser, changed her view, as did Helen Garner, who offered a compelling account of the kind of shift that might take place in the mysterious spaces of reading, taste, and perception. Garner recalled her own early hostility to Hazzard's novels, "back in the 80s":

> Everyone I knew was swept away by them. I tried to read them but they bored me. They made me feel cranky, bolshie and obscurely ashamed. I couldn't hack her elegant women with their

fancy, made-up names, women who were *soignées*, who had their hair done and wore heels and sheer stockings, who trailed their long fingers in fountains and let their bracelets jingle against the marble basin. They (and their creator) shuddered, I knew, at oafish Australians like me, and at the coarse world I came from and was content to live in. I was viscerally insulted by the way she drew her skirts aside from the daggy, rough-grained Australia that I knew I belonged in, the country outside which I already sensed I would never be able to flourish. I don't think I spoke about these thoughts to anyone. I just thought them, resentfully and, though I didn't admit it to myself, sadly.

When Garner returned, decades later, to Hazzard's work, she found her view transformed. She recognised qualities she had, she felt, been "unable to appreciate at the time: the way she handles a sentence, her wit and subtlety, her deep knowledge of the world . . . the fine sensibility, the *adult* sensibility that I was not ready for . . ." This emphatically and thoughtfully "Australian" reading upends the sense that Hazzard's writing is outdated, or out of place in Australia, suggesting as it does that such simple coordinates might not necessarily determine either a reader or a writer.

Returning from Sydney after that last, difficult visit in 2005, Shirley wrote in her diary of "the relief and joy of arrival. Rome. Rome. My room . . . Our days and years here in this hotel. Familiarity. The long and dear and fortunate past." The following year, on the centenary of Francis's birth, she reflected on the continuity created by her own life. She had spent his birthday with Lily Gravino and Lily's cousin Annette, "whom I knew, and closely in 1957. We met in December 1956 in Naples, and they knew me at my Posillipo apartment then. They knew you from 1964 and loved you. On Friday, we sat out on their same terrace as fifty years ago. This is a rare continuity. Lily, Annette, you, I—have no descendants, all that experience will soon evaporate." There was also the continuity of literature and ritual; she read Conrad's *Victory* again, "as ever," on Capri and watched, once more, the procession from the Marina Grande to the church on the Feast of San Costanzo, with "much solitary

sadness at evening." The previous month, she had heard that Muriel
Spark had died: "She was the threshold of my life. She introduced us.
Such memories arise. My cast of characters, my context, begins to depart." Increasingly she was overwhelmed by "the terrible apprestimento
of my approaching departure from all of it, taking with me into oblivion the history of my life." Back in Naples that October, she spent days
with Jonathan Galassi, and a little later Alec's son Peter Vedeniapine
arrived with his son and daughter. In her diary she wrote, "October
1947—we had just met. Fifty-six years ago and he has been dead fifteen
years. And now his son and grandchildren visit me at Naples. Unimaginable, life."

While close friends started to notice occasional lapses, slips of memory or concentration, Shirley was mostly fine, able to manage social
events and conversations and to take pleasure. In October 2005 she went
to Paris, where *Le Grand Incendie* had been published by Gallimard (as
always, impeccably prepared, she spent the weeks leading up to the trip
taking intensive classes at Berlitz to refresh her spoken French). Michael Mallon, now living in Paris, arranged for her to read at the Village
Voice bookshop. At the end of the event, "a terribly *bon genre* French
woman" came up to Shirley and said, "in ever so slightly accented English, 'Madame, you look exactly the way you *should* look.'" She spoke
on beauty and morals at a panel at Columbia University with the poet
Mark Strand, the literary professor Elaine Scarry, and the philosopher
Alexander Nehamas. Edward Hirsch and Michael Collier remembered
an extraordinary lunch, lasting for hours, at L'Absinthe, around the corner from Shirley's apartment. "We just thought we were going to have
lunch with her. Which we did. But it went on and on and on. And no one
wanted to leave. One of the most magical meetings I've ever had. It was
as if we were transported to another place." For Shirley, the opportunity
to talk about, to recite, poetry with poets was a precious combination (also,
to have two younger men to talk to). The conversation was literary, exciting, "personal," but not "confessional." Talk flowed back and forth, with
Shirley always the centre. Collier remembered: "We're deferential. We're
charmed. The wand has been waved over us. It was one of those after-

noons in which you went in when it was bright, and then you came out and the light was different. It had deepened. Not only literally deepened but . . . you just felt that you had moved into another landscape."

There was something ardent for Shirley about poetry. It was bound up with its capacity to move, to express feeling and experience, all this set in motion by reading or hearing, reciting, or even just remembering a poem. Something of that ardour passed to those around her. Hirsch felt this keenly. There was a kind of spark, he said, never suggestive of a literal attraction, but present. "There was never any sense that there would actually be anything . . . I would never have mistaken it for that. I think she would have been shocked if someone did. But it had the lightning electricity of when you meet." At these moments, a "non-erotic friendship" takes on some "erotic component," ardour, falling under a spell. There is a hint of this high and significant feeling in Shirley's other friendships, including with gay men, for instance Donald Keene, who appeared unexpectedly at drinks at the Academy one January, "back this afternoon from Tokyo. I said, 'You were splendid to come.' He said, 'I came because you might be here.'" Through these years, Shirley developed a friendship with Robert Pogue Harrison, another younger literary man, a professor of French and Italian literature at Stanford, with an Italian mother living in Rome. They met in 2003 as she was completing *The Great Fire*, and she saw him thereafter every summer when she passed through Rome on her way south. There was a trace of that same poetic ardour at play in these meetings, recorded in her diaries: "This was quite beautiful"; "These days in Rome were inspired days because of Robert's company. I have learned, perhaps, to enjoy the perfect moment for itself"; "Lunch with RPH at Otello in corner. Talked. Were as one spirit. Walked; parted 3.30 on the Spanish Steps, on a poem of Ezra Pound. This was like love . . . No need for projection or invention. Repose on the occasion. Perfection."

Alongside these pleasures and stimulations, Shirley also began marking, with concern, an increasing incapacity—"lassitude." She noted idleness and "disconnected hours." She had a "demoralizing realisation how crammed and disorderly my apartment—our beloved rooms—have become. I must attempt serious clearance." Sometimes the disorientation was quite literal: "I wonder where I am—perhaps a by-product of having different 'homes.' Perhaps a far more serious shadow of deterioration." It was not simply the fact of adjusting, constantly, to new surroundings and circumstances but also the labour required to pack up and travel three and four times a year, suitcases of clothes and boxes of books, household products, things not available in Capri, which she packaged up and posted. In July 2007 she felt that she no longer wanted "to 'acquire' or add. Only to simplify, divest. I want to do my work. I need to leave something more if I can before I die. I need to leave my costly places." On Capri that spring she had felt the heat bring a "frightening sense of unreality." Resting on her terrace after a day spent with Lily, as the day receded, Shirley felt above all "loneliness, distress. Lily—O my dear friend . . . If I had not been asked out, I might have lost my hold on things today. Very low spirits, dark feelings (on a celestial blue early evening on this terrace—no more beautiful scene in the world). I fear for my equilibrium, my sanity." She was conscious of changes in her demeanour and perspective, conscious of a new "incapacity for prolonged solitude, need of congenial company, at evening. Diminished self-confidence; consciousness of past errors and unworthiness." She decided that she needed to leave Italy, "these places once so loved." All the "splendour," the "cool evenings of blue-gold light" crumbled away in the face of her inability to manage her life. "And I so vague in my mind. The endless details and the inability to focus, to take heed. To put my mind in order. I am pretending to be my conscious comprehending self, while another confused sense of self is rambling in me. I lie on 'my' Posillipo bed reading *War and Peace* (almost every word now familiar). I must pack—and pay—and 'organise,' but remain indolent."

A year or two earlier, Robert Harrison had introduced her to a close friend of his family, Frances Alston. Francie had grown up in Louisiana and moved to New York with her family as a teenager. She had lived in Turkey and then in New York, where she worked for a time as a teacher, then ran consultancies organising child- and eldercare for large corporations. Robert organised a dinner; the two women took immediately to each other, talking till late, then arranging to meet again for lunch the following day. This grew quickly into a warm friendship, with lunches or dinners, outings to the cinema or concerts, or to events at the Century and the Academy. Later, as Shirley's capacity to manage her life began to decline, the friendship continued, shading, gradually, into a relation of care; warm, always, but with increasing responsibility. Francie was a few years older than Shirley, but still lively and far more practical. Early on, when she noticed piles of "unpaid bills, repeated bills" sitting around, she took these over, sorting through them and preparing cheques for signing. From this, other things fell to her, and over the last years of Shirley's life Francie was in the apartment every day, managing, organising, keeping her company. This was, she later reflected, simply what any good friend would have done.

Shirley had been concerned about money for some time, had had a pressing sense that something needed to be done, but had not been able to act. Eventually, when Annabel and Everett took over the management of her finances, they were confronted with the realisation that Shirley was fast depleting her capital. There was very little coming in—small amounts of interest from a few remaining investments, occasional royalty payments, a modest *New Yorker* pension. And Shirley was continuing to live as she and Francis had lived: there was the rent on two apartments, business-class flights to Italy, rooms at the Hassler (at reduced rates, but nonetheless), her drivers in Italy, her generosity to friends. With Shirley's agreement, Annabel assumed power of attorney. She and Everett took Shirley to lunch at the Met to explain how dire the situation was and to convince her that she needed to sell her Capri apartment. Shirley was cross at the interference, as she felt it, and said she would write another novel to make the money she needed. Things continued to deteriorate. In 2007 she was mugged outside her bank in Rome, having just withdrawn thousands of euros to pay the rent at Posillipo. This crystallised things, and, overwhelmed with anxiety, she came round to her friends' point of view: "The calamity of my lost funds. Everything to be re-thought. Much to be sold." She was by now being quite frank, at least within the confines of her diary, about her sense of her capacity to manage things, how she felt "beset by details and forgetfulness. Vagueness of my mind for 'administrative' details. Feeling of losing practical control of daily systems. Frightening."

She was physically very frail. After dinner at the Century one evening, Alec Wilkinson and Sara Barrett walked her to Grand Central so she could take the subway home—"a small, fragile figure, going down the stairs, giving a little wave," Alec recalled, "like an exotic bird blown off course." In Capri in late December 2007, on what turned out to be her last visit, Alison Parente also noticed a new fragility—"She was extremely thin. I kept asking are you getting enough to eat. She looked quite vulnerable"—and confusion. As Alison and Will arrived on the island and walked out of the *funicolare*, they saw her "sitting in the Bar Tiberio and I said, Shirley how lovely to see you. And she didn't quite know who I was, didn't quite know where she was. She looked pretty lost."

A few weeks later Shirley was in Rome. In the late morning, she was making the short walk from the Hassler to the Caffé Greco on Via Condotti, on her way to meet Giulio Colavolpe, when she was knocked to the ground by someone rushing past. Her frailty and general unsteadiness of gait seem to have been almost as much the cause of the fall as the collision. In any event, she was badly hurt. Paramedics were called, and the Ripa di Meanas and Giulio. Vittorio arranged for her to be taken to a private hospital, the Villa Stuart, where doctors confirmed a hip fracture. Shirley stayed there for several weeks, undergoing further surgery. In February, Giulio phoned Francie in New York, saying, "She wants you to come," so Francie came. By then Shirley was able to stand but was still quite shaky. She was keen to return to New York, but it was clear that she could not manage a regular flight, and arrangements were made by friends in New York for a medevac plane. Shirley and Francie went by ambulance to Fiumicino Airport and then began the thirty-hour flight home. The plane was very small: Shirley lay on a stretcher down one side, a nurse and doctor sat at the back, with Francie just in front of them, her knees nearly touching the pilot's back. The plane could fly for only three to four hours before having to refuel, first at Lisbon, then the Azores, then Newfoundland. At each stop, Francie dashed out to the hangar to plug in an electric kettle and make tea. Shirley was in good spirits, chatting and then dozing, but after they spent the night in Newfoundland, Shirley in a hospital, the others at a hotel, she was disoriented and distressed, complaining that her shoes had been taken away, not remembering that she couldn't walk. Back in New York, a program of physical therapy to help her regain mobility was organised, but Shirley resisted. She sent the therapists away when they came to her apartment. "It's not graceful," she told Mary Ellin. After that, Phyllis Lee Levin recalled, "She didn't prosper."

Shirley never walked easily again. She managed first with a walking frame and later used a wheelchair when she went out. But gradually, surely, the limits of her physical world began to contract. She never returned to Italy; Annabel looked after closing up both apartments and, with the help of Mario Coppola, sold the Capri place. Shirley's books were donated to the library at the Centro Caprense Ignazio Cerio, just off the central Piazzetta. The donation was itself a local event, reported in both the Capri and Naples press. The apartment sale came just in time; by now Shirley's funds were so depleted that there was only enough money to cover her costs for a few more months. Money was not her only problem. The moments of fleeting forgetfulness were becoming more and more common. For a few years she continued to go to dinners and events at the Academy and the New York Society Library, most often with Francie, and to see friends at her local restaurants Lumi and L'Absinthe, but eventually even this became too much. In 2011, Michael Collier saw her at the Academy awards reception: "She was not in good shape. At one point I saw her just by herself and no one was talking to her. It broke my heart. I thought most of these people don't know who she is. They don't know who she is." As they waited together in the foyer for the car to take her home, Rosanna Warren arrived. Shirley was buoyed by this, and the three stood there talking for a bit. It was, Collier said, "the last time I saw her." Her longtime friend Robert Pounder saw her at an evening at Ved and Linn Mehta's apartment; again, Shirley seemed disoriented. He took her down to the street, called a taxi, then realised she couldn't manage that either and he would need to go with her to Manhattan House, where the doormen, who had known her now for decades, helped her home. Increasingly, her friends came to her. Sometimes she managed, not always.

For some time she had spoken of a new novel, but most of her friends were sceptical, and there are only the merest fragments in her surviving notebooks. She told Mary Ellin that the book began with a Roman inscription on a wall. Phyllis said, "She wasn't writing. She was talking about writing." In 2008 a collection of her essays on Naples was published by the University of Chicago Press. Publisher Alan Thomas had met her back in 2001, had been charmed, also by her writing, and proposed this collection. Shirley provided an envelope of clippings, but not much more. At the time she had been preoccupied with finishing *The Great Fire*, but after that it became clear that she was simply not able to produce anything new. For all that, *The Ancient Shore* is a luminous book that pays tribute to the complex grace of Shirley's adopted home. She made two last public appearances. In 2010 she was invited by Caro Llewellyn, director of the New York PEN World Voices Festival and a longtime admirer, to speak with the novelist Richard Ford, another admirer, at the 92nd Street Y. Her friends were anxious about her ability to manage, and there were extensive preparations. Bernard Schwartz, director of the Poetry Centre, came to tea at her apartment to give and get a sense of how things would run. Annabel went carefully through the questions Ford was going to ask. Shirley was anxious, even a little frightened. On the night, there was a large crowd, with PEN director Salman Rushdie in the front row. Annabel read extracts from "Harold" and *The Great Fire*. Soothed by Richard Ford's courtesy—he walked with her onto the stage and helped her into her chair, then told her he had read her work "religiously, over the years"—by Annabel's proximity, and by the familiarity of her own prose, Shirley told stories of her life by now retold so many times. Her hands fluttered a little, absently, as she spoke, smoothing her skirt, touching the edges of her collar or her hair. When Ford announced that he was going to read, as conclusion, the opening scene from *Transit*, Shirley said, "I hope it's good; I haven't read it for a long time." He responded, "Oh it's good." There was a standing ovation, and a long line to have books signed. Shirley was very happy; Annabel felt, "We only just got away with it."

Two years later, in September 2012, Shirley attended an event hosted by the New York Society Library to honour her; this would be her last public appearance. She was by now too frail to be included in the planned speakers for the event, but she came, sat in the front row, and at one point addressed the panellists: "Please speak up—I don't want to miss any compliments." Towards the end of the panel discussion, in response to a comment by the writer Jay Parini about the importance of Naples and Vesuvius in her writing, Shirley began to speak. She remained seated but spoke out clearly. There was a kind of insistence to her words, which were weighted with the sense of finality and threat that had latterly consumed her in more private registers. "I feel very much, I have felt increasingly in recent years, that the world has a kind of Vesuvius element now, that we're waiting for something terrible to happen, and we do have an idea what it might be like, but maybe we're pleasing ourselves with that because it might be much more terrifying." Her words were coherent, structured, moving; their sense of devastation and foreboding compelling, its register somehow at once public and utterly personal. Her audience was galvanised by having been present at what was clearly to be her final public appearance.

For the last years of her life Shirley did not leave her apartment. Increasingly bedridden, she alternated between the opacity of dreams and disoriented wakefulness, talking about her years with Francis, then, reaching further back, of her days with Alec. She lay for long hours immobile, eyes closed. On one of Rosanna's visits, she opened her eyes and said, "I'm playing possum." Francie arranged for a live-in nurse, Nelly, who was with her until the end. When funds ran low, friends stepped in and paid for the nursing, and Annabel contemplated selling another painting. Shirley remembered and recognised people some of the time, seemed responsive when friends spoke to her about people and places she had known, but she spoke hardly at all and, with the silence, lay stiller. At one visit Betsy Barlow Rogers saw her stretched out on her bed, looking like marble, "as if she had already been memorialised." Some friends stopped calling; the contrast with the brilliant woman they had known had become too difficult. Francie was there every day, Annabel whenever she came to New York. Everett was now terminally ill and unable to come. Rosanna made her last visit some few months before Shirley died.

> Francie had told me that Shirley wasn't speaking at all and that I shouldn't expect any kind of response. I sat next to her and held her hand and her eyes were closed. I stayed for about forty-five minutes, I think. And I felt sort of intrusive but also this love had meant so much to my whole life that I just chatted at her, feeling kind of stupid, saying things that if she could hear me would mean something to her. I talked about being with her in France, reminding her of Christmases at our family house. Things that if she could hear me, she would remember. And all of a sudden, she opened her eyes and looked at me and said, very distinctly: "I know more than people think I do." It was completely extraordinary. I squeezed her hand, felt some kind of response there, then she closed her eyes again. And that was it.

She died on the evening of December 12, 2016. Annabel had been at a reading at the 92nd Street Y and was just getting into a taxi when she got Francie's call. Nelly was dry-eyed but shaken. Francie was exhausted. Shirley had been increasingly unresponsive for weeks, her breathing weaker each day. There had been what seemed to be strokes. The sadness of death was, inevitably, compounded by its long arrival, and at the same time, there was the release. Annabel said, "One would not have had it go on a minute longer." Valerie had died the previous year, in a Sydney nursing home, also suffering from dementia, contact between the sisters long since ended. Annabel waited at the apartment; the undertakers came and took the body away for cremation. Shirley's ashes were mixed with Francis's and buried together at Francis's family plot in Saint Mary's cemetery in Greenwich, Connecticut.

Shirley had little sentimentality around death and burial. Through her last years, in daily declarations, she had mourned her husband and commemorated their life together, had commemorated too her own achievement of happiness. These were more significant for her by far than burial. And she had imagined and anticipated death through poetry, which had marked and formed her life. One of her last diary entries, from 2007, recorded lines from *Paradise Lost*—"To be no more: sad cure! for who would lose, / Though full of pain, this intellectual being, / Those thoughts that wander through eternity . . ."—to which she added, "I would depart, while in health on such a note." At the same time, mortality was central to her poetic imagination; in her novels, death is everywhere bound to human life, and most of all to love. In an interview a decade before she died, she gave a compelling account of this. She was speaking about the scene in *The Transit of Venus* where Grace meets and falls in love with her son's doctor as they look together at X-ray images of the child. The X-ray, she noted, removes the markers of human individuality, it cuts away the tissue of life and self, "the person . . . the soul, the thinking, the rebellion, the complacency." More than this, it is itself a marker, a fragment, of modernity—"Before x-ray, no one had seen a skeleton unless the person had died"—even as it continues to bear the human weight of memento mori. Most of all, in the scene with Grace and the doctor, the lovers coming together at this moment are facing death. "When their hands meet," she explained, "it is their bones that are meeting, because they are in that moment aware of mortality." It is not just the rare moment of authorial exegesis that is remarkable here, there is also the explicitness, the irreducibility of the image, what she called "seeing the bones." More often in her work, love holds death at bay, or appears to, as in a later scene from *Transit*, with the final meeting of Ted and Caro at the airport, where Ted is reminded of the moment, earlier, "when, on the boat, brightness fell from her hair." The moment and reference, at first just obscurely beautiful, a vision of love, speak in fact to the enormous embrace of death. The line directly recalls Thomas Nashe's "In Time of Pestilence":

*Beauty is but a flower,*
*Which wrinkles will devour;*

*Brightness falls from the air;*
*Queens have died, young and fair;*
*Dust hath closed Helen's eye.*
*I am sick, I must die.*

We are seeing, here again, the bones.

If the irreducibility of human mortality is at the heart of Shirley Hazzard's writing, there is, still, the fact of her own grave, there in Connecticut. There is an anonymity, something deeply private. The cemetery is quiet, surrounded by woods and suburban gardens. Francis's family plot is on a gently sloping ridge, with two imposing but very plain headstones of grey polished granite, bearing only the names STEEGMULLER and TIERNEY, carved large into the stone. When I visit, there are empty, untended receptacles for flowers at each side of both stones, and in the straggled grass in front are sunk the much smaller individual graves. Francis Steegmuller and Shirley Hazzard share a single stone that gives their dates, with her writer's rather than her married name. Saint Mary's is a Catholic cemetery, and the graves around bear mostly Italian, Polish, or Irish names. The Steegmullers and Tierneys buried near to Shirley and Francis are closely tied to their faith and their families, and their homes. Francis too has been returned to his origins, just as in *The Great Fire*, where Aldred Leith speaks of arrangements made for the bodies of fifteen RAF servicemen who had died in China to be returned to British territory, "To their families . . . To their tombs." Shirley Hazzard chose no such return for herself. In the end, she was far from her parents and her sister, their origins obscured and hers cauterised through repeated repudiation. Her grave makes quite literal her severance from both family and country of birth, all cast outside the currents of her life. She had found herself at home in Naples and on Capri, but these too were finally lost to her. There had been a whimsical note in her description of her unaccompanied state in that early letter to Francis in the days of their courting: "She has no accompaniment and is in fact sola solissima." More gravely, now, this had become, in retrospect, a prediction.

She thought how she had been a child beside the sea and then a woman in high rooms, like rooms in dreams, and tangled gardens. She thought of continents and cities, men and women, the beloved . . . As if she listed every graceful moment of her life to offer in extenuation.

# SOURCES

## NOTES ON SOURCES

I have provided full citations of published sources in a source's first note; subsequent references have a short-form citation. The notes provide a full bibliography of all published and unpublished sources used in this book.

Shirley Hazzard's papers are held in the Rare Book and Manuscript Library, Columbia University, in New York. At the time of writing this material was grouped in two collections: Shirley Hazzard Papers 1946–2010, which is partly processed, and a large amount of material that came to the library after her death. This second collection of material includes almost all her diaries and notebooks and is as yet unprocessed. I have distinguished between these two collections in the notes. Francis Steegmuller's papers are also held at Columbia RBML; papers relating to his scholarship and writing are included in the Francis Steegmuller Papers 1877–2002, but additional material is held in the unprocessed Shirley Hazzard material.

Archival citations are listed according to the individual reference systems of these libraries.

## ABBREVIATIONS

APC: "A Place in the Country," in *Collected Stories*, ed. Brigitta Olubas and with a foreword by Zoe Heller (Farrar, Straus & Giroux, 2020).

APVOH: Alexis Piotr Vedeniapine Oral History, recorded December 10, 1987. A copy of this recording was kindly made available to me by Alexis Vedeniapine's family.

AR: Shirley Hazzard, "Autobiographical Remarks About Growing Up in Mosman," unpublished typescript held in Shirley Hazzard Papers (unprocessed papers), University Archives, Rare Book and Manuscript Library, Columbia University Libraries.

AWR: "A Writer's Reflection on the Nuclear Age," in *We Need Silence to Find Out What We Think: Selected Essays*, ed. Brigitta Olubas (Columbia University Press, 2016).

BN: *The Bay of Noon* (Little, Brown, 1970).

CMF: "Canton More Far," in *We Need Silence to Find Out What We Think: Selected Essays*, ed. Brigitta Olubas (Columbia University Press, 2016).

CSHMS: Correspondence of Shirley Hazzard, Muriel Spark, and Francis Steegmuller, 1963–1996. National Library of Australia.

EH: *The Evening of the Holiday* (Knopf, 1966).

EV: "Introduction," in *Elena Vivante: Paintings* (Studio Press, 1995).

FSCDC: Francis Steegmuller Correspondence with Douglas Cooper 1966–1997, Getty Research Institute, Los Angeles (970038).

FSD: Francis Steegmuller's diaries, held in Shirley Hazzard Papers (unprocessed papers), University Archives, Rare Book and Manuscript Library, Columbia University Libraries.

FSP: Francis Steegmuller Papers 1887–2002, University Archives, Rare Book and Manuscript Library, Columbia University Libraries.

GC: *Greene on Capri: A Memoir* (Farrar, Straus and Giroux, 2000).

GD: Shirley Hazzard interviewed by Geoffrey Dutton, August 10, 1984. National Library of Australia, ORAL TRC 3133/7.

GF: *The Great Fire* (Farrar, Straus and Giroux, 2003).

H: "Harold," in *Collected Stories*, ed. Brigitta Olubas and with a foreword by Zoe Heller (Farrar, Straus and Giroux, 2020).

JM: Shirley Hazzard interviewed by James Murdoch, August 23–25, 2000. National Library of Australia, ORAL TRC 4621.

JMM: James Merrill Memorial, in *James Merrill: A Remembrance*, Robin and Mark Magowan, eds. (Academy of American Poets, 1996), 43–44.

LFL: Francis Steegmuller (unpublished typescript), "A book that might be called LOOKING FOR LIVES," in Shirley Hazzard Papers (unprocessed papers), University Archives, Rare Book and Manuscript Library, Columbia University Libraries.

MSC: The National Library of Scotland, TD.3586: the Martin Stannard collection.

NYR: New Yorker Records ca. 1924–1984, MssCol2236, Manuscripts and Archives Division, The New York Public Library.

NYT: *The New York Times.*

P: "Pilgrimage," in Shirley Hazzard and Francis Steegmuller, *The Ancient Shore: Dispatches from Naples* (University of Chicago Press, 2008).

PEH: Papers of Elizabeth Harrower (1937–2005), National Library of Australia.

REP: Ralph Ellison Papers, 1890–2005, Manuscript Division, Library of Congress, Box 1, Folder 96.

SAF: "A Scene of Ancient Fame," in Shirley Hazzard and Francis Steegmuller, *The Ancient Shore: Dispatches from Naples* (University of Chicago Press, 2008).

SHB: Collection of Books from the personal library of Shirley Hazzard, Shirley Hazzard Collection, Mitchell Library, State Library of New South Wales.

SHC: Shirley Hazzard Correspondence and other papers, 1966–ca. 2005, Mitchell Library, State Library of New South Wales, MLMSS 10249.

SHD: Shirley Hazzard's diaries from 1948, 1953, 1954, 1955, and 1956, held in Shirley Hazzard Papers (unprocessed papers), University Archives, Rare Book and Manuscript Library, Columbia University Libraries.

SHDN: Shirley Hazzard's diary notebooks in Shirley Hazzard Papers (unprocessed papers), University Archives, Rare Book and Manuscript Library, Columbia University Libraries.

SHP: Shirley Hazzard Papers 1946–2010, University Archives, Rare Book and Manuscript Library, Columbia University Libraries. At the time of writing, this first tranche of papers had been partially processed.

SHPG: Shirley Hazzard papers, GTMGamms421, Georgetown University Library Booth Family Center for Special Collections, Washington, D.C.

SHPU: Shirley Hazzard Papers (Unprocessed), University Archives, Rare Book and Manuscript Library, Columbia University Libraries. These papers were received by CRBML from Shirley Hazzard's estate after her death. At the time of writing, this second tranche of papers had not yet been processed.

SMH: *Sydney Morning Herald.*

TLS: *Times Literary Supplement.*

TV: *The Transit of Venus* (Viking, 1980).

WR: "Woollahra Road," in *Collected Stories*, ed. Brigitta Olubas and with a foreword by Zoe Heller (Farrar, Straus and Giroux, 2020).

# NOTES

## PROLOGUE

3 *"National Book Awards"*: SHD, Nov. 19, 2003.

4 *"More than two decades"*: Gail Caldwell, "Burning Memories of War and Loss," *Boston Globe*, Oct. 19, 2003.

4 *"For years her admirers"*: Thomas Mallon, "Princess of Discrimination," *The Atlantic*, Nov. 2003.

4 *"For Shirley Hazzard"*: Mel Gussow, "An Old Memory, Not Just Revisited but Also Revised," *NYT*, Oct. 18, 2003.

4 *"In the 22 years since"*: Jamie James, *"The Great Fire," Wall Street Journal*, Oct. 17, 2003.

4 *"Few writers are worth"*: Karen Heller, "A Book That Is Worth a 23-Year Wait," *Free–Lance Star*, Jan. 11, 2004.

4 *"dumbing down"*: Comments by Harold Bloom and others quoted in Renee Tawa, "Hazzard Wins National Book Award; King Honor Causes Stir," *Los Angeles Times*, Nov. 20, 2003.

4 *"What do you think?"*: Quoted in James Campbell, "Dark Art," *NYT*, March 2, 2008.

4 *"I don't think"*: SH, "2003 National Book Award Acceptance," in *We Need Silence to Find Out What We Think: Selected Essays by Shirley Hazzard*, ed. Brigitta Olubas (Columbia University Press, 2016), 183–84.

5 *"is timeless as opposed to timely"*: Ellen Kanner, "Just in Time," *PAGES*, Nov.–Dec. 2003.

5 *"like the last masterpiece"*: James, *"The Great Fire."*

5 "The Great Fire *is a reminder"*: "2004 Miles Franklin Award: *The Great Fire* by Shirley Hazzard," *Antipodes* 18, no. 1 (2004): 81.

5 *"a clarity only possible"*: Alan Wall, "Heat and Dust," *The Guardian*, Nov. 5, 2003.

5 *"shimmers through the prose"*: "75 at 75: Stacy Schiff on Shirley Hazzard," June 19, 2018, at the 92nd Street YMHA; available at www.92y.org/archives/75-75-stacy -schiff-shirley-hazzard.

6   *"never forces a suspension"*: Thomas Mallon, "Princess of Discrimination," *The Atlantic*, Nov. 1, 2003.

6   *The novelist Alice Jolly*: Alice Jolly on the *Backlisted Podcast*, Feb. 23, 2016; available at soundcloud.com/backlistedpod/shirley-hazzard-the-great-fire.

6   *"a special shrine"*: J. D. McClatchy introduced Shirley Hazzard reading from *The Great Fire* at the 92nd Street Y on Nov. 3, 2003; available at www.92y.org/archives /shirley-hazzard-the-great-fire.

6   *"The great novels we get"*: Flannery O'Connor, "Some Aspects of the Grotesque in Southern Fiction," in Flannery O'Connor, *Mystery and Manners: Occasional Prose* (Faber & Faber, 1972), 49–50.

7   *"a hypnotic novel"*: Joan Didion, cover endorsement, *The Great Fire*, by Shirley Hazzard (Farrar, Straus & Giroux, 2003).

7   *"Sunday, grisaille"*: Ibid., 74.

7   *"precariousness"*: Polly Schumann, "Talking with Shirley Hazzard: Rewriting History," *Newsday*, Nov. 16, 2003.

7   *"the feeling of hope"*: Comments by Bloom and others quoted in Renee Tawa, "Hazzard Wins National Book Award; King Honor Causes Stir," *Los Angeles Times*, Nov. 20, 2003.

7   *"I retrieved"*: Ibid.

7   *"The world"*: SH, Reading from *The Great Fire* at the 92nd Street Y, Nov. 3, 2003; available at www.92y.org/archives/shirley-hazzard-the-great-fire.

8   *"a story of falling in love"*: J. D. McClatchy, "Shirley Hazzard: The Art of Fiction no. 185," *Paris Review* 173 (Spring 2005): 188.

8   *"Poetry comes in different forms"*: SH with Richard Ford at the 92nd Street Y, June 26, 2010; available at www.youtube.com/watch?v=ilKEbz0TDT4.

8   *"stupendously beautiful"*: SHDN, Nov. 24, 1982.

9   *"WWW Dot"*: Judith Long, "The Grace of Imagination—Talking with Shirley Hazzard," *Newsday*, March 19, 2000, B11.

9   *"willed to be"*: Jonathan Galassi to BO, March 4, 2021.

9   *"I hate change"*: Interview with Robert Pogue Harrison, Sept. 3, 2020.

9   *"preposterously prim"*: Interview with Steven M. L. Aronson, Nov. 15, 2018.

9   *"Beauty, long since drained"*: GF, 235.

9   *"Some version"*: Interview with Alec Wilkinson, Dec. 13, 2018.

10   *"If a highly intelligent"*: John Russell, Letter to the Committee on Admissions, The Century Association of New York, Oct. 31, 1995, Century Association of New York Archives.

10   *"he thought she was an heiress"*: Interview with Benjamin Taylor, Nov. 3, 2018.

10   *"You would never"*: Interview with Alec Wilkinson, Dec. 13, 2018.

10   *"achieved her life"*: Interview with Alison West, Dec. 17, 2018.

10   *"extraordinary ear"*: Interview with Elizabeth Archibald, April 21, 2020.

10   *"There was a sense"*: Interview with Edward Mendelson, Dec. 7, 2018.

11   *"He had the generous talent"*: SH, James Merrill Memorial, in *James Merrill: A Remembrance*, eds. Robin and Mark Magowan (Academy of American Poets, 1996), 43–44.

11    *"She didn't seem to care"*: Interview with Edward Mendelson, Dec. 7, 2018.

11    *"very very well defended"*: Interview with Matthew Specktor, June 12, 2021.

11    *"being able to hold herself"*: Interview with Amanda Vaill, Dec. 13, 2018.

11    *"There was something so avid"*: Interview with Alec Wilkinson, Dec. 13, 2018.

11    *"a conjugal version"*: Richard Howard, "Fond Memory," in *Literary Lives: The World of Francis Steegmuller & Shirley Hazzard*, ed. Mark C. Bartlett (New York Society Library, 2010), 31.

11    *"He had lent"*: SH, *The Transit of Venus* (Viking, 1982), 190.

12    *"he looked like"*: Eleanor Wachtel, 2003 interview with Shirley Hazzard, CBC radio, available at www.cbc.ca/radio/writersandcompany/shirley-hazzard-writes-of-love -loneliness-and-the-aftermath-of-war-in-the-great-fire-1.2790983.

12    *"I am a lie"*: Francis Steegmuller, *Cocteau: A Biography* (Little, Brown, 1970), 6.

12    *"Francis's worktable"*: Shirley Hazzard, "Lives Well Lived: Francis Steegmuller; Our Reading List," *NYT*, Jan. 1, 1995.

## I. REGGIE'S DAUGHTER

17    *"Auden said"*: Geoffrey Dutton, "Shirley Hazzard: Chance and the Transit of Pleasure," *The Bulletin*, Aug. 28, 1984, 51. The Auden poem is "In Memory of W. B. Yeats."

17–18    *"There was the idea"*: Valerie Lawson, "Hazzard County," *SMH*, June 19, 2004.

18    *"In Italy"*: Desmond O'Grady, "Love's Slow Burn," *SMH*, Nov. 15, 2000.

18    *"In 1960"*: McClatchy, "Shirley Hazzard," 175. *The Order of Release* is a painting by John Everett Millais, depicting the release of an imprisoned soldier.

18    *"It was 1935"*: SH, "Woollahra Road," in *Collected Stories*, ed. Brigitta Olubas and with a foreword by Zoe Heller (Farrar, Straus & Giroux, 2020), 268.

19    *"The front garden"*: WR, 268.

19–20    *"There was what we called the paddock"*: JM.

20    *"a hawker"*: WR, 267.

20    *"She remembered a morning"*: SHDN, no date, 1983.

21    *"I was three"*: JM.

21    *"the tyranny of distance"*: The phrase is from the title of a classic work of Australian history, Geoffrey Blainey, *The Tyranny of Distance*, first published in 1967.

21    *"in perpetual, flagrant violation"*: TV, 31.

21    *"At the very first instant"*: Mark Peel and Christina Twomey, *A History of Australia* (Bloomsbury, 2018), 138.

22    *"The proportions sent out"*: James Jupp, *Immigration* (Oxford University Press, 1998), 15–16.

22    *At Federation*: Peel and Twomey, *History of Australia*, 138.

22    *"We've had racial laws"*: GF, 104.

22    *"instead of repelling"*: Thomas Keneally, *Australians: Flappers to Vietnam* (Allen & Unwin, 2009), 5.

22    *"defensive project"*: Peel and Twomey, *History of Australia*, 170.

22    *"sentimental attachment"*: Ibid., 172.

22  *"the globe marked out in pink"*: JM.

22  *"ignoble endurance"*: Ibid.

23  *"a parched unvisited mystery"*: TV, 32.

23  *"Australia's history"*: Ibid.

23  *its population more than doubled*: Peter Spearritt, *Sydney's Century: A History* (New South Publishing, 2000), 3.

23  *"grinding trams"*: Sydney Ure Smith, *Art in Australia* 20 (1927), quoted in Deborah Edwards and Denise Mimmochi, "Sydney Moderns," in ed. Deborah Edwards and Denise Mimmochi, *Sydney Moderns* (Art Gallery of New South Wales, 2013), 13.

24  *"a great lung"*: Quoted in Spearritt, *Sydney's Century*, 5.

24  *"Golden beaches"*: Basil Burdett, in *The Home*, Feb. 1938, quoted in Spearritt, *Sydney's Century*, 72.

24  *Sydney was in the process*: Spearritt, *Sydney's Century*, 62.

24  *"a dim, presiding figure"*: JM.

24  *By 1933*: Peel and Twomey, *History of Australia*, 179.

24  *"I was lucky"*: JM.

24  *"spectres"*: TV, 34.

24  *"Who or what"*: Ibid., 35.

25  *"with those windows"*: JM.

25  *"I have never lived"*: SH to Rache Lovatt Dickson, April 11, 1962, The Macmillan Archive, Macmillan Publishers International Ltd.

25  *"Australia required apologies"*: TV, 11.

25  *"down a winding road"*: AR.

25  *"All through my life"*: Jan Garrett, "The Transits of Hazzard," *Look & Listen*, Nov. 1984, 36.

25  *"authoritative world"*: WR, 268.

26  *"There was nothing mythic"*: TV, 37.

27  *"light has properties of memory"*: Geoffrey Dutton, "Shirley Hazzard," 50.

27  *"came into sight"*: SH to Elizabeth Harrower, Oct. 3, 1972, PEH.

27  *"scarred for life"*: JM.

28  *"both very good-looking"*: McClatchy, "Shirley Hazzard," 166.

28  *"in their best selves"*: Ibid.

28  *Shirley claimed to have*: JM.

28  *"to the best of my knowledge"*: National Archives of Australia: Australian Imperial Force, Base Records Office; First Australian Imperial Force Personnel Dossiers, 1914–1920, HAZZARD R 63748.

29  *"shrouded in unspeakability"*: JM.

29  *The AIF enlistment forms*: National Archives of Australia: Australian Imperial Force, Base Records Office; First Australian Imperial Force Personnel Dossiers, 1914–1920, HAZZARD R 63748.

29  *"no issue"*: "Death of Mr C. J. Hazzard," *Macleay Argus*, July 22, 1905.

29  *"one of the best collections"*: Ibid.

29 *"she may be termed"*: "District School: West Kempsey Successes at Recent Examinations," *Macleay Argus*, Jan. 24, 1913.

30 *extraordinary stories from the Australian colonies*: For an account of the Tichborne Claimant, see Robyn Annear, *The Man Who Lost Himself* (Constable & Robinson, 2002); for an account of Dyce Murphy in relation to White's novel, see David Marr, *Patrick White: A Life* (Random House, 1991).

30 *Reg's entry*: "Reginald Hazzard," in *Who's Who in Australia: An Australian Biographical Dictionary and Register of Titled Persons*, ed. Joseph A. Alexander, 14th ed. (*The* [Melbourne] *Herald*, 1950), 330.

30 *His second wife, Mary, believed*: Mary Hazzard to SH, Aug. 9, 1973, SHPU.

30 *"The Macleay"*: Ibid.

31 *Interviewed by the local*: "A Boy from the Bush Is a Man of the World," *Macleay Argus*, July 13, 1968.

31 *"he was loyal to her"*: JM.

31 *she kept among her books*: SHB.

32 *tried in 1917*: *New South Wales Police Gazette*, Dec. 19, 1917, 547.

32 *"She came three times a year"*: JM.

32 *"'didn't spare the strap'"*: Ibid.

32 *"A woman had come"*: WR, 270.

32 *"sombre grime"*: TV, 39–40.

33 *"almost in tears"*: JM.

33 *"he didn't know who"*: Ibid.

33 *"country lads"*: Peter Stanley, *Bad Characters: Sex, Crime, Mutiny, Murder and the Australian Imperial Force* (Pier 9, 2010), 109.

34 *The Australian government*: Peter Cahill, "The Expropriation Board in New Guinea 1920–1927," *Journal of Pacific History* 32, no. 1 (1997): 3–28.

34 *"New Guinea had always attracted"*: Ibid., 9.

35 *"My mother's name"*: JM.

36 *"a clever girl"*: Sally Blainey, "The Interpreter," *The Bulletin*, Sept. 20, 2005, 73.

36 *Shirley remembered*: Jan McGuinness, "The Transit of Shirley Hazzard," in *Shirley Hazzard: New Critical Essays*, ed. Brigitta Olubas (Sydney University Press, 2014), 124.

36 *reports of loud church music*: Ibid.

36 *"She could be so sensible"*: JM.

36 *She spoke of an incident*: Interview with Matthew Specktor, June 12, 2021.

36 *Kit claimed*: Catherine Hazzard to SH, no date, SHPU.

36–37 *"a very mild dose of my mother"*: McClatchy, "Shirley Hazzard," 166.

37 *"My mother had grown up"*: JM.

37 *"I CAN ALWAYS DIE"*: TV, 40.

37 *"dark and beautiful"*: WR, 269.

37 *"She couldn't breathe"*: Ibid.

37 *"nice clothes"*: JM.

37 *In return*: Ibid.

38 *"I was very close to her"*: Lacy Crawford, "Shirley Hazzard: A Profile," *Narrative Magazine*, Feb. 2010, 8.

38 *"a man of abilities"*: SH to Peter Vedeniapine, Aug. 30, 2005, SHPU.

38 *"I think I lived"*: JM.

38 *a brief period*: Ibid.

39 *"in the slit of two headlands"*: TV, 36.

39 *"It was high"*: AR.

39 *She recalled her parents*: Ibid.

39 *"well-rounded"*: Gavin Souter, *Mosman: A History* (Melbourne University Press, 1994), ch. 10.

39 *"old, low-lying, weatherboard"*: JM.

39 *"setting off down"*: AR.

40 *"I recall the context"*: Ibid.

40 *visitors to the Stanton Road house*: S. Blainey, "The Interpreter," 74.

40 *"situated on the heights"*: V. M. Medway, *Queenwood: The First Sixty Years 1925–1985* (Macarthur Press, 1986), 6.

40 *"beautiful surroundings"*: Ibid., 225.

40 *Shirley remembered it*: JM.

40 *The girls wore*: Medway, *Queenwood*, 223–25.

40 *She remembered a sheep*: SH to Chris Cooper, Jan. 24, 1983, SHPU.

40 *"enormously good"*: JM.

40 *She was clever*: Interview with Diane Wachman, June 20, 2019.

41 *recalled being lonely*: O'Grady, "Love's Slow Burn," 8.

41 *"quite nasty"*: JM.

41 *"I'm not excusing it"*: Ibid.

41 *"A child whose being"*: SHDN, no date, 1975.

42 *"Caro entered the house alone"*: TV, 78.

42 *"went downhill"*: JM.

42 *"also very nice"*: Ibid.

42 *"smaller, with camelia trees"*: TV, 36.

43 *"an arcadian clearing"*: AR.

43 *"a frangipani bouquet"*: JM.

43 *"innocence, simplicity"*: Ibid.

43 *"declared it his melancholy duty"*: Stuart Macintyre, *A Concise History of Australia* (Cambridge University Press, 1999), 197.

43 *"standing in the local tobacconist's"*: SH, *Coming of Age in Australia* (ABC Enterprises, 1985), 10.

43 *"the war began to have"*: Spearritt, *Sydney's Century*, 78.

44 *"a blazing hot day"*: SH to Donald Keene, Jan. 19, 1983, SHPU.

44 *"a danger zone"*: Medway, *Queenwood*, 29–30.

44 *"across a flat paddock"*: Ibid., 194.

44   *"repelled by the saltless water"*: TV, 45.

44   *other classmates*: Interview with Diane Wachman, June 20, 2019.

45   *Valerie, who became so consumed*: JM.

45   *"The darkness deepened"*: TV, 43.

45   *"Anywhere in the country"*: Susan Wyndham, "Hazzard Ahead," *Weekend Australian*, July 17–18, 2003, 29.

46   *"Italian, even if on our side"*: TV, 44.

46   *"For its construction"*: Ibid.

46   *"these rooms enclosed loveliness"*: Ibid.

46   *"At dusk"*: Ibid.

46   *"In Australia, in wartime"*: Lucy Latané Gordan and T. M. Pasca, "Shirley Hazzard: Back to Basics," *Wilson Library Bulletin* 65, no. 3 (Nov. 1993): 46.

46   *"Buses were soon painted"*: TV, 42–43.

46   *"Without any inhibitions"*: John Curtin, "The Task Ahead," *Melbourne Herald*, Dec. 27, 1941, available at http://john.curtin.edu.au/pmportal/text/00468.html.

47   *"One morning a girl"*: TV, 47.

47   *seconded from his position*: *Who's Who*; JM.

47   *"like the other women"*: JM.

47   *"Oh the dreariness"*: Ibid.

47   *"an old boat"*: Ibid.

48   *"It was terrible"*: Ibid.

48   *"on our shelves"*: SH, *Greene on Capri: A Memoir* (Farrar, Straus & Giroux, 2000), 29.

48   *"very young"*: Catherine Hazzard to SH, May 29, 1967, SHPU.

48   *"learned as if in a renewal"*: SHDN, no date, Nov. 2006.

48   *"I could hardly read"*: McClatchy, "Shirley Hazzard," 170.

48   *"accessible poems by Browning"*: Ibid., 168.

49   *"J'ai plus de souvenirs"*: SH to Elizabeth Harrower, March 10, 1980, PEH.

49   *"whenever I got"*: JM.

49   *"on board ship"*: GC, 67.

49   *"in 1946"*: Ibid.

49   *"There was the gangplank"*: TV, 49.

49   *the Grahame Book Company*: JM.

49   *"artistic Saturday afternoon parties"*: Jill Dimond and Peter Kirkpatrick, *Literary Sydney: A Walking Guide* (University of Queensland Press, 2000), 30.

50   *"distrusted"*: JM.

50   *"romances from the war"*: JM.

50   *Her juvenilia*: "The Track" and "The Nelly Goes Down" were both included in the handwritten "Queenwood Magazine" produced by students in the 1940s. A copy was generously shared with me by the family of her childhood friend Patricia Walmsey. The poem about the Battle of Britain pilot (no title) was included in Medway, *Queenwood: A History*, 236.

50   *"compositions for school"*: JM.

51 *"A pioneer of the skyways"*: Interview with Diane Wachman, June 20, 2019.

51 *"a handful of Australian poets"*: Shirley Hazzard, "When We Were Ten," unpublished ms held in Virago Press Archive 1954–2008, MS 88904, British Library.

51 *"In the circles"*: SH, *Coming of Age in Australia*, 14.

52 *"and Swinburne"*: JM.

52 *"other than Shakespeare"*: McClatchy, "Shirley Hazzard," 169.

52 *"Sundays in Australia"*: JM.

52 *"elderly and careworn"*: SH, "Bread and Circuses: Thought and Language in Decline," *Sydney Papers* 9, no. 4 (1997).

52 *"the genteel suburb"*: GF, 101.

52 *"provincialissimo"*: McClatchy, "Shirley Hazzard," 167.

## 2. A FIRST GLIMPSE OF THE UNKNOWN

53 *"this great conflict"*: GD.

53 *"the warm, drunken Australian night"*: SHD, May 8, 2004.

53 *"coming back drunk"*: Ibid.

53 *"I hardly know why"*: SH, "A Writer's Reflection on the Nuclear Age," in *We Need Silence to Find Out What We Think: Selected Essays by Shirley Hazzard*, ed. Brigitta Olubas (Columbia University Press, 2016), 142.

54 *"fortunate, formative"*: O'Grady, "Love's Slow Burn," 8.

54 *Reg was sent*: S. Blainey, "The Interpreter," 75.

54 *"an entrepôt"*: Boris Schedvin, *Emissaries of Trade: A History of the Australian Trade Commissioner Service* (Commonwealth of Australia, 2008), 115.

54 *As Australia had*: Ibid.

54 *Shirley, still most of a year*: Hazzard kept among her papers a letter from B. L. Rennie, principal of Queenwood, dated May 5, 1947, stating, "Miss Shirley Hazzard has passed the NSW Intermediate Certificate Examination and has completed one year and one term of the two-year course required for the Leaving Certificate and matriculation in New South Wales. She has shown special ability in her English and History studies, while her French Grammar is solid and she has a working knowledge of conversational French. She has also studied Geography and Biology with interest and success. She should be able to attain to any Matriculation standard within a year." SHPU.

54 *"city life!"*: JM.

54 *"little, old, durable ship"*: SH to Donald Keene, Oct. 17, 1999, SHPU.

55 *"in a jungle cove"*: SH, "Pilgrimage," in Shirley Hazzard and Francis Steegmuller, *Ancient Shore: Dispatches from Naples* (University of Chicago Press, 2008), 21.

55 *the* Taiping *was carrying*: AWR, 142.

55 *"with at least two"*: SH to Donald Keene, Oct. 17, 1999, SHPU.

55 *"great departure"*: JM.

55 *"The coast of my native land"*: P, 20–21.

55 *"the thrill of arriving"*: Crawford, "Shirley Hazzard," 3.

55  *"This vast body of water"*: Ibid.

55  *"On an unrepaired road"*: GF, 7.

56  *"They were cast off"*: Ibid., 8–11.

56  *Australian troops*: James Wood, "The Australian Military Contribution to the Occupation of Japan, 1945–1952" (Australian War Memorial, no date); available at www.awm.gov.au/sites/default/files/87111/files/bcofhistory1.pdf.

56  *a compound*: "Japanese Naval Academy Is 'Our Home' to British Commonwealth Occupation Force," *Central Queensland Herald*, Feb. 26, 1948, 3.

56  *"a high narrow room"*: GF, 11.

56  *the principal administration block*: "Japanese Naval Academy."

56  *Beyond the compound*: Ibid.

57  *"the conventional one"*: AWR, 143.

57  *"I didn't even realize"*: Crawford, "Shirley Hazzard," 3.

57  *"the beginning of"*: Denis Welch, "The Fire and the Rose," *New Zealand Listener*, June 18, 2007.

57  *"intuitively"*: GF, 8.

57  *"in numbers"*: Robin Gerster, "Bomb Sites in Japan: Photographing Australian-Occupied Hiroshima," *Meanjin* 74, no. 4 (2015): 89.

57  *"like riding in state"*: TV, 52.

57  *"In the past"*: Ibid., 52–53.

58  *"a lingering memory"*: Edward Stokes, "Introduction," in *Hong Kong as It Was: Hedda Morrison's Photographs*, ed. Edward Stokes (Hong Kong University Press, 2009), 9.

58  *"At that time"*: GD.

58  *"Hong Kong Island"*: Stokes, "Introduction," 9.

58  *"In China, years of"*: Ibid.

59  *"a colony retouching"*: SH, "Prologue," in *Hedda Morrison's Hong Kong*, ed. Edward Stokes (Hong Kong University Press, 2005), xi.

59  *"too much privilege"*: Steve Tsang, *A Modern History of Hong Kong* (I. B. Tauris, 2007), 143.

59  *"not only the end of the war"*: Ibid., 142.

59  *"The Second World War"*: Stokes, "Introduction," 15.

60  *"a wide, covered terrace"*: SH to Peter Vedeniapine, Sept. 4, 2005, SHPU.

60  *"the busiest intersection"*: SH, "Canton More Far," in *We Need Silence to Find Out What We Think: Selected Essays by Shirley Hazzard*, ed. Brigitta Olubas (Columbia University Press, 2016), 149.

60  *"One could not turn"*: Ibid., 150.

60  *"a very tight-knit little" area*: JM.

60  *"Vegetation was as dense"*: SH, "Sir Cecil's Ride," in *Collected Stories*, ed. Brigitta Olubas and with a foreword by Zoe Heller (Farrar, Straus & Giroux, 2020), 327.

61  *"If you were sixteen"*: CMF, 151.

61  *"a colonial life"*: JM.

62  *"the other consular people"*: Ibid.

62 *"There was a man called Eu"*: Ibid.

62 *"loved going out"*: Ibid.

62 *"holding the fort"*: APVOH.

62 *"the green rise"*: SHD, April 13, 2004, SHPU.

62 *"'Portuguese'"*: SH to Peter Vedeniapine, Sept. 4, 2005, SHPU.

62 *She also struck up*: SHD, Jan. 16, 1948; Telegram Rita Xavier to SH with Christmas greetings, SHPU.

62 *"people who had had"*: JM.

63 *"proof"*: Ibid.

63 *Vedeniapine could match*: Interview with Violet Highton, July 29, 2019.

63 *Chris Cooper later described*: McGuinness, "Transit of Shirley Hazzard," 128.

63 *"lovely face"*: Alan Green to BO, Feb. 15, 2018.

63 *Cooper and Green*: Ibid.

63 *Alan Green recalled*: Alan Green to BO, May 26, 2019.

63 *"interpreter to a three-man"*: Ibid.

63–64 *"amusing, clever and literary"*: JM.

64 *"ostensibly keeping her ear to the ground"*: Alan Green to BO, Feb. 15, 2018.

64 *"appeared to sway"*: GF, 120.

64 *Shirley had told him*: Paul French, "Shirley Hazzard's Teenage Spy Career: Paul French on the Late Writer's Brush with Espionage," *Literary Hub*, Dec. 20, 2016, lithub.com/shirley-hazzards-teenage-spy-career/.

64 *"I myself"*: Alan Green to BO, Feb. 15, 2018.

65 *"a two-page report"*: S. Blainey, "The Interpreter," 75; SHD, April 14, 1948, SHPU.

65 *Valerie was working*: "Life Is Never Boring for Hong Kong Journalist," *New Zealand Dominion*, July 4, 1949.

65 *thrilled, like Shirley*: Interview with Hamlin Hazzard Barnes, Nov. 8, 2018.

65 *"the sister who said"*: SCR, 327.

65 *"onto something altogether else"*: JM.

65 *"fiendishly jealous"*: Ibid.

66 *"poetry which was"*: Ibid.

66 *"already a rapturous"*: McClatchy, "Shirley Hazzard," 173.

66 *"I understood"*: JM.

66 *recalled during*: Interview with Matthew Specktor, June 12, 2021.

66 *"The distance between"*: Matthew Specktor, "Shirley Hazzard: 1931–2016," *Paris Review*, Dec. 19, 2016.

66 *"pleasant, mannerly"*: SH to Peter Vedeniapine, Sept. 4, 2005, SHPU.

66 *"was extraordinary"*: Ibid.

66 *"a war hero"*: Alan Green to BO, Feb. 15, 2018.

67 *Alexis Vedeniapine*: APVOH.

67 *"hoping that"*: Ibid.

67 *"local Chinese"*: Ibid.

67 *A favourite pastime*: Interview with Cynthia Vedeniapine, July 30, 2019.

68  *"As a child"*: APVOH.

68  *"In my family"*: Ibid.

68  *The youngest daughter*: Interview with Violet Highton, July 29, 2019.

69  *They finally fled*: APV to RH, Jan. 21, 1950, SHPU.

69  *"Russian Orthodox"*: Interview with Cynthia Vedeniapine, July 20, 2019.

69  *"to repel"*: APVOH.

69  *in Sicily*: He recalled of this: "It didn't make a lot of difference to me because I was doing an officer's work as a sergeant for some time before that." APVOH.

69  *serving as lieutenant*: An account of Vedeniapine's actions appears in the Pegasus Archive, an unofficial history of the British Airborne Forces; available at www.pegasusarchive.org/arnhem/alexis_vedeniapine.htm.

70  *"repeatedly crossed"*: Ibid.

70  *"He personally supervised"*: Ibid.

70  *In his eyes*: Peter Vedeniapine to BO, Oct. 10, 2019.

70  *"A swatch"*: SCR, 332.

70  *"fascinating, sad"*: APVOH.

71  *"I got to know"*: Ibid.

71  *"a man of great courage"*: Ibid.

71  *Chris Cooper recalled*: McGuinness, "Transit of Shirley Hazzard," 127–128.

71  *"more than anyone else"*: Chris Cooper to SH, Feb. 3, 1950, SHPU.

72  *"like himself"*: Ibid.

72  *"He loves England"*: Ibid.

72  *"Crucial reports"*: SH to Peter Vedeniapine, Sept. 4, 2005, SHPU.

73  *"You used to stamp"*: Alec Vedeniapine to SH, May 15, 1949, SHPU.

73  *"Late afternoon"*: SHD, Jan. 16, 1948.

73  *"clarity of sky"*: SHD, Feb. 26, 1999.

73  *"Half day at work"*: SHD, Jan. 1, 1948.

74  *"emotional instability"*: Chris Cooper to SH, Feb. 3, 1950, SHPU.

74  *"serious over me"*: SHD, Jan. 18, 1948.

74–75  *"happy past"*: SHD, Jan. 24, 1948.

75  *"warm . . . and quiet"*: SHD, Jan. 26, 1948.

75  *"felt on the verge"*: SHD, Jan. 31, 1948.

75  *"inexperienced"*: SH to Peter Vedeniapine, Sept. 4, 2005, SHPU.

75  *"Alec called me"*: SHD, Feb. 4, 1948.

75  *"I can't get over"*: SHD, Feb. 5, 1948.

75  *"I was hateful"*: SHD, Feb. 6, 1948.

75  *"Alec and I"*: SHD, May 3, 2004.

75  *"Alec was good"*: SHD, Feb. 16, 1948.

75  *"(Please, God.)"*: SHD, March 27, 1948.

76  *"a lovely day"*: SHD, March 30, 1948.

76  *"I'm struggling"*: SHD, April 5, 1948.

76  *"the eyes of Ahlex"*: SHD, July 9, 1948.

76  *"Alec rang"*: SHD, Aug. 8, 1948.

76  *"A dark-green Humber"*: SCR, 326.

77  *"stateless"*: Ibid., 329.

77  *"But, now the enterprise"*: Ibid., 325.

78  *"The bay appeared"*: Ibid., 328.

78  *"a rather Oxfordian"*: SHD, June 2, 1948.

78  *"Such nonsense"*: SHD, June 6, 1948.

78  *Keats's sonnet*: "Keen, fitful gusts are whisp'ring here and there." *Complete Poems and Selected Letters of John Keats* (Modern Library, 2001), 42.

78  *"Made my mind"*: SHD, Feb. 10, 1948.

78  *"Went to lecture"*: SHD, March 5, 1948.

78  *"Alec had to have"*: SHD, Feb. 28, 1948.

79  *"at a gathering"*: SH, "Translating Proust," in *We Need Silence to Find Out What We Think: Selected Essays by Shirley Hazzard*, ed. Brigitta Olubas (Columbia University Press, 2016), 81.

79  *"rife"*: SH to Peter Vedeniapine, Sept. 4, 2005, SHPU.

79  *two thousand deaths*: Figure reported by the Hong Kong Tuberculosis, Chest, and Heart Diseases Association history, available at www.ha.org.hk/org/antitb/e_greeting.htm.

79  *Valerie had written*: JM.

80  *she was given*: Ibid.; Interview with Hamlin Hazzard Barnes, Nov. 8, 2018.

80  *Reg was to*: SH to Peter Vedeniapine, Sept. 4, 2005, SHPU.

80  *"The last days"*: Ibid.

80  *"the least physical"*: GF, 180.

80  *"trembled in the balance"*: SH to Peter Vedeniapine, Sept. 4, 2005, SHPU.

81  *"Do you want me?"*: GF, 191.

81  *"We sat on the desk"*: SHD, Jan. 26, 1948.

### 3. SEA-GIRT, SOUTHERLY, SUNDERED

82  *"endless sorrow"*: SH to Peter Vedeniapine, Sept. 4, 2005, SHPU.

82  *"limbo of suffering"*: Ibid.

82  *"We reached Manila"*: GF, 253–54.

83  *"Dakota comes down"*: SHDN, no date, 1987.

83  *"One might have been"*: GF, 254.

83  *"Today I walked"*: Ibid.

83  *"posted Alec"*: SHD, Sept. 23, 1948.

83  *"The terrible trip"*: Ibid., Sept. 25, 1948.

83  *"Dreadful days"*: Ibid., Sept. 21, 1948.

84  *"Weep, O Love"*: William Morris, *The Collected Works of William Morris, with Introductions by His Daughter May Morris*, vol. 4, *The Earthly Paradise: A Poem (Part 2)* (Cambridge University Press, 2012), 248.

84  *"vigilant"*: SH to Peter Vedeniapine, Sept. 4, 2005, SHPU.

84  *Valerie reportedly claimed*: McGuinness, "Transit," 128.

84 *Alec's letters*: Alec Vedeniapine to SH, Oct. 4, 1949, SHPU.

84 *"desolate"*: JM.

85 *"I remember walking"*: Ibid.

85 *"very slight tuberculosis"*: SH to Chris Cooper, Sept. 2, 1948, SHPU.

85 *"My mother and Valerie"*: Ibid.

86 *"a new drug"*: GF, 13.

86 *"So you are still"*: Chris Cooper to SH, Aug. 3, 1948, SHPU.

86 *"some tea"*: Alan Green to SH, Sept. 14–16, 1948, SHPU.

86 *"How happy"*: Chris Cooper to SH, Oct. 2–4, 1948, SHPU.

87 *"Between now and you leaving"*: Alan Green to SH, Oct. 31, 1948, SHPU.

87 *"you had better"*: Alan Green to SH, Nov. 17, 1948, SHPU.

87 *in Australia in 1949*: Alison McKinnon, "Early Graduates," in *Encyclopedia of Women and Leadership in Twentieth-Century Australia* (Australian Women's Archives Project, 2014), available at www.womenaustralia.info/leaders/biogs/WLE0432b.htm.

87 *"get a trade"*: SH to Peter Vedeniapine, Sept. 4, 2005, SHPU.

87 *"the last straw"*: JM.

87 *"Misery, foreboding"*: SH to Peter Vedeniapine, Sept. 4, 2005, SHPU.

87 *"As for the shorthand"*: Alec Vedeniapine to SH, Oct. 19, 1948, SHPU.

88 *"Dear Shirley"*: Alec Vedeniapine to SH, Oct. 10, 1948, SHPU.

88 *"You make little"*: Ibid.

88 *"doing what comes naturally"*: Alec Vedeniapine to SH, Feb. 28, 1949, SHPU.

88 *"dull and very disappointing"*: APVOH.

88 *"I live in considerable comfort"*: Alec Vedeniapine to SH, Feb. 28, 1949, SHPU.

88 *"from an army of occupation"*: Alan Green to SH, May 6, 1949, SHPU.

89 *"villages and country lanes"*: Alec Vedeniapine to SH, April 27, 1949, SHPU.

89 *"a slightly better opportunity"*: Ibid.

89 *"Nothing is settled"*: Alec Vedeniapine to SH, March 15, 1949, SHPU.

89 *"I have been offered"*: Alec Vedeniapine to SH, June 20, 1949, SHPU.

89 *Their application*: Interview with Cynthia Vedeniapine, July 30, 2019.

90 *made sure that Shirley understood*: Alec Vedeniapine to SH, Dec. 12, 1949, SHPU.

90 *"last straw"*: SH to Peter Vedeniapine, Sept. 4, 2005, SHPU.

90 *"handsome"*: JM.

90 *"the brilliant airy cleanliness"*: SHDN, no date, 1980s.

90 *the scent from the hills*: Welch, "The Fire and the Rose."

90 *"Air of an uninhabited freshness"*: GF, 233.

91 *"And everything was quiet"*: JM.

91 *"In a way I regret"*: GF, 260.

91 *"just was as dull"*: JM.

91 *"There was such gentility"*: Ibid.

92 *"a pale blue frock"*: "Mr and Mrs Cutler Give Reception for Trade Commissioner," *The Dominion*, March 23, 1949.

92 *"nearly every house then"*: JM.

92  *"... on a height"*: GF, 260–61.

93  *"Weatherboard houses"*: Ibid., 263.

93  *"an adult sadness"*: SHDN, no date, 1980s.

93  *"this is not"*: GF, 268.

93  *"bristled with thick gorse"*: Ibid., 286.

93  *"I was never"*: Ibid., 287.

94  *"the antipodean touch"*: Ibid.

94  *"One thing I had felt"*: JM.

94  *In October:* Alec Vedeniapine to SH, Oct. 4, 1949, SHPU.

94  *"The redeeming thing"*: JM.

94  *"the most beautiful bookshop"*: Quoted in Leonard Bell, *Strangers Arrive: Emigrés and the Arts in New Zealand 1930–1980* (Auckland University Press, 2017), 36.

95  *"I never found"*: JM.

95  *"Fie on you"*: Chris Cooper to SH, no date, Christmas card, 1949, SHPU.

95  *"Chris tells me"*: Alan Green to SH, Dec. 13, 1949, SHPU.

96  *"an older woman"*: JM.

96  *"Norah sounds"*: Alec Vedeniapine to SH, Aug. 15, 1950, SHPU.

96  *"There was no one"*: GF, 254.

96  *"This thing"*: JM.

96  *"I am in our new home"*: Alec Vedeniapine to SH, Oct. 4, 1949, SHPU.

96  *"now tearing about"*: Alec Vedeniapine to SH, Aug. 26, 1949, SHPU.

96  *"middling but adequate"*: Ibid.

97  *"Everything looks fairly clean"*: Alec Vedeniapine to SH, Jan. 8, 1950, SHPU.

97  *"The first livestock"*: Ibid.

97  *"I can fair picture you"*: Alan Green to SH, Feb. 11, 1950, SHPU.

97  *"If you could put"*: Alec Vedeniapine to SH, May 15, 1950, SHPU.

98  *"In order to stave off"*: Alec Vedeniapine to SH, Aug. 26, 1949, SHPU.

98  *"I got your letter"*: Alec Vedeniapine to SH, Oct. 22, 1949, SHPU.

98  *"by then I should have things"*: Alec Vedeniapine to SH, Oct. 29, 1949, SHPU.

98  *"selfish and inconsiderate"*: Alec Vedeniapine to SH, Dec. 12, 1949, SHPU.

99  *"If you are prepared"*: Ibid.

99  *"would have no other"*: Ibid.

99  *"dictated by the feeling"*: Ibid.

99  *"Am I surprised?"*: Chris Cooper to SH, Feb. 3, 1950, SHPU.

100  *"You certainly put your time"*: Alan Green to SH, Feb. 11, 1950, SHPU.

100  *"Of course your family"*: Chris Cooper to SH, Feb. 3, 1950, SHPU.

100  *"Although I might conceivably prosper"*: Alec Vedeniapine to Reginald Hazzard, Jan. 20, 1950, SHPU.

100  *"understandable, sympathetic"*: Alec Vedeniapine to SH, March 2, 1950, SHPU.

100  *"He never really knew"*: SH to Peter Vedeniapine, Sept. 4, 2005, SHPU.

101  *"relax and don't fret"*: Alec Vedeniapine to SH, March 2, 1950, SHPU.

101  *"Your ring is blue"*: Alec Vedeniapine to SH, June 5, 1950, SHPU.

101  *"In order to get you"*: Alec Vedeniapine to SH, April 17, 1950, SHPU.

102  *"When we left Sydney"*: SH to Peter Vedeniapine, Sept. 4, 2005, SHPU.

103  *"I started writing this"*: Alec Vedeniapine to SH, June 5, 1950, SHPU.

103  *His son, Peter, felt*: Peter Vedeniapine to BO, Aug. 8, 2019; Oct. 21, 2021.

103  *"far more foreign"*: Alec Vedeniapine to SH, Jan. 8, 1950, SHPU.

103  *"I am a bit afraid"*: Alec Vedeniapine to SH, March 24, 1950, SHPU.

103  *"determined to keep"*: Alec Vedeniapine to SH, July 16, 1950, SHPU.

103  *"to do all you can"*: Ibid.

103  *"I should probably be"*: Ibid.

103  *"I am afraid"*: Ibid.

104  *"discovered something about myself"*: Alec Vedeniapine to SH, March 24, 1950, SHPU.

104  *"I only wish"*: Alec Vedeniapine to SH, July 16, 1950, SHPU.

104  *"I suppose I oughtn't to mind"*: Alec Vedeniapine to SH, Aug. 15, 1950, SHPU.

104  *"entreating"*: SH, handwritten comment on telegram: Alec Vedeniapine to SH, Oct. 8, 1950, SHPU.

104  *"Reserve judgment"*: Ibid.

104  *"I have been trying"*: Alec Vedeniapine to SH, Oct. 12, 1950, SHPU.

105  *"the unravelling"*: SH to Peter Vedeniapine, Sept. 4, 2005, SHPU.

106  *"an extraordinary man of action"*: Ibid.

106  *she explained that*: Peter Vedeniapine to BO, Aug. 8, 2019.

107  *"You will have to guard"*: Chris Cooper to SH, Feb. 3, 1950, SHPU.

107  *"I saw this lovely photograph"*: Interview with Violet Highton, July 29, 2019.

107  *"the farm was not"*: Interview with Cynthia Vedeniapine, July 30, 2019.

108  *"A story from Thomas Hardy"*: SHD, 1948, pencilled note dated Feb. 17, 1990, SHPU.

109  *"probably an anti-fascist émigré"*: JM.

109  *"They found I could 'say something'"*: Ibid.

109  *"as you would use the word"*: Ibid.

109  *"I had noticed the immigrants"*: Ibid.

110  *"people, interesting to me"*: Ibid.

110  *"[We] sat up on deck"*: GF, 72.

## 4. NEW YORK

113  *"noble scars"*: Ibid.

113  *"come through the East"*: Ibid.

113  *"that great plunder-house"*: Ibid.

113  *"the great austerity"*: Ibid.

113  *"Wendy Hiller"*: Ibid.

114  *"People were terribly polite"*: Ibid.

114  *"achievement"*: TV, 22.

114  *The Australian press reported*: "He'll Get Top Pay," *Melbourne Herald*, Nov. 7, 1951, 2.

114  *"It is so difficult"*: Chris Cooper to SH, Nov. 20, 1950, SHPU.

115  *"heartening to hear you"*: Alan Green to SH, Feb. 24, 1951, SHPU.

115  *"private disappointments"*: Alan Green to SH, July 21, 1951, SHPU.

115  *"We can compare"*: Alan Green to SH, Oct. 1951, SHPU.

115  *"immense change"*: GD.

115  *"When we arrived"*: JM.

116  *"idealistic, like many people"*: GD.

116  *"in its stride"*: E. B. White, *Here Is New York* (Little Bookroom, 2011), 55.

116  *"in armchairs"*: SH, *The Bay of Noon* (Little, Brown, 1970), 73.

117  *"modish"*: David Webster, "Development Advisors in a Time of Cold War and De-colonization: UN Technical Assistance Administration 1950–59," *Journal of Global History* 6, no. 2 (2011): 250.

117  *"on the basis"*: Ibid.

117  *"a poorish Italian film"*: SHD, Jan. 22, 1953.

117  *"I tried to say"*: SHD, Jan. 13, 1953.

118  *"tell lies"*: Anne Fremantle obituary, *The Times* (London), Jan. 24, 2003.

118  *"a generous heart"*: McClatchy, "Shirley Hazzard," 186.

118  *told the story*: Interview with Hugh Fremantle, Oct. 24, 2018.

118  *"When I was first asked"*: "Tribute to W. H. Auden," 92nd Street Y, March 5, 2007; available at www.92y.org/archives/tribute-to-w-h-auden.

119  *had won a scholarship*: "Our London Correspondence: Talks Department," *Guardian*, June 7, 1947, 6.

119  *BBC's North American representative*: "BBC Representative in New York," *Guardian*, Jan. 11, 1949, 3.

119  *responsible for one of only two known recordings*: Michael Crick, "Hearing Guy Burgess's Plummy, Upper-Class Voice for the First Time," Jan. 17, 2014; available at www.channel4.com/news/by/michael-crick/blogs/guy-burgess-winston-churchill-chartwell-munich-3731.

119  *"In the several years"*: SH, "Nothing in Excess," in *Collected Stories*, ed. Brigitta Olubas and with a foreword by Zoe Heller (Farrar, Straus & Giroux, 2020), 137–38.

119  *"I keep thinking"*: SHD, Dec. 22, 1956.

120  *"a Communist-dominated"*: Stanley Meisler, *The United Nations, A History* (Grove Press, 2011), 82.

120  *"infiltration into the UN"*: Trygve Lie, *In the Cause of Peace: Seven Years with the United Nations* (Macmillan, 1954), 388.

120  *"cooperated" with the U.S. government*: Meisler, *United Nations*, 82.

120  *"Such a dreadful newspaper"*: SHD, Jan. 2, 1953.

121  *She also made a point*: SHD, Jan. 5, 1953.

121  *"I felt so terribly sorry"*: SHD, Jan. 7, 1953.

121  *"Oh Christ"*: SHD, Jan. 6, 1953.

121  *"Zablodowsky resigned"*: SHD, Jan. 8, 1953.

121  *"Walter Winchell"*: SHD, Jan. 11, 1953.

121  *"So the prospect"*: Chris Cooper to SH, Jan. 24, 1952, SHPU.

122  *"less than lukewarm"*: SHD, March 5, 1955, SHPU.

122   *"It is exactly like"*: Ibid.

123   *"in New York at last"*: SHD, July 19, 2006, SHPU.

123   *"I am almost incoherent"*: SHD, March 13, 1953, SHPU.

123   *"so outspoken"*: SHD, April 26, 1953, SHPU.

123   *"a magnificent collection"*: SHD, July 6, 1954, SHPU.

123   *"splendid—simple"*: SH to Donald Keene, Aug. 16, 1997, SHP Series II, Box 10.

123   *"simply wonderful"*: SHD, March 5, 1953, SHPU.

123   *"all very cosy"*: SHD, March 26, 1953, SHPU.

123   *"Auden and Marianne Moore"*: SHD, May 13, 1953, SHPU.

124   *"nothing disillusioning"*: "Tribute to W. H. Auden."

124   *"Oh dear"*: SHD, Jan. 21, 1953, SHPU.

124   *"mess and wretchedness"*: SHD, Feb. 6, 1953, SHPU.

124   *"At last"*: Ibid.

125   *"Mommy depressed"*: SHD, Feb. 10, 1953, SHPU.

125   *"Everything has been"*: SHD, Feb. 13, 1953, SHPU.

125   *"Barnes came"*: SHD, Feb. 17, 1953, SHPU.

125   *"Mommy terribly upset"*: SHD, March 2, 1953, SHPU.

125   *"Mommy so upset"*: SHD, March 3, 1953, SHPU.

125   *"I had a lovely"*: SHD, March 8, 1953, SHPU.

125   *"various 'false' attempts"*: SH to Elizabeth Harrower, no date, SHPU.

125   *"Tonight is terrible"*: SHD, May 19, 1953, SHPU.

125   *"I suppose it's not so bad"*: SHD, June 10, 1953, SHPU.

126   *"squalid"*: JM.

126   *"a tear-struck mess"*: Ibid.

126   *"This was a stage"*: SH to Elizabeth Harrower, no date, SHPU.

126   *"I took my mother"*: JM.

127   *"Commissioner Nabbed"*: *Truth*, Dec. 26, 1954.

127   *"putting my hands"*: JM.

127   *"'classics' from lesser known countries"*: Howard Daniel, "The Genesis of the American Edition of *Such Is Life*," *Biblionews* 5, no. 12 (1952). The story is told in David Carter and Roger Osborne, *Australian Books and Authors in the American Marketplace 1840–1940s* (Sydney University Press, 2018).

128   *"vers libre'"*: "New 'Hermes' Editor," *Daily Telegraph* [Sydney], June 21, 1934, 9.

128   *"erotically undernourished"*: *North West Champion* [Moree], July 23, 1934, 2.

128   *"become obsessed"*: Howard Daniel, "Egon Remembered," *Overland* 10 (March 1988): 48.

128   *in 1937*: "Howard Daniel: Complaint Lodged with Foreign Office," *Telegraph* [Brisbane], Aug. 26, 1937, 7.

128   *"real Scarlet Pimpernel stuff"*: "Sydney Says," *Smith's Weekly*, May 25, 1940, 10.

129   *"a fascinating, erudite"*: Lane Morgan to BO, email, Nov. 3, 2019.

129   *"later talk of 'exploitation'"*: SHD, Jan. 1, 1953.

129   *"a rainy Saturday"*: SHD, Jan. 24, 1948.

129   *"I took The Economist down"*: SHD, Jan. 9, 1953.

129   *"Went quite well"*: SHD, Feb. 20, 1953.

130   *"Bohemian guests"*: SHD, Jan. 2, 1954.

130   *"terribly good to me"*: SHD, July 2, 1953.

130   *"true friendship"*: SHD, Jan. 2, 1954.

130   *"The Daniels were very nice"*: Tex Goldschmidt to SH, Oct. 9, 1955, SHPU.

131   *"Oh, why can't I handle"*: SHD, March 31, 1953.

131   *"When we got to 96th"*: SHD, July 15, 1953.

131   *"He made love to me"*: SHD, July 23, 1953.

131   *"He said when was I going"*: SHD, July 30, 1953.

131   *"power couples"*: Landon R. Y. Storrs, *The Second Red Scare and the Unmaking of the New Deal Left* (Princeton University Press, 2012), 10.

131   *"freethinking German immigrants"*: Ibid., 17.

131   *"a combination of scholarships"*: Arthur Goldschmidt (Junior), Memoir. Much of the information about the Goldschmidts was drawn from this unpublished memoir, a copy of which was kindly made available to me by Art Goldschmidt.

132   *Tex then volunteered*: Interview with Arthur Goldschmidt (Junior), Nov. 27, 2018.

132   *"in practice"*: Storrs, *The Second Red Scare*, 245.

132   *"Neither my wife nor I"*: Ibid., 18.

132   *Ann found*: Interview with Ann Richardson, Aug. 3, 2019.

132   *"had promised her"*: Interview with Arthur Goldschmidt (Junior), Nov. 27, 2018.

133   *"I've been unfaithful"*: SHD, July 16, 1954.

133   *remembered Shirley*: Interview with Ann Richardson, Aug. 3, 2019.

133   *"as if she were"*: Interview with Arthur Goldschmidt (Junior) ), Nov. 27, 2018.

133   *"correspondence while the foe"*: SHD, July 8, 1955.

134   *"Wicky seemed"*: SHD, Jan. 15, 1955.

134   *"She had a slow"*: SH, "A Place in the Country," in *Collected Stories*, ed. Brigitta Olubas and with a foreword by Zoe Heller (Farrar, Straus & Giroux, 2020), 14.

134   *"inwardly distraught"*: SHD, Feb. 27, 1955.

134   *In Geneva*: SHD, April 17, 1955.

135   *"scenes, hysterics, violence"*: SHD, May 3, 1955.

135   *Shirley stood her ground*: SHD, June 1, 1955.

135   *"After dinner"*: Ibid.

136   *"It was dark"*: SHD, Aug. 30, 1954.

136   *"deliriously happy"*: SHD, July 8, 1955.

136   *"This surprised"*: Ibid.

136   *"those two little girls"*: Ibid.

137   *"terribly distressed"*: SHD, Aug. 9, 1955.

137   *"She was all right"*: Ibid.

137   *"'Remember . . .' she began"*: APC, 33.

137   *"just terror"*: SHD, Aug. 13, 1956.

137   *"floating on"*: SHD, Oct. 7, 1956.

137   *"Love had not"*: TV, 166–67.

138   *"I didn't want to die"*: SHD, Oct. 7, 1956.

138   *"scarcely the ideal"*: Elizabeth Wickenden Goldschmidt to SH, Sept. 26, 1956, SHPU.

138   *"And this weighed"*: SHD, Oct. 7, 1956.

138   *"We walked down"*: SHD, Dec. 22, 1956.

139   *"Lately it has come"*: SHD, Aug. 25, 1957.


### 5. A LARGER LIFE

140   *"From the first day"*: Susan Wyndham, "Hazzard Ahead," *Weekend Australian*, July 17–18, 1993, 30.

140   *"a whole part of my life"*: Richard Eder, "For Two Writers, Separate Silences," *NYT*, March 26, 1980, T1.

140   *"22 December 1956"*: SHD, Dec. 22, 1956.

141   *"There has been a break"*: Vendela Vida, "An Interview with Shirley Hazzard," *Believer* 15 (July 1, 2004): 80.

141   *"Entirely thanks"*: McClatchy, "Shirley Hazzard," 174.

141   *"realistic and clear"*: SH to Piers Paul Read, Feb. 10, 1963, Papers of Piers Paul Reed, Special Collections & Galleries, Leeds University Library, BC MS 20C Piers Paul Read.

141   *"The traveller equipped"*: P, 22–23.

142   *"a frigid night"*: SHD, Dec. 3, 1996.

142   *"I came here alone"*: SHD, Aug. 25, 1957 (1956 diary).

142   *"one of the good hotels"*: SH, "City of Secrets and Surprises," in SH and FS, *The Ancient Shore: Dispatches from Naples*, 51.

142   *"restaurants, and a pier"*: SH to Valerie Barnes, date illegible, 1957, SHPU.

143   *"a medieval construction"*: CSS, 52.

143   *"vehicle"*: Quoted in Lucy Gordan, "Island Life," *Australian Way Magazine (QANTAS*, October 2000).

143   *"shattered" airport*: Ibid.

143   *returned to their hotels*: SH to UN Personnel, May 13 (no year), "Note for personal file," SHPU.

143   *she had the responsibility*: Ibid.

143   *overwhelmingly sad*: Interview with Lily Gravino, Sept. 20, 2015.

143   *"typical military man"*: Ibid.

143   *"perpetually seething"*: BN, 57.

143   *"Trapped with a handful"*: SHD, Aug. 25, 1957 (1956 diary).

144   *"Your absence"*: Norman Luker to SH, Dec. 19, 1956, SHPU.

144   *"She held a letter"*: SHDN, no date, 1977.

144   *"Angelas and Hilarys"*: BN, 4.

144   *"their term of exile"*: Ibid., 6.

145   *"who lived among men"*: SH, "A Sense of Mission," in *Collected Stories*, ed. Brigitta Olubas and with a foreword by Zoe Heller (Farrar, Straus & Giroux, 2020), 251.

145   *"afraid of women"*: Ibid., 247.

145   *"revisited by ecstasy"*: Ibid., 240.

145   *"the rhythmic crunching"*: Ibid., 242.

145   *"Mysteries"*: Ibid., 244.

145   *"a blitzed town"*: SH, "A Sense of Ancient Fame," in SH and FS, *The Ancient Shore: Dispatches from Naples*, 30.

145   *"recent ravages"*: Shirley Hazzard, *Greene on Capri: A Memoir* (Farrar, Straus & Giroux, 2000), 53.

145   *"those who came to know Naples"*: Ibid.

145   *"The city was the thing"*: GD.

145   *"great dictatorial god"*: Kate Jennings, "Going Against the Grain: Interview with Shirley Hazzard," *Island* 50 (March 1992): 23.

146   *"a love letter"*: McClatchy, "Shirley Hazzard," 181.

146   *"for the city"*: BN, 6.

146   *"'It's the city'"*: Ibid., 51.

146   *"It was necessary"*: GD.

146   *"a revelation"*: Jan Garrett, "The Transits of Hazzard," *Look and Listen*, Nov. 1984, 38–39.

146   *"When I entered"*: Ibid.

147   *"where the city 'splits'"*: CSS, 53.

147   *"a ramp of a street"*: BN, 11.

147   *"standing up"*: Ibid., 65.

147   *"giggling all the way"*: Ibid., 66.

147   *"When I think"*: SHDN, no date, 1966–1968.

148   *"There are accretions"*: Harriet Shapiro, "Hazzard Remembers," in Bartlett, *Literary Lives: The World of Francis Steegmuller & Shirley Hazzard*, 24.

148   *"It is the oddest thing"*: SHDN, no date, 1966–1968.

148   *"A hundred shops"*: BN, 12.

148   *"a deep square"*: BN, 13.

149   *"a few details"*: SH to Patricia Clarke, Aug. 19, 1970, SHPU.

149   *"From here"*: BN, 22.

149   *"The arches and towers"*: Ibid.

149   *"Taxi driver said"*: SHDN, no date, 1966–1968.

149   *"There were many times"*: SHDN, no date, late 1960s.

150   *"high, humid rooms"*: SH, "Italian Hours," in SH and FS, *The Ancient Shore: Dispatches from Naples*, 3.

150   *Villa Mazziotti*: James Merrill to SH, Sept. 4, 1986, SHPU; Carlo Knight to BO, Nov. 4, 2019.

150   *"a red, romantic house"*: SAF, 30.

150   *"In order to reach"*: BN, 53.

150   *"My rooms gave"*: Ibid., 54.

150   *"through the flawed"*: Ibid., 56.

151 *"The window returned"*: Ibid.

151 *"still recognizably close"*: SAF, 30.

151 *"To drive out"*: Ibid.

151 *"seaweedy rocks"*: Desmond O'Grady, *A Word in Edgeways* (Connor Court, 2010), 157.

151 *"Posillipo begins"*: SAF, 31–32.

152 *"The ghosts"*: Ibid., 32.

152 *"with the Vesuvius"*: BN, 47.

152 *"And then there was Capri"*: Lucy Gordan, "Island Life."

152 *"There were no hydrofoils"*: Ibid.

152 *"Blue, brilliant"*: SHD, July 4, 2005.

152 *"Capri's modern prosperity"*: GC, 125–26.

153 *"one of the last"*: James Money, *Capri: Island of Pleasure* (Hamish Hamilton, 1986), 262–63.

153 *"a great beauty"*: SH to Evan Cornog and Ann Goldstein, March 9, 1988, SHPU.

153 *"among friends"*: SHDN, no date, 1968.

153 *"the mountain-face"*: SHD, Oct. 9, 1999.

153 *"I am obsessed"*: SHD, Aug. 25, 1957 (1956 diary).

153 *"memories that were burning"*: Harold H. Martin to SH, Jan. 23, 1957, SHPU.

154 *"each time"*: SHD, Aug. 25, 1957 (1956 diary).

154 *"a privilege"*: Gordan and Pasca, "Shirley Hazzard: Back to Basics," 45.

154 *"Now it grows near"*: SHD, Aug. 25, 1957 (1956 diary).

154 *"in the garden"*: SHD, Aug. 15, 2007.

155 *"Even in the worst"*: BN, 183.

155 *"Below the windows"*: Ibid., 185–86.

155 *using leave*: McClatchy, "Shirley Hazzard," 174.

155 *"weather unexpectedly warm"*: SH to Catherine Hazzard, Oct. 17, 1957, SHPU.

155 *"Seeing that small"*: SH to Donald Keene, July 20, 1986, SHP Series II, Box 10.

155 *"just too lovely"*: SH to Catherine Hazzard, date unclear, SHPU.

156 *"October is one of"*: SH to Patricia Lovell, May 10, 1986, SHPU.

156 *"a rather dilapidated"*: GD.

156 *"the second miracle"*: McClatchy, "Shirley Hazzard," 174.

156 *"bold, elegant"*: SH to FS, March 15, 1963, SHPU.

156 "come a godersi": Roberto Barzanti, "Eugenio Montale e Irma Brandeis a villa Solaia," in Roberto Barzanti and Attilio Brilli, *Soggiorni senesi tra mito e memoria* (Monte dei Paschi di Siena, 2007), 437.

156 *"sand-coloured"*: Arturo Vivante, "Arturo Vivante," in *Contemporary Authors Autobiography Series*, Vol. 12, ed. Joyce Nakamura (Gale Cengage, 1990), 281.

157 *"He came with his characteristic"*: SH to Vera Vivante, Nov. 27, 2004, private collection.

157 *"and thus I met"*: Ibid.

157 *"the girl with eyes"*: SHDN, Nov. 10, 1987.

157 *"The group of trees"*: SHDN, no date.

157 *"perfectly beautiful"*: SH to Catherine Hazzard, June 1958.

157   *"There could not now"*: SH to Vera Vivante, Nov. 27, 2004, private collection.

158   *"If my family had"*: Vivante, "Arturo Vivante," 284.

158   *her work was not*: SH to Ann Goldstein, March 11, 1997, private collection.

158   *the magazine*: *Il Convito* was described by Iris Origo as "the most interesting Italian periodical of the time, which published such works as Carducci's *La Canzone di Legnano*, D'Annunzio's *Le Vergini delle Rocce*, and some of Pascoli's *Poemi Conviviali*." Origo added that "these writers were among the family friends." Iris Origo, *A Need to Testify* (Helen Marx Books, 2001), 52.

158   *Lauro de Bosis*: Ibid., 56.

158   *"because I am not"*: Ibid., 80.

158   *"the destiny of"*: Quoted in ibid., 57.

158   *"I am not counting"*: Ibid., 99.

159   *"Tomorrow, at three o'clock"*: Quoted in Vivante, "Arturo Vivante," 283.

159   *"for me the words"*: Ibid.

159   *"a solitary thinker"*: Arturo Vivante, "Introduction," in Leone Vivante, *Essays on Art and Ontology* (University of Utah Press, 1980), x.

160   *"in the hope"*: Vivante, "Arturo Vivante," 281.

160   *"fascism and the Depression"*: Ibid.

160   *"invited friends"*: Ibid.

160   *there was a flow*: Barzanti writes, *"Solaia, Geggiano, villa Brandi a Vignano e la villa Il Vallone dei Sadun, poco distante, formavano una sorta di sistema, un itinerario che disegnava uno spazio a sé, prediletto da artisti e da personalità in dissenso con il regime."* Barzanti, *Soggiorni senesi*, 445.

160   *whose rooms painted with fruits*: SH to Patricia Lovell, SHPU.

160   *"Parnassus"*: Barzanti, *Soggiorni senesi*, 438.

160   *"his red beard"*: Arturo Vivante's comments quoted in Daniel Pearlman, "Canto 52: The Vivante Passage," *Paideuma: Modern and Contemporary Poetry and Poetics* 10, no. 2 (Fall 1981): 311.

161   *"sharply aware"*: Vivante, "Arturo Vivante," 282.

161   *"telling us with a frown"*: Quoted in Pearlman, "Canto 52," 313.

161   *"No books by Jews"*: Vivante, "Arturo Vivante," 187.

161   *"My father said"*: Ibid. 287.

161   *In 1938*: Interview with Vera Vivante, Nov. 4–5, 2018. This interview was the source for the Vivante family's years in exile from Italy.

162   *"So in the secrecy"*: Elena Vivante's letter read to BO by Vera Vivante during the interview, Nov. 4–5, 2018.

163   *"It was a time"*: Shirley Hazzard, "Introduction," in *Elena Vivante: Paintings* (Studio Press, 1995), 8.

163   *"hidden the silver"*: Vivante, "Arturo Vivante," 295.

163   *The occupying Germans*: Ibid.

163   *"usually friends"*: Ibid.

164  *paying 2,500 lire*: Elena Vivante to Dwight Macdonald, June 10, 1957, Dwight Macdonald Papers MS Series, Manuscripts and Archives, Yale University Library.

164  *"It is an indescribably"*: SH to Chris Cooper, Dec. 19, 1962, SHPU.

164  *"This is paradise"*: Dwight Macdonald to Mary McCarthy, July 24, 1961, in *A Moral Temper: Letters of Dwight Macdonald*, ed. Michael Wreszin (Ivan R. Dee, 2001), 311.

164  *"Every evening"*: SH, "Harold," in *Collected Stories*, ed. Brigitta Olubas and with a foreword by Zoe Heller (Farrar, Straus & Giroux, 2020), 103.

165  *"large and free"*: Dwight Macdonald to Mary McCarthy, July 24, 1961, in Wreszin, *A Moral Temper*, 311.

165  *"fervour in the way"*: Vivante, "Arturo Vivante," 298.

165  *Roberto Barzanti*: Barzanti, *Soggiorni senesi.*

165  "si parlava": Ibid.

165  *"She was tall"*: EV, 7.

166  *"all life"*: Robert Sonkin to Paolo Vivante, no date, 1963, private collection.

166  *"One moonlit night"*: EV, 9.

166  *"To have known her"*: Ibid., 10.

167  *"to make a principled life"*: SHDN, April 30, 1983.

167  *"A distinctive hand"*: EV, 7.

167  *"The light was"*: SH, "The Worst Moment of the Day," in *Collected Stories*, ed. Brigitta Olubas and with a foreword by Zoe Heller (Farrar, Straus & Giroux, 2020), 129.

168  *"paying tribute"*: SHDN, no date, 1983, SHPU.

168  *"The most beautiful change"*: Elena Vivante to SH, no date, SHPU.

168  *"Dear Shirley"*: Paolo Vivante to SH, May 26, 1961, private collection.

168  *"leads the anti-Charis"*: Piers Paul Read to parents, no date, BC MS 20c Piers Paul Read/F1, Literary, Personal and Family Correspondence, Piers Paul Reed Archive, Special Collections, Leeds University Library.

168  *"recopy"*: Arturo Vivante to SH, Jan. 27, 1958, SHB.

169  *"Dearest Shirley"*: Arturo Vivante to SH, no date, SHB.

169  *He had liked*: Arturo Vivante to Dwight Macdonald, Sept. 15, 1957, Dwight Macdonald Papers MS Series, Manuscripts and Archives, Yale University Library.

169  *"there now existed"*: BN, 229–30.

169  *"resolutely heading"*: SH to Elizabeth Harrower, no date, SHPU.

169  *"because I hadn't a penny"*: GD.

170  *"I went to Italy"*: JM.

170  *"I'd been trying to cope"*: Jenny Wiggins, "Accidents Do Happen in Life and War," *Financial Times*, Dec. 11–12, 2004.

170  *"the real risk"*: Ibid.

170  *"It is difficult"*: EV, 10.

170  *"It was there"*: McClatchy, "Shirley Hazzard," 175.

170  *"My idyllic 'childhood'"*: SHD, no date, 1980s.

## 6. Sì, SCRIVO!

171 *"Sat down"*: SH to Evan Cornog and Ann Goldstein, June 22, 1987, private collection.

171 *his mother*: Jan Ligthart to SH, Aug. 26, 1958; Jan Ligthart to SH, Feb. 12, 1960; Gerard Ligthart to BO, June 2021.

171 *"One can't ask"*: WMD, 124.

172 *"Solaia July 1958"*: SHDN, no date.

172 *"lunching in a veritable"*: SHDN, May 27, 1980.

172 *"In your letter"*: Jan Ligthart to SH, Jan. 15, 1959, SHPU.

173 *"in an irritating"*: Piers Paul Read to parents, no date, BC MS 20c Piers Paul Read/ F1, Literary, Personal and Family Correspondence, Piers Paul Reed Archive, Special Collections, Leeds University Library.

173 *"It was the last of"*: McClatchy, "Shirley Hazzard," 186.

174 *"If you're the Robert Sonkin"*: SH interview with Martin Stannard, Feb. 23, 1994, MSC.

174 *"a man of great learning"*: Ibid.

174 *"every second Friday"*: Ibid.

174 *"try to tell people"*: Elena Vivante to SH, May 23, 1960, private collection.

175 *"by nature both"*: in eds. Patricia Clarke and David Footman, *In Memoriam Archie, 1904–1964: A Symposium on Archibald Lauren Lyall by His Friends* (1964), 49.

175 *"One was never surprised"*: Ibid., 50.

175 *"an inspired figure"*: SH to Dwight Macdonald, July 27, no year, Dwight Macdonald Papers MS Series, Manuscripts and Archives, Yale University Library.

175 *"back-handed"*: Clarke and Footman, *In Memoriam Archie*, 51.

175 *"After Archie's death"*: Ibid.

176 *"Algie's last letter"*: "Nothing in Excess," in *Collected Stories*, ed. Brigitta Olubas and with a foreword by Zoe Heller (Farrar, Straus & Giroux, 2020), 153.

176 *"bad poems"*: Jan Ligthart to SH, Aug. 10, 1959, SHPU.

176 *"lovely even though"*: Jan Ligthart to SH, Oct. 6 1959, SHPU.

176 *"I would now"*: Tex Goldschmidt to SH, Jan. 30, 1956, SHPU.

177 *In November 1959*: Jan Ligthart to SH, Nov. 24, 1959, SHPU.

177 *with a letter*: "Success with Short Stories," *SMH*, June 29, 1961.

177 *The following April*: Jan Ligthart to SH, May 9, 1960, SHPU.

177 *Dwight Macdonald had offered*: SH to Dwight Macdonald, Aug. 3, 1960, Dwight Macdonald Papers MS Series, Manuscripts and Archives, Yale University Library.

177 *"a selfless interest"*: Alec Wilkinson, *My Mentor: A Young Writer's Friendship with William Maxwell* (Mariner Books, 2003), 92.

177 *"extremely receptive"*: Interview with Alec Wilkinson, Oct. 16, 2020.

177 *"a near spiritual hunger"*: Wilkinson, *My Mentor*, 92.

178 *"It was the butcher"*: WMD, 125.

178 *"Went to the kitchen"*: SHD, 1960, no date.

178 *"That afternoon"*: Shapiro, "Hazzard Remembers," 25.

178 *"important enough"*: Crawford, "Shirley Hazzard," 12.

178  *"A note to thank you"*: SH to Dwight Macdonald, Aug. 3, 1960, Dwight Macdonald Papers MS Series, Manuscripts and Archives, Yale University Library.

179  *"an astonishment"*: Wyndham, "Hazzard Ahead," *Weekend Australian Magazine*, July 17–18, 1993, 30.

179  *"never asked her"*: Ibid.

179  *"you will have another story"*: William Maxwell to SH, Sept. 6, 1960, SHPU.

179  *"little time it may"*: Jan Ligthart to SH, Dec. 24, 1960, SHPU.

179  *"thought that the whole"*: Henry Robbins to SH, Nov. 29, 1960, Alfred A Knopf, Inc., Records, Box 317, Folder 15, Harry Ransom Humanities Research Center.

179  *"to use this intriguing setting"*: Ibid.

179–80  *"a few small questions"*: Rachel MacKenzie to SH, March 13, 1961, NYR.

180  *"one of the newest"*: "Success with Short Stories."

180  *"a rare bird"*: Shirley Hazzard, obituary for William Maxwell (draft), SHPU.

180  *"English writer"*: Dwight Macdonald to Mary McCarthy, July 24, 1961, in Wreszin, *A Moral Temper*, 311.

180  *"When he had read"*: H, 111.

180  *an incident*: Jan Ligthart to SH, Aug. 10, 1959, SHPU.

181  *"It is nice to think"*: SH to Rachel MacKenzie, July 17, 1961, NYR.

181  *"the new schedule"*: Rachel MacKenzie to SH, Aug. 3, 1961, NYR.

181  *"There was by the way"*: SH to Piers Paul Read, Oct. 27, 1962, BC MS 20c Piers Paul Read/F1, Literary, Personal and Family Correspondence, Piers Paul Reed Archive, Special Collections, Leeds University Library.

181  *"from life"*: SH to Dwight Macdonald, Nov. 1, 1962, Dwight Macdonald Papers MS Series, Manuscripts and Archives, Yale University Library.

181  *"It was with astonishment"*: SH, "Vittorio," in *Collected Stories*, ed. Brigitta Olubas and with a foreword by Zoe Heller (Farrar, Straus & Giroux, 2020), 56.

182  *"for your opinion"*: SH to Rachel MacKenzie, Jan. 31, 1961, NYR.

182  *"in a whiz"*: Rachel MacKenzie to SH, Feb. 6, 1961, NYR.

182  *the offer of*: Rachel MacKenzie to SH, Feb. 9, 1961, NYR.

182  *"the second story"*: Vida, "An Interview with Shirley Hazzard," 81.

182  *"Of course"*: Rachel MacKenzie to SH, March 20, 1961, NYR.

182  *"So you see"*: SH, "Villa Adriana," in *Collected Stories*, ed. Brigitta Olubas and with a foreword by Zoe Heller (Farrar, Straus & Giroux, 2020), 73–78.

183  *"Irish, tall, lean"*: SHDN, no date, 1962.

183  *"It is the pattern"*: SHDN, Feb. 9, 1962.

183  *"We spent an hour"*: SHDN, April 28, 1962.

184  *"Talking of writing"*: Chris Cooper to SH, Feb. 13, 1961, SHPU.

184  *"R came today"*: SHDN, no date, 1961.

185  *"We are asked constantly"*: SHDN, Dec. 17, 1961.

185  *"mournful face"*: SH, "The Party," in *Collected Stories*, ed. Brigitta Olubas and with a foreword by Zoe Heller (Farrar, Straus & Giroux, 2020), 11.

186  *"'I think I told you'"*: APC, 38.

186   *"Upright on her rock"*: Ibid., 119.

187   *"In all events"*: Ibid., 115.

188   *In early 1962*: SH to Rache Lovat Dickson, Jan. 20, 1962; SH to Rache Lovat Dickson, Sept. 19, 1962, The Macmillan Archive, Macmillan Publishers International Ltd.

189   *"'Talk about distant prospects'"*: Shapiro, "Hazzard Remembers," 26.

189   *"most imposing figures"*: Margalit Fox, "Ved Mehta, Writer Who Illuminated India, Is Dead at 86," *NYT*, Jan. 10, 2021.

189   *"Ved would collect"*: SH interview with Martin Stannard, Feb. 23, 1994, MSC.

189   *"by far the best"*: Quoted in Deborah McVea and Jeremy Treglown, "1948–1959: The *TLS* Under Alan Pryce-Jones," *Times Literary Supplement Historical Archive* (Cengage Learning, 2012).

189   *"Alan knew everyone"*: Patrick Leigh Fermor, "Alan Pryce-Jones 1908–2000," *The Spectator*, April 15, 2000, 46.

190   *"for a time it looked"*: Ibid.

190   *"quite the best"*: Rache Lovat Dickson to C. H. Derrick, Jan. 28, 1968, The Macmillan Archive, Macmillan Publishers International Ltd.

190   *"of the genuineness"*: Rache Lovat Dickson to APJ, Feb. 12, 1962, The Macmillan Archive, Macmillan Publishers International Ltd.

190   *"an almost unbelievably clever"*: C. H. Derrick, Reader Report, Jan. 30, 1963, The Macmillan Archive, Macmillan Publishers International Ltd.

190   *"ready for [Muriel]"*: Martin Stannard, *Muriel Spark: The Biography* (Weidenfeld & Nicolson, 2009), 256.

191   *Shortly after*: SH interview with Martin Stannard, Feb. 23, 1994, MSC.

191   *"more arts than beaux"*: Crawford, "Shirley Hazzard," 15.

191   *"all drifted"*: Stannard, *Muriel Spark*, 272.

191   *"Muriel Spark is here"*: SH to Chris Cooper, Dec., no date, 1962, SHPU.

191   *"withheld from almost"*: Muriel Spark to SH, Aug. 6, 1963, cited in Stannard, *Muriel Spark*, 285.

191   *"two-hour calls"*: SH interview with Stannard, Sept. 21, 1993, MSC.

191   *"needed* benzina": Ibid.

191   *"to be closer"*: Ibid.

192   *"Muriel with the x-ray"*: Stannard, *Muriel Spark*, 36.

192   *"She was a very good friend"*: JM.

192   *"a shock"*: SH interview with Martin Stannard, Nov. 1999, MSC.

192   *"Women got more"*: SHDN, Oct. 1962.

192   *"a sourpuss"*: SH interview with Martin Stannard, Feb. 23, 1994, MSC.

192   *"Muriel was very nice"*: Ibid.

193   *"that rather brief"*: SHDN, April 1987.

193   *"reciting poems"*: James Merrill to SH, May 11, 1979, SHPU.

193   *"on the same plane"*: Interview with Steven M. L. Aronson, Nov. 15, 2018.

193   *"It is a perfect delight"*: SH to Ved Mehta, July 11, 1962, Ved Mehta Papers, General Collection, Beinecke Rare Book and Manuscript Library, Yale University.

193 *"Arriving last night"*: Ibid.

194 *"even more distraite"*: SH to Chris Cooper, Dec. 1962, SHPU.

194 *"in the part of Manhattan"*: Ibid.

194 *"a skyscraper-y view"*: SH to Piers Paul Read, Dec. 15, 1962, BC MS 20c Piers Paul Read/F1, Literary, Personal and Family Correspondence, Piers Paul Reed Archive, Special Collections, Leeds University Library.

194 *"my first home"*: SHD, July 3, 2006, SHPU.

194 *"best novel ever"*: Stannard, *Muriel Spark*, 271–72.

194 *"a tiny suite"*: JM.

194 *"this banal thing"*: SH interview with Martin Stannard, Feb. 23, 1994, MSC.

194 *"or mostly forgot"*: JM.

194 *"Thank God"*: SHD, Jan. 26, 1997.

194 *"very tall"*: JM.

194 *"a fawn-coloured greatcoat"*: Gordan and Pasca, "Shirley Hazzard," 48.

195 *"one good armchair"*: JM.

195 *"something destined"*: Ibid.

195 *"an accidental quality"*: Ibid.

195 *"We sat down"*: Gordan and Pasca, "Shirley Hazzard," 48.

195 *"wherever she was going"*: JM.

195 *"Dear Shirley"*: FS to SH, Feb. 6, 1963, SHPU.

196 *"I just had a feeling"*: Crawford, "Shirley Hazzard," 15.

196 *"How is the affair*"*: Muriel Spark to SH, Feb. 21, 1963, FSP, Series IV, Box 104.

197 *"the happiest"*: Crawford, "Shirley Hazzard," 18.

197 *"He is Francis Steegmuller"*: SH to Chris Cooper, Dec. 13, 1963, SHPU.

## 7. FRANCIS

201 *"a very, very fervent"*: "Francis Steegmuller, School Days Remembered," Oral History Interview with Francis Steegmuller by Catherine McNamara (Greenwich Library, 1978). Subsequent quotations are drawn from this source.

203 *"her beautiful English voice!"*: FS, "Vernon Steele," draft typescript, SHPU.

203 *"Miracle!"*: Ibid.

204 *"Hardy country"*: Ibid.

204 *"looked longingly at France"*: Lucy Latane Gordan, "Francis Steegmuller: A Life of Letters," *Wilson Library Bulletin* (January 1992): 63.

204 *"Years later"*: Steegmuller, "Vernon Steele."

204 *"an arresting and contagious"*: Irwin Edman, "Henry K. Dick," *Columbia Alumni News*, Nov. 1953.

204 *"an endless chain"*: Oral History Interview with Winslow Ames, April 29–June 2, 1987, Archives of American Art, Smithsonian Institution; available at: www.aaa.si .edu/collections/interviews/oral-history-interview-winslow-ames-12047.

204 *"chapter by chapter"*: Latane Gordan, "Francis Steegmuller," 64.

204 *He told the story*: Interview with Benjamin Taylor, Nov. 3, 2018.

205   *"because I thought"*: Steegmuller, "School Days."

205   *"Columbia College"*: Jacques Barzun, obituary for Francis Steegmuller, 1995 (draft typescript), SHPU.

205   *"remote and infinitely"*: SH to Jacques Barzun, Aug. 20, 1995, SHPU.

205   *"The first week"*: Latane Gordan, "Francis Steegmuller," 64.

206   *"overwhelming"*: Francis Steegmuller, draft typescript, "A book that might be called LOOKING FOR LIVES," SHPU.

206   *"your excellent book"*: Stefan Zweig to FS, Oct. 23, 1929, from Salzburg to Paris, FSP, Series I, Box 1.

206   *"published just the same"*: FS to EH, no date, 1984, PEH.

207   *"I'm not a teacher"*: "An Interview with Francis Steegmuller, May 14, 1981," for Robert Penn Warren Oral History project, Louie B. Nunn Center for Oral History; available at https://kentuckyoralhistory.org/ark:/16417/xt71rn305997.

207   *"my first and much"*: FS to Jacques Barzun, Jan. 21, 1970, FSP, Box 92.

207   *Harold cut a dashing figure*: Interview with Lucia Hatch, April 4, 2018.

207   *His older sister, Beatrice*: Harold Stein to his grandmother Goldfrank, no date. Letter courtesy of Lucia Stein Hatch.

207   *"to tell stories"*: FS, "Another Storyteller's Story," *New Yorker*, Nov. 8, 1958, 15.

207   *Helen Stein recalled*: Interview with Helen Stein, Nov. 30, 2018.

208   *"may at all times"*: Last Will and Testament of Gerda Goldfrank Stein, SHPU.

208   *"somehow larger than life"*: Interview with Adam Stein, Nov. 17, 2018.

209   *he was central to*: Clark S. Marlor, *The Society of Independent Artists: The Exhibition Record 1917–1941* (Notes Press, 1984), 2–3.

209   *He had first thought*: Walter Pach to Beatrice Steegmuller, May 9, 1927, SHPU.

209   *"Write in French"*: Ibid.

210   *"one of the many young"*: Francis Steegmuller, "About Edna Strasser: A Commemorative Talk," given at the New York Society for Ethical Culture, Sunday, April 4, 1976, SHPU.

210   *"on the Bremen"*: Francis Steegmuller, "Jacques Villon: An Appreciation," draft typescript, SHPU.

210   *"by most standards"*: Steegmuller, "About Edna Strasser."

210   *Francis began work*: Latane Gordan, "Francis Steegmuller."

211   *"a man of some literary"*: Alvin Johnson, director, The New School for Social Research, to Oscar Cox, assistant solicitor general, Department of Justice, Washington, D.C., Box 32, Oscar S. Cox Papers, Franklin D. Roosevelt Presidential Library and Museum.

211   *The novel was read*: LFL.

211   *he felt it did not*: Ibid.

211   *"missed the struggle"*: Ibid.

211   *"It seemed to me"*: Ibid.

211   *"The wedding"*: FS to Stanley Martin, July 3, 1935, SHPU.

211   *"a sunny pleasant apartment"*: Steegmuller, "Jacques Villon."

212   *"When Marcel Duchamp"*: Ibid.

212 *"A landscape hanging"*: FS, "Babes on Fifty-seventh Street," in *French Follies and Other Follies* (Reynal & Hitchcock, 1946), 144.

213 *"As a lover of poetry"*: Steegmuller, "Jacques Villon."

213 *"extraordinary and much debated"*: Stuart Elden, *Understanding Henri Lefebvre: Theory and the Possible* (Continuum, 2004).

214 *"For years Mother has felt"*: Beatrice Steegmuller to Norbert Guterman, Jan. 17, 1937, Norbert Guterman Papers 1920–1984, University Archives, Rare Book and Manuscript Library, Columbia University Libraries, Box 1.

214 *"In letters to his friends"*: LFL.

214 *"and was soon deciphering"*: Ibid.

214 *"Speaking my own language"*: Ibid.

215 *"I'm so full of enthusiasm"*: Lionel Trilling to FS, Feb. 17, 1939, FSP, Series I, Box 1.

215 *"cultivated elevator men"*: FS to Jacques Barzun, Feb. 28, 1939, FSP, Series I, Box 92.

215 *"Oh if I'd only known"*: SH to Donald Keene, Nov. 11, 1995, SHP, Series II, Box 10.

216 *"made the drawings"*: Steegmuller, "Jacques Villon," SHPU.

216 "Il faut rester": Ibid.

216 *"recruited against the requirements"*: Samuel Scrivener, Jr., to R. E. Simpson, Office of Strategic Services, Washington, D.C., Sept. 4, 1944; Steegmuller, Francis J., Personnel Files of the Office of Strategic Services, 1942–ca. 1962, Records of the Office of Strategic Services, 1919–2002, National Archives at College Park, College Park, MD.

217 *"the far East"*: FS to Beatrice Steegmuller, Sept. 1944, SHPU.

217 *"It goes against my nature"*: FS to Beatrice Steegmuller, no date, 1944, SHPU.

217 *a piece he published*: "Babes on Fifty-seventh Street" in FS, *French Follies and Other Follies*, 143–52.

217 *Some members of the Stein family*: Interview with Adam Stein, Nov. 17, 2018.

218 *"to review the subject"*: Eliot Bailen, special assistant to the deputy administrator, to Leigh Danenberg, Foreign Economic Administration, American Embassy, Paris, May 5, 1945, Box 32, Oscar S. Cox Papers, Franklin D. Roosevelt Presidential Library and Museum.

218 *"Air Transport Command bus"*: FS to Beatrice Steegmuller, May 13, 1945, SHPU.

218 *"a room in a queer little hotel"*: Ibid.

218 *"rather fond"*: FS to Beatrice Steegmuller, May 15, 1945, SHPU.

219 *"Floodlighting, beautiful"*: Ibid.

219 *"At the Gare d'Orsay"*: FS to Beatrice Steegmuller, May 19, 1945, SHPU.

219 *"Impossible to describe"*: FS to Beatrice Steegmuller, May 23, 1945, SHPU.

219 *"Visited Simonne [Maubert]"*: FS to Beatrice Steegmuller, May 19, 1945, SHPU.

220 *"matière grasse"*: "Cuisine Française: Summer, 1945," in FS, *French Follies and Other Follies*, 51.

220 *"despite heroic attempts"*: Ibid., 49.

220 *"apologizing for having no other"*: Ibid.

220 *"Stopped in at a show"*: FS to Beatrice Steegmuller, May 30, 1945, SHPU.

220 *The coda to this story*: FS, "Gifts for Sale at the Metropolitan Museum," *NYT*, Oct. 10, 1972, 44.

221   *"the rue de l'Université"*: Harriet Shapiro, "Table Talk," *Threepenny Review* 123 (2010): 4.

221   *"His travels led him"*: Ibid.

221   *Ralph Ellison, who had worked*: Sara Blair, *Harlem Crossroads: Black Writers and the Photograph in the Twentieth Century* (Princeton University Press, 2007), 113.

221   *Francis hired Ellison*: FS to Bob Linscott, March 28, 1949; FS to Ralph Ellison, March 28, 1949, Ralph Ellison Papers, 1890–2005, Manuscript Division, Library of Congress, Washington, D.C., Box 1, Folder 96.

221   *"this hungry young"*: Arnold Rampersad, *Ralph Ellison: A Biography* (Knopf, 2007), ch. 7.

222   *"on my mind when I dedicated"*: Ralph Ellison to FS (no date but 1981 has been added), REP.

222   *"pro-Stalinist"*: Alan Wald, "Inconvenient Truths: The Communist Conundrum in Life and Art," *American Literary History* 21, no. 2 (Summer 2009): 392.

222   *"I put the 'our' in quotation marks"*: FS to Ralph Ellison, July 29, 1947, REP.

222   *"the wonderful vacation"*: Ralph Ellison to FS, Aug. 23, 1947, REP.

223   *"In musing over the difference"*: Ibid.

223   *"Until today"*: Ralph Ellison to FS, June 29, 1948, REP.

223   *"Can I tell you"*: Fanny Ellison to Beatrice Stein, Aug. 11, 1948, REP.

224   *"To catch the sunlight"*: Rampersad, *Ralph Ellison*, ch. 9.

224   *"had I not been"*: Quoted in ibid.

224   *"Our trips were strictly bi-lingual"*: Beatrice Steegmuller to Fanny Ellison, July 24, 1950, REP.

224   *"a most attractive"*: FS to Ralph and Fanny Ellison, no date, REP.

224   *"the handsome, imposing"*: Francis Steegmuller, "Meet Jenny Bradley, a Literary Force Extraordinary," *NYTBR*, Dec. 11, 1960, 5.

224   *"the unemployed youngster"*: Beatrice Steegmuller to Fanny Ellison, July 24, 1950, REP.

224   *The Steegmullers found*: Giles Constable to BO, Jan. 2017.

225   *"We ate in the same"*: Willard Spiegelman, "William Weaver: The Art of Translation No. 3," *Paris Review* 161 (Spring 2002).

225   *"for a 'long' stay"*: FS to Stanley Hyman, April 19, 1951, Papers of Stanley Edgar Hyman, Manuscript Division, Library of Congress, Washington, D.C., Box 16.

225   *"After a spurt of work"*: FS to Stanley Hyman, March 20, 1951, Papers of Stanley Edgar Hyman, Manuscript Division, Library of Congress, Box 16.

225   *"so sticky"*: FS to Stanley Hyman, April 19, 1951, Papers of Stanley Edgar Hyman, Manuscript Division, Library of Congress, Box 16.

225   *"Everyone who writes"*: FS to Gerda Stein, no date, SHPU.

225   *"a most delightful room"*: Ibid.

225   *"the momentary idea"*: Ibid.

225   *"He thinks I could become"*: FS to Beatrice Steegmuller, June 15, 1951, SHPU.

226   *"You interest me"*: Bernard Berenson to FS, no date, FSP, Series I, Box 101.

226   *"ran into [English novelist]"*: FS to Beatrice Steegmuller, May 12, 1951, SHPU.

226   *"Homosexuals make"*: David Pryce-Jones, *Fault Lines* (Criterion Books, 2015), 53.

226   *"a great favourite of Berenson's"*: FS to Beatrice Steegmuller, June 15, 1951, SHPU.

228 *"Most people were courteous"*: Francis Steegmuller Interview, May 14, 1981, Robert Penn Warren Oral History Project, Louie B. Nunn Center for Oral History; available at https://kentuckyoralhistory.org/ark:/16417/xt71rn305997.

229 *"Last year, my wife"*: Francis Steegmuller, "Another Storyteller's Story," *New Yorker*, Nov. 8, 1958, 168.

230 *"Since it needed"*: William Maxwell tribute to FS, April 4, 1995, American Academy of Arts and Letters, 2nd series, no. 46, copy held in SHPU.

230 *"and the four-way friendship"*: Ibid.

230 *"tidy up"*: Barbara Burkhardt, *William Maxwell: A Literary Life* (University of Illinois Press, 2018), 189.

230 *"leaven" the "New York Jewish"*: Richard Cook, *Alfred Kazin: A Biography* (Yale University Press, 2008), 237.

230 *"[Francis Steegmuller] looks"*: Lewis Galantière, Francis Steegmuller recommendation, Century Club, copy held in SHPU.

230 *"Francis Steegmuller and Gustave Flaubert"*: Victor Brombert, Introduction, *Flaubert and Madame Bovary* (New York Review of Books, 2004), vii.

231 *"a kind of goat-like exuberance"*: Richard Match, reviewing *States of Grace* for the *International Herald Tribune*, quoted in "Spring Fiction Roundup, New York City, April 1946."

231 *"an interesting blind alley"*: FS to Jerome Mellquist, Aug. 18, 1947, SHPU.

231 *He had devoted*: John Richardson, "Remembering Douglas Cooper," *NYRB*, April 25, 1985. Patricia Anderson notes that the often-told story about Cooper's wealth having come from sheep-dip was apocryphal: Patricia Anderson, "Douglas Cooper: Our Very Own 'Monuments Man,'" *Daily Review*, June 3, 2014; available at dailyreview.com.au/douglas-cooper-our-very-own-monuments-man/.

231 *"his most assiduous guest"*: John Richardson, "Remembering Douglas Cooper."

232 *"liked it immensely"*: André Maurois to FS, Jan. 2, 1956, Papers of André Maurois, MS8505, Bibliothèque de l'Institut de France, Paris.

232 *In late 1954*: FS to Douglas Cooper, Dec. 4, 1954; FS to Douglas Cooper, Feb. 15, 1955, FSCDC.

232 *"no great lover"*: FS to Douglas Cooper, Jan. 14, 1955, FSCDC.

232 *"Géricault has tempted me"*: Ibid.

232 *"writing about artists"*: Ibid.

233 *"there is going to be"*: Roger Straus to Alfred Knopf, Farrar, Straus & Giroux, Inc. Archive, Manuscripts and Archives Division, The New York Public Library.

233 *"I'm not quite finished"*: John Cheever to FS, Sept. 1957, FSP, Series I, Box 1.

233 *"Dear Francis, it's absolutely marvelous"*: William Maxwell to FS, no date, FSP, Series III, Box 102.

234 *"competing in sales"*: FS interview with William Kennedy, "The Week in Books," Radio Station WEVD, June 8, 1957, FSP.

234 *"One June day"*: Richard Howard, "Fond Memory," in Bartlett, *Literary Lives: The World of Francis Steegmuller & Shirley Hazzard*, 31.

234  *"felt close"*: Shapiro, "Hazzard Remembers," 14.

234  *"this is most unusual"*: Roger Straus to Herbert Lottman, Nov. 6, 1957, Farrar, Straus & Giroux, Inc. Archive, Manuscripts and Archives Division, The New York Public Library.

235  *"La Poussiquette"*: SH to Jacques Barzun, Aug. 20, 1995, Box 99, Folder 10, FSP.

235  *"I told him how"*: Typescript of FS meeting with Pierre Reverdy at Solesmes, Sarthe, Dec. 1, 1957, Francis Steegmuller. Reverdy, Alpha MS 4984, Chancellerie des Universités de Paris—Bibliothèque littéraire Jacques Doucet.

236  *"Beatrice Steegmuller says"*: William Maxwell to Eudora Welty, May 11, 1955, in *What There Is to Say We Have Said: The Correspondence of Eudora Welty and William Maxwell*, ed. Suzanne Marrs (Houghton Mifflin Harcourt, 2011), 80.

236  *Sidney Geist*: Interview with Elizabeth Howard, Dec. 3, 2018.

236  *"General confusion"*: FSD, March 10, 1959, SHPU.

236  *"for professional services"*: Beatrice Steegmuller to FS, Dec. 3, 1969, SHPU.

236  *Liliane would become*: Interview with Rosanna Warren, Dec. 8, 2018.

236–37  *"nice letter"*: Freya Stark to FS, May 29, 1959, SHPU.

237  *"Best visit"*: FSD, June 13, 1959, SHPU.

237  *"Not a picture painted"*: Beatrice Steegmuller to Alfred and Ann Kazin, July 18, 1959, Steegmuller, F. & S., Subseries B: Ann Birstein Papers, Department of Special Collections and Archives, Queens College, City University of New York.

237  *"She rests when she can"*: FS to Roger Straus, Farrar, Straus & Giroux, Inc. Archive, Manuscripts and Archives Division, The New York Public Library.

237  *"As you know"*: FS to Lionello Venturi, June 2, 1960, SHPU.

237–38  *"triumphant at making"*: FS to Douglas Cooper, June 2, 1960, FSCDC.

238  *"any drawing to"*: Beatrice Steegmuller to FS, Dec. 3, 1960, SHPU.

238  Drawings by Beatrice Stein: Jacques Villon to FS, no date, SHPU.

238  *"a distillation"*: Ibid.

238  *"the 'independence'"*: FS to Douglas Cooper, June 5, 1961, FSCDC.

238  *"Bea's strength"*: FS to Douglas Cooper, June 14, 1961, FSCDC.

239  *"Bea . . . spends"*: FS to Douglas Cooper, June 16, 1961, FSCDC.

239  *"Beatrice was an inspiration"*: Joseph Steegmuller to Clara Binswanger, July 5, 1961, SHPU.

239  *"to occupy maid's room"*: FS to Clara Binswanger, July 11, 1961, SHPU.

239  *"stayed in Italy"*: FS to Alfred Kazin and Ann Birstein, Nov. 4, 1961, Steegmuller, F. & S., Subseries B: Ann Birstein Papers, Department of Special Collections and Archives, Queens College, City University of New York.

240  *"I speed to write"*: Roger Straus to FS, Aug. 23, 1962, Farrar, Straus & Giroux, Inc. Archive, Manuscripts and Archives Division, The New York Public Library.

240  *"the old model"*: SH interview with Martin Stannard, Feb. 23, 1994, MSC.

240  *Francis chose canary yellow*: Interview with Evan Cornog, Nov. 2, 2018.

240  *"out of the cold"*: FS to Robert Giroux, May 14, 1962, Farrar, Straus & Giroux, Inc. Archive, Manuscripts and Archives Division, The New York Public Library.

240–41 *"amused that Shirley seemed"*: Interview with Jonathan Burnham, Nov. 6, 2018.

241 *"Francis, like others"*: SH to MS, May 24, 1996, CSHMS.

241 *"Francis was notoriously"*: Penelope Jardine, typed note, undated, CSHMS.

241 *"brought up, once again"*: Michael Mallon, email to BO, Oct. 20, 2021.

241 *John Richardson*: Interview with ADG.

241 *"The experiment of love"*: TGF, 74.

241 *"Bill never made a secret"*: SH quoted in Blake Bailey, *Cheever: A Life* (Knopf, 2009), 174.

## 8. AMITIÉ LITTÉRAIRE

243 *Francis Steegmuller's diary*: FSD, Jan. 1963.

244 *"Dream marvellous"*: FSD, March 17, 1963.

244 *"a party for Names"*: FS to SH, no date, 1963, SHPU.

244 *"My Girl"*: Muriel Spark to SH, March 9, 1963, FSP, Series IV, Box 104.

245 *"a sort of detachment"*: SH to Muriel Spark, March 27, 1963, CSHMS.

245 *"obviously feeling"*: Ibid.

245 *"that FS had been"*: Ibid.

245 *"A writing friend"*: FS to SH, no date, SHPU.

245 *"Lady authoress"*: SH to FS, no date, SHPU.

245 *"I cannot set out"*: SH to FS, March 14, 1963, SHPU.

246 *"You may be"*: FS to SH, Feb. 18, 1963, SHPU.

246 *"much impressed by"*: SH to FS, March 20, 1963, SHPU.

246 *"from a time"*: FS to SH, March 22, 1963, SHPU.

246 *"You'll probably smile"*: FS to SH, March 22, 1963, SHPU.

246 *"Don't know why"*: SH to FS, March 20, 1963, SHPU.

246 *"On Monday"*: Ibid.

247 *"a little at cross purposes"*: SH to FS, March 22, 1963, SHPU.

247 *"thoughts that led to this"*: FS to SH, March 23, 1963, SHPU.

247 *"sad stories"*: FS to SH, March 24, 1963, SHPU.

247 *"you would have entered"*: Ibid.

247 *"Too much has happened"*: Ibid.

247 *"emaciated"*: SH interview with Martin Stannard, Feb. 23, 1994, MSC.

247 *Elena told Shirley*: SHD, April 23, 2002.

247–48 *"The visit to Solaia"*: SH to FS, March 25, 1963, SHPU.

248 *"It seemed to me"*: JM.

248 *"He said he 'could not'"*: SH to Muriel Spark, April 3, 1963, CSHMS.

248 *"a shiver down the spine"*: A. E. Housman, *The Name and Nature of Poetry: and Other Selected Prose*; SH to FS, April 14, 1963, SHPU.

248 *"Surely, dear Shirlers"*: Muriel Spark to SH, April 5, 1963, FSP, Series IV, Box 104.

249 *"He is, though very determined"*: SH to Muriel Spark, April 24, 1963, CSHMS.

249 *"plan your summer"*: Muriel Spark to SH, April 5, 1963, FSP, Series IV, Box 104.

249 *"Il aurait voulu"*: SHDN, April 1963.

249 *"My mother died"*: Paolo Vivante to SH, May 1963, private collection.

249 *"Paolo spent the nights"*: Sophie Lester to SH, May 5, 1963, SHPU.

250 *"Speaking of conversation"*: FS to SH, May 9, 1963, SHPU.

250 *Liliane told him*: Interview with Rosanna Warren, Dec. 8, 2018.

250 *"I still feel slightly odd"*: SH to FS, May 9, 1963, SHPU.

251 *"When we part"*: SHDN, May 31, 1963.

251 *"In the lovely garden"*: SHDN, June 11, 1963.

251 *"From the second day"*: Ibid.

251 *"If this (with me)"*: Ibid.

251 *"swathed in black"*: BN, 200.

251 *"overhung"*: SH to Chris Cooper, Nov. 19, 1987, SHPU.

251 *"very alone among"*: William Maxwell to SH, no date, SHPU.

251 *"dedicated spinsterhood"*: TV, 172.

252 *"A lot of remarks"*: SH to Muriel Spark, June 13, 1963, CSHMS.

252 *"something in a Goya"*: Ibid.

252 *"The Bachelors"*: Ibid.

252 *"He leaves books"*: SHDN, June 11, 1963.

252 *"the ambiguity of F"*: SHDN, October 16, 1963.

252 *"if the depth, the wish"*: SHDN, July 3, 1963.

252 *"Sometimes he is v sweet"*: SH to Muriel Spark, June 26, 1963, CSHMS.

253 *"in the deserted UN garden"*: SHD, July 14, 2002.

253 *"when we began"*: SHD, July 20, 2003.

253 *"it's a wrench"*: Hélène Seiferheld to FS, May 21, 1963, SHPU.

253 *"a married lady"*: Muriel Spark to SH, July 21, 1963, FSP, Series IV, Box 104.

253 *"Why don't you swear"*: Muriel Spark to SH, Aug. 6, 1963, FSP, Series IV, Box 104.

253 *"A great sorrow"*: SH to FS, Aug. 3, 1963, SHPU.

253 *"It seemed the best thing"*: Ibid.

253 *"magnificent as always"*: SH to FS, Aug. no date, 1963, SHPU.

254 *"it is quite hard"*: SH to FS, Aug. 22, 1963, SHPU.

254 *"immediately turned it"*: SH to FS, Aug. 30, 1963, SHPU.

254 *"A lovely drive"*: Ibid.

254 *"I am nearly staggered"*: SH to FS, Aug. 28, 1963, SHPU.

254 *"a lovely spot"*: SH to FS, Aug. 26, 1963, SHPU.

254 *"I said he must come"*: SH to FS, Sept. 3, 1963, SHPU.

255 *"Bill can be great fun"*: FS to SH, Sept. 7, 1963, SHPU.

255 *"Why aren't you here"*: SH to FS, Sept. 13–14, 1963, SHPU.

255 *"It is lovely"*: Ibid.

256 *"I am much alone"*: FS to SH, Sept. 7, 1963, SHPU.

256 *"Long dry autumn"*: SHDN, no date, 1963.

256 *"not that you'd notice"*: SH, "Le Nozze," in *Collected Stories*, ed. Brigitta Olubas and with a foreword by Zoe Heller (Farrar, Straus & Giroux, 2020), 344.

256 *"What a fine book"*: William Maxwell to SH, Oct. 3, 1963, SHPU.

256  *"My word is as good"*: FS to SH, no date, SHPU.

256  *"Shirley and you"*: Catherine Hazzard to FS, Nov. 25, 1963, SHPU.

257  *"This is wonderful"*: Paolo Vivante to SH, Dec. 10, 1963, private collection.

257  *"I keep thinking"*: Muriel Spark to SH, Dec. 14, 1963, FSP, Series IV, Box 104.

257  *"My book appeared"*: SH to Chris Cooper, Dec. 13, 1963, SHPU.

257  *"How fast it is"*: SHD, Dec. 23, 1999.

257  *"We washed up!"*: SHD, no date, Dec. 1994.

258  *"sobbed throughout"*: SH to Elizabeth Harrower, no date, PEH.

258  *"pour patauger"*: FS to Alfred Kazin and Ann Birstein, Jan. 19, 1964, Steegmuller, F. & S., Subseries B: Ann Birstein Papers, Department of Special Collections and Archives, Queens College, City University of New York.

258  *"European rather than African"*: SH, "The Meeting," in *Collected Stories*, ed. Brigitta Olubas and with a foreword by Zoe Heller (Farrar, Straus & Giroux, 2020), 171.

258  *"the ruins were almost covered"*: SH to Patricia Clarke, July 17, 1969, SHPU.

258  *"Bassae, Volubilis"*: SH, "The Sack of Silence," in *Collected Stories*, ed. Brigitta Olubas and with a foreword by Zoe Heller (Farrar, Straus & Giroux, 2020), 349.

258  *"Beach on Atlantic side"*: SHDN, Jan. 11, 1964.

259  *"even after Fez"*: FS to Douglas Cooper, Jan. 25, 1964, FSCDC.

259  *"lure of authority"*: SHDN, no date.

259  *"Analysis, curiously"*: Ibid.

259  *"Lean on sink"*: Ibid.

260  *"combined presence"*: SHDN, May 30, 1964.

260  *"of two women"*: FSD, June 1, 1964.

260  *"To be married"*: SHDN, June 1, 1964.

260  *(Was she perhaps thinking)*: My thanks to Jennifer Livett for this observation.

260  *"The feeling that unfinished"*: FSD, June 2, 1964.

261  *"After Italy"*: Untitled typescript, SHPU.

261  *"hard to believe"*: Ibid.

261  *"Masochist uses analyst"*: FSD, June 5, 1964.

261  *"the foot of Mount Parnassus"*: Untitled typescript, SHPU.

261  *"a cluster of sun-coloured"*: SH, "Out of Itea," in *Collected Stories*, ed. Brigitta Olubas and with a foreword by Zoe Heller (Farrar, Straus & Giroux, 2020), 287.

261  *"The sea, on all sides"*: Ibid., 287–88.

261  *"sloping headland"*: Ibid., 294.

261  *"on the border"*: Ibid.

261–62  *"who had known Schliemann"*: Untitled typescript, SHPU.

262  *"the first friend"*: SHD, Jan. 27, 1996.

262  *"a summer of glorious"*: FS to Robert Penn Warren, Sept. 6, 1964, Robert Penn Warren Papers, Yale Collection of American Literature, Beinecke Rare Book and Manuscript Library.

262  *"The sense of home"*: SHDN, July 26, 1964, SHPU.

262  *"Why don't we split"*: SHDN, no date, 1964, SHPU.

262 *"It is the kind"*: Ibid.

262 *"a beautiful place"*: Ibid.

263 *"It is silent"*: Ibid.

263 *"Why did Sophie walk"*: "Duncan MacDonald Interviews Shirley Hazzard, Author of 'The Evening of the Holiday,'" Feb. 7, 1966, WNYC; available at www.wnyc.org/story /shirley-hazzard/.

264 *"The sadness of losing"*: SHDN, Sept. 1964.

264 *"I can't tell you"*: SH to Cesare Vivante, Oct. 24, 1964, private collection.

264–65 *Cesare told Shirley*: SH to Cesare Vivante, Aug. 19, 1965, private collection.

265 *"bury the hatchet"*: Reginald Hazzard to SH, March 14, 1966, SHPU.

265 *"White Australia Policy"*: SH to Elizabeth Harrower, draft, no date, SHPU.

265 *"quickly or easily"*: Interview with Hamlin Hazzard Barnes, Nov. 8, 2018.

265 *"a dirty old"*: Valerie Barnes to SH, April 5, 1965, SHPU.

266 *"personal abuse"*: Valerie Barnes to SH, April 24, 1965, SHPU.

267 *"confidential"*: FS to Catherine Hazzard, May 3, 1965, SHPU.

267 *"It wasn't this"*: TV, 207.

267 *often recalling the observation*: Interview with Mary Ellin Barrett, Nov. 28, 2018.

267 *"If you cannot be polite"*: Michael Mallon to BO, Sept. 29, 2021.

268 *"Did I tell you how"*: SH to Anthony Hecht, Feb. 7, 1984, Anthony Hecht Papers, 1894– 2005, Stuart A. Rose Manuscript, Archives, and Rare Book Library, Emory University.

268 *"Shirley's New York"*: Crawford, "Shirley Hazzard," 16.

268 *"Civilization is in"*: SHDN, no date, 1975.

269 *"didn't care about this"*: Interview with Benjamin Taylor, Nov. 3, 2018.

269 *"mostly been 'left'"*: SH to Elizabeth Harrower, Nov. 20 1981, PEH.

269 *"had not been communists"*: "An Interview with Francis Steegmuller" for Robert Penn Warren Oral History project, Louie B. Nunn Center for Oral History; available at https://kentuckyoralhistory.org/ark:/16417/xt71rn305997.

269 *"a figure of intellectual grace"*: Cook, *Alfred Kazin: A Biography*, 237–38.

269 *"the Steegmullers had this gift"*: Ibid., 389.

269 *"the magic"*: Alfred Kazin Diary, Nov. 4, 1966, in *Alfred Kazin's Journals*, ed. Richard M. Cook (New Haven and London: Yale University Press, 2011).

270 *"F's snubs"*: Alfred Kazin Diary, June 17, 1982, ibid.

270 *"out to gain advantage"*: Interview with Steven M. L. Aronson, Nov. 15, 2018.

270 *"from the fascist incubus"*: SH, eulogy for Dorle Soria, draft, SHP, Series II, Box 10.

271 *"Her love for music"*: Ibid.

271 *"long and precious"*: SH, Memorial Service for Eleanor Clark, March 9, 1996, SHPU.

271 *"You all have great gifts"*: Robert Penn Warren to FS and SH, Nov. 14, 1966, SHPU.

271 *"I liked getting the prize"*: Robert Penn Warren to FS and SH, Feb. 28, 1967, SHPU.

271 *"I should have known"*: Robert Penn Warren to SH, Dec. 2, 1974, SHPU.

271 *"looked out helplessly"*: GC, 110.

272 *Shirley recalled*: Interview with Rosanna Warren, Dec. 8, 2018.

272 *"This was not"*: Rosanna Warren to BO, Oct. 11, 2020.

272    *"connected imaginatively"*: Ibid.

272    *"part of our family conversation"*: Interview with Rosanna Warren, Dec. 8, 2018.

272    *"I am delighted"*: SH to Elizabeth Harrower, March 10, 1980, PEH.

272    *"an immediate talismanic bond"*: Shirley Hazzard, "William Maxwell," in *We Need Silence to Find Out What We Think*, ed. Brigitta Olubas (Columbia University Press, 2016).

273    *"to put the nurturing"*: Harrriet O'Donovan Sheehy, "William Maxwell and Emily Maxwell," *Guardian*, Aug. 25, 2000.

273    *"a kind of radiance"*: Interview with Alec Wilkinson, Oct. 16, 2020.

273    *"It was an intense"*: Paula Fox, in *A William Maxwell Portrait: Memories and Appreciations*, ed. Charles Baxter, Michael Collier, and Edward Hirsch (W.W. Norton, 2004), 50.

273    *"the most present"*: Interview with Edward Hirsch, Sept. 15, 2020.

273    *"With Bill Maxwell"*: Interview with Benjamin Taylor, Nov. 3, 2018.

273    *"heavy going"*: SH to Rache Lovatt Dickson, Nov. 15, 1962, MA.

273    *"just sublime"*: Interview with Alec Wilkinson, Oct. 16, 2020.

## 9. SMALL MASTERPIECES

277    *"the evening after"*: "Duncan MacDonald interviews Shirley Hazzard."

277    *She felt that*: Ibid.

278    *"wistful music"*: SH, *The Evening of the Holiday* (Knopf, 1966), 152.

278    *"complicated exposition"*: Ibid., 55.

278    *"I would have been"*: Ibid., 28.

278    *"You have told the story"*: Alan Maclean to SH, March 23, 1965, SHPU.

278    *"one of the most beautiful"*: Paul Horgan, inside front cover endorsement, *The Evening of the Holiday* by Shirley Hazzard (Knopf, 1966).

279    *"an almost miraculous"*: Charles Poore, "Books of the Times: Intermezzo," *NYT*, Jan. 15, 1966, 25.

279    *"often as urgent"*: Laurence Lafore, "Nightingale Sang at Last," *NYT*, Jan. 9, 1966.

279    *"half English"*: Poore, "Books of the Times: Intermezzo."

279    *"in this near-perfect"*: *Time*, inside front cover endorsement, *The Evening of the Holiday*, by Shirley Hazzard (Knopf, 1966).

279    *"It is a love story"*: "Duncan MacDonald interviews Shirley Hazzard."

279    *"of a wearily familiar kind"*: Bernard Bergonzi, "Bouillabaisse," *NYRB*, March 17, 1966.

279    *"Much of the book's charm"*: "Books: Elusive Echo," *Time*, Jan. 14, 1966.

279    *"My book came out"*: SH to Howard Moss, June 15, 1966, SHPU.

279    *"an object lesson"*: "A Sort of Vortex," *Spectator*, June 3, 1966, 701.

279    *"one would not want"*: L. V. Kepert, *SMH*, Oct. 15, 1966, 17.

279    *"too heavily on implication"*: Neil Jillett, *The Age*, Aug. 6, 1966, 25.

280    *"neglected character development"*: Suzanne Edgar, *Canberra Times*, Oct. 22, 1966, 12.

280    *"a writer whose fictions"*: Citation held in SHPU.

280    *"The Cocteau story"*: FS to Roger Straus, March 5, 1970, Farrar, Straus & Giroux Inc. Archive, Manuscripts and Archives Division, The New York Public Library.

280    *"found some of the poetry"*: FS to J. Barzun, July 21, 1971, Jacques Barzun Papers,

1900–1999, University Archives, Rare Book and Manuscript Library, Columbia University Libraries.

280  *"played up his own"*: Shapiro, "Hazzard Remembers," 15.

281  *a detailed record*: SHDN, no date.

281  *"An insect was prowling"*: SH to Stephen Walsh, June 9, 2001, SHPU.

281  *"dated type of despair"*: SHDN, July 10, 1965.

281  *"Fine windy day"*: SHDN, July 22, 1966.

282  *"in ugly dark blue"*: SHDN, June 30, 1969, SHPU.

282  *"on an empty curve"*: SHD, July 14, 1998.

282  *"Oleanders, that clear"*: Eleanor Clark to FS and SH, June 14, 1966, FSP.

282  *"hot and pungent"*: Shirley Hazzard, Memorial Service for Eleanor Clark, March 9, 1996, SHPU.

282  *"La mer ne bouge pas"*: SHDN, July 29, 1966.

282  *"not necessarily honorable"*: Shapiro, "Hazzard Remembers," 27–28.

283  *"the revelation of Leger"*: FS to Douglas Cooper, Aug. 11, 1966, FSCDC.

283  *"Will you be mother?"*: SHDN, July 1966.

283  *"'But why not Auden?'"*: SHDN, Aug. 21, 1966.

283  *"The Swedish earth"*: TV, 329–30.

284  *"open with rows"*: Ibid., 330.

284  *"paying my way"*: Catherine Hazzard to SH, Sept. 27, 1965, SHPU.

284  *"I've often thought"*: Ibid.

284  *"an enamel dish"*: Catherine Hazzard to SH, Aug. 13, 1966, SHPU.

284  *"all problems are Relative"*: FS to Douglas Cooper, Oct. 7, 1966, FSCDC.

284  *"finally bearded Doudou"*: FS to SH, Dec. 8, 1966, SHPU.

284  *"Mme Maurois"*: FS to SH, Dec. 1, 1966, SHPU.

285  *"Ten years ago"*: SHDN, Dec. 7, 1966.

285  *"ordinarily that of the Comtesse"*: FS to SH, Dec. 3, 1966, SHPU.

285  *"eating chevreuil"*: FS to Douglas Cooper, Dec. 26, 1966, FSCDC.

285  *"For a last freezing hour"*: "The Tuscan in Each of Us," in *We Need Silence to Find Out What We Think*, ed. Brigitta Olubas (Columbia University Press, 2016), 179.

285  *"in streets and shops"*: Ibid.

285  *"How could I know"*: SHD, July 28, 2003.

285  *"much amity"*: SHDN, no date, 2006.

285  *"All shrouded, shuttered"*: Ibid.

286  *"Proust had often visited"*: Shapiro, "Hazzard Remembers," 15.

286  *"They were captivated"*: Ibid., 19.

286  *"She was frail"*: Ibid., 15.

286  *"The next time he called"*: Ibid.

286  *"no luck with Picasso"*: FS to Douglas Cooper, Feb. 7, 1967, FSCDC.

287  *"thin, drawn, pessimistic"*: SHDN, Jan. 25, 1967.

287  *"French people"*: SHDN, Sept. 30, 1967.

287  *"a figure from another century"*: SH to Chris Cooper, Oct. 29, 1982, SHPU.

287   *"many unlikable things"*: Ibid.

287   *"I decided I couldn't"*: Catherine Hazzard to Elizabeth Harrower, April 27, 1967, PEH.

288   *"Family matters"*: FS to Ved Mehta, June 9, 1967, Ved Mehta Papers. General Collection, Beinecke Rare Book and Manuscript Library, Yale University.

288   *"hour's serpentine drive"*: GC, 104.

288   *"a farmhouse"*: SHDN, no date, 1967–1968.

288   *"Divine here"*: FS to Douglas Cooper, Aug. 28, 1967, FSCDC.

288   *"Characters rarely have"*: Jennings, "Going Against the Grain: An Interview with Shirley Hazzard," 22.

289   *"You remain always conscious"*: Wendy Smith, "Shirley Hazzard," *Publishers Weekly* 23, no. 10 (1990).

289   *"I think we have now covered"*: Alan Maclean to SH, Nov. 3, 1967, SHPU.

289   *"'Why are you so bitter'"*: SHDN, June 1967.

289   *"the comfortable despair"*: Frederic Raphael, "Coming Out Wrong," *NYT*, Oct. 15, 1967, 315.

289   *"The 'review' of Shirley's book"*: FS to the Editor, *NYT* (draft), Oct. 16, 1967, SHPU.

290   *"he made everyone"*: Ved Mehta to SH, June 12, 1967, SHPU.

290   *"from any other buzzing lair"*: Charles Poore, "Books of the Times: Restless Natives of One World," *NYT*, Dec. 13, 1967, 45.

290   *"analogous to"*: Alex Hamilton, *Times* (London), Review, Dec. 16, 1967.

290   *"the demure humour"*: *Times* Saturday Review, May 30, 1970.

290   *"Her turns of phrase"*: *Spectator*, Oct. 20, 1967.

290   *"Some UNO people"*: "Interview with Shirley Hazzard," *Times* (London), Oct. 14, 1967, 21.

290   *"a repetitive pattern"*: Valerie Barnes to SH, Sept. 10, 1966, SHPU.

290   *"a bedsitter"*: Catherine Hazzard to SH, July 5, 1967, SHPU.

290   *"I talk to few"*: Catherine Hazzard to SH, Dec. 17, 1967, SHPU.

291   *"I've always considered"*: Catherine Hazzard to SH, Dec. 17, 1967, SHPU.

291   *"full of woe"*: SHDN, Nov. 22, 1967.

291   *"recurring threats"*: FS to Catherine Hazzard, Feb. 7, 1968, SHPU.

291   *"Personal"*: Catherine Hazzard to FS, Feb. 1968, SHPU.

291   *"something celestial"*: SHD, Dec. 29, 2002.

291   *Ahead of one of these trips*: Interview with Alec Wilkinson, Dec. 13, 2018.

292   *"Your book makes me think"*: SH and FS to Alfred Kazin, Aug. 10, 1982, Alfred Kazin Papers, Henry W. and Albert A. Berg Collection of English and American Literature, The New York Public Library.

292   *"no great individual talent"*: John Darnton, "Harold Acton Is Dead at 89," *NYT*, March 1, 1994, B10.

292   *"half-American"*: Nora Sayre, "Memoires of an Aesthete 1939–1969," *NYT*, May 16, 1971, BR34.

292   *"weapons-grade"*: Guy Adams, "Curse of Brideshead . . . Revisited," *Daily Mail*, July 29, 2019.

292   *"a fabulous name dropper"*: Interview with Alison Parente, Sept. 28, 2018.

292   *"too 'Latin'"*: Harold Acton to FS, April 18, 1967, Harold Acton Papers, La Pietra, New York University.

292   *"shaken my belief"*: Harold Acton to SH, Nov. 6, 1967, Harold Acton Papers, La Pietra, New York University.

293   *"from a Pisan coffee-set"*: SH to Hugh Honour, June 16, 2001, SHPU.

293   *"boring, impervious"*: SHDN, April 20, 1968.

293   *"takes his time"*: SHDN, July 22, 1966.

293   *"a representation"*: SHDN, Aug. 27, 1968.

294   *"Harold's garden"*: SHDN, no date, 1968.

294   *"1/8th Italian"*: SHDN, no date.

294   *"Beautiful English"*: SHDN, July 25, 1968.

295   *She regarded them*: Interview with Benjamin Taylor, Nov. 3, 2018.

295   *"subjecting us to an hour"*: SHDN, no date, 1968.

295   *"Moonlight, Italy, countryside"*: Ibid.

295   *"heavenly countryside"*: Ibid.

295   *"a most delightful person"*: JM.

295   *"in full Cocteau"*: SH to Patricia Clarke, Jan. 25, 1969, SHPU.

296   *"It was unbearably"*: Elizabeth Bowen to SH, April 22, 1969, SHPU.

296   *"We'll go to the length"*: SH to William Meredith, May 14, 1969, William Meredith Papers, Linda Lear Center for Special Collections and Archives, Connecticut College Library.

296   *"she likes my work"*: FS to SH, Dec. 3, 1966, SHPU.

296   *"What a particularly"*: FS, "An Angel, a Flower, a Bird," *New Yorker*, Sept. 27, 1969, 130.

296   *"to spend the day with him"*: SH to Patricia Clarke, Sept. 26, 1969, SHPU.

297   *"the ship so comfortable"*: SH to Patricia Clarke, July 9, 1968, SHPU.

297   *"a torment of letters"*: SH to Patricia Clarke, Jan. 25, 1969, SHPU.

297   *"saying that it would"*: SH to Elizabeth Harrower, June 24, 1967, PEH.

297   *"the really horrendous developments"*: SH to Patricia Clarke, Jan. 25, 1969, SHPU.

297   *"Don't bother"*: SH to Patricia Clarke, Feb. 18, 1970, SHPU.

297   *"The last time"*: Valerie Barnes to SH, June 2, 1969, SHPU.

298   *"Asyngamy"*: BN, 110.

298   *"because I was in love"*: Ibid., 34.

299   *"into detour"*: Peter Brooks, *Reading for the Plot* (Harvard University Press, 1992), 109.

299   *"is immaterial"*: BN, 244.

299   *"At this moment"*: Ibid., 114.

299   *"Like Othello"*: Ibid., 89.

299   "Why am I always": Ibid., 166.

300   *"there and gone"*: Marjorie Garber, *Vested Interests* (Routledge, 1997), 37.

300   *"The engine subsiding"*: BN, 243–44.

300   *"That epoch"*: Ibid., 243.

300  *"on the nerve endings"*: Christopher Lehmann-Haupt, "Books of the Times: A Travelogue as Timeless as Tapestry," *NYT*, March 25, 1970, 45.

300  *"Relics are not the less"*: BN, 243.

301  *"a truly heavenly reception"*: SH to Patricia Clarke, April 18, 1970, SHPU.

301  *"with the misgiving"*: Lehmann-Haupt "Books of the Times: A Travelogue as Timeless as Tapestry," 45.

301  *"The slight plot"*: Claire Tomalin, "Boys in the Corner: Novels," *Observer*, May 10, 1970, 31.

301  *"scratched"*: FS to Douglas Cooper, March 9, 1971, FSCDC.

301  *"Delectable is surely"*: William Maxwell to FS, May 5, no year, SHPU.

302  *"distastefully"*: SHD, July 21, 2002, SHPU.

302  *"'dismissed'"*: Ibid.

302  *"elegant right-wing footlers"*: Martin Stannard, "Meeting Shirley Hazzard," in *Shirley Hazzard: New Critical Essays*, ed. Brigitta Olubas (Sydney University Press, 2014), 141.

302  *"a crater lake"*: SH to Chris Cooper, July 10, 1970, SHPU.

302  *"There is a statue"*: SH to Catherine Hazzard, Aug. 2, 1970, SHPU.

302  *"an abandoned monastery"*: Ibid.

303  *"Sea almost level"*: SHDN, Sept. 2, 1970.

303  *"a wretched little anthology"*: SH to Catherine Hazzard, June 4, 1970, SHPU.

303  *"a mythological version"*: FS to Robert Giroux, June 18, 1970, Farrar, Straus & Giroux, Inc. Archive, Manuscripts and Archives Division, The New York Public Library.

303  *"at the Straus's"*: FS to Ved Mehta, Nov. 26, 1970, Ved Mehta Papers. General Collection, Beinecke Rare Book and Manuscript Library, Yale University.

304  *"Francis Steegmuller, even while"*: Mark Schorer, "Cocteau," *NYT*, Sept. 27, 1970, 4.

304  *"the one Greek word"*: FS to Douglas Cooper, March 9, 1971, FSCDC.

304  *"immortality has been instantly"*: SH to Patricia Clarke, Oct. 31, 1970, SHPU.

304  *"remains the literary hero"*: FS to Jacques Barzun, July 21, 1971, Jacques Barzun Papers 1900–1999, University Archives, Rare Book and Manuscript Library, Columbia University Libraries.

304  *"pretends that the great love"*: Edmund White, quoted in Shirley Hazzard, Letter to the Editor, *Los Angeles Times*, Aug. 20, 2000.

304  *"about the details"*: Ibid.

305  *"the lapse of seven years"*: J. R. Taylor, "The Real Life of an Illusionist," *TLS*, Jan. 15, 1971.

305  *"that the Stravinskys have"*: SH to Catherine Hazzard, Nov. 15, 1970, SHPU.

305  *"a biggish one"*: Catherine Hazzard to SH, Dec. 29, 1970, SHPU.

306  *"an Italianate proclamation"*: FS, "Burial in Venice," *New Yorker*, May 1, 1971, 99.

306  *"a towering Gothic"*: Ibid., 100.

306  *"theatrically handsome"*: Ibid., 101.

306  *"one of Carpaccio's"*: Ibid., 102.

306   *"a gray-haired"*: Ibid., 100.

307   *"His friends in Paris"*: SH to Donald Keene, Aug. 16, 1997, SHP, Series II, Box 10.

## 10. *THE TRANSIT OF VENUS*

308   *"public themes"*: Peter Fuller, "Interview with Shirley Hazzard," *Canberra Times*, May 31, 1991, 23.

308   *"the 'party' mentality"*: SH to Evan Cornog, June 15, 1989, private collection.

308   *"When I was first"*: Ibid.

309   *"so much facile"*: Chris Cooper to SH, Nov. 7, 1951, SHPU.

309   *"I feel as you do"*: SH to Alfred Kazin, April 12, 1966, Alfred Kazin Papers, Henry W. and Albert A. Berg Collection of English and American Literature, The New York Public Library.

309   *"the many thousands of Americans"*: SH and FS, "White House Isolation," *NYT*, Jan. 21, 1968, 46.

309   *"Establishment"*: Quoted in Dwight Macdonald to SH, July 1, 1968, SHPU.

310   *"informed, public indignation"*: Shirley Hazzard, "A Call for UN Reform," *NYT*, Oct. 24, 1970, 30.

310   *"expurgated"*: SH to Patricia Clarke, Nov. 7, 1970, SHPU.

310   *"demi-spheres"*: SH, "A Call for UN Reform."

310   *"a long article"*: SH to Patricia Clarke, Dec. 9, 1970, SHPU.

310   *"the only way"*: SH to Elizabeth Harrower, Oct. 20, 1971, PEH.

311   *"Not getting on"*: SH to Patricia Clarke, Dec. 9, 1970, SHPU.

311   *"Darling if you are intent"*: SH to Catherine Hazzard, June 4, 1970, SHPU.

311   *"like the gnat"*: Catherine Hazzard to SH, March 3, 1970, SHPU.

311   *"in one of the nastiest"*: Valerie Barnes to SH, May 13–June 10, 1970, SHPU.

311   *"details of the disposal"*: Valerie Barnes to SH, Nov. 3, 1970, SHPU.

311   *"The only place"*: SH to Patricia Clarke, Aug. 19, 1970, SHPU.

312   *"like Blanche Dubois"*: Interview with Michelle de Kretser, July 26, 2020.

313   *"a calm and witty"*: SH to Patricia Clarke, April 30, 1972, SHPU.

313   *sent The Watch Tower*: SH to Elizabeth Harrower, June 20, 1972, PEH.

313   *He later told Elizabeth*: FS to Elizabeth Harrower, Oct. 23, 1972, PEH.

313   *she liked only*: Interview with Michelle de Kretser, July 26, 2020.

313   *Elizabeth would later tell*: Ibid.

313   *"yellow pills"*: Elizabeth Harrower to SH, March 19, 1971, SHC.

313   *"'trick' a young doctor"*: Catherine Hazzard to SH, Dec. 19, 1971, SHPU.

313   *"The other day"*: Catherine Hazzard to SH, Feb. 3, 1976, SHPU.

314   *"having two or three friends"*: SH to Patricia Clarke, March 30, 1971, SHPU.

314   *"a v nice evening"*: Alan Maclean to SH, March 6, 1971, SHPU.

314   *"She promises"*: Ibid.

314   *"Bulletins from Tahiti"*: SH to Patricia Clarke, April 22, 1971, SHPU.

315   *"forced our way"*: SH to Elizabeth Harrower, May 30, 1971, PEH.

315   *"They've taken me"*: Catherine Hazzard to Elizabeth Harrower, June 3, 1971, PEH.

315  *"It's funny how"*: TV, 162.

315  *"the right name"*: SH to Patricia Clarke, Aug. 25, 1971, SHPU.

315  *"the trip Has Done"*: Ibid.

316  *"Navy-blue sky"*: SHDN, April 10, 1972.

316  *"a crisis"*: SH to Patricia Clarke, April 28, 1972, SHPU.

316  *"bankrupting myself"*: SH to Patricia Clarke, July 1, 1972, SHPU.

316  *"in amazing tranquillity"*: SH to Elizabeth Harrower, Aug. 9, 1972, PEH.

317  *"England late July"*: SHDNB, no date, 1971.

317  *"frailer and . . . aged"*: SH to Patricia Clarke, Jan. 18, 1973, SHPU.

317  *"spent his last"*: SH to Patricia Clarke, April 19, 1973, SHPU.

317  *"not left alone"*: Ibid.

318  *"Dora would begin"*: SHDN, no date, 1973/4.

318  *"My mater writes"*: SH to Patricia Clarke, July 1, 1972, SHPU.

318  *"good and prominent"*: SH to Patricia Clarke, April 18, 1973, SHPU.

318  *"a tumultuous"*: Christopher Lehmann-Haupt, "Why Pick on the Poor UN?" *NYT*, March 1, 1973, 39.

318  *"a literary feud"*: Michael Knight, "Attack on UN Stirs Literary Row," *NYT*, April 2, 1973, 74.

319  *Cousins eventually responded*: Norman Cousins to SH, Feb. 24, 1976, SHP Series I, Box 1.

319  *"Alfred Kazin"*: SHDNB, no date, 1973.

319  *"laudatory, front-page"*: SH to Patricia Clarke, May 27, 1973, SHPU.

319  *"It is a too-oft"*: Ibid.

319  *"very well"*: SH to Elizabeth Harrower, July 6, 1973, PEH.

320  *"I think all the London thing"*: SH to Elizabeth Harrower, July 1, 1973, PEH.

320  *"hearing her woes"*: SH to Patricia Clarke, Aug. 19, 1973, SHPU.

320  *"Neither F nor S"*: SH to Elizabeth Harrower, Sept. 11, 1973, PEH.

321  *"It is enough imposition"*: SH to Elizabeth Harrower, July 15, 1973, PEH.

321  *"As ever"*: Ibid.

321  *"A bombshell"*: Ibid.

321  *"As we seem determined"*: SH to Elizabeth Harrower, Sept. 14, 1973, PEH.

321  *"enjoying what seems"*: SH to Patricia Clarke, June 5, 1974, SHPU.

321  *"the ghostly glory"*: SHDN, June 15, 1981, SHPU.

321  *"It tolls"*: SH to William Meredith, Oct. 17, 1973, William Meredith Papers, Linda Lear Center for Special Collections and Archives, Connecticut College Library.

322  *"brushed her aside"*: Michael Mallon to BO, Sept. 29, 2021.

322  *"Arendt said Auden"*: SHDNB, Nov. 13, 1973.

322  *"Found myself thinking"*: SHDNB, Feb. 22, 1973.

322  *"marvellous"*: SH to Elizabeth Harrower, Aug. 1, 1973, PEH.

323  *"A trail"*: SH to Patricia Clarke, Oct. 20, 1973, SHPU.

323  *"what is more important"*: SH to Chris Cooper, March 10, 1974, SHPU.

323  *"Thank you"*: William Maxwell to SH, March 20, 1974, SHPU.

323 *"having the acquaintance"*: SH to Patricia Clarke, July 30, 1975, SHPU.

323 *"gently paced"*: Ibid.

323 *"The present owner"*: SH to John Saumarez Smith, Nov. 17, 1978, private collection.

324 *"Everybody walked"*: Interview with Elizabeth Archibald, April 21, 2020.

324 *"a rather awful man"*: SH to Patricia Clarke, July 30, 1975, SHPU.

324 *"We found him"*: Ibid.

325 *"with age"*: GC, 52.

325 *"GG-SH"*: SHDN, no date.

325 *"Joy's cheerful"*: Fondo Shirley Hazzard, Biblioteca del Centro Caprense Ignazio Cerio, Capri.

325 *a new parish priest*: SH to Patricia Clarke, June 5, 1974, SHPU.

325 *"'Protestant' views"*: SH to Graham Greene, May 22, 1975, SHPG.

325 *"There was a fire"*: Ibid.

326 *"intervene"*: SH to Patricia Clarke, June 5, 1974, SHPU.

326 *"800 biting words"*: SH to Patricia Clarke, March 8, 1974, SHPU.

327 *"are sworn"*: SH, "'Gulag' and the Men of Peace," in *We Need Silence to Find Out What We Think: Selected Essays by Shirley Hazzard*, ed. Brigitta Olubas (Columbia University Press, 2016), 112.

327 *"censored"*: Ibid., 116.

327 *"Even I"*: SH to Philip Jessup, March 14, 1974, SHP.

327 *"SH tells"*: SHDN, Nov. 27, 1977.

328 *Morris was thought*: Akeel Bilgrami to BO, April 2010.

328 *"the precious art"*: Ivan Morris to SH, March 17, 1971, SHPU.

328 *"a quiet weekend"*: Ivan Morris to SH, June 20, 1974, SHPU.

328 *"a special nobility"*: Ivan Morris, *The Nobility of Failure: Tragic Heroes in the History of Japan* (Holt, Rinehart & Winston, 1975).

328 *"honouring"*: TV, 16.

328–29 *"The feeling here"*: SHDN, no date, 1973.

329 *"The vulgarest tool"*: Fondo Shirley Hazzard, Biblioteca del Centro Caprense Ignazio Cerio, Capri.

329 *"a strange dichotomy"*: SH to Elizabeth Harrower, Aug. 29, 1974, PEH.

329 *"We'll get to it"*: SH to Elizabeth Harrower, Aug. 1, 1973, PEH.

329 *"a telly"*: SH to Muriel Spark, Sept. 22, 1973, CSHMS.

329 *"As to Watergate"*: SH to Elizabeth Harrower, March 3, 1974, PEH.

329 *"solidarity"*: Phillip McCarthy, "The Reluctant Transit of Shirley Hazzard," *SMH Good Weekend Magazine*, Oct. 27, 1984, 24.

329 *"that anyone"*: SH to Murray Bail, March 13, 1983, Papers of Murray Bail 1950–2001 [manuscript], National Library of Australia.

330 *"Bush, Cheney"*: SHD, Dec. 9, 2005.

330 *"With Whitlam"*: Interview with Thomas Keneally, Dec. 19, 2020.

330 *"recalled for him"*: SH to Elizabeth Harrower, Jan. 5, 1973, PEH.

330 *"hugely civilized"*: SH to Patricia Clarke, July 30, 1975, SHPU.

330 *"Whereas the public library"*: Ibid.

330 *"The election result"*: SH to Elizabeth Harrower, Dec. 17, 1975, PEH.

331 *"occasional grisly threats"*: SH to Patricia Clarke, June 5, 1974, SHPU.

331 *"The country, people"*: SH to Patricia Clarke, May 2, 1976, SHPU.

331 *"Australia is"*: FS to Jacques Barzun, March 12, 1976, Jacques Barzun Papers 1900–1999, University Archives, Rare Book and Manuscript Library, Columbia University Libraries.

331 *"reminded us"*: SH to Patricia Clarke, May 2, 1976, SHPU.

331 *"so that we"*: Ibid.

331 *"I truly believe"*: SH to Patricia Clarke, May 26, 1976, SHPU.

332 *"my old friend"*: Christina Stead (Blake) to SH, Oct. 6, 1976, SHC.

332 *"like the Steegmullers"*: Patrick White to Cynthia Nolan, March 20, 1976, in *Patrick White: Letters*, ed. David Marr (Random House, 1994), 474.

332 *"All Patrick White's books"*: SH, "The New Novel by the New Nobel Prize Winner," in *We Need Silence to Find Out What We Think*, ed. Brigitta Olubas (Columbia University Press, 2016), 72.

333 *"without your suggestions"*: Frances Kiernan to SH, no date, SHPU.

333 *"We hear music"*: SH to Chris Cooper, March 10, 1974, SHPU.

333 *"great love for"*: SH to Elizabeth Harrower, March 9, 1980, PEH.

333 *"in their ambient"*: Interview with Alison West, Dec. 17, 2018.

334 *"Dear Francis"*: Mary McCarthy to FS, June 4, 1964, FSP Series I, Box 1.

334 *"They loved Evan"*: Interview with Ann Goldstein, Dec. 6, 2018.

334 *"a sense of knowing"*: Interview with Alison West, Dec. 17, 2018.

334 *"I'm damn rich"*: SHDN, Oct. 1972, SHPU.

335 *"a charming friend"*: SH to Murray Bail, Dec. 10, 1978, Papers of Murray Bail 1950–2001 [manuscript], National Library of Australia.

335 *"dreary, and dishonest"*: SH to Patricia Clarke, April 19, 1973, SHPU.

335 *"I had the Urquharts"*: Interview with Steven M. L. Aronson, Nov. 15, 2018.

335 *"Like those who now"*: Fondo Shirley Hazzard, Biblioteca del Centro Caprense Ignazio Cerio, Capri.

335 *"She thinks"*: Interview with Steven M. L. Aronson, Nov. 15, 2018.

336 *"parking her chewing"*: SH, "Margaret Mead" (draft), no date, SHPU.

336 *"MM: Listen"*: Ibid.

336 *"greatest philistine"*: SH to Murray Bail, Sept. 6, 1982, Papers of Murray Bail 1950–2001 [manuscript], National Library of Australia.

337 *"a major novel"*: Thomas Lask, "Shirley Hazzard Ends Work on Her Big Novel," *NYT*, May 30, 1979, C24.

337 *"Shirley Hazzard's first novel"*: Press Release, Viking editorial files, Viking Press Archive.

337 *"as many as"*: Michiko Kakutani, "Behind the Bestsellers: Shirley Hazzard," *NYT*, May 11, 1980, 69.

337 *"In America"*: TV, 245.

337 *"the farthest and largest"*: TV, 4.

337   *"Housewives"*: Ibid.

337   *"a dark picture"*: Ibid., 5.

337   *"A little curled"*: Ibid., 8.

338   *"the compulsion to tell"*: TV, 313.

338   *"a fearful current"*: TV, 310.

338   *"in certain music"*: SH tribute to Anthony Hecht (draft typescript), SHPU.

338   *"willingness to destroy"*: Interview with Matthew Specktor, June 12, 2021.

338   *"would take his own"*: TV, 12.

338   *"No one should"*: Wyndham, "Hazzard Ahead," 32.

339   *"would have seemed"*: Michael Gorra, "In Retrospect: Michael Gorra on Shirley Hazzard's *The Transit of Venus*," *Critical Mass: The Blog of the National Book Critics Circle Board of Directors*; available at: bookcritics.org.

339   *"at the perfect moment"*: Geoff Dyer, "Written in the Stars," *New Statesman*, June 28, 2004.

339   *"I was ensnared"*: David Miller, "Book of a Lifetime: *The Transit of Venus*, By Shirley Hazzard," *Independent*, March 18, 2011.

339   *"Why the fuss?"*: Michelle de Kretser, *On Shirley Hazzard* (Black Ink Books, 2019), 71.

339   *"one of the great"*: Akeel Bilgrami to BO, Feb. 12, 2021.

340   *"Ending of book"*: SHDN, no date, 1969.

340   *"the great gasp of ocean"*: SHDN, no date, 1973.

340   *"Stockholm"*: SHDN, no date, 1973.

340   *"(After Stockholm"*: SHDN, no date, 1974.

340   *"Title (The) Transit"*: SHDN, no date, 1976.

340   *"Title: Time Exposure"*: SHDN, no date, 1977.

340   *"business is to break"*: John Leonard, "Books of the Times: *The Transit of Venus*," *NYT*, Feb. 26, 1980, 45.

341   *"A writer of fiction"*: Anthony Hecht, untitled typescript, MSS 926, Box 108: 17, Anthony Hecht Papers ca. 1894–2005, Stuart A. Rose Manuscript, Archives, and Rare Book Library, Emory University.

341   *"Great big novels"*: Valentine Cunningham, "A Chain of Loves and Deaths," *TLS*, April 4, 1980, 382.

341   *"The many allusions"*: SH to John Beston, April 29, 1980, F2358, UQFL429, John Beston Papers, University of Queensland Library, Fryer Manuscripts.

342   *"The didactic side"*: John Malcolm Brinnin to SH, Sept. 10, 1980, SHPU.

342   *"a princely man"*: JM.

342   *"Dear Alan"*: JM.

342   *"a great book"*: Interview with Amanda Vaill, Dec. 13, 2018.

342   *"It says something"*: Kakutani, "Behind the Bestsellers."

343   *"in some ways"*: SH and FS to Patricia Clarke, Jan. 21, 1981, SHPU.

343   *"as someone born"*: SH National Book Critics' Circle Award acceptance speech, typescript, SHPU.

343   *"When Shirley began"*: William Maxwell to FS, Jan. 27, 1981, FSP Series III, Box 103.

343   *"I am in the middle"*: Arthur Miller to William Maxwell, March 21, 1980, SHPU.

343   *"a new degree"*: Jonathan Galassi, "In Praise of Shirley Hazzard," in Bartlett, *Literary Lives: The World of Francis Steegmuller & Shirley Hazzard*, 8.

344   *"APV—Thirty years"*: SHDN, Sept. 4, 1978.

344   *"Good grey suit"*: SHDN, July 19, 1979.

344   *"Look Stranger"*: SHND, no date, 1979.

## 11. A FATED CONNECTION

346   *"Grace has nothing"*: SH to Patricia Clarke, June 16, 1980, SHPU.

346   *"ghastly letters"*: SH to Patricia Clarke, Sept. 15, 1976, SHPU.

347   *"accusing F and S"*: Ibid.

347   *"as if we did not know"*: Ibid.

347   *They would discover*: SH to Patricia Clarke, April 3, 1981, SHPU.

347   *"a barely invited"*: SH to Patricia Clarke, June 24, 1977, SHPU.

347   *Shirley and Francis*: SH to Patricia Clarke, Aug. 22, 1977, SHPU.

347   *"who had humanely gone"*: SH to Patricia Clarke, Sept. 3, 1979, SHPU.

347   *"the world where MM"*: Ibid.

347   *"So you're still"*: SHDN, Nov. 27, 1977.

347   *"sometimes quite lucid"*: SH to Patricia Clarke Aug. 20, 1980, SHPU.

348   *"as she is in"*: Ibid.

348   *"rent man"*: EH typed note, no date, 1980, PEH.

348   *"appalling letters"*: SH to Patricia Clarke, April 3, 1981, SHPU.

348   *"monstrous task"*: SH to Elizabeth Harrower, Sept. 14, 1980, PEH.

348   *"It is almost"*: SH to Edita Morris, no date, 1978, SHPU.

348   *a phone call*: SHDN, May 26, 1980.

348   *"impossible"*: SH to Elizabeth Harrower, Jan. 16, 1983, PEH.

349   *"high refined"*: SH to Murray Bail, March 13, 1983, Papers of Murray Bail 1950–2001 [manuscript], National Library of Australia.

349   *"He was an inveterate"*: SH to Elizabeth Harrower, Jan. 16, 1983, PEH.

349   *Shirley and Francis toasted*: FSD, July 1, 1984.

349   *"Calls me"*: SHDN, March 1, 1979.

349   *"What spirit"*: SH to Elizabeth Harrower, May 15, 1983, PEH.

350   *"what one might imagine"*: Ibid.

350   *"a stern letter"*: SH to Evan Cornog and Ann Goldstein, Feb. 12, 1980, private collection.

350   *"We have no help"*: SH to Elizabeth Harrower, Jan. 1, 1981, PEH.

351   *Alan Maclean and Francis*: Interview with Michelle de Kretser, July 26, 2020.

351   *the first*: SH to Murray Bail, March 4, 1980, Papers of Murray Bail 1950–2001 [manuscript], National Library of Australia.

351   *In June*: SHDN, June 7–11, 1981.

351   *"Vast beauty"*: Ibid.

351   *film rights*: Chris Chase, "At the Movies: The Transit of Shirley Hazzard," *NYT*, Aug. 20, 1982, C8.

351    *"warm and gentle"*: Gillian Armstrong to BO, Aug. 28, 2020.

351    *"inner steel"*: Gillian Armstrong to BO, Nov. 4, 2021.

351–52    *"She is a very nice"*: SH to Donald Keene, June 25, 1985, SHP, Series II, Box 10.

352    *"quite a lot"*: SH to Elizabeth Harrower, Jan. 1, 1981, PEH.

352    *"Title: The Great Fire"*: SHDN, May 1984.

352    *"(shattered!)"*: SHDN, Sept. 15, 1982.

352–53    *"extremely hospitable"*: Ibid.

353    *"this theme"*: Ibid.

353    *Her friend*: Interview with Alison Parente, Sept. 28, 2018.

353    *"thrilling"*: SH to Jacques Barzun, March 31, 1982, FSP, Series I, Box 25.

353    *"Tennysonian"*: SH to Donald Keene, Oct. 22, 1981, SHP, Series II, Box 10.

353    *"studded"*: Victor Brombert to BO, Jan. 28, 2015.

353    *"impressionistic"*: *The Journal of Joyce Carol Oates 1973–1982*, ed. Dora B. Weiner and William R. Keylor, (Harper Perennial, 2008), May 7, 1982.

353    *"infinitely gracious"*: Ibid., April 24, 1982.

354    *"A Jaded"*: SH, "A Jaded Muse," in *From Parnassus: Essays in Honor of Jacques Barzun*, ed. Dora B. Weiner and William R. Keylor (Harper and Row, 1976).

354    *Giles Constable*: Interview with Giles Constable, Jan. 18, 2017.

354    *Edward Said*: Interview with Akeel Bilgrami, Dec. 16, 2018.

354    *"Must it be assumed"*: "Recent Letters to the Editor," *NYT*, Dec. 22, 1963, 11.

354    *"discouraging"*: SH to William Scheick, April 12, 1978, private collection.

355    *"You are very"*: SH to William Scheick, Feb. 11, 1982, private collection.

355    *"one of the most"*: Donald Keene to BO, July 12, 2014.

355    *"signal honors"*: Donald Keene to Elizabeth Harrower, May 31, 1982, SHPU.

356    *"a very entertaining"*: Ibid.

356    *"English ancestors"*: SH to Elizabeth Harrower, May 15, 1983, PEH.

356    *"the sort of people"*: Interview with Carlo Knight, Sept. 24, 2018.

356    *"Magnificent house"*: SHD, June 1984.

356    *"Porte Aperte"*: Eleanora Pasotti, *Political Branding in Cities* (Cambridge University Press, 2009), 110.

356    *"not only the Gulf"*: Interview with Maurizio and Mirella Barracco, Sept. 22, 2018.

356    *"as foreigners' words"*: SH to Elizabeth Harrower, June 17, 1984, PEH.

357    *"Roberto Pane, polymath"*: SH to Chris Cooper, April 13, 1983, SHPU.

357    *"fell in love"*: Interview with Carlo Knight, Sept. 24, 2018.

357    *"Roberto Pane was inveighing"*: SH to Donald Keene, Oct. 28, 1982, SHP, Series II, Box 10.

357    *"A Capri storm"*: SH to Donald Keene, Oct. 4, 1982, SHP, Series II, Box 10.

358    *"Coerenza"*: SH to Donald Keene, Aug. 22, 1987, SHP, Series II, Box 10.

358    *"identified the lost"*: SH to Joe Connors, August 20, 1991, private collection.

358    *"wonderful adventure"*: Interview with Carlo Knight, Sept. 24, 2018.

359    *"Formidable erudition"*: SH, "Papyrology at Naples," in *We Need Silence to Find Out What We Think* ed. Brigitta Olubas (Columbia University Press, 2016), 168.

359    *"The concept of written language"*: Ibid., 170.

359 *"To have entered"*: SH, "Quest for a Fabled Ancient Library," *NYT*, May 10, 1987, B1.

359 *Robert Harrison*: Interview with Robert Harrison, Sept. 3, 2020.

360 *"Yesterday evening"*: SHDN, Nov. 3, 1980.

360 *"Byron to TG"*: Ibid.

360 *"An hour's heavy rain"*: SHDN, July 26, 1982.

361 *"What an unexpected"*: SHD, July 9, 1996.

361 *"by back roads"*: SH to Patricia Clarke, July 25, 1985, SHPU.

362 *"to spend some"*: SH to Donald Keene, Oct. 21, 1998, SHP Series II, Box 10.

362 *"hot summer"*: Ibid.

362 *"fairly breathing"*: SH to Donald Keene, Aug. 3, 1996, SHP Series II, Box 10.

362 *"Here—it is summer"*: SH to Patricia Clarke, Oct. 30, 1982, SHPU.

363 *"A week ago"*: SH to Chris Cooper, Nov. 9, 1980, SHPU.

363 *The concierge*: Interview with Will and Alison Parente, Sept. 28, 2019.

364 *"only rarely"*: SH to Chris Cooper, May 15, 1983, SHPU.

364 *"entered another dimension"*: SH to Elizabeth Harrower, May 15, 1983, PEH.

364 *"Stupendous, Homeric"*: SH to Murray Bail, May 7, 1983, Papers of Murray Bail 1950–2001 [manuscript], National Library of Australia.

364 *"to see the stupendous"*: SH to Chris Cooper, April 13, 1983, SHPU.

364 *"in the same beautiful"*: SH to Elizabeth Harrower, April 9, 1983, PEH.

364 *"The victim carrying"*: FS, "The Incident at Naples," in SH and FS, *The Ancient Shore: Dispatches from Naples*, 74.

365 *"Outside the gate"*: Ibid.

365 *"These summer evenings"*: Ibid., 76.

366 "Professore": Ibid., 92.

366 *"their lovely faces"*: Ibid., 96.

366 *"writer"*: Ibid., 103.

366 *"more compact"*: SHDN, no date, 1984.

366 *"care to see"*: SH to Saul Bellow, Sept. 21, 1984, Saul Bellow Papers, Box 72, Folder 10, Hanna Holborn Gray Special Collections Research Center, University of Chicago Library.

367 *She was consulted*: SHDN, no date, 1984.

367 *"He possibly asked"*: Ibid.

367 *After lunch*: Interview with Benjamin Taylor, Nov. 3, 2018.

367 *"These lectures"*: SH to Donald Keene, June 1984, SHP Series II, Box 10.

367 *"long traditions"*: SH, *Coming of Age*, 38.

368 *"Australians themselves"*: Ibid., 42.

368 *"Australia is not"*: Ibid.

368 *"offering any opinion"*: Michelle de Kretser, *On Shirley Hazzard*, 12.

368 *"bring the truth"*: SH to Elizabeth Harrower, Dec. 17, 1975, PEH.

369 *"an exceptional person"*: SH to Evan Cornog and Ann Goldstein, no date, private collection.

369 *Sumner was known*: Sharon Clarke, *Sumner Locke Elliott: Writing Life* (Allen & Unwin, 1996), 212.

369 *Whitfield Cook told*: Ibid., 212, 286 fn 12. My thanks to Shaun Bell for drawing this story to my attention.

369 *"A great wit"*: Gore Vidal, in *Conversations with Gore Vidal*, ed. Richard Peabody and Lucinda Ebersole (University Press of Mississippi, 2005), 31.

369 *"in an ideal"*: Interview with Evan Cornog, Nov. 2, 2018.

369 *"a current in my life"*: SH to Sharon Clarke, Sept. 3, 1991, in Clarke, *Sumner Locke Elliott: Writing Life*, 251.

369 *"Australian conversations"*: JM.

369 *"Dear Shirl and Frank"*: Sumner Locke Elliott to SH, July 7, 1976, SHPU.

370 *"own sins"*: SH to Geoffrey Dutton, July 19, 1981, SHPU.

370 *"the historic stand"*: SH to David Lange, Feb. 28, 1985, SHPU.

370 *"When I wrote"*: SH to Elizabeth Harrower, July 22, 1981, PEH.

371 *"poor in mementoes"*: SHDN, Jan. 7, 1982.

371 *"No country"*: Gough Whitlam, quoted in National Museum of Australia, "Defining Moments; Blue Poles," available at www.nma.gov.au/defining-moments/resources/blue-poles.

371 *"Ghastly"*: SHD, Jan. 18, 1953.

371 *"subservient to"*: Murray Bail to SH, Aug. 27, 1977, SHPU.

371 *"both thought"*: SH to Murray Bail, July 10, 1977, Papers of Murray Bail 1950–2001 [manuscript], National Library of Australia.

372 *"while given with"*: MB to BO, Feb. 11, 2012.

372 *"Everett quietly"*: SH to Elizabeth Harrower, March 9, 1980, PEH.

372 *"bloody Channing"*: SH to Murray Bail, March 4, 1980, PEH. The original letter Shirley sent to Murray Bail is not included among his correspondence at the National Library of Australia; however, Shirley sent a copy to Elizabeth Harrower, who included it with her correspondence among her papers.

372 *"Australians can't be"*: Ibid.

372 *"As I mentioned"*: Ibid.

373 *"half indignant"*: Murray Bail to BO, Nov. 9, 2020.

373 *"no curiosity"*: SH to Elizabeth Harrower, July 14, 1980, PEH.

373 *"the subject of malevolent"*: SH to Elizabeth Harrower, March 9, 1980, PEH.

373 *"Your rendering"*: SH to Murray Bail, March 4, 1980, PEH.

374 *"enough time"*: Murray Bail to BO, November 9, 2020.

374 *"My toes"*: SH to Murray Bail, June 5, 1981, Papers of Murray Bail 1950–2001 [manuscript], National Library of Australia.

374 *her next letter*: SH to Murray Bail, Sept. 6, 1982, Papers of Murray Bail 1950–2001 [manuscript], National Library of Australia.

374 *"If something exists"*: Quoted in SH to MB, Sept 6, 1982.

374 *"How S's prissy"*: Murray Bail, *Notebooks 1970–2003* (Harvill Press, 2005), 297. Thanks to Moya Costello for drawing Bail's comment to my attention.

374 *"the Australian myths"*: GF, 121.

374 *"I had grown"*: David Marr to SH, 1993, FSP.

375   *"Dear Shirley"*: Patrick White to SH, Dec. 12, 1979, FSP.

375   *"if some of my remarks"*: Patrick White to SH, Jan. 20, 1980, FSP Series V, Box 105.

375   *"feline"*: SH to Murray Bail, March 4, 1980, PEH.

375   *"I hope Shirley's"*: Patrick White to SH, Jan. 4, 1980, FSP Series V, Box 105.

375   *"I don't think Shirley"*: FS to Patrick White, May 4, 1980, FSP Series V, Box 105.

375   *"anything I wrote"*: SH to Elizabeth Harrower, May 11, 1981, PEH.

375   *"so—inadvertent"*: SH to Elizabeth Harrower, July 22, 1981, PEH.

375   *"a violation"*: SH to Elizabeth Harrower, Jan. 16, 1983, PEH.

376   *"In this world"*: SH to Manoly Lascaris, Oct. 19, 1990, FSP Series V, Box 105.

376   *"Patrick's affinity"*: SH to David Marr, July 31, 1993, FSP Series V, Box 105.

377   *"the happiest days"*: SH to Gough Whitlam, Sept. 10, 1984, SHPU.

377   *"The strange thing"*: Quoted in Tim Teeman, "Shirley Hazzard: 'Writing Was Such a Release for Me,'" London *Times*, May 15, 2010.

377   *"because something perhaps"*: SH to Patricia Clarke, July 25, 1984, SHPU.

377   *"an evening of great quality"*: SH to Gough Whitlam, Sept. 10, 1984, SHPU.

377   *"Elizabeth is coming!"*: SH to Donald Keene, Sept. 17, 1984, SHPU.

378   *"As to material"*: FS to Elizabeth Harrower, Aug. 26, 1984 (draft), SHC.

378   *"Alarm was caused"*: FS to Elizabeth Harrower, Sept. 19, 1984 (draft), SHC.

378   as her cousin: Margaret Dick to FS, no date, SHC.

378   *"One purpose"*: SH to Peter Morton, Dec. 2, 1984, Letters from Shirley Hazzard to Peter Morton, Dec. 2, 1984–ca. 1999, MLMSS10163, State Library of New South Wales.

378   *"'One of the many'"*: FS to Elizabeth Harrower, Sept. 19, 1984 (draft), SHC.

379   *"Alan [Maclean]"*: Elizabeth Harrower to SH, Jan. 10, 1971, SHC.

379   *"the animosity"*: SHDN, Dec. 1, 1984.

380   *"seething"*: Ibid.

380   *"amid friendly talk"*: Ibid.

380   *for Elizabeth*: Interview with Michelle de Kretser, July 26, 2020.

380   *"saying—when I"*: SHDN, Nov. 4, 1984.

380   *"in a rage"*: SHDN, Sept. 15, 1982.

380   *Alan related*: Interview with Michelle de Kretser, July 26, 2020.

380   *Alan encouraged*: Ibid.

380   *"I was apprehensive"*: SHDN, no date, 1985.

381   *"far more complicated"*: SH to Donald Keene, Dec. 18, 1984, SHP Series II, Box 10.

381   *"Of course, [Patrick]"*: Elizabeth Harrower to SH, Oct. 10, 1990, SHC.

382   *"most quite beautiful"*: SHDN, no date, 1985.

382   *"playing and replaying"*: Bert Black to SH, Nov. 13, 1984, SHPU.

382   *"for a listener"*: SH to Bert Black, Nov. 1983 (draft), SHPU.

382   *"a speech-day"*: Don Anderson, "Indian-Wrestling a Jellyfish," *National Times*, Dec. 7–13, 1984, 29.

382   *"the best-dressed"*: Peter Pierce, "Conventions of Presence," *Meanjin* 40, no. 1 (1981): 110.

382   *"The book claws"*: John Docker, "Hazzard on Greene," *Australian Book Review* 225 (2000): 12.

383 *"What hatred"*: SHDN, no date, 1985.

383 *"What a dispiriting"*: Ibid.

383 *"long in a world"*: FS to Alfred Kazin, May 23, 1985, Alfred Kazin Papers, Henry W. and Albert A. Berg Collection of English and American Literature, The New York Public Library.

384 *"As to our 'estrangement'"*: SH to Elizabeth Harrower, July 26, 1985, PEH.

384 *"two little girls"*: SHD, July 8, 1955.

384 *"dark she"*: TV, 9.

384 *"my brother and me"*: GF, 264, 266.

384 *"to desolate tears"*: BN, 42–43.

384 *"One of her tragedies"*: SH to Patricia Clarke, July 25, 1985, SHPU.

384 *"You were so good"*: SH to Elizabeth Harrower, May 21, 1985, PEH.

384 *"What almost no one"*: SH to Elizabeth Harrower, July 26, 1985, PEH.

385 *"It is so sad"*: SH to Patricia Clarke, July 25, 1985, SHPU.

## 12. THE ROOM NOT AS I THOUGHT IT WAS

389 *"a deluge"*: SH to CC, Dec. 20, 1986, SHPU.

389 *"unknown to us"*: SH to CC, Jan. 24, 1983, SHPU.

389 *"I have walked"*: SH to Elizabeth Harrower, Nov. 20, 1981, PEH.

390 *"a delightful person"*: SH to Murray Bail, May 9, 1983, Papers of Murray Bail 1950–2001 [manuscript], National Library of Australia.

390 *they had nominated*: Interview with Alec Wilkinson, Dec. 13, 2018.

390 *"good times"*: SH to Elizabeth Harrower, May 15, 1983, PEH.

390 *"We were out"*: SH to Murray Bail, Nov. 9, 1983, Papers of Murray Bail 1950–2001 [manuscript], National Library of Australia.

390 *"the crushing"*: SHDN, April 7, 1987.

390 *"gratuitous"*: SHDN, June 1985.

390 *"Moments—bad hours"*: SHDN, April 7, 1987.

391 *"take things personally"*: Interview with Annabel Davis-Goff, Jan. 9, 2018.

391 *"exposed nerves"*: SHDN, Sept. 7, 1983.

391 *"S with MS"*: Ibid.

391 *"If I could"*: SHDN, April 7, 1987.

391 *"best self"*: SHDN, June 1985.

391–92 *"Early walk"*: FSD, July 8, 1984.

392 *"relating to"*: Document signed and witnessed July 24, 1984, SHPU.

392 *"My confusion"*: FSD, Sept. 24, 1984.

392 *"40–50"*: Viewed at Shirley Hazzard's apartment, Jan. 21, 2017.

392 *"Cognex"*: SHD, Aug. 1, 1994.

392 *"on the downward slope"*: SH to Patricia Clarke, July 25, 1985, SHPU.

392 *"I already dread"*: Ibid.

393 *"It was Francis"*: SH to Chris Cooper, June 27, 1994, SHPU.

393 *"This was a ghastly"*: SHD, Feb. 7, 1983.

394  *Phyllis Lee Levin*: Interview with Phyllis Lee Levin, Dec. 8, 2018.

394  *"the sleeve and cuff"*: SHDN, May 7, 1984, SHPU.

395  *"I had also learned"*: SH to William Shawn, Aug. 12, 1986, SHP.

395  *"unsubstantiated"*: Myra McPherson, "Waldheim," *Washington Post*, Jan. 18, 1980.

395  *"And, having heard"*: SH to Jane Kramer, Nov. 6, 1986, SHP.

395  *"elucidation of Waldheim's"*: SH to William Shawn, Aug. 12, 1986, SHP.

395  *"If Waldheim sued"*: Martin Peretz, "Washington Diarist: Threats," *New Republic*, June 23, 1986, 43.

396  *Shirley spoke*: SH, "What the Waldheim Case Says About the UN," *NYT*, April 7, 1986, 26.

396  *"You deserve"*: Jane Kramer to SH, Oct. 9, 1986, SHP.

396  *"some obligation"*: Wendy Smith, "Shirley Hazzard," *Publishers Weekly* 23, no. 10 (1990).

396  *"I can't go on"*: Ibid.

396  *"sprung"*: SH to Evan Cornog and Ann Goldstein, Sept. 30, 1989, private collection.

396  *"NY night sky"*: SHDN, 1983, no date.

397  *"with mild conspiratory"*: Galassi, "In Praise," 7.

397  *"exceedingly"*: SH to Muriel Spark, no date, "Friday" 1963, CSHMS.

397  *"literary circles"*: Jacques Barzun to SH, Jan. 30, 1990, SHPU.

397  *"So many people"*: Interview with Evan Cornog, Nov. 2, 2018.

397  *"holding forth"*: Interview with Katherine Swett, Dec. 1, 2018.

397  *"her respect"*: Interview with Evan Cornog, Nov. 2, 2018.

397  *"Whether it involved"*: Evan Cornog to BO, Oct. 30, 2021.

398  *"a little girl"*: Interview with Phyllis Lee Levin, Dec. 8, 2018.

398  *"Half day"*: SHDN, June 22, 1979.

398  *Shirley wrote*: Interview with Edward Mendelson, Dec. 7, 2018.

398  *"long festive lunches"*: Annabel Davis-Goff, in eds. Charles Baxter, Michael Collier, and Edward Hirsch, *A William Maxwell Portrait: Memories and Appreciations*, 173.

398  *"quietly joyous"*: Interview with Michael Collier, Sept. 30, 2020.

398  *"wanted to be"*: Interview with Edward Hirsch, Sept. 15, 2020.

398  *"I thought"*: Interview with Alec Wilkinson, Dec. 13, 2018.

399  *"Sitting on the deck"*: Interview with Michael Collier, Sept. 30, 2020.

399  *"sweep and range"*: Interview with Edward Hirsch, Sept. 15, 2020.

400  *She also shared*: Interview with Annabel Davis-Goff, Jan. 12, 2018.

400–401  *Evan Cornog was struck*: Interview with Evan Cornog, Nov. 2, 2018.

401  *"It was characteristic"*: Interview with Jonathan Burnham, Dec. 8, 2018.

401  *"comradely letter"*: Helen Garner to BO, Sept. 11, 2021.

401  *"finding a moment"*: Interview with Annabel Davis-Goff, Oct. 21, 2020.

401  *"more cataract"*: Benjamin Taylor, *Naples Declared: A Walk Around the Bay* (Penguin, 2012), 118.

401  *"this very hard"*: Interview with Ann Goldstein, Dec. 6, 2018.

401  *"what she had to say"*: Michael Mallon email to BO, Sept. 29, 2021.

401 *"nothing to do"*: Interview with Alison West, Dec. 17, 2018.

402 *"wouldn't let stuff"*: Interview with Evan Cornog, Nov. 2, 2018.

402 *"an assassin"*: Interview with Alec Wilkinson, Dec. 13, 2018.

402 *"it would be Shirley"*: Interview with Elizabeth Archibald, April 21, 2020.

402 *Akeel Bilgrami*: Interview with Akeel Bilgrami, Dec. 16, 2018.

402 *"She wouldn't"*: Ibid.

402 *"I woke"*: SHDN, April 14, 1987.

403 *"beautiful house"*: SHDN, June 25, 1984.

403 *"Vast garden"*: SHD, July 6, 1989.

403 *"inhabiting"*: James Merrill to Samuel Lock, Nov. 5, 1986, quoted in Langdon Hammer, *James Merrill: Life and Art* (Knopf, 2015), 718.

403 *"I can see"*: James Merrill to SH, Sept. 4, 1986, SHPU.

404 *Years later*: SH note, added to James Merrill letter, Sept. 4, 1986, SHPU.

404 *a note folded*: SH, James Merrill Memorial, 45.

404 Silenzio e Solitudine: SH note, added to James Merrill letter, Sept. 4, 1986, SHPU.

404 *"emblem"*: J. D. McClatchy to SH, Aug. 26, 2000, SHPU.

404 *"They stood out"*: Interview with Will and Alison Parente, Sept. 28, 2018.

405 *"Stupendous"*: SHD, June 24, 1985.

405 *"probably clearer"*: Interview with Will and Alison Parente, Sept. 28, 2018.

405 *"He rode"*: Leo Tolstoy, *War And Peace* (transl. Rosemary Edmonds) (Penguin, 1978).

405 *"Denisov's"*: Interview with Will and Alison Parente, Sept. 28, 2018.

406 *"a large gathering"*: SH to Evan Cornog and Ann Goldstein, Nov. 19, 1991, private collection.

406 *"Pasquale's sister"*: SHDN, Sept. 30, 1992.

406 *Annabel remembered*: Interview with Annabel Davis-Goff, Dec. 4, 2018.

407 *She knew*: Interview with Will and Alison Parente, Sept. 28, 2018.

407 *"Saint's silver bust"*: SH to Evan Cornog and Ann Goldstein, May 17–19, 1991, private collection.

407 *"settling down"*: William Maxwell to SH and FS, June 6, 1987, FSP, Series III, Box 103.

408 *"there had been"*: James Merrill to SH, Sept. 4, 1986, SHPU.

408 *"dangerous, crazy"*: Interview with Jonathan Burnham, Dec. 8, 2018.

408 *"In Piazza"*: SHD, June 5, 1989.

408 *"The cable boys"*: SH to Elizabeth Harrower, no date, 1973, PEH.

408 *"Palazzeschi"*: FSD, Feb. 16, 1984.

409 *"Lively, youngish"*: SHD, May 16, 1989.

409 *"a charming elderly orthopaedist"*: SH to Evan Cornog and Ann Goldstein, June 15, 1989, private collection.

409 *"These experiences"*: SHD, May 22, 1989.

409 *"The vegetable stalls"*: SH to Evan Cornog and Ann Goldstein, Nov. 7, 1988, private collection.

409 *"as if cut"*: SHD, April 25, 1989.

409 *"At this moment"*: SH to Evan Cornog and Ann Goldstein, June 15, 1989, private collection.

410 *"My one-eyed cat"*: SH to Evan Cornog and Ann Goldstein, July 27, 1988, private collection.

410 *"We've fixed him up"*: SH to Evan Cornog and Ann Goldstein, Nov. 7, 1988, private collection.

410 *"What it means"*: SH to Evan Cornog and Ann Goldstein, July 15, 1990, private collection.

410 *"They usually arrive"*: SH to Evan Cornog and Ann Goldstein, June 15, 1989, private collection.

410 *"his great treat"*: Phyllis Levin to SH, March 30, no year, SHPU.

410–11 *"I had it always"*: Ellen Kanner, "Just in Time," *PAGES*, Nov.–Dec., 2003.

411 *"What an extraordinary"*: William Maxwell to SH, July 19, 1987, FSP Series III, Box 103.

411 *"Alec was as impressed"*: SHDN, July 23, 1988.

411 *"These last words"*: Ibid.

411 *she also published*: "I Wake Alone," *New Yorker*, Nov. 19, 1990, 52; "Even If You Weren't My Father," *New Yorker*, Aug. 6, 1990, 36.

412 *"were it not"*: Camillo Sbarbaro, "I Wake Alone" (transl. Shirley Hazzard), *New Yorker*, Nov. 19, 1990, 52.

412 *"somehow shocking"*: SH to Donald Keene, Oct. 16, 1990, SHP Series II, Box 10.

412 *"Graham Greene"*: SH to Evan Cornog and Ann Goldstein, Oct. 19, 1990.

412 *Shirley remarked*: SH to Michael Richey, Nov. 16, 1992, SHPG.

412 *Joseph Blotner, writes*: Joseph Blotner, *Robert Penn Warren: A Biography* (Random House, 1997), 493.

413 *"Returning together"*: SHDN, June 29, 1991.

413 *"As if one had swallowed"*: Ibid.

413 *"The wish to be away"*: Ibid.

414 *"life of sustained"*: SH to Murray Bail, Nov. 9, 1983, Papers of Murray Bail 1950–2001 [manuscript], National Library of Australia.

414 *"to abandon Flaubert"*: SH to Donald Keene, Aug. 3, 1996, SHP Series II, Box 10.

414 *"We generally have"*: SH to Evan Cornog and Ann Goldstein, Nov. 19, 1991, private collection.

415 *"Nice to see"*: Ibid.

415 *"carried shoulder-high"*: SH to Evan Cornog and Ann Goldstein, Nov. 19, 1991, private collection.

415 *"for sending me"*: Leon Edel to FS, Dec. 20, 1991, SHPU.

415 *"the precise, elegant"*: Julian Barnes, "Unlikely Friendship," *NYRB*, June 10, 1993.

415 *"Dear Doctor Barnes"*: FS to Julian Barnes, July 22, 1984; Sept. 1, 1984, private collection.

415 *"In his later years"*: Julian Barnes, "Francis Steegmuller," *Observer*, Nov. 1, 1994, 41.

416 *"Dreamt that BTS"*: SHD, no date, Sept. 2006.

416 *"It was one of those"*: SH to Donald Keene, Sept. 6, 1992, SHP Series II, Box 10.

416   *"My wife's name"*: FS notes for BBC interview with Miss Jane Bywaters, Jan. 17, 1992, SHPU.

416   *"Great scene"*: SHD, April 4, 1993.

416   *"an interval"*: SHD, April 5, 1993.

416   *"F coraggio"*: SHD, April 15, 1983.

416   *"Your yesterday-today-tomorrow"*: Pat Woolf to SH, no date, SHPU.

417   *"to congratulate"*: SHD, June 17, 1993.

417   *"the death"*: SHD, June 29, 1993.

417   *"Dear Puss"*: SH and FS notes, March 15, 1994, SHPU.

417   *"Is it all right"*: Interview with Bill Hall, March 8, 2020.

418   *"came and put"*: Interview with Robert Pounder, Nov. 20, 2018.

418   *"You look exactly"*: Interview with Jonathan Burnham, Dec. 8, 2018.

418   *"But you* must": Martin Stannard, "Meeting Shirley Hazzard," in *Shirley Hazzard: New Critical Essays*, ed. Brigitta Olubas (Sydney University Press, 2014), 142–43.

418   *"Francis would say"*: Interview with Mary Ellin Barrett, Nov. 28, 2018.

418   *"When I understood"*: SHD, Jan. 24, 1993.

418   *"a writer"*: GC, 7.

419   *"It's a pretty story"*: Michael Richey to SH, Oct. 20, 1992, SHPG.

419   *"The meeting"*: SH to Michael Richey, Nov. 16, 1992, SHPG.

419   *"quite the nicest"*: Michael Richey to SH, Dec. 27, 1992, SHPG.

419   *After his death*: SH to Andrew Roberts, Aug. 11, 2001, SHPG.

419   *"I can scarcely"*: SH to Carlo Knight, June 29, 2007, SHPU.

419   *"Rain en route"*: SHD, April 10, 1994.

419   *"You will know"*: FS to Fanny Ellison, May 30, 1994, Box 1: 68, REP.

419   *Shirley wrote*: SH, "Maestro della luce: La scomparsa del pittore Randall Morgan," *Il Mattino*, April 27, 1995, 8, SHPU.

420   *"unrealising"*: SHD, May 22, 1994.

420   *"May 3"*: SHD, May 3, 1994.

420   *"To Capri"*: SHD, July 7, 1994.

420   *"Heaviness"*: SHD, July 31, 1994.

420   *"Beautiful day"*: SHD, Aug. 25, 1994.

420   *She later carried*: Interview with Frances Alston, Oct. 27, 2018.

420   *"New documents"*: SH to Donald Keene, Sept. 16, 1994, SHP Series II, Box 10.

420   *"no pants"*: SHD, Sept. 30, 1994.

421   *"Essential"*: SHD, July 10, 1994.

421   *"You have beautiful"*: Julian Barnes, *Nothing to Be Frightened Of* (Vintage, 2009), 171.

421   *"deterioration"*: SHD, Oct. 20, 1994.

421   *"to pay bill"*: SHD, Oct. 21, 1994.

421   *"strange days"*: SHD, Oct. 24, 1994.

422   *"I read"*: Leon Edel to SH, Oct. 29, 1994, FSP Series XIV; Edel had been a journalist covering the UN in the late 1940s and early 1950s.

422   *"I have been personally acquainted"*: George ffennell to SH, Jan. 15, 1996, FSP Series XIV.

422 *"You were the climate"*: Willian Maxwell to SH, Oct. 24, 1994, SHPU.

422 *"What an extravagantly"*: Emily Maxwell to SH, Oct. 24, 1994, SHPU.

423 *"great beauty"*: SH to Chris Cooper, July 7, 2004, SHPU.

423 *"'old' room"*: SHD, Oct. 31, 1994.

423 *"punctuated by awful"*: Ibid.

423 *"I remember"*: Michael Mallon to SH, Oct. 21, 1994, SHPU.

423 *"Vines in trees"*: SHD, Nov. 2, 1994.

424 *"Again, memories"*: Ibid.

424 *"at his briskest"*: Ibid.

424 *"Harold Acton"*: SH to Donald Keene, Nov. 8, 1994, SHP Series II, Box 10.

424 *"to Procacci"*: SHD, Nov. 5, 1994.

424 *"only just realising"*: SHD, Oct. 31, 1999.

424 *"Terrific storm"*: SHD, Nov. 7, 1994.

424 *"Storm—sun—storm"*: SHD, Nov. 11, 1994.

425 *"No lights"*: SHD, Nov. 12, 1994.

425 *"The wind rises"*: SHD, Nov. 15, 1994.

425 *saw in her ongoing*: Interview with Robert Harrison, Sept. 3, 2020.

425 *"pouring out libations"*: Virgil, *The Aeneid*, translated by Robert Fagles (Viking, 2006), Book 3, lines 359–360, 113.

425 *"a story that she told herself"*: Interview with Matthew Specktor, June 12, 2021.

425 *"intimate"*: SHD, Nov. 30, 1994.

425 *"I could not restrain"*: SHD, Nov. 28, 1994.

425 *James Merrill came for tea*: SHD, Dec. 6, 1994.

425 *"in the mild evening"*: SH, James Merrill Memorial, 45.

426 *"incredulity"*: SHD, Dec. 27, 1994.

426 *"the lack"*: SHD, Dec. 28, 1994.

426 *"elderly"*: Ibid.

426 *"fear of dark"*: SHD, Feb. 6, 1995.

426 *"As if I wake"*: SHD, March 4, 1995; Henry Reed, "The Door and the Window," in *The Harvill Book of Twentieth-Century Poetry in English*, ed. Michael Schmidt, (Harvill, 2012) 309.

426 *"The first time"*: SHD, Jan. 8, 1995.

426 *"near to death"*: SHD, Jan. 31, 1995.

426 *"a Richter scale"*: SHD, Feb. 2, 1995.

426 *"It is the sadness"*: SHD, March 11, 1995.

### 13. SOLA SOLISSIMA

427 *"Being at James'"*: Allan Gurganus to SH, no date, SHPU.

427 *"Do you ever wonder"*: SH, James Merrill memorial, 43–44.

428 *"the wrong kind"*: SH to Julian Barnes, March 25, 1995, private collection.

428 *"Much about Bea"*: SHDN, April 4, 1995.

428 *"last awful years"*: SHD, May 15, 1996.

428 *"He said, 'Noticeable'"*: SHD, Jan. 19, 1996.

428 *"Things heard"*: SH to Evan Cornog and Ann Goldstein, April 18, 1995, private collection.

429 *her copy*: Fondo Shirley Hazzard, Biblioteca del Centro Caprense Ignazio Cerio, Capri.

429 *"with my pages"*: SH to Evan Cornog and Ann Goldstein, April 18, 1995, private collection.

429 *"deepened and fraught"*: SHD, May 10, 1995.

429 *"I see F"*: SHD, May 11, 1995.

429 *"to see oneself"*: SHD, Oct. 9, 1995.

429 *"divesting"*: SHD, June 16, 1995.

429 *"On the one hand"*: SHD, no date, 1995.

429 *"At this season"*: SHD, June 11 and 14, 1995.

429 *"in moonlight"*: SHD, June 16, 1995.

430 *"essential"*: SH to Donald Keene, Nov. 11, 1995, SHP Series II, Box 10.

430 *"appalling sense"*: SH to Donald Keene, Oct. 21, 1996, SHP Series II, Box 10.

430 *"Strange to have"*: SHD, March 14, 1995.

430 *"lovable, frailer"*: SHD, Feb. 14, 1996.

430 *"We wept"*: SHD, March 1, 1996.

430 *"exhausted and aged"*: SHD, Feb. 21, 1995.

430 *"Coming into"*: SHD, Aug. 3, 1996.

430 *"Memories"*: SHD, Feb. 16, 1996.

430 *Rosanna had come*: Rosanna Warren to BO, Oct. 13, 2020.

430 *"not only for spectacle"*: SH, Memorial Service for Eleanor Clark, 1996, SHPU.

431 *"intelligence, expressiveness"*: SHD, March 8, 1996.

431 *"only work"*: SHD, April 19, 1996.

431 *"for chronic unpunctuality"*: SH to Muriel Spark, May 24, 1996, CSHMS.

431 *"a litany"*: Stannard, "Meeting Shirley Hazzard," 141.

431 *"Francis never"*: SH to Muriel Spark, May 24, 1996, CSHMS.

431 *"Do you remember"*: SH to Evan Cornog and Ann Goldstein, Dec. 12, 1994, private collection.

432 *"After they left"*: SHD, April 21, 1996.

432 *"Alone"*: SHD, July 1, 1996.

432 *"At Sorrento"*: Ms and typescript, SHPU.

432 *"These days"*: SHD, Aug. 9, 1996.

432 *"The light"*: SHD, Aug. 1, 1996.

433 *"How strange"*: SHD, Aug. 28, 1996.

433 *"a kind of 'stroke'"*: SHD, Jan. 24, 1999.

433 *"of such great quality"*: GC, 8.

433 *"Elderly man"*: SHD, June 4, 1996.

433 *"All looms"*: SHD, Sept. 13, 1996.

434 *"This blue and white"*: SHD, June 4, 2007.

434 *"Anne, such a dear"*: SHD, Nov. 28, 1996.

434 *"Some classic moments"*: SHD, Nov. 25, 1996.

434 *"Fuji-like"*: SHD, Dec. 1, 1996.

434 *"What a good"*: SHD, April 25, 1997.

434 *Mary Ellin and Marvin Barrett*: Interview with Mary Ellin Barrett, Nov. 28, 2018.

434 *"the long, long flight"*: SH to Donald Keene, Aug. 16, 1997, SHP Series II, Box 10.

434 *"every 'midwinter' day"*: Ibid.

435 *"dismaying"*: SHD, Aug. 17.

435 *"but I did hear"*: Valerie Barnes to SH, Dec. 9, 1998, SHPU.

435 *"very kind"*: Ibid.

435 *"Waste of being"*: SH to Valerie Barnes, Dec. 20, 1998 (draft), SHPU.

435 *"boredom"*: SH to Elizabeth Harrower, July 26, 1985, PEH.

436 *When Michael Collier*: Interview with Michael Collier, Sept. 30, 2020.

436 *"devotedly"*: Interview with Rosanna Warren, Dec. 8, 2018.

436 *Shirley arranged*: Interview with Edward Mendelson, Dec. 7, 2018.

436 *Katherine Swett*: Interview with Katherine Swett, Dec. 1, 2018.

436 *"like a poem"*: SHD, Nov. 1, 1997.

436 *"on foot"*: Ibid.

436 *"30-odd blocks"*: SHD, Nov. 9, 1997.

436 *"I have such truly"*: SHD, Nov. 11, 1997.

437 *"urgency"*: SHD, April 3, 1998.

437 *"spiritually"*: Ibid.

437 *"my feeling"*: SHD, Oct. 24, 1996.

437 *"I find I take"*: SHD, Jan. 28, 1997.

437 *"more than twice"*: SHD, Jan. 30, 1999.

437 *"I saw Hiroshima"*: SHD, Aug. 3, 1996.

438 *"Image of Avernus"*: SHD, Dec. 1998.

438 *"would have enjoyed"*: SH to Valerie Barnes, Dec. 20, 1998, SHPU.

438 *"glad to have"*: SH to Andrew Roberts, Aug. 11, 2001, SHPG.

439 *"It's a book"*: SH at Bread Loaf Writers' Conference, Middlebury College, Aug. 16, 1999; recording available at archive.org/details/f8_1999-08-16_hazzard.

439 *"'Scrutinizing'"*: Copy of fax, SH to Barbara Epstein, *NYRB*, SHPG.

439 *"Cruauté?"*: Yvonne Cloetta to SH, March 6, 2000, SHPG.

439 *"put herself on the wrong"*: Yvonne Cloetta quoted in Ed Helmore, "Greene's Heart Is Pierced by Poison Pens," *Guardian*, Nov. 20, 2000.

439 *"It is a pity"*: Copy of fax from Yvonne Cloetta to the editors, *NYRB*, July 11–12, 2000, SHPG.

439 *"vituperative"*: Amanda Saunders to the editors, *NYRB*, Jan. 29, 2001, SHPG.

439 *"Greene's reiterated"*: SH to Barbara Epstein, editor at *NYRB*, Oct. 31, 2000, SHPG.

440 *"solace"*: SH, "A William Maxwell Portrait," in *We Need Silence to Find Out What We Think*, ed. Brigitta Olubas (Columbia University Press, 2016), 104.

440 *Throughout these days*: Wilkinson, *My Mentor*, 146.

440 *"Shirley and Bill connected"*: Interview with Alec Wilkinson, Oct. 16, 2020.

440   *"Magnificent day"*: SH to Donald Keene, Dec. 6, 2000, SHP Series II, Box 10.

441   *"remember"*: John Updike to SH, Oct. 23, 2000, SHPU.

441   *"quite good"*: SH to Donald Keene, Dec. 6, 2000, SHP Series II, Box 10.

441   *"unclouded friendship"*: SH, draft of eulogy for William Maxwell, SHPU.

441   *"Those pleasures"*: SH to Hugh Honour, June 16, 2001, SHPU.

441   *"These were reflective"*: SH to Donald Keene, Dec. 6, 2000, SHP Series II, Box 10.

441   *"a sign of how"*: Interview with Will and Alison Parente, Sept. 28, 2018.

442   *Shirley was delighted*: Alison Parente to BO, Oct. 20, 2021.

442   *"How could you"*: Interview with Alice Brinton and Catherine Healey, Sept. 29, 2018.

443   *"That's it"*: Michael Mallon to BO, Sept. 29, 2021.

443   *"filled with remembrance"*: SHD, Aug. 26–30, 2002.

443   *Her "work"*: Ibid.

443   *"The creation"*: SHD, Sept. 6, 2002.

443   *"My homage"*: SHD, Sept. 26, 2002.

443   *"all is changed"*: SHD, Sept. 23, 2002.

443   *"They look estranged"*: SHD, Sept. 3, 2002.

444   *"As to my work"*: SH to Donald Keene, Nov. 7, 2002, SHP Series II, Box 10.

444   *"Reading these excruciating"*: SHD, Sept. 6, 2002.

445   *"How natural"*: SHD, Sept. 3, 2002.

445   *"final touches"*: Anthony Hecht to SH, Nov. 26, 2003, SHPU.

446   *"The island itself"*: GF, 173.

446   *"the distances"*: Ibid., 87.

446   *"AIR, for freedom"*: Ibid., 232.

446   *"repossessed"*: Ibid.

447   *"The scrubby bark"*: Ibid., 222.

447   *"earned elevation"*: John Banville, "Venus in Transit," *NYT*, Oct. 12, 2003.

447   *"with a rather gauzy"*: Gail Caldwell, "Burning Memories of War and Loss," *Boston Globe*, Oct. 19, 2003.

447   *"a kernel"*: Michelle de Kretser, *On Shirley Hazzard*, 92.

448   *"reduced"*: SHD, July 27, 2003.

448   *"losing memory"*: SH to Martin Stannard, Oct. 12, 2003 (draft), SHPU.

448   *"a new wave"*: SHD, July 10, 2002.

448   *"a lovely man"*: SHD, Oct. 4, 2003.

448   *"Memories"*: SHD, Oct. 1, 2003.

448   *"All kind"*: SHD, Oct. 17, 2003.

448   *"delightful"*: SHD, Nov. 7, 2003.

448   *"These long long"*: SHD, Aug. 28, 2004.

448   *"An evening"*: SHD, Sept. 2, 2006.

448   *she told*: Reported by Min Jin Lee, Panel, "On Reading: Shirley Hazzard's *Transit of Venus*," Center for Fiction, March 24, 2021.

449   *"the remnant"*: Valerie Lawson, "Hazzard County," *SMH*, June 19, 2004.

449   *the judges*: Mark Rubbo to BO, Nov. 2, 2021.

450  *"The bequest"*: Quoted in "Hazzard Wins Miles Franklin Award," *The Age*, June 18, 2014.

450  *"so unflattering"*: Jane Sullivan, "Duchess of Hazzard," *SMH*, July 2, 2005.

450  *"I think people"*: Ibid.

450  *"in wonderful ways"*: McClatchy, "Shirley Hazzard," 190.

450  *"Crucial event"*: SHD, July 18, 2004.

450  *"This was for you"*: SHD, Oct. 19, 2004.

451  *"Ted so reduced"*: SHD, Dec. 8, 2004.

451  *"light rain"*: SHD, Dec. 27, 2004.

451  *"fine wanderings"*: SHD, Dec. 29, 2004.

451  *"A beautiful"*: SHD, Jan. 2, 2005.

451  *"of Mariani"*: Ibid.

451  *"Tony heard voices"*: Typescript of SH's memorial for Anthony Hecht, SHPU.

451  *"Fearful of mortgaging"*: SH to Donald Keene, Oct. 8, 2004, SHP Series II, Box 10.

452  *"scratching around"*: SH to Chris Cooper, July 7, 2004, SHPU.

452  *"sentimental"*: SHD, Feb. 27, 2005.

452  *"The coming round"*: SHD, March 5, 2005, SHPU.

452  *"Our parting"*: Ibid.

452  *"utter strangeness"*: SHD, March 7, 2005.

452  *"Sir Cecil's Ride"*: SHD, March 9, 2005.

452  *"Entirely recognisable"*: SHD, March 10, 2005.

452  *"Memory"*: SHD, March 12, 2005.

452  *"scarcely changed"*: SHD, March 16, 2005.

452  *"where one afternoon"*: SHD, March 11, 2005.

452  *"The Bund"*: SHD, March 13–14, 2005.

452  *"white Alaska"*: SHD, March 17, 2005.

453  *"I felt my loneliness"*: SHD, June 3, 2005.

453  *"miserably"*: SHD, June 3, 2005.

453  *"On the hills"*: SHD, July 6, 2005.

453  *David Malouf noticed*: Interview with David Malouf, Jan. 30, 2020.

453  *she mistook*: Interview with Susan Wyndham, Feb. 6, 2020.

453  *Her speech*: Ibid.

453  *"They loved it"*: Interview with David Malouf, Jan. 30, 2020.

454  *David Malouf felt*: Ibid.

454  *Mark Rubbo*: Mark Rubbo to BO, Nov. 2, 2021.

454  *"who looked outwards"*: Michelle de Kretser, *On Shirley Hazzard*, 3.

454  *"In the wake"*: Susan Wyndham, "The Heavenly Brilliance of Shirley Hazzard," *SMH*, Oct. 4, 2019.

454  *"Everyone I knew"*: Helen Garner to BO, Sept. 11, 2021.

455  *"unable to appreciate"*: Ibid.

455  *"the relief"*: SHD, July 14, 2005.

455  *"whom I knew"*: SHD, July 3, 2006.

455  *"as ever"*: SHD, May 14, 2006.

456   *"much solitary sadness"*: Ibid.

456   *"She was the threshold"*: SHD, April 16, 2006.

456   *"the terrible apprestimento"*: SHD, May 27, 2006.

456   *"October 1947"*: SHD, Oct. 13, 2006.

456   *"A terribly* bon genre*"*: Michael Mallon to BO, Sept. 29, 2021.

456   *"We just thought"*: Interview with Michael Collier, Sept. 30, 2020.

456   *"personal"*: Interview with Edward Hirsch, Sept. 15, 2020.

456   *"We're deferential"*: Interview with Michael Collier, Sept. 30, 2020.

457   *"There was never any sense"*: Interview with Edward Hirsch, Sept. 15, 2020.

457   *"back this afternoon"*: SHD, Jan. 17, 1996.

457   *"This was quite"*: SHD, July 17, 2003.

457   *"These days"*: SHD, July 15, 2004.

457   *"Lunch with RPH"*: SHD, Jan. 2–3, 2006.

457   *"lassitude"*: SHD, June 26, 2006.

457   *"disconnected"*: SHD, June 27, 2006.

457   *"demoralizing"*: SHD, April 15, 2006.

458   *"I wonder"*: SHD, May 24, 2007.

458   *"to 'acquire'"*: SHD, June 27, 2007.

458   *"frightening sense"*: SHD, May 24, 2007.

458   *"loneliness, distress"*: SHD, June 29, 2007.

458   *"incapacity for prolonged"*: SHD, Aug. 12, 2006.

458   *"these places"*: SHD, June 29, 2007.

458   *"splendour"*: SHD, June 30, 2007.

458   *"And I so vague"*: Ibid.

459   *"The calamity"*: SHD, June 14, 2007.

460   *"beset by details"*: SHD, July 16, 2007.

460   *"a small, fragile figure"*: Interview with Alec Wilkinson, Dec. 13, 2018.

460   *"She was extremely thin"*: Interview with Alison and Will Parente, Sept. 28, 2018.

460   *In the late morning*: Interview with Giulio Severini Colavolpe, Sept. 20, 2018.

460   *By then Shirley was*: Interview with Frances Alston, Oct. 27, 2018.

461   *Shirley seemed*: Interview with Robert Pounder, Nov. 20, 2018.

462   *She told Mary Ellin*: Mary Ellin Barrett email to BO, Nov. 28, 2018.

462   *"She wasn't writing"*: Interview with Phyllis Lee Levin, Dec. 8, 2018.

462   *"We only just"*: Annabel Davis-Goff to BO, Dec. 28, 2011.

463   *"I feel very much"*: SH, "The New York Society Library Discussion, September 2012," in *We Need Silence to Find Out What We Think*, ed. Brigitta Olubas (Columbia University Press, 2016), 185.

463   *"as if she had"*: Interview with Elizabeth Barlow Rogers, March 7, 2020.

464   *"Francie had told me"*: Interview with Rosanna Warren, Dec. 8, 2018.

464   *"One would not"*: Annabel Davis-Goff to BO, Dec. 15, 2016.

464   *Valerie had died*: Interview with Hamlin Hazzard Barnes, Nov. 8, 2018.

465   *"To be no more"*: SHD, July 1, 2007, SHPU.

465 *The X-ray*: Robert Pogue Harrison, "Shirley Hazzard—A Conversation," *Entitled Opinions*, Jan. 10, 2006; available at www.entitledopinions.stanford.edu/novelist -shirley-hazzard.

465 *"when, on the boat"*: TV, 335.

465 *Thomas Nashe's "In Time of Pestilence"*: *The Oxford Book of English Verse, 1250–1918*, ed. Arthur Quiller-Couch (Clarendon Press, 1939), 207–208.

466 *"To their families"*: GF, 53.

467 *"She thought"*: TV, 335.

# ACKNOWLEDGMENTS

This book could not have been written without the encouragement and generous help of Shirley Hazzard's friends. Meeting the remarkable people who knew her at different stages of her life has been stimulating, a privilege. I want to thank Annabel Davis-Goff for a contribution that went far beyond her executor role; her hospitality quite literally made the New York research possible for me, but even more than that, I value her company and conversation. I also want to thank Francie Alston, whose good cheer has been a great support from my earliest days of rummaging through boxes of papers in the spare room of Shirley's apartment. Over the years of writing this biography, others of Shirley's friends, particularly Alice Brinton and Cathie Healey, and Alison and Will Parente, also extended both hospitality and friendship, enriching the experience of thinking and writing about Shirley's life, turning it all into pleasure.

I was fortunate to be able to interview many friends and others from Shirley Hazzard's circles, some in face-to-face meetings, some via video calls or email, and wish to express my appreciation to them all: Frances Alston, Elizabeth Archibald, Steven M. Aronson, Elizabeth Barlow Rogers, Hamlin Hazzard Barnes, Maurizio and Mirella Barracco, Mary Ellin Barrett, Akeel Bilgrami, Alice Brinton, Jonathan Burnham, Joanna Capon, Giulio Severi Colavolpe, Michael Collier, Mario Coppola, Evan Cornog, Annabel Davis-Goff, Hugh Fremantle, Jonathan Galassi, Vincent Giroud, Arthur Goldschmidt, Jr., Ann Goldstein, Alan Green, Bill Hall, Robert Pogue Harrison, Lucia Hatch, Catherine Healey, Violet Highton, Edward Hirsch, Elizabeth Howard, Tom Keneally, Frances Kiernan,

Carlo Knight, Phyllis Lee Levin, Michael Mallon, David Malouf, Edward Mendelson, Peter Morton, Alison and Will Parente, Robert Pounder, Ann Richardson, Isabella Ripa di Meana, Matthew Specktor, Adam Stein, Helen Stein, Benjamin Swett, Katherine Swett, Benjamin Taylor, Amanda Vaill, Cynthia Vedeniapine, Peter Vedeniapine, Vera Vivante, Diane Wachman, Rosanna Warren, Alison West, Alec Wilkinson, Pat Woolf, Susan Wyndham. My thanks also to those who made available to me their correspondence from Shirley and Francis: Julian Barnes, Joseph Connors, the family of Chris Cooper, Ann Goldstein, Carlo Knight, Peter Morton, Benjamin Taylor, Vera Vivante.

I wish to thank archivists and librarians at the following institutions for their invaluable work and assistance, both before and during the pandemic, which made everything more difficult: Beinecke Rare Book and Manuscript Library, Yale University; British Library; Centro Caprense Ignazio Cerio, Capri; Century Association of New York Archives; Rare Book and Manuscript Library, Columbia University Library; Bibliothèque Littéraire Jacques Doucet, Paris; Georgetown University Library; Getty Research Institute; Harry Ransom Humanities Research Center; Linda Lear Center for Special Collections and Archives, Connecticut College Library; Stuart A. Rose Manuscript, Archives, and Rare Book Library, Emory University; Library of Congress; Macmillan Archive; Yale University Library; National Archives of Australia; National Library of Australia; National Library of Scotland; The New York Public Library; Franklin D. Roosevelt Presidential Library and Museum; Special Collections and Archives, Queens College, City University of New York; Leeds University Library; Viking Press Archive; U.S. National Archives. In particular I want to thank Kevin Schlottman at the Columbia Rare Book and Manuscript Library for his unstinting help in arranging access for me to Shirley Hazzard's unsorted and at times rather unwieldy papers. Carmelina Fiorentino was immensely helpful in arranging access to Shirley Hazzard's library at Centro Caprense Ignazio Cerio in Capri. During 2021, when I was unable to get to Columbia, Aidan Lilienfeld provided invaluable assistance locating photographs and other material there for me.

I want to acknowledge my colleagues in the English program at the University of New South Wales, particularly my fellow Australianists Elizabeth McMahon and Fiona Morrison, and from outside UNSW, Nicholas Birns and Brigid Rooney, with all of whom I've had sustained and inspiring discussions about Shirley Hazzard and her writing. Michelle de Kretser has been another inspired interlocutor on all matters Hazzard. Alice Brinton, Annabel Davis-Goff, Jennifer Livett, and Donna Marcus were astute and attentive early readers; I can't say how grateful I am to them all. Zora Simic generously read and commented on historical aspects of chapter 1. Helen Pringle provided valuable genealogical advice, as did Ann McMahon. I also had genealogical help from the staff at the Kiama Family History Centre, while Bruce Cain from the Kempsey Family History Group shared valuable local historical knowledge. Further afield, I am grateful for information from Roberto Barzanti, Francesca Finetti, Chiara Iacomelli, and Silvia Roncucci in Siena. And I want to thank those friends and colleagues whose generosity and hospitality and wonderful company helped me learn how to navigate New York from my first visit, in particular Nic Birns and Isabella Smalera Birns, Lisabeth During, and Elizabeth A. Wilson.

My research for this book has been supported over the years by funding from various institutions, including an Australian Research Council Discovery grant that enabled me to do the earliest archival work, together with periods of sabbatical leave and research support from the School of the Arts and Media in the Faculty of Arts, Design and Architecture at the University of New South Wales, Sydney. In 2014 I was a visiting scholar at the Oxford Centre for Life Writing, Wolfson College, Oxford University; this was before I had embarked on the biography, but it was a formative experience all the same. In 2018 as I began work on this book, I was a visiting scholar in the Department of English and Comparative Literature at Columbia University.

I have the great good fortune to have Shirley Hazzard's agent and literary executor, Lynn Nesbit, as my agent, and wish to thank her for her support for my work. I have also been unbelievably fortunate with my publishers and wish to thank Jonathan Galassi and Lennie Goodings for having faith in an untried biographer and for their enthusiasm and guidance throughout. I'm also immensely grateful to the impeccable Farrar, Straus and Giroux editorial, design, and production teams for all their work to make this book a reality.

Above all, I want to thank my husband, Bruce Allen, for throwing himself into the world of literary archives with his customary enthusiasm, and for helping make the travelling fun. I am indebted to him and to our daughter, Zoia Olubas, for their patience, good humour, and love. The early months of my work on this book were shadowed by my sister Katharine's illness, and, finally, I want to acknowledge the extraordinary contribution to arranging her ongoing care made by our friend Lindy Weare, which gave me space to write.

# INDEX

Abels, Cyrilly, 313

Abrahams, William, 280, 295

L'Absinthe lunch, 456–57

Abzug, Bella, 335

Acropolis, 237, 261

Acton, Harold, 118, 302; Circolo Tessitore and, 334; Cocteau and, 292; death of, 419, 424; dinner with, 296; English and Italian culture exemplified by, 294; snobbery of, 292

Adelaide Festival Writers' Week, 331

African American spirituals, 228

"After a Journey" (Hardy), 66

Aléramo, Sibilla, 153

Alleanza nazionale, 158

Alston, Frances, 458–59, 460–61

American Academy of Arts and Letters, 230, 343, 355, 461

Amnesty International, 328

*Ancient Shore, The* (Hazzard, Shirley), 462

Anderson, Don, 383

Anderson, Hedli, 123

Angell, Ernest, 132

"Another Storyteller's Story" (Steegmuller, Francis), 229

*Antony and Cleopatra* (Shakespeare), 429

*Apartment, The*, 122

*Apollinaire* (Steegmuller, Francis), 236, 256, 354

Apollinaire, Guillaume, 197, 256, 354; Braque interviewed about, 238; Hart-Davis and, 240; Hazzard, Shirley, reciting, 249; Section d'Or and, 210; Steegmuller, Francis, and, 235, 236, 239, 240, 304

Aprile, Lily, 143, 154

Archibald, Elizabeth, 10, 153, 324, 429

Arendt, Hannah, 322

Armstrong, Gillian, 351

Aronson, Steven M. L., 193, 270, 335

Auden, W. H.: Arendt on, 322; death of, 321–22; on meeting, 118; memorial for, 322; poetry and, 322; on stage, 123–24

Australia: Adelaide Festival Writers' Week, 331; Boyer Lectures, 367–68, 381–83; *Breaker Morant* and, 370; break with, 385; colonial origins, 21–23; connections to, 368–69; criticisms of, 25; disconnection from, 454–55; Glenleigh, 44–46; insularity of, 22; Kempsey, 30–31; last visit to, 453–55; "Letter from Australia," 332, 368; Miles Franklin Award, 449–50, 453; modernity rush of, 23–24; Mosman, 25, 27, 38–39; National Gallery of Australia, 371; nationalism in, 367–68, 382; New Zealand aligned with, 94; non-British immigrants and, 109; populations, 21–22; reputation in,

Australia (*cont.*)
454; return to, 82–83, 265, 315, 331–32;
Tasmania, 297; in *The Transit of
Venus*, 23; unappreciated in, 381–83;
vernacular of, 369–70; White Australia
Policy, 21, 22, 265; World War II and,
43–44; *see also* Sydney, Australia
Australian Academy of Arts and Letters,
454
Australian Commonwealth Literary
Fund, 379
Australian writers in school curriculum, 51

*Bachelors, The* (Spark), 252
Bail, Murray, 368, 369, 371–74
"Ballad of Reading Gaol, The" (Wilde),
151
Banville, John, 447
BAOR, *see* British Army of the Rhine
Barbette (drag aerialist), 296
Barnes, Cathy, 435
Barnes, Hamlin, 265, 435
Barnes, Julian, 415, 428
Barnes, Robbie, 435
Barnes, Robert "Bob": death of, 311;
Hazzard, Valerie, and, 124–26; White
Australia Policy and, 265
Barnes, Valerie: animosity toward
sister, 266–67; death of, 464; living in
Sydney, 265; on possessions of mother,
265–66; suicide of son, 435
Barracco, Maurizio and Mirella, 356
Barrett, Marvin, 268, 434
Barrett, Mary Ellin, 268, 418, 434
Barrett, Sara, 399, 460
Barry, Claud, 62
Barzanti, Roberto, 160, 165
Barzun, Jacques, 205, 397, 430
*Bay of Noon, The* (Hazzard, Shirley):
apartments in, 148–51; brother-sister
desire and, 298–99; Capri and, 315;
conversation used in, 283; desires
crossing in, 298; hepatitis and, 155;
Maxwell, William, on, 300; myth and
comedy in, 299–300; Naples described
in, 146–48; narrative dissolves in, 300;

National Book Award nomination
for, 4; opening of, 141; published,
298; reviews, 301; Rickard and, 110;
siblings idealised in, 384; time sense
and, 148, 300; Villa Mazziotti and,
150–51; Virago securing rights to, 433;
words and, 300
BCOF, *see* British Commonwealth
Occupation Force
Beauty Point, 43
Beauvoir, Simone de, 123
Beaux Arts hotel, 191
Becker, Ginny, 173–74, 255, 302
Becker, John, 173–74, 255
"Bee, the Harp, the Mouse, and the
Bumclock, The" (Irish story), 229
Bell, Caro (fictional character), 11, 23, 26,
27, 37, 41, 42, 45, 46, 49, 137, 251–52,
337–40, 384, 445, 465
Bellow, Saul, 366–67
Berenson, Bernard, 226, 285
Berenson, Mary, 286
Beresford, Bruce, 370
Bergonzi, Bernard, 279
*Best of Everything, The* (Jaffe), 122
Beston, John, 341
Bilgrami, Akeel, 339, 402
Binswanger, Clara, 227, 239, 256, 257
Birstein, Ann, 230, 269
Black, Bert, 382
Blake, Channing, 372
Blanchett, Cate, 449–50
Bloom, Harold, 4
Blotner, Joseph, 412
*Blue Poles* (Pollock), 371
Borghese Gardens, 260
Bosis, Adolfo de, 158
Bosis, Lauro de, 158–59
Boudin, Kathy, 394
Boudin, Leonard, 394–95
Bowen, Elizabeth: death of, 322;
friendship with, 192, 296; Hazzard,
Shirley, compared with, 5, 279; as
literary luminary, 268
Bowen, Marjorie, 48
Boyer Lectures, 367–68, 381–83

Bradley, Jenny, 224
Braque, Georges, 238, 373
Bray, Barbara, 414, 438
*Breaker Morant*, 370
Breunig, LeRoy and Ersi, 262, 430, 440
Bridgeman, Reginald, 283
Brinnin, John Malcolm, 342
Brinton, Alice, 442–43
British Army of the Rhine (BAOR), 88
British Commonwealth Occupation Force
    (BCOF), 56
British Museum, 113
British Parliamentary Group for World
    Government, 319–20
Brodsky, Joseph, 430
Brogan, Hugh, 173, 258
Brombert, Victor, 230–31, 353, 449
Brooke-Rose, Christine, 192
Browning, Robert, 418–19
Bunshaft, Gordon, 227
Burgess, Anthony, 356
Burgess, Guy, 119
Burney, Christopher, 286–87
Burnham, Jonathan, 401, 407, 408, 418
Byron, George Gordon, 329

Cain, Julien, 286
"Call for UN Reform, A" (Hazzard,
    Shirley), 310
Callil, Carmen, 433
cancer, 237–39, 244, 247, 260, 317, 412
*Canopic*, SS, 203–204
"Canton More Far" (Hazzard, Shirley), 64
Capon, Edmund and Joanna, 368, 369
Capri, Italy: apartment purchased in,
    431; Archibald on, 324; *The Bay of
    Noon* and, 315; Bellow in, 366–67;
    Chatwin in, 390; citizenship bestowed,
    441–42; community and, 323; daily
    observations of, 360–61; descriptions
    of, 316, 321; Dunstan in, 389–90;
    expatriatism and, 441; Fahy visiting,
    363–64; first visits to, 152–53; on habit
    and ritual of, 362; Merrill at, 403–404;
    Monte San Michele in, 404–405; priest
    controversy in, 325–26; Ristorante

da Gemma, 407; storms on, 357–58;
    topographical world of, 409–10;
    tourism in, 153; Via Sopramonte
    apartment in, 359; visitor interruptions
    in, 389–90; work interruptions in,
    389–93; *see also Greene on Capri*
Capri tiles, traditional, 433
Caravaggio, 363
Carr, Bob, 435
Carroll, Lewis, 174
Carter, Angela, 347
Carter, Elliott, 401
Carter, Jimmy, 350
Cato, Bob, 434
cats, 410
Catskills, 135–36
Cavendish-Bentinck, Margaret Anne, 404
cemetery, *see* pet cemetery; Saint Mary's
    cemetery
Centro Caprense Ignazio Cerio, 461
Cerio, Laetitia, 324–25, 434
Chanel, Coco, 286
Chapman, Norma, 312
*Château, The* (Maxwell, William), 230, 273
Chatwin, Bruce, 390
Cheever, John, 233, 241
Chelsea, England, 290–91
*Chère Maître*, 438
Chiang Kai-shek, 72
childhood: homes, 18–20; remote location
    of, 20–21; sea and, 25; Sydney and,
    25–27; Vedeniapine, Alexis, on own,
    68; "Woollahra Road" and, 18–20, 32
*Christening Party* (Steegmuller, Francis),
    237
Christoff, Boris, 270, 315
Circolo Tessitore, Il, 334
Clark, Eleanor: death of, 430; friendship
    with, 271–72; Hellman and, 269;
    memorial for, 430–31; on Port-Cros,
    282; *Rome and a Villa* by, 228
Clarke, Patricia, 314; friendship with,
    176; Lyall and, 176, 259
*Cliffs of Fall* (Hazzard, Shirley), 138,
    254, 256, 279
Cloetta, Yvonne, 438, 439, 440

Clyde, Vander, *see* Barbette

*Cocteau* (Steegmuller, Francis): French translation of, 322–23; National Book Award for, 304; *Professional Secrets* and, 303–304; published, 303; sexuality and, 304–305; work begun on, 280–81

Cocteau, Jean: Acton and, 292; Barbette and, 296; Bridgeman and, 283; friends of, 286; Steegmuller, Francis, and, 12, 304

Cohen, Mort, 174, 254

Colavolpe, Giulio, 398, 460

Cold War, 88–89

Coleman, Leo, 241, 431

Collier, Michael, 398, 399, 436, 456–57, 461

Columbia University, 3, 204–205, 309

Columbia University Rare Book and Manuscript Library, 3

Connors, Joseph, 448

Conquest, Robert, 335

Conrad, Joseph, 455

Constable, Giles, 354, 416

Cook, Edwin Crescence, 32

Cook, Whitfield, 369, 425–26

Cook Strait, New Zealand, 90

Cooper, A. W., 143

Cooper, Chris, 184; anti-Americanism and, 309; Foreign Office examination and, 86; on Hong Kong story, 411; letters to, 85–86; on nuptials, 100, 107; at Oxford, 86–87; on professionalism, 121; Vedeniapine, Alexis, and, 66–67, 71–72, 114–15, 352, 413; Wellington correspondences, 95–96

Cooper, Douglas: background, 231; Léger art and, 283; reputation of, 282; Steegmuller, Francis, letter to, 238–39

Coppola, Mario, 441–42, 461

*Coriolanus*, 123

Cornog, Evan: circle of friends and, 397, 400–401; on Elliott, 369; love for, 334; Steegmuller, Francis, gift to, 431–32; on Steegmuller, Francis, 402

Cortesi, Mary Williams, 193

*Countenance of Truth* (Hazzard, Shirley), 335, 396, 401, 411

Cousins, Norman, 319

Craft, Robert, 305, 307

Craig, Gordon, 322

Crea, Enzo, 451

Croce, Benedetto, 403

Cunningham, Valentine, 341

Curtin, John, 46

Curtiss, Mina, 267–68

Daniel, Howard: background, 127–28; in Geneva with, 134; Goldschmidt, Arthur "Tex," and, 130; secret relationship with, 127, 129–30; social connections via, 130; Vivante family and, 156; wartime exploits, 128–29

"Darkling Thrush" (Hardy), 412

Davis-Goff, Annabel, 436; background, 400; Ford interview and, 462; Maxwell, William, and, 400; at Maxwell birthdays, 399, 400; money management by, 459; on monopolised conversations, 401

D-Day sixtieth anniversary, 449

Decter, Midge, 318–19

*Defeat of an Ideal* (Hazzard, Shirley), 318–19

de Kretser, Michelle, 339, 368, 447, 454

Depression, in Sydney, 24–25

Dick, Henry K., 204–205

Dick, Margaret, 348

Didion, Joan, 7

Docker, John, 382

Doerner, Max, 140

*Don Juan* (Byron), 329

Dora (fictional character), 318, 346

d'Orléans, Anne Marie Louise, 232

D'Orsi, Lina and Emanuela, 398

Douglas, Norman, 152

Draper, Ruth, 158, 162

*Drawings by Beatrice Stein*, 238

Driscoll, Helen (fictional character), 74, 80–81, 82–83, 91–93, 96, 384, 443, 445

Duchamp, Marcel, 209–10, 212, 216

Duff, Mountstuart Grant, 117

Dufy, Raoul, 212, 217
Duncan, Isadora, 39, 240, 282, 322, 382
Duncan, Raymond, 282
Dunstan, Don, 368, 369, 389–90
Dutch Bronze Lion medal, 69–70
Dutton, Geoffrey, 368–69, 370
Dutton, Ninette, 368, 369
Dyer, Geoff, 339

East Fifty-First Street apartment, 194
École Normale Supérieure, 309
Edel, Leon, 415, 422
Edgar, Suzanne, 280
Egyptian travels project, 307
"800 biting words" (Hazzard, Shirley), 326
Eliot, T. S., 159, 292
Elliott, Sumner Locke, 368; Australian
    vernacular used by, 369–70;
    background, 369; death of, 412;
    *Fairyland* by, 369
Ellison, Ralph: at cottage in Vermont,
    222–23; death of, 419; at Fifth Avenue
    office, 223–24; Guggenheimer, Ida,
    and, 221–22; *Invisible Man* by, 222;
    Steegmuller, Francis, and, 221–24;
    Stein, Adam, and, 227–28
*Encyclopedia of the Social Sciences*, 211
England: at British Museum, 113;
    Chelsea, 290–91; Hazzard, Kit, return
    to, 314–15, 347; Hazzard, Shirley, on
    London, 253–54; London, 253–54;
    Oxford, 86–87, 115; Southampton, 115,
    204, 314, 347; *Strathaird* bound for,
    109–10; travel delays to, 97–98; two-
    week stay in, 113–15; Vivante family
    in, 161–63; *see also specific cities*
*English Poetry* (Vivante, Leone), 159
Ennis, Lawrence, 24
Eta Jima island, Japan, 56–57
"Even If You Weren't My Father"
    (Sbarbaro), 411–12
*Evening of the Holiday, The* (Hazzard,
    Shirley): atmosphere of, 277;
    complications throughout, 277–78;
    film rights for, 352; happiness in, 246;
    melancholy of, 263–64; plot, 279;

published, 263; reviews, 278–80; time
    thwarted in, 278; title changed to, 250
Ewan, James, 46
Exley, Peter, 411
expatriatism, 441
Experimental College, 206–207
Exposition Internationale des Arts et
    Techniques dans la Vie Moderne, 212
*Eye of the Storm, The* (White, Patrick),
    332–33

Fahy, Everett, 426; background, 333; Bail
    and, 372, 373; in Capri, 363–64; money
    management by, 459; Pope-Hennessy
    funeral, 424; as terminally ill, 463–64;
    walk home with, 436
*Fairyland* (Elliott), 369
Fallowfield, Julie, 433
family life: difficulties in, 265–67,
    287–88, 311–12; extrication from,
    65; Hong Kong photo, 80; misery
    of, 27–28, 94–95; rifts in, 80; status
    elevated in, 114; at Wellington, 94
Fantastici, Agostino, 156
Feast of San Costanzo, 407
*Fécondité* (Redon), 220
feminism, 132, 339
ffennell, George, 136, 422
*First Stone, The* (Garner), 401
Fitzgerald, F. Scott, 215
Flanders, Lowell, 394
Flanner, Janet, 397
*Flaubert's Parrot* (Barnes, Julian), 415
Flaubert, Gustave, 214; as aesthete,
    233; Brombert on, 230–31; letters of,
    351, 375, 414; Maxwell, William, on,
    233–34; Sand and, 414, 438; White,
    Patrick, compared with, 375–76;
    writing about, 307, 413
*Flaubert and Madame Bovary*
    (Steegmuller, Francis), 215, 233
*Flaubert in Egypt* (Steegmuller, Francis),
    317, 354
"Flaubert in Egypt" (Warren, Robert
    Penn), 271
*Flaws in the Glass* (White, Patrick), 375

Fleming, John: death of, 441; friendship with, 293; lunch with, 434; on sexuality of Steegmuller, Francis, 240–41

floor tiles, *see* Capri tiles, traditional

Florence, floods in, 285, 292

*Folded Leaf, The* (Maxwell, William), 273

Fondazione Napoli Novantanove (Naples 99), 356–57

Ford, Richard, 462

Fould, Eugène, 226

Fould-Springer, Poppy, 189

Fox, Paula, 270, 273, 426, 430

France: culture of, 205–206, 212–13; Port-Cros island, 282; *see also* French language

Fraser, Malcolm, 330–31

Fremantle, Anne: background of, 117–18; *Defeat of an Ideal* and, 318–19; UN job of, 118; Mehta and, 189

Fremantle, Christopher, 117–18

French, Paul, 64

French language: *Cocteau* translated to, 322–23; *The Great Fire* published in, 456; "The Owl and the Pussycat" translated to, 422

friends, *see specific individuals*

Galantière, Lewis, 230

Galassi, Jonathan, 9, 343, 397, 433, 456

Galiani, Ferdinando, 414, 415

*Gallipoli Memories* (Mackenzie), 323–24

*Garden of Peonies* (Hart), 65–66

Gargiulo, Anne, 153, 434

Garner, Helen, 401, 454–55

Gauss Seminars, Princeton, 353

Geist, Sidney, 236

Geneva, Switzerland, 134

Georgian farmhouse, 96–97

Géricault, Théodore, 232

Gibbon, Edward, 392–93

Gigante, Marcello, 358–59

Gill, Brendan, 183–84

Gilmore, Myron and Sheila, 285

Giroud, Vincent, 240

Giroux, Robert, 237, 240

Glenleigh, Australia, 44–46

Gloucester Hotel, Hong Kong, 60

Goldfrank, Edna, 210, 224, 225

Goldschmidt, Ann and Arthur, Jr., 132, 133

Goldschmidt, Arthur "Tex," 121; affair, 132–37; affair ended, 137–39; background, 131–32; in Catskills with, 135–36; Daniel and, 130; encouragement of, 176; as first lover, 131; "The Picnic" and, 185–88; "A Place in the Country" and, 186, 188; as progressive, 132

Goldstein, Ann: Cornog friendship and, 334; on Hazzard, Shirley, intellect, 401; Steegmuller, Francis, gift to, 431–32

Goodings, Lennie, 433

Gorra, Michael, 339

Goudeket, Maurice, 284

Gowing, Lawrence, 335

*Grande Mademoiselle, La* (Steegmuller, Francis), 232, 234

Gravino, Lily, 420, 455, 458

Gray, Cleve, 220

Grazia, Sebastian de, 194, 254–55

*Great Fire, The* (Hazzard, Shirley): awards, 448–50; cover of, 352; dialogue of, 5–6; end changed, 445; Eta Jima island and, 56–57; experience of writing, 444–45; firewood pile in, 447; Hecht on, 445; Hiroshima and, 57; hotel in, 91; loss and, 344–45; love affair in, 446; love story and, 7–8, 443–44; as masterly, 445–46; McClatchy, J. D., on, 6–7; Mediterranean described in, 110; Miles Franklin Award, 5, 449–50, 453; National Book Award, 4, 448; New Zealand/Australia aligned in, 94; progress on, 443; prose of, 446–47; published in French, 456; response to, 447–48; reviews, 4, 5; sex and, 81, 241; siblings idealised in, 384; temporal nuances of, 445–46; Thompson Street house and, 92–93; tone of, 410–11; tour and book signings, 448–49; UK launch, 449; Vedeniapine, Alexis, and, 410; Wellington described, 90–91;

Wellington provinciality, 93–94; White Australia policy and, 22

Greece, 261–62

Green, Alan: correspondences to Wellington, 95–96; on farm living, 97; Foreign Office examination and, 86; on Hazzard, Shirley, in Shanghai, 64–65; in Hong Kong, 63; on nuptials, 99–100; at Oxford, 86–87; Oxford visit with, 115; tuberculosis and, 95; Vedeniapine, Alexis, and, 66–67

Greenberg, Martin, 270

Greene, Graham, 123; Browning poem and, 418–19; death of, 412; Egyptian travels project and, 307; friendship with, 325, 438–39; memoir of, 418–19, 420; priest controversy and, 325–26; Renaissance drama essay by, 49

*Greene on Capri* (Hazzard, Shirley): defense of, 439–40; published, 438; rancor surrounding, 438–39; reviews, 382, 439; *The Viper of Milan* and, 48; Warren, Red, quoted in, 271

Greenwich, Connecticut, 202

Guggenheim Fellowship, 326

Guggenheim, Peggy, 283

Guggenheimer, Clara, 208

Guggenheimer, Ida, 209, 221–22

*Gulag Archipelago* (Solzhenitsyn), 326–27

Gurganus, Allan, 427

Guterman, Norbert, 213–14, 240

Hall, Bill, 417–18

*Hamlet* (Shakespeare), 393, 400

Hammarskjöld, Dag, 120

Hardwick, Elizabeth, 334

Hardy, Thomas, 66, 271, 412, 431

"Harold" (Hazzard, Shirley), 180–81, 462

Harold Vursell Award, 343

Harrison, Robert, 9, 359–60, 425, 457

Harrower, Elizabeth, 351; Australian Commonwealth Literary Fund and, 379; background, 312; Bail and, 373; correspondence with, 312–13; falling-out with, 379–81; Hazzard, Kit, and, 312, 313, 314, 317, 320–21; hearing aid and, 321; introductions by, 332; in Italy, 379–80; letters burned by, 348; Maclean and, 380; meeting, 316; pension application and, 320–21; political discussions with, 330–31; Steegmuller, Francis, and, 313; travel reluctance of, 377–79; *The Watch Tower* by, 312; White, Patrick, and, 378–79, 381

Hart, Henry H., 65–66

Hart-Davis, Rupert, 240

Hawke, Bob, 370

Hazzard, Catherine "Kit": birth of, 34; on board *Queen Elizabeth*, 115; books read by, 52; as capricious, 126; in Chelsea, 290–91; Christmas shared with, 317; Daniel and, 127–30; daughters pitted against by, 297–98; death of, 383, 384–85; divorce and, 126–27; Dora character as, 318, 346; early careers of, 36; early life, 34–36; England return of, 314–15; family trust and, 346–47; Harrower and, 312, 313, 314, 317, 320–21; Hazzard, Reg, battling with, 94; Hazzard, Shirley, on, 35, 36–37; Hazzard, Valerie, on, 297–98; on Hazzard, Shirley, engagement, 256–57; hearing aid for, 321; help cries from, 134–35; injured neck and arm, 315; job search, 284; letter burning, 348; lost letter, 102; marriage breaking down, 124–25; marriage of, 27–28, 124–25; mental state, 36–38, 311–12, 313–14, 320; methedrine and, 313–14; money and, 37–38; in nursing home, 348; pension and, 320–21; possessions held by, 265–66; Scots background, 34–35; Spark and, 192–93; Stanton Road house sale and, 42; stroke suffered by, 347–48; suicide threats/attempts, 125, 291; Sydney Harbour bridge and, 24; in Tasmania, 297; uprooted, 290; war endured by, 47

Hazzard, Charles John, 29–30

Hazzard, Margaret, 317

Hazzard, Mary, 30–31

Hazzard, Pauline Amilee, 29–30, 31–32

Hazzard, Reginald "Reg": background, 28–29; birth date, 30; birthplace, 28–29, 31, 33; books read, 52; death of, 317; divorce and, 126–27; early life, 28–34; hatchet buried with, 265; Hazzard, Kit, battling with, 94; Hazzard, Shirley, on, 38; ill health, 287–88; at Kempsey, 30–31; marriage, 27–28, 124–25; military service, 33–34; at Ministry of Munitions, 47; Mosman house and, 38–39; as orphan, 28, 29–30; in Papua New Guinea, 34; at Rabaul, 34; schooling of, 33, 34; Stanton Road house sold by, 42; Sydney Harbour bridge and, 24; trade commissioner posting of, 54; World War II end and, 53; Wycherley affair, 65, 124; yachts and, 47–48

Hazzard, Shirley: academy, relations with, 354–55; on Acton, 419; aging of, 437; aloneness of, 141–42, 429, 432, 436–37, 442–43, 452, 466; animosity toward sister, 266–67; Apollinaire recited by, 249; art tastes, 371–73; Australia left by, 52; authority of, 402; Bail and, 371–74; Barnes, Robert "Bob", and, 124–26; Barrett, Mary Ellin, on, 268; bedridden, 463; Bellow and, 366–67; bereavement, 425–26; bookshops frequented by, 49, 94–95; Boyer Lectures, 367–68; as bully, 41; Burnham on, 401; care burden of, 417–18; childhood, 18–21, 25–27, 32; circles of friends, 268–73, 292–95, 397–98; as civilised, 10–11; Clark memorial, 430–31; cognitive decline, 456, 458, 460, 461, 463; colonial life, 61–62; conversations monopolised by, 401–402; customs and, 407; death of, 464–65; described, 9–11; early writing efforts, 50–51; Elliott and, 369–70; emotional tenors of, 101; engagement, 256–57; England travel delays and, 97–98; erudition of, 397; final public

appearance, 463; frailty of, 460–62, 463; on Fremantle, Anne, 118; funeral of child impressions, 303; Garner on novels of, 454–55; generosity of, 400–401; at Glenleigh, 44–46; in Greece, 261–62; Harrower and, 312–13, 316; on Hazzard, Kit, 35, 36–37; on Hecht, 451; Hellman and, 349–50; hip fracture, 460–61; at Hiroshima, 57–58; Hirsch on, 399–400; Hong Kong described by, 60–61; as humane, 397–98; idealism of, 116; identity resolution of, 262–63; impeccable grooming, 9–10; intelligence unit job, 62–65; Italian studied by, 109; in Japan, 54–58; Jessup, Philip, and, 327; Junior Fortnightly group and, 393–94; Kazin on, 269–70; lassitude of, 457–58; on life history, 437; literary criticism and, 354; literature defining, 48–50, 51–52; on London, 253–54; on loneliness, 141–42; long friendships of, 403; on loss, 264; love and, 7–8, 122; Lowell story, 268; Macdonald remembrance by, 348–49; Marigliano, Salvatore, and, 405–407, 421; marriage of, 11–13, 197–98; marriage plans, 96–97, 101; maturation of, 114; at Merrill memorial, 427–28; miscarriage and hysterectomy, 267; money management, 459–60, 461; on Moravia, 225, 281–82; Morgan, Randolph, and, 238, 403, 414–15, 419, 423; in Morocco, 258; mortality and, 465–66; Mosman house and, 38–39; mother grieved by, 384–85; music and, 123; Naples locals and, 408–409; on New York City, 115–16; *New Yorker* affairs of the heart, 182–84; nonfiction turn, 308; novel writing distractions, 310–11; observational skills, 10, 149, 397, 402, 407; past and, 9; political antipathy, 308–10; political drama and, 329–31; political insight developed by, 73; politics/love connection and, 122; private scholarship and, 355; on professions in novels, 288–89; protest

and, 309, 350–51; psychoanalysis and, 259, 391; public awareness of, 8–9; public letters and, 350–51; public themes and, 328–31; at Queenwood School, 39–41; reading aloud, 392–93; on Reg, 38; return to Australia, 82–83; romantic affairs in New York, 127–34; sailing loathed by, 48; at St. George Hotel, 91; sanatorium trip, 84–85; on Sand, 414; Scheick and, 354–55; secretarial college and, 87; serenity of, 11; sex and, 80–81; on Sitwell, 293–94; socialism and, 269; on Solaia, 164–65, 166, 167–68; Sorrento poem by, 432; in Spain, 250–51; Spark and, 244, 248–49, 301–302; spontaneity of, 402–403; at Stanton Road house, 38–40, 42; Steegmuller, Francis, sexuality and, 240–41; Stein, Martin, and, 391; on Strozzi, 294; stylised correspondence with, 245; suicide contemplated by, 138; TAA appointment for, 116–17; *Taiping* ship and, 54–55; on Trillings, 294–95; UN affairs of the heart, 121–22; UN criticised by, 289, 308, 310–11, 318–20, 326–28, 335–36, 393–94; as unhappy, 41–42; U.S. citizenship, 329; Vedeniapine, Alexis, attraction of, 66–67; Vedeniapine, Alexis, engagement ending for, 104–107; Vedeniapine, Alexis, revisited, 352–53; on Vedeniapine, Alexis, 106; Vedeniapine, Alexis, romance with, 73–76, 84; Vedeniapine, Cynthia, on, 107–108; on Vivante, Elena, 156, 157, 165, 166–67, 168; Waldheim and, 395–96; wedding of, 257; Wellington correspondences, 95–96; Wellington provinciality and, 93–94; White, Patrick, and, 373, 374–77; Wickenden relationship with, 133–34; Wilkinson on, 9, 10, 11, 398–99, 402, 460; *see also specific topics; specific works*
Hazzard, Valerie: Barnes, Robert "Bob", and, 124–26; birth of, 38; engagement of, 125; estrangement from, 383–84; on Hazzard, Kit, inconsistencies, 297–98; in Hong Kong, 65; in Honolulu, 347; marriage of, 126; mother's mental illness impacting, 311–12; Paramount Pictures job of, 124; pregnancy/ miscarriage of, 136–37; sanatorium trip, 84–85; tuberculosis and, 79–80, 84–85; *see also* Barnes, Valerie
Healey, Cathie, 442–43
Heaney, Seamus, 398
Hecht, Anthony, 341, 445, 451
Hellman, Lillian, 269, 319, 349–50, 367
Hemlock Society, 392
hepatitis, 154–55
Herculaneum, Italy, 152, 154
*Hermes* magazine, 128
Heywood Hill bookshop, 323–24
*Hibou et La Poussiquette, Le* (Steegmuller, Francis), 235, 240
Highton, Violet, 107
hip fracture, 460–61
Hiroshima, Japan, 54–55, 56, 57
Hirsch, Edward, 273, 399, 456–57
*History of the Decline and Fall of the Roman Empire* (Gibbon), 392–93
Hong Kong: Central District, 59–60; as centre of earth, 94; departure from, 80–81; Exley and, 411; family photo in, 80; Gloucester Hotel, 60; Hazzard, Shirley, describing, 60–61; Hazzard, Valerie, in, 65; *New Yorker* story set in, 411; official/social functions in, 61–62; postwar, 58–60; Reg as trade commissioner for, 54; return to, 451–52; Stokes describing, 58–60
Honolulu, Hawaii, 347
Honour, Hugh, 240–41, 293, 434, 448
Hooten, Peter, 403–404
Hotel de Perey, 218
Hotel Vesuvio, 142–43
Howard, Richard, 234
Hughes, Robert, 370–71
Hyman, Stanley, 225

Indigenous Australians, 22–23
Institute for Defense Analyses, 309

Intelligence Reform Act, 350
International Congress of Papyrology,
    358–59
"In Time of Pestilence" (Nashe), 465–66
*Invisible Man* (Ellison), 222
*In Youth Is Pleasure* (Welch), 123
Italy: departure from, 169–70;
    expatriatism and, 441; Florence
    floods, 285, 292; Harrower in, 379–80;
    Herculaneum, 152; I Tatti villa in,
    285–86; Lake Nemi, 302; Montalcino,
    254; Monteliscai, 264–65; Rome,
    225, 228; self-rescue in, 18; Solaia in,
    156–57; Sorrento, 432; Sperlonga, 255;
    *see also* Capri, Italy; Naples, Italy
I Tatti villa, 285–86
"I Wake Alone" (Sbarbaro), 411–12

Jackson, Frederick Huth, 117
"Jaded Muse, A" (Hazzard, Shirley), 354
Jaffe, Rona, 122
James, Henry, 404
James, William, 368
Jansen, Edmund, 189
Japan, 54–58
Jardine, Penelope, 241
Jarves, James Jackson, 221, 224, 225, 231
*Java-Java* (Steegmuller, Francis), 206
Jennings, Kate, 434
Jenny (fictional character), 143, 146–151,
    155, 169, 283, 298–300, 384
Jessup, Philip, 327
Jessup, Rebecca, 430
Jillett, Neil, 279–80
Johnson, Samuel, 397
Jolly, Alice, 6
Junior Fortnightly group, 393–94

Kaye, Danny, 271
Kazin, Alfred, 230, 269–70, 309, 319
Keene, Donald, 355, 380, 381, 434, 437,
    457
Keenleyside, Hugh, 117
Keith, David, *see* Steegmuller, Francis
Kempsey, Australia, 30–31
Keneally, Tom, 22, 330

Kennan, George, 280
Kennedy, John F., 257–58
Kennedy, William, 234
Keppert, L. V., 279
Kheel, Theodore, 451
Kiernan, Frances, 333, 334
Kindersley, Richard, 66
King, Stephen, 4
Kit, *see* Hazzard, Catherine "Kit"
Kitt, Eartha, 309
Knight, Carlo, 356, 357, 358, 366
Knight, Ella, 366
Knopf publishing, 295
Korabetski, Lidia (fictional character),
    119
Kramer, Jane, 395, 396

La Capria, Raffaele, 225
Lake Nemi, Italy, 302
Lange, David, 370
Lask, Thomas, 336–37
Laurençin, Marie, 235
"Lead, Kindly Light" (Newman), 110
Lear, Edward, 235
Lecceto monastery, 302
lectures: Boyer Lectures, 367–68, 381–83;
    Gauss Seminars, 353; Sydney Institute,
    434
Lefebvre, Henri, 213, 214
Lefferts, Barney, 183
Léger, Fernand, 283
Leggett, Jack, 268
Lehmann-Haupt, Christopher, 301, 318
Leigh Fermor, Patrick, 189–90
Lenox Hill Bookstore, 448
Leonard, John, 340–41
Leopardi, Giacomo, 151–52, 250, 438
Lester, George and Sophie, 173
"Let Me Confess" sonnet (Shakespeare),
    134
"Letter from Australia" (Hazzard,
    Shirley), 332, 368
"Letter From Venice" (Steegmuller,
    Francis), 305–306
Levin, Phyllis Lee, 393–94, 398
Levy, Andrea, 449

Lewin, Ann, 368
Lewis, Ann, 434
Lie, Trygve, 120
Ligthart, Jan, 171–73, 177, 182
Lippmann, Walter, 293
Lisieux Private Hospital, 84–85
literary criticism, views on, 354
lizards, 410
Llewellyn, Caro, 462
Lodge, David, 439
London, England, 253–54
"Lonely Word, The" (Hazzard, Shirley), 353
Lovat Dickson, Rache, 190
Lovell, Patricia, 351–52
Lowell, Robert, 268
LP records, 123
*Lucia di Lammermoor*, 8
Luker, Norman, 118–19, 144
Lyall, Archibald: Acton on, 292; on author photo, 254; background, 174–75; Clarke and, 176, 259; death of, 259; "Nothing in Excess" and, 176; *People in Glass Houses* and, 175–76

MacArthur, Douglas, 47
Macdonald, Dwight, 174; Columbia students protest and, 309; death of, 348–49; help of, 177, 178–79; on Mead, 336; on Solaia, 164; Ved and, 189; Vivante, Arturo, and, 169
Mackenzie, Compton, 323–24
MacKenzie, Rachel, 179–80, 182, 191–92
MacLaine, Shirley, 122
Maclean, Alan, 278, 314, 351, 380, 448
Macmillan Publishers, 190
MacNeice, Louis, 123
Macpherson, Jessie, 35–36
*Madame Bovary* (Flaubert), 232–34
Mailer, Norman, 269
Mallon, Michael, 401, 423, 424, 425, 456
Mallon, Thomas, 6
Malouf, David, 368, 369, 453, 454
Manhattan House, 196, 227, 228, 259, 264, 433

"Man Who Married the Moon, The" (Indian forest story), 229
Mao Tse-tung, 72–73
Mariano, Nicky, 448
Marigliano, Pasquale, 406
Marigliano, Salvatore, 405–407, 421, 429
Marr, David, 374–75, 376–77
marriage: Cooper, Chris, on pending, 100, 107; delay of, 100–102; Green on pending, 99–100; Hazzard, Kit, and Hazzard, Reg, 27–28, 124–25; of Hazzard, Shirley, 11–13, 197–98; of Hazzard, Valerie, 126; Marigliano, Pasquale, wedding, 406; plans for, 96–97, 101; Reg gives permission for, 100–101; Steegmuller, Beatrice, on, 238; Steegmuller, Francis, and Stein, Beatrice, 211
Marseilles, 110
Martin, Harold H., 153–54
Martin, Stanley, 203–204
Masefield, John, 49
Massine, Léonide, 288
*Matter of Iodine, A* (Keith), 231
Maubert, Simonne, 219
Maugham, Somerset, 226
*Maupassant* (Steegmuller, Francis), 226
Maupassant, Guy de, 221, 268, 304
Maurois, André, 232, 284
Maxwell, Emily: birthday tradition of, 398–400; death of, 440; friendship with, 272–73, 436; Hirsch on, 273
Maxwell, William, 18; background, 177; on *The Bay of Noon*, 300; birthday tradition of, 398–400; on *Cliffs of Fall*, 256; Davis-Goff and, 400; death of, 440; first payment from, 178–79; on Flaubert, 233–34; friendship with, 229–30, 272–73, 436; on *Madame Bovary* translation, 233–34; meeting, 179; memorials for, 440–41; on *New Yorker* debut, 179; Ristorante da Gemma and, 407; sexuality of, 241–42; Shawn and, 180; on "Sir Cecil's Ride,"

Maxwell, William (*cont.*)
323; Steegmuller, Francis, friendship, 229–30, 272–73; Steegmuller, Francis, memorial, 428; Steegmuller, Francis, tribute, 422; *The Transit of Venus* and, 343; *see also specific works*
McCarthy, Joseph, 119–21
McCarthy, Mary, 333–34
McClatchy, J. D. "Sandy", 6–7, 450
Mead, Margaret, 335–36
medevac flight, 460–61
Mediterranean, 110
Medway, Violet, 40, 44
"Meeting, The" (Hazzard, Shirley), 258
Mehta, Ved, 189, 193, 290
Meiklejohn, Alexander, 206–207
melodrama, 337–38
Melville, Herman, 332
memorial: Auden, 322; Clark, Eleanor, 430–31; Hecht, Anthony, 338, 451; Maxwell, William, 440–41; Merrill, James, 427–28; Steegmuller, Francis, 12–13, 428
Mendelson, Edward, 10, 398, 436
Menzies, Robert, 43, 95
Meredith, William, 296
Merrill, James, 11; at Capri, 403–404; death of, 427; friendship with, 193; memorial for, 427–28; "164 East 72nd Street" by, 427; reciting poetry with, 425; Rita poem by, 404
Merrill Business College, 203
methedrine, 313
Miles Franklin Award, 5, 449–50, 453
Miller, Arthur, 343
Miller, David, 339
Milton, John, 465
Ministry of Munitions, 47
Mintz, Morton, 394
Mishima, Yukio, 328
Money, James, 153
*Monkey Grip* (Garner), 454
Monnet, Jean, 217–18
Montalcino, Italy, 254
Monteliscai, Italy, 264–65
Monte San Michele, Capri, 404–405, 431

Monticone, Charles, 46
Moravia, Alberto, 225, 281–82, 412
Morgan, Murray, 128
Morgan, Randolph, 238, 403, 414–15, 419, 423
Morocco, 258
Morris, Ivan, 328, 348, 355
Morris, William, 83–84
Morrison, Hedda, 59
mortality, 465–66
Morton, Peter, 381–82, 435
Mosman, Australia, 25, 27, 38–39
Moss, Howard, 192, 333
"Mount Victoria" (Hazzard, Shirley), 179, 352
Moynihan, Daniel Patrick, 350
Muensterberger, Werner, 236, 238
Murphy, Herbert Dyce, 30
Murray, Albert, 224
Murray, Natalia Danesi, 397
*Musicale, The* (Steegmuller, Francis), 211
Mussolini, Benito, 128, 158
*My Brilliant Career* (film), 351

Naar, Jon, 130
Nabokov, Vladimir, 13
Naples, Italy: affairs in, 153–54; ancientness of, 148; on art treasures, 363; daily observations of, 360–61; described, 145–48, 351; Fahy visiting, 363–64; first lodging in, 142–43; hepatitis contracted in, 154–55; Leopardi and, 151–52; locals in, 408–409; Marigliano, Salvatore, in, 405–406; Morgan, Randolph, and, 403; move to, 140–42; Palazzo Marigliano in, 149; pet cemetery in, 363; Porte Aperte program in, 356; *scippatori* encounter in, 364–66; time sense in, 148; topographical world of, 409–10; as unaltered, 359–60; UNEF and, 142; Via Posillipo and, 150–52; walking in, 146–47
Naples 99, *see* Fondazione Napoli Novantanove

Nashe, Thomas, 465–66
National Book Award: appointment
    diary entry for, 3; *The Bay of
    Noon* nomination withdrawn, 301;
    Hazzard, Shirley, remarks for, 4–5;
    King receiving, 4; nominations, 4;
    Steegmuller, Francis, winning,
    304
National Book Critics Circle Award,
    342–43
National Gallery of Australia, 371
nationalism, in Australia, 367–68, 382
Nehamas, Alexander, 456
"Nelly Goes Down, The" (Hazzard,
    Shirley), 50
Nelson (cat), 410
Nembutal, 392
Nesbit, Lynn, 433
Newfoundland, 460, 461
Newhouse, Edward, 398
Newman, John Henry, 110
New York City: absence from, 144;
    descriptions of, 396–97; intellectual
    enrichment in, 123; romantic affairs
    in, 127–34; social hierarchy of, 115–16;
    UN and, 116
*New Yorker, The*, magazine: affairs of the
    heart at, 182–84; "Another Storyteller's
    Story" in, 229; debut, 179; financial
    stability and, 188; first acceptance
    from, 177–79; first submissions to, 177;
    "Harold" and, 180–81; Hong Kong
    story in, 411; "Letter from Australia"
    in, 332; "Letter from Venice" in,
    305–306; Sbarbaro poetry published
    in, 411–12; "Sir Cecil's Ride" in, 323;
    Spark and, 190; Steegmuller, Francis,
    at, 211; UN criticisms and, 310–11;
    "Woollahra Road" and, 181–82
New York Society Library, 355, 461;
    event at, 463; trustee of, 355
*New York Times, The*: "A Call for UN
    Reform" in, 310; "800 biting words"
    in, 326
New Zealand: Australia aligned with,
    94; Cook Strait, 90; Hazzard family in,

90–108; passage to, 90; Wellington,
    90–96
Nichols, Mike, 400
Nicolson, Harold, 243
nightingales, 166, 250, 278, 428–29
Niles, John Jacob, 228
Nixon, Richard M., 329–30
Noailles, Marie-Laure de, 286
Nobel Prize for Literature, 283
"Nothing in Excess" (Hazzard, Shirley),
    176
"Nozze, Le" (Hazzard, Shirley), 256

Oates, Joyce Carol, 353
O'Connor, Flannery, 6
Office of Strategic Services (OSS),
    216–17
O'Gorman, Ned, 451
"164 East 72nd Street" (Merrill), 427
Orange Prize for Fiction, 449
*O Rare Ben Jonson* (Steegmuller,
    Francis), 204–205, 206
*Order of Release, The* (Millais, John
    Everett), 18, 475
Organization stories, *see People in Glass
    Houses*
Origo, Iris, 438
OSS, *see* Office of Strategic Services
"Out of Itea" (Hazzard, Shirley), 261–62
"Owl and the Pussycat, The" (Lear), 235,
    422
Oxford, England, 86–87, 115, 162

Pach, Walter, 209, 210, 216
Pais, Bram, 397, 418, 430, 440
Palais d'Orsay Hotel, 211–12
Palazzo Marigliano, 149
Pane, Roberto, 357–58
*Papillot, Clignot et Dodo* (Steegmuller,
    Francis and Guterman), 240
Papua New Guinea, 34, 44
*Paradise Lost* (Milton), 465
Parente, Alison, 353, 398, 404–405, 460
Parente, Gaetano, 404
Parente, Will, 398, 404–405
Parini, Jay, 463

Parsonage, Mrs., 315

Parsons Bookshop, 94

"Party, The" (Hazzard, Shirley), 185

Peloponnese, 261–62

PEN World Voices Festival, 462

*People in Glass Houses* (Hazzard, Shirley), 285; Acton and, 292; Korabetski and Wyatt in, 119; Lyall and, 175–76; Organization stories and, 208; published, 288; reviews, 289–90

Peretz, Martin, 395–96

pet cemetery, 363

Phelps, Robert, 303

physical therapy, 461

Picasso, Pablo, 231, 286

"Picnic, The" (Hazzard, Shirley), 185–88

Pierce, Peter, 382

Pissarro, Camille, 217, 373, 430

"Place in the Country, A" (Hazzard, Shirley): affair depicted in, 185–86; lovers' separation in, 137; Macmillan and, 190; unchaperoned in, 135; Wickenden and, 134, 186, 188

Podhoretz, Norman, 318

*Poetical Works of Wordsworth* (Wordsworth), 48–49

poetry: L'Absinthe lunch and, 456–57; ardour for, 457; Auden and, 322; Browning poem, 418–19; buying books of, 123; Crea and, 451; *English Poetry*, 159; expanding appreciation of, 65–66; Hazzard, Shirley, on, 8; love of, 48–49; memory for, 10, 48; Rita poem, 404; Sbarbaro and, 411–12; Sorrento poem, 432; taxi driver reciting, 408–409; as transformative, 17; Unterberg Poetry Center, 6; *see also specific poems*; *specific poets*

Pollock, Jackson, 371

Poore, Charles, 290

Pope-Hennessy, John: Il Circolo Tessitore and, 334; death of, 423; funeral of, 423–24; Hughes and, 371; Lecceto monastery and, 302; on romantic love, 8; Steegmuller, Francis, sexuality and, 241

Porel, Jacques, 287

Port-Cros island, France, 282

Porte Aperte program, 356

Porter, Andrew, 424

*Portrait of Zélide* (Scott), 438

Posillipo apartment, 406; Morgan, Randolph, painting at, 414–15; rental of, 359; Steegmuller, Francis, decline at, 416, 421

Pound, Ezra, 160–61, 306

Pounder, Robert, 193, 240, 461–62

Powell, Anthony, 292

Poynter Fellowship, 328

Pozzino, Il, 291–92

Prata, Hilda, 62

Praz, Mario, 287

*Prime of Miss Jean Brodie, The* (Spark), 190–91

*Princess Casamassima, The* (James, Henry), 404

*Professional Secrets* (Phelps), 303–304

Profumo, John, 324–25

Proust essay, 438

Pryce-Jones, Alan, 189–90, 226, 244

Puffet, Suzanne, 143

purse snatchers, *see scippatori*

*Quartet* (Rhys), 333

*Queen Elizabeth, HMS*, 115

Queenwood School, 39–41, 44

Rabaul, Papua New Guinea, 34

Raphael, Frederic, 289

Rastoff, Rhoda, 121

Read, Piers Paul, 168, 173

Reagan, Ronald, 329–30

Recanati, Italy, 362

Red, *see* Warren, Robert Penn "Red"

Redon, Odilon, 196, 220, 334

Reed, Henry, 426

Reg, *see* Hazzard, Reginald "Reg"

Renaissance drama essay, 49

*Requiem Canticles* (Stravinsky, Igor), 306

Reurs, Helen, 336

Reverdy, Pierre, 235–36

Rhys, Jean, 333
Rich, Dan, 334
Richardson, John, 241
Richey, Michael, 418–19, 438, 449
Rickard, Justin, 110
riggiole, le (traditional Capri tiles), 433
Ripa di Meana, Isabella and Vittorio, 324, 361, 419, 425, 429, 442, 460
Ristorante da Gemma, 407
Rita (cook), 403–404
Ritz Paris Hotel, 286
Robbins, Henry, 179, 295, 352
Roberts, Laurance, 228
Rogers, Betsy Barlow, 463
Rome, Italy, 225
Rome and a Villa (Clark), 228
Rosenthal, Helen, 208
Roycroft Bookshop and Lending Library, 49
Rubbo, Mark, 454
Rubinstein, Nicolai, 293
Ruggiero, Mimi, 323–24
Rushdie, Salman, 462
Russell, John, 10

"Sack of Silence, The" (Hazzard, Shirley), 258
Said, Edward, 354, 402
Saint Mary's cemetery, 466
St. George Hotel, 91
Salt-Water Poems and Ballads (Masefield), 49
Sand, George, 414, 438
Santi Giovanni e Paolo Church, 306
Saunders, Amanda, 439
Sbarbaro, Camillo, 160, 411–12
Scarry, Elaine, 456
Scheick, William, 354–55
Schiff, Stacy, 5
Schwartz, Bernard, 462
scippatori (purse snatchers), 364–66
Scoon, John, 127
Scott, Geoffrey, 438
Second Sex, The (Beauvoir), 123
Section d'Or, 210
Segal, Erich, 304

Seidmann, Dr., 394
Selected Poems (Warren, Robert Penn), 271
"Sense of Mission, A" (Hazzard, Shirley), 145
sente des Pouilleux, Pontoise, La, 217
"Sera del Dì di Festa, La" (Leopardi), 250
Serao, Matilde, 333
Seton, Elizabeth Ann, 244
Severi, Giulio Colavolpe, 361–62
Shakespeare, William, 134, 299, 393, 400, 429
Shanghai, 64–65
Shawn, William, 180, 395, 410
Sheehy, Harriet O'Donovan, 273
Shelley, Percy, 348
"Sir Cecil's Ride" (Hazzard, Shirley): affair in, 108; outing recorded in, 76–78; published, 323; sisters and, 65; war experience in, 70
Sitwell, Osbert, 293–94
Small Island (Levy), 449
Smith, John Saumarez, 323
Smith, Sydney Ure, 23
socialism, 269
Solaia, Villa: described, 156; Hazzard, Shirley, on, 164–65, 166, 167–68; as home, 262; identity resolution at, 262–63; Macdonald on, 164; meeting household at, 157; opened to paying guests, 163–64; social circle and, 173; subject matter provided by, 176–77; ten-year commemoration of, 285; World War II and, 163
Solarz, Stephen, 395
So Long, See You Tomorrow (Maxwell, William), 343
Solzhenitsyn, Alexandr, 326–27
Sonkin, Robert, 166; background, 174; death of, 348; MacKenzie and, 192; as object of desire, 184–85
Sophie (fictional character), 246–47, 263, 277–78
Sorensen, G., 393
Soria, Dorle and Dario, 334; background, 270–71; death of Dario, 348; death of Dorle, 448

Sorrento poem, 432

Southampton, England, 115, 204, 314, 347

*South Wind* (Douglas), 152

Spain, 250–51, 287

Spark, Muriel, 6; *The Bachelors* by, 252; Beaux Arts rooms of, 194–95; break with, 431; Coleman and, 431; Dameship of, 417; death of, 456; falling out with, 192; Flanner and, 397; friendship established with, 190–91; friends in common with, 192; Hazzard, Kit, and, 192–93; Hazzard, Shirley, and, 244, 248–49, 301–302; MacKenzie and, 191–92; *The Prime of Miss Jean Brodie* by, 190–91; relationship advice of, 244, 248–49, 253; Steegmuller, Francis, and, 194, 240–41, 248–49

Specktor, Matthew, 11, 66, 338, 425

Spender, Stephen, 110

Sperlonga, Italy, 255

Springer, Mitzi, *see* Wooster, Mary

Stabb, Violet, 68–69

Stannard, Martin, 190–91, 418, 431

Stanton Road house, 38–40, 42

Stark, Freya, 236–37

Starkie, Enid, 354

*States of Grace* (Keith [Steegmuller, Francis]), 231, 246

Stead, Christina, 51, 332

Steegmuller, Beatrice: art works purchased by, 217, 220; Birstein and, 230; cancer of, 237–39; death of, 239; Guterman and, 214; handicap of, 207, 208, 221, 228, 232; Kazin and, 230; at Manhattan House, 227; on marriage to Steegmuller, Francis, 238; Muensterberger and, 236; Murray, Albert, and, 224; Palais d'Orsay Hotel and, 211–12; Steegmuller, Francis, memorial and, 428; Steegmuller, Joseph, on, 239; as storyteller, 207, 228–29; travels of, 215–16, 221; Warren, Red, and, 228

Steegmuller, Francis, 118; at Acropolis, 237; ambiguity of, 252–53; *amitié littéraire* with, 245, 247, 248; Apollinaire and, 235, 236, 239, 240, 304; appointment diaries of, 3; art history and, 225–26, 232; art tastes of, 371–73; art works purchased by, 217, 220; authority of, 402; awarded Chevalier of the Légion d'Honneur, 234; background, 196; Barbette and, 296; Barzun and, 205; as biographer, 240; biographical subjects compared, 304; Birstein and, 230; birth of, 202; Brombert on, 230–31; cancer and, 237–39; cemetery and, 466; on Chanel, 286; circles of friends, 267–73, 292–95, 397; on *Cliffs of Fall*, 256; Cocteau and, 12, 304; cognitive decline of, 391–92, 417–18; Coleman and, 241; at Columbia University, 204–205; complications with, 196–97; Cooper, Douglas, letter, 238–39; Cornog and Goldstein gift from, 431–32; Cousins and, 319; death of, 421–22; decline of, 391–92, 415–18, 420–21; Dick, Henry, and, 204–205; dreams of, 243–44, 260; Duncan, Isadora, and, 322; Egyptian travels project, 307; Ellison and, 221–24; at *Encyclopedia of the Social Sciences*, 211; Experimental College and, 206–207; on family, 288; family background, 201–202; family trust and, 347; Flaubert and, 214, 230–34, 351; French culture and, 205–206, 212–13; Galantière on, 230; on Géricault, 232; in Greece, 261–62; Greenwich and, 202; grief for, 425–26; grief of, 253, 260; Guterman and, 213–14; Hall caring for, 417–18; Harrower and, 313; at Hotel de Perey, 218; insecurities of, 236; as intransigent, 390–91; Kazin and, 230, 269–70; literary criticism and, 354; long friendships of, 403; *Madame Bovary* translated by, 232–34; at Manhattan House, 227; Marigliano,

Salvatore, and, 405–407, 421; marriage to, 11–13, 197–98; on masochist self, 261; Maurois and, 232; Maxwell, William, and, 229–30, 272–73, 422, 428; at Maxwells' birthday events, 399; meeting, 194–95; memorial for, 12–13, 428; at Merrill Business College, 203; modern art and, 205; Monnet and, 217–18; in Morocco, 258; Murray, Albert, and, 224; Naples locals and, 408–409; National Book Award and, 304; at *The New Yorker*, 211; New York Society Library and, 355, 461; note from, 195–96; obituary of, 415; at OSS, 216–17; paintings sold by, 253; Palais d'Orsay Hotel and, 211–12; in postwar Paris, 217–20, 221; private scholarship and, 354, 355; in psychoanalysis, 243–44, 259; in public school, 202–203; reading aloud to, 392–93; relationship developing with, 243–56; remembrances of, 424–25; resentments toward, 413–14; Rolls-Royce of, 240; *scippatori* attack on, 364–66; Severi and, 361–62; sexuality of, 240–42; socialism and, 269; in Southampton, 204; in Spain, 250–51; Spark and, 194, 240–41, 248–49; Stark and, 236–37; Starkie and, 354; Steegmuller, Beatrice, on marriage to, 238; on Steegmuller, Beatrice, 239; Stein, Beatrice, and, 210, 211; Straus fallout with, 303; Stravinsky, Igor, funeral and, 305–306; stylised correspondence with, 245; "Tasks" and, 391; on *The Transit of Venus*, 338; traveling alone, 224–27; travels of, 215–16, 221; tributes to, 421–22; Venturi and, 225–26, 237; "Villa Adriana" and, 182, 246; Villon and, 210, 212, 213, 220, 250; vivacity rebuffed by, 402–403; Watherston and, 195, 243, 248; Weaver and, 225; wedding with Hazzard, Shirley, 257; White, Patrick, and, 375; Whitlam and, 330; on Wooster, Frank, 227; on

Wooster, Mary, 226; work on *Canopic*, 203–204; on writing, 235–36; *see also specific works*

Steegmuller, Joseph, 202, 296
Steegmüller, Matthew, 202
Steegmuller, Shirley, *see* Hazzard, Shirley
Steele, Muriel and Vernon, 203, 204
Steele, Vernon, 203, 204
Stein, Adam, 227–28, 232
Stein, Beatrice: *Drawings by Beatrice Stein*, 238; family of, 207–208; friends of, 208–209; Pach and, 209; Palais d'Orsay Hotel and, 211–12; Steegmuller, Francis, and, 210, 211; as storyteller, 207; Villon and, 209–10, 212; *see also* Steegmuller, Beatrice
Stein, Catherine, *see* Hazzard, Catherine "Kit"
Stein, Edward, 221
Stein, Gerda Goldfrank, 207–208, 209, 210
Stein, Harold, 207
Stein, Helen, 227
Stein, James, 34, 35–36
Stein, Jessie, 34, 36
Stein, Lucia, 227
Stein, Martin H., 236, 242, 391
Steinberg, Saul, 401, 418
Stokes, Edward, 58–60
"Story of My Death, The" (Bosis, Lauro de), 158–59
Strand, Mark, 456
*Strathaird*, RMS, 109–10
Straus, Roger, 240, 303
Stravinsky, Igor, 94, 281, 305–306
Stravinsky, Vera, 305
streptomycin, 79–80
Strozzi, Uberto, 294
Sulman, John, 24
*Summer and Smoke* (Williams, Tennessee), 123
Swanson, Gloria, 296
Sweden, 283–84
Swett, Katherine, 268, 397, 436
Swift, Dick, 174, 254

"Swoboda's Tragedy" (Hazzard, Shirley), 290

Sydney, Australia: Barnes, Valerie, and, 265; childhood around, 25–27; Depression in, 24–25; Harbour bridge, 24; light and, 27; modernity of, 23–24; returns to, 82–90, 108–109; *The Transit of Venus* on, 26; winter in, 434–35

Sydney Institute lecture, 434

Sydney Writers' Festival, 451

TAA, *see* Technical Assistance Administration

*Taiping* (steamer), 54–55, 58

Tangier, Morocco, 258

Tanner, Mrs., 347

Tasmania, Australia, 297

Taylor, Benjamin, 269, 401

Technical Assistance Administration (TAA), 116–17, 122–23

Thomas, Alan, 462

Thompson Street house, 92–93

Thucydides, 414

Tiberius, 420

Tichborne Claimant, 30

Tierney, Bertha, 201–202

Tierney, Jeremiah, 201–202

*Times Literary Supplement, The,* 189

Tolstoy, Leo, 405

Tomalin, Claire, 301

"To Ned" (Melville), 332

Torcello island, 451

"Track, The" (Hazzard, Shirley), 50

*Transit of Venus, The* (Hazzard, Shirley): Australia described in, 23; boat in, 284; Boudin, Leonard, and, 394; Clarke and, 346; conclusion of, 340; drought recaptured in, 283; epigraph in, 345; feminism and, 339; ferry ride in, 49; film rights for, 351–52; Ford and, 462; genesis of, 339–40; Harold Vursell Award and, 343; Hiroshima and, 57–58; on inland life, 45; isolation described in, 42, 45, 137–38; Lask

and, 336–37; Maxwell, William, and, 343; melodrama and, 337–38; Morris, Ivan, and, 328; mortality and, 465; National Book Award nomination for, 4; National Book Critics Circle Award for, 342–43; people represented in, 346; plot, 337–38; reviews, 340–42, 382; "She thought" excerpt from, 467; siblings idealised in, 384; spinsterhood and, 251–52; Steegmuller, Francis, on, 338; on Sydney, 26; untimely style of, 338–39; Virago securing rights to, 433; White, Patrick, criticism of, 374–75; Williams, Alan, and, 342; Wyndham on, 454

*Trapézistes, Les,* 283

Trilling, Diana, 294–95, 309–10

Trilling, Lionel, 215, 294–95

Tsang, Steve, 59

tuberculosis, 79–80, 84–85, 95

*Twelfth Night* (Shakespeare), 299

*Two Lives of James Jackson Jarves, The* (Steegmuller, Francis), 221, 224, 225, 231

UK, *see* United Kingdom

UN, *see* United Nations

UNEF, *see* United Nations Emergency Force

United Kingdom (UK): *The Great Fire* launch in, 449; on life in, 25; Vedeniapine, Alexis, and, 89; *see also specific countries*

United Nations (UN): affairs of the heart at, 121–22; Boudin, Leonard, and, 394–95; "A Call for UN Reform," 310; censorship and, 326–27; *Countenance of Truth* and, 335; criticism of, 289, 308, 310–11, 318–20, 326–28, 335–36, 393–94; diary on, 120–21; "800 biting words" on, 326; Fremantle, Anne, job at, 118; *Gulag Archipelago* and, 326–27; hounding of, 327–28; Junior Fortnightly group and, 393–94; McCarthyism at, 119–21; Mead and, 335–36; professional prospects at, 154;

resignation from, 188–89; skeptical perspective on, 119–20; TAA of, 116–17; U.S. employees investigated at, 120; Waldheim and, 395–96; White, E. B., on, 116

United Nations Emergency Force (UNEF), 142, 143–45

United States (U.S.): citizenship in, 329; UN employees investigated, 120; Villon in, 216; World War II and, 47–48; see also Greenwich, Connecticut; New York City

*Unromantic Spain* (Praz), 287

Unterberg Poetry Center, 6

Updike, John, 441

Urquhart, Brian, 289, 335

U.S., *see* United States

Vaill, Amanda, 11

Varley, Dimitry, 118, 121, 130

Varmus, Harold, 397

Vedeniapine, Alexis (Alec), 63; attraction to, 66–67; background of, 67–68; BAOR and, 88; at boarding school, 68–69; on childhood, 68; Cold War anxiety of, 88–89; Cooper, Chris, and, 66–67, 71–72, 114–15, 352, 413; death of, 108, 412–13; Dutch Bronze Lion medal awarded to, 69–70; emotional collapse of, 104–106; emotional tenors of, 101; engagement ending for, 104–107; England travel delays and, 97–98; on farm living, 96–97, 99; Georgian farmhouse described by, 96–97; *The Great Fire* and, 410; Green and, 66–67; Hazzard, Shirley, and, 66–67, 73–76, 84, 104–108, 352–53; intelligence work of, 72–73; letters of, 443; long working hours of, 103; lost letter from, 102; marriage plans and, 96–97; micropolitics of Chinese Civil War and, 309; military service of, 69–70; reflection on death of, 413; retirement of, 107–108; reunion with, 344; revisited, 352–53; romance with, 73–76, 84; sex and, 80–81; spiritual

vacuum felt by, 104; Teik Yeo and, 71; UK and, 89; war concerns of, 103–104; writing tone of, 88

Vedeniapine, Cynthia, 107–108, 352–53

Vedeniapine, Peter, 352; letters to, 72–73, 82, 102; visit from, 456

*ventre di Napoli, Il* (Serao), 333

Venturi, Lionello, 221, 225–26, 237

Vernon, Lillian, 158

Veronese, Paolo, 306

Verrazzano, Giovanni da, 302

Via Posillipo, 150–52

Via Sopramonte apartment, 410; on Capri, 359; move into, 433–34; packing up, 429; purchasing new, 431; *le riggiole* for, 433; sale of, 461; walks surrounding, 405

*Victory* (Conrad), 455

Vidal, Gore, 369

Vietnam War, 309, 329, 330–31

"Villa Adriana" (Hazzard, Shirley), 181, 182, 246

Villa dei Papiri, 358–59

Villa Emma, 356

Villa Mazziotti, 150–51

Villon, Jacques: death of, 253; on *Drawings by Beatrice Stein*, 238; as dying, 250; Section d'Or and, 210; Steegmuller, Francis, and, 210, 212, 213, 220, 250; Stein, Beatrice, and, 209–10, 212; in U.S., 216

*Viper of Milan, The* (Bowen, Marjorie), 48

Virago Press, 433

"Vittorio" (Hazzard, Shirley), 181

Vivante, Arturo, 156, 159–60, 161, 162, 168–69

Vivante, Cesare, 160–61, 162, 264–65

Vivante, Charis, 157, 162, 168, 264–65

Vivante, Elena, 163, 417; cancer of, 244, 247; character of, 165; death of, 249–50; in England, 162; grave site of, 254; Hazzard, Shirley, on, 156, 157, 165, 166–67, 168; last visit with, 247–48; meeting, 157; on Sonkin, 174;

Vivante, Elena (*cont.*)
    Sonkin on, 166; as translator, 158;
    tribute to, 438
Vivante, Leone, 157, 159–61, 162, 163,
    168; Pound and, 160–61
Vivante, Paolo: Barbette and, 296; death
    of, 450; death of mother, 249–50; on
    Hazzard, Shirley, engagement, 257;
    on meeting, 157; at Oxford, 162
Vivante family: anti-fascism of, 158–61;
    Daniel and, 156; in England, 161–63;
    return to Italy of, 163

Waldheim, Kurt, 327, 395–96
Walmsley, Patricia, 43, 48
Walpole, Horace, 359
Walsh, Pauline Amilee, *see* Hazzard,
    Pauline Amilee
*Wanganella*, MS, 89–90
*War and Peace* (Tolstoy), 405
Warren, Robert Penn "Red": death of,
    412; "Flaubert in Egypt" by, 271;
    friendship with, 271–72; at Port-
    Cros, 282; *Selected Poems* of, 271;
    Steegmuller, Beatrice, and, 228
Warren, Rosanna: at Academy awards
    reception, 461; death of mother, 430;
    friendship with, 272; last visit with,
    464; memorial for mother, 430–31; in
    Naples, 436
*Waste Land, The* (Eliot), 292
*Watch Tower, The* (Harrower), 312
Watergate, 329
*Waters of the Moon*, 113
Watherston, Margaret, 195, 243, 248
Weatherby, W. J., 332–33
Weather Underground group, 394
Weaver, William: Il Circolo Tessitore and,
    334; decline of, 448; Hazzard, Shirley,
    on, 255; on Rome, 225; translation
    classes, 354
Weintraub, David, 121
Welch, Denton, 123
Wellington, New Zealand: connections,
    96; Cooper, Chris, and Green
    correspondences, 95–96; described,

90–91; family life at, 94; provinciality
    of, 93–94; social life in, 91–92
Wentworth Falls, 84
West, Alison, 10, 333, 334, 401–402
Wheelock, John Hall, 173
White, E. B., 116
White, Edmund, 304–305
White, Patrick, 10; arguments with,
    374–75, 376–77; death of, 381,
    412; dinner with, 373–74; Flaubert
    compared with, 375–76; Harrower
    and, 378–79, 381; Nobel Prize
    awarded to, 332–33, 408; tribute to,
    376
White Australia Policy, 21, 22, 265
Whitlam, Gough, 330, 371, 377
Wickenden, Elizabeth, 131; affair ended
    by, 137–39; background, 132; Hazzard,
    Shirley, relationship with, 133–34;
    "The Picnic" and, 185–88; "A Place in
    the Country" and, 134, 186, 188
Wilde, Oscar, 151
Wilkinson, Alec, 273; on Hazzard,
    Shirley, 9, 10, 11, 398–99, 402, 460;
    on Maxwell, William, 177
Williams, Alan, 342
Williams, Fred, 371
Williams, Freddy, 78
Williams, Tennessee, 123
Willoughby, 18–20
Wolff, Judith, 128
Woolf, Pat, 416–17
"Woollahra Road" (Hazzard, Shirley),
    18–20, 32, 181–82
Wooster, Frank, 227
Wooster, Mary, 226
Wordsworth, William, 48–49
*World of Books, The* (radio program),
    234
World War I, 24
World War II: Australia and, 43–44; end
    of, 53–54; Keene and, 355; Ministry of
    Munitions and, 47; Papua New Guinea
    and, 44; Queenwood School and, 44; as
    routine, 46; Solaia and, 163; U.S. and,
    47–48

"Worst Moment of the Day, The"
  (Hazzard, Shirley), 181, 182
Wyatt, Algie, 119
Wycherley, Mary, 65, 124
Wyndham, Susan, 434, 453,
  454

Xavier, Rita, 62

yachts, 47–48
Yeats, William Butler, 440
Yeo, Teik, 71

Zabel, Frances, 49
Zablodowsky, David, 120
Ziegel, Liliane, 236, 250
Zweig, Stefan, 206

# PERMISSIONS ACKNOWLEDGMENTS

Grateful acknowledgment is made for permission to reprint the following material:

Lines from "On This Island" by W. H. Auden. Copyright © 1935 by W. H. Auden, renewed. Reprinted by permission of Curtis Brown, Ltd. All rights reserved.

Excerpts from unpublished letters by John Cheever. Copyright © John Cheever, used by permission of The Wylie Agency LLC.

Lines from "Le Dernier Poème" by Robert Desnos. Used by permission of Jacques Fraenkel.

Excerpts from unpublished letters by William Maxwell. Copyright © William Maxwell, used by permission of The Wylie Agency LLC.

Excerpts from an unpublished poem by James Merrill. Copyright © the Literary Estate of James Merrill at Washington University, used by permission of The Wylie Agency LLC.

Extracts from unpublished letters by James Merrill. Copyright © the Literary Estate of James Merrill at Washington University.

Excerpt from an unpublished letter by Arthur Miller. Copyright © Arthur Miller, used by permission of The Wylie Agency LLC.

Lines from "Canto LII" by Ezra Pound, from *The Cantos of Ezra Pound*, copyright © 1940 by Ezra Pound. Reprinted by permission of Faber and Faber Ltd.

Excerpts from unpublished letters by Muriel Spark © Copyright Administration Limited, used by permission of David Higham Associates.

Excerpts from unpublished letters by John Updike. Copyright © John Updike, used by permission of The Wylie Agency LLC.

Excerpts from unpublished letters by Valerie Barnes. Used by permission of Hamlin Barnes.

Excerpts from unpublished letters by Chris Cooper. Used by permission of Antony Cooper.